D0984111

INTERNATIONAL HANDBOOK OF MATHEMATICS EDUCATION

Kluwer International Handbooks of Education

VOLUME 4

International Handbook of Mathematics Education

Part 2

Edited by

Alan J. Bishop
Monash University, Clayton, Victoria, Australia

Ken Clements
Universiti Brunei, Darussalam

Christine Keitel
Freie Universität Berlin, Germany

Jeremy Kilpatrick
The University of Georgia, U.S.A.

Colette Laborde
Université Joseph Fourier, Grenoble, France

KLUWER ACADEMIC PUBLISHERS
DORDRECHT / BOSTON / LONDON

A C.I.P. Catalogue record for this book is available from the Library of Congress

ISBN 0-7923-3533-3

Published by Kluwer Academic Publishers,
P.O. Box 17, 3300 AA Dordrecht, The Netherlands.

Kluwer Academic Publishers incorporates
the publishing programmes of
D. Reidel, Martinus Nijhoff, Dr W. Junk and MTP Press.

Sold and distributed in the U.S.A. and Canada
by Kluwer Academic Publishers,
101 Philip Drive, Norwell, MA 02061, U.S.A.

In all other countries, sold and distributed
by Kluwer Academic Publishers Group,
P.O. Box 322, 3300 AH Dordrecht, The Netherlands.

Printed on acid-free paper

Printed in the Netherlands

Table of Contents

Teaching & Learning Mathematics
Colette Laborde – Section Editor

Perspectives & Interdisciplinary Contexts
Ken Clements – Section Editor

Social Conditions & Perspectives on Professional Development
Christine Keitel – Section Editor

Chapter 19: Critical Issues in the Distance Teaching of Mathematics and Mathematics Education

STEPHEN ARNOLD, CHRISTINE SHIU, NERIDA ELLERTON
The University of Newcastle, Australia, The Open University, United Kingdom and the Edith Cowan University, Australia

ABSTRACT

Distance modes of teaching and learning have proved to be increasingly pop-ular, worldwide, during the last three decades of this century, especially in the areas of mathematics and mathematics education. This chapter critically ex-amines the distance education phenomenon in relation to several key varia-bles: the nature and purposes of both mathematics and distance teaching; the current and potential roles of computer technology in the flexible delivery process; and the particular implications of these factors in relation to interac-tions between so-called 'developed' and 'developing' countries. Case studies of current practice are presented to exemplify several of these key issues in relation to course development and delivery. Finally, a framework for future discussion is provided in the form of eight possibly contentious propositions which call for stronger theoretical and practical relationships to be developed between educators in the fields of distance education, mathematics and math-ematics education.

1.   CHANGING CONCEPTS OF DISTANCE EDUCATION

In the mid-1980's Keegan (1986) defined distance education as a form of ed-ucation with the following five properties:
1) The physical separation of teacher and learner throughout most of the learning process — although occasional face-to-face meetings between students and tutors may occur;
2) the influence of an educational organisation in the planning and preparation of learning materials for the provision of student support services;
3) the use of media for the delivery of learning content;
4) the provision of two-way communication; and
5) the absence of the learning group so that people are usually taught as individuals and not in groups.

A.J. Bishop et al. (eds.), International Handbook of Mathematics Education, 701 - 753

Interestingly, the magnitude and rate of conceptual change in the field of distance education has been sufficiently great that although each of the above five properties is still, to a certain extent, pertinent, taken as a whole, the five properties no longer provide an adequate description of what contemporary distance educators are trying to achieve.

Although the first and the fifth properties emphasise physical separation, taken together the two properties tend to give a wrong impression of where contemporary distance education is moving – because, with advances in interactive videoconferencing the physical separation of learner and teacher is no longer necessarily a feature of distance education. The second property called for a strong curriculum and course design components for distance education programs, but some distance educators – see, for example, Ellerton and Clements, 1990 – eschew hierarchical centre-to-periphery models of distance education which emphasise the need for 'professional' course designers to work with 'expert' course teams at the curriculum design and developmental phases. The third and fourth properties imply the use of transmission modes of learning, supported by teacher/lecturer feedback, but many distance educators are now calling for less teacher-directed, yet more interactionist, forms of distance education.

There are still many educators who think of distance education as a motley collection of 'second-best' correspondence forms of education which are adopted to overcome barriers which restrict educational parity between urban centres and remote communities. However, as Kia (1995) has pointed out:

> As distance learning technologies have evolved, it has become apparent that the audio and visual capabilities and the one-to-one interactivity offered by many of today's state-of-the-art technologies can have a much greater impact on the learning process than any individual teacher can achieve in a traditional classroom. As a result, distance learning is not only viewed as the best method to deliver quality education to rural and remote communities, but the best method to deliver quality education, period.

Kia's statement bears ample testimony to the fact that some educators tend to become excited when they reflect on the potential of harnessing hi-tech multimedia developments to education, and especially to policies and practices in the realm of distance education.

There is no shortage of impressive data, though, to support the contention that the future of education will be with the evolving methods and concepts of distance education. In this Internet age – with communication satellites circling our globe and such ideas as videoconferencing, electronic mail, and virtual campuses no longer in the realm of science fiction – distance education, it seems, presents unparalleled opportunities for making the world a better place for more people. Never before has it been possible to bring together so many people, in so many parts of the world, so quickly and so easily.

At the tertiary level, for example, there has been a dramatic increase in the use of forms of distance education, so that today, less than thirty years after the establishment of the Open University in the United Kingdom (Perry, 1972), the ten largest universities in the world use distance methods as their major mode of operation. Modern communication systems, assisted by dazzling advances in technology, enable profitable links to be established between students on the same campus, or between students at different locations. It is relatively easy for students to interact, through technology, with other students anywhere in the world. Indeed, the establishment of a global campus, linked by internationalised curricula (Oldham, 1989), is a vision held by an increasing number of educators.

Even a cursory glance at advertisements on the Internet for tertiary education programs will draw attention to the large number of 'paper-free' academic courses which have been developed. Prospective students are being told that all they have to do is to enrol in a course, and they will then be able to qualify for higher degrees without ever having to put pen or pencil to paper (Clements, 1996). The enrolment itself can be completed electronically, course fees can be paid electronically, the syllabuses and text 'books' can be communicated electronically, and all assessment tasks can be submitted electronically. Comments by lecturers who assess students' submissions would be conveyed to the students by electronic means. Throughout the course students would be able to interact with each other, and with their lecturers, electronically.

The high profile which has been accorded by educators and politicians to the hi-tech gadgetry of distance education can be misleading, however. It needs to be remembered that in the mid-1990's most of the world's distance education is still carried out almost totally through the print medium, complemented occasionally by radio, audiotapes and, perhaps video-tapes (Purwanto, 1995). Difficulties of access can be associated with social, cultural as well as geographical factors and some are related to the particular needs of disabled or disadvantaged students. Distance education has a role to play with respect to meeting these needs.

1.1   From Open Universities to Open Schooling

Since early in the 20th century, and probably before then, various forms of distance education have been developed to cope with the needs of school-age pupils living in remote regions (Mukhopadhyay, 1995). However, the development of new multi-modal forms of distance education suggest that the earlier dominance of the print medium is gradually giving way to interactive technologies and learning modalities within an overall framework of multi-

703

channel learning. The traditional concept of a school as a fairly insular institution where groups of 30 to 40 students are taught by one teacher in one room, for 5 hours a day, is likely to become obsolete – even in large cities.

In 1994 in the State of Victoria (Australia), for example, all government primary and secondary schools were fitted with satellite dishes and decoders to access curriculum delivered by interactive satellite television – a new form of education at a distance. The network, called 'SOF Net', is used to disseminate programs in three categories: curriculum, corporate information, and teacher professional development. It is intended that in Victoria, systems of computers will be installed in all classrooms in government schools (Peck, 1995).

It would be foolish, however, to assume that solutions to education problems in one country or context are appropriate to other countries or contexts. Syarief and Seligman (1995), in commenting on efforts to provide hi-tech answers to the problems of increasing participation in junior secondary education in Indonesia stated:

Looked at from [the perspective of] a developing country it appears to be a good solution – for somebody else. It is too hi-tech, too expensive and totally inaccessible to the vast majority of children, even if the infrastructure for provision was there.

The same point was made, graphically, by Hareng, Ali, Sadjad and Johari (1995), who described education systems in Eastern Indonesian States:

In the mid-1980's, a USAID-assisted project called the 'Rural Satellite Project' determined to use an interactive audio-conferencing system together with an interactive graphic system and a dial-up telephone system to assist Eastern Indonesian universities to reach students in more effective ways.

However, according to Hareng et al. (1995):

The system was totally designed without any involvement of the local technical team. The original designed system consisted of pieces of equipment granted by USAID which turned out to be inappropriate choices for the environment. Thus, in the later phase, we are forced to redesign the system to use full indigenous technology, appropriately. From experience we learned that local equipment... has been more appropriate.

In fact, the original system lasted for a year only – the graphic system did not function at all – before a local technical team moved to develop new equipment to meet the specific needs of the project.

Clearly, such examples are needed to counter the rhetoric coming from technocrats who believe that schools as we know them will not be needed in the new millennium.

An article published in Malaysia's major national English-language newspaper, the *New Straits Times*, on August 23, 1995, informed readers that sixth-grade school children living in remote parts of Iowa, in the United States of America, were participating in education programs which enabled them, through the use of advanced fibre-optic networks, to provide interactive voice and video links between classrooms and instructors hundreds of kilometres apart. The children were talking directly with NASA rocket scientists and engineers.

Readers were told that this was but an illustration of future trends in education. A technology analyst of Link Resources Corporation was quoted as saying that 'it is the calm before the storm', and that what was beginning to happen in distance learning 'mimics the movements in PCs in schools in the mid-80's'. A Sony Corporation representative was quoted as saying that various companies were determined to cope with the demand, and that despite the massive competition, Sony Corporation expected to sell US$25 million in distance education equipment per year by the year 2000 (up from US$15 million in 1995). Some idea of the scope and pace of expected change could be gained from the fact that although in 1995 only 17 schools in the State of Indiana were 'on line' for fibro-optics programs, it was hoped that within six years over 500 schools in that State would be wired. The cost would range from US$25 000 to US$40 000 per classroom.

Although the anticipated costs were large, school systems in the United States were, the *New Straits Times* article stated, determined to go ahead. This was because they recognised that the new technology would provide students with learning opportunities which previously had not been available. Thus, for example, Spirit Lake High School, in Spirit Lake, Iowa, which, had not offered Russian language classes for two years because of cost considerations, was now once again offering Russian classes – this time with the aid of the fibre-optic network, which enabled Spirit Lake students to tune into a Russian language class being held at Marshalltown High School, 410 km away, in Des Moines.

The *New Straits Times* article made one thing particularly clear: no longer were the startling advances in distance education being confined to tertiary education. Schools in developed countries were also prime targets for ambitious education policy makers keen to display their ability to incorporate the latest expensive hi-tech gadgetry into school systems. In the late 1990's there is an international shortage of teachers qualified to teach senior secondary mathematics classes, and some education makers have already moved to use satellite technology to beam the same standard senior mathematics lessons into schools across a state or a nation (Peck, 1995).

It is a short step from that scenario to another described by Kia (1995), of the Canadian Communication Consortium:

> Ideally, and ultimately, courseware should be developed locally in the country where it is intended. Due to the high costs involved in establishing production facilities and producing education videos and computer software, this may not always be the most practical solution upon implementation of a distance learning system. If this is the case there is a wealth of educational television programming and interactive multi-media CD-ROM's available on the market today. The majority of this courseware can be easily adaptable to meet the cultural, language and educational requirements of the local population. By acquiring affordable dubbing, subtitling, studio and editing equipment, an operator can establish special courseware production workstations to modify and add advanced learning features to existing courseware. With the appropriate equipment, special learning 'flashback' systems can be put onto CD-ROM's to help improve student retention and learning, and a data signal can be integrated into a standard broadcast television program to turn this into an interactive medium.

One implication to be drawn is that technology has brought education into a brave new world in which all concerned with education administration, curriculum development, and teaching and assessment, will need to face up to the challenges of flexible modes of course delivery.

Another conclusion is that in the rush towards hi-tech education systems, principles concerning the importance of developing education systems in which co-operation is encouraged, cultures and languages are respected, and equity fostered, are in danger of being overlooked, ignored, or avoided. The dangers are especially relevant in the domain of mathematics education, for mathematics is commonly thought to be culture-free territory.

The application to multi-channel forms of education at the school level would not be confined to wealthy schools in developed nations. Indeed, education administrators in developing countries, and officials formulating and supervising education aid packages sponsored by UNESCO, World Bank, Asian Development Bank, etc., see distance education as a major means of achieving the 'Education for All' objective articulated by the Jomtien Conference (1990) and the Delhi Summit of heads of Nine High-Population countries (1993). There are far-reaching implications for curriculum and for a commitment to equity in education. India, for example, has projected setting up 20 open schools offering programs in 16 languages with an annual intake capacity of 4 to 5 million students (Mukhopadhyay, 1995). Indonesia's 'Universal 9-Year Basic Education Program' is expected to have an enrolment of over 2 million distance students by the year 2010 (Rahardjo, 1995).

Brotosiswojo (1995), the Rector of The Indonesian Open Learning University, has pointed out that for countries like Indonesia, providing education in a traditional way by using classroom models, with face-to-face interaction between students and teachers, turns out to be 'very expensive', both in the sense of funding and also in terms of the time frame. He asked, candidly:

Starting with limited number of qualified teachers/experts to educate a very large population, how long are we willing to wait? Five years, ten years, twenty-five years, or perhaps one hundred years?

According to Brotosiswojo (1995), between 1968 and 1995 the secondary school enrolment in Indonesia increased from a 10% to a 40% participation rate. Even so, there was a long way to go to achieve 100% participation, with many of the remaining 60% to be reached living in remote regions. In an attempt to educate the teachers needed, Brotosiswojo's Indonesian Open Learning University currently has about 200 000 teachers enrolled in its courses. In 1995, only 5% of its enrolled students were younger than 26-years-of-age. Many of the enrolled students were taking a mathematics subject.

It will be argued that, although it would be foolish to turn away from the challenges and to deny the possibilities, it needs to be recognised that those seeking to apply the new technologies in mathematics education settings face many dangers. During this time of rapid change, especially, we need to stop and reflect on the questions: 'Where are we going with distance education, and why? And, what are the particular advantages and pitfalls for mathematics teaching and learning?' This chapter represents a first step in that questioning process.

2. ESTABLISHING PRIORITIES IN DISTANCE EDUCATION

2.1 Three Fundamental Principles

Clements, a mathematics educator, has argued that despite the huge potential of distance forms of education for maximising the value of international co-operation in education, it is important that mathematics educators keep the following three fundamental principles in mind (see Clements, 1995, 1996):

1. *The co-operation principle.* A distance mathematics education program developed in New York, say, is unlikely to be suited to students in Indonesia unless the development of the program was marked by substantial and equal co-operation between educators from the different countries. Rich forms of collaboration need to take place at all stages of the planning, development, implementation, and

evaluation of programs. The dangers of educational colonialism are everpresent and must be *consciously* avoided.
2. *The culture and language principle.* There is a need to make sure that cultural and linguistic considerations are fully taken into account at all stages in curriculum development and implementation.
3. *The equity principle.* Despite the impressive and rapid developments in technology, curriculum developers, teachers, education administrators and policy makers, and politicians involved in formulating policies and developing courses, for distance education programs need to keep equity considerations in the forefront of their mind. In particular, they need to take account of the tendency of technocrats to want to use too much technology, too soon. Teachers and students need to be ready to avail themselves fully of the benefits of programs which are offered.

These three principles suggest that the development of efficient distance education networks ought to be accompanied by corresponding large-scale professional development programs for teachers, lecturers, curriculum developers, and education administrators. Unless this occurs the potential of distance education to improve the teaching and learning of mathematics, and in particular, to create more equitable systems of mathematics education, is not likely to be realised. In fact, a pendulum-effect reaction against distance forms of education could occur.

2.2 Distance Education at the Market Place: Possibilities, Attractions and Challenges

Clements's (1995, 1996) three principles need to be seen in the context of an ever-increasing tendency towards the operation of market forces in education. As we move towards a new century, new universities and old universities alike are looking towards establishing fundamentally different forms of programs which will enable them to remain educationally and financially viable in an increasingly competitive higher education market. It is recognised that there is an important message in the fact that in the mid-1990's enrolment numbers at the Open University in the United Kingdom are surpassed only by other 'distance universities' – in China, Indonesia, India, and Thailand, for example. Incredibly, some of these universities have enrolments approaching half a million students.

Furthermore, national curriculum thrusts in a number of Western countries (for example, Australia, Canada, New Zealand, the United Kingdom, and the United States of America) have generated neo-behaviourist outcomes-based forms of curriculum which, if badly used, could precipitate a lowest-common-denominator reversion to transmission emphases in distance teaching and learning of mathematics (Ellerton and Clements, 1994).

It needs to be recognised, too, that distance education agencies are being driven by the competitive urge to gain a market advantage. Not only is there within-country competition to attract students, but there is also competition to attract full-fee-paying students who live in other countries. It is likely that these overseas students will spend at least a fraction of their courses based in their 'home countries', studying by distance means.

Interestingly, the move by many universities in well-to-do countries towards developing high quality distance education programs is being welcomed by the governments of developing nations. These governments are often struggling to provide enough secondary education and higher education facilities for their people. Therefore, a policy which encourages students to enrol in 'quality' overseas distance programs is likely to achieve the twin result of reducing pressure on their own institutions while simultaneously keeping currency at 'home'. In comparison with students who go abroad for on-campus study, the families of distance students who remain at 'home' will spend less money outside of the home countries – for there will be substantial savings in travel and accommodation costs.

The fact that students who remain largely in their home environments will not be subjected to forces which create potential conflict from a cultural perspective is not lost on governments, either. Distance education students are less likely to leave their home countries permanently (as a result of marriage or other factors).

The perceived advantages of distance forms of education present both economic and educational opportunities for the universities with impressive distance education facilities. Furthermore, positive feelings towards the developed nations and their education institutions are likely to be developed by alumni who participated in distance education programs, but would have been unable to afford to leave their countries for on-campus enrolments.

It makes good sense, then, for developed nations to establish appropriate working partnerships, in the realm of distance education, with education institutions and governments in developing nations. The trend towards marketplace economics in education means that conscious acceptance and adherence to the three principles previously elaborated should be a priority for mathematics educators wishing to make greater use of distance concepts and methods.

How close are we to delivering hi-tech, multimedia, quality mathematics education programs at a distance? The answer is clear: we are not just close – in fact, we are actually there. For at least a decade, multi-campus universities in many countries have held staff meetings, via videoconferences, involving staff located at different campuses. In 1995, those attending a conference held at Monash University in Melbourne on 'Regional Collaboration in Mathematics Education' interacted with educators who were in the United States (attending the American Education Research Association Conference), in a videoconference on the theme 'Assessment Alternatives in Mathematics Education.'

On another day at the Monash University Conference, Professor Colette Laborde – attending the Conference from France – led a master-class on *Cabri Geometry* for which the learners were secondary students located in Hong Kong. Laborde, watched by Conference participants in Melbourne, was able to see, hear and interact with Hong Kong students located many thousands of kilometres away.

An Edith Cowan University (Perth) brochure on its Virtual Campus Project states:

> The Virtual Campus gives isolated students the electronic equivalent of on-campus facilities. They are able to post mail to each other and to their tutors, read notice boards, submit and receive files of work, explore remote data bases, and engage in real-time conversations with others on the system. The Virtual Campus provides 'just-in-time' contact and support. Students can enter the campus at any time, day or night, and avail themselves of the many services provided for them.

In 1994 one of the authors (Ellerton) attended a UNESCO-sponsored conference held in Perth where one of the keynote speakers was the Vice-Chancellor of the University of Hong Kong. The Vice-Chancellor read his address from an office in his own University, but his image and his words were simultaneously seen and heard by all the conference participants in Perth. After his address he answered questions put to him directly by conference participants.

Most universities in developed countries, and many universities in other countries, would be able to achieve what has just been described.

3.   MATHEMATICS AND DISTANCE EDUCATION

There is a sense in which no other discipline is as clearly defined by its traditions and practices as mathematics. Despite the burgeoning interest in ethnomathematics, situated cognition, and cultural and linguistic influences on mathematics education – see chapters on these themes in Section 3 of this *Handbook* – it is nonetheless fair to say that from the United States to Asia, from the European Economic Community to the isolated 'bush' of Australia, 'mathematics classrooms' have recognisable similarities. Asking students (and their teachers) to 'describe a typical mathematics lesson' can lead to disturbingly consistent responses, seemingly regardless of age, gender, socioeconomic standing, nationality or even (in many cases) cultural background.

This pan-cultural phenomenon of school mathematics is being challenged by the startling growth of distance education concepts in the closing decades of this century. While there are many who would not mourn the passing of the

710

'introduction/worked example/seatwork/recapitulation' pattern of mathematics teaching (Clarke, 1984; Stodolsky, 1988, Cuban 1993), the fact is there are still strong societal pressures on teachers to teach according to that pattern.

Not the least of these pressures is the literature on effective teaching, which tends to look favourably on the standard pattern (see, for example, Killen, 1996). One of the significant issues associated with the growth of alternative structures which call into question the central role of face-to-face personal interactions between teacher and student is that teachers, students, and indeed society believe that well-ordered mathematics teaching based on that pattern has a good chance of generating quality learning outcomes.

The possibility that assumptions and values implicit in hi-tech, multimedia approaches to mathematics education may be inconsistent with existing mathematics curricula and assessment practices, and with the findings of mathematics education research, needs to be taken seriously. In particular, it could be argued that if educators wish to establish effective networks which maximise the potential of flexible forms of education, then they will need to recognise that mathematics and mathematics education are not, and never can be, culture-free or 'neutral'. Furthermore, they will need to be wary of subtle forces which push education administrators and curriculum developers towards adopting hi-tech yet culturally inappropriate curricula and practices.

This chapter considers these issues and implications as they relate to both mathematics teaching and learning, and the preparation and professional development of mathematics educators. In doing so, it seeks to locate mathematics and mathematics education within the context of high technology and flexible delivery educational developments, in which distance education approaches are increasingly advocated and defined.

The characteristics of distance mathematics teaching and learning spring from two roots – there are those which emerge from the practice of distance teaching and learning and those which emerge from the enterprises of teaching and learning of mathematics and of mathematics education. The purpose of this chapter is, on the one hand, to identify, exemplify and examine the current and emergent developments in distance teaching and learning as manifest in the particular discourses of mathematics education. At the same time, the chapter aims to expose and analyse some of the assumptions which underlie distance teaching and learning of mathematics and mathematics education.

4.   THE NATURE OF DISTANCE EDUCATION

At the present time most people who study at a distance are adults, and most of the courses provided come from institutions offering formal and informal education programs. Some universities – such as Indira Gandhi University in India, the Allama Iqbal Open University in Pakistan in Pakistan, Sukhothai

University and Ramkamhaeng University in Thailand, the Open University of Indonesia, and the Open University in the United Kingdom – are dedicated distance teaching institutions. Many traditional higher education institutions provide a mixture of conventional teaching for on-campus students and distance teaching for external or off-campus students. Some students in a dual institution will receive a mixture of face-to-face teaching and distance teaching, and even in a distance-taught course there may be face-to-face elements such as local tutorials or short residential schools.

Several major reasons for the existence of distance education can be identified: access courses for adults who have missed or failed aspects of school level education; difficulty in physical access to institutions of higher learning; the need to gain or upgrade specific qualifications; and the professional development of practising teachers. As more and more distance materials are produced for school subjects, the viability of including elements of distance teaching in traditional on-campus school programs also increases.

With increased mobility of the workforce and greater competition for employment, many adults find that they need to be able to undertake formal study as well as sustain full-time employment. Distance education provides one solution for this category of student.

Sometimes the notion of distance education is linked with that of open learning. The Open University in the United Kingdom, for example, was deliberately established to be the 'university of the second chance': a second chance to study a desired course whether for personal satisfaction or in pursuit of extrinsic goals such as career change or development. Students are registered in order of application regardless of previous qualifications. Although there is an important strand of advice and counselling incorporated into student support, the decision to enrol in a particular course remains with the student, subject only to limitations of numbers.

5.   DISTANCE TEACHING OF MATHEMATICS

5.1   Two Common Assumptions About Mathematics Education at a Distance

For reasons of economy, both of time and of materials, it is often assumed that the discipline of mathematics is more or less culture free. It is a common assumption, for example, that the content and methods used to teach mathematics in one part of the world are (or should be) the same as those which are appropriate for another. Furthermore, the idea that quality distance education materials which are prepared in one country can readily be used in another country, with only a few changes, is widely accepted (Ellerton and Clements, 1989, p. 4).

It is also commonly assumed that the ability to acquire scientific and technological skills depends upon having an adequate grounding in mathematics

(Briggs, 1987, p. 27), and that more widespread use of the distance mode of teaching might be an appropriate way of addressing the problem of the world-wide scarcity of qualified mathematics teachers in schools and universities (Briggs, 1987, p. 26).

Post-secondary distance teaching of mathematics is a major enterprise around the world. A report on *Commonwealth Co-operation in Open Learning* (Coffey, Hubbard, Humphries, Jenkins and Yates, 1988), for example, indicated that, of 306 institutions which responded to a questionnaire, 114 (i.e. 37%) said that they offered distance teaching of mathematics; economics/business studies (120 institutions, i.e. 39% of respondents) was the only subject area which was offered, in the distance mode, by more institutions.

It is tempting to suggest that the popularity of this distance mode for the teaching of mathematics arises because of the effectiveness of this mode in this process. It is, however, more likely that the widespread use of the distance mode in this area has arisen because:

a) distance education methods are most commonly used with adult learners (Coffey et al., 1988, p. 11) and many adults feel the need to upgrade their mathematical knowledge and qualifications; and

b) across the world there is a serious shortage of personnel qualified to take up employment requiring specific scientific and technological skills.

Bishop (1988), in his book, *Mathematical Enculturation*, has emphasised that the teaching of mathematics should always take full account of local cultural influences, both with respect to the nature of mathematics and to how mathematics is learnt. In the light of his argument, the use of curriculum materials developed by institutions set in one culture for implementation in mathematics courses taught in distance mode in another culture, is likely to be problematic and should only be attempted after due consideration of the likely implications.

Despite this, a paper prepared for the first Board meeting of the Commonwealth of Learning argued that there are distance education materials already in existence which can be used to provide effective education and training in science and engineering in many developing countries which need to train more scientists, technologists and engineers (Commonwealth of Learning, 1988, p. 2). Similar arguments have been applied in the area of mathematics education.

5.2   A Study Into Distance Teaching of Mathematics in Commonwealth Post-Secondary Institutions

In 1988, Ellerton and Clements undertook, for the Commonwealth of Learning, a study of distance teaching of mathematics in Commonwealth post-secondary institutions, and produced a report which addressed the following four questions:

1. Are there needs in the teaching of mathematics at the post-secondary level which are common across a variety of Commonwealth countries?
2. To what extent are approaches to the teaching of mathematics and to curriculum development in mathematics sufficiently similar in different Commonwealth countries to permit or encourage the sharing of materials?
3. Which pre-existing mathematics materials could be made available for wider distribution?
4. What kind of difficulties have been encountered by distance-teaching institutions in the teaching of mathematics?

Ellerton and Clements added a fifth question to their agenda:

5. To what extent is the discipline of mathematics a culture-free phenomenon?

Ellerton and Clements's (1989) final report (entitled 'Teaching Post-secondary Mathematics at a Distance') to the Commonwealth Secretariat, made eight recommendations, most of which ran counter to prevailing distance education theories and to the aspirations of those distance education bodies which saw themselves as key providers of curriculum materials, course designs, and expertise for a burgeoning international distance education market. The eight recommendations were:

1. Tertiary institutions not already offering distance programs in mathematics should not be encouraged to do so unless they are prepared to commit, on a continuing basis, adequate funds and staffing to the development of high quality, *locally produced* courses.
2. In carrying out its advisory role on the establishment of distance programs in mathematics, the Commonwealth of Learning should encourage institutions to adopt action research policies. In this way the responsibility for planning and developing courses, and for the continuing provision of resources will, from the beginning, lie within the institutions, and will foster co-operative course team structures.
3. In view of Recommendation 2, the Commonwealth of Learning's policy on the role of consultants (from bodies such as the British Council, the World Bank, UNESCO, and even the Commonwealth of Learning itself) who are asked to advise on the establishment of distance courses in mathematics, should be one of facilitating within local institutions the operation of action research procedures. Generally speaking, such consultants should not recommend the adoption, in whole or in part, of overseas programs, unless the genesis of the idea for such adoption comes from within the local institution.

4. Notwithstanding anything stated in Recommendations 1, 2 and 3, the Commonwealth of Learning should, in accord with Paragraph 22 of the Daniel Report (1988), act as a clearing-house for information and resources which will generally facilitate the development of distance education courses in mathematics. Copies of syllabuses, assessment procedures, printed materials and multi-media resources of all kinds should be located both at the Commonwealth of Learning headquarters in Vancouver, and in selected regional centres around the world (especially in third-world countries). In particular, succinct written and diagrammatic descriptions of a variety of successfully implemented models for the development of distance programs in mathematics should be available, supplemented if possible by video-tapes illustrating how these models were established.

5. The Commonwealth of Learning should offer to co-ordinate regional seminars and workshops at which any or all of those models of distance education courses in mathematics (see Recommendation 4) in which local institutions have expressed interest would be surveyed, illustrated and discussed. In general, the Commonwealth of Learning should make itself available to assist institutions to plan and implement models which they feel are appropriate to their particular situations (see Recommendations 1, 2, and 3).

6. The Commonwealth of Learning should bring together a committee charged with the task of investigating the allegation, often heard in third-world countries, that mathematics degree qualifications from certain institutions in third-world (and other) countries are not being accorded their due international recognition. This committee should consist of a balanced representation of third-world and other countries in the Commonwealth. Furthermore, the Commonwealth of Learning should take steps to ensure that degrees based on distance education programs in tertiary mathematics in Commonwealth countries should be accorded similar status to degrees derived solely or partly from on-campus studies.

7. In view of the controversy surrounding the notion of mathematics as a culture-free phenomenon, statements in future Commonwealth of Learning reports should not imply that the discipline of mathematics is more-or-less culture-free.

8. When an institution agrees to make materials which it has developed for its tertiary mathematics distance programs available for use by institutions elsewhere, the price asked should not normally be much more than the total for printing (excluding course production), handling and postage costs.

(Ellerton & Clements, 1989a, pp. 33-35)

In order to place these recommendations within a more theoretical context, it will be useful to outline some mathematical, philosophical and historical considerations which bear on the issue of whether mathematics is culture free. In particular, the issue of whether the teaching and learning of mathematics at a distance can realistically be based on more or less the same materials, prepared in one country, will be discussed.

6.   SOME BROADER PERSPECTIVES

For Ludwig Wittgenstein, the Austrian/English philosopher, mathematics was not something entirely independent of reality, and no statement was true *a priori*. For Wittgenstein, Western mathematics was a product of history, of social transmission processes at work, and had been shaped by evolutionary, 'survival of the fittest' processes. The particular forms of mathematics which were accepted, developed, and utilised by a powerful group were passed on not only to children in the group, but also to other groups. When a new kind of problem arose, an extension of existing mathematical knowledge was called for in order that a solution might be obtained; this, in turn, was socially transmitted, and came to be recognised as 'mathematical truth' (Del Campo and Clements, 1990). So, reducing Wittgenstein's thesis to its simplest form – although physical reality and biological dispositions imposed certain constraints on conventions which were developed and included within the ambit of mathematics, there is no mathematical reality that guarantees the results which are obtained (Wittgenstein, 1956, p. 90).

The idea of mathematics as a socially constructed body of knowledge has gained increasing credibility in contemporary philosophy (Lakoff, 1987, p. 354). After David Hilbert, Bertrand Russell and others had, early this century, attempted to lay the foundations of mathematics solidly as a formal system, where all truths could be proved and only truths could be proved (see Russell, 1974), Gödel showed that this formalistic philosophy of mathematics was unattainable. Gödel proved that even within such a basic structure as first order predicate calculus, together with axioms sufficient to model fully the natural numbers, there are statements which cannot be proved, even though they have been constructed so that they would be true (see Rucker, 1982, for detailed comments on Gödel's celebrated theorem).

Gödel's stunning proof led to a questioning of the nature of mathematics: Gödel, who was himself a dedicated Platonist, was quoted as saying that either 'mathematics is too big for the human mind, or the human mind is more than a machine'. In a similar vein, Herrman Weyl is reputed to have said: 'God exists because mathematics is undoubtedly consistent and the devil exists because we cannot prove the consistency' (quoted in Herlihy, 1986, p. 15). Other statements such as 'mathematics is the only branch of theology that has a proof that it is a branch of theology' were made, and the embarrassment among mathematicians is reflected in the following comment from Morris Kline (1980) in the Preface to his book, *Mathematics: The loss of certainty:*

> Many mathematicians would perhaps prefer to limit the disclosure of the present status of mathematics to members of the family. To air these troubles in public may appear to be in bad taste, as bad as airing one's marital difficulties. But intellectually oriented people must be fully aware of the powers of the tools at their disposal. Recognition of the limitations, as well as the capabilities, of reason is far more beneficial than blind trust, which can lead to false ideologies and even to destruction.

If the domain of mathematics is not as logically self-contained as was formerly believed to be the case, then it is interesting to consider what the implications of this might be for the teaching and learning of mathematics, in general, and for distance education programs in mathematics, in particular.

6.1   Gödel's Death Blow to Formalism

In 1930, shortly before Gödel announced his proof, Hilbert, when giving a lecture on the nature of human reason, had exclaimed, 'We must know! We must know!' Absolute knowledge was the stated goal of the Hilbertian formalist school. But then came Gödel's startling proof.

The far-reaching implications of Gödel's proof were not lost on mathematicians and philosophers. Herrman Weyl was led to say that although 'the question of the ultimate meaning of mathematics remains open, we do not know in what direction it will find its final solution, nor even whether a final objective answer can be expected at all' (quoted in Kline, 1979, p. 1207). Wittgenstein, a contemporary of Gödel, commented that 'there is no religious denomination in which the metaphysical expression has been responsible for so much sin as it has in mathematics' (quoted in Shanker, 1987, p. vii). He went on to say that he believed the twentieth century would witness a rejection of the logic of Leibniz, Gottlob Frege, and Bertrand Russell.

Many late 20th-century mathematicians and philosophers — though certainly not all — believe that Wittgenstein was right. Karl Popper's fallibilist philosophies followed, and suggested that a scientific theory could never be proved, only refuted. In mathematics, these ideas were taken up by Imré Lakatos (1976) in his book *Proofs and Refutations*. Lakatos described the long history of disputes within mathematics about the properties of polyhedra, and argued that many mathematicians, in defending the view that mathematics is a form of absolute knowledge, had defined and redefined the term 'polyhedron' to fit their goals.

In the 1990's many philosophers of science and education have come to view the characteristic thinking patterns of mathematicians as fundamentally similar to human thought as embedded in other domains. Indeed, mathematics is no longer seen as involving the discovery of truths existing outside the realm of human activity. Rather, mathematics is seen as domain-specific, context-bound, and as procedurally rooted as any other form of knowledge. Mathematics educators, and especially those who hold constructivist ideas (see, for example, von Glasersfeld, 1989) tend to label the Platonist notion that 'mathematical objects somehow exist independently of human experience' as, at best, unprovable, and at worst, extremely improbable.

Not all mathematicians and philosophers accept the relativistic position on the nature of mathematics (for a counter statement, in which a neo-Platonist position is elaborated and defended, see, for example, Bigelow and Pargetter, 1990). Nevertheless, all mathematicians and mathematics educators are agreed that there exists a body of mathematical knowledge accumulated 'over the years, and that this body of knowledge can be found in books, in journals, and in the exchanges in the many different communities of mathematicians' (Bergeron and Herscovics, 1990, p. 125).

Bishop (1988, pp. 56-57) termed the internationally accepted body of knowledge that is the domain of professional mathematicians as 'Mathematics' (with a capital M), and added that, in using such a term, he did not mean to imply that there was just *one* mathematics. Bishop (1988) noted that there are many different mathematics (with a small m), such as 'Chinese mathematics, Greek mathematics, Roman mathematics, African mathematics, Islamic mathematics, Indian mathematics and Neolithic mathematics' (p. 56). The term Mathematics (with a capital M) refers to an internationalised discipline which is nonetheless a specific line of knowledge development which has been cultivated by certain culture groups until it has reached the particular form that we know today. As Stillwell (1988), an Australian mathematician, has observed, 'Probably ninety-nine percent of mathematicians are now in agreement over what is a number, what is a function, etc., and there is a similar consensus over what has and what has not been proved' (p. 6)

In the sense that different cultures will have different forms of 'small-m' mathematics, it is only to be expected that mathematics teaching and learning should not be uniquely immune to the influence of culture. Rather, it ought to be as culturally-bound as learning in any other domain (Stigler and Baranes, 1988, p. 258). Education philosophers such as Evers and Walker (1983) have argued that since mathematical knowledge is only one aspect of a seamless web of knowledge, mathematics should not be taught as if it is an 'out-there' objective form of knowledge.

6.2 Implications for the Teaching and Learning of Mathematics at a Distance

Despite the well-developed relativist arguments on the nature of mathematics, in the 1990's most education bureaucrats, curriculum developers, and distance education course developers, cling to an image of mathematics as an atomised body of facts, skills, definitions, proofs and theorems which are absolutely true, independently of human reasoning. If pressed most would concede that there remains a sense in which mathematics can be seen as the pinnacle of human reason – however, they would also be adamant that that view of mathematics is not something with which distance mathematics programs should be greatly concerned. Rather, these influential persons believe that the main task of any mathematics education course is for the teacher/lecturer/writer to enable the learner to acquire basic knowledge and skills.

This kind of pragmatic orientation gives rise to the notion that mathematical curricula, and especially mathematics curricula for distance programs, should be hierarchical in nature and that mathematics teachers should stress the importance of students acquiring basic mathematical facts and skills, and making correctly sequenced verbal and written statements (Ellerton and Clements, 1990).

Distance education – in any subject area – has tended to seek hierarchy in curriculum design, and frequently structures texts by declaring explicit aims and (largely behavioural) objectives – or in modern parlance, student outcome statements together with 'pointers' or 'indicators'. The underlying assumption is often that the course will be followed in a wholly linear manner, and that 'templates' for model answers will be found in the text. Interaction with respect to the subject matter will be mainly or solely with tutors and fellow students on the same course. Such a tendency has been particularly prevalent in course designs for mathematics programs to be offered at a distance.

However, changes in emphasis and belief which have lead educators away from behaviourism, towards constructivism and reflective learning present strong challenges to objectives-driven course design (Chambers, 1995, Thorpe, 1995). At the same time, technological developments which allow non-linear course design through the use of *hypertext* and multimedia (Burge 1995, Rominszowski 1995), and unmediated access to information through the internet, enable students to pursue idiosyncratic paths through material. Electronic communications permit and encourage students to participate in individual discussion and conferencing involving an ever-wider community.

Finally, there are social, cultural and practical pressures which spring from the context in which and for which distance teaching materials are prepared. As distance education becomes more prevalent and its outcomes widely recognised, it moves from a minority enterprise in which teachers and learners are relatively free to experiment and innovate, into a situation where it is subject to the forces experienced by mainstream institutions. As Bates (1995) has argued:

All educational institutions, conventional or dual mode, autonomous distance teaching universities or training organisations, are undergoing tremendous pressure for change, mainly due to external circumstances over which they seem to have little control. (p. 42)

In the next two sections particular responses to these pressures in the design and presentation of distance courses in mathematics and mathematics education are presented as case studies.

7.   DISTANCE MATHEMATICS TEACHING – A CASE STUDY

The traditional educational milieu is the classroom and the image of mathematics teaching is typically embedded in such a setting. One teacher and a group of students meet together in a dedicated room to focus together on the common topic of mathematics. In distance education teacher and students are separated – at a distance – and students separated from each other. There is no dedicated classroom and individuals' place of study may be used for many other purposes both by the students themselves or by their families or colleagues.

Nevertheless many of the ingredients of traditional classroom education have their counterparts in distance education, and the typical and particular concerns of the mathematics teacher have their counterparts in distance mathematics teaching – however different the superficial aspects of their manifestation might be. In this section significant educational aspects of distance education are examined and illustrated by examples drawn from mathematics entry courses offered by the Open University of the United Kingdom (OU-UK).

OUUK is an autonomous distance teaching university. All its courses are designed *ab initio* for distance students rather than adaptations of existing conventional courses. There are rules for combining courses to produce a degree profile leading to the award of an Open University degree containing a minimum of six credits. All students study on a part-time basis and the 'normal' rate of progress is one credit per year.

7.1   Who Are the Students?

One of the features of distance education is its relatively long preparation and course production phases. For new educational ventures the prospective students are almost invariably unknown to those preparing the courses and logically the prospective students themselves are unlikely to know that they are indeed prospective students. (Evans, 1995, p. 69)

When preparing a course, a very early question to be addressed is who are the students and what are their needs and aspirations?

Early courses were successful in giving opportunities to those who were conscious of having missed a university education and as they did this gained both word of mouth publicity from these students and incidental media publicity from 'drop-in' viewers and listeners to course television and radio programs which were broadcast on public broadcasting, albeit at somewhat unsocial hours. Thus the pool of prospective students both grew and changed in composition. By 1994 the 4000 students who registered for the introductory mathematics course at OUUK had a very wide range of previous educational qualifications.

In fact 2% had no previous educational qualification (in any subject), 20% had qualifications at the level of a sixteen year-old school leaver (not necessarily including mathematics), 55% had a qualification for the 18-21 age group that might have gained them a place in a conventional degree course (again not necessarily including a specialist mathematics qualification), while 20% had some previous higher education (HE) qualification whether certificate, diploma or degree. (No data was available for the remaining 3%). There was variation in pass rates on the assessment, with the lowest rates obtained by the group with no qualifications and most of the higher rates by those with an HE qualification.

However, flexibility in adapting to distance study skills seems at least as important as previous knowledge as a predictor of success, and there were and are many examples of excellent performance among those who enter with minimal or non-existent formal qualifications. Indeed the description of the course in the undergraduate courses 'newspaper' specifically comments on the difference between possessing specific knowledge and using well-developed thinking skills:

'Use your head to learn the subject - use the subject to learn to use your head' (G. Polya, twentieth-century mathematician). What is mathematics, and what can it do? In this course we set out to answer that question by helping you to understand mathematics and to use it. But understanding mathematics requires doing mathematics. It also requires the development of a certain degree of intellectual maturity and a willingness to do some thinking for yourself.

This means that a mathematics course, however modest its dependence on previous knowledge, presents you with a real intellectual challenge. We have tried to organise the course to help you meet this challenge. The intention is to get you doing mathematics in order to help you understand the ideas underlying the development of this important subject. (Open University, 1995)

An intention of the new suite of courses which have resulted from evaluation and revision of the initial courses is to broaden access to university study still further and in particular to attract and support 'non-traditional' mathematics students. Enrolment in the introductory mathematics course has remained at a stubborn 25% women and 75% men, so an intention of *Open Mathematics* is to attract a higher proportion of female students. At the same time it is recognised that there will be significant numbers of students entering with considerable mathematical knowledge and skill.

7.2 Curriculum Design

Curriculum design in distance teaching operates at many levels and is often extremely overt. In OUUK the design of a course needs to fit within larger study programs and within the institutional systems for presentation, the course itself is prepared by a multi-functional team and the components prepared by different members of the team need to be integrated, and the resulting materials themselves are visible in the public domain and hence subject to external scrutiny.

Distance courses at university level must meet perceptions of what is proper university study. In a discussion of the nature of higher education Perraton (1995) quotes Barnett (1990) who reveals a broad consensus of a cluster of aims and values associated with higher education ranging from the 'pursuit of truth and objective knowledge' to 'preserving society's culture'. Perraton concludes that 'if the search for legitimacy in distance education is to get beyond bland assertions, then one productive line of research may be to examine how far distance education can or does achieve any of these purposes'.

What particular meaning has legitimacy in the context of mathematics courses? It may be helpful to consider the process of curriculum design in mathematics through the framework proposed for the school mathematics curriculum by Howson and Wilson (1986):

> First it is essential to draw attention to the three levels on which the content of the school mathematics can be viewed:
>
> a) the *intended* curriculum: what is prescribed in national and examination syllabuses;
>
> b) the *implemented* curriculum: what teachers teach; and
>
> c) the *attained* curriculum: what students learn. (Howson and Wilson's emphases)

722

The course materials are an embodiment of the 'intended curriculum' as conceived by the course team. But a broad view of curriculum design must also consider implementation of the curriculum, that is how it is transformed by the students as they work on the material, and how this transformation is mediated by the tutors who are consulted (whether by telephone, electronic communications or face-to-face) and who mark and comment on students' assignments, and the attained curriculum – the outcomes for students – both in terms of assessment results and preparedness for further study of mathematics.

In the case of distance mathematics teaching curriculum development takes place within the same climate as other mathematics curriculum design. Debates on the nature of mathematics as outlined earlier in this chapter, the aims and purposes of mathematics education, and rise and fall of standards of achievement in mathematics all impinge on the enterprise. There is then a potential tension between the immediate learning needs of students and the demands of intellectual rigour within the peer academic community. Changes in the balance of this tension are well illustrated in the history of mathematics entry courses.

The course team which designed the first mathematics entry course for this program, M100, was the whole of a young faculty fresh from conventional universities and eager to establish the academic credentials of the new institution. There was much concentration on content and rigour of presentation. They produced a course consisting of 36 units to be studied at the rate of one per week (by part-time students). The interdependencies of the 36 units formed a complex structure, though one which was dependent on a number of key but abstract ideas, notably that of morphism.

Many students responded with enthusiasm to the challenge of engaging with the material, though there was some suggestion that the team had not only met but exceeded its targets of legitimacy, for in a review of the course materials Hirst (1972) wrote:

> I would judge that the course would make considerable demands on the students, and I have no doubt about the work being of university standard. Many first year students at other universities would be hard pressed to gain anything like a real understanding of all the material in the course of one year of study.

The second entry course, M101, recognised that the assumptions made by M100 were too demanding for a significant proportion of the students for whom it aspired to cater. M101 was first offered in 1978 and was divided into six blocks of study paced through the year, but quite quickly became the subject of a rolling rewrite in which it was replaced block by block. A continual process of adjustment was completed and a stable form was achieved in 1986, which has remained substantially unchanged for ten years.

As the time approached to plan the replacement of M101 in the overall OU plan, much had changed in the pool of prospective students and in the social and cultural context in which the replacement was to be offered. Now there was to be a definite attempt to attract the non-traditional student, an attempt informed by explicit notions of equity, and the desire to meet the needs of an increasing pool of aspiring students.

At the same time other forces operated to constrain and influence the intended curriculum. There were national pressures to recruit in the areas of mathematics, science and technology. There was also an internal need to rationalise mathematics provision for entry students whether their planned profile was in mathematics itself or in science or technology. And significantly there was a new national system of vocational qualifications. Within this system a set of general core skills were defined in the areas of:

- application of number
- communication
- improving own learning and performance
- problem solving
- use of information technology
- working with others

Criteria for the appropriate achievement in these core skills, at different educational levels including undergraduate and postgraduate degrees, were specified by the National Centre for Vocational Qualifications (NCVQ).

With the exceptions of working with others and the oral component of communication, this list seemed highly relevant for students who were trying to develop distance learning skills within the context of a mathematics course, though the dangers of reification and hence introducing a new kind of behavioural objective was recognised. The curriculum design of the revised courses therefore incorporated planned opportunities for progression towards these criteria, through reflective learning which would be controlled by the students. Students are responsible for recording evidence of their own progression against the published criteria within a (provided) learning file, and may choose whether or not to submit this evidence for assessment and accreditation in the core skills, in addition to the normal course assessment.

By these means the use of the core skills framework was seen as a move which both gave a means of encouraging and rewarding the effective development of learning skills and an independent set of referents by which the standard of the courses might be judged.

7.3 The Teaching Materials

Much of the teaching intention in distance education is carried by the materials supplied to students. These materials may be a mixture of text of various kinds, software and audio-visual components. Although there are increasing moves towards integrating such materials into multi-media format, many courses remain mixed-media and are largely text driven. The text both provides learning material in its own right and directs students to the use of other materials.

Text. When text is itself the learning medium the challenge is to initiate active learning as opposed to passive reading. Particular techniques have become established for this purpose, as described by Lockwood (1995) who writes of 'the integration of questions within the teaching material, the opportunity for learners to respond and the provision of a corresponding answer or discussion'. He goes on to report that the effectiveness of this strategy has traditionally been tested in experimental studies which have frequently returned very positive results. However few students study under the conditions set up in experiments.

> Recent studies suggest that when the experimental controls are relaxed, or more real-life material and conditions are allowed, the previously identified findings are undermined. For example many of the experimental studies allowed the learner unlimited time to study material prior to a criterion test. When the time allowed is restricted, which is typical in real learning situations, previously noted effects disappear.

Nevertheless more quantitative approaches to evaluating activity initiating questions tend to support their use, and suggest that students make reasoned decisions about how and when to respond. According to Lockwood (1995):

> Learners perceive both the benefits to their study that activities offer and recognise the potential cost of responding to them. When learners reconcile the potential cost offered by activities with the costs they are likely to incur in responding to them, they operate a cost-benefit analysis. Analysis revealed that the majority of learners operated a balance responding to some activities and not others as study time pressures and the perceived value of benefits varied. (pp. 205-206)

Activities were incorporated into the texts for both M100 and M101. The description of M101 draws explicit attention to this:

> One of the most important aims of the course is to help you discover something of how mathematics is learned and to acquire the confidence you need to go on to further studies in mathematics. For this reason we have chosen to emphasise the directed activity approach, engaging you in doing mathematics. If you learn to study independently and to tackle problems effectively, then you acquire self-confidence and gain a foundation for extending your knowledge. (Open University, 1995)

The same basic strategy is being used in the revised Mathematics Entry Suite. However, in addition to direct teaching activities there are reflective activities in each chapter which encourage students to work on more general study skills though with particular emphasis on learning and communicating mathematics. Although the overt reward is that mentioned earlier of generating evidence towards the award of GNVQ core skills, the teaching intention is to establish reflective learning in the context of distance education, in a way which can be applied in later mathematics courses.

The notion of keeping a learning file is introduced in the revised program and students read that the 'Learning File is to encourage you to keep a record of your work through the course and provide a filing system for your notes on the 'reflection' you will be doing as you study. Most learning takes place when actively processing information and the activities in the text are designed with this in mind'. Four kinds of activities were described:

> **Core skills activities** [are] fundamental to your learning and are intended to help you think about, evaluate and improve your own learning and performance in mathematics.
>
> **Handbook activities** are concerned with specific topics in mathematics. [Y]ou will be creating your own mathematical handbook, so you build up a useful reference source.
>
> **Investigations** are primarily concerned with solving problems, using and applying the mathematics you have learned in a different situation or to answer a particular question.
>
> **Exercises** are useful in helping you develop and become confident in a particular skill or technique.

Although the content of the text is crucial, design and layout have an important part to play in the support of distance learning. These issues were already evident – and appreciated – in the design of the initial course. The recognition that text consists of much more than mere words and symbols is also important in relation to distance teaching materials. As Lowe (1995) argued:

> It is widely accepted that, compared with materials for classroom instruction, the textual components in distance education materials need to be both more explicit with respect to the presented content and more supportive with respect to instructional guidance that is provided for the learner. A similar expectation is typically not held for the illustrations in such materials. This may be a consequence of the secondary role that illustrations have traditionally served while text carried most of the responsibility for presentation of content. However in our increasingly visually oriented society, such a role for illustrations seems inappropriate. This chapter is based on the assumption that the illustrations used in distance education materials should also be more

explicit and supportive than would be considered appropriate for other modes of instruction. [p. 288)

In mathematics, of course, the use of diagrams and figures is customary in text, and these frequently present much of the information about a mathematical situation. However the reading of such diagrams or their production by students to communicate understanding is not always addressed explicitly and this may be beneficially addressed through reflective activities.

7.4   Graphics Calculators and Software

This visual orientation impinges not only on textual materials but also on a variety of potential support technologies used singly or in partnership with other course components. The new entry suite is designed around the use of versatile but reasonably financially accessible computing power. Thus in *Open Mathematics* costings have incorporated a graphics calculator within the basic course cost and this is supplied as part of the course materials. This also means that course authors know that all students will be using the same model and they can therefore design course and assessment materials which make reference to explicit key sequences.

In a number of courses students need to obtain access to a personal computer. In many cases this will mean direct purchase. although a low cost rental scheme will be provided for some students. A multi-application software package *(Mathcad 5.0)* is provided. Some students activities are incorporated in prepared files often involving exploration of mathematical ideas. Other activities will demand direct use of *Mathcad* as a calculating tool.

As in all mathematics teaching the use of software and graphics calculators allows interaction with the visual display – students can vary parameters, and combinations, zoom in and out or move objects on the screen in order to create personalised set of examples from which to conjecture and generalise. In distance education it also gives focus to decisions about when to use a more or less interactive mode or medium.

7.5   Audio-visual Materials

Audio-visual materials have traditionally played a key role in distance teaching, and this is certainly true of OUUK mathematics courses. In current plans software is used wherever students' interaction with the screen image is to be maximised. When a more directed approach is judged appropriate, for example, when it is desired that the student pays full attention to a structured sequence of graphic images, video may be used. Video allows the facility to pause and to replay but not to alter sequence or structure.

Traditional television 'programs' are still used as a means of presenting distant or inaccessible scenarios. It provides motivation, context, and enrichment both in terms of contrast to text and other materials, and economically in time by allowing much contextual information to be provided by the synchronous use of sound and visual image.

Paradoxically audio tape also has its place within a visual culture. It can be used alone as a vivid means of promoting imagery, or as a guide either to the interpretation of text, or to the use of other resources. All of these are incorporated into the mathematics entry suite.

Thus teaching possibilities are enhanced by the variety of media available, but there remains a danger of being dazzled by the possibilities, and overwhelming students with the demands of managing resources. If such demands become too great, some resources will be neglected or even ignored and those parts of the intended curriculum which depend on them will not be implemented.

7.6   Student Support

A crucial link in a chain which runs from the production course team to the student, is the tutor. OUUK appoints part-time tutors to a course on a regional basis. Tutors are responsible for maintaining contact with students and familiarity with the course ethos and materials. They receive and grade students' assignments, and use these as the basis for individual written teaching comments. They also plan and run local tutorials, though the degree of 'localness' depends on the location and spread of students within a region. With entry courses, tutors also undertake an important educational counselling role which includes the induction of new students to distance study and OU practices, and the maintenance of study and career advice for continuing students. Ideally students will retain their first tutor as their counsellor throughout their OU program, though distance education shares, with its face-to-face counterpart, many possible reasons for breaks in continuity of teaching.

Many students have traditionally initiated further contact with their tutors by telephone and this will continue for many in the new suite. However the inclusion of a personal computer as a necessary piece of technology for studying certain courses opens up new possibilities for communication. Students who identify themselves as unable to attend tutorials for whatever reason — remoteness, disability, family responsibilities, unusual work patterns, etc. — will be able to opt in to electronic tutor groups. The usual mode of interaction with their tutor and fellow students will be through conferencing and e-mail software. In addition they will be able to submit their assignments and receive feedback through file transfer. Given the current rate of general increase in electronic communication it is anticipated that these facilities will need to be available to almost all students within a very few years.

7.7 Assessment

As in face-to-face study assessment is a major determinant of the implemented curriculum. Like most OU courses mathematics entry courses are assessed by a mixture of continuous assessment (using both tutor-marked assignments (TMAs) and computer-marked assignments (CMAs) and an end of course examinable component. Students must pass in both assessment elements to gain course credit. Students commonly, and reasonably, embark on their study of a unit by inspecting associated assessment questions.

Research suggests that student behaviour then diverges into TMA dominated action, in which material considered irrelevant to the question is either skipped or given cursory attention, and TMA aware action in which course materials are studied for reasons other than their contribution to the assignment. The challenge as in all mathematics assessments is to find ways of assessing that which is considered important, rather than assessing that which is easily measurable. In particular if engagement with a specific course resource is to be encouraged, then it is necessary to set questions which can only be answered in the required form by using the software or by drawing on the kind of reflections for which the Learning File has been provided.

7.8 Evaluation

A final issue in distance education is evaluation of the materials and their presentation, and this is a traditional aspect of course design and follow up. One strategy is 'building good quality in rather than inspecting bad quality out' (Koumi, 1995), and the open university has procedures whereby from an early stage academics work with designers and media producers on the course components (material-focused evaluation). However the judgments of the course team can be considerably enhanced by early field testing by groups representing the populations from which tutors and students will be drawn (expert-focused and student-focused evaluation).

Sometimes, especially when innovations are proposed, the three modes of evaluation can produce conflicting evidence. For example student-focused responses to Learning File activities were different from expert-focused ones, and careful decisions about the formality of the design of prepared Learning File sheets had to balance the points made.

Another phase of evaluation is carried out at the end of the first presentation when the first cohort of students is surveyed for feedback on their experience of the course. Although many course components (such as television programs) may be difficult to modify, this feedback can be used to inform tuition and assessment strategies. In other words, the intended curriculum is, in the main, preserved, but the implemented and attained curricula can still be affected.

8.   DISTANCE TEACHING OF MATHEMATICS TEACHER EDUCATION WITHIN
     A TECHNOLOGICALLY-RICH CONTEXT

If mathematics itself has been readily adaptable to distance modes of teaching
and learning, the same could not be said of mathematics teacher education –
at least until relatively recently. Teaching itself has long been recognised as
a complex craft, poorly suited to traditional text-based modes which have
been associated with distance learning in the past. The rapid growth of new
technologies for learning, however, is rapidly transforming the nature and
purposes of distance education, and the discipline of mathematics teacher education provides a most suitable example of this transformation. Mousley and
Sullivan (1996) make this point strongly in the introduction to their *Learning
About Teaching* project:

> Merseth and Lacey (1993) argue that the potential of multimedia
> includes the possibility of introducing the complexity of teaching to
> novices. Its non-linear capability, they claim, distinguishes multimedia
> from conventional video-tape since it allows the use of multiple
> perspectives and opportunities to review situations. we have found that
> the variety of media available in these productions, as well as the ability
> to navigate between a range of perspectives, allows users to explore the
> richness and multidimensionality of teachers' work in classrooms.

Recent developments in computer-based technologies for learning offer exciting opportunities for mathematics educators. Access to the internet, the potential of CD-ROM technology, the redefinition of instructional design
premised by *hypertext* facilities, and the increasing mathematical power
available in pedagogically appropriate computer software potentially redefine significant aspects of the roles of mathematics teacher educators. The
same principles of quality still apply: students must be exposed to broad and
deep mathematical and pedagogical experiences, within contexts characterised by models of good practice and reflective teaching.

At the same time, the ways in which such experiences may be offered are
currently the subject of some negotiation. Traditional school-based experiences remain essential and yet problematic: within general climates of increasing budgetary restraint, faculties of education can no longer afford to
give preservice teachers as much time in schools as they might like. Universities clamour for more and more students, and yet are prepared to devote
fewer and fewer resources to the preparation as teachers, resulting in growing
class sizes and increased face-to-face teaching expectations. Distance education appears attractive as an avenue for increased enrolment beyond traditional catchment areas.

This section outlines three innovations involving computer technology
currently being trialed in Australia. The first involves the use of the world

wide web browser, *Netscape Navigator*, as a front-end for distance education materials offered both via internet access and by CD-ROM, making them accessible to a majority of potential students, with or without web access.

The second innovation arises from an ongoing project involving the development of a simulated algebra learning environment using *HyperCard*. Instructional modules from beginning algebra to calculus have been developed (Arnold, 1993). Computer algebra, graph plotting and tables of values are available and their use is encouraged within the program. Probes and prompts encourage student teachers, not only to engage mathematically with the materials, but to reflect on their pedagogical implications. Responses are elicited and a full text record of the progress of each individual is kept by the program.

Such a model offers much within the context of mathematics teacher education, exposing students to the range of available software tools and to a variety of contexts within which their use may be seen to be appropriate. It also offers a flexible instructional format, within which students are free to access the materials at any time and to complete both instructional and assessment requirements. The model is particularly appropriate for distance education modes. Both these innovations are being trialed within the Faculty of Education at the University of Newcastle.

Finally, a recurrent problem of teacher education centres on exposure of preservice teachers to the complexities and richness of classroom situations in such a way that they are able to draw meaning from these experiences. An interactive CD-ROM developed by the *Learning About Teaching* Project (Mousley, Sullivan and Mousley, 1996) – a cooperative venture of Deakin University and the Australian Catholic University – would appear to have considerable implications for distance learning. By linking lesson video-tapes with transcripts and probe questions within the context of research-based 'components of quality teaching', this model offers control over the complexities of the teaching experience and engages the learner actively in studying the process from a rich variety of perspectives.

8.1   Mathematics Teacher Education at a Distance

Developments in the electronic transmission of information using the Internet and, more recently, world wide web facilities, have ushered in a new era for education which universities have been quick to capitalise upon. The growing importance of electronic mail for academics appears to be the tip of the iceberg. Already, there are 'virtual universities' offering 'virtual courses' towards 'virtual degrees'.

In 1996 the Faculty of Education at the University of Newcastle offered its first electronic distance education subject in mathematics education. The subject *(Teaching Mathematics Through a Problem-posing and Problem-solving Approach)* is available in three forms: traditional text-based materials, in CD-

ROM format and via the world wide web. Apart from a set text, all readings for the subject are available electronically: in both Macintosh and Windows formats and in HTML form which may be read using the *Netscape* browser, again in either *Macintosh* or *Windows* platform.

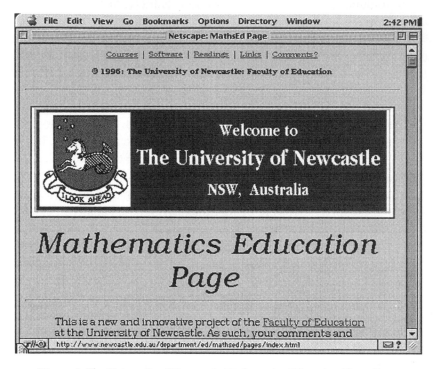

Figure 1. The University of Newcastle Mathematics Education Home Page.

The original concept for this course began with the idea of offering it via the internet, and so the choice of *Netscape* was an obvious one. Upon further reflection and discussion, it emerged that the majority of potential students are, as yet, unlikely to have full access to the facilities required for web browsing, and the idea of offering a CD-ROM option was considered. Although created as a web browser, *Netscape* is capable of functioning effectively as a viewer for local materials, as well as for those 'on-line'. By resetting the 'home page' within Netscape's preferences, the program can be easily configured to open at any selected page upon start-up. Figure 1 shows the *Mathematics Education Home Page* which greets students of the course.

Although this home page is available on-line, it was initially offered within the course CD-ROM. Students had the option of working through the course materials directly from the CD-ROM, or copying the appropriate files onto their own hard drives. Access to all remaining course information and materials is then available using hypertext links, placed throughout the materials and, importantly, at the top and bottom of each page, assisting the process of navigation through the myriad paths available.

This powerful hypertext facility is just one of the significant features of this approach to the development of distance education materials. The ease with which web pages may be created makes the process accessible to anyone with a little patience and the desire to learn. Increasingly, of course, there are programs designed to assist in this process, and it is a simple matter to take almost any word processor file (complete with formatting and graphics) and convert it directly into HTML form. The language itself, however, is quite transparent and offers the added advantage of working with ASCII text files, which may be readily transferred across any of the major platforms.

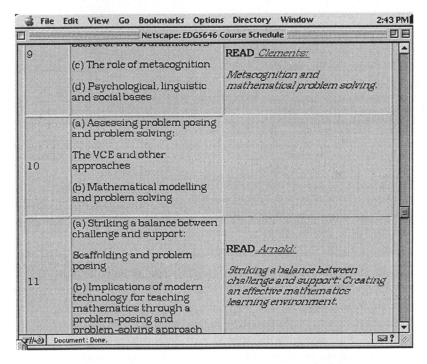

Figure 2. Excerpt from the EDGS646 Course Schedule.

The possibilities offered by hypertext facilities are challenging, essentially redefining existing approaches to instructional design. It is easy to get 'lost in hyperspace', and good page design and links must serve to minimise this problem. In addition to hypertext and cross-platform facilities, a web browser such as *Netscape* offers powerful multimedia capabilities (especially sound and video) which can serve to enhance the learning experience. In addition to the learning of mathematical concepts, of course, video options greatly enhance access to the teaching process for preservice teachers.

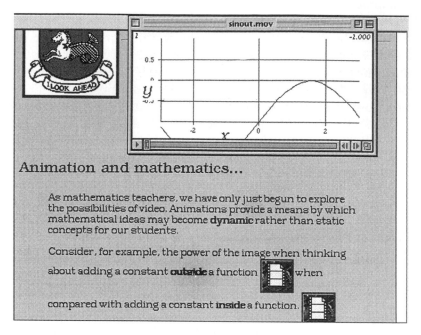

Animation and mathematics...

As mathematics teachers, we have only just begun to explore the possibilities of video. Animations provide a means by which mathematical ideas may become **dynamic** rather than static concepts for our students.

Consider, for example, the power of the image when thinking about adding a constant **outside** a function when compared with adding a constant **inside** a function.

Figure 3. Netscape as a Quicktime Viewer.

It is possible to configure Netscape to access other software packages. These 'helper' applications usually include video and sound players, file decompression programs and text editors. A wide range of other software applications, however, may also be defined as helpers, allowing Netscape to be used to access, for example, sample mathematical software, as in Figure 3, where the Macintosh freeware package *xFunctions* may be opened by clicking on its underlined name. The possibilities for creating interactive tutorial and instructional modules using this approach are still being explored.

An important advantage of the use of Netscape as a viewer for instructional materials is that it is free for educational purposes. Materials developed for students are accessible by them, free of charge. It seems clear that this approach to course development has much to offer teacher educators, and the potential is not limited to distance education. Consider, for example, transferring existing course materials (much of which is already in word processed form and so readily convertible) into HTML form and taking advantage of the cost and availability features of CD-ROM technology. Multimedia capabilities using such an approach are accessible to a far greater audience than just the programs of the past.

8.2 A Simulated Algebra Learning Environment

Over the past three years, a computer-based package called Exploring Algebra (Arnold, 1993) has been developed using HyperCard on the Macintosh, providing access to a range of mathematical software tools within algebra learning contexts spanning the secondary school years. This package tracks the progress of the user, probes thinking and understanding concerning key mathematical and pedagogic concepts, and saves the session record as a text file for analysis. In addition to use with secondary school students, the package has been trialed with several groups of preservice teachers as part of their study of technology in mathematics education and is to be used in distance mode with post-graduate students as a medium for professional development.

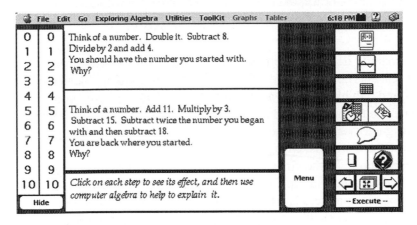

Figure 4. Introducing variables within Exploring Algebra.

The use of a simulated technology-rich algebra learning environment offers several advantages for preservice teacher education, in both distance and traditional modes. The modules offer a model of good practice for both algebra learning and the use of technology in mathematics learning. Students are provided with opportunities to use powerful mathematical software tools (many of which are free for educational purposes and so may be copied and used later in schools) within appropriate and thought-provoking contexts. Further, the materials themselves contain reflective prompts which engage the user in metacognitive activity, applying to the mathematical experience a range of pedagogical concerns. Of course, the flexibility of this approach offers some significant advantages in itself for both students and teachers, effectively removing the need for face-to-face teaching and lending itself ideally to distance modes of learning.

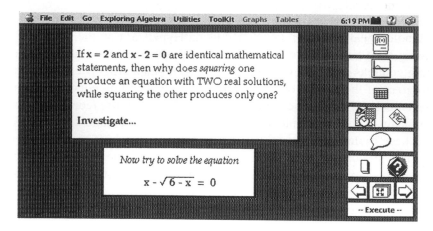

Figure 5. An interesting mathematical problem.

One interesting issue to arise from the research data gathered from the pre-service teachers concerned the distinction between 'thinking like a mathematician' and 'thinking like a mathematics teacher'. Two groups were introduced to the package and the supporting software tools, and both groups were assigned assessment tasks which required them to work through specific aspects of the materials, engage in the appropriate activities, and complete a reflective report. In the final analysis, however, it was clear that the two groups had responded quite differently: The first had engaged primarily in an evaluation of the materials from a teaching point of view (as they had been instructed). However, this group had failed to engage *mathematically* with the problems and activities – they appeared to have thought like 'mathematics teachers' in the sense that they did not see it as their role to engage in active problem solving.

When this was recognised from an initial analysis of the data, mathematical problem solving was made an explicit assessment priority for the second group. While this group, too, evaluated the materials from a teaching point of view, they attempted to come to grips with both the problems presented and the use of the software tools. Problems such as that illustrated in Figure 5 became the subject of active and persistent investigation on the part of the participants. The available software tools were used thoughtfully and mathematical insight was a common outcome of the process.

Clearly, the distinction between the mathematical and pedagogical thinking of preservice teachers is an important one. A significant aspect of the powerful new tools available for mathematics teaching and learning is the extent to which they empower the users (both teachers and students) mathematically, and the ways by which the technology facilitates the process whereby students and teachers become co-learners through the act of problem solving.

As a model for distance learning in the context of mathematics teacher preparation, the development of such simulated learning environments promises much if used thoughtfully. When coupled with the powerful mathematical software tools already available in areas such as computer algebra, dynamic geometry and interactive statistics, opportunities are provided for active engagement with the learning materials, both mathematically and pedagogically.

8.3   Learning about Teaching at a Distance

Potentially the most powerful influence of CD-ROM and multimedia approaches to teaching and learning will arise from their non-linear nature. The audio and video enhancements which have been an increasingly significant aspect of distance teaching over the past two decades provide *linear* access to their content. By contrast, CD-ROM provides *random* access, in which any section of the material may be accessed at any time and in any sequence. This technology offers significant implications for active and reflective approaches to learning, in which the user may 'interrogate' the materials easily and with unprecedented control. The innovative *Learning About Teaching* CD-ROM (Mousley, Sullivan and Mousley, 1996) makes full use of this technology in providing a means of studying and learning about the complexities of the teaching process.

Recent research by the authors of this program has identified six key components of quality teaching (Sullivan and Mousley, 1994):
  − Building understanding
  − Communicating
  − Engaging
  − Nurturing
  − Organising for learning
  − Problem solving

The *Learning About Teaching* program supports detailed analysis of a single lesson in terms of these and other significant concerns, using not only video but a broad range of interactive options (Figure 6 captures an excerpt from the video). For example, users wishing to explore 'patterns of communication' in a mathematics lesson would be able to call up such features as:
  − the teacher outlining her aims for the lesson, including her intention to have the children share their developing understandings;
  − patterns of verbal and non-verbal communication across an entire one-hour lesson;
  − individual interactions between the teacher and each pupil (as well as with the class and with small groups);
  − discussions between children as they investigated a problem;

- questions asked by each pupil of the teacher and of each other;
- a transcription of the lesson (with the ability to cross to the video at any point to check inflection and non-verbal aspects, etc.);
- children reporting back to the class what their groups had done and what they had learned;
- some recent journal articles about types of communication in classrooms;
- some specially written papers about specific aspects of communication (such as types of questions);
- some articles about certain purposes for classroom communication (such as engaging children in higher-level thinking);
- teacher responses to particular students' comments and questions;
- graphed data about aspects of communication (such as the number of interactions each child had with the teacher);
- a map of the classroom (with the ability to click on a group of desks to view the children's interactions;
- the teacher talking after the lesson about how students' contributions were the subject of formative evaluation; and
- a range of other resources. (Mousley and Sullivan, 1996)

Although mathematics teacher education is not alone in benefiting significantly from the influence of technology, it serves as an example of the potential for the redefinition of the teaching and learning process made possible by such advances.

9.   POTENTIAL DANGERS ASSOCIATED WITH DISTANCE EDUCATION

What, then, of the problems? The possibilities and potential benefits are exciting indeed, but the dramatic growth in distance modes of education alone in recent years gives cause for concern. Alongside the positive features there are significant dangers in the unbridled growth in this area, particularly as applied to the interactions between 'developed' and 'developing' nations.

9.1   Stage of Readiness for Technology

Some of the nations of the Asia/Pacific region have many well equipped education institutions which own, or have access to, sophisticated hardware and software. These institutions also have staff, or have access to staff, who are well trained not only in how to use modern technology but also in how to create effective learning environments which maximise the educational potential of the technology. Other nations in the Asia/Pacific region are not nearly at that stage, however. In some, the provision of electricity is not yet constant or reliable, and the repair and maintenance of hardware can present major problems.

Figure 6. An Excerpt from Learning about Teaching.

It makes no sense to assume that education institutions should all move at the same pace to incorporate the use of hi-tech, expensive equipment into their curricula. It may well be better to introduce well designed, more traditional courses which, in the short term, are mainly based on the print medium. Experience of institutions such as the Open University, in the United Kingdom, and a number of Australian universities, has shown that effective distance education programs can be developed which do not *necessarily* depend on access to advanced technology.

There is a danger that the education policy makers of some nations, dazzled by the apparent power of modern technology, will allow hi-tech distance education programs to be designed and implemented which are unsuited to the economic and technological stages of development of those nations. Consultants from more developed nations need to be wary of the temptation to recommend to less developed nations that they move immediately to develop hi-tech distance education programs, when these are not what are needed at the present time.

Furthermore, as Michael Grant (1995) of Edith Cowan University, has written 'bad graphics, bad sound, bad video, or bad design will not be made better by the multimedia technology – in fact they may be made worse!' For hi-tech distance education programs to be effective, educators will not only need to have reliable access to well-maintained equipment, but they will also need to appreciate how this equipment can be used effectively in education settings.

9.2   Colonialism and Distance Education – Learning From Mathematics Education

Most educators would accept the view that one of the aims of education is to enhance learners' knowledge and appreciations of local institutions and society, and that local cultures, religions, languages, and history need to be respected. However, it is also the case that many educators believe that the content and the methods for *some* subjects in a curriculum should not vary significantly from country to country. It is often assumed, for example, that the ability to acquire mathematical, scientific and technological skills is, or should be, dependent on having an adequate grounding in those more or less culture-free skills which are associated with internationalised understandings of mathematics, science and technology.

For example, a paper prepared for the first Board meeting of the Commonwealth of Learning pointed to the fact that since many developing countries are particularly short of scientists, technologists and engineers, high quality distance-teaching materials already in existence in developed countries should be used to provide effective education and training in mathematics, science and engineering (Commonwealth of Learning, 1988). Implicit in this view is the idea that provided they are suitably modified, quality distance education materials prepared in one country can readily be used in another country.

Such assumptions are accepted by many educators throughout the world. Their acceptance is particularly strong among educators in those countries which are often referred to as 'developing nations' (Ellerton and Clements, 1989). However, such attitudes are likely to generate *more* rather than *less* inequality in educational achievement. Higher enrolments, achieved largely through compulsory attendance regulations, will be offset by failure and rejection of formal education systems by students who find the so-called 'culture-free' education offerings irrelevant to their needs (Clements, Grimison, and Ellerton, 1989).

740

It may also be argued that the assumption that certain subjects within a curriculum can be culture-free represents a 'colonialist' way of thinking. Colonialism in education has been defined as:

> ... an attitude of mind accepted by both the leaders and representatives of the colonising power and by those who are being colonised, that what goes on 'at home' should also take place in the colonies. While this 'acceptance' is sometimes a conscious act, more often it is unconscious – people behave in a colonialist way simply because that is the way they have learnt to behave.
>
> (Clements, et al., 1989, p. 72)

In regard to this statement, it is important to note that the concept of 'colonialism' is being used in its *educational* rather its *political* sense. Australia, for example, might be regarded as having allowed itself to be colonised in its educational thinking and practices by both the United Kingdom and the United States of America.

Often, political and educational forms of colonialism have acted in parallel. For example, in Commonwealth countries there has always been a tendency among educators in the colonies to mimic what has been happening in schools in England (Clements et al., 1989). Thus, those attempting to explain why the payment-by-results system (Dear, 1975) – with all its attendant instrumental effects on school mathematics – was introduced into the Australian colonies in the 1860's need not look far beyond the fact that the system was introduced in England just before its introduction in Australia. It should also be observed that the same system was adopted later in the nineteenth century in many British Commonwealth colonies including India, Ceylon, East Africa and Malaya (Watson, 1982).

9.3   The Case of Mathematics

Clearly, a form of colonialism has been shaping the curricula, assessment policies and indeed the perceived *raison d'etre* of school and university mathematics in many countries around the world. Such thinking has not been confined to countries politically regarded as colonies, or to the nineteenth or early twentieth century. Rather, it has been and continues to be evident in the relationship between many developing countries and so-called 'advanced' nations, such as the United States of America, the United Kingdom, and Russia. In order to appreciate how colonialist ideas can have an impact on those responsible for developing distance education policies and practices, it will be useful to consider the effects of colonialism on mathematics education. Much has been written about such matters elsewhere (see, for example, Ellerton and Clements, 1988).

Despite the best intentions of all concerned, the employment of education consultants from 'advanced' countries for the purpose of advising on curricula in developing countries has nurtured, developed and maintained colonialist attitudes and policies in schools and universities. So, for instance, after the 'New Math(s)' was introduced in the United States, France, and the United Kingdom, in the late 1950's and 1960's, it was inevitable that versions of the same 'New Math(s)' would subsequently be introduced in many other countries, despite the fact that it was meeting with only limited success in those countries where it had been originally introduced (Moon, 1986). Similar arguments could be developed with respect to PSSC Physics, and certain other curriculum packages.

One is reminded of Paulo Fréire's (1985) words: 'Propaganda, slogans, myths are the instruments employed by the invader to achieve his objectives: to persuade those invaded that they must be the objects of his action, that they must be the docile prisoners of his conquest'. Fréire (1985) added that 'it is incumbent on the invader to destroy the character of the culture which has been invaded, nullify its form, and replace it with the by-products of the invading culture' (p. 114), and argued for the establishment of dialogue which avoids cultural invasion. Some may regard Fréire's views as extreme, but we believe that his sentiments need to be noted by all involved in the export of education, especially through forms of distance education.

9.4   An Illustrative Example

The folly of trying to impose fairly common mathematics courses on students at any level, and from different cultures, has become increasingly evident. Such attempts inevitably result in learners from major groups (including, for example, females, the working classes, and ethnic and racial groups) being disadvantaged, yet this happens in a social climate aiming to achieve 'equality of educational opportunity' (Clements, 1992).

This point was amplified in the mid-1970's by data obtained in a large investigation into the literacy and numeracy skills of Australians aged 10 and 14 years carried out by the Australian Council for Educational Research (ACER). The sample for this study included subsamples of tribal Aborigines, mainly from the Northern Territory, and urban Aborigines from different parts of Australia. The urban Aborigines performed significantly less well on the numeration tests when compared with non-Aboriginal children of the same age, and the tribal Aboriginal children showed next to no understanding of the written tasks. Bourke and Parkin (1977), in reporting these findings, concluded that the questions on the literacy and numeracy tests involved ideas which were largely foreign to the tribal Aboriginal children's cultures, a point emphasised by writers with an empathy for Aboriginal cultures (for example, Harris, 1987, 1989, 1991; Watson, 1988, 1989).

742

One example from the 1975 ACER study will serve to illustrate this point. Both the 10- and 14-year-old students who were tested were asked to write down the time shown on a watch-face: the watch used for the younger students had Arabic numerals on its face, but that used for the older students had only strokes. The times shown were 11:35 and 4:40 for the 10- and 14-year-olds, respectively, and results obtained are set out in Table 1. Bourke and Parkin (1977), in commenting on the very small percentage of tribal Aboriginal respondents who gave correct answers to these time questions, stated that the tasks themselves were 'certainly outside the experience of many' (p. 149).

Age Group	% of Correct Responses for ...		
	Tribal Aboriginal Children	Urban Aboriginal Children	Australia Overall
10 year olds	2	25	71
14 year olds	3	73	89

Table 1. Performance on Time-Telling Tasks by Three Groups of Students.

Harris's (1991) report on Aboriginal time, space and money concepts lends strong support to the view that what is regarded as 'basic' in one culture can be irrelevant in another. Many Aborigines do not make use of Western notions of time. It follows that the very existence of an internationalised curriculum is likely to be sufficient to ensure that many teachers and lecturers will waste much time trying to help unprepared and increasingly disaffected students acquire skills that although described as 'basic' are, for these learners, almost meaningless. And that will be true no matter how much hi-tech is employed in the delivery of the curriculum.

IN CONCLUSION: EIGHT PROPOSITIONS FOR MATHEMATICS EDUCATION AT A DISTANCE

This chapter concludes with the statement of eight propositions which arise from the previous discussion. Derived from the research of Ellerton and Clements (1989, 1996), they provide a framework within which the current and potential growth of distance education and flexible modes of teaching and learning should be considered.

1. Assumptions Influencing Current Developments in Mathematics Education Involving Flexible Modes of Learning Urgently Need to be Identified

The face of primary, secondary and tertiary education around the world changed dramatically during the twentieth century. In 1900, less than 1 per cent of the world's population had gained a secondary education, and an even smaller proportion went on to study at a university (Connell, 1980). In most countries school and tertiary mathematics courses were based on rigid, externally prescribed curricula, formal textbooks, and written examinations, and it was accepted that only the best students should go on to higher mathematical studies (Clements, 1992).

As the twentieth century progressed, universal elementary education became a reality in many countries, and an increasing proportion of the population gained access to secondary and higher education. Recent trends, especially with respect to flexible modes of delivery, make it certain that the number of students studying mathematics in secondary schools will increase dramatically over the next few decades. It is also clear that many prospective or practising teachers of mathematics will want to study mathematics and/or mathematics education at a distance. The largest universities in the world are now distance education institutions, and many of those enrolled are teachers, seeking to upgrade their qualifications.

This first proposition calls for the identification of the underlying assumptions from which education policies – and, in particular, mathematics education policies – have been developed. Implicit in the proposition is the question: What needs to be done to reduce, and ultimately eliminate, the prevalence and force of unwarranted assumptions?

Proposition 1. Many inadequate assumptions influence ways in which mathematics teaching and learning at a distance is organised and practised. The identification of those assumptions which most urgently need to be questioned represents the first, and perhaps most important, *problématique* of contemporary distance education as it relates to mathematics.

It may be argued that, increasingly, during the twentieth century, many on-campus school and university curricula – and in particular mathematics curricula – were of questionable relevance for most learners (Ellerton and Clements, 1988). More generally, those assumptions which had most influence on those responsible for planning, teaching and assessing mathematics programs were inherited from nineteenth century patterns of education. These assumptions, and corresponding expectations for what mathematics education programs should achieve, increasingly did not fit the new circumstances of the twentieth century. Yet, they have been applied to most contemporary flexible mode education programs. Such assumptions are likely to be hopelessly inadequate, and indeed inappropriate, for the 21st century.

A word of warning concerning this first proposition is in order: it is unlikely that any set of unwarranted assumptions would be culture-free. In other words, what is educationally appropriate (or inappropriate) in one culture will not necessarily be appropriate (or inappropriate) in another.

2. Flexible Mode Mathematics Education Programs Should Do More Than Merely Prepare Students for the Next Highest Level of Education

With traditional on-campus modes of education, the curriculum and standards of learners at any level have traditionally been linked with those at the next level, and these expectations have not changed much over time. Given the increasingly diverse range of backgrounds of students, and the increasing use of flexible modes, distance educators need to take up the challenge of developing curricula and practices which genuinely meet the needs of individual learners, of all ages and in all cultures.

That is to say, formal education institutions should not only be *open* to all who wish to learn, but their curricula should be *appropriate* to their needs. That philosophy has been fundamental to the establishment of 'open universities' around the world. However, it is not an easy task for institutions of higher learning, even those which carry the word 'open' in their name, to be truly 'open'. Tensions inevitably arise in trying to achieve an acceptable balance between, status, quality, and curriculum relevance.

It is open to question whether it is reasonable for mathematics and science departments in tertiary faculties to continue to use fixed curricula which expect each successive group of incoming students to have with the same basic mathematical knowledge, year after year, and be able to do the same kind of activities, at about the same levels. In particular, individual, cultural, and social factors should be vital considerations in mathematics curriculum development, implementation, and evaluation processes.

Many universities have introduced 'bridging programs' to bring 'deficient' mathematics students to an 'acceptable' level; others have chosen simply to fail greater proportions of students. The possibility that schooling no longer provides the best preparation for many first-year tertiary mathematics education programs needs to be taken seriously.

Attempts by school systems and universities to reform their mathematics curricula have often been opposed by education policy makers and higher education institutions on the grounds that new courses might not prepare students as well for existing programs. This desire to maintain 'standards' may not be rationally based, and should be subjected to scrutiny through research.

This is the basis for the second proposition:

Proposition 2. Preparation for a culture-free internationalised education agenda should not be the primary concern of those concerned with developing flexible-mode mathematics education programs for adults.

In particular, the quality of mathematics education programs should not be judged by how many students subsequently proceed to the next year of their tertiary studies.

3. Language Factors Should be of Central Concern in Mathematics Education Taught and Learned at a Distance

Our third proposition is in line with comments made by Secada (1988) on how cultural minorities and students in many so-called developing countries have been tacitly regarded as only of marginal relevance in much education research. Secada pointed out that in much of the world it is normal to be bilingual, yet most mathematics education research has focused on monolingual children – with bilingual children being regarded as likely to need special attention.

Secada's point is well made. In many countries, including industrialised Western countries, there are children (in some cases, a majority of school children) who are required to learn in classrooms where the language of instruction is not their first language. Sometimes young children sit in classrooms for years without understanding what the teacher or textbook writer or examiner is saying. Ironically, it is often claimed that in order to achieve 'equality of educational opportunity' the language of instruction and the curriculum should be the same for all, or most, children attending schools in the same country. With distance education, communication is obviously of primary importance, and therefore distance educators, faced with the challenge of creating new cultures and expectations, in education, need to pay careful attention to language issues.

This leads to the third proposition:

Proposition 3: In this age of flexible delivery modes, the implications for educators – and particularly for mathematics educators – of the fact that many learners are bilingual or even multilingual urgently need to be explored.

Many linguistic factors impinge upon learning, and although much has been done in regard to identifying and relating these factors, more research is needed, especially in relation to distance education programs in mathematics and/ or mathematics education (Ellerton and Clements, 1991).

746

4. Education Policy Makers Responding to the Challenges of Flexible Delivery Modes Need to be Conscious of the Dangers of Cultural Imperialism

According to Bishop (1990), almost all educators falsely believe that 'western mathematics' is neutral. A similar neutrality is often attributed to imported distance education programs. The mystique and values of western education systems and high technology have readily been accepted by most local and national leaders, for it is thought that somehow they hold the key to economic and educational development.

The fourth proposition is:

Proposition 4: The assumption that it is reasonable to accept forms of distance education in mathematics and/or mathematics education which result in a large proportion of learners following a linear, behaviourist curriculum, and being subjected to narrow assessment procedures should be rejected. Alternative forms of distance education for mathematics, by which greater value would be accorded to the cultural and linguistic backgrounds of learners, should be explored.

In relation to Proposition 4, it is recognised that mathematics education must always be political – in the sense that it inevitably will impose certain values on students and compel them to be involved in certain activities (Harris, 1991; Mellin-Olsen, 1987).

5. Cultural Biases Implicit in Existing Education Theories Need to be Questioned

It is extremely unlikely that the domain of education, in general, and of mathematics education in particular, is controlled by culture-free laws which can be progressively identified through research.

The influence of certain theories – such as the Piagetian epistemologies and stages of learning, Vygotskyan ideas on scaffolding, the SOLO taxonomy, Skinner's behaviourism, notions of outcomes-based-education, and certain information processing models – on the thinking of mathematics education researchers, may or may not have advanced the quality of mathematics teaching and learning around the world over the past decades. However, powerful figures who have insisted that research based on such theoretical models is superior to research in which more exploratory approaches are preferred, have succeeded in creating restricting, and sometimes arguably colonialist, even racist, mindsets within an influential section of curriculum developers.

Proposition 5: The idea that the best mathematics education programs are those based on coherent, internationally developed theoretical frameworks of learning (like, for example, Piagetian, or Vygotskyan, or Outcomes-Based-Learning frameworks) should be subjected to careful scrutiny.

Clements and Ellerton (in press) have pointed to the dubious methods used by some to defend their own theoretical positions. For example, rhetorical statements such as Kurt Lewin's 'there is nothing as practical as good theory and nothing as theoretical as good practice' are often thrown at those who argue that at the present moment education needs *more* reflective, more culture-sensitive, and more practice-oriented research, and *less* theory-driven research. While accepting the second part of Lewin's statement ('... there is nothing as theoretical as good practice'), Clements and Ellerton (in press) have offered an alternative to the first part of Lewin's statement: 'In mathematics education there is nothing so *dangerous* as speculative theory based on small-sample data – or indeed, mere reflection – of influential individuals in a single culture'.

The advent of distance education, with all its multi-modal communication challenges involving high technology, provides educators with the perfect opportunity to rethink their educational theories and, indeed, to question long-accepted relationships between theory and practice. A process of deconstruction and reconstruction is called for. Given the troubled history of mathematics education in the 19th and 20th century, distance education is providing mathematics educators with an opportunity to redefine their domain.

6. New Epistemological Frameworks for Curricula Offered Through Flexible Delivery Modes Need to be Developed

The sixth proposition concerns the need to establish new epistemological frameworks for mathematics education programs, especially those offered by flexible delivery modes. Such frameworks would need to emphasise the importance of recognising the histories and cultures of learners.

Proposition 6: A suitable framework for achieving a more unified and systematic approach to developing mathematics education programs incorporating flexible modes of delivery is needed. One possible approach would focus on co-ordinated curricula and programs which

a) linked the histories and development of curricula, within local, national, and international contexts;

b) took into account the influences of culture on the curricula, and in particular recognised the impact of home, schooling, and society on learners' thinking and learning processes.

A framework based on Proposition 6 need not be unduly restrictive. However, it is essential that local educators are fully involved in any curriculum development exercise.

7. New Methods for Monitoring and Assessing Learning Need to be Developed

It should be obvious that distance educators face a major problem so far as the valid assessment of mathematics learning is concerned. The new technologies obviously provide educators with the opportunity to develop more authentic methods by which students' progress can be monitored and assessed. Given the reality of flexible modes of course and program delivery, it would be difficult to sustain an argument that assessment of students enrolled in education programs of any kind, and at any level, would be best done through short-answer and multiple-choice pencil-and-paper forms of testing.

Proposition 7: Closer scrutiny needs to be given to the issue of how performance is best defined and measured for mathematics education programs being offered at all levels. Pressure should be exerted on education authorities to apply contemporary findings of research into assessment alternatives.

In other words, politicians, education bureaucrats, educators (including mathematics educators) should begin to pay more than lip service to the truism that, in education, what is assessed is what is valued, and that what is valued is what is assessed. The question is, of course, how to do this and yet at the same time be seen to be maintaining 'standards'. It is important that, in time, graduates of distance mathematics programs be regarded as no less qualified – and perhaps even more qualified – as graduates of traditional on-campus programs.

8. The Inalienable Right to Lifelong Mathematics Education

None of the above propositions touches on the important principle that all people, regardless of age, gender, race, or creed, should have full opportunity to participate in both formal and informal mathematics education. Practices which attempt to maximise the potential contributions of *all* participants in mathematics educational activity at *all* stages of that activity, including the design and reporting stages, need to be become commonplace.

Proposition 8: All people, regardless of age, gender, race, or creed, should be free to participate fully in formal and informal mathematics education programs. Furthermore, the views of lecturers, teachers, and students involved in the programs should be sought and taken seriously by those who frame education policies. Mathematics education policies should not be developed *solely* by 'experts' outside the cultures of learners.

Just as centre-to-periphery models of curriculum change are likely to be actively resisted by teachers and lecturers, so too are curriculum decisions emanating from persons who are perceived, by students, teachers and lecturers to be too remote to understand the pressures which shape what is possible in mathematics education programs.

In particular, effective partnerships need to be developed in which all partners have equal status. Steps should be taken to implement policies which empower local educators to provide high quality mathematics education programs.

REFERENCES

Arnold, S.M.: 1993, *Exploring Algebra: A Computer Based Approach,* Australian Association of Mathematics Teachers, Adelaide.
Bates A.W.: 1995, 'Creating the Future: Developing Vision in Open and Distance Learning', in F. Lockwood (ed.), *Open and Distance Learning Today*, Routledge and Kegan Paul, London, 42-51.
Bergeron, J.C. and Herscovics, N.: 1990, 'Kindergartners' knowledge of the preconcepts of number', in L. P. Steffe and T. Wood (eds.), *Transforming Children's Mathematics Education: International Perspectives,* Lawrence Erlbaum, Hillsdale, NJ, 125-134.
Bigelow, J. and Pargetter, R.: 1990, *Science and Necessity,* Cambridge University Press, Cambridge, UK.
Bishop, A.J.: 1988, *Mathematical Enculturation,* Kluwer, Dordrecht.
Bishop, A.J.: 1990, 'Western Mathematics: The Secret Weapon of Cultural Imperialism', *Race & Class* 32(2), 51-65.
Bourke, S.F. and Parkin, B.: 1977, 'The Performance of Aboriginal Students', in S.F. Bourke and J.P. Keeves (eds.), *Australian Studies in School Performance: Volume 3, The Mastery of Literacy and Numeracy,* Australian Government Printing Service, Canberra, 1977, 131-155.
Briggs, Lord: 1987, *Towards a Commonwealth of Learning,* Commonwealth Secretariat, London.
Brotosiswojo, B.S.: 1995, *An Experience in Managing a Large System of Distance Education,* Paper given at the First International Symposium on 'Networks into the 21st Century: Prospects for Distance Education', held in Yogyakarta, Indonesia, November 1995.
Burge, L.: 1995, 'Electronic highway or Weaving Loom? Thinking About Conferencing Technologies for Learning', in F. Lockwood (ed.), *Open and Distance Learning Today*, Routledge and Kegan Paul, London, 151-163.
Chambers, E.: 1995, 'Course Evaluation and Academic Quality', in F. Lockwood (ed.), *Open and Distance Learning Today*, Routledge and Kegan Paul, London, 343-353.

Clarke, D.J.: 1984, 'Secondary Mathematics Teaching: Towards a Critical Appraisal of Current Practice', *Vinculum* 21(4), 16-21.

Clements, M. A.: 1992, *Mathematics for the Minority: Some Historical Perspectives of School Mathematics in Victoria,* Deakin University, Geelong.

Clements, M.A.: 1995, *Maximising the Potential of International Co-operation Through Distance Education,* Paper given at the First International Symposium on 'Networks into the 21st Century: Prospects for Distance Education', held in Yogyakarta, Indonesia, November 1995.

Clements, M.A.: 1996. 'Linking Australian and Southeast Asian Education Through Distance Education', in A. Barthel (ed.), *Intercultural Interaction and Development: Converging Perspectives,* University of Technology, Sydney, 12-28.

Clements, M.A. and Ellerton, N.F.: in press, *Mathematics Education Research: Past, Present, and Future,* UNESCO, Bangkok.

Clements, M.A., Grimison, L. and Ellerton, N.F.: 1989, 'Colonialism and School Mathematics in Australia 1788-1988', in N.F. Ellerton and M.A. Clements (eds.), *School Mathematics: The Challenge to Change,* Deakin University Press, Geelong, 1989, 50-78.

Coffey, J., Hubbard, G., Humphries, C., Jenkins, J. and Yates, C.: 1988, *Commonwealth Co-operation in Open Learning: Summary Report,* Commonwealth Secretariat, London.

Commonwealth of Learning: 1988, *Programme Activities,* Board of Governors' Paper BG1/10,

Connell, W.F.: 1980, *A History of Education in the Twentieth Century World,* Curriculum Development Centre, Canberra.

Cuban, L.: 1993, *How Teachers Taught: Constancy and Change in American Classrooms 1890-1990,* Teachers College Press, New York.

Dear, K.E.: 1975, 'Payment by Results' and the Status of Teachers in Victoria 1862-1872, in S. Murray-Smith (ed.), *Melbourne Studies in Education 1975*, Melbourne University Press, Melbourne, 66-93.

Del Campo, G. and Clements, M.A.: 1990, 'Expanding the Modes of Communication in Mathematics Classrooms', *Journal für Mathematik-Didaktik.* **11**(1). 45-79.

Ellerton, N.F. and Clements, M.A.: 1988, 'Reshaping School Mathematics in Australia 1788-1988', *Australian Journal of Education* 32(3), 387-405.

Ellerton, N.F. and Clements, M.A.: 1989, *Teaching Post-secondary Mathematics at a Distance: A Report to the Commonwealth Secretariat,* Deakin University, Geelong.

Ellerton, N.F. and Clements, M.A.: 1990, 'Culture, Curriculum and Distance Teaching of Mathematics', in T. Evans (ed.), *Research in Distance Education,* Deakin University Press, Geelong (Victoria), 200-218.

Ellerton, N. F. and Clements, M.A.: 1991, *Mathematics in Language: A Review of Language Factors in Mathematics Learning,* Deakin University, Geelong.

Ellerton, N.F. and Clements, M.A.: 1994, *The National Curriculum Debacle,* Meridian Press, Perth.

Ellerton, N.F. and Clements, M.A.: 1996, 'Locating Mathematics, Science, and Technology Education Within the Context of High Technology and Flexible Delivery Education Programmes', *Journal of Science and Mathematics Education in Southeast Asia, 19*(1), 21-32.

Evans, T. D.: 1995, 'The Potential of Research with Students to Inform Development', in F. Lockwood, *Open and Distance Learning Today,* Routledge and Kegan Paul, London, 1995, 67-75.

Evers, C.W. and Walker, J.C.: 1983, 'Knowledge, Partitioned Sets and Extensionality: A Refutation of the Forms of Knowledge Thesis', *Journal of the Philosophy of Education* 17(2), 155-170.

Fréire, P. : 1985, *Education for Critical Consciousness,* Sheed and Ward, London.

Grant, M.: 1995, *... It Makes it Hard to Turn the Machine Off.* Unpublished paper, Edith Cowan University.

Hareng, H., Ali, T., Sadjad, R. and Johari, R.: 1995, *Eastern Indonesian Distance Education Satellite System: Lessons Learned and Future Prospects.* Paper presented at the First International Symposium on 'Networking into the 21st Century', held in Yogyakarta, Indonesia.

Harris, P.: 1987, *Measurement in Tribal Aboriginal Communities,* Northern Territory Department of Education, Darwin.

Harris, P.: 1989, 'Contexts for Change in Cross-cultural Classrooms', in N.F. Ellerton, and M.A. Clements (eds.), *School Mathematics: The Challenge to Change,* Deakin University., Geelong, 1989, 79-95.

Harris, P.: 1991, *Mathematics in a Cultural Context: Aboriginal Perspectives of Space, Time and Money,* Deakin University, Geelong.

Herlihy, P.: 1986, 'Letter to the Editor', *Vinculum.* 23(4), 15-16.

Hirst K.E.: 1972, 'The Open University?Mathematics Foundation Course', *Mathematics Teaching* 60, 59-62.

Howson G and Wilson, B.: 1986, *School Mathematics in the 1990's.* ICMI Study Series, Cambridge University Press.

Keegan, D.: 1986, *The Foundations of Distance Education,* Croom Helm, London.

Kia, A.: 1995, *Finally, a Practical and Affordable Distance Learning System,* Paper given at the First International Symposium on 'Networks into the 21st Century: Prospects for Distance Education', held in Yogyakarta, Indonesia, November 1995.

Killen, R.: 1996, *Effective Teaching Strategies,* Social Science Press, Wentworth Falls, NSW.

Kline, M.: 1979, *Mathematics in Western Culture,* Penguin, Harmondsworth.

Kline, M.: 1980, *Mathematics: The Loss of Certainty,* Oxford University Press, Oxford.

Koumi, J.: 1995, 'Building Good Quality In, Rather than Inspecting Bad Quality Out', in F. Lockwood, *Open and Distance Learning Today,* Routledge and Kegan Paul, London, 1995.

Lakatos, I.: 1976, *Proofs and Refutations: The Logic of Mathematical Discovery,* Cambridge University Press, Cambridge, UK.

Lakoff, G.: 1987, *Women, Fire and Dangerous Things: What Categories Reveal About the Mind,* University of Chicago Press, Chicago.

Lockwood, F. (ed.): 1995, 'Students' Perception of, and Response to, Formative and Summative Assessment Material', in F. Lockwood (ed.), *Open and Distance Learning Today,* Routledge and Kegan Paul, London, 197-207.

Lowe, R.: 1995, 'Using Instructional Illustrations for Distance Education', in F. Lockwood (ed.), *Open and Distance Learning Today,* Routledge and Kegan Paul, London, 288-300.

Marsh, C.J.: 1994, *Producing a National Curriculum: Plans and Paranoia,* Allen and Unwin, Sydney

Mellin-Olsen, S.: 1987, *The Politics of Mathematics Education,* Reidel, Dordrecht.

Moon, B.: 1986, *The 'New Maths' Curriculum Controversy,* Falmer Press, Barcombe, East Sussex.

Mousley, J. and Sullivan, P.: 1996, *The Learning About Teaching Project.* Accompanying documentation, Deakin University, Geelong.

Mousley, J., Sullivan, P. and Mousley, P.: 1996, *Learning About Teaching*, Deakin University, Geelong.

Mukhopadhyay, M.: 1995, *Shifting Paradigms in Open and Distance Education,* Paper given at the First International Symposium on 'Networks into the 21st Century: Prospects for Distance Education', held in Yogyakarta, Indonesia, November 1995.

Oldham, E.: 1989, 'Is There an International Mathematics Curriculum?' in B. Greer and G. Mulhern (eds.), *New Directions in Mathematics Education*, Routledge, London, 185-224.

Open University.: 1995, *Undergraduate Courses, 1996,* The Open University (UK), Milton Keynes, UK.

Peck, F.: 1995, *Classrooms of the Future Program.* Paper presented at the First International Symposium on 'Networking into the 21st Century', held in Yogyakarta, Indonesia.

Perraton, H.: 1995, 'A Practical Agenda for Theorists of Distance Education', in F. Lockwood (ed.), *Open and Distance Learning Today,* Routledge and Kegan Paul, London, 13-22.

Perry, W.: 1972, *The Early Developments of the Open University,* The Open University, Bletchley, Bucks.

Puwanto: 1995, *The Growth of Diploma 2 By Air (D2 Air).* Paper given at the First International Symposium on 'Networks into the 21st Century: Prospects for Distance Education', held in Yogyakarta, Indonesia, November 1995.

Rahardjo, R.: 1995, *SMP Terbuka: A Distance Learner Sampler at the Junior Secondary Level,* Paper given at the First International Symposium on 'Networks into the 21st Century: Prospects for Distance Education', held in Yogyakarta, Indonesia, November 1995.

Romiszowski: 1995, 'Use of Hypermedia and Telecommunications for Case-study Discussions in Distance Education', in F. Lockwood (ed.), *Open and Distance Learning Today*, Routledge and Kegan Paul, London.

Rucker, R.: 1982, *Infinity and the Mind,* Harvester Press, London.

Russell. B.: 1974, *History of Western Philosophy,* Unwin, London.

Secada, W.G.: 1988, 'Diversity, Equity, and Cognitivist Research', in E. Fennema, T.P. Carpenter, and S.J. Lamon (eds.).: *Integrating Research on Teaching and Learning Mathematics,* University of Wisconsin-Madison, Madison, 1988, 20-58.

Shanker, S.: 1987, *Gödel's Theorem in Focus,* Croom Helm, London.

Stigler, J.W. and Baranes, R.: 1988, 'Culture and Mathematics Learning', in E.Z. Rothkopf (ed.), *Review of Research in Education, 15, 1988-89,* American Educational Research Association, Washington, 253-306.

Stillwell, J.: 1988, 'The World of Mathematics', *Vinculum.* 25(1), 6-8.

Stodolsky, S.: 1988, *The Subject Matters: Classroom Activity in Math and Social Studies,* University of Chicago Press, Chicago.

Sullivan, P. and Mousley, J.: 1994, 'Quality Mathematics Teaching: Describing Some Key Components', *Mathematics Education Research Journal.* 6(1), 4-22.

Syarief, H. and Seligman, D.: 1995, *Human Resource Development Through Distance Learning Networks.* Paper presented at the First International Symposium on 'Networking into the 21st Century', held in Yogyakarta, Indonesia.

Thorpe, M.: 1995, 'The Challenge Facing Course Design', in F. Lockwood (ed.), *Open and Distance Learning Today*, Routledge and Kegan Paul, London, 175-184.

von Glasersfeld, E.: 1989, 'Cognition, Construction of Knowledge, and Teaching', *Synthese* 80(1), 121-140.

Watson, H.R.: 1988, 'The Ganma Project: Research in Mathematics Education by the Yolngu Community in the Schools of the Laynhapuy: N.E. Arnhemland', In R.P. Hunting, (ed.), *Language Issues in Learning and Teaching Mathematics,* La Trobe University, Melbourne.

Watson, H.R.: 1989, 'A Wittgensteinian View of Mathematics: Implications for Teachers of Mathematics', in N.F. Ellerton and M.A. Clements (eds.), *School Mathematics: The Challenge to Change,* Deakin University, Geelong, 18-30.

Watson, K.: 1982, 'Colonialism and Educational Development', in K. Watson (ed.), *Education in the Third World,* Croom Helm, London, 1-46.

Wittgenstein, L.: 1956, *Remarks on the Foundations of Mathematics,* Basil Blackwell, Oxford.

Chapter 20: Adults and Mathematics (Adult Numeracy)

GAIL E. FITZSIMONS, HELGA JUNGWIRTH, JEURGEN MAAß AND
WOLFGANG SCHLOEGLMANN
Swinburne University of Technology, Australia and Johannes Kepler University, Linz, Austria

ABSTRACT

This chapter investigates the current state of knowledge of teaching and learning involving adults currently or potentially participating in educational activities where mathematics (or numeracy) is involved. It addresses relevant educational issues from socio-economic, technological, and personal perspectives of participants, educators and the general community (including business and industry). These include the complexity of defining the concepts of numeracy and mathematics education, the state of adults' knowledge and understanding of mathematics in both cognitive and affective domains, and the organisational structures (courses, curriculum, teachers, participants, teaching-learning processes) prevalent in further education. The heterogeneity of the field makes it impossible to provide a comprehensive overview, but the chapter provides a range of perspectives, and attempts to identify gaps in our current knowledge. This burgeoning field is resistant to definitive categorisation, but is being recognized as one of increasing importance to all stakeholders. We have suggested but a few of the substantial array of directions for future research, which could be informed by the disciplines of history, philosophy, psychology, and sociology, to name a few. Information was gathered from a literature review, comprised mainly of journal articles, books and conference proceedings, as well as authors' own collective experience.

1. INTRODUCTION

1.1 Numeracy and Mathematical Education – Two Terms for One Subject

The attempt to describe basic features of the field 'adults and mathematics' leads primarily to realising the great heterogeneity of this field: Heterogeneity is the very term for its description. Scholarship shows, of course, diversity within the field 'children/young people and mathematics' – especially when international comparisons are made. There is, however, a unique term used to specify the subject: It is always mathematics, or the children's relationships to mathematics. This is not the case with adults, where two main terms are

A.J. Bishop et al. (eds.), International Handbook of Mathematics Education, 755 - 784

used to describe the subject: mathematics and numeracy; other variations include mathematical literacy and critical numeracy. Whether the topic of interest is adults' relationships to mathematics, or adult numeracy, probably depends on the socio-cultural surroundings in which the research takes place. It is difficult to know which factors will determine the label of the subject. On one hand, the peculiarities of the school or learning place – and the educational system as a whole – may play a role, on the other hand, special cultural features may be important; for instance, the extent to which more pragmatic approaches are pursued in relation to those which are more theoretically-oriented and sophisticated.

In the German-speaking countries, for example, only the term 'mathematics' is used in scholarship and in public discussion – the questions are: how well adults are educated in mathematics, the extent of their mathematical knowledge, the requirements this knowledge should meet, etc. It is not clear what being mathematically well-educated really means. There are different interpretations of this term, and the following adopts a very broad perspective. According to this, being mathematically well-educated firstly means to have a sound mathematical knowledge, i.e. to know important concepts and methods and to be able to apply them in an appropriate way to various problems. Secondly, a mathematically well-educated person has acquired knowledge about concepts and methods typically utilized in mathematics – about their power, and about their limitations. Such knowledge about mathematics is very important; for instance, when results gained by mathematical means have to be evaluated, such as forecasts of the economic situation, or the outcomes of opinion polls. Having knowledge about mathematics implies knowing about the limits of the application of mathematics, too. Underlying a narrow concept of mathematics this kind of knowledge is called meta-knowledge. Thirdly, being mathematically well-educated includes having a clear picture of, and a critical, yet not too critical – in the sense of disapproving mathematics as a whole – stance on mathematics. Such a person has thought about his/her subjective experiences with mathematics and all the emotional involvement entailed, and about its value of utilization and of its meaning in our society as well.

In the Anglo-American area, however, the subject often is termed 'adult numeracy'. The meaning of numeracy also varies greatly (see, for example, Gal 1993; Galbraith, Carss, Grice, Endean & Warry 1992). In the Crowther Report (1959), where the term was used for the first time, it means 'the minimum knowledge of mathematics and scientific subjects which any person should possess in order to be considered educated' (quoted in Withnall 1994, p. 11). Nowadays too, being numerate means having developed certain basic mathematical skills applicable to various situations in everyday life. Within this framework, however, distinct aspects are stressed.

Firstly, there are differences with regard to how the subject is perceived. On the one hand, there is a societal focus: Numeracy is primarily related to socio-economic change and the technological development of society: It should correspond to these and serve the progress of society as a whole. On the other hand, numeracy is linked to the individual's life: The focus is on the individual. This approach is given great importance in the Cockcroft Report where the value of numeracy for a person's everyday life is the crucial aspect:

> We would wish the word 'numerate' to imply the possession of two attributes. The first of these is an 'at-homeness' with numbers and an ability to make use of mathematical skills which enables an individual to cope with the practical mathematical demands of his everyday life. The second is an ability to have some appreciation and understanding of information which is presented in mathematical terms, for instance graphs, charts or tables or by reference to percentage increase or decrease.
>
> (Cockcroft 1982, p. 11)

Another difference in the understanding of the term 'numeracy' refers to the role emancipation has within this concept. On the one hand, numeracy is understood as a means of helping people cope with their life-situations. Withnall (1994) calls 'functional numeracy' a concept of numeracy which emphasizes its role for people's functioning according to the needs of the given society. On the other hand, numeracy is considered a means to gain insight into the structures of society and to enable people to take an active part in political decision-making. This aspect is stressed in particular by Evans in his concept of 'critical citizenship' which means 'engagement with discussions and debates about individual, family and public well-being, and about describing, appreciating, evaluating, deciding on future directions of public policy' (Evans & Thorstad 1994, p. 65). Other scholars taking this view are, for example, Webber (1988), and Yasukawa, Johnston & Yates (1995). Webber built on the notion of developing a critical stance. According to her, numeracy means 'developing the ability to grapple with a problem until we come to a critical understanding of it' (Webber 1988, p. 7).

A third aspect which is seen differently by scholars is the question as to whether numeracy is context-bound or not. Is numeracy a set of skills that can be separated from the practical situations in which they are used, or is numeracy always linked to the everyday context in which it occurs? Evans and Thorstad (1994) in particular, but other scholars too, argue that the numerate aspects of everyday activities cannot be separated from the general purposes and goals of these activities, nor from the social dimension of acting. The situation as a whole has to be taken into account. This implies that numeracy can be learned and developed within specific contexts only. Besides, the question arises as to whether it is possible to transfer numerate ideas and skills rooted in one context to another. In any case it is open to question as to what purpose would be served by teaching numeracy concepts in isolation, even if they could be taught that way.

Finally, it should be mentioned that there is no agreement as to whether numeracy includes attitudinal factors. (This is also a question which has arisen in discussions about mathematical education in general.) On the one hand, scholars argue that education always covers attitudes, or even has to comprise them because cognition and affect cannot be separated from each other; on the other hand, some stress the differences and argue against their integration (McLeod & Adams 1989).

1.3   Numeracy and Mathematical Education – Is There Really a Difference?

Considering the fact that the use of the two terms – numeracy and mathematics education – has become customary, it is somewhat surprising that it is unclear where the dividing line between numeracy and mathematical education should be drawn. Protagonists of the duality often argue that numeracy is a restricted mathematical education – it is seen as a low-level mathematics, often taught by non-mathematicians, to people who have no aspiration to be mathematicians. At first sight it seems obvious to reduce numeracy to 'elementary' skills or abilities, and in practice numeracy is often understood in this way – that is, as having a good command of the four rules, fractions and percentages, being familiar to some extent with statistical description, or with the interpretation of (cartesian) graphs. But numeracy is not necessarily to be restricted to the skills or abilities mentioned above. If the thesis of its dependence on the context is taken seriously in certain cases, even an understanding of differentiation might be classed with numeracy – when it is helpful in the given context. For example, in discussions about economical issues certain facts, such as marginal rates, can be described exactly by the use of the concept of the derivative.

A second argument in favour of the duality of mathematics and numeracy is that numeracy means quantitative, spatial, etc. ideas in the context of a practice other than school mathematics or professional mathematics. The problem with this separation is that it is counterproductive to all efforts aimed at producing an understanding of mathematics where its use in everyday situations is an essential part. Besides, it is not always possible to discriminate between the context of school or professional mathematics and other practical contexts. Finally the question arises as to whether it is sensible to differentiate between numeracy and mathematics in further education; present day ethnomathematicians do not do so.

1.4 Differences in the Approach to the Subject

There are differences as well with regard to the general framework in which the scholarly discussion about adults and mathematics (or numeracy) takes place. There is a culturally oriented approach which understands the relationship of mathematics as a part of the manifestations of the mind and which is interested in the analysis of this relationship as far as it provides insight into our culture. The other approach to adults and mathematics (or numeracy) is motivated more by educational issues and perceived educational deficits. It is differentiated within itself: Positions vary from a general interest in adults' education, to a more pragmatic approach which deals with the subject within the context of development and organization of courses in further education in mathematics, to a focus on the role of mathematics in our society and on combating inequalities through advocating adequate mathematical education for all. The last position is held very strongly by adult educators who wish to see society change, and use this emancipatory approach to guide the curriculum (see, for example, Frankenstein, 1990).

The complexity of the field 'adults and mathematics' and of the scholarly approaches to this field is mirrored in this review. Hence, it is not possible in a chapter such as this to provide an overall perspective, or a definite focus.

1.5 Reasons for the Relevance of the Subject

Before going into the main aspects of the field 'adults and mathematics (or numeracy)' we want to deal with the question as to why this subject can claim to be relevant. Actually, mathematics didactics does not pay as much attention to adults learning mathematics as to the relationship of children to mathematics. This can be seen easily from the respective numbers of publications. We hold the opinion that it will be necessary in future to take more notice of the relationship of adults to mathematics, especially with reference to the structure of our society and the role mathematics plays in this society. We are aware that society and the (relative) importance of mathematics may be, and actually are, perceived and commented on quite differently; yet we think that the following description will be shared widely and therefore we base the argument for the relevance of our subject upon it.

The German philosopher Huelsmann (1985) calls western industrial society the 'Technological Formation'. This means that it is a dynamic system, in which an integrative structure works, combining government, capital, labour, and research — to name some of the most important factors of society only. This integrative structure is technology; in contrast to former ones, present society is constituted by the technology being produced and applied in it. Mathematics is a basic structure of the Technological Formation. This holds all the more if a broader concept of mathematics than usual is taken as a basis.

According to this, mathematics is a social phenomenon, firmly embedded in social context, a functional form of communication. Two aspects can be discerned — the means aspect and the system aspect:

> Mathematics provides a *means* for individuals to explain and control complex situations of the natural and the artificial environment and to communicate about those situations. On the other hand, mathematics is a *system* of concepts, algorithms and rules, *embodied in us*, in our thinking and doing; we are subject to this system, it determines parts of our identity.
>
> (Fischer 1993, p. 113; accentuation in the original text)

In detail the following factors make us regard mathematics as a basic structure of the Technological Formation:

> [Mathematics] is the basis of all new technologies because algorithms are the basis of software and materialized mathematical logic is the basis of hardware for computers and microprocessors. Mathematical theories and models are becoming increasingly important as the basis of a variety of forward-looking alternatives in simulating planning and knowledge in economic and technical fields, for example in control, optimization, and construction, or in the fields of politics or social science through the use or misuse of statistics. Mathematics has long been established as the scientific core of the natural sciences and, increasingly, of the social sciences as well.
>
> (Maaß & Schloeglmann 1988, p. 295)

We want to emphasize, however, that mathematics being a basic structure of the Technological Formation — and the Technological Formation itself as well — is not a given state: This 'fact' is established by the day by day acting of the members of society. Without having in mind a certain social order, a certain era, or a certain subject, Schuetz in his phenomenology (1971-1972) as well as the ethnomethodology of Garfinkel (1967) and the symbolic interactionism of Blumer (1969) all stress this idea of 'making' society's structures. According to them the world in which we live has been constituted by social acting. The (everyday) world is established by the society members' mutual acts of giving and interpreting meaning. Therefore the Technological Formation and the importance attached to mathematics are the result of such processes. Inherent necessities to develop and apply more and more technology and to use more and more mathematics that occur in our society — we do not want to deny this at all — are always results of former acting.

In this society the relationship of people to mathematics is of great importance. Mathematics has to be acknowledged as an inherent approach to things, and people should be able to make use of mathematics — but sensibly;

that is, without absolutizing mathematics. As mathematics is applied in our society on very different levels and in very different contexts, the mathematics-related requirements with which people find themselves confronted vary greatly, too. Considering all of this, it is a prominent task to deal with the mathematical education (or numeracy) of adults – to analyse the state of the art, to reflect on it, and to take steps for change whenever indicated. Further mathematics education programs demand particular attention in this context. There are many courses in which mathematics is taught on various levels – aiming at the acquisition of basic skills within numeracy programs, or that of selected knowledge at university level within further education for scientists and engineers – and the demand for such courses is increasing. Therefore encouraging research in this field – the development of didactical conceptions, the evaluation of given courses, the analysis of the effects of learning etc. – is of eminent importance.

There is, however, a question which remains problematic: the question of which kind of mathematics is really necessary, and in which context, in order that people can cope with the situations they encounter, or can alter them according to their needs. Much too little is known about this. Although the relevance of mathematics in our society is an undisputed fact in principle, and hence it is easy to argue for an appropriate mathematical education (or numeracy) being essential, our knowledge about the concrete use of mathematics in context, especially in professional life, and even more the requirements made on the mathematical qualifications of (adult) people, is very small. Thus, for example, Buckingham (1994) claimed that we do not have a good understanding of the ways mathematics is used or might be used in trade and production. Foyster (1990) noted with respect to trade-based calculations that the skills a given worker may use at any particular stage of their career, although possibly easy to define, are likely to be different from those required at different stages, and also differ according to the particular area of the trade operated in. It seems as if the common empirical way of positivist research is not practicable in this case, or at least does not lead to results useful in the sense that general education programs could be based on them (see, for example, Bardy 1985). Interviews often reveal rather strange ideas about the role and the concrete uses of mathematics. For example, employers, when asked which mathematical skills were important, frequently nominated arithmetic skills, even when they were no longer vocationally relevant. When adults describe which kinds of mathematics they use in professional and private life the results are often meagre (for possible reasons see below). Ethnographically oriented studies (described below) analysing adults' everyday use of mathematics show that mathematical activities are interwoven with all other acting. Other methodologically similar studies investigating the mathematical requirements in certain professions (Damerow, Elwitz, Keitel & Zimmer 1974) state the importance of the context as well, and arrive at very abstract descriptions only when trying to characterize the requirements without taking the context into account.

2. THE SITUATION AS IT IS

2.1 Adults' Mathematical Knowledge and Understanding

Two different approaches can be identified within research on the mathematical knowledge and understanding of adults. The first relates to school mathematics, and the second to non-educational contexts.

2.1.1 Knowledge and Understanding of School Mathematics

The first approach is interested in the knowledge and understanding of mathematical topics which are, in general, part of school mathematics. Research typically takes the form of laboratory studies, where subjects are given certain tasks outside the situations in which they normally encounter mathematical topics. It is important to note that this kind of research design indicates an interest to the subjects in their performance on the given (school) mathematics. Mathematics is the reference point, not only for the scholars, but also for the subjects. They see themselves being confronted with (school) mathematical tasks, even if these are application problems. Within this approach we can differentiate between the two following branches.

2.1.1.1 Focus on Statistical Data

The first branch investigates adults' school-mathematical knowledge and tries to establish causes of lack of knowledge and misunderstanding. The interest in knowledge here is centred on the relevance this knowledge has within the numerous courses in further education in mathematics. In these courses learners explicitly, or at least implicitly, deal with school-mathematics, or are introduced to new concepts or methods based on school-mathematics. Methodologically common test instruments are used, analysis makes use of (advanced) statistics, and this branch aims at results being universally valid, at least in some respects. It should be mentioned that investigating the mathematical knowledge of adults is somewhat more laborious than for children and young people. Firstly, it involves specific organizational problems as there are no institutions like schools from which subjects could be recruited easily. Secondly, the interpretation of the data may be more complicated as the factors influencing the state of knowledge increase with age. Findings in the UK and in the German-speaking countries (ACACE 1982; Ekinsmyth &

Bynner 1994; Schloeglmann 1993) indicate that about nine out of ten adults have no problems with the four fundamental operations of arithmetic if natural numbers are not too large. Similarly for decimal numbers, in easier cases, for example if the numbers of places after the decimal points are all the same. If tasks include additional hurdles, like brackets, very large or very small (decimal) numbers, or arithmetic operations on different hierarchy levels like addition and multiplication, the rate of mistakes rises fairly dramatically. Calculating with fractions and transforming units seems to be problematic for about fifty percent of adults; working with variables and powers is problematic for a majority of people. Not unexpectedly, Kirsch, Jungeblut, Jenkins, and Kolstad (1993) found that adults' mathematical performance is higher when they have completed school or vocational training, and it increases with educational level. Interestingly people at an advanced age do not perform worse than younger people: Sometimes test scores are even higher (Southwell 1994). This finding might be due to several factors, like changes in the objectives of teaching mathematics, the frequent use of calculators etc. It should be mentioned, however, that people showing low performance on such tests do not necessarily have problems with mathematics when it occurs in everyday situations (see below). Yet it may be that a poor knowledge in school-mathematics can have an adverse effect on the chances for success in vocational retraining – the relevance here is that this measure affects an increasing number of people in our society.

2.1.1.2 Focus on Subjective Interpretations of Tasks

Typical of the second branch of research on adults' mathematical knowledge and understanding is that the focus is on the subjective reading of the tasks by the subjects. Their understanding of mathematical concepts, their interpretations of the task assignments, their subjective solutions etc. are worked out. The goal is to reveal the subjective logic underlying the treatment of the given task; the question whether this is contrary to the mathematically correct one is only of marginal importance in this branch (unlike in the first one). In this design 'open' tasks are frequently used, that is, tasks without an obviously optimal method of solution, or even with no unique solution at all. Methodologically this branch, with its aim of reconstructing subjective perspectives, belongs to the area of interpretative research. Until recently this second branch was not widely used within research on adults and mathematics, and the studies carried out are very different with respect to the mathematical topics analysed. Examples include the investigation of adults' treatment of word problems (Wildt 1993), their interpretations of a real-world graph (Jungwirth 1995c), and their understanding of concepts and procedures in the elementary algebra (Moeller 1989). Because of the small number of studies and because of the heterogeneity of the subjects analysed it is not possible to say whether

there are adult-specific ways of understanding mathematical concepts, procedures, representations etc. Findings indicate that there are very different individual solutions and approaches.

2.1.1.3   Focus on Respondents' Reports about Their Use of Mathematics

Studies asking adults about their use of mathematics in their professional and
private lives provide additional insight into mathematical knowledge and understanding (see, for example, Harris 1991; Hind 1994; Jungwirth 1995a;
Knight, Arnold, Carter, Kelly & Thornley 1992; Sewell 1981). These studies
can be counted among those which are oriented towards school-mathematics
because the subjects are told that the question is about mathematics, and their
answers refer to their own conceptions of mathematics; in general they identify mathematics with school-mathematics. Findings indicate that adults use
pragmatically acquired methods in order to solve the problems they are faced
with in their everyday life; these are rather simple in comparison with the application of methods used in school-mathematics. Sewell (1981, p. 70) found,
for example, that adults were 'adding instead of subtracting. For example 105
- 97 was seen as adding 3 to 97 to make 100, then 5 more to make 105; 3 and
5 make 8'. Another method was 'taking half and half again to obtain an approximate 'share'. For example, 40 minutes pay at 5 pounds an hour was seen
as a bit less than 3/4 hour's pay (that is 1/2 hour + 1/4 hour)'. Another finding
is that, for the most part, interviewees refer to arithmetical operations only –
the four fundamental operations are performed using integers, decimal numbers, or money units; percentages are calculated, etc. Very frequently all this
is embedded in the context of shopping – people estimate roughly the amount
which has to be paid, or check the sums on sales slips. Furthermore, they often mention private financial transactions, and doing craftsman's work in the
home (such as painting walls). Gender differences also emerge in their reports: For example, it is primarily women who quote the context of cooking
and preparing meals. It is remarkable that the descriptions are often strangely
vague, and those of the professional use of mathematics are even more unclear. This leads to the assumption (Foyster 1990) that adults do not recognize
their use of mathematics as such in any case. Additional support is given to
this assumption by the observation that they derogate their mathematical
skills – for example, Hind (1994, p. 74) noted 'my respondents talked about
'figure work'' – and that they give the impression that these activities are not
worth mentioning. This is further confirmed by Harris (1991) who asked
young workers about mathematical and other skills they used on the job. They
often denied using mathematical methods when asked by the mathematics
questionnaire but simultaneously their answers to the general skills questions
indicated that, in fact, they do use these methods: 'Hairdressers, for example,
denied that they used ratio and proportion when asked about them as mathe-

matical skills, yet used the word 'proportion' when they explained the necessity for mixing hair tints accurately, in responses to questions about their practical skills' (Harris 1994, p. 19). Whether people's failing to recognise mathematics in their everyday activities is considered a problem or not, depends on the concept of mathematics that is adopted by the researcher. As the conceptualization of mathematics broadens, it would appear that people's ideas of mathematics increasingly deviate from those of the researcher's, and this could be problematic.

2.1.2 People's Ways of Using Mathematics in Non-Educational Contexts

The second of the two approaches to the research on mathematical knowledge and understanding of adults tries to grasp how they deal with mathematics in the contexts beyond the educational ones (see, for example, Carraher, Carraher & Schliemann 1985; Grier 1994, 1995; Lave 1988; Lave & Wenger 1991; Millroy 1992; Nunes, Schliemann & Carraher 1993). Adults are observed in their everyday life, or everyday situations are simulated within the investigation. The crucial thing is that an interest is shown in how they manage their affairs, and not in their application of certain school-mathematical methods. According to its aim, this research is ethnographically oriented. The most important finding is that the mathematical – this term mirrors the scholars' perspective, not necessarily that of the subjects – activities are integrated in the context. The management of everyday affairs – vocational ones like street selling, or doing carpenter's work, and private ones, like shopping in the supermarket, housekeeping, or preparing meals – is characterized by a permanent interlinking of various aspects: perception of the situation and acting in the situation, acting and reflecting, thinking about solutions and putting them into practice etc. The mathematics involved goes without saying, it is, so to speak, something natural: People do not recall certain methods stemming from school-mathematics in order to apply them. Besides, mathematics is not as important as might be assumed. For instance, carpenters preferred comparison, using the senses of touch and sight, to measuring; yet they also used several mathematical concepts, such as congruence, symmetry, proportion (Millroy 1992). Referring to mathematics in shopping Lave (1988, p. 157) stated:

> Quantitative relations are assembled in various forms in grocery shopping, among which are price and quantity comparisons. These occur at the end of largely qualitative decision-making processes when a person-acting faces a dilemma and the elimination of alternative grocery items comes to a halt before a choice has been made. It was pointed out ... that if arithmetic is utilized, it is employed when the number of choices still under consideration is not greater than three and rarely greater than

two, and precisely at moment when shoppers have no strong qualitative preferences (Murtaugh 1985a). Arithmetic problem solving is both an expression of and a medium for dealing with these stalled decision processes. It is, among other things, a move outside the qualitative characteristics of a product to its characterization in terms of a standard of value, money.

It is therefore not surprising that, as stated above, inquiries about the everyday use of mathematics often yield fairly scanty results. The use of mathematics is embedded in the course of action; it is not something outstanding that is paid particular attention. Besides, in general, people – from the mathematics they experienced in school – are not familiar with such integration of context and therefore do not identify this context-bound mathematics with mathematics they have learned at school.

Several examples show that people act differently depending on how they interpret the given situation – as an everyday situation, or a school-mathematical one (Clarke & Helme 1993; Grier 1995). A specific everyday perspective has also been revealed in a study about the handling of technical drawings. Technical drawers described drawings presented to them in a professional-like context from perspectives closely related to those of their everyday professional activities (Bromme, Rambow & Sträßer 1995). Another important finding is that people could solve mathematical tasks within the context, yet failed to do so when the tasks – although being mathematically identical – were presented to them as abstract mathematical tasks. For example, street vendors could solve about 92 per cent of the tasks in context, but only about 37 per cent of these as modified, formal tasks (Carraher, Carraher & Schliemann 1985).

2.1.2.1   Consequences for the Pedagogical Discussion

Higher mathematical performance within an everyday-life context is noteworthy for the following reasons. Firstly, it brings a new aspect into the discussion about adults' mathematical knowledge and understanding. Within everyday contexts, beyond those of school-mathematics, adults are obviously able to solve (certain) problems – and this means that they can do this where it actually matters. This fact is likely to qualify the findings about their knowledge and understanding obtained by tests. Furthermore, the question arises as to whether success in academic mathematics is a valid measure of mathematical power. It is, however, still open to question whether such a performance difference occurs at every mathematical level; in particular if the mathematics involved is at college or university level. It might be that the context improves performance only if the abstraction and complexity of mathematics do not exceed a certain limit. Additionally, however, there are indications

(Schliemann & Acioly 1989) that mathematical performance as such does not necessarily increase with schooling, whereas a more general ability to analyse and to explain mathematical relationships and models does.

Secondly, the indications that performance is better within context provoke reflection about the teaching of mathematics – not only in further education but in school, too. What do these findings mean for the teaching and learning of mathematics? Should mathematics – at least on elementary levels – be taught in context whenever possible, for instance within projects? But – this question might arise here – would it then still be mathematics that is taught and learned? It is no accident that people operating within an everyday context do not recognize their mathematical activities as such. Would this way of teaching and learning mathematics thus meet with the 'character' of mathematics? This is in doubt presuming that a basic feature of mathematics is that it is a general means of problem solving, abstracting from the specificities of the given application. Should we abandon showing students – as is done in school – universal ways of solving problems, strategies to enable them to organize their thinking (Grier 1994), but which, however, they often do not use, and apparently do not need to use at all, in order to manage the mathematical aspects of their everyday affairs? Or should mathematics teaching lay much more emphasis than it does nowadays on the development of the ability to link mathematics and its application in context? That is, – to use Bauersfeld's concept of the 'subjective domains of experience' (Bauersfeld 1985) – to enable the (adult) learners to construct a third, mediating subjective domain of experience linking mathematics and everyday actions. Or, is poor test performance primarily caused by an aversion to mathematics negatively affecting mathematical thinking? In this case changing attitudes to mathematics would be the first task.

2.2 Adults' Beliefs about and Attitudes towards Mathematics

In this section we deal with adults' ideas of mathematics and their emotional relationship to mathematics. We hold the opinion that both aspects cannot be separated in the end, but we think that it is helpful to distinguish between them in a review like this. We use the terms 'belief' and 'attitude' as indicators of each. Some investigations dealing with adults' beliefs about and attitudes towards mathematics have been carried out (see, for example, Benn 1994; Burton 1987; Crawford, Gordon, Nicholas & Prosser 1993; FitzSimons 1993; 1994a; 1995; Galbraith & Chant 1993; Jungwirth 1994; 1995a; Wood & Smith 1993); these often take the form of case studies. Studies of attitude and belief are often embedded in the organization and evaluation of further education programs in mathematics, and so there is a wide variation in the type of questions posed. There are however, attempts to develop more standardized instruments for the analysis of adults' beliefs about and attitudes towards mathematics (see, for example, Galligan, Surman & Harris 1994; Taylor 1995). Findings differ in detail; in particular, differences emerge when studies go into adults' mathematics life histories. Additionally, it has to be taken into account that people, or groups of people, differ in attributes relevant for their relationship to mathematics at school, or in their professions. In general the subjects in theses studies are participants of courses in further education in mathematics, not just people in the street, selected at random. Despite this certain tendencies can be identified.

Firstly, adults when asked about their beliefs about mathematics tend to identify mathematics with arithmetic. Doing mathematics is doing some sort of calculation; they often hold the conception of mathematics as numbers, rules and formulae although they do not always consider these things as really constitutive of mathematics. A second trend is that adults claim to be convinced of the importance of mathematics in our society. According to the findings, the relevance is ascribed on the one hand to the overall use of mathematics in society – including personal everyday life – and to the benefits from the application of mathematics. However, Gellert (1995) found that student teachers, while accepting the importance of mathematics for society, excluded its value to their personal lives. On the other hand, the relevance of mathematics is traced back to a connection with mental processes: Mathematics – it is said – enhances reasoning, or else doing mathematics is considered thinking as such. Many believe that there is an inherent natural ability for mathematics. Some findings indicate that the conviction that society benefits from mathematics has the status of a dogma as it is not based on an appropriate knowledge about applications (Jungwirth 1995a). It is remarkable that an unreserved appreciation of mathematics can be stated only if school-mathematics and subjective experiences with mathematics education are out of the focus. The more school is the reference point, the more the usefulness and the aim and object of mathematics are questioned. Additionally, and in connection with the latter, a third tendency is indicated; especially in studies working with in-depth interviews. Findings show that adults' relationship to mathematics in school, particularly beyond elementary school, has often been emotionally strained, even that anxiety has become the dominant feeling. Many adults say that they had to work hard and did not experience success, that in the course of time their confidence in learning mathematics flagged and (therefore) they lost interest in mathematics; and often they could not make sense of the mathematical subjects they were taught. For many, learning mathematics was rote-learning, and some people report a very instrumental approach to the mathematics they learn in further education programs as well. They are interested only in applying formulae and procedures; deductions and proofs are – from their point of view – of no use and only take up precious time (Schloeglmann 1994; Sträßer & Dreyfus 1989; Toerner & Grigutsch 1994).

Summing up we can say that people seem to have a relatively limited conception of mathematics; on the one hand, they appreciate and perhaps even overestimate the value of mathematics, and on the other hand, they take up a sceptical stance or try to avoid mathematics whenever possible. The attitude towards mathematics that emerges cannot be called negative but is not clearly positive either. But what does negative and positive really mean in this context? Is enthusiasm for mathematics positive in any case, and turning away from mathematics absolutely negative? The answer depends on the normative foundation.

2.2.1 A Classification of People's Relationships to Mathematics

We think that the following model, originally developed within the analysis of human relations, provides an appropriate basis for judging an attitude towards mathematics because it considers extreme positions as problematic and intends a balanced stance. In this model relations can take on three states: the state of dependence, the state of counterdependence, and the state of interdependence. In the state of dependence a person acknowledges another person as an absolute authority. In the state of counterdependence the person rebels against the authority; the important thing is simply to say 'no', not to do something specific. Therefore – one could say – in this state a dependent position is still maintained. In the state of interdependence the person develops her/his own position. It might contradict authority, or it might not; this does not matter any more. This third state is considered the utmost, the mature state, dependence and counterdependence both indicate immaturity.

Applying this model to the analysis of people's relationship to mathematics (Jungwirth 1994) we can say: In the state of dependence mathematics is considered an undisputed authority. There is a boundless confidence in the capacity of mathematics, results attained by mathematical means are never questioned, mathematics is admired. Characteristic of the counterdependent state is the defiance against mathematics. Mathematics is flatly refused, admiration has changed into disdain. In the state of interdependence the specificities of mathematics are appreciated, but not absolutized. A person in this state is aware that mathematics can do much, and at the same time, that the capacity of mathematics is limited. There is neither an implicit faith in mathematics nor a condemnation of it. Whether the use of mathematics is sensible or not is a question that has to be answered from case to case.

The present findings indicate that many respondents vary between dependence and counterdependence; their relationship to mathematics is often ambivalent. But it seems that this is true for society as a whole. On the one hand, it is a relief to be finished with this 'odd' school-mathematics, and on the other hand, mathematics is the very means to underpin one's own assertions and to attack those of an opponent. Mathematics seems to guarantee reliability, even indisputability.

2.2.2 Consequences for the Teaching of Mathematics

From the model presented above there are certain consequences for the teaching of mathematics. The basic question as to whether mathematics teaching could change adults' relationship to mathematics at all does not need to be discussed further in this context, as several studies show that this is the case (see, for example, Burton 1987; FitzSimons 1993). According to the three stage model above, mathematics education should enable people to overcome the counterdependent state and the dependent as well. In order that this can be achieved mathematics teaching must be two-fold: It is necessary that it, on the one hand, provides support to overcome aversion, and, on the other hand, develops a distance towards mathematics. What should be given priority depends on the learners' relationships to mathematics in each particular case. Taking into account the tendency of people to vary between dependence and counterdependence, mathematics education will often have to provide both. Compared with current practice of mathematics teaching this probably means a shift in orientation towards achieving more detachment from mathematics. Today's mathematics education seems to aim at overcoming aversion in the first place — for example, using real-world problems to demonstrate the usefulness of mathematics. It is, however, no less important to support emancipation from a dependence on mathematics — by pointing out that the power of mathematics is limited and therefore is its relevance.

2.3 Further Education in Mathematics

Adults learn mathematics in very different educational channels, institutions, and courses, with very different goals and in very different ways. Many project and research reports documenting programs of further education in mathematics are listed in the literature. To name only a few titles here — in order to save space — would be presumptuous in our opinion. Diversity is much greater in further education than in education at the primary and secondary levels. In the following paragraph we outline typical structures (institutions, curricula, types of courses), look at teachers and participants, and finally turn to the teaching and learning process itself. Interesting questions for further studies emerge from research undertaken in all these aspects.

2.3.1 General Structures

The most outstanding feature of further education in mathematics (or numeracy) is the diversity of agencies offering programs and single courses: state-run institutions of adult education, communal services (for example, the 'Volkshochschulen' in the German-speaking countries), neighbourhood houses, services for vocational education run by the trade union or by federations of industry, universities, industrial enterprises, banks, insurance companies, education departments of public or private service enterprises. Further education institutions comparable to schools have not everywhere been founded by governments. The agencies actually organizing further education in mathematics in a given country depend on the structure of its educational system as a whole. Funds are sometimes provided by the government or by local communities (for example, for retraining courses for the unemployed), but some participants have to pay (sometimes high) tuition fees. There are indications that adult education, particularly at the grassroots level, is heavily reliant on the 'contribution and commitment of volunteers and people who work long hours beyond those they are paid for' (Aulich Report 1991, p. 49). Related to the limited funding for employment of staff is the limited funding for purchase of resource materials to support the teaching of numeracy. Similarly providers of Access or Bridging courses in vocational colleges and universities find it harder to attract funding than their more high profile industrial or professional departments.

2.3.2 Types of Courses

One way to classify the numerous courses and programs is to distinguish between 'mathematical' and 'mathematics-related' further education (Maaß 1993). The term 'mathematical' in further education means that explicit mathematics teaching takes place. This happens primarily in programs which award formal credentials, for example evening classes for working people, courses offering alternative pathways to gain university admission, training for factory foremen etc. In these programs mathematics is one subject among many. Explicit mathematics teaching takes place as well in workplace education, or in university courses for professionals, where mathematics learning is oriented to practical needs. Numeracy courses also are classed with this type of further education. 'Mathematics-related' further education, on the other hand, is the term for courses in which mathematical concepts and methods are actually used but which are not, however, called 'mathematical' in preliminary announcements, nor in the title, neither mention mathematics in the list of contents. Examples of these are computer-aided design (CAD) courses, or courses offering training on computer numeric controlled (CNC)

771

machines, and those which refer to basic geometry, or software training, such as for bankers to calculate compound interest rates.

A second way of classification is to differentiate between courses (primarily) leading to formal credentials and courses aiming at competency enhancement without awarding any credentials. Within English speaking countries, an important topic of debate in this context is 'competency-based training' (see, for example, Bagnall, 1994; Jackson, 1993). Typical of competency-based training and assessment is the subdivision of programs into modules; each module is detailed in terms of:

a) elements, described as segments within which a competency can be demonstrated and assessed;

b) performance criteria, which specify what the student is expected to do;

c) the range and/or conditions which apply during the learning and assessment process; and

d) examples of assessment tasks.

The periods of time that courses and programs run vary greatly, too. Some courses last hours, and other programs like grammar school evening classes run for years. In terms of the mathematical levels there is a spectrum from elementary mathematics (for example, in numeracy courses) to university mathematics (in courses for professionals such as scientists, or engineers).

2.3.3 Issues Associated with Curriculum Design

If a course leads to a recognized credential and if it is financed by public funds the responsible authorities will have to agree to the curriculum, or at least to have it formally documented. The development of such curricula is generally done by a project team (or commission) after consultation with national business and industry organisations. Otherwise the institution offering a course decides on the content of the curriculum. Often the selection of content is influenced by the demand from outside – it is oriented to the 'needs of the practice'. In many cases the market situation is the decisive factor for the design of a course with its specific goals, content, and ways of teaching. From the pedagogical perspective the fact that the market situation is so important can be problematic as it may happen that courses which meet the perceived demands of prospective students and employers are questionable in some respect when compared to principles concerning people's relationships to mathematics, their attitudes or their values.

A related problem is the trend towards instrumentalization. Vocational further education as a whole is tending to be viewed from a merely functional perspective. In an era of economic rationalism, public authorities tend to emphasize this perspective more than, for example, an emancipatory one. Further education programs providing formal qualifications run the risk that the mathematical part is seen as a necessary evil, attended only because it is compulsory. This then negates the idea that learning mathematics can contribute to the personal development of people and can be of use in our society.

Adopting an instrumentalist perspective may also result in negative consequences for course design: One persistent problem for numeracy educators is the tendency by employers to use selection tests which are qualitatively different from the prescribed curricula, such as asking for decontextualised basic skill operations, which are either not relevant to the vocation, or would normally be solved by using a calculator. The dilemma is whether to prepare students for such tests or whether to remain faithful to recent, technologically-based curricula which focus more on the types of thinking skills actually preferred by employers. Further education in mathematics is confronted with different and partly contradictory demands to a large extent: On the one hand, it should meet the specific practical needs of the participants (customer orientation is a basic principle in all adult education), and these vary already, and on the other hand it should comply with demands arising from the conception of mathematics in society and the role which is ascribed to mathematics.

2.3.4 Teachers

Heterogeneity is characteristic of the teachers in further education in mathematics. On the one hand, school teachers, trade teachers, university teachers, students, or practitioners (engineers, craftsmen, economists etc.) deliver mathematics or mathematics related courses as a sideline to their primary occupation. On the other hand, there are full-time teachers. Considering this heterogeneity it is not surprising that the mathematical qualifications of teachers vary widely, too. There are mathematically highly qualified teachers as well as teachers who – in the first place – are well qualified pedagogically. However in Australia, for example, numeracy classes are often conducted by literacy teachers or tutors who integrate the two curriculum areas. It frequently happens that these teachers and tutors have a limited background in the discipline of mathematics, and feel inadequately prepared to deliver numeracy programs (see, for example, Gal & Schuh 1994). To overcome this problem there have been a series of professional development programs and packages devised to assist literacy teachers preparing to teach numeracy subjects. By contrast, teachers working in non-pedagogical fields like technics in their first occupation may have difficulties with teaching itself and its specificities in the context of further education. It is important that these people develop an awareness of the special needs of the students, and what factors can cause difficulties for learners, no matter how well motivated. Teachers with experience limited to teaching school children need to develop new skills in the teaching of adults, sometimes referred to as andragogy. Some further education institutions have reacted to pedagogical problems by offering teacher training in pedagogy and didactics. However, these courses may be very general and fail to address specific issues which emanate from research into mathematics education, and which form an important part of teacher education for the school sector.

2.3.5 *Participants*

Participants in further mathematics education are heterogeneous, too. They differ in educational background, mathematical knowledge and beliefs about mathematics, and occupations and hence in vocational experience with mathematics (Maaß & Schloeglmann 1991). Their motives to enrol in further education courses vary: In numeracy courses some students enrol of their own volition, others are compelled or strongly encouraged by their employer to attend classes, while others are required to attend in order to maintain unemployment or social security payments. Students choose to enrol in numeracy classes for a variety of reasons. They may need social interaction, intellectual stimulation, and/or self-fulfilment through completing an education which has been previously denied them. Justifications are often phrased in terms of being able to help children with their homework, being a good role model for children, preparing for further study or employment, enhancing the possibility of promotion or maintaining employment through developing a wider skills base, and becoming a better informed citizen (FitzSimons, 1993; 1994b). In work-oriented courses motives are particularly related to the occupation – for example to changes in the scope of duties, to career aspirations, or to maintaining the position presently held (Sefton, Waterhouse & Deakin, 1994). It should be mentioned that in further education people may find themselves confronted with social barriers or problems keeping them from participating in a course or from completing it successfully. These include the financial ability to pay initial enrolment fees and then to purchase stationery, texts and other requisites; the continuing availability and affordability of appropriate child-care; reliable, affordable transport, accessibility of the venue in terms of transport, parking and wheelchair access; and the timing of the class to fit in with arrangements for school children and other dependants, or employment responsibilities.

It should be noted that the prejudice is still held that adults, particularly older ones, are no longer able to learn. However, the findings of learning theory (Baltes, Dittmann-Kohli & Dixon 1984) state that only the ability to remember isolated facts decreases with age; the ability to put things into context even increases. There are indications that this applies to the learning of mathematics, too. Additionally, adults' thinking – because of job-related experiences and life-experience as a whole – seems to be more likely to be context-bound than children's. Presumably this is an important reason why they often refuse to accept formalized knowledge typical of mathematics

(Schloeglmann 1994). Furthermore, their attitude to learning seems to be specific: They often have reservations about ways of learning typical of the school sector. In some cases there is a problematic relationship to mathematics, as well (see above), and adults often have forgotten methods of systematic learning, if they ever developed them, and therefore their ways of learning are not as efficient as they could be.

Of course – one might say – participants in further education courses expect them to be practically-oriented; that is, that they can benefit from these courses in private life (for example, from numeracy courses), or in their jobs (for example, from workplace education). However, the demand for practical orientation is not as unproblematic as it may seem at a first sight – because of the great heterogeneity of the participants, and because of the principal difficulty in establishing precisely which kind of mathematics is actually needed in a given field of practice. Summing up we can say that teaching adults mathematics is an ambitious task, having at least in part a quality other than teaching mathematics to children and young people. But the participants, too, deserve respect. Adults returning to study are almost always making a sacrifice. It may be in terms of payment for courses and equipment, childcare costs, lost time from the workplace, or restrictions on leisure time. It is essential that any research undertaken with adult learners shows the greatest respect for the additional sacrifice of time, energy and emotion required of them: There should be benefits for both sides.

2.3.6 Teaching and Learning Processes

It is important to have a profound knowledge of classroom processes in order to gain a better understanding of people's relationship to mathematics. So-called 'thick descriptions' of what happens in the mathematics classroom are very informative, as numerous examples in the research on children's relationship to mathematics demonstrate. Aspects investigated i. studies of the microstructures of teaching and learning mathematics are very different: Attention can be directed to the emotional climate in the classroom, as well as to academic teacher-student interactions, or the ways students co-operate during group work.

Within the research on adults and mathematics, however, this branch is still in its embryonic state. There are only a few rich descriptions giving insight into the events and processes in classroom life. Helme (1995) investigated the impact of task context on the responses of adult women students to a range of mathematical tasks. She concluded that students' construction of mathematical understanding will be facilitated by tasks which are carefully chosen to support and encourage their social and cultural values, promote metacognitive skills, and stimulate discussion, argument, and reflection. FitzSimons (1994b) analysed how women attending a basic mathematics course actually learn mathematics. She found that these women preferred to learn through discussion, using multiple representations – for example drawing graphs or diagrams, building or using models, using a calculator or a computer, or by actual measurement of people or objects – and also liked to have plenty of practice through worksheets. Another interesting finding is that learning in the class under analysis – which was based on a constructivist perspective of teaching and learning – changed the students' views of the role of the teacher and of themselves as learners. At the beginning of the course the teacher was regarded as a provider of knowledge, and their own part was to listen, copy, understand, remember and reproduce. Later on, the women saw the teacher as a facilitator, providing optimal conditions for learning and their role as to think, explore ideas and reflect on their own and others' ideas.

Jungwirth (1995b) investigated teachers' and participants' perceptions of the teaching, and the structure of interaction and the practices by which it was established. The courses analysed were formal qualifying programs, and the findings show that mathematics teaching was seen as preparation for the examinations. The interaction took place in the form of a guided and standard development of the task-solutions intended to serve as models for those required in the final examination. The teachers contributed to this pattern by decomposing the solution process into a sequence of small activities, and by giving hints to the expected answers. The participants contributed to it by paying attention to the hints and answering in a form related only to the small aspect which was actually the focus of the question, often in verbally reduced form. It is remarkable that the pattern of interaction in these mathematics classes is the same as in mathematics teaching at school (Voigt 1989). Because the present analyses are only case-studies it is an open question as to whether this pattern is as typical of further education in mathematics as it is of mathematics teaching at school. Mathematics teaching in school showing this pattern is suspected of hindering the development of mathematical abilities on higher cognitive levels. Further discussion is warranted about possible negative consequences of following this pattern in further education.

McRae (1995) investigated the aspect of initial assessment of students. She described how, on a one-to-one basis, she assesses students entering Adult Basic Education programs. Her method allows for active participation by the student, whereby knowledge and experience are placed in context. Initially she asks questions giving insight into the student's confidence, self-esteem, and readiness to join a numeracy program. She also asks questions about the extent of the student's everyday use of mathematics. As part of the same conversation McRae discusses information about courses, what is expected from the student, comparing and contrasting social constructivist views of mathematics and how it is learned with the student's previous experiences. The assessment then continues with more mathematically probing contextual questions, where the student determines whether they could answer, whether they would need some help, and whether they wish to answer. This process appears beneficial to both student and teacher, as it allows the teacher to have a clear idea of suitable placement for the student and how to structure the beginning of the program, and it allows the student to know what to expect in the first few lessons.

3.   PERSPECTIVES ON FUTURE RESEARCH

Mathematical (or numeracy) education of adults is an issue of great, and in future, even increasing importance because – as explained in the introduction – mathematics is a basic structure of our society. The survey review of research on the subject, however, shows that many aspects require further analysis. Adults' relationship to mathematics and the teaching of mathematics to adults are not paid as much attention within the didactics of mathematics as they should be. More research on adults and mathematics (or numeracy) would be advisable; subsidizing this branch of research from public funds could be an important impetus. In detail, the following aspects should be investigated.

3.1   The Everyday Use of Mathematics in Professional and Private Life

Our research-based knowledge about this is rather fragmentary. Present findings indicate that the use of mathematics is interwoven with other activities. This restricts the validity of statements to the context analysed; similarly future research is likely to lead to domain-specific results, yet without lessening their relevance. The fact that we do not have good knowledge about the concrete uses of mathematics in our society implies that the empirical basis for the discussion about the socially desirable mathematical qualifications of people, or groups of people, is insufficient as well. Discussions, particularly about numeracy, propose definitions of numeracy and estimations of its role in people's lives. We do not assert that the question as to which mathematical qualification, or numeracy, is appropriate to the needs of society could ever be settled empirically – basic convictions, valuations, and objectives set up previously always will play a very important role in this process as the numeracy debate shows – but more studies about the concrete uses of mathematics could be helpful.

In this context the question arises as to which would be the appropriate way to ascertain the actual state of mathematical knowledge and understanding of adults. One approach is to analyse school-mathematical knowledge. The main goals of this approach are: To gain insight into the effectiveness of mathematics teaching at school, and to establish the knowledge that participants in further education mathematics courses possess, in order to be in the position to develop an appropriate course design. Within the discussion of the (necessary) mathematical qualification, however, this approach is questionable: It is not clear whether such analyses can ascertain the mathematical abilities which are actually relevant as they do not take into account the everyday uses of mathematics which are linked with the other activities within the given context. There are some indications that performance is higher within private or professional practice. Another approach to people's use of mathematics tries to analyse its use within everyday situations. A very important task would be to conduct further studies which compare the everyday use of mathematics and the learning in educational settings.

3.2 The Long-Term Effect of the Mathematics Teaching at School

Our present knowledge is restricted by the focus of most studies on elementary mathematics; mathematics at higher levels is — with few exceptions — not the subject of investigation. Yet it would be interesting to gain insights into knowledge and understanding of higher mathematics as well. Furthermore, it would be important to have more studies documenting not only how much mathematics adults know — on whatever level — but also revealing subjective interpretations of mathematical tasks, and their relationship to the learner's affective domain.

3.3 The Relation between Computerization and Use of Mathematics in Society

In what respect or to what extent does the increasing computerization of professional life change the use of mathematics, even people's relationship to mathematics as a whole? This aspect has hardly been investigated. In this context the issue of mathematical qualification (or numeracy) should be discussed, too. There are some indications that mathematical knowledge and understanding — perhaps contrary to the assumptions held by many people — do not principally lose their relevance; intensive studies have yet to be conducted. A related issue which warrants further investigation is the impact of technology on the teaching of numeracy and mathematics. Further studies relating to issues of equity of access to technology could be undertaken.

3.4 Further Education in Mathematics

One aspect that has not been dealt with sufficiently is the orientation to the needs of 'practice', a common demand of courses in further education. With respect to this several questions arise. Which sort of practice should be the reference point? That is how to deal with the diversity of practice and the changes taking place. What are the real needs of practice? We do not know much about the actual use of mathematics in practice; and whether conflicts arise between this practical demand and mathematics being a general means of problem solving abstracting from concrete applications. Finally, we know little about the resolution of such conflicts.

3.4.1 Teaching and Learning Processes

Teachers have reported anecdotal evidence of a rapid acceleration of learning in adults once they have found their confidence. This phenomenon, which is found typically (but not only) in classrooms which operate under constructivist principles should be investigated, as should adults' beliefs in what mathematics is, and how it is learned. Recent research literature suggests that the affective domain is no less important than the cognitive domain, and further work needs to be done here. Additionally, it would be worth investigating whether, or to what extent, the teaching of mathematics succeeds at overcoming dependence on mathematics. The development and evaluation of courses aiming at both overcoming the dependent and the counterdependent state, should be intensified as an ambivalent stance to mathematics is a problematic phenomenon that is widespread in society. Furthermore, there is a lack of research analysing the interactions in adult mathematics classrooms. This is important because respective analyses of mathematics classes at school indicate that certain structures of interaction may retard the development of independent understanding on the part of the learners.

3.4.2 Assessment

Cummins (1994, p. 4) asserted that 'assessment is now the most significant issue confronting the basic education sector'. Increased funding means that adequate documentation of student progress must occur, and yet in some countries teachers in this sector, like teachers in other sectors, are inadequately prepared to address contemporary assessment issues. The student base is non-typical, population performance characteristics are ill-defined and known to be highly contextualized, and there is a lack of coherent assessment practice. Traditional assessment practices are thus inappropriate and meaningless, according to Cummins.

3.5 School-Related Research

An additional task for the future would include reference to the findings of the school-related research within the discussion about the ways mathematics courses in further education should be designed. Although there are didactically relevant differences between the respective groups – children and young people on the one hand, adults on the other – it would be worth referring more to this research. For example, conceptions stemming from school-related didactics could be given more consideration.

In summary, there is a need for more research into adults returning to study mathematics and numeracy, focusing on both cognitive and affective domains. Implications for teaching should be drawn, and attention paid to the professional development, both initial preparation and continuing education, of practitioners in the field.

ACKNOWLEDGEMENT

We wish to thank the reviewers, Jeff Evans and Marilyn Frankenstein, for their helpful comments on an earlier draft. The opinions expressed, however, are solely those of the authors.

REFERENCES

Advisory Council for Adult and Continuing Education (ACACE): 1982, *Adults' Mathematical Ability and Performance*, ACACE, Leicester.

Aulich, T. G. (Chair): 1991, *Come in Cinderella: The Emergence of Adult and Community Education. Report by the Senate Standing Committee on Employment, Education & Training*, Commonwealth of Australia, ACT.

Bagnall, R.: 1994, 'Pluralising Continuing Education and Training in a Postmodern World: Whither Competence?', *Australian & New Zealand Journal of Vocational Education Research, 2*(2), 18-39.

Baltes, P. B., Dittmann-Kohli, F. & Dixon, R.: 1984, 'New Perspectives on the Development of Intelligence in Adulthood', in: Baltes, P.B., Brim, O.G. (eds.): *Life-Span Development and Behaviour,* New York, Academic Press, 33-76.

Bardy, P.: 1985, 'Mathematische Anforderungen in Ausbildungsberufen', in: Bardy, P., Blum, W., Braun, H.G. (eds.): *Mathematik in der Berufsschule – Analysen und Vorschlage zum Fachrechenunterricht*, Giradet Verlag Essen, 37-48.

Bauersfeld, H.: 1985, 'Contributions to a Fundamental Theory of Mathematics Learning and Teaching', in C. Verhille (ed.), *Proceedings of the 1985 Annual Meeting of Canadian Mathematics Education Study Group* (CSMEG), Universite Laval, Quebec, 1-27.

Benn, R.: 1994, 'Mathematics: Breaking down the Barriers', in: D. Coben (ed.), *ALM - 1, Proceedings of the Inaugural Conference of Adults Learning Mathematics – A Research Forum*, University of London, London, 24-29.

Blumer, H.: 1969, *Symbolic Interactionism. Perspective and Method,* Prentice-Hall, Englwood Cliff, NJ.

Bromme, R., Rambow, R., & Straesser, R.: in press, *Jenseits von 'Oberflaeche' und 'Tiefe': Zum Zusammenhang von Problemkategorisierungen und Arbeitskontext bei Fachleuten des Technischen Zeichnens, im Druck.*

Buckingham, E.: 1994, December, *Theoretical Underpinnings and Methodology of a Study of Industrial Workers' Evaluation Of Education.* Paper presented at conference Mathematics, Science and the Environment, Deakin University (Burwood Campus), Vic.

Burton, L.: 1987, 'From Failure to Success: Changing the Experience of Adult Learners of Mathematics', *Educational Studies in Mathematics, 18*(3), 305-316.

Carraher, T., Carraher, D., & Schliemann, A.: 1985, 'Mathematics in the Streets and in the Schools', *British Journal of Psychology 3*, 21-29.

Clarke, D. & Helme, S.: 1993, *Context as Construct*. Paper presented at the 16th annual conference of the Mathematics Education Research Group of Australasia, Brisbane, Qld., July 9-13.

Cockroft, W. H. (Chairman): 1982, *Mathematics Counts: Report of the Committee of Inquiry into the Teaching of Mathematics in Schools*, Her Majesty's Stationery Office, London.

Crawford, K., Gordon, S., Nicholas, J., & Prosser, M.: 1993, 'Learning Mathematics at University Level: Initial Conceptions of Mathematics', in B. Atweh, C. Kanes, M.Carss, & G. Booker (eds.), *Contexts in mathematics education*, Mathematics Education Research Group of Australasia, Brisbane, Qld., 209-214.

Crowther Report.: 1959, *15 to 18: A Report of the Central Advisory Council for Education*, Her Majesty's Stationery Office, London.

Cumming, J. J.: 1994, October, *Issues in the Assessment of Core Literacy and Numeracy Performance in Adult General and Vocational Education Programs in Australia*. Paper presented at the Conference of the International Association for Educational Assessment, Wellington, New Zealand.

Damerow, P., Elwitz, U., Keitel, C., & Zimmer, J.: 1974, *Elementarmathematik: Lernen für die Praxis? Ein exemplarischer Versuch zur Bestimmung fachüberschreitender Curriculumziele*, Klett Verlag, Stuttgart.

Ekinsmyth, C., & Bynner, J.: 1994, *The Basic Skills of Young Adults. Some Findings from the 1970 British Cohort Study*, Social Statistics Research Unit, London.

Evans, J. & Thorstad, I.: 1994, 'Mathematics and Numeracy in the Practice of Critical citizenship', in D. Coben (ed.), *ALM - 1: Proceedings of the Inaugural Conference of Adults Learning Mathematics — A Research Forum*, University of London, London, 64-70.

Fischer, R.: 1993, 'Mathematics as a Means and as a System', in S. Restivo, J. P. van Bendegem, & R. Fischer (eds.), *Math Worlds: Philosophical and Social Studies of Mathematics and Mathematics Education*, State University of New York, New York, Press, 113-133.

FitzSimons, G.: 1993, 'Constructivism and the Adult Learner: Marieanne's Story', in B. Atweh, C. Kanes, M. Carss, & G. Booker (eds.) *Contexts in Mathematics Education*, Mathematics Education Research Group of Australasia, Brisbane, Qld., 247-252.

FitzSimons, G. E.: 1994a, 'TAFE Students: The Affective Domain and Mathematics', in G. Bell, B. Wright, N. Leeson, & J. Geake (eds.), *Challenges in Mathematics Education: Constraints on Construction*, Mathematics Education Research Group of Australasia, Lismore, NSW, 233-241.

FitzSimons, G. E.: 1994b, *Teaching Mathematics to Adults Returning to Study*, Deakin University Press, Geelong, Vic.

FitzSimons, G. E.: 1995, July, *The Inter-Relationship of the History and Pedagogy of Mathematics for Adults Returning to Study*. Paper presented at the conference of the International Study Group for the Relations of History and Pedagogy of Mathematics, Cairns, Qld.

Foyster, J.: 1990, 'Beyond the Mathematics Classroom: Numeracy on the Job', in S. Willis (ed.), *Being Numerate: What Counts?*, Australian Council for Educational Research, Melbourne, Vic., 119-137.

Frankenstein, M.: 1990, 'Incorporating Race, Gender, and Class Issues into a Critical Mathematical Literacy Curriculum', *Journal of Negro Education, 59*(3), 336-347.

Gal, I.: 1993, *Issues and Challenges in Adult Numeracy*, National Center on Adult Literacy, Philadelphia.

Gal, I. & Schuh, A.: 1994, *Who Counts in Adult Literacy Programs? A national survey of numeracy education*, National Center on Adult Literacy, Philadelphia.

781

Galbraith, P. L., Carss, M. C., Grice, R. D., Endean, L., & Warry M. C.: 1992, 'Towards Numeracy for the Third Millenium: A Study of the Future of Mathematics and Mathematics Education', *Educational Studies in Mathematics 23,* 569-593.

Galbraith, P. L., & Chant, D.: 1993, 'The Profession, the Public, and School Mathematics', in B. Atweh, C. Kanes, M. Carss, & G. Booker (eds.), *Contexts in Mathematics Education,* Mathematics Education Research Group of Australasia, Brisbane, Qld., 267-273.

Galligan, L., Surman, P., & Harris, P.: 1994, 'Measurement of Metacognition in Adult Students of Mathematics. A Report on Initial Investigations', in *Australian Bridging Mathematics Network Conference Proceedings, Vol. II,* University of Sydney, Sydney, NSW., 20-30.

Garfinkel, H.: 1967, *Studies in Ethnomethodology,* Prentice-Hall, New Jersey.

Gellert, U.: 1995, July, *Challenging Student Teachers' Views on Mathematics and Mathematics Education by Confronting them with a Non-Eurocentric Approach to its History.* Paper presented at the conference of the International Study Group for the Relations of History and Pedagogy of Mathematics, Cairns, Qld.

Grier, S.: 1994, 'The Situatedness of Adults' Numerical Understandings', in G. Bell, B. Wright, N. Leeson, & J. Geake (eds.), *Challenges in Mathematics Education: Constraints on Construction,* Mathematics Education Research Group of Australasia, Lismore, NSW., 315-322.

Grier, S.: 1995, 'What is Mathematics? What is not Mathematics? What may be Mathematics?' In R. P. Hunting, G. E. FitzSimons, P. C. Clarkson, & A. J. Bishop (eds.), *Regional Collaboration in Mathematics Education 1995,* Monash University, Melbourne, Vic., 291-300.

Harris, M.: 1991, 'Looking for the Maths in work', in M. Harris, (ed.), *Schools, Mathematics and Work,* Falmer Press, London, 132-144.

Harris, M.: 1994, 'Finding Common Threads: Researching the Mathematics in Traditionally Female Work', in: D. Coben (ed.), *ALM - 1: Proceedings of the Inaugural Conference of Adults Learning Mathematics – A Research Forum,* University of London, London, 18-23.

Helme, S.: 1995, 'Maths Embedded in Context: How do Students Respond?', *Numeracy in Focus, 1,* 24-32.

Hind, G.: 1985, 'The Role of Informal Learning in Adult Numeracy', in D. Coben (ed.), *ALM - 1: Proceedings of the Inaugural Conference of Adults Learning Mathematics – A Research Forum,* University of London, London, 71-84.

Huelsmann, H.: 1985, *Die technologische Formation – oder: lasset uns Menschen machen,* Verlag Europaeische Perspektiven, Berlin.

Jackson, N.: 1993, 'Competence: A Game of Smoke and Mirrors?', in C. Collins (ed.): *Competencies: The Competencies Debate in Australian Education and Training,* Australian College of Education, Canberra, ACT., 154-161.

Jungwirth, H.: 1994, Erwachsene und Mathematik – eine reife Beziehung, *Mathematica Didactica, 17*(1) 69-89.

Jungwirth, H.: 1995a, 'Subjektive Theorien uber Mathematik bei Erwachsenen', in H. Jungwirth, J. Maasz, & W. Schloeglmann, *Mathematik in der Weiterbildung. Final Project-Report,* Institut fur Mathematik, Johannes Kepler University, Linz.

Jungwirth, H.: 1995b, 'Lehr – Lern – Prozesse in der mathematischen Weiterbildung', in H. Jungwirth, J. Maasz, & W. Schloeglmann, *Mathematik in der Weiterbildung. Final Project-Report* Institut fur Mathematik, Johannes Kepler University, Linz.

Jungwirth, H.: 1995, 'Das Loesen von anwendungsbezogenen Aufgaben im Schnittpunkt von Mathematik und umgebender Realitat', in *Beitraege zum Mathematikunterricht,* Franzbecker, Hildesheim, 284-287.

Kirsch, I. S., Jungeblut, A., Jenkins, L., & Kolstad, A.: 1993, *Adult Literacy in America: A First Look at the Results of the National Adult Literacy Survey,* Educational Testing Service, Princeton, NJ.

Knight, G., Arnold, G., Carter, M., Kelly, P., & Thornley, G. 1992, *The Mathematical Needs of New Zealand School Leavers: A Research Report*, Massey University, Palmerston North.

Lave, J.: 1988, *Cognition in Practice: Mind, Mathematics and Culture in Everyday Life,* Cambridge University Press, Cambridge.

Lave, J. & Wenger, E.: 1991, *Situated Learning: Legitimate Peripheral Participation*, Cambridge University Press, Cambridge.

Maasz, J.: 1993, 'Mathematische und mathematikhaltige Weiterbildung', in *Beitraege zum Mathematikunterricht*, Franzbecker, Hildesheim, 271-274.

Maasz, J. & Schloeglmann, W.: 1988, The Mathematical World in the Black Box – Significance of the Black Box as a Medium of Mathematizing' *Cybernetics and Systems: An International Journal, 19*, 295-309.

Maasz, J. & Schloeglmann, W.: 1991, 'Der Hochschullehrgang 'Mathematische Methoden fur Anwender' am IFF-Studienzentrum in Bregenz', *Weiterbildung in Wirtschaft und Technik, 2,* 20-24.

McLeod, D. B. & Adams, V. M. (eds.): 1989, *Affect and Mathematical Problem Solving. A New Perspective*, New York, Springer.

McRae, A.: 1995, Assessing Students in Numeracy Programs. *Numeracy in Focus, 1,* 15-19.

Millroy, W. L.: 1992, *An Ethnographic Study of the Mathematical Ideas of a Group of Carpenters*, National Council of Teachers of Mathematics, Reston, VA.

Moeller, R.: 1989, *Mathematik in der Weiterbildung. Eine Fallstudie zu einem Algebrakurs der University of Maryland*, Franzbecker, Bad Salzdetfurth.

Nunes, T. Schliemann, A. & Carraher, D.: 1993, *Street Mathematics and School Mathematics*, Cambridge University Press, Cambridge.

Schliemann, A. D. & Acioly, N.-M.: 1989, 'Mathematical Knowledge Developed at Work: The Contribution of Practice versus the Contribution of Schooling', *Cognition and Instruction, 6*(3), 185-221.

Schloeglmann, W.: 1993, 'Mathematikkenntnisse von Erwachsenen', in *Beitraege zum Mathematikunterricht*, Verlag Franzbecker, Hildesheim, 319-322.

Schloeglmann, W.: 1994, 'Mathematiklernprozesse bei Erwachsenen', in *Beitraege zum Mathematikunterricht* Verlag Franzbecker, Hildesheim, 326-329.

Schuetz, A.: 1971-1972, *Gesammelte Aufsatze. Band I-III,* Nijhoff, Den Haag.

Sefton, R., Waterhouse, P., & Deakin, R. (eds.): 1994, *Breathing Life into Training: A Model of Integrated Training*, National Automotive Industry Training Board, Doncaster, Vic.

Sewell, B.: 1981, *Use of Mathematics by Adults in Daily Life*, The Advisory Council for Adult and Continuing Education, Leicester.

Southwell, B.: 1994, 'A Comparison of the Mathematical Understandings of Primary Teacher Education Entrants', in G. Bell, B. Wright, N. Leeson, & J. Geake (eds.), *Challenges in Mathematics Education: Constraints on Construction*, Mathematics Education Research Group of Australasia, Lismore, NSW., 547-554.

Straesser, R. & Dreyfus, T.: 1989, 'Mathematics in Adult Education, Including. Distance Education', *Zentralblatt fur Didaktik der Mathematik, 21*(6), 191-216.

Taylor, J. A.: 1995, 'Attitude to Mathematics of Adults Returning to Tertiary Study in the Distance Mode', in R. P. Hunting, G. E. FitzSimons, P. C. Clarkson, & A. J. Bishop (eds.), *Regional Collaboration in Mathematics Education 1995*, Monash University, Melbourne, Vic., 685-694.

Toerner, G., & Grigutsch, S.: 1994, "Mathematische Weltbilder' bei Studienanfangern – eine Erhebung', *Zentralblatt fur Mathematikdidaktik, 15*(3/4), 211-251.

Voigt, J.: 1989, 'Social Function of Routines and Consequences for Subject Matter Learning', *International Journal of Educational Research, 13*, 647-656.

Webber, V.: 1988, 'Maths as a Subversive Activity', *Education Links, 32*, 6-9.

Wildt, M.: 1993, *Kognitive Aktivitaten aus der Naehe betrachtet – Erwachsene loesen mathematische Sachaufgaben*, Verlag Franzbecker, Hildesheim.

Withnall, A.: 1994, 'Towards a Definition of Numeracy', in D. Coben (ed.), *ALM - 1: Proceedings of the Inaugural Conference of Adults Learning Mathematics – A Research Forum*, University of London, London, 11-17.

Wood, L. N. & Smith, N. F.: 1993, 'Students' Ideas about Mathematics', in B. Atweh, C. Kanes, M. Carss, & G. Booker (eds.), *Contexts in Mathematics Education*, Mathematics Education Research Group of Australasia, Brisbane, Qld., 593-597.

Yasukawa, K., Johnston, B., & Yates, W.: 1995, 'Numeracy as a Critical Constructivist Awareness of Maths. Case Studies from Engineering and Adult Basic Education', in R. P. Hunting, G. E. FitzSimons, P. C. Clarkson, & A. J. Bishop (eds.), *Regional Collaboration in Mathematics Education 1995,* Monash University, Melbourne, Vic., 815-825.

Chapter 21: Popularization: Myths, Massmedia and Modernism

PAUL ERNEST

University of Exeter, School of Education, Exeter, Devon, United Kingdom

ABSTRACT

This chapter looks critically at the popularization of mathematics, which is distinguished from the public understanding of mathematics. After a brief review of the history of popularization materials, the intended audiences of projects are considered. A selection of popularization projects is discussed, chosen to illustrate the possible range of audiences, objectives and media. Two conclusions are reached. First, for high quality popularization productions directed at a mass audience, collaboration among media, mathematics and educational professionals is needed. Second, most projects are not evaluated. Systematic data on effectiveness is needed.

The second part of the chapter explores myths about mathematics, and in particular negative myths that are widespread in society, circulated through the massmedia. It is argued that these myths are supported by modernism in the philosophy of mathematics and mathematics. Also, that the source of the maths myths is the stereotyped experience of school mathematics shared by many. It is claimed therefore that to eradicate negative maths myths will involve the reform of school mathematics. This raises the issue of aims for the popularization of mathematics and strategies for achieving them. The chapter concludes with questions for further research on the topic.

1. THE POPULARIZATION OF MATHEMATICS

One of the clarion cries in the late 20th century west is for the popularization and public understanding of mathematics and science. These great engines of modern civilization are crying out for human resources to supply the always increasing needs of education, science, medicine, industry, commerce and administration in the modern world. Couple this with the commonly negative perceptions of mathematics, and in some countries the unpopularity of science and technology too, there is a need for the popularization of these subjects. In particular, there is a need for the popularization of the language of science, technology and computers: namely, mathematics, as well as an increased public understanding of the subject.

A.J. Bishop et al. (eds.), International Handbook of Mathematics Education, 785 - 817
© 1996 Kluwer Academic Publishers, Printed in the Netherlands

An immediate question arises: What is the popularization of mathematics and what does or might it mean? The valuable ICMI study on the topic (Howson and Kahane 1990) suggests four key features of the popularization of mathematics.

- It consists in sharing mathematics with a wider public
- It includes encouraging people to be more active mathematically
- It must provide mathematical activity in freedom, not by compulsion
- It brings mathematics into human culture, providing mathematics for all.

Implicit in these features is another goal which is worth making explicit: to improve the popular image of mathematics and popular attitudes to it.

The popularization of mathematics should be distinguished from another overlapping area of study, the public understanding of mathematics. By analogy with the public understanding of science this includes public:

- Knowledge of the facts, skills, concepts and strategies of mathematics.
- Knowledge and beliefs about the role of mathematics and its relationships with science, technology, culture, history, commerce, industry and other areas of human knowledge and activity.
- Beliefs about the nature of mathematics as a discipline, the activities of mathematicians, the means of testing and warranting mathematical knowledge and its status.
- Distortions of knowledge and misconceptions in the above areas.
- Knowledge and beliefs about the teaching and learning of mathematics and its assessment.

The public understanding of mathematics is concerned to discover and describe public knowledge and beliefs about mathematics, whereas the central concern of the popularization of mathematics is to enhance public attitudes to and involvement with mathematics. However, improving the public's knowledge of mathematics and its role in education and society, may also lead to the popularization of mathematics.

Although the popularization of mathematics takes place against widespread negative images of mathematics and mathematicians, there are also many features of modern life that provide support for it.

- The public love of puzzles and games, often with a mathematical component.
- The growing interest and fascination with computers and computer based activities including games and simulations, computer-generated patterns and fractal geometry, virtual reality and the information superhighway.
- Press interest in breakthroughs in mathematics and science, as the media coverage of Andrew Wiles' proof of the Fermat Conjecture and interplanetary exploration showed.

- Increased interest in 'edutainment': knowledge and information presented as entertainment, such as the growing range of CD-ROM titles and TV quiz and puzzle shows.
- Reform movements worldwide in mathematics teaching aimed at making mathematics more accessible and the learning experience more active, enjoyable and effective.

These spontaneous areas of interest and independent activities suggest that developments and projects for the popularization of mathematics can draw upon many media, artefacts and forms of communication. The following categories are indicative of some of the means that have been so employed:

- **Celebrations, festivals and events,** including well publicized annual mathematics weeks; mathematics months, and mathematics years, such as the year 2000, the International Year of Mathematics. These can be local, regional, national and international. They are usually coordinated with broadcast media launches, exhibitions, lectures, competitions and other programmes of events, including environment related activities, such as mathematics trails
- **Exhibitions,** including mathematical exhibits in science or other museums (e.g. the Italian exhibition of Mathematical Machines organised by M. Bartolini-Bussi); touring mathematics shows; 'hands-on' activity or exploratory exhibits; displays of mathematical toys, games and puzzles; displays of mathematical books and materials at book shops or in libraries or in exhibitions.
- **Lectures,** including mathematics enrichment lectures, masterclasses and visiting mathematician speakers, lectures on the history of mathematics, ethnomathematics, games, puzzles, demonstrations of mathematical apparatus; calculating prodigies; school mathematics evenings for parents.
- **Computing and Computer Activities.** Popular computer activities include games, recreations and simulations; software for generating or exploring mathematical patterns, symmetries, fractals, etc.; programming and other mathematics computer activities; bulletin boards for sharing and discussing mathematical ideas and challenges.
- **Games, manipulatives, toys and puzzles** with mathematical content such as mathematical board games; cryptanalysis and code kits; calculators and electronic learning toys.
- **Print materials** include books of mathematical games, puzzles and recreations; children's fiction with mathematical content; popular books on mathematics and its history, philosophy and cultural contexts; puzzle 'corners' and features in magazines and newspapers; mathematical magazines and serial publications for young people; posters with mathematical content and patterns. For example, in France there are some very good comics 'bande dessinee' for educated adults treating

mathematical themes such as *Les aventures d'Anselme Lanturlu* (about non-Euclidean geometries) by the physicist Jean Pierre Petit, which was a popular success in the late-1970's and 1980's.
— **Audio-visual and broadcast media** including TV programmes with mathematical puzzles and games; educational programmes for children with mathematical content, cartoons and films with mathematical content, news updates on mathematical developments in science programmes; programmes about mathematicians and the history and philosophy of mathematics; mathematical radio programmes; music and songs with mathematical content; parent education programmes; adult education programmes, both advanced and numeracy orientated (Chapter 20 in this volume by Jungwirth *et al.* treats adult numeracy).

1.1   The History Of Popularization Materials In Mathematics

Popularization materials have been around for a long time, in the form of problem books and mathematical games. Singmaster (1994) argues that these originate in recreational mathematics which is intended to be both fun and popular, and can be traced back at least 4000 years to the Rhind Papyrus of North Africa (Egypt). This contains a problem leading to adding 7 + 49 + 343 + 2401 unrelated to the other problems in the papyrus and most likely inserted for recreational purposes. It is almost analogous to the following problem found in Fibonacci and in medieval Britain but reproduced here from a present day book of children's rhymes.

As I was going to St. Ives,
I met a man with seven wives,
Each wife had seven sacks,
Each sack had seven cats,
Each cat had seven kits:
Kits, cats, sacks, and wives,
How many were there going to St. Ives?

(Kincaid and Kincaid 1975: 58)

Singmaster's review indicates how extensive the history of recreational mathematics is, and thus implicitly, how important a role it has played in the popularization of mathematics. If there has been a modern shift in the field, it has been towards more systematic attempts to popularize mathematics, and the direction of such attempts towards specific target audiences, rather than simply making recreational resources available to the public, and especially, enthusiasts.

1.2   Audiences

One of the central issues that arises in a consideration of the popularization of mathematics is the question of audiences. Thus the ICMI study asks in a heading 'To whom, what, by whom?' (Howson and Kahane 1990; p.11). Another question may be appended: 'To what end?' A number of different audiences for projects for the popularization of mathematics can be imagined. For each popularization project it is necessary to ask: What are the objectives and desired outcomes of the popularization project? Who is the intended audience? What is their relationship with mathematics? Which of their characteristics should be accommodated in such a project? What kinds of topics or experiences are needed to achieve the planned outcomes for the target audience?

Table 1 below offers an indicative set of objectives for possible popularization projects, and target audiences.

OBJECTIVE OF POPULARIZATION PROJECT	TARGET AUDIENCES
1. To show mathematics as a creative and exciting subject, rich with patterns and connections to the world of the child	1. Younger children.
2. To show mathematics as a creative and exciting subject, rich with pattern and applications, exemplifying how it can be communicated to children	2. Primary school teachers, parents.
3. To involve in mathematical activity, develop a fascination with the subject, and encourage further study of mathematics	3. Older children who like mathematics.
4. To overcome traditional negative views of mathematics as a cut-and-dried, uncreative subject accessible only to a minority	4. Older children who are neutral to or dislike mathematics.
5. To show how mathematical thinking permeates everyday and shopfloor life and current affairs	5. Adult workers.
6. To broaden knowledge of mathematics as a central element of culture, art and life, present and past	6. Retired persons.
7. To involve in challenging and creative mathematical problem solving and show that it is open to all	7. General public.
8. To show how mathematics permeates and underpins science, technology and all aspects of human culture	8. Informed citizens.

Table 1. Possible Objectives for Popularization Projects and Target Audiences.

OBJECTIVE OF POPULARIZATION PROJECT	TARGET AUDIENCES
9. To show changing views of the nature of mathematics and controversy over the foundations of its knowledge, and theories of its relation to culture, history and society.	9. General public (especially the more educated public).

Table 1. Possible Objectives for Popularization Projects and Target Audiences.

Naturally it is not exhaustive. Table 1 is simply intended to illustrate the breadth and variety of possible objectives and target audiences for popularization projects.

2.   SAMPLE POPULARIZATION PROJECTS

The following is a sample of illustrative popularization projects and initiatives. Each is successful and indicative of good practice, although systematic data of impact is mostly absent. The sample is based on opportunity, which inevitably skews it towards projects in Britain and anglophone countries. For every project reported there must be scores of equally good ones around the world not mentioned. Additional examples of popularization projects are reported in Howson and Kahane (1990).

2.1   Primary Mathematics Year, 1988.

In Great Britain 1988 was designated Primary Mathematics Year through the initiative of the Primary Initiatives in Mathematics Education (PrIME) Project, in collaboration with other supporters and providers. This project focused on investigational and problem solving approaches to mathematics in the elementary school, with special emphasis on calculators and computers. The aim of Primary Mathematics Year was to encourage children in primary schools to share with their parents and the public their enjoyment of mathematics, and their confidence in mathematical investigational and problem solving. It was heralded by the distribution of many thousands of copies of a quarterly newsletter outlining ways of raising awareness and providing details of the planned events. It was launched on 29 February at Birmingham Town Hall through TV and guest appearances of 'personalities' such as Johnny Ball, a dynamic and popular ex-teacher TV presenter known nationally on children's TV for his enthusiasm for puzzles and the popularization of mathematics. Many thousand primary school children and others around the country participated through maths fairs, exhibitions, competitions, displays of pupil's work, parent workshops, maths trails, and other events. McDonalds, the fast food chain, participated by sponsoring school projects, and many stories were carried in newspapers under banners like 'Making maths fun', 'Adding fun to maths', and 'On the Maths Trail' (PrIME 1988a)

The event seems to have been a great success in stimulating enthusiasm and mathematical awareness among younger school children and their teachers and parents.

2.2 April, NCTM Mathematics Education Month

Every year the North American National Council of Teachers of Mathematics celebrates April as Mathematics Education Month. The aim is to celebrate the beauty and utility of mathematics and to promote mathematics awareness in the home, classroom and community. The slogan of this event is 'Math Power for All' and in 1994 NCTM provided members who ask for it with a free 'Math Power Kit'. This included an NCTM presidential proclamation certificate, an activities calendar, an account of mathematics reform efforts, 'Math Power for All' promotional items, a mathematics poster and parental involvement materials. In 1995 NCTM a similar 'Mathematics Heritage Kit' was available free to members, to promote awareness and appreciation of mathematics.

A strength of this initiative is the reach of NCTM, with several hundred thousand members in North America, all of whom have the opportunity to ask for a free kit annually to use in their school and community to promote and popularize of mathematics. However I know of no evaluation of the take up or effectiveness of this initiative.

2.3 The Pop Maths Roadshow

The Pop Maths Roadshow was a lively interactive exhibition sponsored by the Royal Society and other scientific and mathematical bodies, which toured over twenty cities in Britain in 1989-90. During the opening week at Leeds there were interactive displays including 'Frontiers of Chaos', Johnny Ball on 'Funtastic Maths', Mazes and Puzzles; Juggling; Mathematics and Magic; Knots; Soap Bubbles; a mathematical 'Any Questions', a children's corner, and other events and displays including an exhibition shop selling a range of mathematical products. There were also demonstrations, talks and lectures open to the public and school parties, free of charge. The touring show was very well attended, especially by schoolchildren, and had 200 000 visitors in six months (PrIME, 1988b).

A maths trail which guided participants around the centre of Melbourne observing mathematically significant aspects of the environment was set up in 1985 (Blane and Clarke 1985). This was designed to support the Australian and New Zealand Association for the Advancement of Science meeting. Trail followers are guided along a set route where they are invited to look out for interesting shapes, symmetries, structures, patterns and other mathematical features of the built environment, and to solve environment related maths problems. The aim is to combine a pleasurable outdoor activity with a set of pursuits that sharpen perceptions of the mathematics of the environment, as well as to break down a 'ghetto' perception of mathematics as something belonging only to the classroom.

The trail was intended mainly for parents and children during one particular week of school vacation. However the trail has continued to be supported, and since its inception over 10,000 copies of the trail guide have been issued. Blane (1992) also reports that an 'Environmental Mathematics Trail' has been developed at Western Plains Zoo in New South Wales which raises current environmental problems and issues as well as the activities described above.

Mathematics trails have been developed in many other countries including Canada and Britain. They provide an opportunity for adults and children to develop a mathematical appreciation of their environment, as well as an environmental appreciation of mathematics. If successfully implemented, they represent a means of bringing an awareness of mathematics into everyday life. At Exeter the design of local mathematics trails has been used as an exercise for student teachers, to broaden their conceptions of mathematics and its links with the environment. Testing their draft trails on groups of children provides a valuable induction into some of the skills of the teacher.

Reports of mathematics trails rarely include any research or evaluation data beyond participation counts and anecdotal reports of enthusiastic reception by small numbers of participants. To ascertain their impact on public perceptions of mathematics more systematic research is required.

2.5   Zeeman's Lectures and Masterclasses

The mathematician Christopher Zeeman has played a leading role in the Britain in the popularization of mathematics by means of lectures. In 1978 he gave the Royal Institution Christmas Lectures on mathematics, contributing to a tradition in the popularization of science which dates back to Faraday. This series of 6 annual lectures is televised on public access TV on successive days in the Christmas vacation and is thus accessible to the majority of Britain population. How many actually chose to view the programmes is not known, but may be around the one million mark. An important aspect of Zeeman's presentations is that he offered mathematical proofs to the public, on the grounds that mathematics is about theorems and proofs, and to omit this central part would be to misrepresent mathematics, and to leave out a central aesthetic feature. His criteria for the choice of which proofs to popularize are interesting, and are reproduced below. They closely resemble Hardy's (1941) view of what makes a mathematical theorem interesting.

1) A theorem should be noble. In other words, it should capture the quintessence of some mainstream branch of mathematics.
2) Results should be surprising and intriguing, sufficient to capture the imagination and hold the attention.
3) Proofs should be elegant, rigorous, complete and understandable.
4) Each proof should fit onto a single [overhead] transparency. (Howson and Kahane 1990: 196)

Zeeman also contributed to the founding of the Royal Institution annual Mathematics Masterclasses. These aim to offer enrichment to mathematically talented 13 year olds, who are invited to attend 10 weekly 2 ½ hour sessions, comprising talks and problems sessions. Topics treated include perspective, gyroscopes, gears, knots and links, curves of constant diameter, and spherical geometry. Zeeman suggests that such content should be chosen not only to match the above four criteria, but also the following:

– Worksheets should contain both theory and computation, and should stimulate discovery and creativity.
– Applications should be useful
– Experiments should be surprising, robust, easy to do, and easy to repeat at home with home-made equipment. (Howson and Kahane 1990: 201)

Such masterclasses have spread to over 20 locations in Britain. Significantly, a follow-up study was undertaken four years after a series of such classes at Warwick University, to assess their impact on the participants. Watson (1989) found that all the participants he contacted reported that the masterclass experience had greatly increased their confidence and their problem-solving ability both in mathematics and in all other branches of science.

2.6   Sharing Maths with Parents

A number of initiatives worldwide aim to involve parents in their children's mathematics. The British Mathematical Association (1987) produced an imaginative guide to informing and involving parents in mathematics including workshops, stalls, displays of resources and children's work, out of school mathematical activities, and so on.

Project IMPACT aims to involve parents in shared mathematical activity with their children. It draws upon informal and out-of-school knowledge and builds links with written school mathematics. More than 600 primary schools in Britain participate, and local implementers are encouraged to evaluate their impact. It is a very successful project, to judge by its take-up (Merttens and Vass, 1990). It has also spread to number of other countries. Detailed data concerning its effects are sparse, but independent critical evaluations of the project are underway (Brown 1992).

A comparable project in the USA is FAMILY MATH, which aims to create whole family enjoyment of mathematics in an out-of-school setting and teaches parents how to encourage their children at home. The project offers classes for parents, leadership workshops for educators and parents who wish to give classes to other parents, and games, handouts and activity packs for family use in the home.

A number of evaluation studies have been carried out (De la Cruz and Thompson, 1992). The most dramatic finding concerns perceptions of the nature of mathematics. Most parents interviewed regarded mathematics as a very difficult study made up of drill, practice and memorization. After attending 12-16 hours of FAMILY MATH classes parents perceptions changed.

There were dramatic changes in attitudes towards mathematics and perceptions of the subject...parents were surprised that the classes were not only interesting but fun...they were surprised at the learning that took place during the cooperative activities and games...and...that problems can be approached in a variety of ways rather than in just one correct way. (De la Cruz and Thompson 1992: 2)

FAMILY MATH has proved successful with dominant and ethnic minority groups across the USA, and to facilitate its use by Hispanic families the materials are available in Spanish. The project has also been transferred with apparent success to many other countries, and in total over a quarter of a million parents and children have participated. However no evaluation data from implementations outside the USA is reported.

IMPACT and FAMILY MATH both encourage mathematics among primary school aged children and their parents. Both have grown large by training leaders and trainers to spread the project further. There are indications that both may impact positively on children's and families' perceptions' of mathematics, including building strong links with out-of-school activities. There are claims that both also improve the knowledge, confidence and problem-solving skills of their participants, but more systematic data is needed to substantiate this claim.

One negative feature of both programs is that they have developed a capitalized brand name (IMPACT and FAMILY MATH) which is marketed like a product, and participant loyalty to the 'brand' is encouraged. Although this may facilitate the successful spread of the program, over-emphasizing the identity of the project at the expense of mathematics itself may impede the transfer of positive gains in confidence and perceptions to school mathematics.

2.7 Fractals in Youth Computer-Culture

The Mandelbrot set and computer generated fractal images can be seen in popular music videos, record covers, magazines, Tee-shirts, posters, and in club and set decor. Many consumers of these images may have only a slim notion that these are mathematical in origin. More significantly, computer software that generates such patterns and allows the operator to zoom in endlessly on details have been widely distributed commercially, and as shareware and freeware. Since the 1980's a computer subculture has blossomed among the youth, particularly in industrialized countries. Fractal geometry images have been a popular part of this, presumably due to their stunning visual beauty and the possibility of exploring them inexhaustibly. Some of the young enthusiasts involved in this culture master recursion and the programming techniques necessary to create such displays. The relationship between such pursuits and attitudes to and participation in academic mathematics is unknown, and anecdotal evidence suggests that some of the participants who delve deepest into the associated mathematics are school students who have already chosen to specialize in mathematics, computing and the physical sciences.

Apart from the limited take-up of the programming language Logo, in which recursion is a central concept, little of this enthusiasm appears to have been exploited by schools or incorporated into the mathematics curriculum.

2.8 Enactive and Displacement Games

There are numerous popular physically enactive and displacement games which might be termed mathematical. A well known example is Rubik's cube, which sold millions in the 1980's. To 'solve' the Rubik cube, involves returning it to the original state after an arbitrary physical permutation of its elements in 3 dimensions. However, in doing this, the mathematics is usually hidden under a set of specific procedures and strategies.

A similar but earlier game is 'the fifteen puzzle' in which 15 numbered unit squares are permuted by displacement within a 4x4 grid. This was probably invented in the USA in 1878 (Thiele 1994). The problem that captured the public imagination is that of exchanging only the pieces 14 and 15. This can be proved to be impossible using a theorem of Bézout. However the proof of impossibility has not put the public off from continuing to attempt the challenge.

It is not clear how much games which can be analysed or solved mathematically contribute to the public popularization of mathematics, although they can be asset to the mathematics classroom. For such games may well be perceived in concrete and game-specific terms, rather than as embodiments of mathematical knowledge. The popular books published for enthusiasts showing how to solve them usually do so in concrete non-mathematical terms.

Once a game catches the public imagination, as the game of Nim did after Alain Renais' film *L' Année Dernière à Marienbad*, in the early 1960's, then there may be an opportunity to popularize the mathematical analysis or solution, and hence mathematics itself. But this is a secondary strategy, dependent on the exploitation of a cultural opportunity.

2.9 Children's books

There is a growing number of children's fiction books in which mathematics plays a significant or central part, but which are read by children out of fascination for the story. Finding mathematical topics in an imaginative story often imbues them with interest and attractiveness. An example is *Dot and Line* by Norton Juster. This classic mini-book is the story of the love affair between a dot and a line. It is imaginative, fantastical and beautifully illustrated, which made it my daughter Jane's favorite book when she was 6 or 7 years old. The complex mathematical shapes and words like 'dodecahedron' and 'parallelepiped' held a mystery and magic for her.

2.10 Mathematics Magazines

In many countries, there are mathematics magazine directed at students, teachers and others, such as the following.

The Mathematical Digest, from the University of Cape Town circulates throughout South Africa and further afield. This contains puzzles, challenges and articles, and is directed at school children. It is claimed to have served as the model on which *Plus Magazine* published by Mathematical Association in Britain is based, also circulated among schoolchildren.

Nyanssapow magazine, from Accra, Ghana is intended to be a light, interesting read and contains articles, puzzles, problems and games related to mathematics and science. It is primarily directed at teachers, and is intended to feed and keep alive their interests in these subjects.

Tangente: L'Aventure Mathematique is a mathematical magazine from France. The typical September-October 1993 issue contains an article about mathematics in comic strips, other articles about Andrew Wiles and the history of the Fermat's 'Last Theorem', the mathematics of tax, as well as mathematical problems, humor and news. It looks like a professionally presented and interesting commercial newsstand magazine with mathematics as its special theme.

Another French magazine is *Maths & Malices: Le Magazine de Mathématiques Pour Tous*. One issue contains the life story of Maria Agnesi, puzzles, mathematical jokes, an article on Escher-like tessellations, a mathematical Tin-Tin story, and an explanation of how two negatives make a positive in multiplication in terms of 'an enemy of an enemy is a friend'. Again an eye catching and interest holding magazine. There are regular features treating themes in the history of mathematics, mathematics in literature (including fiction, plays and movies), mathematics in art, mathematics in life, games and puzzles, logic games, mathematical problems (including genuinely open mathematical problems), and in each issue there are several pages of exercises for the classroom with solutions and a discussion of their meaning and purpose.

This magazine is estimated to have a circulation of the order of 10 000 copies per issue. It speaks well of the public appreciation of mathematics in French culture that such magazines are commercially viable. What their impact is on their readership is unknown, and this needs investigation. However one can imagine that they would appeal to young persons with an interest in mathematics and might help to round out their incidental knowledge and foster recreational interest in the subject.

2.11 Mathematical Puzzle and Recreation Books

There is a long history of mathematical puzzle and recreations going back to ancient times. Mathematical puzzle and recreation book can be found in most literate civilizations and cultures. For example, the Kama Sutra, the Ancient Indian guide to sexual etiquette in its unexpurgated edition (as George Gheverghese Joseph terms it) contains mathematical problems and puzzles for use during love making. In modern times mathematical recreations and puzzle books have been very popular, as the enormous sales of Martin Gardner's books show. Schaaf's (1978) bibliography of recreational mathematics had reached four volumes, when last seen.

Mathematical puzzles and recreations in the public domain raise the same issue as mathematical games. Are the persons puzzling doing mathematics, or aware that they are doing mathematics, or are they just solving puzzles? Mathematical puzzle and recreation books involve mathematical knowledge, skills and creative strategic thought, in their solutions, rather than just the physical manipulation that some games or toys require. Ainley (1988) argues that the mathematical thinking involved in games and puzzles is closer to the activity of a mathematician than that in routine school mathematics exercises. Such puzzle and recreation books are often popularly identified as mathematical too. So they do seem to make a real and positive contribution to the popularization of mathematics.

2.12 Square One TV

Square One TV is a television series for children, broadcast daily on public service TV in the USA since 1987. It is aimed at 8-to-12-year-old children viewing at home after school. There are over 200 half-hour shows made up of segments which are parodies of television shows, including: dramas, musicals, game shows, commercials, and music videos. For example, one segment 'General Mathpital' is a parody of 'General Hospital', a popular soap opera. In it, surgeons operate on an asymmetric shape so as to reassemble the pieces into one that is bilaterally symmetric. In doing so, the surgeons discuss the concept and explore several solutions to the problem. Similarly a series of segments called 'Mathnet' parodies 'Dragnet', the popular TV detective series of the 1950's. Many segments use the music video format and various musical genres, including: blues, heavy metal, rock and roll, country & western, rap, and others, in recognition of the diversity of taste and subcultures in the USA (Schneider 1994).

An investigation was carried out to determine the impact on children's mathematics. The study examined changes that might occur in children's
1) attitudes towards mathematics, and
2) use of problem solving strategies.

An experimental test design was used in the study, with the experimental group watching 30 half hour programmes. The experimental subjects gained significantly more than those in the control group on both measures, and the gains were made by subjects irrespective of gender, socio economic status or previous mathematics achievement (Esty and Schneider 1990).

This TV program for children is important in several respects. Children choose to watch it for entertainment purposes in open competition with commercial TV programs. It benefits all groups of students (within the target age range), including the traditional groups who are educationally deprived. An evaluation study suggests that it is beneficial both with regards to children's attitudes to mathematics and problem solving skills. These benefits seem to flow from the fact that the series is broadcast widely at an appropriate time for its intended audience, it is well designed with well integrated mathematics content, there are high production values and the series is adequately funded.

Fun and Games is a televised mathematical game show presented in prime viewing time (7:00 pm) by Celia Hoyles, professor of mathematics education, and Johnny Ball or Rob Buckman. Mathematical problems are presented using eye-catching props, and small groups of contestants solve them. Contestants are given hints by Hoyles if they get stuck. Typically, discrete process-type problems are used, so that different arrangements and strategies can be employed and represented visually. The program 'had ordinary people participate in non-trivial mathematics. They were able to find complex, beautiful, intriguing, counter-intuitive strategies for various puzzles and games, all without rehearsal.' (Pollak 1994: 320). The series ran for four years on British commercial TV beginning in 1987, and attracted 8 or 9 million viewers at its peak (over 15 per cent of the entire population). It was well reviewed with favourable comments including the following: 'Beneath its relentless high spirits Fun and Games is intellectually unique among game shows and quizzes. It demands answers actually worked out by mental agility rather than by recall.' and 'packed with puzzles, conundrums, brain teasers and games Fun and Games aims to shake the cobwebs out of mathematics' (Hoyles 1990: 131)

The impact of the program on its viewers was investigated. After the 1989 series a representative sample were asked in a questionnaire if having seen Fun and Games they had changed their view of mathematics. 20 per cent responded affirmatively. Although the program producers were disappointed that this figure is low, as Hoyles says, if almost 2 million viewers changed their view of mathematics as a consequence of viewing the program this would be a most dramatic result for the popularization of mathematics. However welcome they are, such conclusions must be treated with caution as a flawed and superficial methodology was used to gather this data.

The success of Fun and Games is an important step forwards in the popularization of mathematics. A large adult audience chose to watch it in prime-time, and were encouraged to try to solve non-routine mathematical problems, and to watch others do so with evident enjoyment. It also featured a woman as representing mathematical expertise, which is an important step in challenging gender stereotypes. Like with Square One TV, the message seems to be that if the purseholders choose to support mathematics on TV with funding equivalent to other programming, then expertise can be found to make high quality effective and popular programmes on mathematics with viewer appeal. The main obstacle seems to be the resistance of the program makers. The head of science programming of the TV company that made the program thought that the image of mathematics might kill it, and needed strong persuasion to proceed.

Images of schooling abound in movies world wide such as in the films of Jean Vigo, Francois Truffaut, Satyajit Ray and the St. Trinian's series. However 'Stand and Deliver', released by Warner Brothers in 1988, is unique because it is a successful Hollywood movie whose hero is a mathematics teacher. The drama revolves around getting a class of disadvantaged Hispanic teenagers to study calculus and pass the Advanced Placement Test in mathematics for college entrance. It is based on the inspiring true story of teacher Jaime Escalante, who is played by Edward James Olmos.

The film is a gripping contemporary drama depicting schooling in East Los Angeles in which the usual problems of drug-abuse and gang violence arise, but are treated in a non-exploitative way. The film contains a number of important messages about mathematics and schooling, such as that no learners should be written off, and that advanced mathematics is open to anybody if they are taught well and try hard enough. A notable quote is that 'Students rise to the level of your expectations.' The teacher also reminds the Hispanic students that they own mathematics: 'Your ancestors the Mayans invented the concept of zero.' He uses vivid analogies and methods to link mathematics with the student's interests and culture, and to make the subject meaningful for them. He builds powerful personal relationships with the students which inspire them to exceed their self-expectations.

Unfortunately the pedagogy illustrated in the film is very traditional, as the title 'Stand and Deliver' suggests. It is confined to teacher boardwork and student seatwork, and the students' success is implicitly ascribed to the teacher's giftedness in explaining, and his unparalleled motivation in getting the students to apply themselves, in and out of scheduled-school time. There is little recognition of the necessity for active learning by students and the vital roles of experience, multiple forms of representation, and discussion in the construction of mathematical meaning. Nevertheless, the film challenges myths about the inaccessibility of mathematics, and must have offered this message to an audience of tens of millions worldwide.

How much impact it would have on the received view of mathematics and mathematical ability is impossible to say. One might speculate that it would have little lasting effect, as the events it portrays could be regarded as untypical, and attributed to an exceptional teacher. Popular conceptions and stereotypes appear to be able to survive counterexamples, which are assimilated as 'the exception that proves the rule'. The fact that the film ends by claiming to be a true story and listing the increasing number of students who pass the Advanced Placement Test in subsequent years at the school is a device that has been weakened by its use in many made-for-TV movies. Nevertheless, the film is an important first for Hollywood's contribution to the popularization of mathematics.

This brief review raises a number of issues concerning the mathematical content of projects; project objectives and intended audiences; the evaluation of the outcomes and effectiveness of the projects; the range of extant popularization of mathematics projects; and funding for such projects and the necessity of collaborating with media producers.

In looking over the range of sample popularization projects it appears that the depth and complexity of the mathematical content is inversely proportional to the scale and scope of the projects. Many of the larger projects address knowledge of arithmetic and the elementary applications of arithmetic, measures and geometry in the world. Next in popularity comes the solving of mathematical puzzles and recreations, which concerns processes and strategies rather than substantial mathematical content. The treatment of deeper mathematical concepts and ideas such as algebraic relationships, proofs, mathematical models and infinity is something found only rarely. It is a sad fact that many of the most attractive features of mathematics, such as the beauty and elegance of its concepts, theories and results cannot be appreciated without a deeper treatment of mathematical content, and few popularization projects take the risk of addressing this area.

The objectives of the sample popularization projects include most of those listed in Table 1. One of the listed objectives not exemplified in any projects is no. 5. To show how mathematical thinking permeates everyday and shopfloor life and current affairs. This aim may be better treated in adult numeracy (see Chapter 20) or critical mathematical literacy programmes.

Another set of objectives less thoroughly treated in the projects listed above are those concerning knowledge and appreciation of mathematics in culture, art, science, technology and philosophy. These are among the most difficult objectives to address because they require in-depth knowledge of the role of mathematics in culture as well as in-depth and possibly expensive media treatment.

One aim tackled infrequently is that of addressing critical mathematics literacy, i.e. the mathematics needed by citizens in order to participate fully and critically in modern democratic society (Skovsmose, 1994). It is all too rare that relevant issues, such as underlying economic forecast models, the effects of voting systems on democracy, or ecological risk models, are discussed critically. When they are discussed in the mass media, the scientific and technical details are usually kept to a minimum. In the rare cases where such technicalities are discussed, usually the topic is seen as social comment or political critique, with no relevance to mathematics. Perhaps none of this is surprising, in view of the widespread perceptions of mathematics as neutral and devoid of social and political values, throughout the popular, academic and educational domains (Ernest, 1991).

The intended audiences of the projects illustrated above vary from a few, specifically targeted groups to offerings for the full, general public. The targeted groups are mainly younger children at home, parents of primary school children, primary school teachers and their pupils, and older children who like, and have displayed a talent for, mathematics. These are all linked to, but not a direct part of, formal education, and the initiatives offer pre-school or out-of-school support for institutionalized mathematics teaching. This is primarily with the aim of enriching children's mathematics-related experiences and improving attitudes to and involvement in mathematics. These are clearly important functions. But do they also point to problems with or inadequacies in formal school mathematics?

Several projects are offered to the general public and it is a self-selected minority who choose to watch or participate. Thus the degree of take-up is an important indicator of success. This will depend on many presentational factors that go beyond mathematical content. What the sample projects illustrate is the importance of collaboration between mathematicians and educators, on the one hand, and producers, journalists and other media professionals, on the other. Because of the costs and scale of funding needed for the production of professional quality mass-media productions, as well as the degree of professional production expertise required, full collaboration with media producers is essential. Programme series like 'Square One TV' could only have been produced through large scale commitment of funds and professional expertise. This leaves the popularizers of mathematics with a vicious cycle to break into. Until mathematics becomes more popular, the mass media are not likely to invest or give much attention to popularization of mathematics programmes. But until more effort is directed towards popularization of mathematics projects, especially in the mass-media, mathematics is unlikely to gain in popularity.

It is evident, however, that there is a growing effort by mathematicians, mathematics educators, teachers, and others to mount projects for the popularization of mathematics. The most effective involve co-operation with media producers and professionals, civic interests, and commercial sponsors, who see involvement as both a part of their civic duty and as a marketing strategy to children, parents and schools. Such cooperation is a necessity for mathematicians, educators and teachers wishing to promote mathematics popularization projects with any hope of large-scale and significant impact, whether targeting a specific group or a general audience.

3. MYTHS ABOUT MATHEMATICS

The question that has been avoided until now, is 'why are projects for the popularization of mathematics necessary?' The answer is that mathematics has a bad press, with a widespread public image of being difficult, cold, abstract, and in many cultures, largely masculine. It also has the image of being remote and inaccessible to all but a few super-intelligent beings with 'mathematical minds'. This myth is the prevailing public image in Western Anglophone countries, where many persons operating at high levels of competency in numeracy, graphicacy, computeracy in their professional life happily admit to being no good at mathematics. There is a widespread public acceptability in being 'bad at maths' (Adult Learning and Basic Skills Unit 1994). In contrast to the shame associated with illiteracy, innumeracy is sometimes almost a matter of pride amongst educated persons in these countries.

Many persons making such claims are not innumerate at all, and it is school or academic mathematics not everyday or business mathematics that they feel they cannot do. Numeracy, contextual mathematics, even ethnomathematics are perceived to be quite distinct from school and academic mathematics, and the latter is understood to be 'real' mathematics. Thus the popular image of mathematics sets it apart from daily concerns of the public, despite the many social applications of mathematics referred to daily in the mass-media, from sports and weather to economic and social indicators. The widespread public image of mathematics is largely a negative and remote one, alien to many persons' professional and personal concerns and their self-perceived abilities. An indication of this stereotyped public image of mathematics can be found in the massmedia including films, TV shows, magazines, newspapers, children's comics, games, puzzles and cartoons. The following example illustrates this.

Figure 1 shows a puzzle given away in the breakfast cereal Sugar Puffs in 1992, which probably reached many thousand children in Britain and elsewhere. It is a 4 piece jigsaw puzzle that reassembles to show a different and luminous pattern. The main puzzle image shows an angry male teacher, hair protruding wildly at the sides, raising or shaking an admonishing finger at the viewer, who is playfully positioned as a schoolchild. Over his shoulder on the chalkboard is the incorrect sum 2+2=5 symbolizing Falsehood. It represents an elementary error by the viewing child, a moral lapse, the dereliction of the duty of study and the obligation to elementary correctness. This is an archetypal set of associations for mathematics, in a humorous context: overbearing masculine authority, the inferior positioning of the pupil, the mathematics classroom, absolute knowledge, and errors and failure.

As in this example, for many people the image of mathematics is associated with anxiety and failure. When Sewell (1981) was gathering data on adult numeracy for the Cockcroft Report she asked a sample of adults on the street if they would answer some questions. Half of them refused to answer further questions immediately when they understood it was about mathematics, indicating negative responses to mathematics.

Figure 1. Free 1992 puzzle from Nabisco cereal 'Sugar Puffs'.

Such reactions reflect the widespread public and massmedia myth of mathematics as difficult, cold, abstract, theoretical, ultra-rational, isolated and inaccessible (Ernest 1995, Buerk 1984). This is not a new view. According to Ascham (1570: 34) 'Mark all Mathematical heads, which be only and wholly bent to those sciences, how solitary they be to themselves, how unfit to live with others, and how unapt to serve in the world.' In the last century Flaubert wrote: 'Mathematics. Dries up the heart.' A recent newspaper article stated: 'Of all the subjects built to a greater degree on number than on words, Gauss's Queen of the Sciences is considered the most likely to instill terror, or at least glaze eyes, outside the zealous ranks of the converted.' (Katz 1995: 33)

There is no doubt about it. In most developed countries the public image of mathematics is bad. Jokes appear in the newspapers; stereotyped, incorrect views on mathematics abound. 'All problems are already formulated', 'Mathematics is not creative', 'Mathematics is not a part of human culture', 'The only purpose of mathematics is for sorting out students', 'Mathematics may be important to other people, not to me'...Even when it seems positive, the image is usually wrong: Mathematics is always correct, providing absolute truth, solid and static. The image of mathematicians is still worse: arrogant, élitist, middle class, eccentric, male social misfits. They lack social antennae, common sense, and a sense of humor.' (Howson and Kahane 1990, p. 2-3)

Unfortunately little systematic research has been undertaken on such myths and the popular image of mathematics, except for limited investigations into the views of students and females. For example Kouba and McDonald (1987, 1991) found that students regard mathematics as an exclusive domain, school based and isolated from other areas of study. Preston (1975) found a substantial subgroup of students who see mathematics as an algorithmic, mechanical and stereotyped subject. Erlwanger's (1973) seminal case study of a successful 12 year old studying an individualized scheme uncovered a view of mathematics as an irrational 'wild goose chase' searching for many unrelated and arbitrary rules, sanctioned only by the dictates of authority.

This and other evidence suggests that children construct powerful stereotyped images of mathematics for themselves, apparently based on their classroom learning experiences. Any impact of massmedia or other popular images of mathematics are harder to discern, as students' classroom experiences seem to be the dominant influences.

Much of the research on girls/women and mathematics is concerned with the stereotypical perceptions of mathematics as a male domain. Such views are prevalent, especially in Western Anglophone countries. It is claimed that parents play a key role in communicating such perceptions to their children and in encouraging boys more than girls to learn mathematics. According to Walkerdine (1988) and others, stereotyped popular views of gender identify mathematics as masculine and femininity as antithetical to mathematics.

The mass-media and the market-place are also arenas where gendered conceptions of mathematics are evident. An interesting case is that of the talking Barbie doll produced by Mattel Inc. in the USA in 1993. This speaks a number of phrases including 'Math class is tough!', suggesting that because 'Barbie' represents a girl, she find school mathematics difficult. Following a public outcry, the doll was modified so that this phrase no longer occurs.

In Britain, a 1994 government advertisement for teacher training used a girl's socks to represent academic attainment. One sock, corresponding to English, Science and Technology, was correctly pulled up. The other sock labelled Maths had fallen down, linking girls with under-achievement in mathematics. This stereotypical image was ironic in the first year in which British girls out-performed boys in mathematics examinations at the end of compulsory schooling.

As these examples illustrate, stereotypical gendered (i.e. masculine) images of mathematics are widespread, and probably contribute to the problem of female underparticipation in mathematics. However this problem is not the same in all countries. For example, there are proportionately five times as many female scientists in Latin American countries as there are in Anglo-Saxon (Pile 1993).

The central issue is that there are widespread false myths and negative images of mathematics circulating in society, and these create the need for the popularization of mathematics. In many developed countries, mathematics is either unpopular or insufficiently popular with a significant section of the public. This is an issue of concern both for utilitarian and social justice reasons, because mathematics serves as a 'critical filter' controlling access to many areas of advanced study and better-paid and more fulfilling professional occupations. This not only concerns those occupations involving scientific and technological skills, but also extends far beyond this domain to many other occupations, including education, the caring professions and financial services. In addition, many adults leaving full-time education have not been empowered by their mathematics education as mathematically-literate citizens who are able to exercise independent critical judgements with regard to the mathematical underpinnings of democratic modern society and its crucial processes of social and political decision-making.

4.   MODERNISM AND MATHEMATICS

The central argument made below is that the widespread negative myths about mathematics, centrally bound up with the popularization problem, find support in the philosophy of mathematics. There is a recent tendency in this field commonly termed Modernism. Descartes is regarded as having founded Modernism with his 'dream of reason' (Davis and Hersh 1988). This envisaged the building of indubitable structures of thought based on a logical masterplan, the Euclidean paradigm. This is the Ancient Greek model for an axiomatic theory, first used for geometry almost two and a half thousand years ago. Francis Bacon called Euclid's theory the only true science, and in Modernism it became the model for all science, reasoning and rationality. Physics (e.g. Newton), philosophy (e.g. Spinoza) and mathematics (e.g. Frege, Peano, Russell), as well as other disciplines, fashioned their theories in its image.

These traditions are termed Modernist because they are characterized by a shared overall design based on one overarching scheme or central concept, namely the Euclidean paradigm. This approach sweeps away history, traditions and the human sides of mathematics (and knowledge in general) as obsolete, and is built up instead from 'clear and simple ideas' and 'explicitly stated postulates', as used in axiomatics. Modernism is foundationalist, because it believes that certainty can be conferred on knowledge when grounded through its axiomatic form.

Early twentieth century philosophy of mathematics adopted this descendent of mathematical form as its paradigm. It reapplied the model to mathematics in the quest for absolutely certain foundations for knowledge. This was the foundationalist program of the Logicist, Formalist, and to a lesser extent the Intuitionist schools in the philosophy of mathematics. However the failure of the prescriptive programs of these schools to achieve this aim is well documented. For technical and other reasons it is not possible to formally axiomatize all of mathematical knowledge, nor to gain absolute certainty even for a large part of mathematics (Tiles 1991, Tymoczko 1986). However the failure of the foundationalist programme has not spelled the end of Modernism (or absolutism as it is also called), in philosophy of mathematics as a legitimate way of interpreting mathematics (Ernest 1991).

Absolutism is primarily an epistemological position concerned with how to best justify mathematical knowledge, but it has consequences for views about the nature of mathematical knowledge. In simplified terms, absolutist perspectives describe mathematical knowledge as an objective, absolute, certain and incorrigible body of knowledge. According to absolutism mathematical knowledge is timeless, although we may discover new theories and truths to add; it is superhuman and ahistorical, for the history of mathematics is irrelevant to the nature and justification of mathematical knowledge; it is pure isolated knowledge, which happens to be useful because of its universal validity; it is value-free and culture-free, for the same reason.

The outcome therefore is a philosophically sanctioned image of mathematics as objective, fixed, pure, abstract and wholly logical, in short, the traditional image and often negative myth described above. If this is how many philosophers, mathematicians and teachers describe their subject, small wonder it lends support to the public myth. Although absolutist philosophies of mathematics can be defended as rational, they are often incorrectly associated with negative myths and irrational beliefs about mathematics and this connection must be severed.

For example, an analogous but irrational view of mathematics is that of Dualism. Perry (1970) distinguished a number of belief systems or stages in intellectual development including that of Dualism, which has been applied to views of mathematics by researchers (Copes 1982).

The Dualist view of mathematics, in brief, is that it is a fixed and absolute set of truths and rules laid down by authority. Mathematics is exact and certain, 'cut and dried', and there is always a rule to follow in solving problems. Thus mathematical knowledge is in final form, and its foundations are permanent and eternally secure, and if a human error in mathematics is uncovered it means that the questioned parts were not knowledge after all.

This is more or less the widespread negative myth about mathematics described above. Whatever its origins, this view receives support from Modernist conceptions and philosophies of mathematics. However there is an opposing set of philosophies of mathematics which can be used to support a more positive view of mathematics.

4.1 Post-Modernism

A new Post-Modernist and fallibilist tradition has been emerging in the philosophy of mathematics (Lakatos 1976, Tiles 1991, Davis and Hersh 1980). It is Post-Modernist because of its rejection of absolutism, foundationalism and the associated logical meta-narratives of certainty. Mathematical knowledge is understood to be fallible and eternally open to revision, both in terms of its proofs and its concepts. Post-Modernism is committed to a multidisciplinary account of mathematics as a set of socially distributed practices. It embraces the practices of mathematicians, the history and applications of mathematics, and the place of mathematics in human culture, including issues of values and education. In short Post-Modernism fully admits the human face and basis of mathematics as a legitimate philosophical concern. This perspective draws inspiration and intellectual support from other currents of thought, including the history and sociology of mathematics (e.g. S. Restivo), and from cultural studies and semiotics (e.g. B. Rotman). The rejection of Modernism also finds echoes in mathematics education in radical constructivism (e.g. E. von Glasersfeld), feminist critiques (e.g. V. Walkerdine) and in ethnomathematics (e.g. U. D'Ambrosio).

Post-Modernism proposes a reconceptualised view of the nature of mathematics. It is no longer seen as defined by a body of pure and abstract knowledge which exists in a superhuman, objective realm. Instead mathematics is associated with sets of social practices, each with its history, persons, institutions and social locations, symbolic forms, purposes and power relations. Thus academic research mathematics is one such practice (or rather a multiplicity of shifting, interconnected practices). Likewise each of ethnomathematics and school mathematics is a distinct set of such practices. They are intimately bound up together, because the symbolic productions of one practice may be recontextualized and reproduced in another.

As in the previous case, one of Perry's (1970) categories, that of Relativism, fits well with this perspective. The Relativist view applied to mathematics, in brief, is that it is a dynamic, problem-driven and continually expanding field of human creation and invention, in which patterns are generated and then distilled into knowledge. This view places most emphasis on mathematical activity, the doing of mathematics, and it accepts that there are many ways of solving any problem in mathematics. It also stresses that mathematical knowledge must be evaluated relative to its context, which are multiple, and is not given in absolute, once-for-all-time form.

Using the Dualist-Relativist distinction to classify people's conceptions of mathematics is of course a simplification. If views can be classified in terms of a single distinction it will be along a continuum, rather than at the two poles. For some purposes it is important to go beyond this simple framework, and to characterize peoples' beliefs multi-dimensionally. Nevertheless, the distinction is an important one, and has been usefully applied to by a number of researchers including Cooney (1988) and Carré and Ernest (1993). Keeping to a simple dichotomy allows the important analogy with the philosophy of mathematics to be made.

Some of the curriculum reform movements in mathematics have promoted views of mathematics that fit this classification. On the one hand, the Back-to-Basics movement which emphasises basic numeracy as knowledge of facts, rules and skills, to be learned through practice and rote, with little regard for meaning or problem solving, can be regarded as promoting a Dualist view of mathematics (Ernest 1991). On the other hand, the emphasis on problem solving and investigational work in mathematics, in the Cockcroft Report (1982) and the National Curriculum Council's (1989) *Non-Statutory Guidance in Mathematics* supports a Relativist view of mathematics. For example, the latter contrasts 'closed' mathematical tasks (single fixed answer) from those which are not-Closed (these have multiple answers, some times an unlimited number). A Dualist view of mathematics would not regard children posing their own problems as anything to be encouraged or tolerated. In contrast, a Relativist view of mathematics would regard such activity as potentially a valuable contribution to mathematical proficiency.

An important issue for the popularization of mathematics is the relationship between ethnomathematics and academic mathematics. The absolutist view is that mathematics is specialist knowledge produced by mathematicians which is applied to real world problems by applied mathematicians and scientists. Mathematicians own the pure 'essence' of mathematical knowledge, and ethnomathematics, street-mathematics, and all the forms of informal mathematics which permeate work, culture and leisure are very 'dilute' versions not worthy of the name. This view alienates the public from the applications of mathematics that surround them in their daily lives, whether they are technical, utilitarian or even aesthetic applications. Thus mathematics is perceived as belonging to the knowledge 'ghettos' of school and the academy, and not a part of the popular activity.

In contrast, a Post-Modern or cultural (or Relativist) view is that mathematics is an intrinsic part of most people's cultural activities (Bishop 1988). Academic mathematicians have appropriated and decontextualised it, until it seems quite separate from the cultural activities and diverse applications that give rise to it. These cultural origins and uses should be recognised as a legitimate part of the locus of mathematics.

5.   MYTHS, MASSMEDIA AND MODERNISM

Academic philosophies of mathematics and personal views of the nature of mathematics differ in a number of ways. The former are explicit, clearly defined and well defended philosophical systems. The latter may be tacit, vague, imagistic and possibly unconscious systems of beliefs manifested variously through attitudes, opinions, prejudices, choices and actions. Nevertheless, I wish to argue that significant relations exist between them. However, despite the analogy indicated above, there is no simple correspondence between beliefs and philosophies of mathematics. Absolutism and fallibilism cannot simply be equated with Dualism and Relativism, respectively. Both an absolutist and a fallibilist philosophy of mathematics can be associated with a Relativist belief-system. Thus an absolutist might promote a Relativist view of mathematics including, for example: mathematicians are liable to error and to publish flawed proofs, humans can discover mathematical knowledge through a variety of means, the concepts of mathematics are historical constructs (but its truths are objective), a humanized approach to the teaching and learning of mathematics is advisable. Where the link is strong, I would argue, is in the association of a Dualist view of mathematics with absolutism. A Dualist view, with its irrational reliance on Authority, cannot tolerate the relativistic aspects of fallibilism.

Thus absolutism in the philosophy of mathematics can be misused to justify Dualism. However there is no logical connection. Dualism implies some of the objectivist properties associated with absolutism, but absolutism is independent of Dualism and can be equally associated with Relativism, as illustrated above.

In ascertaining the impact of philosophies of mathematics and beliefs it is important to consider:

1) Teachers' views of mathematics and school mathematics
2) The image of mathematics realized in the classroom and experienced by students
3) The general public's views of mathematics

It is widely argued that there is a connection between 1) and 2), in, for example Thompson (1984) and Cooney (1988). The connection is not a simple logical or causal one. Rather it is a correlation which is greatly influenced by educational values and contextual factors. The influence of the social context may in fact neutralize or overpower such influence (Ernest 1995).

More importantly with regard to the popularization of mathematics, and less frequently discussed is 3). I wish to claim that there is a strong influential relationship between 2) and 3), and in particular, that the experience of school mathematics often makes a decisive contribution to the general public's views of mathematics. This claim is plausible because all members of the general public in modern industrialized societies spend many years as students of school mathematics, and many recount these experiences in strong and emotionally charged terms.

Students' views of school mathematics 2) depend on the sum of their classroom experiences of mathematics, including the quality of the relations they have with their teacher, institutionalized classroom competition, the extent of negative weight placed on errors, the degree of public humiliation experienced in consequence of failure, and other such factors which powerfully impact on the young learners, self-esteem and self-concept as learners of mathematics. Dualistic views of mathematics can be communicated by giving students a myriad of unrelated routine mathematical tasks which involve the application of memorized procedures, and by stressing that every task has a unique, fixed and objectively right answer, coupled with disapproval and criticism of any failure to achieve this answer. Unfortunately the experience many learners have during their years of schooling confirms the negative Dualistic image of mathematics as cold, absolute, inhuman and rejecting. Such an image is frequently associated with negative attitudes to mathematics. This is verified in studies of adults' attitudes and responses to mathematics, such as Buerk (1984) and Sewell (1981).

Thus my claim is that experiences in school mathematics form the basis for the image of mathematics constructed by learners, especially negative ones. These in turn are a major source – perhaps often the dominant source for the public's image of mathematics. Of course only a portion of classroom experiences or images of mathematics are negative. And just as a single bad experience can produce a negative image of mathematics, so too a single good experience can provide the basis for the development of a positive image of mathematics. Womack (1983) illustrates this when he describes his personal experience in which an interest in pursing a single mathematics problem in school led to success, teacher encouragement and the growth of a fascination with mathematics which resulted ultimately in his choice of a career in mathematics education.

There is evidence then that there are two sources of the myths, images and conceptions of mathematics, which obstruct the popularization of mathematics. First of all, the ubiquitous presence of these myths in the popular, educational and academic domains means that they reproduce themselves. Teachers, parents, colleagues, and the massmedia pass on these myths, forming and reinforcing them in the young and others with whom they communicate. This would not be enough to sustain them if, as the mathematics community claims, they are false. Secondly, the myths are maintained by many persons' experiences in learning mathematics in schools and colleges. This is recognised by reform movements in mathematics education worldwide, which are promoting Relativistic and humanistic views of mathematics in school (Cockcroft 1982, National Council of Teachers of Mathematics 1989, National Curriculum Council 1989). The weight of informed educational opinion has supported such progressive reforms, but this image of mathematics still exists more in the realm of rhetoric than in practice, where little evidence for it exists outside of a few exceptional classroom situations.

Mathematics, in its public persona, is a discipline that is riddled with contradictions. As E. T. Bell described it, it is both the queen and servant of science, which is an impossible combination in the realm of human social roles. It is known and used by all, but understood by few. The justification of its knowledge is purely rational, by logical argument, and it is open to challenge by any, irrespective of their station in life. Yet mathematics is widely experienced as the most arbitrary of all school subjects, comprising rules imposed solely by the dictate of authority. Many of these contradictions arise from the tension between the public and private personae of mathematics: mathematics as it is perceived, experienced and used throughout our culture versus the mathematicians' mathematics. Davis and Hersh (1980) in their account of mathematics contrast the inner and outer issues. Hersh (1988) elaborated this dichotomy with his claim that mathematics has both a visible front and a hidden back.

Mogens Niss points to another contradiction in mathematics: its hidden but ubiquitous formatting power (Skovsmose 1994). In modern society, especially in industrialized countries, mathematical concepts, algorithms and models now underpin every aspect of daily life. In the domains of virtually all organised activity including transport, commerce, communications, healthcare, industrial production, leisure, government, education and social security, for example, it is no exaggeration to say that all functioning depends on deeply embedded mathematizations. In other words, peoples' total activity is formatted by mathematics, largely hidden mathematics. The paradox is that this ubiquitous mathematics is invisible, hidden in the workings of 'black boxes' driving the social mechanisms, so that the populace is largely unaware of this basis. This is reinforced by the tendency for mathematicians and others to describe as mathematical only that which is labelled mathematics in the academic and school contexts. The outcomes are myths about mathematics and a mathematically disempowered citizenry.

This raises the question: Why promote the popularization of mathematics? What are the goals of this activity?

First of all, there are utilitarian and mathematics-centred goals. Mathematics underpins the workings of modern industrial society, providing the basis for science, technology and the information revolution. Therefore to aid development and progress in all countries a numerate populace is necessary. This both helps the economic development of the country and helps individuals enhance their careers and economic possibilities.

However, contrary to the utilitarian argument, as mathematics becomes more submerged in the 'formatting' mathematization of modern society, only a diminishing group of mathematical experts is needed for industry. Only a few more students in the areas of mathematics, science and technology are needed to bolster the economy, and improving the public image of mathematics as in the projects discussed above, and possibly using advertising or public relations consultants suffices to solve this problem.

The mathematics-centred argument is that the institution of mathematics needs public support both in terms of able new recruits and finance both for utilitarian and cultural reasons. Mathematics is a central and essential element in human history and culture, and it must be supported, and its popularity enhanced because of the central contribution of mathematics to humanity's intellectual tradition and development.

To pursue the cultural argument, some reform of the institution of mathematics is needed, to bring out its cultural and historical role. Typically, the public's encounters with school and academic mathematics is largely devoid of cultural elements, so a reform of mathematics teaching at all levels is required. In particular, the development of mathematical appreciation is needed (akin to musical appreciation) rather than mathematical competency or capability (paralleling the ability to make music). Although this is a goal of some popularization projects, appreciation is not an aim currently addressed in institutionalized mathematics education.

A second set of goals for the popularization of mathematics are to provide widespread personal pleasure through mathematics as well as to achieve general critical mathematical literacy.

Mathematics is an aspect of human activity and culture which can bring pleasure, enjoyment and fascination, and all persons should have the opportunity to have such positive experiences. Popularization should bring personal pleasure to a broader segment in society, giving more people a positive experience of mathematics which is rewarding in itself. However, it appears that the engagement with mathematics in school is for many not intrinsically rewarding, and so a reform of the populace's encounters with mathematics in school and college is called for, if this aim is to be achieved. Such a reform needs to stress the *personal* relevance of mathematics, including both the personal satisfaction in solving problems and puzzles and pursuing investigations within mathematics, and the motivation and pleasure derived from seeing the power of mathematics in applications.

In a healthy democratic society all citizens need to be critically mathematically literate. This means they should be confident in applying mathematical knowledge and acquiring any needed skills, and be able to use their knowledge and skills to interpret and critically evaluate the mathematics embedded in social and political systems and claims, from advertisements to government pronouncements, from national lotteries to the stock market. Critical mathematical literacy for all as a goal of the popularization of mathematics requires the reform of mathematics teaching, as well as its popular treatments, so that mathematics is taught and presented in an outward looking way. The content must include socially relevant questions and projects, authentic social statistics, accommodate social and cultural diversity, and use' local cultural resources. The introduction of mathematical concepts and methods needs to be seen in the light of their power to illuminate the students' lives, understood to include economic, cultural, political and other global contextual factors (Skovsmose 1994).

To achieve the various goals for the popularization of mathematics a number of strategies are required, including the following.

- Getting mathematics a better press and more positive media coverage
- Offering the public more opportunities to participate in mathematics
- Reforming the content and pedagogy of school and college mathematics to reflect the above goals as educational aims
- Changing the views of mathematics of the public and mathematicians to include ethnomathematics and social applications of mathematics as well as 'pure' mathematical activities.

6.1 Questions for Research

There are many areas related to the popularization of mathematics in which further research and evidence would be valuable.

What is and what should be the relationship of the popularization of mathematics with the popularization of science?

Many mathematicians love not the utility but the timeless beauty of mathematics with its perfect symmetries and awe-inspiring structures. Can such differences between mathematics and science be exploited to popularize mathematics?

What goals should projects for the popularization of mathematics address? Which are most feasible?

How is collaboration among media, mathematics and educational professionals and practitioners for joint work towards the popularization of mathematics best achieved?

What further types of the popularization projects are being deployed world-wide?

What are the most effective popularization projects for mathematics? How is their impact best evaluated?

What range of attitudes, images and conceptions of mathematics are held by the general public, teachers, students and mathematicians?

For different segments of society, what is the public understanding of mathematics, including knowledge, skills and appreciation of the discipline as a whole?

What experiences and influences lead to the formation of the such views and attitudes? What is the role of the mass media, parental influences, peer influence, and school and college experiences?

Are school experiences a primary causal factor in forming the public's view of mathematics? To what extent would different school reforms help to improve the popularity of mathematics?

What are the correlations, if any, between specific attitudes to and conceptions of mathematics and divisions of society defined in terms of gender, age, social class, occupation, ethnicity, cultural grouping, language or country?

What theoretical constructs, conceptual frameworks and research methodologies are best employed for answering the above questions and for analysing the issues raised?

The popularization of mathematics is an under-investigated area, and further research is needed. Gaining answers to the above questions would be a start in solving some of the problems that have been identified and discussed. However, it must not be forgotten that the problems of popularization vary greatly from culture to culture, although for some reason they are most acute in the anglophone West. It might be speculated that this is a consequence of the culture of late twentieth century capitalism, with its emphasis on consumption and immediate self-gratification, as opposed to the consistent hard work that mastering mathematics requires. However, there is no evidence to support this. What the cultural variation does show is that there cannot be any universal, culture-free solutions. Each society must identify and solve its own popularization problems. Even so, from the perspective of the institutions of mathematics and mathematics teaching, the issue of the popularization of mathematics is everywhere of vital importance. For unless significant numbers of young persons choose to specialize in mathematics, where will the mathematicians and mathematics teachers of the twenty-first century come from?

REFERENCES

Adult Literacy and Basic Skills Unit (1994) *Basic Skills*, London: ALBSU.
Ainley, J. (1988) Playing Games and Real Mathematics, in Pimm, D. Ed. (1988) *Mathematics, Teachers and Children,* Kent: Hodder & Stoughton, 243-248.
Ascham, R. (1570) *The Schoolmaster*, Aldersgate, London: John Daye (Reprint edited by E. Arber, Constable and co., London, 1923)
Bishop, A. J. (1988) *Mathematical Enculturation,* Dordrecht: Kluwer.
Blane, D. C. (1992) Changing the Image of Mathematics through using the Environment, paper presented at Working Group 21: The Public Image of Mathematics and Mathematicians, *7th International Congress on Mathematical Education*, Quebec 17-23 August 1992.
Blane, D. C. and Clarke, D.J. (1985). *A Mathematics Trail Around the City of Melbourne*, Melbourne: Monash University.
Brown, A. J. (1992) Participation, Dialogue and the Reproduction of Social Inequalities, in Merttens, R. and Vass, J. Eds (1992) *Partnership in Maths: Parents and Schools,* London, The Falmer Press.
Buerk, D. (1982) An Experience with Some Able Women Who Avoid Mathematics, *For the Learning of Mathematics,* Vol. 3, No. 2, 19-24.
Carré, C. and Ernest, P. Performance in Subject Matter Knowledge in Mathematics, in S. N. Bennett and Carré, C., Eds *Learning to Teach*, London: Routledge, 1993, 36-50.
Cockcroft, W. H. Chair (1982) *Mathematics Counts*, London: HMSO.
Cooney, T. J. (1988) The Issue of Reform, *Mathematics Teacher*, Vol. 80, 352-363.

Copes, L. (1982) The Perry Development Scheme: A Metaphor for Learning and Teaching Mathematics, *For the Learning of Mathematics,* Vol. 3, No. 1, 38-44.

Davis, P. J. and Hersh, R. (1980) *The Mathematical Experience*, Boston: Birkhauser.

Davis, P. J. and Hersh, R. (1988) *Descartes' Dream*, London: Penguin Books.

De la Cruz, Y. and Thompson, V. (1992) Influencing Views of Mathematics through the FAMILY MATH program, paper presented at *7th International Congress on Mathematical Education*, Quebec 17-23 August 1992.

Erlwanger, S. (1973) Benny's conception of Rules and Procedures in IPI Mathematics, *Journal of Children's Mathematical Behaviour*, 1(2), 8-25.

Ernest, P. (1991) *The Philosophy of Mathematics Education*, London, Falmer Press.

Ernest, P. (1995) Values, Gender and Images of Mathematics: A Philosophical Perspective, *International Journal for Mathematical Education in Science and Technology*, 26 (3) 449-462.

Esty, E. and Schneider, J. (1990) Square One TV: A Venture in the Popularization of Mathematics, in Howson and Kahane (1990), 103-111.

Grattan-Guiness, I. Ed. (1994) *Companion Encyclopedia of the History and Philosophy of the Mathematical Sciences*, 2 Vols, London: Routledge.

Hardy, G. H. (1941) *A Mathematician's Apology*, Cambridge: Cambridge University Press.

Hersh, R. (1988) Mathematics has a Front and a Back, paper presented at Sixth International Congress of Mathematics Education, Budapest, July 27-August 4, 1988.

Howson, A. G. and Kahane, J.-P. (1990) *The Popularization of Mathematics*, Cambridge: Cambridge University Press.

Hoyles, C. (1990) Mathematics in Prime-Time Television: The study of Fun and Games, in Howson and Kahane (1990), 124-135.

Katz, I. (1995) Fame by Numbers, *The Guardian Newspaper*, Weekend Supplement, 8 April: 33-34, 38-42.

Kincaid, L. and Kincaid, E. (1975) *Time for a Rhyme: A collection of Nursery Rhymes*, Cambridge: Brimax Books.

Kouba, V. and McDonald, J. L. (1987) Students' Perceptions of Mathematics as a Domain, in Bergeron, J. C., Herscovics, N. and Kieran, C. Eds (1987) *Proceedings of PME 11 Conference*, Montreal: University of Montreal. Volume 1, 106-112.

Kouba, V. and McDonald, J. L. (1991) What is Mathematics to children? *Journal of Mathematical Behaviour*, 10, 105-113.

Mathematical Association (1987) *Sharing Maths With Parents,* Cheltenham: Stanley Thornes.

Merttens, R. and Vass, J. (1990) *Sharing Maths Cultures: IMPACT Inventing Maths for Parents and Children and Teachers,* London, The Falmer Press.

National Curriculum Council (1989) *Non-Statutory Guidance in Mathematics*, London: Her Majesty's Stationery Office.

Perry, W. G. (1970) *Forms of Intellectual and Ethical Development in the College Years: A Scheme*, New York: Holt, Rinehart and Winston.

Pile, S. (1993) King's College: what went wrong with the bluestocking revolution? *The Daily Telegraph*, 15 March 1993, page 19.

Pollak, H. O. (1994) 'The Popularization of Mathematics' in Gaulin, C., Hodgson, B. E., Wheeler, D. H. and Egsgard, J. H. Eds (1994) *Proceedings of the 7th International Conference on Mathematical Education*, Sainte-Foy, Quebec: Laval University Press, 319-322.

Preston, M. (1975) *The Measurement of Affective Behaviour in C. S. E. Mathematics* (Psychology of Mathematics Education Series), London: Centre for Science Education, Chelsea College.

PrIME (1988a) *Primary Mathematics Year Newsletter 3,* Cambridge: PrIME Project.

PrIME (1988b) *PrIME Newsletter 10*, Cambridge: PrIME Project.

Schaaf, W. L. (1978) *Bibliography of Recreational Mathematics* (4 vols), Reston, Virginia: National Council of Teachers of Mathematics.

Schneider, J. (1994) Issues for the Popularization of Mathematics, *Proceedings of the International Congress of Mathematicians*, Zurich, August 1994.

Sewell, B. (1981) *Use of Mathematics By Adults In Everyday Life,* Leicester: ACACE.

Singmaster, D. (1994) Recreational Mathematics, in Grattan-Guiness (1994) Vol. 2, 1568-1575.

Skovsmose, O.(1994) *Towards a Philosophy of Critical Mathematics Education*, Dordrecht: Kluwer.

Thiele. R. (1994) Mathematical Games, in Grattan-Guiness (1994), Vol. 2, 1555-1567.

Thompson, A. G. (1984) The Relationship Between Teachers' Conceptions of Mathematics and Mathematics Teaching to Instructional Practice, *Educational Studies in Mathematics*, 15, 105-127.

Tiles, M. (1991) *Mathematics and the Image of Reason*, London: Routledge.

Tymoczko, T. Ed. (1986) *New Directions in the Philosophy of Mathematics*, Boston: Birkhauser.

Walkerdine, V. (1988) *The Mastery of Reason*, London: Routledge.

Watson, S. (1989) *Warwick University Mathematics Masterclasses, An Evaluation*, unpublished MA Thesis, Warwick University.

Womack, D. (1983) *'Seeing the Light'*, Times Educational Supplement, 8 April 1983.

817

Section 3

Perspectives & Interdisciplinary Contexts
Ken Clements – Section Editor

Introduction to Section 3

KEN CLEMENTS
Universiti Brunei, Darussalam

HISTORICAL PERSPECTIVES

Although the term 'new math(s)' is normally reserved for the movement which affected school mathematics around the world during the period 1955-1970, there is a sense in which the 20th century witnessed three international 'new math(s)' movements – one during the first decade of the century, one during the period 1955-1970, and one occupying the last two decades of the century (see Howson, 1982; Stanic, 1987; Clements, 1992; Kilpatrick, 1992). This third section of the *Handbook* is primarily concerned with identifying and linking the elements of the *third* of these revolutions.

Around 1980, following a sharp 'back-to-the-basics' backlash against the perceived excesses of the 1955-1970 'new math(s)' period, there emerged a vanguard of reformers within the developing international mathematics education community who were once again, ready to ask, and attempt to answer, fundamental questions about school mathematics. Some of these questions concerned mathematics classrooms: should the teaching of mathematics be different from that which had prevailed in times when school mathematics had been mainly for children of the élite?

Other questions concerned mathematics education research. Around 1980 there were some who seriously questioned the validity of quantitative research in which inferential statistical procedures were applied to analyse data derived from contrived education settings (Carver, 1978). Did it make sense to ask, and expect generalisable answers to, questions such as 'is it better to teach elementary algebra by method A or by method B?' Even more fundamentally, did it make sense to use probabilistic, inferential techniques to seek after 'truth' in mathematics education, as if best teaching methods, best curricula, best methods of assessment, and so on, were somehow, out there, waiting to be discovered by rigorous researchers.

Over the past two decades mathematics education reformers have been increasingly concerned with what goes on in mathematics teaching/learning situations, especially in classrooms. What kind of teaching/learning/curriculum arrangements are needed to cope with the fact that in many nations a large proportion of children are now staying on at school and proceeding to study senior secondary mathematics?

Reflections on this and other issues brought about a growing awareness that mathematics education research needed to develop in new directions. From that perspective, a study by Erlwanger (1975) into the effects of a mas-

A.J. Bishop et al. (eds.), International Handbook of Mathematics Education, 821 - 825
© *1996 Kluwer Academic Publishers, Printed in the Netherlands*

tery learning mathematics program on children at one grade level in one elementary school, can be regarded as a landmark. Erlwanger's study, which brought into the open many mathematics classroom issues which, although everpresent, had not previously been the stuff of formal research investigations, represented the thin edge of the wedge. Henceforth, new methods — springing from different ideas about the purpose of, and procedures for collecting and interpreting data — would become more and more acceptable within the international mathematics education research community.

What Erlwanger's study did was to draw attention to what was going on below the surface in mathematics classrooms, to inbuilt assumptions, to the ways by which a mastery program had produced children who were happy merely to get right answers, irrespective of whether they understood what they doing.

Bauersfeld's (1980) seminal paper entitled 'Hidden Dimensions of the So-called Reality of a Mathematics Classroom' continued this new quest to understand the sub-cultures of mathematics classrooms. Bauersfeld acknowledged the efforts of Jack Easley, who had supervised Erlwanger's study and other like studies, and described Erlwanger's dissertation, and another dissertation by Shirk (1972), as a cornerstone 'for the discussion of human interaction in the mathematics classroom' (Bauersfeld, 1980, p. 25).

It would be inappropriate here to continue the above summary of significant events in the recent history of school mathematics, mathematics education, and mathematics education research. It suffices to say that the chapters in section 3 of this *Handbook* need to be placed in the context of a period in which much soulsearching has taken place within the international mathematics education community. It is that soulsearching which is the essence of this third 'new math(s)' period. There is a new determination to go beyond tinkering at the edges of curriculum. It is increasingly being recognised that we need to identify, deconstruct, and reconstruct assumptions and practices in all aspects of mathematics education.

Chapter 22, by Anna Sierpinska (Canada) and Stephen Lerman (United Kingdom), addresses the fundamental epistemological issue of what it means to say we 'know' anything in mathematics education. In our quest for truth in mathematics education, how can we be sure anything is true? This inevitably leads to a consideration of the glosses which culture can place on supposed 'truths'. Sierpinska and Lerman emphasise that it is the qualities of persistent interaction patterns in mathematics classes — which are vitally influenced by the hidden dimensions, or the cultures, of classrooms — which fundamentally influence what the teacher teaches, and what the students learn. The paths which mathematics educators took in order to achieve this state of enlightenment led them through the domains of problem solving, metacognition, and various forms of constructivism.

The question whether the idea of 'proof' still remains at the heart of mathematics is the focus of Chapter 23, written by Gila Hanna (Canada) and H.

Niels Jahnke (Germany). Despite the fact that the worlds of mathematics and mathematics education are being increasingly influenced by relativist philosophies, by technological advances, and by cultural considerations, are those who claim to teach mathematics being true to their calling if they are not stressing the need to prove? In the new world of high technology, has the concept of proof remained constant? What is proof, and what are the implications of this question for mathematics curriculum and teaching practices?

In keeping with the recognition that culture is such a vital force in mathematics education, Chapter 24, by Paulus Gerdes, of Mozambique, provides a comprehensive review of the development and growing influence on mathematics educators of the major concepts of ethnomathematics. Gerdes makes it clear that many of the issues on which ethnomathematics researchers are focusing urgently need to be taken into consideration by educators. Four such issues are: Should mathematics curricula incorporate the special mathematics of local communities? Should Bishop's (1988) six universal mathematical activities – counting, locating, measuring, designing, playing, and explaining – be used as a basis for investigating mathematics inherent in cultural practices? Or is there a danger by so doing of subjugating the essence of a culture to blunt and inappropriate classification criteria which, in fact, deny the cultures their right to define their own parameters? What are the implications of the findings of ethnomathematics research for the teaching and learning of mathematics?

In Chapter 25, on gender and mathematics, the Australian mathematics educators Gilah Leder and Helen Forgasz combine with Claudie Solar, of Canada, to report the good news that increasingly during the 20th century females across the world were able to become serious students of mathematics, and to show that they were as capable as males of studying all forms of mathematics. The chapter points to how qualitative, critical research has complemented the more traditional quantitative research in demonstrating to the world that 19th century beliefs about the subordinate role of women with respect to mathematics, and the idea that women had less capacity than men for higher mathematics, were false. Leder, Forgasz and Solar concentrate on the qualities of intervention programs most likely to break down many of the old gender stereotypes.

The various strands which have often unconsciously been taken to constitute the domain for the expression 'language factors in mathematics learning' have been brought together in Chapter 26. The authors of this chapter, Nerida Ellerton and Philip Clarkson – both from Australia – argue that culture, communication, and language are intimately connected, and that the issue of what is 'basic' in school mathematics needs to be considered from a linguistic/cultural perspective rather than from a narrow, instrumentalist algorithmic viewpoint.

Many of the issues which arise in Chapters 22 through 26 with respect to cultural and linguistic influences on mathematics and mathematics education are raised again by Bill Barton, in Chapter 27. Barton, a New Zealander, argues that the discourses of pure and applied mathematics are different from discourses *about* mathematics and about how mathematics relates to other areas of human endeavour, and that this fact should have implications for both mathematics education practices and mathematics education research.

In order to avoid floundering in dark and difficult territory, mathematics educators have made persistent calls for the development and application of appropriate theories of mathematics education. Issues associated with the use and misuse of theories are discussed in Chapter 28, written by John Mason (United Kingdom) and Andrew Waywood (Australia). Mason and Waywood argue that different structuralist and constructivist theories not only affect mathematics teaching and learning, but also mathematics education research. They call for a sensible blend of theory and practice in which issues are investigated from multiple theoretical perspectives.

CONCLUDING COMMENT

One of the great achievements by the international community of mathematics educators over the past two decades has been to bring to centre-stage the premise that the teaching and learning of mathematics, and indeed all forms of mathematics education, are inevitably surrounded by cultural constraints and forces. Research is now attempting to identify, to harness, and to prioritise – and where necessary, to by-pass – these constraints and forces, in order that answers to compelling questions will be provided. At issue, though, is *how* these questions can be *best* answered, so that the answers will not only throw light on local settings, but also on the pressing problems which are being faced across the world, as more people than ever before are being becoming teachers and learners of mathematics.

The seven chapters in this third section of this first *International Handbook of Mathematics Education* should provide a stimulating basis for the further discussion and critique needed to generate more equitable and intellectually satisfying frameworks for mathematics education in the 21st century.

REFERENCES

Bauersfeld, H.: 1980, 'Hidden Dimensions in the So-called Reality of a Mathematics Classroom', *Educational Studies in Mathematics* **11**(1), 23-41.
Bishop, A.J.: 1988, *Mathematical Enculturation: A Cultural Perspective on Mathematics Education,* Dordrecht, Kluwer.
Carver, R.P.: 1978, The Case Against Statistical Significance Testing. *Harvard Educational Review* 48, 378-399.

Clements, M.A.: 1992, *Mathematics for the Minority,* Second Edition, Deakin University, Geelong.

Erlwanger, S.H. 1975, *Case Studies of Children's Conceptions of Mathematics*, unpublished PhD Dissertation, University of Illinois, Urbana-Champaign. (Reprinted in *Journal of Children's Mathematical Behavior* 1, 157-281).

Howson, G.: 1982, *A History of Mathematics Education in England,* Cambridge University Press, Cambridge, UK.

Kilpatrick, J.: 1992, 'A History of Research in Mathematics Education', in D. Grouws (ed.), *Handbook of Research on Mathematics Teaching and Learning,* Macmillan, New York, 3-38.

Shirk, G.B.: 1972, *An Examination of Conceptual Frameworks of Beginning Mathematics Teachers,* unpublished PhD dissertation, University of Illinois, Urbana-Champaign.

Stanic, G.M.A.: 1987, 'Mathematics Education in the United States at the Beginning of the Twentieth Century', in T. Popkewitz (ed.), *The Formation of School Subjects: The Struggle for Creating an American Institution,* The Falmer Press, New York, 145-175.

Chapter 22: Epistemologies of Mathematics and of Mathematics Education

ANNA SIERPINSKA AND STEPHEN LERMAN
Concordia University, Canada and South Bank University, United Kingdom

ABSTRACT

This chapter addresses issues concerning epistemology, as they relate to mathematics and education. It commences with an examination of some of the main epistemological questions concerning truth, meaning and certainty, and the different ways they can be interpreted. It examines epistemologies of the 'context of justification' and of the 'context of discovery', foundationalist and non-foundationalist epistemologies of mathematics, historico-critical, genetic, socio-historical and cultural epistemologies, and epistemologies of meaning.

In the second part of the chapter, after a brief look at epistemology in relation to the statements *of* mathematics education, epistemologies *in* mathematics education become the main focus of attention. Controversial issues within a number of areas are considered: the subjective-objective character of mathematical knowledge; the role in cognition of social and cultural context; and relations between language and knowledge. The major tenets of constructivism, socio-cultural views, interactionism, the French *didactique*, and epistemologies of meaning are compared. Relationships between epistemology and a theory of instruction, especially in regard to didactic principles, are also considered.

1.   EPISTEMOLOGIES OF MATHEMATICS AND OF MATHEMATICS
     EDUCATION

Our intention in this chapter is to clarify what is meant by 'epistemology' in the various settings in which it is used within the international mathematics education community, to elaborate critically the origins, meanings and uses of those notions of epistemology, and to reflect on our practices as researchers and educators in relation to the epistemological theories upon which we draw. We shall not attempt to be exhaustive in our study of epistemologies of mathematics and mathematics education, neither in a historical sense nor in our examination of current theories.

The chapter has been written primarily for mathematics educators – not for philosophers of mathematics – and we shall confine our study to those areas

A.J. Bishop et al. (eds.), International Handbook of Mathematics Education, 827 - 876

that we consider relevant to our audience (and ourselves). Although our review of the research done in mathematics education in relation to epistemology will not be exhaustive, nonetheless major epistemological issues are addressed.

The chapter commences with an overview of the basic questions of epistemology and the many different ways in which they can be interpreted. In fact, the first part of the chapter ('Epistemologies of Mathematics') attempts to 'sort out' epistemologies. In particular, we evoke historical discussions related to the distinction between epistemology on the one hand, and psychology, sociology and history of science, on the other. This leads us to speak about epistemologies of the 'context of justification' and epistemologies of the 'context of discovery'. Reference is made to foundationalist and non-foundationalist epistemologies of mathematics, as well as to historico-critical, genetic, socio-historical and cultural epistemologies, and to epistemologies of meaning.

In the second part of the chapter ('Epistemologies of Mathematics Education') we proceed to an examination of the use and role of epistemologies in mathematics education. We argue that constructivist, socio-cultural, interactionist and anthropological approaches are founded on different epistemologies of knowledge. We also discuss approaches that focus on epistemological analyses of the meaning of particular mathematical concepts. We end with a reflection on relations between epistemology and theories of instruction which necessarily incorporate systems of values or principles. This discussion will include the issues of complementarity and eclecticism.

1.1 Epistemologies of Mathematics

In this chapter we shall be concerned with the clarification of the notion of epistemology itself, its various meanings, questions considered epistemological and not, and different interpretations of these questions.

1.1.1 Sorting Out Epistemological Questions

Epistemology as a branch of philosophy concerned with scientific knowledge poses fundamental questions such as: 'What are the origins of scientific knowledge?' (Empirical? Rational?); 'What are the criteria of validity of scientific knowledge?' (Able to predict actual events? Logical consistency?); 'What is the character of the process of development of scientific knowledge?' (Accumulation and continuity? Periods of normal science, scientific revolutions and discontinuity? Shifts and refinement in scientific programs?).

These questions can be interpreted in various ways. They can be asked in their full generality, as above, or they can be made more specific with respect to some particular domain of scientific knowledge, for example, mathematics. One can also be interested in knowledge from various perspectives. One can ask: what are the origins of the validity of our beliefs? Or, what are the sources of meaning of knowledge, and how is the meaning constituted? These are different questions because meaning and truth are different categories. One can also ask: what is the ontogenesis of knowledge? and speak of the development of 'cognitive structures', for example. Or the question can be posed about the 'phylogenesis' of discursive systems of knowledge such as mathematics or its parts.

Some prefer to approach epistemological questions in a philosophical way, and others in a more scientific way. The former ask: How can a scientific result be rationally explained on the basis of what it was obtained from? The latter ask: How was a given scientific result actually obtained?

These questions discriminate between the attitudes towards epistemology of mathematical foundationalists and mathematics educators. Mathematics educators are generally less interested in studying grounds for the validity of mathematical theories than in explaining the processes of growth of mathematical knowledge: their mechanisms, the conditions and contexts of past discoveries, the causes of periods of stagnation and claims that, from the point of view of present day theory, appear to be, or have been, erroneous.

Mathematics educators are also interested in observing and explaining the processes of mathematical discovery in the making, both in expert mathematicians and in students. Ultimately, as practitioners, they research ways of provoking such processes in teaching. If questions of certainty occupy mathematics educators, it is often in the context of discussing the concept of error, its different categories and the possible undertakings of the teacher in reaction to students' errors, misconceptions or conceptions departing from those accepted or expected. However, as will be shown, there have been a number of studies of the significance of philosophical issues for mathematics education.

All mathematics educators do not share the same epistemology, even if they are concerned with similar epistemological questions. We shall see in the second part of this chapter that the lines of division lie along issues such as the subjective-objective character of knowledge, the role in cognition of the social and cultural context, and the relations between language and knowledge.

1.1.2 Epistemology of the Context of Justification and Foundationalism in the Philosophy of Mathematics

The above concerns of mathematics educators would have been regarded, by certain philosophers of science from the first half of the century, as not belonging to epistemology proper but to psychology, history, sociology or semiotics. For example, Carnap (1928/1966), and Reichenbach (1938/1947) proposed that epistemology occupies itself with a 'rational reconstruction' of scientific thought processes, that is to say with the description of how scientific processes would develop if 'irrational factors' did not interfere. 'Rational reconstructions' were meant to be descriptions of the thinking processes of scientists not when they are discovering something, but when they are trying to communicate and justify their findings. They were meant to be accounts of the 'context of justification' of scientific thought. The 'context of discovery' or the actual processes of scientific discovery and the impact on them of cognitive, social and cultural-historical factors belongs, according to these authors, not to epistemology but to the empirical domains of psychology, sociology and history of knowledge.

Karl Popper (1972) understood epistemology in an 'anti-psychologistic' way. Imre Lakatos, a disciple and critic of Popper, extended the domain of epistemological reconstruction to those parts of the discovery process that he felt could be rationalised. His *Proofs and Refutations* (1976) provided a rational reconstruction of processes of discovery and justification of a certain part of topology. But Lakatos' epistemology remains programmatically anti-psychologistic. His notion, for example, of the 'proof-generated concept' is a methodological tool in rational reconstructions, not a generalisation of historical or psychological facts.

A 'context of justification' approach to epistemology in the philosophy of mathematics is known as 'foundationalism'. The foundationalist approach to the questions of growth of mathematics is a-historical and a-social: 'the history of mathematics is punctuated by events in which individuals are illuminated by the new insights that bear no particular relation to the antecedent of the discipline' (Kitcher, 1988).

Answers to the question of origins of knowledge have been traditionally put into two categories: apriorism and empiricism. Foundationalist philosophies of mathematics whose main concern is to find some 'first mathematics, some special discipline from which all the rest must be built' (Kitcher, 1988, p.294) are necessarily aprioristic. Otherwise, says Kitcher, there would be no point in their concerns. Of course, apriorism appears as a sensible solution, if empiricism, especially a naive empiricism, is seen as the only epistemological alternative. Empiricism is simply unacceptable for an epistemology of mathematics. Richard (1907) provided an argument against empiricism from a foundationalist point of view: 'if experience alone can prove the truth of axioms, how can we know that they are true everywhere?'

There can be other arguments for apriorism, given from different perspectives. For example, from an ontogenesis of knowledge perspective, in which apriorism is identified with innatism, there is a known argument by C. G. Hempel, cited by Jerry Fodor (in M. Piatelli-Palmarini, 1979, p.380). The argument is as follows: suppose in a measurement the following pairs of numbers were obtained: (0, -1), (1, 0) and (2, 1). There are infinitely many possibilities for generalisation (for example,

$$y = x-1; y = (x-1)^3; y = (x-1)^{2n} \cos 1(1-x/2) \ for \ n = (1,2,\ldots)$$

If knowledge was a result of the individual's experiences then, in principle, all these generalisations would be equivalent. But there is an order of preference in the choice of the function model, which makes y = x - 1 the obvious choice. Fodor commented: 'One can call it simplicity, or the a priori order of functions, or innatism'.

1.1.2.1   Epistemology of the context of discovery: Poincaré and the French tradition in epistemology.

French philosophy of science is regarded as traditionally psychologistic and historicist (see, for example, Largeault, 1994). Accounts of actual processes rather than their rational reconstructions were attempted. In the field of the epistemology of mathematics, the works of Brunschwicg (especially *Les Etapes de la Philosophie Mathématique,* published in 1912), and the philosophical writings of Poincaré – published in articles in *L'Enseignement Mathématique* (see, for example, Poincaré, 1899, 1908a) and then in his well known books such as *Science et l'Hypothèse* (1906), and *Science et Méthode* (1908b) – have had an important influence. Cavaillès, Bachelard and Piaget were Brunschwicg's students.

The psychologism of the epistemologies of Poincaré, Bachelard and Piaget is evident. Bachelard's (1938) *La Formation de l'Esprit Scientifique* was a search for the 'psychological conditions of the progress of science'. Poincaré started an article by saying that the problem of the genesis of mathematical invention should inspire the most lively interest of a psychologist (Poincaré, 1908a). According to Poincaré, the 'context of discovery', or rather 'invention' (Poincaré was not a Platonist), was something worth studying because by reflecting on this process one could find reasons for errors in mathematics.

Although psychologistic, Poincaré's epistemology was nonetheless concerned with the origins of validity of our beliefs and not with the psychogenesis or history of scientific knowledge. Poincaré found these origins in the mathematician's synthetic a priori intuition and in his/her 'experience' or effective construction which allows him/her to verify if a postulated object exists. But intuition is fallible; a sudden illumination that has flattered the mathematician's aesthetic sense may turn false when submitted to the test of logical examination (1908a). Thus, in the construction of mathematical laws, intuition and logic interact; one in the invention process, the other in its verification.

There are, unexpectedly, many common features between the epistemological reflections of Poincaré and those of Dieudonné (1992), in spite of the link of Dieudonné to Bourbaki and its acclaimed logicism.

Dieudonné professed a 'structuralist' epistemology of mathematics, in the sense that he viewed mathematics as an 'interplay and comparison of patterns' (Anglin, 1995, p.52). Ontology of mathematical objects (whether they exist, and whether they exist independently of the human mind) is not important: 'For a structuralist, what is important is not the metaphysics of, say, the Unique Factorisation Domains, and the Primary Ideal Domains, but the fact that every structure of the first kind is, *a fortiori,* a structure of the second kind' (p.52).

Structure being the focus of the structuralist view of mathematics, the nature of elements in any given situation or problem quickly fades into the background and broad generalisations take their place. Transformations of particular figures in the plane are replaced by transformations of the plane regarded as a structure of a particular kind; the general notion of group supersedes various particular groups of geometric transformations; the notion of mapping supplants the activity of change of variables, etc.

For Dieudonné (1992), the method of validation of mathematical statements is certainly deductive proof. In this sense, the basis for the acceptance of a statement is in the acceptance of axioms. However, Dieudonné does not say that there can be no mathematical knowledge prior to axiomatisation. Axioms are not, genetically, first. They can play various roles in the evolution of mathematics. They help reorganise mathematical knowledge, and they play an important part in understanding and the development of intuitions.

Like Poincaré, Dieudonné (1992) was not interested just in the context of justification. In fact, he stated that the question of validity of mathematical knowledge is simple: a true statement is a proved statement, although rigorous proofs are possible only in axiomatised theories. All mathematical theorems are true. Hence the evaluation of mathematical results cannot be based on their truth. Other criteria must be used, such as non-triviality, generality, depth. But what these evaluative terms mean changes from one epoch to the other and depends on fashions and fads. Thus the criteria for the evaluation of a mathematical work are, according to Dieudonné (1992), 'unavoidably subjective, a fact which makes some people say that mathematics is much more an art than a science' (p.28).

Dieudonné (1992) remarked that the proof that is sometimes thought of as constituting the birth of mathematics (incommensurability of a side of a square and its diagonal) is actually a proof of impossibility (p.34). This makes us reflect on the specificity of mathematical statements and concerns. Proofs of impossibility are a trademark of a mathematical frame of mind. In sciences one is interested in explaining phenomena, not in proving that some phenomena are impossible. There are also other questions that can be considered as typical of mathematics; for example, to describe all possible objects satisfying a certain condition, such as: all regular polyhedrons; all possible forms of a crystal; all simple groups, that is to say all cases, not just typical cases, or prototypes. In solving a mathematical problem it is seen as important to take into account all the possible cases, not just those that are most likely to occur in applications. This drive towards 'having a complete picture' can explain certain general definitions like the one of linear independence of a set of vectors which includes the case of the set composed of one single vector. Mathematics educators sometimes think such definitions are nitpicky and formalist. But it may well be that mathematics has grown that way, driven by the overriding concern to present the whole picture, the full structure described in all detail.

Dieudonné mentioned another typically mathematical concern, namely to have a set of different ways of speaking of a given concept: translations from one setting to another; geometric to algebraic to analytic and vice versa. It is enough to evoke the history of linear algebra, which has grown by way of the development of and a dialectic interaction between synthetic geometric, analytic and structural languages (Sierpinska, Defence, Khatcherian and Saldanha, in press).

As a structuralist, Dieudonné (1992) viewed mathematics as a unified whole, in which the meaning and significance of every part is a function of the role it plays in this whole. From this perspective, the work of synthesis, the bringing together and organisation of results for the purposes of communication is very important. Dieudonné, one of the founders of the Bourbaki group, went as far as to claim that it was in such expository works that the basis of an account of evolution in mathematics was to be found. For evolution in mathematics consists in generalisation, reformulation in a new or different language, reorganisation, axiomatisation. Ever since Euclid, said Dieudonné (1992), expository works have consolidated transformations in the conception of mathematics, and affirmed the new ways of thinking (p.162).

Dieudonné (1992) did not see evolution in mathematics in a dramatic fashion, such as would be implied by Kuhn's theory of revolutions, or Lakatosian reconstructions of the history of mathematics. There is no question of discontinuity in the history of mathematics. Dieudonné is not alone in holding this view. Many working mathematicians see the development of mathematics as occurring in a more or less continuous way. They have very good reasons for that (Sfard, 1994). Changes are in the meta-mathematics and ways of thinking, not in the technical mathematical layer. Mathematicians tend to stress the technical layer: there are no revolutions there, so there are no revolutions.

Mathematics educators, on the other hand, are more likely to see the history of mathematics in a more dramatic fashion because they are and must be more concerned with the meta-mathematical layer. This is where the learners get stuck. Mathematicians, in their day to day practice, do not bother themselves with meta-mathematical questions. They go on with their investigations hoping that 'la foi leur viendra'. They can disagree on certain subtleties of philosophical nature, but they are at least willing and sometimes even able to change their ways of approaching problems. They can be intuitionists or constructivists on the metamathematical level, but this will not prevent them from understanding the mathematics written by people with other views. It may be different for students for whom the technical level of mathematics can be totally interwoven with questions of a philosophical nature (Sierpinska, 1990).

1.1.2.3   The genetic and historico-critical approaches to epistemology in Piaget's works.

The restriction of epistemology to the context of justification and to rational reconstructions of the processes of scientific research has been contested by some philosophers, who have postulated the necessity of serious philosophical analyses of discovery processes and actual methods of control and validation used by real scientists (Kuhn, 1962; Feyerabend, 1978).

While Kuhn and Feyerabend relied, in their analyses, on historical data and sociological considerations, Piaget was the first to coordinate the 'logic of scientific discovery' with psychological data in a systematic and methodologically clear way. For Piaget, the objects of epistemology are mechanisms involved in the processes of the constitution of knowledge in the frame of particular scientific disciplines (not the origins of the validity of beliefs or the methods of justification of scientific claims). Two complementary methods can be used in the identification and study of these mechanisms: one looking at them from a synchronic perspective, the other from a diachronic perspective. In the synchronic perspective, a logico-mathematical analysis is used to define the 'epistemological significance' of a given conceptual tool: how it 'functions within an actual, synchronic system of cognitive interactions' (Piaget and Garcia, 1989, p.1). In the diachronic perspective, a psychogenesis and a historical genesis of an area of scientific thought are constructed. Both perspectives are necessary to put forward and explain the 'epistemological significance' of an item of knowledge, as, according to Piaget, knowledge is not independent from the process of its formation, and, therefore, 'the most advanced constructions conserve partial links with their most primitive forms' (Piaget and Garcia, 1989, p.3).

Piaget stressed the common features of psychogenesis and history of science. For him, both developments were 'sequential', in the sense that they are not random and one can distinguish stages in the advancement of the development. Each next stage is at once 'a result of the possibilities opened up by the previous one and a necessary condition for the following one. In addition, each stage begins with a reorganisation, at another level, of the principal acquisitions that occurred at the preceding stages' (Piaget and Garcia, 1989, p.2). This sequentiality justified, Piaget maintained, the claim that the most primitive constructions are 'integrated' in the most advanced ones. This integration, however, concerns not so much the content of knowledge nor even its structure, as the instruments and mechanisms of its constitution. The 'truly universal factors in any kind of cognitive development ... are functional in kind rather than structural' (Piaget and Garcia, 1989, p.25).

It should be noted, however, that what allowed Piaget to claim this specific 'parallelism' of psychological development and history of science, is an approach to the study of these processes that, while not falling into straight 'logicism', is nevertheless free of 'factual' references and considerations. He spoke of the psychogenesis and the historical genesis of knowledge and not of factual processes. He posed the question of constitution of knowledge in terms of cognitive norms at different stages or levels of development. He ignored the factual aspects of individual development such as the behaviour on a psychophysiological level (material mechanisms of action, states of consciousness, memory, mental images, etc.). He left aside historical facts such as who has proved what at a given time.

> The history of a concept gives some indication as to its epistemic significance only insofar as the question of this relationship is posed 'in terms of 'trends' – that is, in terms of the evolution of norms at a scale that makes it possible to discriminate stages rather than in factual terms of how one author influences another; or, particularly, in terms of the controversial if somewhat uninteresting problem concerning the role of precursors in the creation of a new system ... This is a psychological problem much more than an epistemological one.
>
> (Piaget and Garcia, 1989, p.5).

This way, Piaget was not simply bringing psychology and history of science into epistemology. While allowing himself to use results of experiments to solve certain questions in epistemology (for example, whether the notion of solid is an empirical datum) or to justify certain choices in the construction of his theory, he endeavoured to justify the statements of his theory on the basis of admitted assumptions and other statements. What allowed him to say that he had avoided logicism in his theory was the fact that he studied 'the cognitive norms of the subject and not of the logician' (Piaget and Garcia, 1989, p. 5).

1.1.3 Sociological Views of Mathematics

1.1.3.1 Naturalism.

Constructivism is an alternative to genetic apriorism on the one hand, and empiricism on the other. Constructivism focuses on the internal, cognitive or conceptual development of the mind or the discipline as a whole. Other epistemologies turn their attention to the more external, and social aspects of the growth of knowledge. Some of these epistemologies propose a view of mathematics that underlines its similarity to natural sciences. Kitcher (1988) called his epistemology 'naturalist'. Lakatos spoke of 'a quasi-empiricist' philosophy of mathematics.

An interesting set of arguments concerning the experimental aspects of mathematics can be found in Dreyfus (1993).

Kitcher's naturalism has as a goal to break loose from the foundationalist philosophies (Kitcher, 1988, p.294). Naturalism finds no need to regress to axioms in the search for the origins of mathematical knowledge. In fact, from the naturalist point of view, axioms of a theory are not its beginning. Rather, they are a result of a systematisation of a 'prior corpus of claims' about the objects of the theory 'that had been tacitly or explicitly employed in reasoning'. The work of axiomatisation shows that these claims 'could be derived from [certain] principles ... selected as basic'. Kitcher stated that when Cauchy founded mathematical analysis on the concept of limit, it was not because he was suddenly enlightened by some kind of Platonic intuition or because this notion forced itself upon his intuition as a necessary construction: rather, it was because he found it especially useful in his endeavour to structure the vast domain of knowledge called Calculus.

Kitcher (1988) stressed that the way axioms are justified 'is exactly analogous' to the way in which a scientist would explain the introduction of a 'novel collection of theoretical principles on the grounds that they can explain the results achieved by previous workers in the field' (p.295). We find here a kinship with Lakatos' idea of mathematics as a 'quasi-empirical science' (Lakatos, 1978).

Naturalism brings a historical dimension into the questions of genesis and justification of knowledge and makes them inseparable from the question of the growth of knowledge. Mathematical knowledge is a historical product.

Kitcher (1988) adopted the following line of argument in his naturalist account of mathematical knowledge. The origins of mathematical knowledge are in the 'primitive, empirically grounded practice', and 'perceptual experiences in situations where [people] manipulate their environments (for example, by shifting small groups of objects)'. What counts as a justification differs from one 'mathematical practice' to another. This notion of 'mathematical practice' relativises the problem of growth of mathematical knowledge both historically and culturally. According to Kitcher, a mathematical practice comprises, aside from the 'technical level' (we borrow the term from E.T. Hall – see Sierpinska, 1994) of language and accepted statements, 'a set of questions that [the practitioners] regard as important and as currently unsolved, a set of reasonings that they use to justify the statements they accept', and a 'meta-mathematics' (cf., Sfard, 1994), that is to say 'a set of mathematical views embodying their ideas about how mathematics should be done, the ordering of mathematical disciplines, and so forth' (Kitcher, 1988, p.299). Kitcher continued:

> Contemporary mathematical knowledge results from the [primitive, empirically founded practice] ... through a chain of interpractice transitions, all of which are rational ... Each generation transmits to its successor its own practice. In each generation, the practice is modified by the creative workers in the field. If the result is knowledge, then the new practice emerged from the old by a rational interpractice transition. (p.299)

The 'naturalist' epistemology of mathematics, as proposed by Kitcher, has certain important features – in particular its social and historical character and the importance attached to practice – in common with Vygotsky's general account of the foundations of [scientific] knowledge.

1.1.3.2   Wittgenstein and Lakatos, and other sociological views on mathematics.

Ludwig Wittgenstein, whose early work *Tractatus Logico-Philosophicus* (1974) had attempted to provide a foundation for knowledge in the correspondence between language and reality, and had made him a hero of the Vienna Circle, produced a later philosophical position in direct criticism of most of the *Tractatus*. In this later work, Wittgenstein denied that mathematical statements referred to objects at all. In doing mathematics, he argued, one is transforming expressions from one form into another and the correctness or otherwise is determined by how people use those expressions and what is called 'correct'. The process of the generation of mathematical statements, rather than being either a mechanical operation (logicism and formalism) or a correspondence with intuition (intuitionism) is about the social activity of 'obeying a rule' (Wittgenstein, 1953, p.202). Mathematics is normative, it tells what one ought to do, and its objectivity is in the publicly exhibited, rule-following processes that social groups call mathematics.

It is likely that Lakatos had read and was influenced by Wittgenstein's work. Lakatos elaborated his approach to the development of mathematical knowledge in his *Proofs and Refutations*. In other writings on the nature of mathematics Lakatos (1978) proposed that the classical positions called Logicism, Intuitionism and Formalism were Euclidean programs, designed to develop mathematics as systems ensuring the transmission of truth from indubitable axioms, through certain deductive procedures, to equally certain statements. He argued that, on the contrary, mathematics proceeds in a way similar to science, a quasi-empiricism, in that the falsity of counterexamples to conjectures re-transmits to axioms and definitions. If something that is considered as a basic statement turns out to be false by virtue of the admitted axioms and definitions, rather than rejecting the statement, the axioms and definitions are changed to accommodate it.

Although the 'classroom' in Lakatos' (1976) *Proofs and Refutations* was perhaps not intended to suggest that mathematics proceeds by negotiation, or that the heuristics are the essence of mathematics, not the outcomes, it has been taken in that sense by mathematics educators.

As we mentioned above, most mathematicians do not support a Lakatosian or Wittgensteinian view of mathematical activity. Hersh (1979) has explained this in terms of the 'security' of the working mathematician, who believes in the existence of mathematical objects when s/he is working with them, but falls back on formalism at weekends, when asked to justify her/his belief.

Another interpretation might be that the history of the achievements of mathematics in science, technology and within mathematics itself are such that notions of the potential fallibilism of its results seem pedantic (although see Grabiner, 1986; Gillies, 1992). Yet another might be that the notion of mathematics as certain, as engaging with the paradigms of the signifiers 'truth' and 'proof', supports a privileged position for mathematics and its academics. It is clearly not in the interests of mathematicians, or scientists, to undermine their position and status by challenging certainty, proof or truth in mathematics. Such studies and critiques are for those weekends, or they are categorised as external sociologies, that is sociologies of mathematicians or of false directions in the development of mathematical knowledge. 'True' mathematics needs no sociology.

Often those who write about such things as the 'sociology of mathematics' are dismissed by practising mathematicians as scientists and mathematicians, and others, who have either finished their productive life within science or mathematics, or have never really been mathematicians at all: all such people can do, it is alleged, is write *about* science or mathematics. They are no longer capable or never were capable, of doing mathematics. The same types of arguments can of course be made for the Lakatosian position and the interests served.

It is certainly the case, however, that the dichotomy into Euclidean programs and quasi-empiricist or sociological programs has strong links with the views of mathematics teachers about their enterprise and there is a considerable body of research examining these links (Dawson, 1969; Rogers, 1978; Nickson, 1981; Thompson, 1982; Lerman, 1983; Cooney, 1985; Ernest, 1985; Moreira, 1992; Monteiro, 1993; Seeger, 1994). Put briefly, mathematics is identified either as a particular body of knowledge, a subset of which is deemed appropriate for all school students and a somewhat larger subset for those who may go into higher education in mathematical subjects, or it is identified by particular kinds of activities that are called mathematising, including modelling, pattern-recognition, generalising, proving, etc. The latter view is not intended to ignore the body of mathematical knowledge-as-experience that has developed through mathematising. In practice, national curricula, which largely or exclusively specify content, obviate any choice, and this is further confused with the issue of teaching strategies or principles which we address below.

The move to heuristics, the processes of doing mathematics as the pivotal characteristic of the subject, rather than its content, has led to and supported problem solving and investigational work as a major focus of school mathematics since the 1970's. The growing interest in Popper, Lakatos, Kuhn and others was parallelled by the growth of problem solving and investigational work in schools by teachers in such groups as the Association of Teachers of Mathematics in the United Kingdom. As an approach to the teaching of mathematics it was given impetus first by Polya (1945) and later by many other writers, in particular Mason, Burton and Stacey (1984) and Schoenfeld (1985). That it is now a view of mathematical knowledge is due to writers and advocates such as Hersh (1979), Agassi (1982), Lerman (1983, 1986), Davis and Hersh (1980), and Ernest (1991). It is overtly an attempt to draw together the contexts of discovery and of justification. For example, Davis and Hersh (1980) wrote:

- Fact 1: Mathematics is our creation; it is about ideas in our minds.
- Fact 2: Mathematics is an objective reality, in the sense that mathematical objects have definite properties, which we may or may not be able to discover. (pp.408-409)

And Ernest (1991) wrote:

Social constructivism links subjective and objective knowledge in a cycle in which each contributes to the renewal of each other ... from subjective knowledge (the personal creation of the individual), via publication to objective knowledge (by intersubjective scrutiny, reformulation and acceptance). (p.43)

Stronger sociological presentations of mathematical knowledge and its development have been given by Bloor (1976, 1983) and Restivo (1985, 1992). In perhaps the most developed sociological description of mathematical knowledge and its justification, Restivo (1992) engages with such issues as: How one can account for the different kinds of mathematics that developed in different societies; mathematical abstraction; the unreasonable applicability of mathematical results; the hegemony of Western mathematics; Western mathematics' unique involvement with truth and proof, and so on. For instance, in relation to abstraction, Restivo's (1992) argument is as follows:

For the objects with which mathematicians deal are activities of mathematicians. In building upon the operations already in existence, and making them symbolic entities upon which further operations can be performed, mathematicians are self-consciously building upon previous activities in their intellectual community. (p.84)

Restivo (1992) drew attention to a history of mathematical competitions and rivalry that set those activities in context and thus offered a fully sociological rationale for generalising in mathematics. He described types of mathematical development, drawing on historical studies of different countries or regions – the factors leading to those types being presented as dependent largely on the nature of the mathematical community in terms of its cohesiveness, size, sources of patronage, longevity, relation to religion, etc. Thus the mathematics of China was described as a mathematics of survival; of India, as episodic; and of Japan as about commercial revolution.

Restivo (1992) was aware of the limitations of available translations and extant documents, but his aim was to offer possible sociological analyses of different kinds of mathematical developments, as against an explanation through a metaphysical internal logic of mathematics itself. Thus he pointed out that other descriptions of those historical periods are equally valid. In the final part of his book he developed a case for a strong sociology of mathematics, arguing from the notion that mind is itself a social structure, in that 'selves, minds and ideas are not merely social products; nor are they merely socially constructed; they are social constructs' (p.132).

Restivo's (1992) case began with a rationale for the conjecture that mathematical representations are social constructions. He then argued that so-called 'pure ideas' can be given social and material foundations – indeed that it makes no sense to claim that mental states and products can be non-social or a-social – and ended with a discussion of the social relations of pure mathematics.

A sociological view is particularly concerned with the justification of socially valued knowledge, this being the process by which communities validate themselves and establish and retain power. This applies also to an academic community and to the sub-communities within it. We have referred above to the investment mathematicians have in the status of mathematics in society, and it is certainly the case for mathematics educators and the status given to mathematics in school curricula all over the world. Similarly, within the community of mathematics education one can identify sub-groups with investments of different kinds in research perspectives, teaching styles, and so on.

1.1.4 Epistemologies of Meaning

Epistemology of meaning can be indistinguishable from the epistemology of validity for those who, like Frege (1892/1952), equate meaning with truth conditions – although Frege (1892/1952) suggested that 'sense' should be distinguished from meaning, the former having social origins.

But is it sensible to equate meaning with truth conditions? Clearly, it is not difficult to find sentences which have meaning but to which questions of truth do not apply (like, for example, interrogative sentences, orders, etc.). Moreover, there exist sentences whose truth conditions are identical, yet they carry different meanings. For example, 'Fortunately, Gauss is dead' and 'Unfortunately, Gauss is dead, or 'p and not q' and 'p but not q' (Strawson, 1971). Theoreticians of communication – at least some of them – claim, however, that in every sentence there is a core of meaning that can be explicated either through truth conditions or some related notion (like, for example, 'fulfilment', in the case of a wish).

The equating of meaning with truth conditions is unacceptable for anybody who is concerned not so much with the creation of a coherent theory of communication but with successful communication in the practice of teaching. Even if, in mathematics education, we are interested in the building of theories, we should never lose sight of the ultimate goal of these theories, which is the improvement of practice. A theory of meaning which would allow one to claim that statements such as 'p and not q' and 'p but not q' have the same meaning would not be able to take into account and explain many of the students' problems related to the understanding of mathematical language (Girotto, 1989).

Mathematics educators are as much concerned with the communication of meaning as they are with truth, and they are more concerned with teachers' and children's thoughts than they are with the sentences the teachers and students utter. They are also as interested in the change and growth of mathematical meanings in mathematical classrooms as they are in the accumulation of mathematical truths that might be taking place there. This explains why some mathematics educators are likely to understand epistemology as the study of 'the status, structure, and meaning of knowledge' (Steinbring, 1994, p.93), and base their epistemological analyses of the mathematical subject matter on a theory of meaning. Thus, for example, Steinbring (1994) used a systemic approach to the notion of 'concept' inspired by Ogden and Richard's 'semiotic triangle': meaning is a triad of thoughts, words and things. This theory allowed him to explain the difficulty of the communication of mathematical concepts, and at the same time to propose certain necessary conditions for this communication. There exist other explanations of difficulties in mathematical communication (see, for example, Thomas, 1987; Fischer, 1988).

A comprehensive review of philosophical perspectives on meaning and a discussion of the relevance of these perspectives for the psychology of cognition can be found in Ernest (1990).

1.2 Epistemologies in Mathematics Education

1.2.1. Epistemologies 'in' or 'of' Mathematics Education?

Before embarking on an examination of particular theoretical orientations which have been called epistemologies of mathematics education, we will dwell for a moment on what might be meant by the notion of 'epistemology of mathematics education'. If epistemology is the theory of knowledge, and epistemology of mathematics is the theory of mathematical knowledge, then epistemology of mathematics education must concern the same study, but of the propositions of mathematics education rather than those of mathematics. We would want to examine the body of so-called knowledge in that domain and ask what are the sources of that knowledge, how is it justified, and how does it develop? Answers might range over whether it is empirical or rationalist, and so on. We might expect a symmetry of answers across epistemologies of mathematics and mathematics education.

Piaget claimed that logico-mathematical knowledge comes about entirely through reflective abstraction, whereas scientific knowledge requires both empirical and reflective abstraction, which might suggest that the contexts of justification for these two kinds of knowledge might be different. On the other hand, sociologists of knowledge (like, for example, Bloor and Restivo) would argue that symmetrical analyses need to be made of all domains of cultural knowledge in terms of factors such as the social relations of members of those communities in different places and times, and the interests served by the 'ownership' of bodies of knowledge. The study of the radical constructivists or post-structuralists as social/knowledge groups within the mathematics education community would be as important as that of the logicists or formalists within the mathematics community.

From many points of view education is a derivative activity dependent on many other domains of knowledge, including psychology, sociology, anthropology, history, philosophy and, in our case, mathematics. As an explicit institutional structure, it certainly has a varied history across the world. Where it has been institutionalised, education has of course always served purposes specific to particular social-cultural groups and governments and as such has necessarily been concerned with values, expressed in terms of teaching principles. In terms of curriculum content, these have been as crude as the mass schooling in England in the nineteenth century, when boys were taught sufficient arithmetic to enable them to function as workers in industrial society but not so much as to make them challenge that society. Girls were taught only such arithmetic as they might require to enable them to manage the economics of their family.

One would expect, however, that epistemologies concerned with the origins of knowledge – that is to say, genetic epistemologies – would approach mathematics education knowledge and mathematical knowledge in a unified way. Similarly, sociologically oriented theories would also treat pedagogical knowledge symmetrically with other knowledge. On the other hand, some epistemologies of mathematical knowledge do not engage with the issue of the acquisition of that knowledge. This is especially true for foundationalist epistemologies of mathematics and those approaches that reduce epistemology to the study of the context of justification, which explains why these epistemologies have had such a small impact on mathematics education. Attempts were made in this direction – the articles published in *L'Enseignement Mathématique* at the beginning of the century testify for that. There were also Felix Klein's reform proposals to build a curriculum on and around the fundamental concept of function (the so-called 'Meran program' – see Gray and Rowe, 1993). But the effect was not noticeable.

If the foundationalist ideas of structuralism in mathematics found their way into mathematics education at large in the sixties (Modern Mathematics or New Math reforms), it could be argued that this was only because they were backed up by the structuralist genetic epistemology elaborated by Piaget and popularised in books such as *Structuralism* (1970) *and Science of Education and the Psychology of the Child* (1972). Piaget was speaking about how children come to know mathematics and not only how mathematical statements are justified and best organised into consistent wholes, or how adult mathematicians come to make mathematical discoveries or inventions.

Mathematics education, which deals not only with the possible worlds of mathematical subject matter but also with the actual minds of children and teachers, all embedded in a socially complex world of the educational institution, was badly in need of a genetic epistemology, of a sociology and a theory of culture. All these needs are reflected in the interpretations that mathematics educators and researchers have been making of the Piagetian constructivist epistemology, theories inspired by Vygotsky and Bruner, the 'polemic epistemology' of Bachelard, and other epistemological views. In this section, we shall have a look at some of these interpretations, the avenues they open and their limitations.

1.2.2 Constructivism

Constructivists have endeavoured to develop a rationale for the activities of a teacher which could be said to conform to the tenets of constructivist learning theory. For constructivists, there are no direct connections between teaching and learning, since the teacher's knowledge cannot be conveyed to the students, the teacher's mind is inaccessible to the students and vice versa, and the notion of the knowledge of the community of mathematicians runs up against the impossibility of internalisation by the individual.

Some social constructivists argue for a process of enculturation, separate from and in addition to the child's constructions and sense-making. Bauersfeld (1995), for example, has suggested that 'the core part of school mathematics enculturation comes into effect on the meta-level and is 'learned' indirectly,' and Cobb (1989) has claimed that children's mathematical constructions are 'profoundly influenced by' social and cultural conditions. Given the very precise language in which Piaget, von Glasersfeld and Steffe describe the child's construction of knowledge, the social constructivist explanation of enculturation in terms of unspecified meta-levels, indirect learning and profound influence might be described as rather unclear (Lerman, 1996). Placing social interactions on a par with sensori-motor and graphical interactions as those factors which generate perturbations for the individual, as do Steffe and von Glasersfeld, and the social-cultural milieu as the specific limit of the range of possible interactions, is consistent. The desire to retain such a view of mathematical (and other) construction but to wish to give a much greater and indeed formative role to socio-cultural influences, leads to the need for another, but unspecifiable, process of learning.

For radical constructivists, at the most general level, the first principle is that the teacher recognises that she is not teaching students about mathematics, she is 'teaching them how to develop their cognition' (Confrey, 1990, p.110), and that she is 'a learner in the activity of teaching' (Steffe and D'Ambrosio, 1995, p.146). It follows from this that teaching is 'a task of inferring models of the students' conceptual constructs and then generating hypotheses as to how the students could be given the opportunity to modify their structures so that they lead to mathematical actions that might be considered compatible with the instructor's expectations and goals' (von Glasersfeld, 1990, p.34).

Following constructivist principles does not just imply an approach to what students do in their learning: 'the basic tenets enter into human activity through the principle of self-reflexivity, which means that we apply the basic tenets first and foremost to ourselves in our activities' (Steffe and D'Ambrosio, 1995, p.146).

At a more detailed level, constructivist mathematics educators have attempted, through teaching experiments (see, for example, Steffe, 1992), to illustrate how researchers might make sense of students' behaviours in terms of their possible existing conceptual structures, in order to predict what might be suitable activities to extend their structures mathematically. At least three important issues are implicit in this:

a) that researching in a teaching experiment situation is not the same as teaching a class of students;

b) that the process of extending structures needs to be analysed, particularly in terms of assimilation and/or accommodation; and

c) an analysis needs to be carried out into 'what is meant by a more powerful and effective construction' (Confrey, 1990, p.111), since the aim of the mathematics teacher is to extend her students mathematically.

Concerning the first of the above issues, Steffe and D'Ambrosio (1995) have drawn on Maturana's (1978) notion of nonintersecting phenomenal domains of interaction in which a distinction was made between the study of the phenomena of the components of a unity and the study of the phenomena of the unity itself. In relation to the mathematical concepts and structures of individual students they argued that the first is the domain of psychological phenomena, and the second the domain of sociological phenomena. The class teacher must unavoidably focus on the latter, and researchers, even in teaching experiments, must avoid confusing the former with the latter. This is completely consistent with the notion that, at the level of the individual, constructivists view learning as the accommodations students make in their conceptual schemes.

At the level of groups of students, Steffe and D'Ambrosio (1995) described constructivist teaching as interacting with students in a learning space whose design is based, at least in part, on a working knowledge of students' mathematics. This learning space consists of three elements, the posing of situations, the encouragement of reflection and interactive mathematical communication. (It is worth noting, in this regard, that Kilpatrick (1987) suggested that particular strategies of teaching are neither exclusive to, nor indicative of particular epistemologies.) Reflection serves two purposes: it enables the individual to step outside of the particular experience and see it as an object in its own right, and it can offer the possibility of another voice for other students, enabling them to compare and contrast with their own view. Teaching actions, of course, are in the domain of social interactions and hence the encouragement of interactive mathematical communication, verbal and other, can encourage reflection and 'enact their mathematical knowledge in appropriate and timely ways' (Steffe and D'Ambrosio, 1995, p.156)

On the second issue, Steffe and D'Ambrosio (1995) distinguished between situations and problems or tasks (Simon, 1995), arguing that in their use of the former they were attempting 'to bring forth, sustain and encourage, and modify the mathematics of students' (p.157). They advocated 'situations that involve assimilating generalisation', which they suggest is the constructivist way of speaking of transfer of knowledge (Steffe and Wiegel, 1994). The emphasis is on the neutralisation of perturbations. The latter, problems and tasks posed by the teacher at key points where she considers it necessary, aim rather at accommodation through setting up cognitive conflicts for students. 'I tried in different ways to promote disequilibrium so the students would reconsider the issue' (Simon, 1995, p.129). This is an area of debate within constructivism (see the first three papers in the March 1996 issue of the *Journal for Research in Mathematics Education* (Volume 26).

Let us now reflect on the third issue. If learning in this context cannot be couched in terms of appropriating the cultural tools of the mathematics community, as it would be, for a view inspired by Vygotsky's or Jean Lave's works, constructivists must face the problem of specifying the direction in which mathematics learning should proceed for every individual. Since all learning is a process of constructing, students will be doing so in whatever classroom situation exists.

Constructivist classrooms have been distinguished as those which encourage the construction of powerful and effective constructions in mathematics (Confrey, 1990; Simon, 1995). In addressing the issue of how students might construct such powerful mathematical ideas, Confrey suggested that, first, students must believe in their knowledge since that belief in what they construct implies knowledge, from a constructivist perspective. Thus the issue of student autonomy is crucial. Given this, Confrey (1990) argued that one can list what makes a powerful and effective construction from a mathematical point of view:

1) A structure with a measure of internal consistency;
2) An integration across a wide variety of concepts;
3) A convergence among multiple forms and contexts of representations;
4) An ability to be reflected on and described;
5) A historic continuity;
6) Ties into various symbol systems;
7) An agreement with experts;
8) A potential to act as a tool for further constructions;
9) A guide for future actions; and
10) An ability to be justified and defended. (pp.111-112)

Teaching programs can then be designed with the aim of facilitating the development of these features of mathematical activity, as Confrey's (1991) work in multiple representations demonstrated.

1.2.3 Socio-Cultural Views

The label 'socio-cultural' is used here to denote epistemologies which view the individual as situated within cultures and social situations such that it makes no sense to speak of the individual or of knowledge unless seen through context or activity. Knowledge is cultural knowledge taken as socially produced, always potentially changeable, bound up with social values and socially regulated. Thus what constitutes mathematical knowledge is a social norm: 'If there is confusion in our operations, if everyone calculated differently, and each one differently at different times, then there isn't any calculating yet' (Wittgenstein, 1956, V. 2), and 'if rule became exception and exception became rule; or if both became phenomena of roughly equal frequency – this would make our language-games lose their point' (Wittgenstein, 1953, 142).

A feature of the changing trends in research in mathematics education during recent years has been the growing interest in and focus on the social context of the mathematics classroom (Bishop, 1988; Keitel, 1989; Nickson and Lerman, 1992; Nickson, 1992; Lerman, 1994). The role played by the social context in the development of the individual or of groups has been theorised, implicitly or explicitly, in many ways; what demarcates current interests is a move away from the identification of social factors as the realm of the affective to a concern with the part that the social and cultural environment plays as a whole in the development of the child. In relation to knowledge, these interests reflect moves away from knowledge as a priori but also away from knowledge as what is individually constructed to knowledge as socially constructed and justified.

Lave (1988) developed the notion of knowledge-in-action in contrast to a cognitive perspective, and located mathematics in various contexts in which people act. Her studies have been largely of 'mathematical' practices in everyday and workplace situations. In her few comments on school mathematics she emphasised its orientation towards generalisable techniques and skills which are supposed to be applicable in daily life and she was, of course, critical of that approach.

> Practices common to both cognitive research and schooling treat arithmetic, logic, and monetary calculations as exemplars of 'rational thought' … Math practice is described as general mental exercise. Math in conventional pedagogical guises is presented in the form of capsule puzzles – 'problems' – with explicit, prefabricated goals, employing only 'factual' information; procedures are construed to be value-free, technical means.
>
> (Lave, 1988, pp.172-173)

Neither Wittgenstein nor Lave engaged in any depth with pedagogical issues. Vygotsky and his followers, on the other hand, were centrally concerned with learning (and teaching). In fact, Vygotsky did not deal with issues of the nature of mathematics or any other form of knowledge (except for psychology which he attempted to redefine and restructure as a materialistic science, building on but essentially rejecting behaviourism). For Vygotsky, all knowledge was considered to be just what it is at any time and in any place, and the purpose of education is to pass on that cultural knowledge to the next generation. Following Marx, Vygotsky regarded consciousness as a product of time and place, in particular economic relationships and one's position within them, and, particularly in Vygotsky's re-formulation, also of one's cultural situation(s).

Thus Vygotsky's (1978) concern was with the nature of consciousness and in particular with its development. For him, communication drove consciousness and, therefore, the process of learning was integral to communication. He identified two types of thinking, everyday or spontaneous thinking and scientific or theoretical thinking. The latter was the conscious, intended teaching-and-learning which led to the child's appropriation of cultural knowledge. The former came into being informally through the interactions of the child with peers and adults – although Vygotsky, in his short working life as a psychologist, had very little to say about this stage.

Vygotsky (1978) identified a region which he termed the 'zone of proximal development', which was the difference between what a child could do on her or his own and what she or he could do with the aid of a more experienced peer or adult. This fundamental concept established all learning as taking place with others, and that learning pulls each person along, so that what he or she sees others doing today, he or she will do with them tomorrow and alone after that. Learning leads development, an approach which Vygotsky pointed out was in direct contrast to the writings of Piaget for whom development, in the form of the stages of development of the child, led learning. Vygotsky suggested that this left the child practising its knowledge of yesterday.

The process of internalisation was another fundamental feature of Vygotsky's thought. For Vygotsky, 'the process of internalisation is not the transferral of an external to a pre-existing, internal 'plane of consciousness'; it is the process in which this plane is formed' (Leont'ev, 1981, p.57). Thus there is a unification of teaching and learning, at the school stage.

An important feature of Vygotsky's approach, and of considerable relevance to this chapter, is the sense in which the world, and the individuals in it, are products of their time and place. In particular, the psychology of the individual, expressed as consciousness, is formed through the mediation of tools, which are expressions of the social-historical-cultural situation. This brings subject and object together, overcoming Cartesian duality. It also implies that there are no grounds to claim that there is a parallel between historical epistemological obstacles in mathematics, for instance, and cognitive obstacles to learning. New knowledge and knowledge structures lead to a shift in the 'world'; it is not the same as it was before.

For example, according to Western histories of mathematics, the development of the concept of negative number was fraught with epistemological obstacles; many mathematicians, even as late as the nineteenth century, were reluctant to accept the concept (although it seems clear that the Babylonian authors of some of the clay tablets of around 1500 BC found it much easier to accept such numbers). We now regard the negatives as part of the integers, and young children can learn the nature of them without having to recreate that (partial) history; there is no reason, except an apriori assumption, why there should be such a parallel (Lerman, 1995).

In a similar vein, following a study of the birth of modern algebraic geometry seen as a reaction against the Italian classical school, Bartolini-Bussi and Pergola (in press) also drew a distinction between historical studies and the teaching-learning process.

Going back to the past does not mean to identify individual and classroom learning with recapitulation of history: first, process is collective and depends on innumerable individual and social factors from inside as well as from outside mathematics; because of this very complexity it is not a good candidate to modelise the whole of learning process ... Learning in school cannot be reduced to creating anew; it has to be conceived also as appropriation, that is the process that has as its end result the individual's reproduction of historically formed human properties, capacities and modes of behaviour (Leont'ev, 1981). To realise appropriation the introduction of mediation tools (Vygotsky, 1978: physical objects as well as symbolic systems) is crucial: this introduction is realised from outside by the representative of culture in the classroom, i.e. the teacher, who can speed, mix up, break off and even reverse, if necessary, any possible recapitulation of the historical process.

In research terms, perhaps the most developed approach along these lines has been in Activity Theory (Garnier, Bednarz and Ulanovskaya, 1991). Although Vygotsky pointed out the centrality of the notion of the acting person, he emphasised 'meaning' as the mediation between the individual and the world. Through tools, and cultural tools in particular, society and culture are mediated for the child ('It is the world of words which creates the world of things' – Lacan, 1966, p.155). In particular, thought and language were to be seen as being dialectically related. Language offers the child inherited historical-cultural meanings but each participant in the conversation or other activity uses those tools intersubjectively to re-shape meanings in communication and action. It is often pointed out that Leont'ev emphasised activity as the mediation, but it should be clear from the previous sentence that Leont'ev's focus is very close to Vygotsky's formulation.

According to Leont'ev's view, the activity orients the participants and provides the initial meaning and motivation. Meanings are socially-centred, whereas sense is the individual's perspective. Actions of individuals within the activity are always motivated by sense, which incorporates cognition, culture and affect. Finally, there are operations or the specific moves that individuals make in response to specific phenomena. To take a well-known example of Leont'ev's, in a group activity of hunting, one person, the beater, will have the role of circling around the prey to beat the undergrowth and usher the prey towards the hunters. The actions of that person only make sense within the context of the activity. If there is a boulder in the way, the beater will go around it; this is an operation.

The final features of Vygotsky's approach which will be described here, were drawn from Marx and further developed by Davydov. These are the ascent from the abstract to the concrete in the development of scientific concepts in the zone of proximal development, and the significance of the dialectic in analysing structures of thinking. In mathematics, Davydov drew on these notions and empirical studies to question the familiar expectation that children must engage in concrete activities before they can generalise towards the abstract. He reported on a number of experiments which he had carried out with elementary school-age children working with algebra. He emphasised the general features of children's language even when they appeared to be engaging at a concrete level, as well as the dialectical nature of concrete/abstract as distinct from a linear progression from one to the other (see Cobb, Perlwitz and Underwood, 1994; Lompscher, 1994). Davydov's work has been developed, in mathematics education, by, among others, Lins (1994).

1.2.4 Interactionist Views

Interactionism could be listed as one of those approaches to developmental research and theory that promotes a socio-cultural view on the sources and growth of knowledge. What distinguishes it from other approaches, however, is that interactions (of various kinds) are not regarded as mere auxiliary and helpful factors of development (Voigt, 1995, p.164). Development and interactions are seen as inseparable. It is stressed that the focus of study is not the individual but interactions between individuals within a culture (Bruner, 1985; Bruner and Bornstein, 1989). Language (or, rather, 'languaging') is very important: it is seen as an 'active molder of experience', not a 'passive mirror of reality' (cited in Bauersfeld, 1995, p.283). Interactionists often quote Wittgenstein's statement: 'the speaking of language is ... a form of life' (Wittgenstein, 1974, cited in Bauersfeld, 1995, p.279).

Interactionist approaches in mathematics education draw their genealogy from, among others, the symbolic interactionism of Mead (1934) and Blumer (1969), the ethnomethodology of Garfinkel (1967), Goffmann's (1974) frame analysis, the philosophy of language of the later Wittgenstein, and the theory of language acquisition of Bruner and his collaborators. Also the works of Lave (1988), Lave and Wenger (1991), Walkerdine (1988), and Edwards and Mercer (1993) are often quoted. We find these references and an exposition of interactionist views in the writings of Bauersfeld, Voigt, and Krummheuer (for example, in Cobb and Bauersfeld, 1995). There are other researchers working within a core of similar assumptions, some making explicit their kinship with interactionism and some not (Steinbring, 1989; Yackel, Cobb, and Wood, 1991; Cobb and Yackel, 1995). Epistemological ideas close to interactionism sometimes appear under a different name – like, for example, the social constructionism proposed by Gergen (1995).

Some former constructivist researchers started leaning towards interactionism in trying to resolve, for themselves, the dilemma between the idea of mathematical knowledge as a subjective construction of the mind and its conception as an entity objectively existing outside of the mind. For example, Paul Cobb's reflection was:

> The most inviting way out that I see is to complement cognitive constructivism with an anthropological perspective that considers that cultural knowledge (including language and mathematics) is continually regenerated and modified by the coordinated actions of members of communities. This characterisation of mathematical knowledge is, of course, compatible with findings that indicate that self-evident mathematical practices differ from one community to another ... Furthermore, it captures the evolving nature of mathematical knowledge revealed by historical analysis ...
>
> (Cobb, 1990, p.214, cited in Steinbring, 1991a)

For an interactionist mathematics educator, learning is not just an endeavour of the individual mind trying to adapt to an environment, nor can it be reduced to a process of enculturation into a pre-established culture. In the mathematics classroom, the individual construction of meanings takes place in interaction with the culture of the classroom while at the same time it contributes to the constitution of this culture (Cobb and Bauersfeld, 1995, p.9).

This property of the relation between the students' individual activity and the classroom culture is called reflexivity. The notion of reflexivity is quite central to interactionist approaches. One important implication of the assumption of reflexivity is that what is eventually learned by individual students in the classroom depends on the type of microculture they have participated in developing.

While the teacher's and the students' individual understandings contribute to the elaboration of mathematical meanings characteristic of a given classroom culture, it may not be possible to attribute the authorship of a meaning to anyone in particular. The meanings are elaborated through negotiations whereby the group comes to agree on certain conventions in the interpretation of signs, situations, and behaviours. The final result of these negotiations has emergent properties: through interaction, the individual contributions may add up to something nobody in particular has thought about and anticipated (Voigt, 1995).

Another important stance of interactionism is that people learn indirectly, through participating in a culture and its discursive practices. In particular, students learn what counts as mathematical thinking by observing what is attended to (for example, quantitative and spatial relations) and what kind of solutions are distinguished by the teacher and other students as 'insightful', 'simple' or 'elegant' (Voigt, 1995, p.197).

The interactionist orientation to language distinguishes it from both the constructivist and the Vygotskian perspectives, although it shares with them a rejection of a representationist view of language ('language as a representation of the world'). In constructivism, language is an expression of thought ('Language is moulded on habits of thought' – Piaget, 1959, p.79). Vygotsky saw in language a medium of cultural transmission. Interactionism ceases to see language as a separate object – a tool – that can be used for one purpose or another (and that, in principle, could be replaced by something else: some other means of communication). People are not so much speaking a language as they are 'languaging' (Bauersfeld, 1995). Language creates a reality; languaging is living in this reality. Or, according to Gergen (1995):

> We employ language not as a means of world reflection or self-expression, but (following Wittgenstein) as we might move within a game. We use language to carry out actions within the game, and others might respond to these actions by virtue of the locally established rules of the game. To illustrate, when I say, 'I know this to be the case', the term *know* is not a picture of my mental condition. It invites you to treat my saying with respect and authority; it indicates that if you question me I will stand by what I have said. (p.27)

Related to this attitude toward language is the postulate of the discursive character of knowledge. In particular, mathematics is seen as a special type of discourse. 'Discourse', however, is not just 'language'; it is language-in-action, or language as a means for accomplishing cognitive, social, and other ends. It is 'a vehicle for doing things with and to others' (Bruner, 1985). As a discourse, mathematics establishes a certain universe: mathematics is a way of seeing the world, and thinking about it. As this universe is established through communication and the building up of conventions and shared understandings of contexts (Bruner, 1985), the type of mathematical knowledge that students develop depends on the characteristics of the communication situations in which they develop it.

This assumption about knowledge leads to looking at education as 'a communicative process that consists largely in the growth of shared mental contexts and terms of reference through which the various discourses of education (the various 'subjects' and their associated academic abilities) come to be intelligible to those who use them' (Edwards and Mercer, 1993, p.62). The aim of communication in education is, from this perspective, seen as the establishing of certain shared ways of understanding and knowing.

Constructivism, which criticises 'the idea of knowledge as representing an 'external' reality supposed to be independent of the knower' (von Glasersfeld, 1993) does not go so far as to claim that knowledge is a discourse. According to constructivism, the primary function of language is to express individual thoughts, not to create cultural objects. Thoughts constitute knowledge in an individual. These thoughts are a function of the subject's operational schemas which, while not being copies of an 'outside reality', are still 'representations' in the sense of models of the subject's actions upon some physical or mental reality. These models are not assumed to bear any 'resemblance' to these actions – their relation to the actions is symbolic rather than iconic – but they are not supposed to have a linguistic character either.

In some accounts of the interactionist position, the conventional character of knowledge is stressed (see, for example, Bauersfeld, 1995; Gergen, 1995). 'Conventional', however, does not mean 'arbitrary', or 'formal'. The qualification refers to the connotations of 'convention' such as 'agreement' or 'consensus' on a set of matters. It points to the assumption that meanings are achieved through negotiation (Bauersfeld, 1995, p.277).

The notions of consensual domain, and taken-as-shared activities or meanings, account for, in interactionism, a phenomenon that Piaget explained by saying that the intra- and the inter-individual coordination of actions 'constitute a single and identical process' (Piaget, 1972, p.71). Vygotsky also assumed the existence of a cultural fact or an attribute of the 'collective mind': namely the phenomenon of the apparent 'objectivity' of knowledge or the belief that knowledge exists outside individuals' minds.

The taken-as-shared meaning is not some kind of intersection (in the set-theoretic sense) of the individual understandings of the interlocutors; rather it is an interpretation that they may not be conscious of, but which makes them interact smoothly and make successful predictions with respect to the others' actions and moves. 'They act as if they were thinking of the same thing [although in fact] several interpretations could be assumed' (Voigt, 1995, pp.172-173). In his explication of the term, Voigt refers to Blumer (1969): 'The meaning of a thing [for me] grows out of the ways in which other persons act [toward me] with regard to the thing'.

The taken-as-shared meanings belong to the so-called 'working interim' or 'a kind of interactional modus vivendi' (Goffman, 1959, p.9): 'together, the participants contribute to a single overall definition of the situation which involves not so much a real agreement as to what exists but a real agreement as to whose claims, concerning what issues will be temporarily honored'.

In interactionism, culture has a special position. It is neither ignored nor taken for granted: it is the most basic object of study. Some of the central problems that interactionism sees for mathematics education are:
- How are mathematical meanings interactively constituted in the different cultures of the mathematics classroom?
- How do these meanings become stabilised?
- What are these meanings and how do they depend on the kind of classroom culture in which they evolve?

Interactionists claim that their theory can explain both the fact that cultures change (which, they argue, the Vygotskian approaches fail to do), and the fact that they are identifiable, that is to say present a relative stability (which, they argue, the individualistic approaches such as constructivism fail to do). The properties of reflexivity and emergence account for the cultural change; patterns, routines and formats of interaction, and the recurrence of themes of discourse account for the stability of cultures.

Repeatable patterns of interaction are a consequence of a natural tendency to make human interactions more predictable, less risky in their organisation and their evolution. Research has identified various patterns of classroom interaction, such as the 'funnel pattern', 'elicitation', 'recitation' (Bauersfeld, 1995), 'focusing pattern' (Wood, 1992), 'formats of argumentation' (Krummheuer, 1992), various 'thematic patterns of interaction' (Voigt, 1995), the concrete-to-abstract pattern of interaction (Steinbring, 1993), and others. Brousseau's (1986b) notions of 'effet Topaze' and 'effet Jourdain' could also be seen as results of an analysis of interactional patterns in the mathematics classroom.

Some interactionists have seen complementarity, if not compatibility, between constructivism and interactionism, or between Vygotsky's theory and interactionism. With regard to the first pair of approaches, Bauersfeld (1995), for example, stated that while the individual has to construct meanings for him or herself, this process of construction is based on interpretations that have their source not in the individual alone but in his or her interactions with others within a culture (p.274). The individual's attention is directed and oriented by what other people say and do. One of the main functions of languaging is exactly such an orienting activity. Cobb and Yackel (1995), after expressing a need for a theoretical effort to coordinate the interactionist and constructivist perspectives, came up with the idea of an 'emergent approach' (p.24).

It has also been said that constructivism and interactionism are complementary in the sense that they take different perspectives on people's knowing. Constructivism is the point of view of the individual as he or she tries to make sense of the world. Interactionism is the point of view of an observer of the social life; it looks at people sharing meaning and at the functioning of language as it creates meanings.

However, there are deep differences between the two approaches, especially those pertaining to the way they view language and communication, and knowledge (see Gergen, 1995, p.33).

Both Gergen and Bauersfeld see the approaches they promote (social constructionism and interactionism, respectively) as theoretical steps in overcoming an epistemological dualism. For Bauersfeld, interactionism is a way out of the dilemma between individualistic and collectivistic views on the sources of meaning. According to interactionism, meanings are generated neither by individual minds nor are they an attribute of some historically founded 'collective mind' of a society, but they are continually constituted in interactions whose patterned character accounts for the relative stability of cultures.

Gergen (1995) sees social constructionism as an epistemology that overcomes the traditional opposition between what he calls the exogenic (world centred and empiricist) and the endogenic (mind centred and rationalist) orientations to knowledge. For him, knowledge starts with language:

> As we assay the culture's accumulation of what we take to be knowledge, we primarily find a repository of linguistic artifacts: texts, documents, and journals … If we assay what we take to be the transmission of knowledge in the classroom, again we primarily find our focus is on language: lectures, discussions, overhead projections, and the like. (pp. 23-24)

Two final remarks for this section will be in order. The first one is a word of caution with respect to the interactionist view of knowledge which stresses its linguistic and conventional character. Interactionists are not trying to undermine the power of knowledge. They recognise that things can be done with words that are not so easily undone, if they can be undone at all. These can be very beneficial things, but they can also be very harmful. Scientific knowledge may well be a kind of discourse, but it has implications on our lives that are not just words. Nuclear power, spacecrafts, as well as the many utilities of daily life (like the computers we are using to write this chapter) are products of a scientific and theoretical effort that have transcended the sphere of discourse.

The other remark is that interactionism brings back or rehabilitates some of the 'old-fashioned' values in education. Bauersfeld (1995), for example, has stressed the role of the quality of the culture in which one lives for personal upbringing, and has reminded us of the fact that imitative learning 'is the most common form of learning in a culture' (p.283). He thus views the teacher as having to play an important, indeed, a crucial part in the educational process: 'As an agent of the embedding culture, the teacher functions as a peer with a special mission and power in the classroom culture. The teacher, therefore, has to take special care of the richness of the classroom culture – rich in offers, challenges, alternatives, and models, including languaging' (p.283).

Voigt (1995) also stressed the role of the teacher, in particular, as he or she is setting the socio-mathematical norms, thus implicitly defining what will count as mathematical thinking (p.197). Interactionism, in fact, finds good reasons to support certain patterns of classroom interaction that have been much criticised in recent times, as putting too much stress on skills and 'rote learning' and not enough on understanding (Merttens, 1995).

1.2.5 An Anthropological Approach to Epistemology in French Didactique

Mathematics educators working within a tradition that has been developing in France since mid-seventies have devoted much space in their work to a reflection on the epistemology of mathematics education, that is to say on the nature of this knowledge – which they have named 'didactique des mathématiques' – on its object as a field of scientific research, on its place among other disciplines, on the ways in which this knowledge is constructed and validated (see, for example, Brousseau, 1986a, b; Balacheff, 1990a; Artigue, 1991; Chevallard, 1991, 1992; Vergnaud, 1991; Arsac, 1992; Artigue, Gras, Laborde and Tavignot, 1994; see also Sierpinska, 1995). They have also done substantial research on the epistemology of specific mathematical notions and domains. The way they approach epistemological questions, however, hardly fits into any one of the three broad perspectives that we have outlined so far. This is why we decided to devote a separate section to it.

The two most cited authors in this domain are Guy Brousseau and Yves Chevallard, the former for his 'théorie des situations', the latter for the concept of 'transposition didactique'. These theories have known a rapid development in the eighties and, at the beginning of the nineties, Chevallard proposed a more general theoretical framework, 'anthropologie des savoirs', of which the theory of didactic transposition formed a part.

1.2.5.1 Chevallard's position.

Chevallard's 'anthropology of knowledge' (our free translation) is an extension of epistemology, in the sense that, traditionally, the object of study in epistemology was the production of scientific knowledge, while anthropology of knowledge is assumed to occupy itself not only with the mechanisms of the production but also with practices related to the use or application of scientific knowledge, its teaching, and its transposition, that is to say the treatment of knowledge which makes certain aspects of it fit to function in various types of institutions (school is one of them) (Arsac, 1992, p.26). It is worthy of noting that, had we accepted Chevallard's extended understanding of epistemology, the title of our chapter could be shortened to 'On various approaches to the anthropology of mathematical knowledge'. In this perspective, the study of the phenomena of teaching and learning mathematics becomes a part of an anthropology of mathematical knowledge or its epistemology in this extended sense.

The notion of didactic transposition, in its beginnings (Chevallard, 1985, 1990), made certain more or less tacit assumptions about mathematical knowledge that distinguished it sharply from epistemological constructivism. It was assumed that there is some such identifiable object called 'savoir savant mathématique', against which the subject matter of the mathematics as taught at school could be compared and judged as 'legitimate' or not. Already the existence of knowledge outside of the minds of individuals is inexplicable from a constructivist point of view. It is also tacitly assumed in the theory of didactic transposition that what is taught will be ultimately learned, with some delay, of course, and maybe not by all students. Therefore, there is some ideal (or 'expert') 'state of knowledge' to which teaching and learning should and could converge. This, again, is contrary to how constructivists view the processes of teaching and learning.

Given the assumptions of constructivism, it is impossible to define what constitutes 'the novice' or the 'expert' states of knowledge in general (Lesh and Kelly, 1994, p.281). What a given student comes with to the classroom depends on his or her previous mathematical experiences and personal ways of approaching problems. The teacher can only organise rich learning environments and facilitate the development of students' mathematical thinking by offering challenging activities, promoting the construction by students of their own mental models, exploring the properties of these models, testing the range of their application and their validity in new situations (p.283).

The end product of these activities may be different for each student in terms of mental constructions, and, as such, it cannot be planned. It also cannot be judged with respect to some external entity called 'mathematical knowledge'; the criterion of evaluation is the internal coherence of each particular student's mental model or system of models.

Although Brousseau (1986a, b) also argued that there is a need to design and organise challenging activities, he claimed that the target knowledge can and even must be planned. His 'didactic situations' are meant to construct, in students, an 'artificial genesis' of specific mathematical ideas whose historical genesis and various aspects in the present day theory are understood and known.

The theory of didactic transposition has been criticised for, among other things, the vagueness of the notion of 'savoir savant mathématique' (Freudenthal, 1986). A response to this criticism (found in Arsac, 1992) revealed the socio-cultural order of the notion: society recognises the existence of a certain group of professionals who produce knowledge which, in the culture, is considered 'knowledgeable' (savant) or 'scientific' (in the broad sense which does not reduce science to natural sciences only). This understanding of knowledge is closer to what Vygotsky tacitly assumed (and left unquestioned) and perhaps even more to the epistemology inherent in Bruner's approach to language acquisition.

In more recent developments of the theory, it has been proposed to shift from comparing different types of knowledge (research mathematicians' knowledge versus the school subject of mathematics) to a much larger domain of comparing different types of social practices (Martinand, 1989, in Arsac, 1992). Chevallard (1991) was looking at relations between the social practice of research in mathematics and the social practice of institutionalised teaching and learning of mathematics at school. Different pairs of practices involving mathematics have drawn the attention of other researchers. For example, Lave (1988) and Walkerdine (1988) studied the lack of congruence between the functioning of mathematical thinking at school and in out-of-school spheres of practice such as home management, parenting, and work.

By focusing on social practices and institutions, rather than on 'knowledge', Chevallard extended his theory to the dimensions of an anthropology. He assumed that all knowledge is knowledge of an institution. Professional research in mathematics is one institution, school is another, family is yet another. Mathematics also 'lives' in business and industry. It can live in each of these institutions, but, through adaptation, it becomes different mathematics. Epistemological studies of mathematics should investigate the sources, ways of control, and mechanisms of growth of mathematics in all the 'institutional niches' in which it lives.

This 'anthropological approach' to epistemology brought Chevallard to adapt the notion of the individual's knowledge or knowing. There is no question of mental structures or models in this notion, but of an attitude ('un rapport'), a relationship to and functioning with respect to what an institution defines as being its knowledge. One 'knows' (or doesn't) only relative to an opinion of an institution, not in an absolute sense (Arsac, 1992).

In view of the new developments in the theory of didactic transposition, one may wonder if it still makes sense to use the language of 'epistemological correctness' that characterised the discourse of this theory in its early versions: 'to measure the deviation ('écart') between 'savoir savant' and 'savoir enseigné'; to exert an 'epistemological vigilance'; 'to call into question the legitimacy of a curriculum' if it departs too much from the mathematics of the mathematicians, etc.

But, from the beginning, the theory of didactic transposition has brought forward certain useful or sensitising epistemological distinctions. We need not claim that school mathematics ought to be 'legitimised' through reference to the mathematics of the university mathematicians, but we have to admit that the two knowledges are, epistemologically, very distinct objects. They grow from different sources and they grow in different ways. While the development of research mathematics is problem-driven, the motive power of the progress of learning mathematics at school is a kind of dialectic between the 'old material' and the 'new material'.

Moreover, the differences between the institutional contracts, within which the two knowledges are inscribed, are such that certain 'research-type' mathematical behaviours may be difficult to obtain in the classroom. This is especially true in the case of the activity of proving. The kind of interactional format that establishes itself in the mathematics classroom lends itself more to 'argumentative behaviours', where the aim is to reach an agreement, than to proving, which endeavours to establish the truth of a statement (Balacheff, 1990b). A change in this situation would require a re-negotiation of the rules of the contract with the students. This may prove difficult, however:

We have to realise that most of the time students do not act as theoreticians but as practical men. Their task is to give a solution to the problem the teacher has given to them, a solution that will be acceptable with respect to the classroom situation. In such a context the most important thing is to be efficient, not to be rigorous. It is to produce a solution, not to produce knowledge ... This means that beyond the social characteristics of the teaching situation we must analyse the nature of the target it aims at. If the students see the target as 'doing' more than 'knowing' then their... argumentative behaviours could be viewed as being more 'economic' than behaving mathematically.

(Balacheff, 1990b)

Another useful distinction brought forth by the theory of didactic transposition is that between the teacher's knowledge (the knowledge to be taught) and the knowledge that the students are made responsible for (the knowledge to be learned). For example, the teacher will be responsible for the theory of the systems of linear equations, while the students will have to demonstrate that they know how to solve them. The distinction between these two different epistemological rules in the didactic contract imposes conditions on what is going to be considered as 'teachable'. A frequent answer is that a piece of knowledge is teachable if it can be algorithmised (Chevallard, 1991).

The theory of didactic transposition proposed many other epistemological constructs, among them, the notions of 'depersonalisation' and 'decontextualisation' of knowledge. The process of didactic transposition starts when the mathematician prepares to communicate his result to fellow mathematicians. This process leads to stripping the result of the personal history of its discovery, its heuristics, and the context of the particular questions and problems within which it was born. The author will try to establish his or her result on a more abstract and general level. When the result is published, it is 'depersonalised' and 'decontextualised', it is public, open to scrutiny and new generalisations and applications in different contexts.

In the process of learning, a reverse process must take place. The learner has to make the result his or her own, by creating a personal path for its understanding and embedding it into the context of problems he or she is presently working on. Knowledge must become personal knowledge.

The anthropological approach proposed by Chevallard and interactionism in mathematics education share certain points of view and concerns. Certainly, both see education from cultural and social perspectives. Both give prominence to processes of creation of 'consensual domains' or 'milieus' whereby certain elements of the culture become 'taken-as-shared' or 'allant de soi, transparents'. These processes are seen as mechanisms that account for the relative stability of cultures. Both approaches are concerned with the mechanisms of change. Interactionists are interested in looking at teaching and learning at the micro-level – from inside the classroom – and attribute an important role to the individual contributions of teachers and students: the notions of 'reflexivity' and 'emergence' account for the change in classroom cultures. For Chevallard, who studied 'didactic systems' at the macro-level, the source of change is in the work of the 'noosphere' or the interface between schools and the society at large, where the organisation, the contents, and the functioning of the educational process are being conceived.

Noosphere involves groups such as mathematicians, ministerial commissions, parents, and head teachers. It occupies itself with the 'manipulation' of knowledge according to the priorities that emerge in the society at a given time. At one time, there is a feeling that mathematics taught at school should be closer to the mathematics of the university mathematicians. At another time, it is proposed that mathematics education at school prepares students for the applications of mathematics in the workplace, and problem solving in everyday life. Chevallard does not ascribe a greater role in the process of change to regular classroom teachers, whose work, for him, is limited to the 'editing of the text of knowledge which is determined (albeit not written) by the noosphere' (Arsac, 1992, p.17).

1.2.5.2   Brousseau's theory of situations.

Brousseau's (1986a, b) theory of situations has been extensively studied and applied by researchers in France and elsewhere (see Perrin-Glorian, 1994). At the basis of this theory is the epistemological assumption that 'knowledge exists and makes sense for the cognising subject only because it represents an optimal solution in a system of constraints' (Brousseau, 1986b, p.368). There is a similarity here with the Piagetian idea of knowing as an adaptive activity that we find in constructivist declarations such as the following, from von Glasersfeld (1995):

> From the constructivist perspective, as Piaget stressed, knowing is an adaptive activity. This means that one should think of knowledge as a kind of compendium of concepts and actions that one has found to be successful, given the purposes one has in mind. (p.7)

The act of knowing is thus 'situated' in a system of constraints which, through feedback to the subject's actions, signal to him or her the cost of trials, errors, and learning, where the latter is understood as a change in the subject's 'rapport au milieu'. Learning occurs when the application of previously constructed notions becomes too costly, and the subject is compelled to make adaptations or even rejections.

Briefly, a concept will not develop, if the subject never has a need for it. If all the functions that a student has ever dealt with are everywhere continuous, it is likely his understanding of the expression 'limit of the function at the point x = a' will be reduced to 'value of the function at x = a'. If all vector spaces a student has ever seen are the R^n spaces, then proving that in an arbitrary vector space the zero vector is unique will appear senseless to him. For a given target concept, the task of the didactician is to organise situations or systems of constraints for which the given concept will appear as an optimal (less costly) solution.

Where does one find guidelines for situations adapted for the teaching of a given mathematical concept? Brousseau (1981, p.48) suggested an 'epistemological study' of the concept, comprising research on

- the meanings of the concept within the structure of the present-day theory;
- the historical and cultural conditions of the emergence of the concept (its various intermediary forms, conceptions and perspectives that created 'obstacles' with respect to the evolution of the concept, as seen from the perspective of the present-day theory, problems that led to an 'overcoming' of these obstacles and allowed for a further development);
- the study of the psychogenesis of the concept (or its 'genetic epistemology');
- a 'didactic analysis', that is to say a study of the meanings of the concept as intended and/or conveyed by its teaching, presently and in the past (including the study of the didactic transposition or a comparison with the results of the above 'structural' and 'historical' analyses).

The aim is not to have students recapitulate, in their learning, a historico-cultural process of a concept's development. The aim is to find a balance between a 'historical' approach that would make the child repeat many of the forgotten conceptions of the past, and a direct teaching of the concept as it appears in the structure of the present day, without trying to build the concept on today's students' conceptions as they evolve within the frame of a culture and schooling (Brousseau, 1981, p.48). Brousseau proposed here a whole research program for didactics of mathematics involving epistemological studies, design of didactical situations, experimentation, comparison of the design with the actual processes, revision of the epistemological studies and of the design, and study of the conditions of the reproducibility of the situations.

Brousseau proposed that the design of didactic situations related to a given mathematical concept be aimed at the construction of its 'artificial genesis' which would simulate the different present aspects of the concept for the students, and which, without reproducing the historical process, would nevertheless lead to similar results (Brousseau, 1981, p.50).

Possibly inspired by the work of Lakatos on rational reconstructions of historical geneses of mathematical concepts, Brousseau identified several types of didactic situations, or states of a didactic contract, which, for him, create a general schema of a 'didactic sequence' of situations provoking an 'artificial genesis' of a mathematical concept: situations focused on 'action', where students make their first attempts to solve a problem proposed by a teacher (examples can be found in Brousseau, 1981, p.61); situations focused on 'communication', where students communicate the results of their work to other students and the teacher; situations focused on 'validation', where theoretical rather than empirical arguments must be used; and situations of institutionalisation, where the results of the negotiations and conventions in the previous phases are summarised, attention is focused on the 'important' facts, procedures, ideas, and the 'official' terminology. Starting from the phase of institutionalisation, the meaning of terms is no longer an object of negotiation, but of correction, by reference to accepted definitions, notation, theorems, procedures. Within each of these situations, there is an 'a-didactic' component, that is to say, a time and space where the management of the situation falls entirely on the students. This is considered to be the most important part, as, in fact, the ultimate goal of teaching is what Brousseau called 'dévolution du problème aux étudiants', which Bruner named the 'handover' of a competence from the teacher to the students (Bruner, 1983; Edwards and Mercer, 1993).

The research program sketched by the theory of situations was aimed at an elaboration of a certain number of 'fundamental situations' related to the basic mathematical concepts taught at school, that would, in a way, guarantee their acquisition by students regardless of the personality of the teacher (Berthelot and Salin, 1995).

The basic assumption of Brousseau's theory of situations is that knowledge constructed or used in a situation is defined by the constraints of this situation, and that, therefore, by creating certain artificial constraints the teacher is able to provoke students to construct a certain type of knowledge. This assumption is certainly closer to constructivism (see Laborde, 1989) than it is to approaches which derive from the Vygotskian notion of the zone of proximal development.

1.2.6 Approaches Based on Epistemologies of Meaning

In some research in mathematics education, epistemology is understood mainly as an epistemology of meaning (in mathematics). It is seen as a reflection on the nature of mathematical concepts, on the processes and conditions for their development, on the characteristics of present as well as past mathematical activity, and on what makes the specific nature of one mathematical domain or another.

This is certainly the case of studies related to the 'epistemological triangle' theory of meaning, mentioned above in the discussion of the work of H. Steinbring. The research program outlined in Brousseau's theory of situations encouraged this type of epistemological work, and, more specifically, studies centred around the notion of epistemological obstacle, borrowed from Bachelard (1938).

The notion of epistemological obstacle is grounded in an antipositivistic philosophy of science, and the assumption that the process of growth of knowledge is basically discontinuous, non-cumulative marked by 'ruptures', 'thresholds' and important redefinitions in the foundations of theories. Following this program, some mathematics educationists embarked on studies of epistemological obstacles related to various mathematical notions (see for example, Cornu, 1983; Sierpinska, 1985a,b, 1990; Schneider-Gilot, 1988).

But epistemological analyses of mathematical concepts or domains have been done outside of Brousseau's program, without using the notion of epistemological obstacle and/or without taking a historical perspective. For example, Anna Sfard's epistemology of algebraic thinking, based on the idea of a dialectic between the operational and the structural modes of thinking, made no reference to the concept of epistemological obstacles but supported its claims with historical arguments (Sfard, 1991).

Other researchers have looked at how various mathematical concepts function in contemporary theory and culture. Marc Legrand was able to explain student difficulties in mathematical analysis by comparing the algebraic and the analytic modes of thinking in the context of, for example, the relation of equality (thinking in terms of identity of values versus thinking in terms of 'approximation, majoration, minoration' — see Artigue, 1995). The 'tool-object dialectic' theory developed by Régine Douady was not a consequence of a historical study, but a result of an analysis of contemporary mathematical activity (Artigue, 1995).

The epistemological studies of Heinz Steinbring have also been grounded in a reflection on contemporary mathematical theory. Steinbring (1991a, b) looked at the inevitable conflicts that arise in the teaching of mathematics when teachers try to introduce mathematical concepts as 'concrete generalisations', thereby neutralising the distinction between socially-achieved conventional explanations and the fundamentally theoretical or 'self-referent nature of mathematical objects'. In analysing how basic probabilistic concepts are introduced in teaching, Steinbring provided an example of a classroom interaction where students were observing a discrepancy between the theoretical expectations of the outcome of a random process (a gambling game) and the actual empirical results. Theoretically, a loss was the most probable, yet in the actual playing of the game a gain was obtained. Students explained this conflict by asserting that the results had been due to 'chance' or 'luck', and the teacher reinforced this view by emphasising the expression 'chance', and then conveying the feeling that that settled the matter. By doing that the teacher established an 'interactional frame' (Goffman, 1974) which provided the word 'chance' with a general and all-explanatory power. This way the difference between experience and theory was neutralised and an obstacle for the construction of the mathematical concepts of the random event and probability as a measure of randomness was created.

Steinbring made a remark which is interesting from the point of view of epistemology of mathematics and the relations between the subjective and the social dimensions of knowledge. He stated that such conventional 'universal objects' obtained through 'concrete generalisation' of a social reaction to a phenomenon are especially inaccessible to students' understanding. Such social constructs cannot be personalised: they operate only on the level of social interaction, they seem to be 'pure convention or completely pre-constructed by the teacher's methodical intentions'. 'Only theoretical knowledge', Steinbring stated, 'is open for individual or personally subjective access'.

1.2.7 Epistemology and a Theory of Instruction

Morf (1994), in reflecting on the difficulties that a theory of instruction ('théorie didactique') has, so far, in integrating the constructivist epistemology with itself, considered the impact of a given epistemology on the theory and practice of teaching of mathematics. The two domains were seen to have totally different objects of study, orientation, aims and tasks. They look at phenomena from different points of view.

Complexity is an important consideration. While an epistemology studies knowledge as a relation between a subject and an object, a theory of instruction, as soon as it takes into account the didactic activity, must deal with at least two types of knowledge, the knowledge of the student (to be transformed) and the knowledge of the teacher (to be used in this transformation). In the practice of teaching, the situation is even more distant from epistemology than the theory of instruction, because knowledge is no longer conceived of as a relationship between a subject and an object but becomes an aspect of the psychological subject – to teach means to transform the subject cognitively. A theory of instruction which tried to incorporate a constructivist epistemology has attempted to reduce the complexity by putting aside the knowledge of the teacher and occupying itself solely with the knowledge of the student. Restoring the role of the teacher in constructivist theory requires a serious effort of theorisation (see, for example, Simon, 1995).

Another problem which besets attempts to incorporate genetic epistemological notions (such as Piagetian genetic epistemology) – which focus essentially on the genesis of knowledge – into a theory of instruction is that 'the theory of instruction has to give an account of knowledge itself, and orient the action to the specific transformations of this knowledge' (Morf, 1994, p.33). Morf commented that 'the chances of founding a theory of instruction on purely structural epistemological models are doubtful'. Indeed, while a psychologist would be content with the statement that a child has developed certain instruments of knowledge, such as (reversible) operations, and is therefore considered ready to tackle such and such mathematical problems, a teacher's concern is to ensure that the child actually gains the experience of solving these mathematical problems.

Morf (1994) postulated that the object of study of a theory of instruction is knowledge and its functioning 'in an arbitrary subject'. Like epistemology, didactic theory should put aside the psychological subject. Assuming, of course, that 'knowledge depends on a cognitive system which can be an individual subject, a group, a culture, or any system which can assign a meaning to an object or an event', the theory should nevertheless postulate that the specific features of this system should not intervene in the description of the knowledge.

Knowledge, in relation to a theory of instruction, should be regarded as a 'potential of action developed through experience'. The orientation of an epistemology can be descriptive; a theory of instruction must be action-directed, or didactic. Instead of building theories based on assumptions and verification of hypotheses, pedagogy creates theories based on principles, and the elaboration of didactic interventions which match the spontaneous transformation of knowledge and guarantee a synergy between the action of the teacher and the functioning of the potential of action in students.

Whether or not one accepts Morf's (1994) postulates, it is impossible to ignore the fact that theories of instruction are, or are expected to be, both theories *of* action and theories *for* action, and therefore are likely to be based on principles rather than axioms. Having to take into account phenomena of a very heterogeneous nature, these principles are likely to draw not on one single and coherent system of epistemological assumptions but possibly on a range of them applied to different contexts. Bartolini-Bussi (1994) accepted this view when she spoke of the unavoidable necessity of using multiple theoretical perspectives in any research in mathematics education whose purpose is action and not only knowledge. The result is not eclecticism: she preferred to evoke complementarity. Bartolini-Bussi (1994) provided examples of different classroom situations which probably should not be analysed from the same epistemological basis; some would be better explained from the Piagetian perspective, and others, from a Vygotskian perspective.

Cooney (1994) did not hesitate to speak about eclecticism in theories of mathematics education. In fact, he proposed viewing theory in a way that would allow one to say 'eclectic theory' without committing an oxymoron.

While we are quick to use the word theory in discussing issues in mathematics education, we would be wise to view theory as something other than a monolithic concept rooted in a notion of objectivity defined by a sense of reality. Snow ... maintains that theory has many forms, ranging from a set of well-defined propositions as suggested by 'traditional' science, to conceptual analyses, even to the inclusion of metaphors that reflect and influence our thinking. Given the nature of our field, it is difficult to imagine that theory in mathematics education is likely to result in a set of interdependent propositions. In fact, we might be wiser to conceptualize theory development as an exercise in revealing the human ingenuity, insight and compassion of which Feyerabend ... speaks. (p.105)

The concern with the issue of what constitutes a theory in mathematics education has fairly recent origins, and it is not evenly spread in the international mathematics education community. In many countries or groups of mathematics educators, a 'theory of instruction' is still a set of principles which are value laden, and imply recommendations for action.

According to some educationists the theoretical framework of interactionism, together with its ethnographic methodological orientation could be a favourable meeting place for the researcher and the teacher. This is where the activities of the researcher and the teacher might profitably complement each other. As Kawecki (1993) has argued, both ethnographic researchers and teachers investigate and prepare for what they will do, they analyse and organise, and they present the results of their work in the form of a commentary about certain aspects of the human life. Both give accounts of their activities by 'telling a story' (Woods, 1986, 1992; Cooney, 1994, p.105). The teacher describes his or her own experience, and the ethnographer tries to describe teaching and learning processes from the point of view of the participants of these processes. Both the professional practice of teaching and the ethnographic research are considered to have features such as 'style', 'insight', and 'sensitivity' which are characteristic more of an art than of orthodox scientific method.

CONCLUSION

Our assignment was to write a chapter titled 'Epistemologies of mathematics and of mathematics education'. The second 'of' was quite puzzling and we spent some time thinking about what kind of work we would have to do in order to take the second part of the title seriously. Should we study the origins of the validity of our beliefs about the teaching and learning of mathematics? Should we study the psychological and historical genesis of these beliefs? Should we discuss the methods of justification of statements about the teaching and learning of mathematics?

We did not feel ready to study the genetic and methodological epistemology of mathematics education. We decided, therefore, to take an 'inside view', from within mathematics education, and not from a meta-level of methodologies and sociologies of research in mathematics education. We reasoned that if we took the meta-level approach, it would be very difficult for us to make a link between what we write and the study of epistemologies

866

of mathematics, which was the first part of the assignment. We would have ended up with two parallel, non-intersecting studies. Thus, our interpretation of the title was: 'Epistemologies of mathematics and their role in mathematics education'.

As we have seen, epistemologies of mathematics could find their way to mathematics education only via genetic, social and cultural, and historico-critical epistemologies. Moreover, it has become quite clear over the years, that epistemologies do not translate directly into theories of instruction and do not make recommendations for the practice of teaching. Studies of the processes of learning, the elaboration of theories of learning have all been very valuable, but there is a need to create original theories of mathematical instruction and original theories of the practice of mathematics teaching. There already exists a non-negligible body of research in this direction and an effort has been made to make explicit the epistemological assumptions under-lying theories of instruction and theories of the professional knowledge of teachers that have been elaborated.

It is useful to be more aware of what epistemologies can and cannot do. Some epistemologies do ask the question: 'What does it mean to instruct a child?' Certainly, interactionism does, for example, but it does not, by itself, define what is good instruction. There is no such thing as 'an interactionist mathematics classroom' like there is 'a constructivist mathematics class-room' (Burton, 1993). If interactionism has any implications for teaching it is in the form of an awareness that different formats of interaction produce dif-ferent types of knowledge. The choice of the type of knowledge we, as edu-cators, want our students to achieve, is a matter of ideological values, not of learning theory. On the other hand, the matching of a format of interaction with the preferred type of knowledge is a matter of study and experimenta-tion. A Vygotskian approach, however, necessarily draws teaching and learn-ing into a unified activity.

There is much debate within the international community of mathematics educators about theoretical approaches and their underlying epistemological issues. Constructivist, socio-historical and interactionist stances are com-pared, set against each other or brought together as complementary points of view in discussions that go far beyond the immediate concerns of mathemat-ics teaching and learning. Are these philosophical and theoretical considera-tions essential in shaping directions for worthwhile research in mathematics education and for making recommendations for the practice of teaching?

Researchers tend to respond in the affirmative to this question. The clari-fication of theoretical assumptions is essential for establishing the means of justification, control and evaluation of didactical proposals. On the other hand, educational policy makers, curriculum designers and textbook authors seem to rely, in their work, on principles usually implicit, rather than on some coherent theory of instruction built on definite epistemological assumptions.

Some mathematics educators have seen a danger in this. Tietze (1994), for example, commented on the danger of principles tending to be interpreted in exaggerated and oversimplified ways. For example, the principle of isolating difficulties resulted in a disintegration of the subject matter: mathematics appeared as a collection of separate topics best characterised by its 'typical exercises'. Another often-heard 'principle', the need to make extensive use of a variety of visual representations, does not rest easily with the now equally well known fact that the meanings of diagrams and graphs are not transparent and that 'iconic language can cause considerable additional difficulties in comprehension' (Tietze, 1994). In Tietze's view, 'the main problem with didactic principles is the lack of a sound analysis of their descriptive and prescriptive components, which are often compounded'. The same could be said of setting mathematical concepts in 'real-life' contexts.

Sorting out the descriptive parts and recommendations for action could certainly help to avoid certain unwelcome practices. But it seems that an even clearer view of the value and possible consequences of such principles could be obtained if such analysis was topped up by a study of their underlying epistemological assumptions.

Mathematics education is undoubtedly a developing academic discourse in its own right, but it is not unaffected by its surrounding 'contributing disciplines' which Higginson (1980) lists as mathematics, philosophy, psychology and sociology. In our investigation of epistemologies of mathematics and mathematics education we have been most concerned with the ways in which we in mathematics education use the term 'epistemology' or in which we draw implicitly on epistemological assumptions, and we have looked outwards from there. We have examined epistemologies of mathematical knowledge; we have examined what might be termed epistemologies of psychology, at least in the sense that for psychology the central issue is the epistemic subject and how he or she comes to know; and we have examined the manner in which sociologists might address the term 'epistemology'. Perhaps one of the main outcomes of this chapter is that, for mathematics educators, epistemologies of mathematics and assumptions about the epistemic subject cannot be divorced. For some they are the same.

The mathematics classroom is a social institutional creation and we have been at pains to point out that the shift from any kind of epistemological description, be it of the body of mathematical knowledge that occupies many shelves of books in the library or be it the knowing of every individual, to prescriptions about teaching necessarily draws beliefs and values into the debate. These beliefs may be about what students should learn, what social relationships they should experience or which forms of classroom organisation and teaching styles will best enable students to construct/appropriate/gain that mathematical knowledge or those mathematical ways of thinking.

Thus notions such as 'development', 'hierarchy', 'growth', 'rich construction', 'higher mental functions' all necessarily imply a sense of the normal child and therefore of the abnormal, or deviant. There is no avoiding such discourses in education, which are inevitably repressive. We would want to argue that an explicit engagement with the underlying epistemological assumptions of education, mathematics, teaching, learning and the child is an ethical requirement of the researcher and the teacher and others involved in education. 'Power and knowledge directly imply one another .... There is no power relation without the correlative constitution of a field of knowledge, nor any knowledge that does not presuppose and constitute at the same time power relations' (M. Foucault, quoted in Sheridan, 1980).

ACKNOWLEDGMENT

The writing of this paper was supported by the Canadian Social Sciences and Humanities Research Council grant no. 410-93-0700. We would also like to acknowledge the assistance of Michelle Artigue, who contributed some of the ideas, and Mariolina Bartolini Bussi, Alan Bishop and Astrid Defence for their comments on an earlier draft. The responsibility for the ideas in this final version, however, is entirely ours.

REFERENCES

Agassi, J.: 1982, 'Mathematics Education as Training for Freedom', *For The Learning of Mathematics* 1(1), 28-32.
Anglin, W.S.: 1995, *The Invisible Art: An Introduction to the Philosophy of Mathematics*, unpublished manuscript, Concordia University, Montréal.
Arsac, G.:1992, 'The Evolution of a Theory in Didactics: The Example of Didactic Transposition', in R. Douady and A. Mercier (eds.), *Research in Didactique of Mathematics. Selected Papers*, La Pensée Sauvage éditions, Grenoble.
Artigue, M.: 1991, 'Epistémologie et Didactique', *Recherches en Didactique des Mathématiques* 10 (2-3), 241-286.
Artigue, M.: 1995, 'Epistemology and Mathematics Education', paper presented at the Annual Meeting of the Canadian Mathematics Education Study Group, London, Ontario, May 26-30.
Artigue, M., Gras, R., Laborde, C., and Tavignot, P. (eds.): 1994, *Vingt Ans de Didactique des Mathématiques en France. Hommage à Guy Brousseau et Gérard Vergnaud*, La Pensée Sauvage éditions, Grenoble.
Bachelard, G.: 1938, *La Formation de l'Esprit Scientifique*, Presses Universitaires de France, Paris.
Balacheff, N.: 1990a, 'Towards a Problématique for Research on Mathematics Teaching', *Journal for Research in Mathematics Education* 21 (4), 258-72.
Balacheff, N.: 1990b, 'Beyond a Psychological Approach: The Psychology of Mathematics Education', *For the Learning of Mathematics* 10 (3), 2-8.
Bartolini-Bussi, M.-G.: 1994, 'Theoretical and Empirical Approaches to Classroom Interaction', in R. Biehler, R.W. Scholz, R. Sträßer, and B. Winkelman (eds.), *Didactics of Mathematics as a Scientific Discipline*, Kluwer Academic Publishers, Dordrecht.

Bartolini-Bussi, M.-G. and Pergola, M.: (in press), 'History in the Mathematics Classroom: Linkages and Kinematic Geometry', in H.N. Jahnke, N. Knoche and M. Otte (eds.), *Geschichte der Mathematik in der Lehre,* Vandenhoeck & Ruprecht: Gottingen.

Bauersfeld, H.: 1995, ''Language Games' in the Mathematics Classroom: Their Function and their Effects', in P. Cobb and H. Bauersfeld (eds.), *The Emergence of Mathematical Meaning: Interaction in Classroom Cultures,* Lawrence Erlbaum Associates, Publishers, Hillsdale, NJ.

Berthelot, R. and Salin, M.-H.: 1995, 'Savoirs et Connaissances dans l'Enseignement de la Géométrie', in G. Arsac, J. Gréa, D. Grenier, and A. Tiberghien (eds.), *Différents Types de Savoirs et leur Articulation,* La Pensée Sauvage éditions, Grenoble.

Bishop, A.: 1988, *Mathematical Enculturation: A Cultural Perspective on Mathematics Education,* Kluwer, Dordrecht.

Bloor, D.: 1976, *Knowledge and Social Imagery,* Routledge, London.

Bloor, D.: 1983, *Wittgenstein: A Social Theory of Knowledge*, Macmillan, London.

Blumer, H.: 1969, *Symbolic Interactionism: Perspective and Method,* Prentice-Hall, Englewood Cliffs, NJ.

Brousseau, G.: 1981, 'Problèmes de Didactique des Décimaux', *Recherches en Didactique des Mathématiques* 2(1), 37-128.

Brousseau, G.: 1986a, 'Fondements et Méthodes de la Didactique des Mathématiques', *Recherches en Didactique des Mathématiques* 7(2), 33-115.

Brousseau, G.: 1986b, *'Théorisation des Phénomènes d'Enseignement des Mathématiques',* Thèse de Doctorat d'Etat ès Sciences, Université de Bordeaux I.

Bruner, J.S.: 1983, *Child's Talk,* Oxford University Press, London.

Bruner, J.S.: 1985, 'The Role of Interaction Formats in Language Acquisition', in J.P. Forgas (ed.), *Language and Social Situations,* Springer-Verlag, New York.

Bruner, J.S. and Bornstein, M.H.: 1989, 'On Interaction', in J.S. Bruner and M.H. Bornstein (eds.), *Interaction in Human Development,* Lawrence Erlbaum Associates, Publishers, Hillsdale, NJ.

Brunschwicg, L.: 1912, *Les Étapes de la Philosophie Mathématique,* F. Alcan, Paris.

Burton, L.:1993, *The Constructivist Classroom* (video), Edith Cowan University, Perth, Western Australia.

Carnap, R.: 1928/1966, *Der Logische Aufbau der Welt,* F. Meiner, Hamburg.

Chevallard, Y.: 1985, *Transposition Didactique du Savoir Savant au Savoir Enseigné,* La Pensée Sauvage Éditions, Grenoble.

Chevallard, Y.: 1990, 'On Mathematics Education and Culture: Critical Afterthoughts', *Educational Studies in Mathematics* 21(1), 3-28.

Chevallard, Y.: 1991, *La Transposition Didactique du Savoir Savant au Savoir Enseigné,* La Pensée Sauvage éditions, Grenoble.

Chevallard, Y.: 1992, 'Concepts Fondamentaux de la Didactique: Perspectives Apportées par une Approche Anthropologique', *Recherches en Didactique des Mathématiques* 12(1), 73-112. (There exists an English translation: 1992, 'Fundamental Concepts in Didactics: Perspectives Provided by an Anthropological Approach', in R. Douady and A. Mercier (eds.), *Research in Didactique of Mathematics.* Selected papers, La Pensée Sauvage éditions, Grenoble).

Cobb, P.: 1989, 'Experiential, Cognitive and Anthropological Perspectives in Mathematics Education', *For the Learning of Mathematics* 9(2), 32-43.

Cobb, P.: 1990, 'Multiple Perspectives', in L.P. Steffe and T. Wood (eds.), *Transforming Children's Mathematical Education: International Perspectives,* Lawrence Erlbaum Associates, Publishers, Hillsdale, NJ.

Cobb, P. and Bauersfeld, H. (Eds.): 1995, *The Emergence of Mathematical Meaning: Interaction in Classroom Cultures,* Lawrence Erlbaum Associates, Publishers, Hillsdale, NJ.

Cobb, P. Perlwitz, M. and Underwood, D.: 1994, 'Construction Individuelle, Acculturation Mathématique et Communauté Scolaire', in M. Larochelle and N. Bednarz (eds.), *Constructivisme et Education: Revue des Sciences de l'Education. Numéro Thématique* 20(1), 41-61.

Cobb, P. and Yackel, E.: 1995, 'Constructivist, Emergent and Sociocultural Perspectives in the Context of Developmental Research', *Proceedings of the Seventeenth Annual Meeting of the North American Chapter of the International Group for the Psychology of Mathematics Education,* October 21-24, Columbus, Ohio, 3-29.

Confrey, J.: 1990, 'What Constructivism Implies for Teaching', in R.B. Davis, C. A. Maher, and N. Noddings (eds.), *Constructivist Views on the Teaching and Learning of Mathematics,* Journal for Research in Mathematics Education, Monograph No. 4, 107-122.

Confrey, J.: 1991, 'The Concept of Exponential Functions: A Student's Perspective', in L.P. Steffe (ed.), *Epistemological Foundations of Mathematical Experience,* Springer-Verlag, New York.

Cooney, T.J.: 1985, 'A Beginning Teacher's View of Problem Solving', *Journal for Research in Mathematics Education* 16, 324-336.

Cooney, T.J.: 1994, 'On the Application of Science to Teacher and Teacher Education', in R. Biehler, R.W. Scholz, R. Sträßer and B. Winkelman (eds.), *Didactics of Mathematics as a Scientific Discipline,* Kluwer Academic Publishers, Dordrecht.

Cornu, B.: 1983, *Apprentissage de la Notion de Limite: Conceptions et Obstacles.* Thèse de Doctorat présentée au Département des Mathématiques Pures de l'Université Scientifique et Médicale de Grenoble.

Davis, P.J. and Hersh, R.: 1980, *The Mathematical Experience,* Birkhauser, Boston.

Dawson, A.J.: 1969, *The Implications of the Work of Popper, Polya and Lakatos for a Model of Mathematics Instruction,* unpublished doctoral dissertation, University of Alberta.

Dieudonné, J.: 1992, *Mathematics — The Music of Reason,* Springer-Verlag, Berlin/Heidelberg/New York.

Dreyfus, T.: 1993, 'Didactic Design of Computer-based Learning Environments', in C. Keitel and K. Ruthven (eds.), *Learning from Computers: Mathematics Education and Technology,* Springer-Verlag, Berlin/Heidelberg/New York.

Edwards, D. and Mercer, N.: 1993, *Common Knowledge: The Development of Understanding in the Classroom,* Routledge, London and New York.

Ernest, P.: 1985, 'The Philosophy of Mathematics and Mathematics Education', *International Journal for Mathematical Education in Science and Technology* 16(5), 603-612.

Ernest, P.: 1990, 'The Meaning of Mathematical Expressions: Does Philosophy Shed Any Light on Psychology?', *British Journal of Philosophy and Science* 41, 443-460.

Ernest, P.: 1991, *The Philosophy of Mathematics Education,* Falmer, Basingstoke.

Feyerabend, P.: 1978, 'In Defence of Aristotle: Comments on the Conditions of Content Increase', in G. Radnitzky and G. Andersson (eds.), *Progress and Rationality in Science,* D. Reidel Publishing Company, Dordrecht.

Fischer, R.: 1988, 'Didactics, Mathematics, and Communication', *For the Learning of Mathematics* 8(2), 20-30.

Frege, G.: 1892/1952, *Translations from the Philosophical Writings of Gottlob* Frege, P. Geach and M. Black (eds.), Blackwell, Oxford.

Freudenthal, H.: 1986, 'Review of Y. Chevallard, *Transposition Didactique du Savoir Savant au Savoir Enseigné,* La Pensée Sauvage Éditions, Grenoble, 1985', *Educational Studies in Mathematics 17,* 323-327.

Garnier C., Bednarz N. and Ulanovskaya I. (eds): 1991, *Aprés Vygotski et Piaget: Perspectives Sociale et Constructiviste. Ecoles russe et occidentale,* Bruxelles: De Boeck - Wesmael.

Garfinkel, H.: 1967, *Studies in Ethnomethodology,* Prentice-Hall, Englewood Cliffs, NJ.

Gergen, K.J.: 1995, 'Social Construction and the Educational Process', in L.P. Steffe and J. Gale (eds.), *Constructivism in Education,* Lawrence Erlbaum Associates, Publishers, Hillsdale, NJ.

Gillies, D. (ed.): 1992, *Revolutions in Mathematics,* Clarendon, London.

Girotto, V.: 1989, 'Logique Mentale, Obstacles dans le Raisonnement Naturel et Schémas Pragmatiques', in N. Bednarz and C. Gernier (eds.), *Construction des Savoirs, Obstacles et Conflits,* C.I.R.A.D.E., Agence d'Arc Inc. (les éditions), Ottawa, Ontario.

Goffman, E.: 1959, *The Presentation of Self in Everyday Life,* Doubleday, New York.

Goffman, E.: 1974, *Frame Analysis: An Essay on the Organisation of Experience,* Harvard University Press, Cambridge, Massachussetts.

Grabiner J.: 1986, 'Is Mathematical Truth Time-Dependent?' in T. Tymoczko (ed.), *New Directions in the Philosophy of Mathematics,* Birkhauser, Boston.

Gray, J.J. and Rowe, D.E.: 1993, 'Felix Klein at Evanston: Learning, Teaching and Doing Mathematics in 1893', *For the Learning of Mathematics* 13(3), 31-36.

Hersh, R.: 1979, 'Some Proposals for Reviving the Philosophy of Mathematics', *Advances in Mathematics* 31(1), 31-50.

Higginson, W.: 1980, 'On the Foundations of Mathematics Education', *For The Learning of Mathematics* 1(2), 3-7.

Kawecki, I.: 1993, *Etnografia i Szkola,* Wydawnictwo Panstwowej Wyzszej Szkoly Sztuk Plastycznych w Lodzi, Lodz.

Keitel, C. (ed.): 1989, *Mathematics Education and Society,* UNESCO Document Series No. 35.

Kilpatrick, J.: 1987, 'What Constructivism Might Be in Mathematics Education', *Proceedings of the Eleventh Conference of the International Group for the Psychology of Mathematics Education,* Vol. 1, 3-27.

Kitcher, P.: 1988, 'Mathematical Naturalism', in W. Aspray and P. Kitcher (eds.), *History and Philosophy of Modern Mathematics,* Minnesota Studies in the Philosophy of Science, Volume XI, University of Minnesota Press, Minneapolis.

Krummheuer, G.: 1992, 'Formats of Argumentation in the Mathematics Classroom', paper presented at the Sixth International Congress of Mathematics Education, Québec.

Krummheuer, G.: 1995, 'The Ethnography of Argumentation', in P. Cobb and H. Bauersfeld (eds.), *The Emergence of Mathematical Meaning, Interaction in Classroom Cultures,* Lawrence Erlbaum Associates, Publishers, Hillsdale, NJ.

Kuhn, T.S.: 1962, 'The Structure of Scientific Revolutions', *in The International Encyclopedia of Unified Science* II(2), The University of Chicago Press, Chicago.

Laborde, C.: 1989, 'Audacity and Reason: French Research in Mathematics Education', *For the Learning of Mathematics* 9(3), 31-36.

Lacan, J.: 1966, *Ecrits 1,* Seuil, Paris.

Lakatos, I.: 1976, *Proofs and Refutations,* Cambridge University Press, Cambridge.

Lakatos, I.: 1978, 'A Renaissance of Empiricism in the Recent Philosophy of Mathematics', in J. Worrall and G. Currie (eds.), *Mathematics, Science and Epistemology,* Cambridge University Press, London/New York.

Largeault, J.: 1994, 'Compte Rendu du Livre de Janet Folina, Poincaré and the Philosophy of Mathematics, Macmillan, London, 1992', *Archives de Philosophie* 57(4), 717-719.

Lave, J.: 1988, *Cognition in Practice: Mind, Mathematics and Culture in Everyday Life,* Cambridge University Press, Cambridge.

Lave, J. and Wenger, E.: 1991, *Situated Learning: Legitimate Peripheral Participation,* Cambridge University Press, Cambridge.

Leont'ev, A.N.: 1981, 'The Problem of Activity in Psychology', in J.V. Wertsch (ed.), *The Concept of Activity in Soviet Psychology,* Sharpe, Armonk, New York.

Lerman, S.: 1983, 'Problem-Solving or Knowledge-Centred: The Influence of Philosophy on Mathematics Teaching', *International Journal of Mathematical Education in Science and Technology* 14(1), 59-66.

Lerman, S.: 1986, *Alternative Views of the Nature of Mathematics and their Possible Influence on the Teaching of Mathematics,* unpublished doctoral dissertation, University of London.

Lerman, S. (ed.): 1994, *Cultural Perspectives on the Mathematics Classroom,* Kluwer, Dordrecht.

Lerman, S.: 1996, 'Intersubjectivity in Mathematics Learning: A Challenge to the Radical Constructivist Paradigm?' *Journal for Research in Mathematics Education* 27(2), 133-150.

Lesh, R. and Kelly, A.E.: 1994, 'Action-theoretic and Phenomenological Approaches to Research in Mathematics Education: Studies of Continually Developing Experts', in R. Biehler, R.W. Scholz, R. Sträßer, and B. Winkelman (eds.), *Didactics of Mathematics as a Scientific Discipline,* Kluwer Academic Publishers, Dordrecht.

Lins, R.: 1994, 'Eliciting the Meanings for Algebra Produced by Students: Knowledge, Justification and Semantic Fields', in J.P. da Ponte and J.F. Matos (eds.), *Proceedings of the Eighteenth Meeting of the International Group for the Psychology of Mathematics Education,* Lisbon, vol. 3, 184-191.

Lompscher, J.: 1994, 'The Sociohistorical School and the Acquisition of Mathematics', in R. Biehler, R.W. Scholz, R. Sträßer, and B. Winkelman (eds.), *Didactics of Mathematics as a Scientific Discipline,* Kluwer Academic Publishers, Dordrecht.

Martinand, J.L.: 1989, 'Pratiques de Référence, Transposition Didactique et Savoirs Professionnels en Sciences et Techniques', *Les Sciences de l'Education* 2, 23-29.

Mason, J., Burton, L. and Stacey, K.: 1984, *Thinking Mathematically,* Addison Wesley, London.

Maturana, H.R.: 1978, 'Biology of Language: The Epistemology of Reality', in G.A. Miller and E. Lennenberg (eds.), *Psychology and Biology of Language and Thought: Essays in Honour of Eric Lannenbers,* Academic Press, New York, 27-63.

Mead, G.H.: 1934, *Mind, Self and Society,* University of Chicago Press, Chicago.

Merttens, R.: 1995, 'Teaching not Learning: Listening to Parents and Empowering Students', *For the Learning of Mathematics* 15(3), 2-9.

Monteiro, B.: 1993, *Factors Affecting Mathematics Teachers' Use of Computers and Software in Secondary Schools,* unpublished doctoral dissertation, University of Oxford.

Moreira, C.: 1992, *Primary Teachers' Attitudes Towards Mathematics and Mathematics Teaching with Special Reference to a Logo-Based In-Service Course,* unpublished doctoral dissertation, University of London Institute of Education.

Morf, A.: 1994, 'Une Épistémologie pour la Didactique: Spéculations Autour d'un Aménagement Conceptuel', *Revue des Sciences de l'Education* 20(1), 29-40.

Nickson, M.: 1981, *Social Foundations of the Mathematics Curriculum,* unpublished doctoral dissertation, University of London Institute of Education.

Nickson, M.: 1992, 'The Culture of the Mathematics Classroom: An Unknown Quantity?', in D. Grouws (ed.), *Handbook of Research on Mathematics Teaching and Learning,* Macmillan, New York, 101-114.

Nickson, M. and Lerman, S. (eds.): 1992, *The Social Context of Mathematics Education: Theory and Practice,* South Bank Press, London.

Perrin-Glorian, M.-J.: 1994, 'Théorie des Situations Didactiques: Naissance, Développement, Perspectives', in M. Artigue, R. Gras, C. Laborde, and P. Tavignot (eds.), *Vingt Ans de Didactique des Mathématiques en France,* La Pensée Sauvage éditions, Grenoble.

Piaget, J. and Garcia, R.: 1989, *Psychogenesis and the History of Science,* Columbia University Press, New York.

Piaget, J.: 1959, *The Language and the Thought of the Child,* Routledge and Kegan Paul Ltd, London.

Piaget, J.: 1970, *Structuralism,* Basic Books, Inc., New York.

Piaget, J.: 1972, *Science of Education and the Psychology of the Child,* The Viking Press, New York.

Piatelli-Palmarini, M. (ed): 1979, *Théories du Langage, Théories de l'Apprentissage, Le Débat Entre Jean Piaget et Noam Chomsky,* Editions du Seuil, Paris.

Poincaré, H.: 1899, 'La Logique et l'Intuition dans la Science Mathématique', *Enseignement Mathématique* 1, 157-162.

Poincaré, H.: 1906, *La Science et l'Hypothèse,* Flammarion, Paris.

Poincaré, H.: 1908a, 'L'Invention Mathématique', *Enseignement Mathématique* 10, 357-371.

Poincaré, H.: 1908b, *Science et Méthode,* Flammarion, Paris.

Polya, G.: 1945, *How To Solve It* (second edition), Doubleday Anchor, New York.

Popper, K.R.: 1972, *La Connaissance Objective,* Editions Complexe, Bruxelles.

Reichenbach, H.: 1938/1947, *Experience and Prediction: An Analysis of the Foundations of Structure of Knowledge,* University of Chicago Press, Chicago.

Restivo, S.: 1985, *The Social Relations of Physics, Mysticism and Mathematics,* Reidel, Dordrecht.

Restivo, S.: 1992, *Mathematics in Society and History,* Kluwer, Dordrecht.

Richard, J.: 1907, 'Sur la Nature des Axiomes en Géométrie', *L'Enseignement Mathématique* 9, 463-473.

Rogers, L.: 1978, 'The Philosophy of Mathematics and the Methodology of Teaching Mathematics', *Analysen* 2, 63-67.

Russell, B.: 1989, *Principles of Mathematics,* Norton, New York.

Schneider-Gilot, M.: 1988, *Des Objets Mentaux 'Aire' et 'Volume' au Calcul des Primitives,* Dissertation présentée en vue de l'obtention du grade de Docteur ès Sciences, Université Catholique de Louvain, Faculté des Sciences, Louvain-la-Neuve.

Schoenfeld, A.H.: 1985, *Mathematical Problem Solving,* Academic Press, London.

Seeger, F.: 1994, 'Capturing Regularities and the Theory of Practice' in L. Bazzini (ed.), *Proceedings of the Fifth International Conference on Systematic Cooperation Between Theory and Practice in Mathematics Education,* Grado, Italy, 211-220.

Sfard, A.: 1991, 'On the Dual Nature of Mathematical Conceptions: Reflections on Processes and Objects as Different Sides of the Same Coin', *Educational Studies in Mathematics* 22(1), 1-36.

Sfard, A.: 1994, 'Mathematical Practices, Anomalies, and Classroom Communication Problems', in P. Ernest (ed.), *Constructing Mathematical Knowledge: Epistemology and Mathematics Education,* The Falmer Press, London.

Sheridan, A.: 1980, *Foucault: The Will to Truth,* Tavistock, London.

Sierpinska, A.: 1985a, 'La Notion d'Obstacle Épistémologique dans l'Enseignement des Mathématiques', *Actes de la 37e Rencontre de la C.I.E.A.E.M.,* 73-95.

Sierpinska, A.: 1985b:, 'Obstacles Épistémologiques Relatifs à la Notion de Limite', *Recherches en Didactique des Mathématiques* 6(1), 5-68.

Sierpinska, A.: 1990: 'Some Remarks on Understanding in Mathematics', *For the Learning of Mathematics* 10(3), 24-36.

Sierpinska, A.: 1994, *Understanding in Mathematics,* The Falmer Press, London.

Sierpinska, A.: 1995, 'Some Reflections on the Phenomenon of French Didactique', *Journal für Mathematik Didaktik* 16(3/4), 163-192.

Sierpinska, A., Defence, A., Khatcherian, T., and Saldanha, L.: in press, 'A Propos de Trois Modes de Raisonnement en Algèbre Linéaire', to appear in J.-L. Dorier (ed.), *État de l'Art de la Recherche Internationale sur l'Enseignement Universitaire en Algèbre Linéaire,* La Pensée Sauvage éditions, Grenoble.

Simon, M.A.: 1995, 'Reconstructing Mathematical Pedagogy from a Constructivist Perspective', *Journal for Research in Mathematics Education* 26(2), 114-145.

Steffe, L.P.: 1992, 'Schemes of Action and Operation Involving Composite Units', *Learning and Individual Differences* 4, 259-309.

Steffe, L.P. and D'Ambrosio, B.: 1995, 'Toward a Working Model of Constructivist Teaching', *Journal for Research in Mathematics Education* 26(2), 146-159.

Steffe, L.P. and Weigel, H.: 1994, 'Cognitive Play and Mathematical Learning in Computer Microworlds', *Educational Studies in Mathematics* 26, 111-134.

Steinbring, H.: 1989, 'Routine and Meaning in the Mathematics Classroom', *For the Learning of Mathematics* 9(1), 24-33.

Steinbring, H.: 1991a, 'Mathematics in Teaching Processes. The Disparity Between Teacher and Student Knowledge', *Recherches en Didactique des Mathématiques* 11(1), 65-108.

Steinbring, H.: 1991b, 'The Concept of Chance in Everyday Teaching: Aspects of a Social Epistemology of Mathematical Knowledge', *Educational Studies in Mathematics* 22, 503-522.

Steinbring, H.: 1993, 'Problems in the Development of Mathematical Knowledge in the Classroom: The Case of a Calculus Lesson', *For the Learning of Mathematics* 13(3), 37-50.

Steinbring, H.: 1994, 'Dialogue between Theory and Practice in Mathematics Education', in R. Biehler, R.W. Scholz, R. Sträßer, and B. Winkelman (eds.), *Didactics of Mathematics as a Scientific Discipline,* Kluwer Academic Publishers, Dordrecht.

Strawson, P.F.: 1971, 'Meaning and Truth', in P.F. Strawson (ed.), *Logico-Linguistic Papers,* Methuen, London.

Thomas, R.S.D.: 1987, 'Cartesian and non-Cartesian Thinking: Reflections on the Learning in Mathematics', *For the Learning of Mathematics* 7(1), 23-29.

Thompson, A.G.: 1982, *Teachers' Conceptions of Mathematics: Three Case Studies,* unpublished doctoral dissertation, University of Georgia, Athens, USA.

Tietze, U.-P.: 1994, 'Mathematical Curricula and the Underlying Goals', in R. Biehler, R.W. Scholz, R. Sträßer, and B. Winkelman (eds.), *Didactics of Mathematics as a Scientific Discipline,* Kluwer Acadamic Publishers, Dordrecht.

Vergnaud, G.: 1991, 'La Théorie des Champs Conceptuels', *Recherches en Didactique des Mathématiques* 10(2/3), 133-170.

Voigt, J.: 1995, 'Thematic Patterns of Interaction and Sociomathematical Norms', in P. Cobb and H. Bauersfeld (eds.), *The Emergence of Mathematical Meaning. Interaction in Classroom Cultures,* Lawrence Erlbaum Associates, Publishers, Hillsdale, NJ.

von Glasersfeld, E.: 1990, 'Environment and Communication', in L.P. Steffe and T. Wood (eds.), *Transforming Children's Mathematics Education: International Perspectives,* Lawrence Erlbaum Associates, Publishers, Hillsdale, NJ, 30-38.

von Glasersfeld, E.: 1993, 'Learning and Adaptation in the Theory of Constructivism', *Communication and Cognition* 26(3/4), 393-402.

von Glasersfeld, E.: 1995: 'A Constructivist Approach to Teaching', in L.P. Steffe and J. Gale (eds.), *Constructivism in Education,* Lawrence Erlbaum Associates, Hillsdale, NJ.

Vygotsky, L.: 1978, *Mind in Society,* Harvard University Press: Cambridge, MA.

Walkerdine, V.: 1988, *The Mastery of Reason: Cognitive Development and the Production of Rationality,* Routledge, London and New York.

Wittgenstein, L.: 1953, *Philosophical Investigations,* Basil Blackwell, Oxford.

Wittgenstein, L.: 1956, *Remarks on the Foundations of Mathematics,* Basil Blackwell, Oxford.

Wittgenstein, L.: 1974, *Tractatus Logico-Philosophicus,* Routledge and Kegan Paul, London.

Wood, T.: 1992, 'Funneling or Focusing? Alternative Patterns of Communication in Mathematics Class', paper presented at the Sixth International Congress of Mathematics Education, Québec.

Woods, P.: 1986, *Inside Schools: Ethnography in Educational Research,* Routledge and Kegan Paul, London.

Woods, P.: 1992, 'Symbolic Interactionism: Theory and Method', in M.D. LeCompte, W.L. Millroy, J. Preissle (eds.), *The Handbook of Qualitative Research in Education,* Academic Press, San Diego.

Yackel, E., Cobb, P. and Wood, T.: 1991, 'Small-Group Interactions as a Source of Learning Opportunities in Second-Grade Mathematics', *Journal for Research in Mathematics Education* 22, 390-408.

Chapter 23: Proof and Proving

GILA HANNA AND H. NIELS JAHNKE

The Ontario Institute for Studies in Education of the University of Toronto, Canada and Institut für Didaktik der Mathematik der Universität Bielefeld, Germany

ABSTRACT

Proof is an essential characteristic of mathematics and as such should be a key component in mathematics education. Translating this statement into classroom practice is not a simple matter, however, because there have been and remain differing and constantly developing views on the nature and role of proof and on the norms to which it should adhere.

Different views of proof were vigorously asserted in the reassessment of the foundations of mathematics and the nature of mathematical truth which took place in the nineteenth century and at the beginning of the twentieth, a reassessment which gave rise to well-known and widely divergent philosophical stands such as logicism, formalism and intuitionism. These differences have now been joined by disagreements over the implications for proof of 'experimental mathematics', 'semi-rigorous mathematics' and 'almost certain proofs', concepts and practices which have emerged on the heels of the enormous growth of mathematics in the last fifty years and the ever-increasing use of computers in mathematical research. If these and earlier controversies are to be reflected usefully in the classroom, mathematics educators will have to acknowledge and become familiar with the complex setting in which mathematical proof is embedded. This chapter aims at providing an introduction to this setting and its implications for teaching.

It is not merely as a reflection of mathematical practice that proof plays a role in mathematics education, however. Proof in its full range of manifestations is also an essential tool for promoting mathematical understanding in the classroom, however artificial and unnatural its use there may seem to the beginner. To promote understanding, however, some types of proof and some ways of using proof are better than others. Thus this chapter also aims at providing an introduction to didactical issues that arise in the use of proof.

The chapter first discusses the great importance accorded in mathematical practice to the communication of understanding, pointing out the place of proof in this endeavour and the implications for mathematics teaching. It then identifies and assesses some recent challenges to the status of proof in mathematics from mathematicians and others, including predictions of the 'death of proof'. It also examines and largely seeks to refute a number of challenges to the importance of proof in the curriculum that have arisen within the field

A.J. Bishop et al. (eds.), International Handbook of Mathematics Education, 877 - 908

of mathematics education itself, sometimes prompted by external social and philosophical influences.

This chapter continues by looking at mathematical proof, and the mathematical theories of which it is a part, in terms of their role in the empirical sciences. There are important insights into the use of proof in the classroom that may be garnered through a deeper understanding of the mechanism by which mathematicians, nominally practitioners of a non-empirical science, make an indispensable contribution to the understanding of external reality.

Later sections examine the use of proof in the classroom from various points of view, proceeding from the premise that one of the key tasks of mathematics educators at all levels is to enhance the role of proof in teaching. The chapter first reports upon some ambivalent but nevertheless encouraging signs of a strengthened role for proof in the curriculum, and turns to a discussion of proof in teaching, offering a model defining its full range of potential functions. The important distinction between proofs which prove and proofs which explain is then introduced, and its application is presented at some length with the help of examples.

1.   PROOF AND UNDERSTANDING

The most significant potential contribution of proof in mathematics education is the communication of mathematical understanding. One comes to appreciate the importance of this seemingly trite determination if one examines critically the view of proof adopted by the 'new math' movement of the 1950's and 1960's.

The belief implicit in the 'new math' was that the secondary-school mathematics curriculum better reflects mathematics when it stresses formal logic and rigorous proof. This belief rested upon two key assumptions:

a)   that in modern mathematical theory there are generally accepted criteria for the validity of a mathematical proof; and

b)   that rigorous proof is the hallmark of modern mathematical practice.

Both of these beliefs can be seen to be false (Hanna, 1983). First of all, even a cursory revisiting of the major accounts of the nature of mathematics (logicism, formalism, intuitionism and quasi-empiricism) makes it obvious that these significant schools of mathematical thought hold widely differing views on the role of proof in mathematics and on the criteria for the validity of a mathematical proof.

Second, an examination of mathematical practice shows clearly that in the eyes of practising mathematicians rigour is secondary in importance to understanding and significance, and that a proof actually becomes legitimate and convincing to a mathematician only when it leads to real mathematical understanding. According to Hanna (1983), mathematicians accept a new theorem only when some combination of the following holds:

1) They understand the theorem (that is, the concepts embodied in it, its logical antecedents, and its implications) and there is nothing to suggest it is not true;

2) The theorem is significant enough to have implications in one or more branches of mathematics, and thus to warrant detailed study and analysis;

3) The theorem is consistent with the body of accepted results;

4) The author has an unimpeachable reputation as an expert in the subject of the theorem;

5) There is a convincing mathematical argument for it, rigorous or otherwise, of a type they have encountered before (p.70).

Subsequent studies of a number of cases have confirmed the appropriateness of these criteria (Neubrand, 1989; Berggren, 1990). In light of both the theory and the practice of mathematics, then, teachers can be assured that they would be imparting to students a greater understanding of proof itself, not to mention the mathematical topic under consideration, if they were to concentrate upon the communication of meaning rather than upon formal derivation. A mathematics curriculum which aims to reflect the real role of rigorous proof in mathematics must present it as an indispensable tool of mathematics rather than as the very core of that science.

Several mathematicians have expressed similar points of view quite explicitly (Manin, 1977; Kline, 1980; Davis and Hersh, 1981, 1986). Particularly interesting in this regard is a more recent paper by William Thurston (1994). Along with 15 other mathematicians, Thurston was responding to an article by Jaffe and Quinn (1993), who had cautioned against weakening the standards of proof. Jaffe and Quinn had proposed that heuristic work in mathematics be labelled 'speculation' or 'theoretical mathematics', to distinguish it from what they regard as proper mathematics, in which theorems are proven rigorously.

Thurston maintained that in attempting to answer the question 'What is it that mathematicians can accomplish?', one should not begin with the question 'How do mathematicians prove theorems?'. He pointed out that the latter question carries with it two hidden assumptions:

a) that there is a uniform, objective and firmly established theory and practice of mathematical proof; and

b) that the progress made by mathematicians consists of proving theorems (p.161).

According to Thurston (1994), neither of these assumptions will stand up to careful scrutiny. One will note that these hidden assumptions are in effect the same as the assumptions of the 'new math' discussed above.

Thurston (1994) also dismissed as a caricature the popular view of mathematical progress usually referred to as the definition-theorem-proof (DTP) model. For Thurston the right question to ask was: 'How do mathematicians advance human understanding of mathematics?'. And he added: 'We [mathematicians] are not trying to meet some abstract production quota of definitions, theorems and proofs. The measure of our success is whether what we do enables people to understand and think more clearly and effectively about mathematics' (p.163).

It is perhaps necessary to point out that stressing the importance of understanding is not in any way a criticism of formal proof as such. Thurston himself made this clear:

> I am not advocating the weakening of our community standard of proof; I am trying to describe how the process works. Careful proofs that will stand up to scrutiny are very important. ... Second, I am not criticizing the mathematical study of formal proofs, nor am I criticizing people who put energy into making arguments more explicit and more formal. These are both useful activities that shed new insights on mathematics (p.169).

Not all agree with Thurston on this point, however. A number of recent developments in the practice of mathematics, all of them reflecting in some way the growing use of computers, have caused some mathematicians and others to call into question the continuing importance of proof.

1.1 Challenges to Proof from Mathematics

The computer has acted as a leavening agent in mathematics, reviving an interest in algorithmic and discrete methods, leading to increased reliance on constructive proofs, and making possible new ways of justification, such as those that make use of computer graphics (Davis, 1993). The striking novelty of its uses, on the other hand, has lent a tone of urgency to the discussions among mathematicians about its implications for the nature of proof (Tymoczko, 1986; Jaffe and Quinn 1993; Thurston, 1994).

Indeed, the use of the computer has led some to announce the imminent death of proof itself (Horgan, 1993). On the basis of interviews with several mathematicians, Horgan made this prediction in a thought-provoking article entitled 'The death of proof' that appeared in the October 1993 issue of *Scientific American*. He claimed that mathematicians can now establish the validity of propositions by running experiments on computers, and maintained that it is increasingly acceptable for them to do mathematics without concerning themselves with proof at all.

One of the developments that prompted Horgan's announcement is the use of computers to create or validate enormously long proofs, such as the recently published proofs of the four-colour theorem (Appel and Haken) or of the solution to the party problem (Radziszowski and McKay). These proofs required computations so long they could not possibly be performed or even verified by a human being. Because computers and computer programs are fallible, then, mathematicians will have to accept that assertions proved in this way can never be more than provisionally true.

A second and particularly fascinating development is the recently-introduced concept of zero-knowledge proof (Blum, 1986), originally defined by Goldwasser, Micali and Rackoff (1985). This is an interactive protocol involving two parties, a prover and a verifier. It enables the prover to provide to the verifier convincing evidence that a proof exists without disclosing any information about the proof itself. As a result of such an interaction, the verifier is convinced that the theorem in question is true and that the prover knows a proof, but the verifier has zero knowledge of the proof itself and is therefore not in a position to convince others. (In principle, a zero-knowledge proof may be carried out with or without a computer.)

Here is an illustration of this concept taken from Koblitz (1994). Assume a map is colourable with three colours and the prover has a proof, that is, a way of colouring the map so that no two countries with a common boundary have the same colour. The prover wants to convince another person that there is a proof (a way of colouring the map) without actually revealing it, by letting the other person verify the claim in another way.

The prover first translates the problem into a graph consisting of vertices (countries) and edges (common boundaries). This means that the prover has a function f: $V \rightarrow \{R, B, G\}$ that assigns the colours R (red), B (blue), and G (green) to vertices (countries) in such a way that no vertices joined by an edge have the same colour. The prover also has two devices: Device A, which sets each vertex to flash a colour (R, B, or G), and Device B, which chooses a random permutation of the colours and resets each vertex accordingly. (A permutation might cause all green vertices to switch to blue and all blue vertices to red, for example).

The interaction between prover and verifier then proceeds as follows. To convince the verifier that there is a proof, the prover keeps the colours hidden from the verifier's view, but allows the verifier to grab one edge at a time and see the colours displayed at the two ends (the vertices) by Device A. The verifier starts by grabbing any edge, looking at the colours at the ends and noting that they are different. The prover then uses Device B to permute the colours randomly; the permutation is unknown to the verifier. After the permutation, the verifier again grabs any edge and verifies that the colours at the ends are different. The prover again permutes the colours. The two repeat these steps until the verifier is satisfied that the prover knows how to colour the map (has a proof).

This interaction does not tell the verifier how to colour the graph, nor does it reveal any other information about the proof. The verifier is convinced that the prover does have a proof, but cannot show it to others. Perhaps the significant feature of the zero-knowledge method, in fact, is that it is entirely at odds with the traditional view of proof as a demonstration open to inspection. This clearly thwarts the exchange of opinion among mathematicians by which a proof has traditionally come to be accepted.

Another interesting innovation is that of holographic proof (Cipra, 1993; Babai, 1994). Like zero-knowledge proof, this concept was introduced by computer scientists in collaboration with mathematicians. It consists of transforming a proof into a so-called transparent form that is verified by spot checks, rather than by checking every line. The authors of this concept have shown that it is possible to rewrite a proof (in great detail, using a formal language) in such a way that if there is an error at any point in the original proof it will be spread more or less evenly throughout the rewritten proof (the transparent form). Thus to determine whether the proof is free of error one need only check randomly selected lines in the transparent form.

By using a computer to increase the number of spot checks, the probability that an erroneous proof will be accepted as correct can be made as small as desired (though of course not infinitely small). Thus a holographic proof can yield near-certainty, and in fact the degree of near-certainty can be precisely quantified. Nevertheless, a holographic proof, like a zero-knowledge proof, is entirely at odds with the traditional view of mathematical proof, because it does not meet the requirement that every single line of the proof be open to verification.

Zero-knowledge proofs, holographic proofs and the creation and verification of extremely long proofs such as that of the four-colour theorem are feasible only because of computers. Yet even these innovative types of proof are traditional, in the sense that they remain analytic proofs. More and more mathematicians appear to be going beyond the bounds of deductive proof, however, using the computer to confirm mathematical properties experimentally.

Horgan quotes several mathematicians who concede that experimental methods, though perhaps not new, have acquired a new respectability. They have certainly received increased attention and funding following the development of graphics-oriented fields such as chaos theory and non-linear dynamics. As a result, more mathematicians have come to appreciate the power of computational experiments and of computer graphics in the communication of mathematical concepts.

They are going well beyond communication, however. In a clear departure from previous practice, it now seems to be quite legitimate for mathematicians to engage in experimental mathematics as a form of mathematical justification that does not include pencil-and-paper proof. Horgan (1993) has claimed, in fact, that some mathematicians think 'the validity of certain propositions may be better established by comparing them with experiments run on computers or real-world phenomena' (p.94).

A case in point is the University of Minnesota's Geometry Centre, where mathematicians examine the properties of four-dimensional hypercubes and other figures, or study transformations such as the twisting and smashing of spheres, by representing them graphically with the aid of computers. Horgan also cited the so-called computer-generated video proof called 'Not Knot', prepared by the mathematician William Thurston at Berkeley.

Exploration itself is not inconsistent with the traditional view of mathematics as an analytic science. But in drawing general conclusions from such explorations these mathematicians would appear to be turning to the methods of the empirical sciences. Indeed, the Geometry Centre has helped found a new journal called *Experimental Mathematics*. Such a radical shift in mathematical practice is entirely justified, according to Philip Davis, a mathematician who strongly advocates greater use of computer graphics. He has argued that the concept of visual proof is an ancient one that was unfortunately overshadowed by the rise of formal logic, and deserves to regain its important place in mathematics (Davis, 1993).

One must admit that visual proofs and other experimental methods are easier to grasp than some new methods such as holographic proof. Babai (1994) himself has pointed out that holographic proofs 'may not provide either insight or illustration'. On the other hand, as Babai added, they do enjoy the advantage of yielding near-certainty, and in this respect they 'differ fundamentally from experimental mathematics' (p.454).

The developments described here certainly pose intriguing questions for practitioners and philosophers of mathematics (Horgan, 1993; Krantz, 1994). In discussing zero-knowledge and holographic proofs, for example, Babai (1994) asked the following questions: 'Are such proofs going to be the way of the future?', 'Do such proofs have a place in mathematics? Are we even allowed to call them proofs?'.

Others have posed similar questions. Should mathematicians accept mathematical propositions which are only highly probably true as the equivalent of propositions which are true in the usual sense? If not, what is their status? Should mathematicians accept proofs that cannot be verified by others, or proofs that can be verified only statistically? Can mathematical truths be established by computer graphics and other forms of experimentation? Where should mathematicians draw the line between experimentation and deductive methods?

Mathematicians continue to debate these and other questions in meetings, on the Internet and in the Forum section of *the Notices of the American Mathematics Society*. Yet the very existence of this debate is a confirmation of the central role that proof is seen to play in mathematics. It is difficult to know just how mathematicians will eventually answer such questions, and in any case one should not expect unanimity. If a loose consensus does evolve, it will undoubtedly redefine the concept of proof to some degree. Perhaps this consensus will recognise a multiplicity of types of justification, perhaps even one that is hierarchically ordered.

But the point we must not lose sight of is that the existence of such a new consensus, even one with large remaining areas of disagreement, would not create a situation which would differ in principle from that which has prevailed up to now. As discussed above, there has never been a single set of universally accepted criteria for the validity of a mathematical proof. Yet mathematicians have been united in their insistence on the importance of proof. This is an apparent contradiction, but mathematics has lived with this contradiction and flourished. Why would one expect or want this to change?

That is why Horgan's (1993) 'The Death of Proof' article is mistitled. It actually provides evidence that proof is thriving, albeit under a number of exciting disguises. To be sure, some of the things being done today, in the name of proof, or as an alternative to proof, may in the end lose the battle for general acceptance, but proof itself appears to be alive and well. In using the power of technology, mathematicians are certainly creating new ways of proving and even new ways of thinking about mathematics. But by no means are they abandoning the idea of proof.

2.   CHALLENGES TO PROOF FROM MATHEMATICS EDUCATION

2.1   The Influence of Educational Theories

Until the introduction of the 'new math' the teaching of proof in mathematics education was limited to geometry. It was in geometry classes that students were introduced to concepts such as axiom, conjecture, theorem, and deductive method. Even in geometry, proof was somewhat of a necessary evil, a ritual to be followed rather than a source of deeper mathematical understanding. In many instances classical proofs were simply memorised.

This changed with the curriculum reforms of the late 1950's. Influenced by the tremendous growth in mathematics and in particular by the emergence of set theory as a unifying concept, primarily through the work of Bourbaki, the 'new math' introduced into the mathematics curriculum a new emphasis on axiomatic structure and proof which went well beyond geometry. This reform, like others, aimed at the improvement of mathematical understanding, but failed to live up to its expectations.

Since the demise of the 'new math', with its exaggerated emphasis on formal proof, there has been a gradual decline – in school mathematics curricula around the world – in the use of any kind of proof at all. This can be attributed in large part to the curriculum reforms and the theories of mathematics education which have come to dominate the scene since the 1960's. In their views of proof, mathematics educators have probably been influenced more by these developments in their own field than by innovations in mathematics itself.

The first important influence was the back-to-basics movement, based upon a behavioural learning model and associated with the work of Bloom (1956), Gagné (1967), and Ausubel and Sullivan (1970). It attempted to set precise behavioural objectives and promoted 'mastery learning', a programmed method that focused upon very specific skills such as arithmetical calculation, the execution of an algorithm, and the step-by-step solution of word problems. This focus came at the expense of proof and other forms of justification, and thus at the expense of the level of understanding they can provide. It is interesting to note that the behavioural approach was attacked from the very beginning by a number of important critics, who argued that 'mastery learning' did not imply any real understanding of what was learned (Skemp, 1976; Freudenthal, 1979).

Following a decline in the popularity and acceptance of the back-to-basics approach a number of other approaches emerged – such as instruction by discovery, cooperative learning, learning through problem-solving, and classroom interaction. None was ever universally accepted, but all exercised significant influence on the curriculum. While none of them attacked the teaching of proof specifically, they did shift the emphasis away from it, relegating it to heuristics (Polya, 1973; Silver, 1985).

The most influential theory of mathematics education at present, judging by the attention it has received from mathematics educators, is undoubtedly constructivism in its various forms – all of which subscribe to the central tenet that knowledge cannot be transmitted, but must be constructed by the learner (von Glasersfeld, 1983; Cobb, 1988; Kieren and Steffe, 1994). It too may come to be seen as having had a deleterious effect on the teaching of proof, if only because it has been interpreted in a way that undermines the importance of the teacher in the classroom.

Paradoxically this has happened at the very time that a number of experimental studies have confirmed just how important the teacher really is. In exploring new ways to teach proof, these studies have shown the value of such approaches as debating, restructuring, and preformal presentation, all of which posit a crucial role for the teacher in helping students to identify the structure of a proof, to present arguments, and to distinguish between correct and incorrect arguments.

Let us first review some of the new approaches to teaching proof, beginning with classroom debate. Alibert (1988) designed an experimental study in which teachers had students engage in debate among themselves to help them understand a mathematical justification. Most of the students viewed this favourably. Balacheff (1988) also investigated the use of classroom debate *(débat socio-cognitif)* to teach proof and its uses. He described a three-stage method in which the teacher guided the students through discussions in which they come up with a conjecture, perform appropriate measurements to test it, and then create a proof in support of their conjecture. He came to the conclusion that this method is superior to the one traditionally used in French schools.

In other studies, Movshovitz-Hadar (1988) and Leron (1983) showed that there are a number of techniques to make proofs more meaningful to students. The same theorem, for example, can be proved in the same class in more than one way. A proof can be restructured to make its overall structure clear, before each step is looked at in detail. Or a proof by contradiction can be avoided, where possible, by substituting a constructive one. Blum and Kirsch (1991) investigated teaching students to understand and produce proofs by using what they call a preformal presentation, in which the teacher leaves out formal details while explaining the overall structure of a proof.

These interesting new methods not only encourage students to interact with each other, but they also require the active intervention of the teacher. They are thus inconsistent with the passive role sometimes attributed to constructivist theories. Where classroom practice is informed by these theories, there is evidence that teachers tend not to present mathematical arguments or take a substantive part in their discussion. They tend to provide only limited support to students, leaving them in large measure to make sense of arguments by themselves. The idea clearly seems to be to let students 'form their own intuition about the structures of mathematics' without the intervention of the teacher (Pirie, 1988; Koehler and Grouws, 1992).

Lampert, Rittenhouse and Crumbaugh (1994), for example, reported with approval a classroom in which fifth graders engaged in group discussion and where the context of instruction was such that it was possible, as they put it, 'for the teacher to step out of the role of validator of ideas and into the role of moderator of mathematical arguments'.

One must question the idea of the teacher as impartial moderator. We want to see students develop their own ability to state and defend positions, of course, but we also know they need direction along the way. One has to be apprehensive about leaving the task of validation to their exclusive judgement. Is it educationally productive to ask them to 'negotiate meaning' and 'share their knowledge', to use the terms of this report, without the help of a teacher? In encouraging students to 'share their knowledge', might we not be simply encouraging them to share their ignorance?

It should also be said that there does not appear to be anything in the constructivist theory of learning itself that would deny to the teacher an active role. In fact Cobb (1994), one of its proponents, decried just such an interpretation of constructivist theory, and added:

Pedagogies derived from constructivist theory frequently involve a collection of questionable claims that sanctify the student at the expense of mathematical and scientific ways of knowing. In such accounts, the teacher's role is typically characterised as that of facilitating students' investigations and explorations. Thus, although the teacher might have a variety of responsibilities, these do not necessarily include that of proactively supporting students' mathematical development. Romantic views of this type arise at least in part because a maxim about learning, namely that students necessarily construct their mathematical and scientific ways of knowing, is interpreted as a direct instructional recommendation. As John Dewey observed, it is then a short step to the conclusion that teachers are guilty of teaching by transmission if they do more than stimulate students' reflection and problem solving (p.4).

Indeed, Yackel and Cobb (1994) have been quite specific about the active role of the teacher:

When students give explanations and arguments in the mathematics classroom their purpose is to describe and clarify their thinking for others, to convince others of the appropriateness of their solution methods, but not to establish the veracity of a new mathematical 'truth'. ... The meaning of what counts as an acceptable mathematical explanation is interactively constituted by the teacher and the children (p.3).

Yet the constructivist theory of learning has been translated into classroom strategies which are inimical to the teaching of proof. As mentioned, recent studies confirm that it is crucial for the teacher to take an active part in helping students understand why a proof is needed and when it is valid. A passive role for the teacher also means that students are denied access to available methods of proving. It would seem unrealistic to expect students to rediscover sophisticated mathematical methods or even the accepted modes of argumentation.

Current theories of mathematics education have undoubtedly made us more aware of the construction of knowledge by the learner, of the social and cultural environment, and of the need to foster among students a critical perspective. But we must be cognisant of what we might lose if we do not constantly cast a critical eye on how such theories are implemented in the classroom. We need to ensure that students develop the ability to assess each step in a proof and make an informed judgment on the validity of a mathematical argument as a whole. It would seem unwise to avoid methods that promise to help do this effectively, simply because they require active intervention by the teacher.

The foregoing discussion examined challenges to the status of proof inherent in some general trends in mathematics education. But there is another factor which has contributed to the attrition of this status: the misguided interpretation of Lakatos' ideas on the nature of mathematics.

Some current initiatives influenced by the work of Lakatos (1976) and set out by NCTM in the *Professional Standards for Teaching Mathematics* advocate classroom discourse among students. As pointed out earlier, this idea can unfortunately be interpreted in such a way as to downplay the role of the teacher. But there is also an inherent problem with these initiatives, in that they recommend having students develop among themselves 'agreed upon rules' for appropriate mathematical behaviour. Underpinning this approach is the belief that it is possible and desirable to emulate in the classroom the heuristic proof analysis described by Lakatos in *Proofs and Refutations*.

The publication of *Proofs and Refutations* provoked much discussion among philosophers, mathematicians and mathematics educators. Fascinated by this new and engaging way of looking at mathematical discovery, however, mathematics educators may have assumed that Lakatos' approach is more widely applicable than in fact it is. The case for heuristic proof analysis as a general method rests only upon its successful use in the study of polyhedra, an area in which it is relatively easy to suggest the counterexamples which this method requires (Hacking, 1979; Steiner, 1983; Anapolitanos, 1989). Should one really generalise from a sample of one?

It is not difficult, in fact, to find examples where the way in which a proof is found or a mathematical discovery is made would be radically different from the process of heuristic refutation described in *Proofs and Refutations* (Pickert 1984). Even the proof of Euler's theorem cited by Lakatos, for example, is a case in which refutation is redundant; as soon as adequate definitions are formulated the theorem can be proved for all possible cases without further discussion. In fact, whenever mathematicians work with adequate definitions (or with an adequate 'conceptual setting', to use Bourbaki's term), the process of proof is not one of heuristic refutation. In 'A Renaissance of Empiricism in the Recent Philosophy of Mathematics', Lakatos (1978) himself stated:

> Not all formal mathematical theories are in equal danger of heuristic refutation in a given period. For instance, elementary group theory is scarcely in any danger: in this case the original informal theories have been so radically replaced by the axiomatic theory that heuristic refutations seem to be inconceivable. (p. 36)

There are issues associated with the application of Lakatos' ideas to the classroom which are problematical. One must question, for example, the extent to which a group of students can emulate during the course of a lesson, or even over a series of lessons, the drawn-out process of examination and discussion through which new mathematical results are subjected to potential refutation (Hanna and Jahnke, 1993).

More relevant here, however, is that the application of Lakatos' ideas may convey in the classroom a misleading picture of mathematical practice. His concepts of 'informal falsifiers' and of the 'fallibility' of mathematics seem to have led many mathematics educators to believe that we should eliminate any reference to 'formal' mathematics in the curriculum and in particular that we should downplay formal proof (Ernest, 1991; Dossey, 1992).

This attitude is surely misguided. In the first place, formal proof arose as a response to a persistent concern for justification, a concern reaching back to Aristotle and Euclid, through Frege and Leibniz. There has always been a need to justify new results (and often previous results as well), not always in the limited sense of establishing their truth, but also in the broader sense of providing grounds for their plausibility. Formal mathematical proof has been and remains one quite useful answer to this concern for justification.

Second, it is a mistake to think that the curriculum would be more reflective of mathematical practice if it were to limit itself to the use of informal counterexamples. The history of mathematics clearly shows that it is not the case, yet Lakatos seemed to imply that only heuristics and other 'informal' mathematics are capable of providing counterexamples. The reality is that formal proofs themselves have often provided counterexamples to previously accepted theories or definitions. For instance, as Steiner (1983) pointed out, Peano provided a counterexample to the definition of a curve as 'the path of a continuously moving point' by showing formally that a moving point could fill a two-dimensional area.

Gödel's famous incompleteness proofs provide another example, albeit with an interesting and ironic twist. In this case formal proofs were employed to demonstrate that the axiomatic method itself has inherent limitations. Gödel could not have produced these proofs without using a comprehensive system of notation for the statements of pure arithmetic and a systematic codification of formal logic, both developed in the *Principia* for the purpose of arguing the Frege-Russell thesis that mathematics can be reduced to logic. His proofs could certainly not have been produced in informal mathematics or reduced to direct inspection.

Nor does it seem reasonable to assume that Gödel's conclusions could have been arrived at through a discovery of counterexamples ('monster-barring') followed by a denial ('monster-adjusting'), or by finding unexplained exceptions ('exception-barring') or unstated assumptions ('hidden-lemmas'). Ironically, when some mathematics educators make a case that formal proof and rigour should be downplayed in the curriculum they rest their case on the most formal of Gödel's proofs.

Informal methods have an important place in the mathematics curriculum, and it is clearly commendable to teach heuristics, as Lakatos advocates. But those who would insist upon the total exclusion of formal methods run the risk of creating a curriculum unreflective of the richness of current mathematical practice. In so doing they would also deny to teachers and students accepted methods of justification which in certain situations may also be appropriate and effective teaching tools.

2.3   The Influence of Social Values

Proof has also been challenged by the claim that it is a key element in an authoritarian view of mathematics (Ernest, 1991; Confrey, 1994; Nickson, 1994). This claim owes much, including its terminology, to Lakatos (1976), who was attempting to offer what he saw as a 'long overdue challenge' to the 'Euclidean programme', as he termed it, a programme which in his opinion aimed to create an 'authoritative, infallible, irrefutable mathematics'.

Supporters of this claim would argue that the so-called 'Euclidean' view of mathematics is in conflict with the present values of society, which dictate that we not bow down to authority and not regard knowledge as infallible or irrefutable. They appear to see proof in general, and rigorous proof in particular, as a mechanism of control wielded by an authoritarian establishment to help impose upon students a body of knowledge that it regards as predetermined and infallible.

Now, it may be true that mathematics has sometimes been presented as infallible and taught in an authoritarian way, but there has certainly been no recent consensus among educators that it should be. Whatever the case, it is rather strange that proof should have become the main target of what in the end may be no more than a misguided desire to impose a sort of political correctness on mathematics education.

It is not clear, in the first place, what it means to say that mathematics or a mathematical proof is 'authoritative', to use a term taken from Lakatos. Certainly a proof offered by a very reputable mathematician would initially be given the benefit of the doubt, and in that sense the fact that this mathematician is considered an 'authority' by other mathematicians would play some role in the eventual acceptance of the proof. But the contention seems to be that the very use of proof is authoritarian, and one is at a loss to understand such a claim.

In fact the opposite is true. A proof is a transparent argument, in which all the information used and all the rules of reasoning are clearly displayed and open to criticism. It is in the very nature of proof that the validity of the conclusion flows from the proof itself, not from any external authority. Proof conveys to students the message that they can reason for themselves, that they do not need to bow down to authority. Thus the use of proof in the classroom is actually anti-authoritarian.

Of course one could claim that the use of proof requires that the students accept certain 'authoritative' rules of deduction, and so move the argument to a new, meta-mathematical plane. But one would hope that those who challenge the role of proof are not also challenging the very idea of rules of reasoning. It would be disturbing to see mathematics teachers ranging themselves on the side of a revolt against rationality.

It has also been claimed that the use of proof strengthens the idea that mathematics is infallible. Looking at this first from the point of view of theory, however, it is clear that any mathematical truth arrived at through a proof or series of proofs is contingent truth, rather than absolute or infallible truth, in the sense that its validity hinges upon other assumed mathematical truths (and upon assumed rules of reasoning). If we look at this claim from the point of view of mathematical practice, we know that mathematicians, much as they would like to avoid errors, are as prone to making them as anyone else, in proof and elsewhere. The history of mathematics can supply many examples of erroneous results which were later corrected. Thus it is hard to see how proof strengthens 'infallibility' in any way.

The use of proof in the classroom has also been called into question on the grounds that it would encourage the idea that mathematics is an a priori science. The supporters of this claim appear to see a conflict between this idea and their view that mathematics is 'socially constructed' (Ernest, 1991). Their use of the term 'a priori' is not clear, but one suspects that what they reject is not the idea that mathematics is a priori in the sense of being analytic, non-empirical. One presumes that what they have in mind is a priori in the sense of given, pre-existing, waiting to be discovered, a view of mathematics which of course they might well see as standing in opposition to 'socially constructed'.

But as Kitcher (1984) has stated, the pursuit of proof and rigour does not carry with it a commitment to looking at mathematics as a body of a priori knowledge. Nor does the value of proof in mathematics education hinge upon a resolution of this ongoing philosophical debate. As Kitcher (1984) put it: 'To demand rigour in mathematics is to ask for a set of reasonings which stands in a particular relation to the set of reasonings which are currently accepted' (p.213). Whether the set of reasonings currently accepted is regarded as given a priori or as socially constructed has no bearing on the value of proof in the classroom.

Those who challenge the use of proof in general would challenge even more strongly the use of rigorous proof in particular. Yet rigour is a question of degree, and in mathematical practice the level of rigour is often a rather pragmatic choice. Kitcher (1984) maintained that it is quite rational to accept unrigorous reasoning when it has proven its worth in solving problems (as has been the case in physics). He added that mathematicians begin to worry about defects in rigour only when they 'come to appreciate that their current understanding ... is so inadequate that it prevents them from tackling the urgent research problems that they face' (p.217).

Mathematics educators could profitably ask themselves the question Kitcher asked about mathematicians: When is it rational to replace less rigorous with more rigorous reasoning? Kitcher's answer is: 'when the benefits it [rigorisation] brings in terms of enhancing understanding outweigh the costs involved in sacrificing problem-solving ability'. A more rigorous mathematical argument may sometimes be more enlightening. It is the teacher who must judge when more careful proving might be expected to promote the elusive but most important classroom goal of understanding.

In sum, it is difficult to take seriously those who challenge the use of proof in the classroom as an expression of authoritarianism and infallibility. There are no grounds for the belief that proof is in conflict with present-day social values or with the reality of mathematics as a human enterprise open to error. Nor does a significant role for proof in the classroom require mathematics educators to embrace a specific a priori view of mathematics.

3.   MATHEMATICAL PROOF AND THE EMPIRICAL SCIENCES

So far the discussion has considered proof from the internal viewpoint of mathematics. It is both useful and necessary, however, to examine it from the external viewpoint of the empirical sciences as well. To modify Thurston's (1994) question, quoted earlier, one might ask: 'How do mathematicians advance human understanding of reality?', and in answering this question the role of mathematical proof must also be considered.

Proof is the way by which mathematics establishes truth, but truth in mathematics is certainly different from truth in the empirical sciences. This is an entirely appropriate distinction that reflects the everyday operation of these different disciplines. But to deny that there is a connection between these different notions of truth would be completely unsatisfactory. In addressing the meaning of mathematics one cannot neglect its relationship to reality and the empirical sciences.

There are also educational reasons for an external view. It is a commonplace that the relationship of mathematics to reality should play a key role in teaching and learning, and that in this relationship one should not ignore proof and the specific type of truth it produces. This applies especially to geometry, of course, which in the classroom has an undeniable empirical dimension. There is an ongoing interplay between the figures students draw and those entities which are the subjects of the geometrical theorems they prove.

Students are frequently asked to measure the angles of a triangle, for example. After they find that their sum is always nearly equal to 180 degrees, they are told that measurement can establish this fact only for individual cases and that they will have to prove it if they really want to be sure that it is true for all triangles. This explanation may have been obvious at the time of Plato and Euclid, but it must seem unsatisfactory at a time when experiment and measurement are considered the foundation of scientific methodology. To avoid contradiction, the students are, of course, told that the triangles they draw are fundamentally different in nature from the triangles that play a role in geometrical theorems – the latter are ideal or theoretical entities, whereas the former are empirical. As valid as this distinction may be, teachers themselves still assume that one can be sure about the sum of the angles of empirical triangles only after the respective theorem for ideal triangles has been proved, and they cannot help conveying this conviction to their students.

In physics lessons, however, the message is exactly the other way round. One would never seriously entertain the idea that a natural law might be established by a theoretical proof. One would insist that all such laws are founded upon experiment and measurement, even in domains so fundamental and so much a part of everyday experience as statics (the law of the lever) and gravity. It is well known that this view is historically recent, however, and that well into the 18th century most people believed in a purely rational mode of cognition through which one might state and derive natural laws independent of experience. In the 18th century there was even a sharp distinction between the rational sciences (geometry, mechanics) and the empirical sciences (natural history in the widest sense). This distinction was eliminated only in the 19th century, with non-Euclidean geometry playing an important role in the amalgamation of rational and empirical cognition.

In a sense, this dichotomy has survived in the language of modern mathematics. On the one hand, we have what one might call the Platonist-Euclidean vocabulary. This is the language we use when we speak about truth, proof and intuition. It is the language of rationalism and conveys a background message of absolute certainty. It is most closely associated with elementary geometry, but has been transferred by way of paradigm to all branches of mathematics. Most mathematicians are conscious that in a philosophical sense this language may not be entirely satisfactory, but it is useful and convenient when we speak as internalists (that is to say, when we speak as mathematicians about mathematics).

Another language is spoken, however, when it comes to applications. Its vocabulary comprises the concepts of model, modelling, application, interpretation, mathematisation and so on. The idea underlying this language is that mathematical theories provide, in principle, models for certain domains of phenomena. Certainty is restricted to the internal mechanism of these models, while the models as a whole remain open to revision in the light of new phenomena. An important step in the evolution of this language was the reformulation of the axiomatic method by Hilbert and others at the end of the nineteenth century, as reflected in Einstein's (1921) famous dictum: 'Insofar as the theorems of mathematics refer to reality they are not certain, and insofar as they are certain they do not refer to reality' (p.123, our translation).

Mathematicians get along quite well in both languages, but it is not clear that the same is the case for students. In principle, Einstein's dictum also applies to the constant sum of angles discussed above. But very seldom do teachers convey to their students an adequate idea of the empirical meaning of geometric theorems, even though the epistemological relationship of geometry to our surrounding reality has long been made clear by the development of non-Euclidean geometry. Geometry offers us different models of the spatial relations around us, and deciding which model to use is a matter of experiment and measurement. This means that it is really measurement rather than proof that determines the sum of the angles in real triangles, and that proof has only a circumscribed, though important, role in this decision (Jahnke, 1978). As discussed later, it is possible to convey this message even to younger students when they are introduced to geometric proofs.

Mathematics teachers should not use the Platonist-Euclidean language exclusively. They should even avoid the admittedly convenient habit of professional mathematicians, who use this vocabulary when they are speaking about mathematics as internalists, switching to the language of modelling and mathematisation only when it comes to applications.

The external view of proof, however, is not limited in its implications to the introduction of lessons from the philosophy of science into mathematics teaching. It is a viewpoint, rather, which considerably deepens and enriches the whole picture of proof, epistemological, psychological and educational. In particular, it permits one to deal much more satisfactorily with the thorny relationship between certainty and relativity posed by proof. As mentioned, one can really accept neither the Platonist claim of absolute certainty in mathematics nor the messages of total relativism so fashionable nowadays. The external view offers a third way.

The standard view of proof, stemming from the Euclidean paradigm, is that it transfers truth to a new theorem from axioms which are intuitively true and from theorems which have already been proven. A new insight is reduced to insights already established. This view is not only an epistemological claim, but also a true reflection of the subjective feelings of a mathematician producing a proof or of a person who is learning a mathematical theory but is already quite at home with it. It does not reflect the feelings of beginners, however. And in new areas of mathematics, in applications and at the borderlines between disciplines, this view of proof is not always adequate, as will now be shown.

An example of the inadequacy of this view is Newton's proof of Kepler's laws. When, in his *Philosophiae Naturalis Principia Mathematica* (1687), Newton derived Kepler's laws of planetary motion from his own law of gravity, he based empirically well-established laws upon an uncertain hypothesis. Newton's law of mass attraction was in fact a subject of contention at the time, for two reasons. First, it introduced the idea of action at a distance, a concept which was at odds with the ideal of reducing all mechanical phenomena to the interaction of bodies through direct contact. Second, the specific mathematical form of this law appeared to be quite arbitrary: Why should the attraction between two masses be inversely proportional to the square of their distance?

Thus Newton's proof cannot be described as having provided certainty to laws which until that time had been based only upon measurements (using the rationale often given to students when they prove geometrical theorems). Rather, the reduction of Kepler's laws to the law of gravity meant that Kepler's laws lost their purely descriptive character and were placed in a broader context. Moreover, this broader context was not purely theoretical, but in fact made it possible to connect the laws with measurements in totally different areas. Simply put, Kepler's laws were 'generalised'. They became an instance of a whole manifold of dynamic phenomena. Newton achieved this by introducing concepts of a higher order, mass and force, whose interplay could explain the movement of the planets as well as some terrestrial phenomena. By providing in this way a 'theoretical explanation' for Kepler's laws, Newton made it possible to draw new conclusions, explain additional empirical facts, and formulate new predictions.

In this manner a theoretical explanation or a proof may often have the effect of deriving a well-known, immediately comprehensible and empirically well-established fact from something which, though more general, is also less known, less comprehensible and less certain. In so doing, the proof may lend more credibility to the assumption from which it proceeds than to the conclusion derived. In the case at hand, for instance, the more general concepts of mass and force acquired meaning, and the law of gravity credibility, by being applied to Kepler's laws. The special form of the Newtonian law of forces which was a focus of debate was undoubtedly justified, in Newton's eyes, by the very fact that he was able to derive Kepler's formulae from it. At a certain stage in the development of a theory, then, that which is proved serves to legitimise the assumptions from which it is derived.

After the law of gravity had been applied successfully to sufficiently many cases, however, it was accepted by the scientific community as one of the foundations of mechanics. From that point in the development of the theory, proving something to be a consequence of the law of gravity did mean the transfer of truth or certainty from the assumption to the consequence.

From these considerations one can derive a static and a dynamic picture of a mathematised empirical theory and the role of proof within it. In the static picture an empirical theory can be seen as a network of laws (theorems) and measurements. The laws are connected by deductive relationships established by proofs. But a law is a statement about measurements, and its validity is enhanced by a proof, not via reduction to absolute certainty, but only in the following way. When an empirical law becomes part of a theory by virtue of a proof, it is tested and confirmed not only by those measurements which refer to it directly, but also by other measurements which confirm other laws of the same theory. The theory as a whole is confirmed by all the measurements it explains, and this yields far greater certainty than any individual test of an individual law.

As discussed, the wider the application of Newton's law of gravity, the stronger the foundation it provides for Kepler's laws. The same relationship applies to geometry, viewed as a science describing the spatial relations of the world around us. We measure the angles of triangles and see that we always get a sum near 180 degrees. Then we prove this result as a theorem. And in fact this proof does have an important function. It enhances our conviction of the truth of this result, not because mathematics has a mysterious power to make statements about triangles, a power that goes beyond that of measurement, but because it connects the measurements of angles in triangles with a wealth of other measurements which taken together confirm that Euclidean geometry viewed as an empirical theory is one of the most well-established theories of all.

A dynamic picture of a mathematised empirical theory would stress that there are different stages in the evolution of such a theory and that the meaning of a proof may vary considerably from stage to stage, epistemologically, psychologically and educationally. In the infancy of a theory a proof may serve more to test the credibility, plausibility or fruitfulness of the assumptions from which it proceeds than to establish the truth of the result derived. Later on, when the theory has been incorporated into a body of accepted knowledge (or when the student has come to feel at home in it), the meaning of proof will change and it will play the (Euclidean) role of transferring truth (or conviction) from the assumptions to the theorem proved.

This dynamic view has many features that apply to purely intra-mathematical situations as well and facilitate a deeper understanding of proof in general. In school and university mathematics, proofs are often carried out using concepts which, though formally defined, cannot become completely clear to the student at the time. Theorems and proofs involving such concepts are often hard to understand. Consider, for instance, the theorem that the set of all natural numbers is equivalent to the set of all square numbers. Confronted with this theorem for the first time, learners will sense a paradox. And they will certainly not think that the proof has deduced a new truth from an old one. What they will probably do is look for the source of the paradox and eventually ask whether the definition of set-theoretical equivalence used in the proof (and which in case of finite sets does in fact lead to the expected results) is really an appropriate one. Rather than transferring truth from the conditions to the proved theorem, the proof actually has the effect of calling the conditions themselves into question. It is only in the course of further work that the meaning and usefulness of the concept of set-theoretical equivalence can become clear to the student (Jahnke, 1978).

896

The dynamic view sketched here also helps explain many phenomena observed by teachers when students are introduced to proof. Often students do not see why a fact has to be proved, because in their view it is either obvious or sufficiently justified by actual measurements. And even after students have been shown a proof they often remain unconvinced of the theorem's general validity and ask for the additional testing of specific examples (Fischbein, 1982). Experience also shows that in other cases students do not think a geometrical argument is sufficient, and will accept only symbolical reasoning as proof (Wittmann and Müller, 1988). All these phenomena reflect the fact that proofs really do have different meanings in different contexts, and show that students are frequently unsure about the relationship of a deductive argument to its area of application and to measurements. This behaviour, which so often leads to disappointment on the part of the teachers, is in most cases quite reasonable from the viewpoint of the students and simply reflects the variety of meanings that proof has in reality.

The most important conclusion from these considerations is that the teaching of proof should reflect this variety of meanings. One would not demand that the empirical meaning of a proof be discussed in every case, nor would a complete abandonment of Platonist-Euclidean language be reasonable. On the other hand, the teaching of proof should be freed from the unfruitful supposition that in the school we operate in a deductive system. Rather, one should apply Freudenthal's idea of 'local organisation' and decompose the subject matter into small units. When proofs appear in such units they may assume a variety of roles. Sometimes, in line with the established view, a proof will act to transfer truth from the assumptions to the theorem proved. Sometimes a proof will serve to explain the assumptions by showing that such and such consequences can be drawn from them. Sometimes a proof will explain a theorem, sometimes generalise it, sometimes show a new and unexpected feature. And sometimes a proof might make possible a reference to the empirical dimension of geometry or mathematics in general.

As examples of the latter type, let us consider two proofs of the theorem that the sum of the angles in a triangle is equal to two right angles. One was suggested by Fischbein (1982). He proposed the following intuitive argument. One starts with a segment AB, draws the triangle ABP and the perpendiculars MA and NB to AB. If then AP and BP are rotated towards MA and NB, a sequence of triangles is generated. It can easily be seen that the angle APB will gain whatever is lost by the angles MAB and NBA (p.17).

This is an argument of compensation. Under variable conditions the sum of the angles remains invariant, because the increase in the angles at the base is compensated for by a corresponding decrease in the angle at the apex. Finally, AP and BP change into AM and BN, and since each of the angles MAB and NBA is equal to a right angle, the theorem is proved. Fischbein was right in emphasising that notwithstanding its undoubtedly empirical element this reasoning is very different from simply measuring individual triangles.

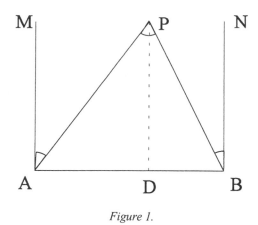

Figure 1.

In classroom teaching, the argument might be carried out in different ways: one might show the compensation qualitatively, or make actual measurements. The students would be convinced empirically of the compensation in either case, but a gap would still remain.

What happens in the limiting case of the transition from the triangle to the original configuration with the two parallels? Will compensation be preserved in this case as well? The students might ask themselves whether there are other measurements, possibly with other figures, that would help clarify this case. But, whatever turn the discussion might take, in the end it will become clear that we have to make an hypothesis at this point. One cannot prove that exact compensation is also preserved in the limiting case when AP and BP change into AM and BN, since this is equivalent to the parallel axiom.

There is no reason why students, even young ones, should not be told that one can formulate other hypotheses, that this was done in the nineteenth century, and that a different hypothesis will lead to a different geometrical theory. Then not only the proof will take on a different meaning, but so too will the measurements of the sum of the angles as well. The fact that our measurements always yield values near 180 degrees for the sum of the angles will show that exact compensation in the limiting case is at least a very good hypothesis.

Another proof could arise out of a focus on an investigation into whether polygons in general have a constant sum of interior angles, or, an even better question, which polygons have this property and which do not. This question is bound to arise as soon as one has determined the answer for triangles by taking measurements. One could explore this question empirically without having proved the theorem for triangles. The students may well come to the realisation that quadrangles, pentagons, hexagons and so forth all must have constant sums of interior angles if triangles do. They might even find a convincing argument for this by decomposing polygons into triangles.

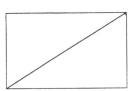 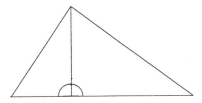

Figure 2.

Then the whole question would depend on the case of triangles. This case, however, could in turn be resolved by reference to special polygons. One could start with a rectangle and decompose it into two right triangles by one of its diagonals. Because the two triangles are congruent, a fact which could be established in an informal way, it would follow that the sum of their interior angles is equal to two right angles. From this would follow the theorem for right triangles in general, because for every right triangle it is possible to construct the corresponding rectangle. But if the theorem is true for all right triangles then it is also true for all triangles, since every triangle can be decomposed into two right triangles.

The procedure used to reduce the case of polygons to that of triangles eventually serves to resolve the problem of triangles themselves. Is this reasoning circular? Obviously not. What the proof does is to connect a series of statements about the sum of the angles of polygons, each of which can be empirically tested. To tie all these statements together into a local theory about the sum of angles is an enormous achievement, one which lends enhanced credibility to each individual statement.

4.   PROOF IN THE CLASSROOM

As described above in some detail, there have been a number of challenges to proof from both mathematics and mathematics education, but despite these challenges there is reason for optimism with regard to the status of proof in the curriculum. This is evidenced by the NCTM *Standards,* an influential curriculum reform document published in 1989 by the National Council of Teachers of Mathematics (NCTM) in the United States. (The authors are conscious of the great differences among the countries of the world from the point of view of curriculum, and have chosen to discuss the situation in the United States as indicative of direction rather than present status.)

Though this document did not stress proof as such, it did recommend that students be encouraged to make conjectures, to explain their reasoning, to validate their assertions and to discuss and question their own thinking and that of others. It also suggested a shift of emphasis in the teaching of geometry, where proof has traditionally resided in the United States. It recommended that less emphasis be given to two-column proofs and to Euclidean geometry as a complete axiomatic system. But seven topics are recommended for greater emphasis, among them two which have a flavour of proof:

a)   the development of short sequences of theorems; and

b)   deductive arguments expressed orally and in sentence form (National Council of Teachers of Mathematics, 1989, pp.126-127).

The NCTM *Standards* document does seem to shy away from the explicit use of the word proof, however. For example, it states in the section 'Standard 3: Mathematics as Reasoning' that:

In grades 9-12 the mathematics curriculum should include numerous and varied experiences that reinforce and extend logical reasoning skills so that all students can ...

– make and test conjectures;
– formulate counterexamples;
– follow logical arguments;
– judge the validity of arguments;
– construct simple valid arguments;

and so that, in addition, college-intending students can ...

– construct proofs for mathematical assertions, including indirect proofs and proofs by mathematical induction. (p.143)

It makes similar recommendations in another of its parts, 'Standard 14: Mathematical Structure', where it suggests that college-intending students:

– prove elementary theorems within various mathematical structures, such as groups and fields;
– develop an understanding of the nature and purpose of axiomatic systems. (p.184)

In the *Standards* document there is only one explicit reference to proof, and it applies only to 'college-intending' students. But proof is implicit in the rest of the recommendations as well, even though its wording does suggest a certain ambivalence. If one is willing to consider a focus on the testing of conjectures, the formulation of counterexamples and the construction and examination of valid arguments as evidence of an intention to teach mathematical proof, then the existence of the NCTM *Standards* might lead one to believe that proof is not about to disappear from the mathematics curriculum.

Of course these recommendations do not guarantee a significant presence of proof in the curriculum, even in the United States. We do not know the extent to which they have been implemented over the past five years or how they may have been interpreted in classroom practice.

Certainly such recommendations are needed. Research undertaken before their publication showed that students' understanding of proof and its value was deficient. Senk (1985), for example, investigated the proof-writing ability of students studying Euclidean geometry. Her survey of 1,520 high-school students, from five of the U.S. states, showed that only about 30 per cent of them had reached a 75 per cent mastery level in writing proofs and only 3 per cent had received a perfect score. A study by Schoenfeld (1994) at about the same time found that students had very little aptitude for proof or appreciation of its importance. Fischbein (1982) found that high-school students who had learned and presumably understood the proof of a proposition nonetheless thought that further checks on its truth would be desirable, demonstrating thereby that they had failed to grasp the function of proof as a transmitter of truth.

Silver and Carpenter (1989) reported in the *Fourth National Assessment of Educational Progress* (NAEP) that most 11th-grade students demonstrated little understanding of proof. Fewer than 50 per cent of the students were able to select an appropriate counterexample, and fewer than 25 per cent were able to identify correctly the meaning of an axiom. Other studies (Williams, 1980; Martin and Harel, 1989; Schoenfeld, 1989; Chazan, 1993) also documented students' lack of appreciation for proof, as well as their inability to identify false deductive arguments or to distinguish between empirical evidence and proof.

5. THE FUNCTIONS OF PROOF IN TEACHING

To draw conclusions for the teaching of proof from the complex setting discussed here, one must take into consideration the fundamental difference between scholarly mathematics and school teaching. Research mathematicians take as given the explicit and implicit assumptions behind their mathematical work. These assumptions are determined in part by the division of labour between mathematics and the other sciences, and in part by a consensus, maintained by force of habit, among the experts in the field. In particular, mathematicians confine themselves largely to the deductive aspects of proof. In passing judgment on a proof, they may discuss potential applications and consider other issues of fruitfulness, but their main concern is whether the proof is syntactically correct and the theorem in question thus conclusively demonstrated. For them the primary issue is whether the complexity of the mathematics in the narrower sense has been successfully mastered.

In teaching and learning, on the other hand, many issues which the practising mathematician can often afford to ignore assume the greatest importance. In particular, proof cannot be taught or learned without taking into consideration the relationship of mathematics to reality. Teachers must weigh the contribution that a proof can make to our understanding of the physical and intellectual world around us. While mathematicians can afford to focus almost exclusively upon mathematical complexity, teachers have to deal with a high level of epistemological complexity. Mathematics education is faced in this regard with a genuine scientific and philosophical challenge.

Teachers cannot avoid this challenge by simply conveying the concepts of modern axiomatics. On the contrary, for each new mathematical topic they have to interpret afresh the complex relationship between deductive reasoning and the application of mathematics. They have to teach at different levels simultaneously. In no topic is this as important as in that of proof. But this is extraordinarily hard to achieve, because one has to develop arguments and examples relating a proof and its applications for which there is often no model in scholarly mathematics.

Despite the fundamental difference between scholarly mathematics and school teaching, it is useful, when attempting to set out the role of proof in the classroom in a systematic fashion, to consider the whole range of functions which proof performs in mathematical practice. In the long run, proof in the classroom would be expected to reflect all of them in some way. But these functions are not all relevant to learning mathematics in the same degree, so of course they should not be given the same weight in instruction (de Villiers, 1990; Hersh, 1993).

This range of functions is quite broad; mathematicians clearly expect more of a proof than justification. As Manin (1977) pointed out, they would also like it to make them wiser. This means that the best proof is one that also helps readers to understand the meaning of the theorem being proved: to see not only that it is true, but also why it is true. Of course such a proof is also more convincing and more likely to lead to further discoveries. A proof may have other valuable benefits as well. It may demonstrate the need for better definitions, or yield a useful algorithm. It may even make a contribution to the systematisation or communication of results, or to the formalisation of a body of mathematical knowledge.

Expanding on Bell's distinction among the functions of proof (1976), de Villiers (1990) presented what he and his colleagues believed to be a useful model:
  − verification (concerned with the truth of a statement)
  − explanation (providing insight into why it is true)

- systematisation (the organisation of various results into a deductive system of axioms, major concepts and theorems)
- discovery (the discovery or invention of new results)
- communication (the transmission of mathematical knowledge) (p.18)

One should add to this model the functions of:
- construction of an empirical theory
- exploration of the meaning of a definition or the consequences of an assumption
- incorporation of a well-known fact into a new framework and thus viewing it from a fresh perspective.

Such a richly differentiated view of proof is the product of a long historical and educational development, however. Just as it has taken humankind a long time to reach such a high level of sophistication, so must every individual entering the world of mathematics go through a process of growth. Such a process must start with fundamentals, and the fundamental question that proof addresses is 'why?'. (This question is not peculiar to mathematics, of course; it forms the point of departure for all human thought.) In the educational domain, then, it is natural to view proof first and foremost as explanation, and in consequence to value those proofs which best help to explain. Wittmann and Müller (1988), for example, have pointed out the value of the *inhaltlich-anschaulicher Beweis,* in which the demonstration makes use of the meaning of the terms employed rather than relying on abstract methods.

Because the key goal is understanding, any justification chosen must also be appropriate in its form to the grade level and the context of instruction. It could well be a calculation, a visual demonstration, a guided discussion observing accepted rules of argumentation, a preformal or informal proof, or even a proof that conforms to strict norms of rigour. Related ideas have been put forward by Blum and Kirsch (1991), in their plea for 'doing mathematics on a preformal level'. The classroom context and the level of experience of the students may also make it appropriate to emphasise some points at the expense of others, or even to leave out some points entirely where that can be done without loss of integrity.

5.1 Proofs that Prove and Proofs that Explain

A proof that we propose to use in the classroom must be well structured, and almost any proof could presumably be restructured to make it more teachable. Yet proofs do differ greatly in their inherent explanatory power, and it is useful to make a distinction between proofs that prove and proofs that explain (Hanna, 1989, 1990). This distinction has been expressed in different ways by many others, and goes back at least to the 18th-century mathematician

Clairaut (Barbin, 1988). A proof that proves shows that a theorem is true. A proof that explains does that as well, but the evidence which it presents derives from the phenomenon itself. In the words of Steiner (1978):

> An explanatory proof makes reference to a characterizing property of an entity or structure mentioned in a theorem, such that from the proof it is evident that the result depends on the property. It must be evident, that is, that if we substitute in the proof a different object of the same domain, the theorem collapses; more, we should be able to see as we vary the object how the theorem changes in response.

As an illustration, let us look at different ways of proving that the sum of the first n positive integers, S(n), is equal to n(n+1)/2. As we know, this theorem can easily be proved by mathematical induction. Such a proof has little explanatory value, however. It demonstrates that the theorem is true, but gives the student no inkling of why it is true.

A proof that explains, on the other hand, could show why the theorem is true by basing itself upon the symmetry of two representations of that sum, as follows:

$$S(n) = 1 + 2 + ... + n$$
$$S(n) = n + (n - 1) + ... + 1$$
$$2S(n) = (n + 1) + (n + 1) + ... + (n + 1)$$
$$= n(n + 1), \text{ since there are } n \text{ lots of } (n + 1)$$

Another explanatory proof of this same theorem is, of course, the geometric representation of the first n positive integers by an isosceles right triangle of dots; here the characteristic property is the geometrical pattern that compels the truth of the statement. We can represent the sum of the first n integers as triangular numbers (see Figure 3).

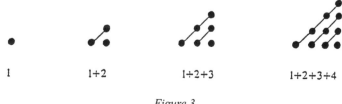

| 1 | 1+2 | 1+2+3 | 1+2+3+4 |

Figure 3.

The dots form isosceles triangles containing $S(n) = 1 + 2 + 3 + ... + n$ dots.

Two such sums, $S(n) + S(n)$, give a square containing n^2 dots and n additional dots, because the diagonal of n dots is counted twice.

904

Therefore:

$$2S(n) = n^2 + n$$
$$S(n) = (n^2 + n)/2$$

Another explanatory proof would be the represen̶t̶a̶t̶i̶o̶n of the first n integers by a staircase-shaped area as follows. A rectangle with sides n and n+1 is divided by a zigzag line (see Figure 4).

The whole area is $n(n+1)$, and the staircase-shaped area, $1+2+3+\ldots+n$ only half, hence $\dfrac{n(n+1)}{2}$

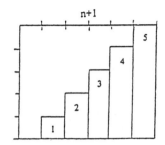

Figure 4.

We have seen that even the most experienced mathematicians prefer a proof that explains. For teachers it is all the more important to take the time to search out those proofs which best promote understanding. Such a proof is much more likely to yield not only 'knowledge that', but also 'knowledge why'. Unfortunately there is no guarantee that every theorem we might like to use will have a proof that explains. But let us reserve non-explanatory proofs for those limited situations in which we simply cannot find a proof that makes us wiser.

ACKNOWLEDGMENT

Preparation of this paper was supported in part by NATO under a Collaborative Research Grant, and by the Social Sciences and Humanities Research Council of Canada.

REFERENCES

Alibert, D.: 1988, 'Towards New Customs in the Classroom', *For the Learning of Mathematics* 8(2), 31-35, 43.

Anapolitanos, D.A.: 1989, 'Proofs and Refutations: A Reassessment', in K. Gavroglu, Y. Goudaroulis, and P. Nicolacopoulos (eds.) *Imre Lakatos and Theories of Scientific Change.* Kluwer, Dordrecht, 337-345.

Ausubel, D. P. and Sullivan, E. V.: 1970, *Theory and Problems of Child Development,* Grune & Stratton, New York.

Babai, L.: 1994, 'Probably True Theorems, Cry Wolf?', *Notices of the American Mathematical Society* 41(5), 453-454.

Balacheff, N.: 1988, *Une Étude des Processus de Preuve en Mathématiques chez Les Élèves de Collège,* Thèse d'État, IMAG, LSD2, Université Joseph Fourier, Grenoble.

Barbin, E.: 1988, 'La Démonstration Mathématique: Significations Epistemologiques et Questions Didactiques', *Bulletin de l'A.P.M.E.P.* no. 366, 591-619.

Bell, A.: 1976, 'A Study of Pupils' Proof-explanations in Mathematical Situations', *Educational Studies in Mathematics* 7, 23-40.

Berggren, J.L.: 1990, 'Proof, Pedagogy and the Practice of Mathematics in Medieval Islam', *Interchange* 21(1), 36-46.

Bloom, B.: 1956, *Taxonomy of Educational Objectives: Cognitive Domain,* David O. McKay, New York.

Blum, M.: 1986, 'How to Prove a Theorem So No-one Else Can Claim It', *Proceedings of the International Congress of Mathematicians,* 1444-1451.

Blum, W. and Kirsch, A.: 1991, 'Preformal Proving: Examples and Reflections', *Educational Studies in Mathematics* 22(2), 183-204.

Chazan, D.: 1993, 'Empirical Evidence and Proof', *Educational Studies in Mathematics* 24(4), 359-387.

Cipra, B.: 1993, 'New Computer Insights From 'Transparent' Proofs', *What's Happening in the Mathematical Sciences* 1, 7-12.

Clairaut: 1986, *Elements de Géometrie* (Originally published in 1765), Republished Siloë, Laval.

Cobb, P.: 1988, 'The Tension Between Theories of Learning and Instruction in Mathematics Education', *Educational Psychologist* 23, 87-104.

Cobb, P.: 1994, 'Constructivism in Mathematics and Science Education', *Educational Researcher* 23(7), 4.

Confrey, J.: 1994, 'A Theory of Intellectual Development', *For the Learning of Mathematics* 14(3), 2-8.

Einstein, A.: 1921, 'Geometrie und Erfahrung', Sitzungsberichte der Preußischen Akademie der Wissenschaften, Jahrgang 1921, 1. Halbband, Berlin, 123-130.

Davis, P.J.: 1993, 'Visual Theorems', *Educational Studies in Mathematics* 24(4), 333-344.

Davis, P.J. and Hersh, R.: 1981, *The Mathematical Experience,* Houghton Mifflin, Boston.

Davis, P.J. and Hersh, R.: 1986, *Descartes' Dream,* HBJ Publishers, New York.

de Villiers, M.: 1990, 'The Role and Function of Proof in Mathematics', *Pythagoras* 24, 17-24.

Dossey, J.: 1992, 'The Nature of Mathematics: Its Role and its Influence', in D. Grouws (ed.), *Handbook of Research on Mathematics Teaching and Learning,* Macmillan, New York, 39-48.

Ernest, P.: 1991, *The Philosophy of Mathematics Education,* Falmer, London

Fischbein, E.: 1982, 'Intuition and Proof', *For the Learning of Mathematics* 3(2), 9-18, 24.

Freudenthal, H.: 1979, 'Ways to Report on Empirical Research in Education', *Educational Studies in Mathematics* 10(3), 275-303.

Gagné, R. M.: 1967, 'Instruction and the Conditions of Learning', in L. Siegel (ed.), *Instruction: Some Contemporary Viewpoints,* Chandler, San Francisco, 291-313.

Goldwasser, S., Micali, S. and Rackoff, C.: 1985, 'The Knowledge Complexity of Interactive Proof-systems', *Proceedings of the 17th ACM Symposium on Theory of Computing,* 291-304.

Grouws, D. (ed.).: 1992, *Handbook of Research on Mathematics Teaching and Learning,* Macmillan, New York.

Hanna, G.: 1983, *Rigorous Proof in Mathematics Education,* OISE Press, Toronto.

Hanna, G.: 1989, 'Proofs that Prove and Proofs that Explain', in G. Vergnaud, J. Rogalski, and M. Artigue (eds.), *Proceedings of the International Group for the Psychology of Mathematics Education,* Paris, Vol. II, 45-51.

Hanna, G.: 1990, 'Some Pedagogical Aspects of Proof', *Interchange* 21(1), 6-13.

Hanna, G. and Jahnke, H.N.: 1993, 'Proofs and Applications', *Educational Studies in Mathematics* 24(4), 421-437.

Hersh, R.: 1993, 'Proving is Convincing and Explaining', *Educational Studies in Mathematics* 24(4), 389-399.

Horgan, J.: 1993, 'The Death of Proof', *Scientific American* 269(4), 93-103

Jaffe, A. and Quinn, F.: 1993, "Theoretical Mathematics': Towards a Cultural Synthesis of Mathematics and Theoretical Physics', *Bulletin of the American Mathematical Society* 29(1), 1-13.

Jahnke, H.N.: 1978, Zum Verhältnis von Wissensentwicklung und Begründung in der Mathematik – Beweisen als didaktisches Problem. Bielefeld: Materialien und Studien des IDM, 10.

Kieren, T. and Steffe, L.: 1994, 'Radical Constructivism and Mathematics Education', *Journal for Research in Mathematics Education* 25(6), 711-733.

Kitcher, P.: 1984, *The Nature of Mathematical Knowledge,* Oxford University Press, New York.

Kline, M.: 1980, *The Loss of Certainty,* Oxford University Press, Oxford.

Koblitz, N.: 1994, *A Course in Number Theory and Cryptography,* Springer-Verlag, New York.

Koehler, M. and Grouws, D.: 1992, 'Mathematics Teaching Practices and Their Effects', in D. Grouws, (ed.), *Handbook of Research on Mathematics Teaching and Learning,* Macmillan, New York, 115-126.

Krantz, S. G.: 1994, 'The Immortality of Proof', *Notices of the American Mathematical Society* 41(1), 10-13.

Lakatos, I.: 1976, *Proofs and Refutations,* Cambridge University Press, Cambridge.

Lakatos, I.: 1978, 'Mathematics, Science and Epistemology', in J. Worrall and G. Currie, (eds.), *Philosophical Papers,* Vol. 2, Cambridge University Press, Cambridge, UK.

Lampert, M., Rittenhouse, P. and Crumbaugh, C.: 1994, 'From Personal Disagreement to Mathematical Discourse in the Fifth Grade', Paper presented at the annual meeting of the American Educational Research Association, New Orleans.

Leron, U.: 1983, 'Structuring Mathematical Proofs', *American Mathematical Monthly* 90(3), 174-185.

Manin, Yu.: 1977, *A Course in Mathematical Logic,* Springer-Verlag, New York.

Martin, W.G. and Harel, G.: 1989, 'Proof Frames of Preservice Elementary Teachers', *Journal for Research in Mathematics Education* 20(1), 41-51.

Movshovitz-Hadar, N.: 1988, 'Stimulating Presentations of Theorems Followed by Responsive Proofs', *For the Learning of Mathematics* 8(2), 12-19.

National Council of Teachers of Mathematics: 1989, *Curriculum and Evaluation Standards for School Mathematics,* Commission on Standards for School Mathematics, Reston, VA.

Neubrand, M.: 1989, 'Remarks on the Acceptance of Proofs: The Case of Some Recently Tackled Major Theorems', *For the Learning of Mathematics* 9(3), 2-6.

Newton, I.: 1687, *Philosophiae Naturalis Principia Mathematica,* J. Streater, London.

Nickson, M.: 1994, 'The Culture of the Mathematics Classroom: An Unknown Quantity', in S. Lerman (ed.), *Cultural Perspectives on the Mathematics Classroom,* Kluwer, Dordrecht, 7-36.

Pickert, G.: 1984, 'Erzeugung Mathematischer Begriffe Durch Beweisanalyse', *Journal für Mathematik Didaktik* 5(3), 167-187.

Pirie, S.: 1988, 'Understanding: Instrumental, Relational, Intuition, Constructed, Formalised ...? How Can We Know?', *For the Learning of Mathematics* 8(3), 2-6.

Polya, G.: 1973, *How to Solve It: A New Aspect of Mathematical Method,* Princeton University Press, Princeton, NJ.

Resnik, M.D.: 1992, 'Proof as a Source of Truth', in M. Detlefsen (ed.), *Proof and Knowledge in Mathematics,* 6-32. Routledge, London, 6-32.

Schoenfeld, A.: 1989, 'Explorations of Students' Mathematical Beliefs and Behaviour', *Journal for Research in Mathematics Education* 20(4), 338-355.

Schoenfeld, A.: 1994, 'What Do We know About Curricula?', *Journal of Mathematical Behavior* 13(1), 55-80.

Senk, S.L.: 1985, 'How Well Do Students Write Geometry Proofs?', *Mathematics Teacher* 78(6), 448-456.

Silver, E.A. (ed.):1985, *Teaching and Learning Mathematical Problem Solving: Multiple Research Perspectives,* Lawrence Erlbaum Associates, Hillsdale, NJ.

Silver, E. A. and Carpenter, T. P.: 1989, 'Mathematical Methods'. In M.M. Lindquist (ed.), *Results from the Fourth Mathematics Assessment.* National Council of Teachers of Mathematics, Reston, VA.

Skemp, R.: 1976, 'Relational Understanding and Instrumental Understanding', *Mathematics Teaching* 77, 20-26.

Steiner, M.: 1978, 'Mathematical Explanation', *Philosophical Studies* 34, 135-151.

Steiner, M.: 1983, 'The Philosophy of Imre Lakatos', *The Journal of Philosophy* LXXX, 9, 502-521.

Thurston, W.P.: 1994, 'On Proof and Progress in Mathematics', *Bulletin of the American Mathematical Society* 30(2), 161-177.

Tymoczko, T.: 1986, 'The Four-colour Problem and Its Philosophical Significance', in T. Tymoczko (ed.), *New Directions in the Philosophy of Mathematics,* Birkhauser, Boston, 243-266.

Vinner, S.: 1991, 'The Role of Definitions in the Teaching and Learning of Mathematics', in D. Tall (ed.), *Advanced Mathematical Thinking,* Kluwer, Dordrecht, 65-79.

Vollrath, H.-J.: 1994, 'Reflections on Mathematical Concepts as Starting Points for Didactical Thinking', in R. Biehler, R.W. Scholtz, R. Strässer and B. Winkelmannn (eds.), *Didactics of Mathematics as a Scientific Discipline,* Kluwer, Dordrecht, 61-72.

von Glasersfeld, E.: 1983, 'Learning as a Constructive Activity', in J.C. Bergeron and N. Herscovics (eds.), *Proceedings of the North American Chapter of the International Group for the Psychology of Mathematics Education,* 1, PME-NA, Montreal, 41-69.

Williams, E.: 1980, 'An Investigation of Senior High School Students' Understanding of the Nature of Mathematical Proof', *Journal for Research in Mathematics Education* 11(3), 165-176.

Wittmann, E.C. and Müller, G.: 1990, 'When is a Proof a Proof? *Bulletin Soc. Math. Belg.* 1, 15-40.

Yackel, E. and Cobb, P.: 1994, 'The Development of Young Children's Understanding of Mathematical Argumentation', Paper presented at the annual meeting of the American Educational Research Association, New Orleans.

Chapter 24: Ethnomathematics and Mathematics Education[1]

PAULUS GERDES

Department of Mathematics, Universidade Pedagógica, Maputo, Mozambique

ABSTRACT

This chapter analyses the emergence of ethnomathematics as a field of research. It starts with the work of some isolated forerunners like Wilder and Raum, and moves to D'Ambrosio's ethnomathematical research program, and the simultaneous gestation of other concepts, like indigenous, socio-, informal, spontaneous, oral, hidden, implicit, and people's mathematics. It compares various conceptualisations and paradigms of ethnomathematics. The influence of Freire's ideas on a series of scholars working in the field of ethnomathematics is stressed. The second part of the chapter presents an overview of ethnomathematical literature, continent by continent. The third and final part discusses some of the basic assumptions associated with the use of ideas from ethnomathematics in education. Some complementary and partially overlapping trends in educational experimentation are considered from an ethnomathematical perspective.

1.   HISTORY OF ETHNOMATHEMATICS: AN OVERVIEW

This chapter analyses the emergence of ethnomathematics as a field of research, and then presents an overview of ethnomathematical literature continent by continent. It concludes with some illustrations of educational experimentation and research within an ethnomathematical perspective.

1.1   Early Advocates of Ethnomathematics

Ethnomathematics, which may be defined as the cultural anthropology of mathematics and mathematical education, is a relatively new field of interest, one that lies at the confluence of mathematics and cultural anthropology. Traditionally, the dominant view saw mathematics as a 'culture-free', 'universal' phenomenon, and ethnomathematics emerged later than other ethnosciences. Among mathematicians, ethnographers, psychologists and educationalists, Wilder, White, Fettweis, Luquet and Raum may be registered as the principal forerunners of ethnomathematics.

A.J. Bishop et al. (eds.), International Handbook of Mathematics Education, 909 - 943

In an address entitled 'The cultural basis of mathematics', delivered in 1950 to an international congress of mathematicians, Raymond L. Wilder stated that it was not new to look at mathematics from a cultural perspective: 'Anthropologists have done so, but as their knowledge of mathematics is generally very limited, their reactions have ordinarily consisted of scattered remarks concerning the types of arithmetic found in primitive cultures' (Wilder, 1950, p.260). However, Wilder (1950) said, there were noteworthy exceptions – like, for example, the arguments put forward in an article entitled 'The Locus of Mathematical Reality: An Anthropological Footnote' written by the anthropologist L. White (1947). Wilder (1950) summarised his ideas in the following way:

> In man's various cultures are found certain elements which are called *mathematical*. In the earlier days of civilization, they varied greatly from one culture to another so much that what was called 'mathematics' in one culture would hardly be recognized as such in certain others. With the increase in diffusion due, first, to exploration and invention, and, secondly, to the increase in the use of suitable symbols and their subsequent standardization and dissemination in journals, the mathematical elements of the most advanced cultures gradually merged until ... there has resulted essentially one element, common to all civilized cultures, known as mathematics. This is not a fixed entity, however, but is subject to constant change. Not all of the change represents accretion of new material; some of it is a shedding of material no longer, due to influential cultural variations, considered mathematics (pp.269-270).

Wilder pointed out that there are some 'borderline' practices and concepts which are difficult to place either in mathematics or outside mathematics. Later Wilder elaborated his ideas in two books, *Evolution of Mathematical Concepts* (1968) and *Mathematics as a Cultural system* (1981).

White started his study by asking the question 'Do mathematical truths reside in the external world, there to be discovered by man, or are they man-made inventions?' (White, 1947/1956, p.2349). In seeking an answer, he asserted that 'mathematics in its entirety, its 'truths' and its 'realities', is part of human *culture*' (p.2351), and concluded with the statement that mathematical truths 'are discovered but they are also man-made'. He went on to assert that although mathematical truths are 'the product of the mind of the human species', they 'are encountered or discovered by each individual in the mathematical culture in which he grows up' (p.2357). For White, mathematics did not originate with Euclid and Pythagoras – or even in ancient Egypt or Mesopotamia – but is 'a development of thought that had its beginning with the origin of man and culture a million years or so ago' (p.2361).

Wilder and White did not seem to be aware of the studies by the German mathematician, ethnologist and pedagogue, Fettweis (1881-1967)[2] on early mathematical thinking and culture, or of the reflections of the French psychologist Luquet on the cultural origin of mathematical notions (Luquet, 1929). Likewise, Raum's (1938) book, *Arithmetic in Africa*, was not known among the mathematicians and anthropologists of his time. It contained the substance of a course given in the Colonial Department of the University of London Institute of Education. The foreword stated that education 'cannot be truly effective unless it is intelligently based on indigenous culture and living interests' (Raum, 1938, p.4). One of the principles of good teaching 'lays down the importance of understanding the cultural background of the pupil and relating the teaching in school to it' (Raum, 1938, p.5).

Other mathematicians, anthropologists and educators were slow to take up these early reflections of Wilder, White, Fettweis, Luquet and Raum. The prevailing idea in the first half of the century was that of mathematics as universal, basically aprioristic form of knowledge. A reductionist tendency tended to dominate mathematics education, with culture-free models of cognition in the ascendency.[3]

1.2   Ubiratan D'Ambrosio: Intellectual Father of the Ethnomathematical Program.

In the 1970's several pervasive factors combined to stimulate reflection not only on the place of mathematics in school curricula but also, more generally, within society. Simultaneously, questions about the role of mathematics education research, and any implications of such research for curriculum development and for teaching and learning, began to be asked. Among these pervasive factors were:

a)   the failures of the hasty transplantations of 'New Mathematics' curricula from the North to the South in the 1960's;

b)   the importance attributed in the newly politically independent states of the Third World to the concept of 'education for all', including mathematics education, in the quest for economic independence; and

c)   public unrest about the involvement of mathematicians and mathematical research in the Vietnam war.

At the end of the 1970's and the beginning of the 1980's, a growing awareness of the societal and cultural aspects of mathematics and mathematical education began to emerge within the ranks of mathematicians.[4] Evidence to support this statement can be found in the summaries of sessions at various international meetings of mathematicians, mathematics educators, and education policy makers in which the societal objectives of mathematical education were earnestly considered – for example, at the 1976 International Congress on Mathematical Education (ICME3, Karlsruhe, Germany), the

1978 Conference on Developing Mathematics in Third World Countries (Khartoum, Sudan) [see El Tom, 1979], the 1978 Workshop on Mathematics and the Real World (Roskilde, Denmark) [see Booss and Niss, 1979], the session on Mathematics and Society at the 1978 International Congress of Mathematicians (Helsinki, Finland), the 1981 Symposium on Mathematics-in-the-Community (Huaraz, Peru), and the 1982 Caribbean Conference on Mathematics for the Benefit of the Peoples (Paramaribo, Surinam).

Ubiratan D'Ambrosio, a Brazilian mathematician and mathematics educator, played a dynamic role in all these initiatives. It was during that period that he launched his 'ethnomathematical program', and, at the Fourth International Congress of Mathematics Education in 1984 (ICME4, held in Adelaide, Australia), he presented in the opening plenary lecture his reflections on the 'Socio-cultural Bases for Mathematics Education' (D'Ambrosio, 1985a).

D'Ambrosio (1990) proposed an ethnomathematical program as a 'methodology to track and analyse the processes of generation, transmission, diffusion and institutionalization of (mathematical) knowledge' in diverse cultural systems (p.78). D'Ambrosio (1985b) contrasted 'academic mathematics', that is to say the mathematics which is taught and learned in the schools, with 'ethnomathematics', which he described as the mathematics 'which is practised among identifiable cultural groups, such as national-tribal societies, labour groups, children of a certain age bracket, professional classes, and so on' (p.45).

According to D'Ambrosio (1985b), the 'mechanism of schooling replaces these practices by other equivalent practices which have acquired the status of mathematics, which have been expropriated in their original forms and returned in a codified version' (p.47). Before and outside school almost all children in the world become 'materate' − that is to say, they develop the 'capacity to use numbers, quantities, the capability of qualifying and quantifying and some patterns of inference' (D'Ambrosio, 1985a, p.43). In school 'the 'learned' materacy eliminates the so-called 'spontaneous' materacy. An individual who manages perfectly well numbers, operations, geometric forms and notions, when facing a completely new and formal approach to the same facts and needs creates a psychological blockage which grows as a barrier between different modes of numerical and geometrical thought' (D'Ambrosio, 1985a, p.45). As a consequence, 'the early stages of mathematics education offer a very efficient way of instilling in the children a sense of failure and dependency' (D'Ambrosio, 1985a, p.45).

D'Ambrosio (1985a) asserted that:

> the mathematical competencies, which are lost in the first years of schooling, are essential at this stage for everyday life and labour opportunities. But they have indeed been lost. The former, let us say spontaneous, abilities have been downgraded, repressed and forgotten while the learned ones have not been assimilated either as a consequence

of a learning blockage, or of an early drop-out, or even as a consequence of failure or many other reasons' (p.46).

The question which arose, then, was what to do about this disempowering effect of schooling: 'Should we ... give up school mathematics and remain with ethnomathematics? Clearly not' (D'Ambrosio, 1985a, p.70). In D'Ambrosio's view (1985a) one should 'compatibilize' cultural forms. By that he meant the mathematics curriculum in schools should incorporate ethnomathematics in such a way that they facilitate the acquisition of knowledge, understanding, and the compatibilization of known and current popular practices. Furthermore, in order to be able to incorporate ethnomathematics into the curriculum it will be necessary to 'identify within ethnomathematics a structured body of knowledge' (D'Ambrosio, 1985b, p.47).

Let us now briefly review other concepts which have been proposed and are related to D'Ambrosio's ethnomathematics.

1.3   Gestation of New Concepts

Colonialist education presented mathematics generally as something rather 'western', 'European', or as an exclusive creation of 'white men'.[5] An important aspect of the hasty curriculum transplantations – during the 1960's – from the highly industrialised nations to 'Third World' countries, was the implicit negation of Aboriginal Australian, African, Asian, American-Indian, Polynesian, and other forms of mathematics.

During the 1970's and 1980's, this negation was increasingly seen to be the culmination of racist and (neo-) colonialist prejudices, and there emerged among teachers and mathematics educators in developing countries, and later also in other countries, a growing resistance to the negation (see, for example, Njock, 1985).[5] The thesis that before and beyond the 'imported school mathematics' there existed other forms of mathematics, was gradually given greater credence, even in industrialised nations.

In this context, various concepts have been proposed to provide a contrast between ethnomathematics and the academic 'school mathematics' which had been transplanted into the school systems of developing nations. A range of terms – some of which will now be presented – were introduced:

  – *indigenous mathematics*, was used by, for example, Gay and Cole (1967) and Lancy (1978). Gay and Cole (1967), in critiquing the education of Kpelle children in 'western-oriented' schools in Liberia in the 1960's, stated that children were 'taught things that have no point or meaning within their culture' (p.7). Gay and Cole proposed a creative mathematical education that used indigenous mathematical concepts and practices as a starting point;

- *socio-mathematics,* was a term employed by Zaslavsky (1973). According to Zaslavsky, socio-mathematics not only referred to the mathematics used every day by African people, but also to the influence that African institutions had upon the evolution of their mathematics[6];
- *informal mathematics,* which, according to Posner (1978, 1982) is the mathematics which is transmitted and is learned outside the formal system of education;
- *mathematics in the (African) socio-cultural environment,* an expression used to describe the integration of the mathematics of African games and craft work with a social-cultural environment that encompasses children and the mathematics curriculum (Doumbia, 1989; Touré, 1984);
- *spontaneous mathematics,* a term used by D'Ambrosio (1982) to express the idea that each human being and each cultural group spontaneously develops certain mathematical methods[7];
- *oral mathematics,* which expresses the idea that within all human societies there exists mathematical knowledge which is transmitted orally from one generation to the next (Carraher, Carraher and Schliemann, 1982; Kane, 1987);
- *oppressed mathematics:* in class societies (like, for example, 'Third World' countries during colonial occupation) there exist mathematical elements in the daily life of the populations which are not recognised as mathematics by the dominant ideology (Gerdes, 1982);
- *non-standard mathematics:* Carraher et al. (1982), Gerdes (1982, 1985a) and Harris (1987) are among those who have used this term to express the idea that beyond the dominant standard forms of 'academic' and 'school' mathematics there has developed – and will continue to develop – in each culture in all parts of the world, unique, qualitatively different, local forms of mathematics;
- *hidden* or *frozen mathematics:* Although, probably, most of the mathematical knowledge of formerly colonised peoples has been lost, one may try to identify, reconstruct, and thereby 'unfreeze' the mathematical thinking which is 'hidden' or 'frozen' in old techniques (like, for example, basket making) (Gerdes, 1982, 1985a, b);
- *folk mathematics* is the mathematics which is embodied in everyday work activities. Although it is often not recognised as mathematics, it may serve as a starting point in the teaching of mathematics (Mellin-Olsen, 1986);
- *people's mathematics,* was an expression coined for a component of the education of people in the context of the struggle against apartheid in South Africa (Julie, 1989);
- mathematics *codified in know-how* (Ferreira, 1991);
- *implicit* and *non-professional mathematics* (Ascher and Ascher, 1981; Zaslavsky, 1994).[8]

914

The concepts associated with these terms were provisional. They arose in the context of indigenous 'Third World' thinking and later found their expressions in other countries.[9]

The various aspects illuminated by the aforementioned provisional concepts have been gradually united under the more general 'common denominator' of D'Ambrosio's ethnomathematics. The process of unification was accelerated by the creation, in 1985, of the *International Study Group on Ethnomathematics* [ISGEm].[10]

2.   ETHNOMATHEMATICS AS A FIELD FOR RESEARCH

In the previous section, the concept of ethnomathematics was linked with the mathematics of certain (sub)cultures. In that sense, so-called 'academic mathematics' is also a concrete example of ethnomathematics. If all ethnomathematics is mathematics, then why call it ethnomathematics? Why not simply refer to the mathematics of this and that (sub)culture?

One answer is to allow the special term 'ethnomathematics' to be defined at another level, as a research field in its own right, a field that reflects an acceptance and a consciousness of the existence of many forms of mathematics, each particular in its own way to a certain (sub)culture.

As a research field, ethnomathematics may be defined as the cultural anthropology of mathematics and mathematical education. Even more generally, the concept of 'ethnoscience' might be developed. D'Ambrosio (1977) described this concept as 'the study of scientific and, by extension, technological phenomena in direct relation to their social, economic and cultural background' (p.74). In this sense, ethnoscience includes 'the study of mathematical ideas of non-literate peoples', which was Ascher and Ascher's (1986) definition of ethnomathematics.

Among ethnographers and anthropologists the concept of 'ethnoscience' has been used since the end of the nineteenth century. Their use of the concept seems to have been more restricted and has carried different ideological connotations from the concept with the same name which is now used by mathematicians and others interested in ethnomathematics.

In Panoff and Perrin's (1973) dictionary of ethnological terms, two definitions of the concept of ethnoscience were presented. According to the first, ethnoscience was a branch of ethnology which dedicated itself 'to the comparison between the positive knowledge of exotic societies and the knowledge that has been formalized in the established disciplines of western science' (p.68). This definition raises immediately some questions, like: 'What is *positive* knowledge?', 'In what sense is a society *exotic?*, 'Does there exist a *western* science?' According to the second definition, ethnoscience could be regarded as 'each application of one of the western scientific disciplines to natural phenomena which are understood in a different way by indigenous thinking' (p.68).

Both definitions belong to a tradition that traces back to colonial times, when ethnography was born in the most 'developed' countries as a 'colonial science', for the purpose of referring to, and systematising studies into the cultures of subjected peoples. It represented a world view of 'science' that saw so-called 'primitive' thinking as somehow absolutely different from 'western' thinking.

Other ethnographers tend to view ethnoscience in a very different way. Favrod (1977), for example, in his introduction to social and cultural anthropology, characterises ethnolinguistics as the attempt 'to study language in its relationship to the whole of cultural and social life' (p.90). If this characterisation of ethnolinguistics is translated to the domain of ethnomathematics, then, by analogy, ethnomathematics may be regarded as an attempt *'to study mathematics (or mathematical ideas) in its (their) relationship to the whole of cultural and social life'*.

According to Crump (1990), the term 'ethnoscience' became popular among ethnographers in the 1960's and 'may be taken to refer to the 'system of knowledge and cognition typical of a given culture' (p.160). In Crump's (1990) book, *The anthropology of number* there were only a few references to the work of 'ethnomathematicians'. He pointed out that 'first, few professional mathematicians have any interest in the cognitive assumptions in their work; second, few anthropologists are numerate in the sense of being able to realize how significant the numbers that occur in the course of their field work might be in the local culture' (Crump, 1990, p.viii). The review of the history of ethnomathematics presented in the last section suggests, however, that in the 1990's anthropologists, historians of science, and mathematicians are becoming more aware of each other's work, and that they realised that by working together they would be better able to develop and synthesise the field of ethnomathematics as an anthropology of mathematics and mathematics education.[11]

There is another interpretation of ethnomathematics to which attention should be drawn. Ferreira and Imenes (1986) characterised ethnomathematics as the 'mathematics incorporated in the culture of a people' (p.4), and defined ethnomathematics as a part of ethnology, in which ethnoscience is a *'method to arrive at the concepts of the institutionalized sciences'*. This idea had also been stressed in the following editorial comment in the first issue of *ISGEm-Newsletter*:

Ethnomathematics: what might it be? ... examples of Ethno-mathematics derived from culturally identifiable groups, and related inferences about patterns of reasoning and models of thought, can lead to curriculum development projects that build on the intuitive understandings and practised methods students bring with them to school. Perhaps the most

916

striking need for such curriculum development may be in Third World countries, yet there is mounting evidence that schools in general do not take advantage of their students' intuitive mathematical and scientific grasp of the world

(ISGEm-Newsletter, 1985, Vol.1, No. 1, p.2).

Such a viewpoint pointed to the need to achieve expressions of the pedagogical implications of D'Ambrosio's ethnomathematical research program in actual education programs: that is to say, there is a need to recognise and incorporate the concepts and principles of contemporary ethnomathematics into mathematics curricula around the world.

2.1   Ethnomathematical Movement

Many scholars who are engaged in ethnomathematical research are highly committed to the basic concepts and importance of the domain which they are researching. In this sense we might speak of an *ethnomathematical movement* (cf., Gerdes, 1989a),[12] and of researchers involved in the movement as *ethnomathematicians*. The ethnomathematical movement may be characterised as follows:

- Ethnomathematicians adopt a broad concept of mathematics, including, in particular, counting, locating, measuring, designing, playing, and explaining (Bishop, 1988a)[13];
- Ethnomathematicians emphasise and analyse the influences of sociocultural factors on the teaching, learning and development of mathematics;
- Ethnomathematicians argue that the techniques and truths of mathematics are a *cultural product;* and stress that all people – every culture and every subculture – develop their own particular forms of mathematics. Mathematics is considered to be a *universal, pan-human activity*. As a cultural product, mathematics has a history. Under certain economic, social, and cultural conditions, it emerges and develops in certain directions; under other conditions, it emerges and develops in other directions. In other words, the development of mathematics is *not unilinear* (cf, Ascher and Ascher, 1986).
- Ethnomathematicians emphasise that the school mathematics of the transplanted, imported 'curriculum' is *apparently* alien to the cultural traditions of Africa, Asia, and South America. Apparently this mathematics comes completely from the outside of the 'Third World'. *In reality*, however, a great part of the contents of this 'school mathematics' is of African and Asian origin. First, it became expropriated in the process of modes of colonisation which destroyed the scientific cultures of the oppressed peoples.[14] Then colonialist

ideologies ignored or despised the surviving themes and concepts of African, Asian and American-Indian mathematics. The mathematical capacities of the peoples of the 'Third World' became negated or reduced to rote memorisation. This tendency was reinforced by curriculum transplantation (especially 'New Math' in the 1960's) from the highly industrialised nations to 'Third World' countries.

— Ethnomathematicians try to contribute to and affirm the knowledge of the mathematical realisations of the formerly colonised peoples. They look for cultural elements which have survived colonialism and which reveal mathematical and other scientific thinking. They try to *reconstruct* the original mathematical modes of thinking, concepts, and principles.

— Ethnomathematicians in 'Third World' countries look for mathematical traditions which survived colonisation, especially for mathematical activities in people's daily. They try to develop ways of incorporating these traditions and activities into the curriculum.

— Ethnomathematicians also look for other *cultural elements and activities* that may serve as a *starting point* for doing and elaborating mathematics in the classroom.

— In the educational context, ethnomathematicians generally favour a socio-critical view and interpretation of mathematics education which enables students to reflect on the realities in which they live, and empowers them to develop and use mathematics in an emancipatory way. The influence of Paulo Freire, the radical 'Third World' pedagogue, is visible.

This characterisation of ethnomathematicians, which was developed by Gerdes (1989a), was accepted by Ferreira (1991, 1993) as the *ethnomathematical paradigm.*

3.   PAULO FREIRE AND ETHNOMATHEMATICS

A series of scholars working in the field of ethnomathematics (see, for example, Frankenstein, 1981, 1983, 1989; Mellin-Olsen, 1986; Borba, 1987a; Ferreira, 1992; Frankenstein and Powell, 1994) have paid tribute to the writings and work of the Brazilian pedagogue Paulo Freire. His ideas, in particular, those enunciated in his books *Pedagogy of the Oppressed* (1970) and *Education for Critical Consciousness* (1973) have had a profound influence on ethnomathematicians. In Mellin-Olsen's (1986) words: 'If knowledge is related to culture by the processes which constitute knowledge – as Freire expresses it – this must have some implication for how we treat knowledge in the didactic processes of (mathematical) education' (p.103). Freire included the paper 'Ethnomathematics: the mathematics of a 'favela' (slum) in a pedagogical

918

proposal' – written by his and D'Ambrosio's student, Borba – in the book *In the School We Make ... An Interdisciplinary Reflection on People's Education* (Freire, Nogueira and Mazza, 1987).

Frankenstein and Powell (1994) have argued that the movement among educators to reconsider what educators value as mathematical knowledge, to recognise the effect of culture on mathematical knowledge, and to uncover the distorted and hidden history of mathematical knowledge, have been the significant contributions of a Freirean, ethnomathematical perspective. This perspective calls for a reconceptualisation of the discipline of mathematics and the pedagogical practices of the mathematics education (Frankenstein and Powell, 1994). The use of Freire's dialogical methodology is seen as essential in developing 'the curricular praxis of ethnomathematics by investigating the ethnomathematics of a culture to construct curricula with people from that culture and by exploring the ethnomathematics of other cultures to create curricula so that people's knowledge of mathematics will be enriched' (Frankenstein and Powell, 1994, p. 32).

4.   AN OVERVIEW OF ETHNOMATHEMATICAL LITERATURES

In the following section, a brief overview of ethnomathematical literature will be presented, continent by continent.

4.1   Americas

In 1981, M. and R. Ascher, mathematician and anthropologist, respectively, published their *Code of the Quipu: A Study in Media, Mathematics and Culture*, which among other things revealed how Peruvian pieces of string served to embody a rich, logical, numerical tradition. In the preface to Closs's (1986) edited collection on *Native American Mathematics* (1986), the editor stated that 'native American mathematics can best be described as a composite of separate developments in many individual cultures' (p.2). The book analysed number systems, numerical representations in rock art, calendrial systems, tallies and ritual use of number and some aspects of geometry. The use of appropriate ethnomathematical research methodologies was a point of concern. Closs remarked that the papers in the edited collection provided some idea on the form which the history of mathematics must take if it is to incorporate material outside of its traditional boundaries'. According to Closs (1986) a form was needed 'in which an almost total reliance on the historical approach is supplemented or replaced by drawing on the resources and methodologies of other disciplines such as anthropology, archaeology and linguistics' (p.2).

Pinxten, van Dooren, and Harvey (1983) studied the 'geometrical' world view of the Navajo and formulated suggestions for mathematics education (see also, Pinxten, 1989; 1994). Moore (1986) analysed the use of string figures for 'Native American mathematics education' (cf., Moore, 1987; 1994), and Marschall (1987) elaborated an 'atlas' of American Indian geometry.

Ferreira (1988, 1989) and his students at Campinas State University in Brazil have analysed mathematics and mathematics teaching among Indian communities in Brazil (for example, Paula and Paula (1986) reported on the use of string figures by Tapirapé Indians).

A series of important studies have been carried out and reported by D'Ambrosio's students. Borba (1987) analysed the mathematics in the daily life of the population of a slum in Campinas; Nobre (1989a, b) studied the mathematics of the popular animal lottery and wrote a masters thesis entitled *Social and Cultural Aspects of Mathematics Curriculum Development* (1989a); Buriasco (1989) completed a masters thesis on *Mathematics Outside and Inside School: From Blockage to Transition;* Knijnik's (1995) doctoral thesis was on the mathematics used by landless peasants in the southern Brazilian state Rio Grande do Sul in their struggle to live (cf, Knijnik, 1993); Leite presented a M.Ed. thesis *Playing is Serious: Studies about Playing, Learning, and Mathematics,* based on extended ethnographic research involving children aged between 5 and 8 years old. She analysed mathematical elements in spontaneous children's play. Bello submitted a dissertation *'Indigenous Mathematical Education – An Ethnomathematical Study of the Guarini-Kaiova Indians in the State of Southern Mato Grosso'* (cf., D'Ambrosio, 1995a).

In Pernambuco (north-eastern Brazil), important research on the borderline between ethnomathematics and cognitive psychology has been done by T. Carraher (Nunes), D. Carraher, and A. Schliemann. Schliemann (1984), for example, analysed the mathematics used by apprentice carpenters; T. Carraher (1988) compared street mathematics and school mathematics; and Carraher, Carraher, and Schliemann (1987) analysed the differences between written and oral mathematics; Saxe (1988) reported on candy selling and math learning. The first edition of the Brazilian journal *A Educação Matemática*, published in 1993, was dedicated to ethnomathematics. It contained contributions from D'Ambrosio, Ferreira, Meira, Knijnik, and Borba.

In Colombia, Albis (1988) analysed some aspects of ritual geometry among Indian populations. Cossio and Jerez (1986) published a study on mathematics in the Quichua (Ecuador) and Spanish language. Cauty and his collaborators analysed possibilities of mathematics education in the context of what they call the ethnoeducation of the indigenous populations of Colombia (cf., Cauty 1995a,b). Gerdes (1989b) conducted a study into the arithmetic and geometrical decoration of Indian baskets from Brazil. In March 1996, the Goeldi Museum (in Belém, Brazil) organised a conference on the teaching of mathematics and science in Amazonian languages.

Among the early workers in the field of ethnomathematics in the United States of America were Ginsburg and his students, Petitto and Posner. In 1978 his students concluded their PhD theses on mathematical knowledge employed in professional groups such as cloth merchants and tailors and by workers in two ethnic groups in Côte d'Ivoire, and did comparative testing. In his paper entitled 'Poor Children, African Mathematics and the Problem of Schooling', Ginsburg argued: 'The moral for American researchers is clear. If poor children do badly on some tests, the likelihood is greater that there is a problem with the test than with the child' (Ginsburg, 1978, p.41). 'Therefore', he continued, 'teaching of basic skills could be more effective if the curricula were oriented to the particular styles of each culture'. 'For African children, the answers seem obvious: to be effective, curricula must be responsive to local culture'. Ginsburg maintained that 'the same is likely to be true for subgroups of the American poor (Ginsburg, 1978, pp.42, 43).

The *Newsletter* of the International Study Group on Ethnomathematics published a series of short articles on ethnomathematical research and education in North America. Orey (1989) presented an analysis of 'Ethnomathematical perspectives on the NCTM *Standards*'; Gilmer (1990) outlined an 'Ethnomathematical approach to curriculum development'; Lumpkin (1990) commented on possibilities for 'A multicultural mathematics curriculum'; Zaslavsky (1989) argued a case for 'Integrating math with the study of cultural traditions', and for 'World cultures in the mathematics class'; Shirley (1991) analysed mathematics in 'kid culture' in 'Video games for math: A case for 'kid culture''. Stigler and Baranes (1988) published a review of research on culture and mathematics learning.

In the context of the influence of the earlier discussion on the influence of Paulo Freire reference was made to the work of Frankenstein and Powell. Their Critical Mathematics Educators Group is involved in activities which are aimed at mathematically empowering 'non-traditional' students (cf., Frankenstein and Powell, 1989). They have recently edited a book, entitled ·*Ethnomathematics: Challenging Eurocentrism in Mathematics Education*, which comprises a collection of 'classical' ethnomathematical papers (Frankenstein and Powell, 1996).

The multiculturalisation of the mathematics curriculum is one way to increase (cultural) self-confidence among non-traditional students (Wilson, 1992). M. Ascher (1991) joined and adapted a series of her earlier papers on mathematical ideas in 'non-western' societies in her book, *Ethnomathematics: A Multicultural View of Mathematical Ideas*. The book contains chapters on numbers, graphs in the sand, logic of kin relations, chance and strategy in games and puzzles, organisation and modelling of space and symmetric strip decorations. Gilmer, Thompson and Zaslavsky (1992) prepared multicultural mathematical activities for children from Kindergarten through Grade 8 (cf., Zaslavsky, 1992). Ratteray's (1992) account of an African-centred approach to developing a multicultural curriculum included a section on mathematics. Several mathematics books emphasising the value of emphasising multicultural aspects of mathematics were published in 1995: *Multicultural Science and Math Connections – Middle School Projects and Activities* (Lumpkin and

Strong, 1995), *African Cultural Materials for Elementary Mathematics* (Lumpkin, 1995), *The Multicultural Math Classroom: Bringing in the World* (Zaslavsky, 1995), *Math Across Cultures* (Bazin and Tamez, 1995). Lumpkin and Powell (1995) also published the booklet *Math: A Rich Heritage,* which was intended to motivate African-Americans to study mathematics.

4.2 Asia, Oceania and Australia

Souviney (1989) described the results of the Indigenous Mathematics Project which was started in 1976 in Papua New Guinea. Earlier, Lancy (1983) had published a book *Cross-cultural Studies in Cognition and Mathematics* in which results of cognitive testing in Papua New Guinea and in the USA were compared (cf., Lancy, 1978). Bishop (1978, 1979) analysed spatial abilities, Clements and Lean (1981) investigated influences on mathematics learning in four different provinces of Papua New Guinea, and Saxe (1981, 1982a, 1982b) conducted a series of studies of body counting and arithmetic among the Oksapmin of Papua New Guinea (see also, Lean, 1986).

Lean's (1992) PhD thesis was on *The Counting Systems of Papua New Guinea and Oceania.* The Papua New Guinea University of Technology, where Lean worked, recently published 24 volumes of his summaries of more than 2000 counting systems (Lean, 1995). Lean's documentation was based on a combination of field notes, recorded interviews, secondary source data, and responses to questionnaires, accumulated over a period of more than 25 years.[15]

Ascher (1995) studied mathematical ideas of modelling and mapping embodied in the stick charts of the Mashallese navigation tradition (Ascher, 1995). Ascher (1988a) and Nissen (1988) analysed mathematical aspects of sand drawings in the New Hebrides.

Crawford (1984, 1989), Graham (1988), Harris (1980, 1984, 1989, 1991, 1992), Jones, Kershaw and Sparrow (1995) and Watson (1987, 1989) addressed mathematics education issues in Australian Aboriginal communities, and Hunting's (1985) book *Learning, Aboriginal World View and Ethnomathematics* specifically applied ethnomathematical principles to educational issues (cf., Hunting, 1987). Peard (1994) investigated, from an ethnomathematical perspective, the effects of social background on the probabilistic concepts of senior secondary mathematics students in Queensland, Australia.

Knight (1982a,b) published two papers on the geometry of Maori art, in the contexts of weaving and rafter patterns, and more recently has argued that Maori people have been culturally alienated from mathematics, and that 'attempts to overcome this must go beyond the superficial introduction of elements of Maori culture into a traditional presentation of mathematics'

(Knight, 1994, p.284). Ascher (1987) studied mathematical aspects of a Maori game.

Barton (1990) wrote a paper entitled 'Using the Trees to see the Wood: An Archaeology of Mathematical Structure in New Zealand'. He is currently preparing a PhD. thesis on the theme 'A Philosophical Justification for Ethnomathematics and Some Implications for Education' (see also his 1992 discussion paper with the same title, and his 1995 paper on cultural issues in New Zealand mathematics education). Together with Fairhall, he edited the book *Mathematics in Maori education* (Barton and Fairhall, 1995).

Gerdes (1989c; 1993-4, 1995) investigated mathematical aspects of Tamil threshold designs, called 'kolam', in India, and Nagarajan is preparing a doctoral thesis on these 'kolam' designs (personal communication, 1994). Mukhopadhyay – who did fieldwork in India – is preparing a paper, entitled *Mathematics and Culture: The Möbius strip*, on mathematics in everyday contexts versus mathematics as a formal school subject.

Zepp (1989) dedicated the last chapter of his book *Language and Mathematics Education* (which was published in Hong Kong) to a theoretical discussion of ethnomathematics. In a series of studies, Turner (1992) analysed primary mathematics education and ethnomathematics in Bhutan in the eastern Himalayas, and Fasheh (1982, 1989) analysed cultural conflicts arising in mathematics education on the West Bank of occupied Palestine.

4.3 Europe

In 1985 Mellin-Olsen and his colleagues at the Bergen Institute of Education organised a seminar on 'Mathematics and Culture' which included participants from the Scandinavian countries, Great Britain, France, Mexico and Mozambique (cf., Bonilla-Rius, 1986). It seems to have been the first European meeting with the specific theme of cultural issues in mathematics education.

M. Harris (1987) argued that ethnomathematical research in Africa has stimulated critical reflection on mathematics education in the English setting, especially in relation to the emancipation of women, the 'working class' and minority groups. Her 'Maths in Work Project', based at the University of London Institute of Education, attempted to 'make a reconciliation between school ideal and work practice by bringing mathematically rich activities of daily life into school as resources to be developed mathematically by teachers' (Harris and Peashooter, 1991, p.278). Textiles and textile activities are seen to be an example of a 'very rich mathematical resource, one that is common and natural to all cultures and both sexes' (Harris, 1988, p.28). According to Harris and Paechter (1991), if pupils of both sexes and all social and cultural backgrounds 'become self confident in their recognition of mathematics as some thing they do and enjoy as part of everyday working life, then there is surely more chance of them developing the positive and confident attitudes that employers say they want' (p.282) (cf., Evans, 1989; Smart and Isaacson, 1989).

Interest in multicultural issues in mathematics education is growing in France. In 1992 a French edition of the *Newsletter* of the International Study Group on Ethnomathematics was launched by the Institute for Research in Mathematics Education. At the 1993 European Summer University on History and Epistemology in Mathematics Education, D'Ambrosio was invited for the plenary lecture (D'Ambrosio, 1995b), and Cauty (1995b), Doumbia (1995), and Soto (1995) presented papers on 'Mathematics and Ethno-education in Colombia', 'Games and Mathematics Education in Côte d'Ivoire', and 'Mathematics Education Among Chilean Peasants', respectively.

Damerow (1992) emphasised the need for German educators to reflect on ethnomathematical issues. Shan and Bailey (1991) and Nelson, Joseph and Williams (1993) argued that if British educators genuinely desire to establish education programs which will work towards the establishment of a more just and equal society in the British context, then there is a need to develop more balanced multicultural emphases in mathematics education programs. Skovsmose (1994) argued that ethnomathematical studies can make an important contribution to the development and realisation of a 'critical mathematics education' agenda. Contreras presented a Ph.D dissertation at the University of Granada, in Spain, on 'Ethnomathematics in the Artisanal Work in Andalusia: Its Integration in a Model for Pre-service Teacher Education and in Innovation of School Mathematics Curricula' (cf., D'Ambrosio, 1995a).

4.4   Africa[16]

The present chair of the African Mathematical Union Commission on Mathematics Education, M. El Tom from Sudan, sees ethnomathematical education research and experimentation as a necessary activity in a context in which most African countries attempt to imitate major curriculum reforms in the West (El Tom, 1995).

As mentioned earlier in this chapter, where reference was made to Raum's (1938) *Arithmetic in Africa,* Gay and Cole's (1967) *The New Mathematics in an Old Culture,* and Zaslavsky's (1973) *Africa Counts,* there is a rich tradition of ethnomathematical investigation in Africa.

Lea (1987; 1989a,b; 1990) and her students at the University of Botswana have collected information from the San hunters in Botswana. Her papers describe counting, measurement, time reckoning, classification, tracking and some mathematical ideas in San technology and craft. Educational suggestions arising from this research can be found in Stott and Lea (1993). Garegae-Garekwe has concluded a study on 'Cultural games and mathematics teaching in Botswana'.

924

Numerous research investigations into spoken and written numeration systems in Africa have being carried out over the past two decades (see, for example: in Nigeria, Ale (1989); in Botswana, Lea (1987, 1989a,b, 1990); in Côte d'Ivoire, Tro (1980) and Zepp (1983); in Senegal (Kane, 1987); in Central Africa (Mubumbila, 1988); and in Mozambique (e.g. Gerdes, 1993)).

Ascher (1990) analysed mathematical-logical aspects of story puzzles from Algeria, Cape Verde Islands, Ethiopia, Liberia, Tanzania and Zambia. Kubik (1990) recorded 'arithmetical puzzles' from the Valuchazi (eastern Angola and northwestern Zambia). Doumbia (1993, 1994) conducted teaching experiments in Côte d'Ivoire in the context of traditional verbal and cowry games (cf., Doumbia and Pil, 1992). Ondo (1990) published a study on two 'calculation games' – the 'Mancala' games – and Owani (Congo) and Songa (Cameroon, Gabon, Equatorial Guinea) (cf., Deledicq and Popova, 1977) have also carried out ethnomathematical investigations. The Faculty of Education at the Ahmadu-Bello-University (Zaria, Nigeria) has been active in carrying out ethnomathematical investigations. Shirley (1988), for example, has studied the mathematics used by unschooled children and adults in daily life, and has considered the possibility of embedding this knowledge in mathematics education programs.

At the regional conference on 'Mathematics, Philosophy, and Education' held in Yamoussoukro, Côte d'Ivoire, in January 1993, Doumbia (Côte d'Ivoire) and Gerdes (Mozambique) jointly conducted a workshop on the didactic uses of traditional African games, drawings and craft work. The Association for Mathematics Education in South Africa (AMESA) included, as part of its first national congress in 1994, a round-table discussion on ethnomathematics and education. In the same year AMESA formed a study group, coordinated by D. Mosimege, on ethnomathematics. Mosimege himself is researching the educational use of string figures and other traditional games from the north of South Africa. Millroy (1992), conducted an ethnographic study into the mathematical ideas which are embedded in everyday woodworking activities of a group of carpenters in Cape Town.

In Mozambique ethnomathematical research started in the late 1970's. As most 'mathematical' traditions which survived colonisation and most 'mathematical' activities in the daily life of the Mozambican people are not explicitly mathematical, in the sense that the mathematics is partially 'hidden', the first aim of this research was to 'uncover' the 'hidden' mathematics. The first results of this 'uncovering' are included in the book *On the Awakening of Geometrical Thinking* (Gerdes, 1985b,c). The main thesis was slightly extended in *Ethnogeometry: Cultural-anthropological Contributions to the Genesis and Didactics of Geometry* (Gerdes, 1991a). In the book *African Pythagoras: A Study in Culture and Mathematics Education,* Gerdes (1992a, 1994b; cf., 1988b) showed how diverse African ornaments and artefacts can be used to create a rich context for the discovery and the demonstration of the so-called Pythagorean Theorem and of related ideas and propositions. Gerdes included a series of earlier papers (e.g. Gerdes, 1988a in the books *Ethnomathematics: Culture, Mathematics, Education* (Gerdes, 1991b) and *Ethnomathematics and Education in Africa* (1995a). In *SONA Geometry: Reflections on the Tradition of Sand Drawings in Africa South of the Equator*, Gerdes (1993-4, 1994c, 1995c, 1996) reconstructed mathematical components of the Tchokwe drawing-tradition (Angola)[17] and explored their educational, artistic and scientific potential (cf., Gerdes, 1988c). In his book *Lusona: Geometrical Recreations of Africa*, Gerdes (1991c) included recreational activities inspired by the geometry of the sand drawing tradition. The booklet *Living Mathematics: Drawings of Africa* (Gerdes, 1990), was directed at the interests of children aged between 10 and 15 years.

In recent years students and colleagues of Gerdes have also participated in ethnomathematical research. Papers produced include 'The Origin of the Concepts of 'Even' and 'Odd' in Macua Culture (Northern Mozambique)' (Ismael, 1994), 'Popular Counting Practices in Mozambique' (Ismael and Soares, 1993; Soares and Ismael, 1994), 'A Children's 'Circle' of Interest in Ethnomathematics' (Cherinda, 1994a b), and 'Mental Addition and Subtraction in Mozambique' (Draisma, 1994). Two edited collections – *Numeration in Mozambique: Contribution to a Reflection on Culture, Language and Mathematical Education* (Gerdes, 1993) and *Explorations in Ethnomathematics and Ethnoscience in Mozambique* (Gerdes, 1994d) – included papers by Cherinda, Ismael, Soares, Mapapá, Uaila and Draisma. Gerdes and Bulafo (1994) published a book on the geometrical knowledge of the mostly female weavers of the *sipatsi* hand bags. This investigation of the mathematical knowledge of a particular group of women was part of a larger series of studies into women and geometry in Southern Africa, the main reports of which (Gerdes 1995b, 1996) contain suggestions for further research.

5.   EDUCATIONAL EXPERIMENTATION: BASIC ASSUMPTIONS AND POSSIBLE
      TRENDS

It seems that thus far most ethnomathematical research has been directed towards identifying and studying various cultural 'forms' of mathematics which differ from dominant, standard 'academic' and 'school' Mathematics. Bishop (1994) distinguished between the following three major approaches used in ethnomathematical research:

  – *Investigating mathematical knowledge in traditional cultures*. This research has been informed by *anthropological* approach which emphasised the uniqueness of particular knowledge and practices. Towards this end, language factors have been deemed to be especially worthy of study in these studies, as have the values and customs of the groups concerned.

— *Investigating mathematical knowledge in non-Western societies.* This approach has had more of an *historical* flavour, with a major emphasis being on the analysis of key historical documents rather than on present practice.

— *Investigating the mathematical knowledge of different groups within the same society.* The emphasis in this type of research has been *socio-psychological*, with the focus being on elaborating how the particular mathematical knowledge associated with the actual practices of groups being investigated has been socially constructed.

Whatever the principal focus and methodology used, the research findings stimulate the reflection on the history of mathematics and science in general. As D'Ambrosio (1995a) stated: 'We can hardly fit knowledge recognized in a variety of cultural environments into the current academic classification of knowledge which comes from the civilisations around the Mediterranean. With the increasing attention to – and respectful attitude towards – different cultures, broader epistemologies are needed (p.4). This need has found expression in the organisation of international symposia such as 'Ethnomathematics, Ethnoscience, and the Recovery of World History of Science' and 'Ethnoscience and Ethnomathematics: The History of the Evolution of Modes of Thought in the Last Five Hundred Years', which were the respective themes at the 19th International Congress of History of Science (held in Zaragoza in 1993) and the 20th Congress (to be held in Liège in 1997) (cf., D'Ambrosio and Gerdes, 1994). At the 1996 Oberwolfach History of Mathematics Meeting on the theme 'Significant Changes in our Picture of Mathematics' Past', special attention was paid to ethnomathematical research.[18]

Ethnomathematical-educational research, including the study of possible educational implications of ethnomathematical research, is still in its infancy. Bishop (1994) has argued that in order to experiment, a basic and radical *assumption* needs to be recognised: specifically, 'all formal mathematics education is a process of cultural interaction, and that every child (and teacher) experiences some degree of cultural conflict in that process' (p.16). Established theoretical constructs of mathematics education are not based on this assumption. For example, it has never been made clear what teachers and students should do in mathematics educational task situations where there is obviously cultural dissonance between out-of-school and in-school cultural norms.

Ethnomathematical research findings suggest that mathematics educators need to reflect on, and take actions with respect to certain fundamental mathematics educational questions: Why teach mathematics? What and whose mathematics should be taught, by whom and for whom?, Who participates in curriculum development?, etc. Abreu (1993) suggested that one of the most pressing problems arising from her ethnomathematical studies among sugar cane families in rural Brazil was: 'How should school practices be organised in order to minimize the effects of the disruptive relationship between home and school mathematics?' (cf., Bishop, 1995b).

In the following discussion, examples of complementary and partially overlapping trends arising from the application of the findings of ethnomathematical research in education settings will be briefly presented.

A   *Incorporation into the curriculum of elements belonging to the socio-cultural environment of the pupils and teachers, as a starting point for mathematical activities in the classroom, is likely to increase the motivation of both pupils and teachers.*

Example: Cowry games in Côte d'Ivoire

In 1980 a seminar on the theme 'Mathematics in the African Socio-cultural Environment' took place at the Mathematical Research Institute of Abidjan (IRMA) in Côte d'Ivoire. The seminar was directed by Doumbia, and one of the interesting themes analysed by her and her colleagues was the mathematics of traditional West-African games. Their work deals with the classification of the games, with the solutions of mathematical problems inherent in the games, and with the exploration of the possibilities of using games such as *Nigbé Alladian* in the mathematics classroom.

One plays *Nigbé Alladian* with four cowry shells. There are two players, and each takes turns in casting the cowry shells. When all four land in the same position, that is to say all are 'up' or all are 'down', or when two land in the 'up' position and the other two in the 'down' position, the player gets points. In the other cases – one 'up' and three 'down', or, three 'up' and one 'down' – a player does not get points. The IRMA researchers calculated experimentally the chance that a cowry shell fell in the 'up' position is 2/5, and were therefore able to demonstrate that the rules of the game had been chosen in such a way that the probability of winning points was (almost) the same as that of getting no points. Doumbia (1989) concluded that 'without any knowledge of calculation of probability, the players had managed to adopt a clever counting system, in order to balance their chances (p.175). This and other games are embedded into the secondary school curriculum as an introduction to probability theory and computer simulation. Interesting examples are given by Doumbia and Pil (1992) and by Doumbia (1993).

B   *Alerting future mathematics teachers and teacher educators to the existence of mathematical ideas – understood by people with little or no formal education – which are similar to, or different from, those in standard textbooks; learning to respect and to learn from other human beings in other social/cultural (sub)groups.*

Example: Market women in Mozambique

Lecturers and students of the master's degree program in mathematics education for primary schools at the Beira Branch of Mozambique's Universidade Pedagógica have analysed arithmetic used inside and outside of school. On interviewing illiterate women to determine how they find sums and differences, it was found that the women solved easily nearly all the problems, using essentially methods of oral/mental computation, that is to say, computation based on the spoken numerals. The methods used were often similar to those suggested in current primary school mathematics syllabuses, but there were some interestingly different approaches (Draisma, 1992). For instance, 59 per cent of the interviewed women calculated mentally 62 - 5 = ... by first subtracting 2 and then 3. That is to say, they used the same method which was emphasised in the school textbooks. Another 29 per cent of the women subtracted first 5 from 60 and then added 2, and 12 per cent subtracted first 10 from 62, and added the difference between 10 and 5 (i.e., 5).

Did these women *(re)invent* their method? Did they *learn* them? From whom and how?

When multiplying, most of the interviewed women solved the problems by doubling. An example illustrates the process 6 x 13 = ... Schematically the most common approach was as follows: 2 x 13 = 26; 4 x 13 = 2 x 26; 2 x 26 = 52; 6 x 13 = 26 + 52; 26 + 52 = 78 (Draisma, oral communication, 1992). Does each of these women (re)invent the doubling method spontaneously? Or does there exist a tradition? If so, how was the method taught and learnt?

C   *Preparation of future mathematics teachers who will investigate mathematical ideas and practices of their own cultural, ethnic, linguistic communities and who will look for ways to incorporate their findings into their own teaching.*

Example: Peasants in Nigeria

Shirley (1988) and his students at the Ahmadu Bello University in Nigeria conducted oral interviews with unschooled, illiterate members of the students' home communities. They found that although some of the (arithmetical) algorithms used by the informants were similar to those taught in schools, other interesting non-standard techniques were also used. Shirley advised teachers to work with their students in finding the (ethno)algorithms used in their communities – by the literate or illiterate, rural or urban inhabitants. 'Too often', Shirley (1988) stated, 'school lessons leave the impression that there is only one way to do a given task' (p.9).

D   *Incorporation into the curriculum of material, from several cultures,*
    thereby valuating the cultural backgrounds of all pupils and enhancing
    the self-confidence of all and calling for respect for all human beings
    and cultures. This 'helps all children in the future to negotiate more
    effectively in a multicultural environment' (Nelson, Joseph and
    Williams, 1993, p.6), and at the same time broadens their
    understanding of what mathematics is all about and its relationship to
    human needs and activities.

Examples of such a multicultural perspective, by which the world is brought
into the classroom, can be found in the writings of — for example — Ascher,
Joseph, Lumpkin, Nelson, Shan and Bailey, and Zaslavsky.

E   *Incorporation into teacher education programs of mathematical ideas*
    of various cultural/linguistic groups of a country or region, and/or
    developed by various social groups such as basket weavers, potters,
    and house builders, in order to contribute to mutual understanding,
    respect and valuing of (sub)cultures and activities.

Examples are provided in the work of Bulafo, Uaila, and Cherinda (basket
weaving techniques); Saide (Yao pottery); Soares (traditional house building); and Mapapá and Ismael (games in Mozambique) and Mosimege (games
in South Africa).

F   *Use of ideas embedded in the activities of certain cultural or social*
    (marginalised) groups within a society to develop a mathematical
    curriculum for and with/by this group.

Examples are provided in the work of Knijnik (with landless peasants in
southern Brazil); of Borba (with the community of a *favela* in Brazil); of Cauty (with Sierran Indians in Colombia); of Hernanéz (with the Mixes of Mexico (cf., D'Ambrosio and Gerdes, 1994); of Harris and Paechter (with women
in Great Britain); and of Ale (with the nomadic Fulani in Nigeria, where 'the
mathematics curriculum that will be acceptable [to the Fulani] must be centred on their vocation which is cattle-rearing' (Ale, 1989, pp. 35-36).

G   *Introduction in textbooks of cultural elements that facilitate learning*
    by being recognised and appreciated by (most of) the pupils as
    belonging to their culture.

An important example is provided in the experimental school textbook series
for African countries which use French as the language of instruction. The series is coordinated by Touré of Côte d'Ivoire. For instance, the popular Awalé

game is used in the study of symmetry, and of multiples and divisors (cf., Touré, 1993, 1994).

H   *Elaboration of materials on the mathematical heritage of the forefathers/mothers of the pupils, and the introduction of these in teacher education programs and/or in school curricula.*

Examples are provided in the work of Morales (1994) in Guatemala with Mayan mathematics, and in the writings of Gilmer, Lumpkin, Powell, Ratteray, Strong, Thompson, and Zaslavsky.

I   *Elaboration of materials that explore possibilities for mathematical activities starting with artistically appealing designs belonging to the culture (possibly in a broad sense) of the students or of their forefathers/mothers.*

Examples are to be found in the work of Stott and Lea (Botswana); and Gerdes (1992b, 1994c) and Doumbia on the Pythagorean Theorem. Langdon (1989) explored the symmetries of 'adinkra' cloths (in Ghana) for the purpose of using them in the classroom. From a similar perspective, M. Harris (1988) described and explored not only the printing designs on plain woven cloths from Ghana, but also symmetries on baskets from Botswana and 'buba' blouses from the Yoruba (Nigeria).

ENDNOTES

1. An earlier version of a paper was presented at the Annual Meeting of the American Association for the Advancement of Science (AAAS, Boston, 11-16 February 1993).
2. For a list of his publications, see Reich, Folkerts and Scriba (1989).
3. Cf., D'Ambrosio's (1987, p.80) analysis.
4. Cf., the bibliographic guide by Wilson (1981).
5. See, for example, studies by Anderson (1990) and Joseph (1987, 1989, 1991).
6. D'Ambrosio (1976) used the same term in the context of Brazil.
7. Students and colleagues of D'Ambrosio, including Carraher, Schliemann, Ferreira and Borba, published many interesting examples of 'spontaneous' mathematics.
8. At the end of their book 'Code of the Quipu', Ascher and Ascher (1981) present the following comments on the development of mathematics and of mathematical activities: 'Mathematics arises out of, and is directly concerned with, the domain of thought involving the concepts of

number, spatial configuration, and logic. In Western culture a professional class, called mathematicians, ..., deals solely and exclusively with these concepts. Examples of other groups involved in mathematical endeavours are accountants, architects, bookies, construction engineers, landscape designers, navigators, and system analysts. Non-professional mathematics, as practised by these groups ... may often be implicit rather than explicit. When these mathematical endeavours are implicit, they are nonetheless, mathematics. Because of the provincial view of the professional mathematicians, most definitions of mathematics exclude or minimize the implicit and informal. It is, however, in the nature of any professional class to seek to maintain its exclusivity and to do this, in part, by recreating the past in terms of unilinear progress towards its own present' (pp.158-159).

9.   In the context of his historical research on Ancient Mesopotamia, Høyrup (1994) introduced the concept of 'subscientific mathematics'.

10.   The ISGEm *Newsletter* may be obtained from the editor P. Scott, College of Education, University of New Mexico.

11.   D'Ambrosio sometimes uses the expression 'anthropological mathematics' (see, for example, D'Ambrosio, 1985b; cf., Gerdes, 1985c).

12.   A special 1994 issue of the journal *For the Learning of Mathematics* was dedicated to ethnomathematics. U. D'Ambrosio and M. Ascher were guest editors for this issue, which included contributions from C. Zaslavsky, C. Moore, A. Bishop, P. Gerdes, R. Pinxten, V. Katz, R. Bassanezi, M. Ascher and U. D'Ambrosio.

13.   See the chapter 'Environmental activities and mathematical culture' in Bishop (1988a). See also Bishop's forthcoming book *Mathematical Acculturation – Cultural Conflicts in Mathematics Education,* where it is assumed that all mathematics education is in a process of cultural interaction, and that every child experiences some degree of cultural conflict in the process (cf., Bishop, 1994).

14.   Bishop (1990, 1995a), for example, has argued that it is ironic that although many different non-western cultures and groups – the Egyptians, the Chinese, the Indians, the Moslems, and the Greeks – contributed when Western cultural imperialism imposed its version of Mathematics on colonised societies, it was rarely recognised or acknowledged as anything to which these societies might have contributed.
anything to which these societies might have contributed.

15.   Glen Lean died in 1995, only weeks after finalising his 24-volume documentation of the counting systems of Papua New Guinea and Oceania.

16.   For a bibliography on ethnomathematics and the history of mathematics in Africa south of the Sahara, see Gerdes (1994b).

17.   See also Ascher (1988b) and chapter 2 of Ascher (1991).

18. The Conference was held from November 4-8, 1996, at Oberwolfach (Germany). P. Gerdes and M. Ascher were invited speakers on the implications of ethnomathematical research.

REFERENCES

Abreu, G. and Carraher, D.: 1989, 'The Mathematics of Brazilian Sugar Cane Growers', in C. Keitel, P. Damerow, A. Bishop and P. Gerdes (eds.), *Mathematics, Education, and Society*, UNESCO, Paris, 68-70.
Abreu, G.: 1993, *The Relationship Between Home and School Mathematics in a Farming Community in Rural Brazil*, PhD thesis, University of Cambridge, Cambridge, UK.
Albis, V.: 1988, *La Division Ritual de la Circunferencia: Una Hipótesis Fascinante*, Bogotá (mimeo).
Ale, S.: 1989, 'Mathematics in Rural Societies', in C. Keitel, P. Damerow, A. Bishop and P. Gerdes (eds.), *Mathematics, Education, and Society*, UNESCO, Paris, 35-38.
Anderson, S.: 1990, 'Worldmath Curriculum: Fighting Eurocentrism in Mathematics', *Journal of Negro Education* 59(3), 348-359.
Ascher, M.: 1984, 'Mathematical Ideas in Non-western Cultures', *Historia Mathematica* 11, 76-80.
Ascher, M.: 1987, 'Mu Torere: An Analysis of a Maori Game', *Mathematics Magazine* 60(2), 90-100.
Ascher, M.: 1988a, 'Graphs in Culture: A Study in Ethnomathematics I', *Historia Mathematica* 15, 201-227.
Ascher, M.: 1988b, 'Graphs in Cultures (II): A Study in Ethno-mathematics', *Archive for History of Exact Sciences* 39(1), 75-95.
Ascher, M.: 1990, 'A River-Crossing Problem in Cross-cultural Perspective', *Mathematics Magazine* 63(1), 26-29.
Ascher, M.: 1991, *Ethnomathematics: A Multicultural View of Mathematical Ideas*, Brooks, Pacific Grove, Ca.

Ascher, M.: 1995, 'Models and Maps from the Marshall Islands: A Case in Ethnomathematics', *Historia Mathematica* 22, 347-370.

Ascher, M. and Ascher, R.: 1981, *Code of the Quipu: A Study in Media, Mathematics and Culture*, University of Michigan Press, Ann Arbor.

Ascher, M.: 1986, 'Ethnomathematics', *History of Science* 24, 125-144.

Ascher, M.: 1994, 'Ethnomathematics', in I. Grattan-Guinness (ed.), *Companion Encyclopedia of the History and Philosophy of the Mathematical Sciences*, Routledge, London, 1545-1554.

Ascher, M. and D'Ambrosio, U.: 1994, 'Ethnomathematics: A Dialogue', *For the Learning of Mathematics* 14(2), 36-43.

Barton, B.: 1990, *Using the Trees to See the Wood: An Archaeology of Mathematical Structure in New Zealand,* Auckland (mimeo).

Barton, B.:1992, *A Philosophical Justification for Ethnomathematics and Some Implications for Education,* Auckland (mimeo).

Barton, B.: 1995, 'Cultural Issues in NZ Mathematics Education', in J. Neyland (ed.), *Mathematics Education: A Handbook for Teachers* (Vol. 2), Wellington College of Education, Wellington, NZ, 150-164.

Barton, B. and Fairhall, U. (eds.): 1995, *Mathematics in Maori Education*, University of Auckland, New Zealand.

Bazin, M. and Tamez, M.: 1995, *Math Across Cultures*, Exploratorium Teacher Activity Series, San Francisco.

Bishop, A.: 1978, *Spatial Abilities in a Papua New Guinea Context*, Papua New Guinea University of Technology, Lae (mimeo).

Bishop, A.: 1979, 'Visualising and Mathematics in a Pre-technological Culture', *Educational Studies in Mathematics* 10, 135-146.

Bishop, A.: 1988a, *Mathematical Enculturation: A Cultural Perspective on Mathematics Education*, Kluwer, Dordrecht.

Bishop, A. (ed.): 1988b, *Culture and Mathematics Education*, Kluwer, Dordrecht.

Bishop, A.: 1990, 'Western Mathematics: The Secret Weapon of Cultural Imperialism', *Race & Class* 32(2), 51-65.

Bishop, A.: 1994, 'Cultural Conflicts in Mathematics Education: Developing a Research Agenda', *For the Learning of Mathematics* 14(2), 15-18.

Bishop, A.: 1995a, 'Western Mathematics: The Secret Weapon of Cultural Imperialism', in B. Ashcroft, G. Griffiths and H. Tiffin (eds.), *The Post-colonial Studies Reader*, Routledge, London, 71-76.

Bishop, A.: 1995b, *Constructing a Mathematical Education Between Ethno-mathematics and Technology*, paper presented at the IVth Pan-African Congress of Mathematicians, Ifrane, Morocco, September 1995.

Bonilla-Rius, E.: 1986, 'Seminar on Mathematics and Culture. A Viewpoint of the Meeting', *Zentralblatt für Didaktik der Mathematik* 2, 72-76.

Booss, B. and Niss, M.: 1979, *Mathematics and the Real World*, Birkhäuser, Basel,

Borba, M.: 1987a, *Um Estudo em Etnomatemática: Sua Incorporação na Elaboração de Uma Proposta Pedagógica Para o Núcleo-Escola da Favela de Vila Nogueira e São Quirino* (M.Ed. thesis) São Paulo State University, Rio Claro.

Borba, M.: 1987b, 'Etnomatemática: A Matemática da Favela em Uma Proposta Pedagógica', in P. Fréire, A. Nogueira and D. Mazza (eds.), *Na Escola que Fazemos ... Uma Reflexão Interdisciplinar em Educação Popular*, Editora Vozes, Petrópolis, 71-77.

Buriasco, R.: 1989, *A Matemática de Fora e de Dentro da Escola: do Bloqueio à Transição,* (M.Ed thesis) UNESP, Rio Claro.

Carraher, T.: 1988, 'Street Mathematics and School Mathematics', *Proceedings of the 12th International Conference on the Psychology of Mathematics Education*, Veszprem, 1-23.

Carraher, T., Carraher, D. and Schliemann, A.: 1982, 'Na Vida, Dez; Na Escola, Zero: Os Contextos Culturais da Aprendizagem de Matemática', *Cadernos de Pesquisa* 42, 79-86.

Carraher, T., Carraher, D. and Schliemann, A.: 1987, 'Written and Oral Mathematics', *Journal of Research in Mathematics Education* 8, 83-97.

Cauty, A.: 1995a, 'What Sort of Mathematics for Amerindians?', *Proceedings of the ORSTOM-UNESCO Conference '20th Century Science Beyond the Metropolis'*, ORSTOM-UNESCO, Paris.

Cauty, A.: 1995b 'Regards Echangés Avec les Naturels de Colombie – Conditions de l'Ethnoéducation en Langues Vernaculaires', in *First European Summer University Proceedings: History and Epistemology in Mathematics Education*, IREM, Montpellier, 535-548.

Cherinda, M.: 1994a, 'Mathematical-educational Exploration of Traditional Basket Weaving Techniques in Children's 'Circle of Interest'', in P. Gerdes (ed.), *Explorations in Ethnomathematics and Ethnoscience in Mozambique*, ISP, Maputo, 16-23.

Cherinda, M.: 1994b, 'Children's Mathematical Activities Stimulated by an Analysis of African Cultural Elements', in C. Julie, Z. Davis and D. Angelis (eds.), *Proceedings of the 2nd International Conference on the Political Dimensions of Mathematics Education: Curriculum Reconstruction for Society in Transition*, Maskew Miller Longman, Cape Town, 142-148.

Clements, M. and Lean, G.: 1981, *Influences on Mathematical Learning in Papua New Guinea – Some Cross-cultural Perspectives*, Working Paper 17, Indigenous Mathematics Project, Port Moresby.

Closs, M. (ed.): 1986, *Native American Mathematics*, University of Texas, Austin.

Cossio, C. and Jerez, A.: 1986, *Elementos de Analisis en Matematicas Quichua y Castellano*, Pontifica Universidad Catolica, Quito.

Crawford, K.: 1984, 'Bicultural Teacher Training in Mathematics Education for Aboriginal Trainees from Traditional Communities', in P. Damerow, M. Dunkley, B. Nebres and B. Werry (eds.), *Mathematics For All*, UNESCO, Paris, 101-107.

Crawford, K.: 1989, 'Knowing What Versus Knowing How: The Need for a Change in Emphasis for Minority Group Education in Mathematics', in C. Keitel, P. Damerow, A. Bishop and P. Gerdes (eds.), *Mathematics, Education, and Society*, UNESCO, Paris, 22-24.

Crump, T.: 1990, *The Anthropology of Number*, Cambridge University Press, Cambridge.

D'Ambrosio, U.: 1976, 'Matemática e Sociedade', *Ciência e Cultura* 28, 1418-1422.

D'Ambrosio, U.: 1982, *Mathematics for Rich and for Poor Countries*, CARIMATH, Paramaribo (mimeo).

D'Ambrosio, U.: 1985a, *Socio-cultural Bases for Mathematics Education*, UNICAMP, Campinas.

D'Ambrosio, U.: 1985b, 'Ethnomathematics and its Place in the History and Pedagogy of Mathematics', *For the Learning of Mathematics* 5(1), 44-48.

D'Ambrosio, U.: 1987, *Etnomatemática: Raízes Socio-culturais da Arte ou Técnica de Explicar e Conhecer*, UNICAMP, Campinas.

D'Ambrosio, U.: 1990, *Etnomatemática: Arte ou Técnica de Explicar e Conhecer*, Editora Ática, São Paulo.

D'Ambrosio, U.: 1995a, 'Recent Theses & Dissertations on Ethnomathematics', *ISGEm Newsletter* 11(1), 3-4.

D'Ambrosio, U.: 1995b, 'Ethnomathematics, History of Mathematics and the Basin Metaphor', in *First European Summer University Proceedings: History and Epistemology in Mathematics Education*, IREM, Montpellier, 571-580.

D'Ambrosio, U. and Gerdes, P.: 1994, 'Ethnomathematics, Ethnoscience, and the Recovery of World History of Science – Zaragoza Symposium Report', *Physis, Rivista Internazionale di Storia della Scienza* XXXI(2), 570-573.

Deledicq, A. and Popova, A.: 1977, *'Wari et Solo': Le Jeu de Calculs Africain*, Cedic, Paris.

Doumbia, S.: 1989, 'Mathematics in Traditional African Games', in C. Keitel, P. Damerow, A. Bishop and P. Gerdes (eds.), *Mathematics, Education, and Society*, UNESCO, Paris, 174-175.

Doumbia, S.: 1992, *Les Jeux Verbaux au Côte d'Ivoire*, paper presented at ICME7, Université Laval, Québec (August).

Doumbia, S.: 1993, 'Jeux Verbaux et Enseignement Traditionnel en Afrique: Les Jeux de Cauris', *Actes du Séminaire Interdisciplinaire Mathématiques-Philosophie et Enseignement*, Ministère de l'Éducation Nationale, Yamoussoukro, 92-101.

Doumbia, S.: 1994, 'Les Mathématiques dans l'Environnement Socioculturel Africain, et l'Exposition 'Jeux Africains, Mathématiques et Société', *Plot* 69, 1-31.

Doumbia, S.: 1995, 'L'Expérience en Côte d'Ivoire de l'Etude des Jeux Traditionnels Africain et de Leur Mathématisation', in *First European Summer University Proceedings: History and Epistemology in Mathematics Education*, IREM, Montpellier, 549-556.

Doumbia, S. and Pil, J.: 1992, *Les Jeux de Cauris*, IRMA, Abidjan.

Draisma, J.: 1992, 'Arithmetic and its Didactics', in *Report of the First Year of the Master's Degree Program in Mathematics Education for Primary Schools (August 1991- July 1992)*, Instituto Superior Pedagógica, Beira, 1992, 89-129 (mimeo).

Draisma, J.: 1993, 'Numeração Falada Como Recurso na Aprendizagem da Aritmética', in P. Gerdes (ed.), *A Numeração em Moçambique*, ISP, Maputo, 134-150.

Draisma, J.: 1994, 'How to Handle the Theorem $8 + 5 = 13$ in (Teacher) Education?', in P. Gerdes (ed.), *Explorations in Ethnomathematics and Ethnoscience in Mozambique*, ISP, Maputo, 30-48; reproduced in C. Julie, Z. Davis and D. Angelis (eds.), *Proceedings of the 2nd International Conference on the Political Dimensions of Mathematics Education. Curriculum Reconstruction for Society in Transition*, Maskew Miller Longman, Cape Town, 196-207.

El Tom, M. (ed.): 1979, *Developing Mathematics in Third World countries*, North-Holland, Amsterdam.

El Tom, M.: 1995, *The State and Future of Mathematics Education and Mathematical Research in Africa*, paper presented at the Third World Academy of Sciences.

Evans, J.: 1989, 'Mathematics for Adults: Community Research and the "Barefoot" Statistician', in C. Keitel, P. Damerow, A. Bishop and P. Gerdes (eds.), *Mathematics, Education, and Society*, UNESCO, Paris, 65-68.

Fasheh, M.: 1982, 'Mathematics, Culture and Authority', *For the Learning of Mathematics* 3(2), 2-8.

Fasheh, M.: 1989, 'Mathematics in a Social Context: Math Within Education as Praxis Versus Within Education as Hegemony', in C. Keitel, P. Damerow, A. Bishop and P. Gerdes (eds.), *Mathematics, Education, and Society*, UNESCO, Paris, 84-86.

Favrod, C.: 1977, *A Antropologia*, Publicações Dom Quixote, Lisbon.

Ferreira, E.S.: 1988, *The Teaching of Mathematics in Brazilian Nature Communities*, UNICAMP, Campinas (mimeo).

Ferreira, E.S.: 1991, 'Por Uma Teoria da Etnomatemática', *BOLEMA* 7, 30-35.

Ferreira, E.S.: 1992, *A Matemática no Pensamento de Paulo Freire*, UNICAMP, Campinas, 8 pages (mimeo).

Ferreira, E.S.: 1993, 'Cidadania e Educação Matemática', *A Educação Matemática em Revista* 1(1), 12-18.

Frankenstein, M.: 1981, 'A Different Third R: Radical Maths', *Radical Teacher* 20, 14-18.

Frankenstein, M.: 1983, 'Critical Mathematics Education: An Application of Paulo Freire's Epistemology', *Journal of Education* 165, 315-339.

Frankenstein, M.: 1989, *Relearning Mathematics: A Different Third R – Radical Maths*, Free Association Books, London.

Frankenstein, M. and Powell, A.: 1989, 'Mathematics Education and Society: Empowering Non-traditional Students', in C. Keitel, P. Damerow, A. Bishop and P. Gerdes (eds.), *Mathematics, Education, and Society*, UNESCO, Paris, 157-159.

Frankenstein, M. and Powell, A.: 1994, 'Towards Liberatory Mathematics: Paolo Freire's Epistemology and Ethnomathematics', in P. McLaren and C. Lankshear (eds.) *The Politics of Liberation: Paths from Freire*, Routledge, London, 74-99 (preprint 1991).

Frankenstein, M. and Powell, A. (eds.): 1996, *Ethnomathematics: Challenging Eurocentrism in Mathematics Education*, SUNY, New York.

Freire, P., Nogueira, A. and Mazza, D. (eds.): 1987, *Na Escola que Fazemos ... Uma Reflexão Interdisciplinar em Educação Popular*, Editora Vozes, Petrópolis.

Gay, J. and Cole, M.: 1967, *The New Mathematics in an Old Culture: A Study of Learning Among the Kpelle of Liberia*, Holt, Rinehart & Winston, New York.

Gerdes, P.: 1982, *Mathematics for the Benefit of the People*, CARIMATH, Paramaribo (mimeo).

Gerdes, P.: 1985a, 'Conditions and Strategies for Emancipatory Mathematics Education in Underdeveloped Countries', *For the Learning of Mathematics* 5(3), 15-20.

Gerdes, P.: 1985b, *Zum Erwachenden Geometrischen Denken*, Eduardo Mondlane University, Maputo (mimeo).

Gerdes, P.: 1985c, 'How to Recognize Hidden Geometrical Thinking? A Contribution to the Development of Anthropological Mathematics', *For the Learning of Mathematics* 6(2), 10-12, 17.

Gerdes, P.: 1986, 'On Culture, Mathematics and Curriculum Development in Mozambique', in S. Mellin-Olsen and M.J. Hoines (eds.), *Mathematics and Culture, a Seminar Report*, Caspar Forlag, Radel, 15-42.

Gerdes, P.: 1988a, 'On Culture, Geometrical Thinking and Mathematics Education', *Educational Studies in Mathematics* 19(3), 137-162 (reproduced in A. Bishop (ed.) *Mathematics Education and Culture*, Kluwer, Dordrecht, 1988, 137-162).

Gerdes, P.: 1988b, 'A Widespread Decorative Motif and the Pythagorean Theorem', *For the Learning of Mathematics* 8(1), 35-39.

Gerdes, P.: 1988c, 'On Possible Uses of Traditional Angolan Sand Drawings in the Mathematics Classroom', *Educational Studies in Mathematics* 19, 3-22.

Gerdes, P.: 1989a, 'Zum Konzept der Ethnomathematik', in P. Gerdes, *Ethnomathematische Studien* 1, 4-11.

Gerdes, P.: 1989b, 'Sobre Aritmética e Ornamentação Geométrica: Análise de Alguns Cestos de Indios do Brasil', *BOLEMA*, Special no. 1, 11-34, reproduced in *QUIPU*, 1989, 6, 171-187.

Gerdes, P.: 1989c, 'Reconstruction and Extension of Lost Symmetries: Examples from the Tamil of South India', *Computers & Mathematics with Applications* 17(4-6), 791-813.

Gerdes, P.: 1990, *Vivendo a Matemática: Desenhos da África*, Editora Scipione, São Paulo.

Gerdes, P.: 1991a, *Ethnogeometrie. Kulturanthropologische Beiträge zur Genese und Didaktik der Geometrie*, Verlag Franzbecker, Bad Salzdetfurth (Germany).

Gerdes, P.: 1991b, *Etnomatemática: Cultura, Matemática, Educação*, Instituto Superior Pedagógico, Maputo [preface by U. D'Ambrosio].

Gerdes, P.: 1991c, *Lusona: Geometrical Recreations of Africa*, Instituto Superior Pedagógico, Maputo [preface by A. Kuku].

Gerdes, P.: 1992a, *Pitágoras Africano – Um Estudo em Cultura e Educação Matemática*, Instituto Superior Pedagógico, Maputo.

Gerdes, P.: 1992b, *Sobre o Despertar do Pensamento Geométrico*, Universidade Federal de Paraná, Curitiba, [preface by U. D'Ambrosio].

Gerdes, P.: 1993-1994, *Geometria Sona: Reflexões Sobre Uma Tradição de Desemho em Povos da África ao Sul do Equador*, Instituto Superior Pedagógico, Maputo (3 volumes).

Gerdes, P. (ed.): 1993, *A Numeração em Moçambique – Contribuição Para Uma Reflexão Sobre Cultura, Lingua e Educação Matemática*, Instituto Superior Pedagógico, Maputo.

Gerdes, P.: 1994a, 'Mathematics in the History of Sub-Saharan Africa', *Historia Mathematica* 21, 345-376.

Gerdes, P.: 1994b, *African Pythagoras – A Study in Culture and Mathematics Education*, Instituto Superior Pedagógico, Maputo.

Gerdes, P.: 1994c, *SONA Geometry: Reflections on the Tradition of Sand Drawings in Africa South of the Equator*, Instituto Superior Pedagógico, Maputo, Vol. 1 (translation by A. Powell).

Gerdes, P. (ed.): 1994d, *Explorations in Ethnomathematics and Ethnoscience in Mozambique*, Instituto Superior Pedagógico, Maputo.

Gerdes, P.: 1995a, *Ethnomathematics and Education in Africa*, University of Stockholm Institute of International Education, Stockholm.

Gerdes, P.: 1995b, *Women and Geometry in Southern Africa: Suggestions for Further Research*, Universidade Pedagógica, Maputo.

Gerdes, P.: 1995c, *Une Tradition Géométrique en Afrique – Les Dessins sur le Sable*, L'Harmattan, Paris (3 volumes).

Gerdes, P.: 1996, *Femmes et Géométrie en Afrique Australe*, L'Harmattan, Paris.

Gerdes, P.: in press (a), 'On Ethnomathematics and the Transmission of Mathematical Knowledge in and outside Schools in Africa South of the Sahara', in *20th Century Science Beyond the Metropolis*, ORSTOM-UNESCO, Paris.

Gerdes, P.: in press (b), *Sona Geometrie – Reflektionen über eine Sandzeichentradition im Südlichen Zentralafrika*, Bibliographisches Institut, Mannheim.

Gerdes, P. and Bulafo, G.: 1994, *Sipatsi: Technology, Art and Geometry in Inhambane*, Instituto Superior Pedagógico, Maputo (translation by A. Powell) (also published in Portuguese and French).

Gilmer, G.: 1990, 'Ethnomathematical Approach to Curriculum Development', *ISGEm-Newsletter* 5(2), 4-5.

Gilmer, G., Thompson, M. and Zaslavsky, C.: 1992, *Building Bridges to Mathematics: Cultural Connections*, Addison-Wesley, San Francisco.

Ginsburg, H.: 1978, 'Poor Children, African Mathematics and the Problem of Schooling', *Educational Research Quarterly*, Special Edition 2(4), 26-43.

Graham, B.: 1988, 'Mathematical Education and Aboriginal Children', in A. Bishop (ed.), *Culture and Mathematics Education*, Kluwer, Dordrecht, 119-136.

Harris, M.: 1987, 'An Example of Traditional Women's Work as a Mathematics Resource', *For the Learning of Mathematics* 7(3), 26-28.

Harris, M.: 1988, 'Common Threads, Mathematics and Textiles', *Mathematics in School*, 24-28.

Harris, M. et al.: 1988, *Cabbage, Mathematics in Work*, Institute of Education, University of London, London.

Harris, P.: 1980, *Measurement in Tribal Aboriginal Communities,* Northern Territory Department of Education, Darwin.

Harris, P.: 1984, 'The Relevance of Primary School Mathematics in Tribal Aboriginal Communities', in P. Damerow, M. Dunkley, B. Nebres and B. Werry (eds.), *Mathematics For All*, UNESCO, Paris, 96-100.

Harris, P.: 1989, 'Contexts for Change in Cross-cultural Classrooms' in N. Ellerton and M. Clements (eds.), *School Mathematics: The Challenge to Change,* Deakin University, Geelong, 79-95.

Harris, P.: 1991, *Mathematics in a Cultural Context: Aboriginal Perspectives on Space, Time and Money,* Deakin University, Geelong.

Harris, M. & Paechter, C.: 1991, Work reclaimed: status mathematics and non-elitist contexts, in M. Harris (ed) *Schools, mathematics and work*, Falmer Press, London, U.K.

938

Harris, P.: 1992, 'Australian Space – Pushing Back the Frontiers', in B. Southwell, B. Perry, and K. Owens (eds.), *Space – The First and Final Frontier,* Mathematics Education Research Group of Australasia, Sydney, 55-72.

Høyrup, J.: 1994, *In Measure, Number, and Weight – Studies in Mathematics and Culture,* State University of New York, Albany.

Hunting, R.: 1985, *Learning, Aboriginal Worldview and Ethnomathematics,* Western Australia Institute of Technology, Perth, WA.

Hunting, R.: 1987, 'Mathematics and Australian Aboriginal Culture', *For the Learning of Mathematics* 7(2), 5-10.

Ismael, A.: 1994a, 'On the Origin of the Concepts of 'Even' and 'Odd' in Makhuwa Culture', in P. Gerdes (ed.), *Explorations in Ethnomathematics and Ethnoscience in Mozambique,* ISP, Maputo, 9-15.

Ismael, A.: 1994b, 'Motivations for the Learning of Mathematics – In View of Mozambique's Historical, Social and Cultural Development', in C. Julie, Z. Davis, and D. Angelis (eds.), *Proceedings of the 2nd International Conference on the Political Dimensions of Mathematics Education: Curriculum Reconstruction for Society in Transition,* Maskew Miller Longman, Cape Town, 53-56.

Ismael, A. and Soares, D.: 1993, 'Métodos Populares de Contagem em Moçambique', in P. Gerdes (ed.), *A Numeração em Moçambique,* ISP, Maputo, 114-120.

Jones, K., Kershaw, L., and Sparrow, L.: 1995, *Aboriginal Children Learning Mathematics,* Edith Cowan University, Perth.

Joseph, G.: 1987, 'Foundations of Eurocentrism in Mathematics', *Race & Class* 28(3), 13-28.

Joseph, G.: 1989, 'Eurocentrism in mathematics: The Historical Dimensions', in C. Keitel, P. Damerow, A. Bishop and P. Gerdes (eds.), *Mathematics, Education, and Society,* UNESCO, Paris, 32-35

Joseph, G.: 1991, *Crest of the Peacock: Non-European Roots of Mathematics,* Tauris, London

Julie, C. (ed.): 1989, *Proceedings of a Conference on the Politics of Mathematics Education,* NECC Mathematics Commission, Cape Town.

Julie, C, Davis, Z. and Angelis, D. (eds.): 1994, *Proceedings of the 2nd International Conference on the Political Dimensions of Mathematics Education: Curriculum Reconstruction for Society in Transition,* Maskew Miller Longman, Cape Town.

Kane, E.: 1987, *Les Systèmes de Numération Parlée des Groupes Ouest-Atlantiques et Mande. Contribution à la Recherche sur les Fondaments et l'Histoire de la Pensée Logique et Mathématique en Afrique de l'Ouest,* PhD thesis, Lille

Katz, V.: 1994, 'Ethnomathematics in the Classroom', *For the Learning of Mathematics* 14(2), 26-30.

Keitel, C., Damerow, P., Bishop, A. and Gerdes, P. (eds.): 1989), *Mathematics, Education, and Society,* UNESCO, Paris.

Knight, G.: 1982a, 'The Geometry of Maori Art – Rafter Patterns', *The New Zealand Mathematics Magazine* 21(2), 36-40.

Knight, G.: 1982b, 'The Geometry of Maori Art – Weaving Patterns', *The New Zealand Mathematics Magazine* 21(3), 80-87.

Knight, G.: 1994, 'Mathematics and Maori Students: An Example of Cultural Alienation?' in J. Neyland (ed.), *Mathematics Education: A Handbook for Teachers* (Vol. 1), Wellington College of Education, Wellington, NZ, 284-290.

Knijnik, G.: 1993, 'An Ethnomathematical Approach in Mathematics Education: A Matter of Political Power', *For the Learning of Mathematics,* 13(2), 23-25.

Knijnik, G.: 1995, *Exclusão e Resistência: Educação Matemática e Legitimidade Cultural,* Ph.D. thesis, Artes Médicas, Porto Alegre.

Kubik, G.: 1990, 'Visimu Vya Mukatikati – Dilemma Tales and "Arithmetical Puzzles" Collected Among the Valuchazi', *South African Journal of African Languages* 10(2), 59-68.

Lancy, D. (ed.): 1978, 'The Indigenous Mathematics Project', *Papua New Guinea Journal of Education* 14, 1-217.

Lancy, D.: 1983, *Cross-cultural Studies in Cognition and Mathematics*, Academic Press, New York.

Langdon, N.: 1989, 'Cultural Starting Points for Mathematics: A View from Ghana', *Science Education Newsletter* 87, 1-3.

Lea, H.: 1987, 'Traditional Mathematics in Botswana', *Mathematics Teaching* 119

Lea, H.: 1989a, 'Informal mathematics in Botswana', *Proceedings of the 41st CIEAEM Meeting of the International Commission for the Study and Improvement of Mathematics Teaching*, Brussels, 43-53.

Lea, H.: 1989b, *Mathematics in a Cultural Setting*, University of Botswana, Gaberone (mimeo).

Lea, H.: 1990, 'Spatial Concepts in the Kalahari', *Proceedings of the 14th International Conference on Psychology of Mathematics Education*, Oaxtepec, Mexico, Vol. 2, 259-266.

Lean, G.: 1986, *Counting Systems of Papua New Guinea*, Papua New Guinea University of Technology, Lae.

Lean, G.: 1992, *Counting Systems of Papua New Guinea and Oceania*, PhD thesis, Papua New Guinea University of Technology, Lae.

Lean, G.: 1995, *Counting Systems of Papua New Guinea and Oceania*, Third edition, 24 volumes, Papua New Guinea University of Technology, Lae.

Lumpkin, B.: 1990, 'A Multicultural Mathematics Curriculum', *ISGEm-Newsletter* 6(1), 2.

Lumpkin, B.: 1995, *African Cultural Materials for Elementary Mathematics*, Educational Equity Services, Chicago.

Lumpkin, B. and Powell, A.: 1995, *Math: A Rich Heritage*, Globe Fearon Educational Publisher, Upper Saddle River, NJ.

Lumpkin, B. and Strong, D.: 1995, *Multicultural Science and Math Connections – Middle School Projects and Activities*, Weston Walch Publisher, Portland.

Luquet, G.: 1929, 'Sur l'Origine des Notions Mathématiques: Remarques Psychologiques et Ethnographiques', *Journal de Psychologie* 733-761

Mapapá, A.: 1994, Symmetries and Metal Grates in Maputo – Didactic Experimentation', in P. Gerdes (ed.), *Explorations in Ethnomathematics and Ethnoscience in Mozambique*, ISP, Maputo, 49-55.

Mapapá, A. and Uaila, E.: 1993, 'Tabelas e Mapas Comparativos Relativos à Numeração Falada em Moçambique', in P. Gerdes (ed.), *A Numeração em Moçambique*, ISP, Maputo, 121-132.

Marschall, J.: 1987, 'An Atlas of American Indian Geometry', *Ohio Archaeologist* 37(2), 36-49.

Mellin-Olsen, S.: 1986, 'Culture as a Key Theme for Mathematics Education: Postseminar Reflections', in *Mathematics and Culture: A Seminar Report*, Caspar Forlag, Radal, 99-121.

Mellin-Olsen, S.: 1987, *The Politics of Mathematics Education*, Kluwer, Dordrecht.

Mellin-Olsen, S. and Hoines, M. (eds.): 1986, *Mathematics and Culture: A Seminar Report*, Caspar Forlag, Radel

Millroy, W.: 1992, *An Ethnographic Study of the Mathematical Ideas of a Group of Carpenters*, NCTM, Reston, Virginia.

Moore, C.: 1986, *The Implication of String Figures for Native American Mathematics Education*, Flagstaff(mimeo).

Moore, C.: 1987, 'Ethnomathematics', *Science* 236, 1006-1007.

Moore, C.: 1994, 'Research in Native American Mathematics Education', *For the Learning of Mathematics* 14(2), 9-14.

Morales, L.: 1994, *Matemática Maya*, La Gran Aventura, Guatemala.

Mubumbila, V.:1988, *Sur le Sentier Mystérieux des Nombres Noirs*, L'Harmattan, Paris.

Mve Ondo, M.: 1990, *L'Owani et le Songa: Deuz Jeux de Calculs Africains*, CCF St Exepéry/ Sépia, Libreville (Gabon).

Nelson, D., Joseph, G. and Williams, J.: 1993) *Multicultural Mathematics: Teaching Mathematics from a Global Perspective*, Oxford University Press, Oxford.

Nissen, P.: 1988, 'Sand Drawings of Vanuatu', *Mathematics in School* 10-11.

Njock, G.: 1985, 'Mathématiques et Environnement Socio-culturel en Afrique Noire', *Présence Africaine* 135(3), 3-21.

Nobre, S.: 1989a, *Aspectos Sociais e Culturais no Desenho Curricular da Matemática*, M.Ed thesis UNESP, Rio Claro.

Nobre, S.: 1989b, 'The Ethnomathematics of the Most Popular Lottery in Brazil: The 'Animal Lottery'', in C. Keitel, P. Damerow, A. Bishop and P. Gerdes (eds.), *Mathematics, Education, and Society*, UNESCO, Paris, 175-177.

Orey, D.: 1989, 'Ethnomathematical Perspectives on the NCTM Standards,' *ISGEm-Newsletter* 5(1), 5-7.

Panoff, M. and Perrin, M.: 1973, *Dicionário de Etnologia*, Lexis, São Paulo.

Paula, L. and Paula, L.: 1986, *XEMA'EAWA, Jogos de Barbante Entre os Índios Tapirapé*, UNICAMP, Campinas (mimeo).

Peard, R.: 1994, *The Effect of Social Background on the Development of Probabilistic Concepts*, Ph.D thesis, Deakin University, Geelong.

Pinxten, R.: 1989, 'World View and Mathematics Teaching', in C. Keitel, P. Damerow, A. Bishop and P. Gerdes (eds.), *Mathematics, Education, and Society*, UNESCO, Paris, 28-29.

Pinxten, R.: 1994, 'Ethnomathematics and its Practice', *For the Learning of Mathematics* 14(2), 23-25.

Pinxten, R., van Dooren, I. and Harvey, F.: 1983, *The Anthropology of Space: Exploration into the Natural Philosophy and Semantics of the Navajo*, University of Pennsylvania.

Pompeu, G.: 1992, *Bringing Ethnomathematics into the School Curriculum*, PhD Thesis, University of Cambridge, Cambridge, UK.

Posner, J.: 1982, 'The Development of Mathematical Knowledge in Two West African Societies', *Child Development* 53, 200-208.

Ratteray, J.: 1992, *Center Shift: An African-centered Approach for the Multicultural Curriculum*, Institute for Independent Education, Washington, DC.

Raum, O.: 1938, *Arithmetic in Africa*, Evans Brothers, London.

Reich, K.; Folkerts, M. and Scriba, C.: 1989, 'Das Schriftenverzeichnis von Ewald Fettweis: (1881-1967) samt einer Würdigung von Olindo Falsirol', *Historia Mathematica* 16, 360-372.

Saxe, G.: 1981, 'Body Parts as Numerals: A Developmental Analysis of Numeration among Remote Oksapmin Village Populations in Papua New Guinea', *Child Development* 52, 306-316.

Saxe, G.: 1982a, 'Developing Forms of Arithmetical Thought Among the Oksapmin of Papua New Guinea', *Developmental Psychology* 18, 583-594.

Saxe, G.: 1982b, 'Culture and Development of Numerical Cognition: Studies Among the Oksapmin of Papua New Guinea', in *Children's Logical and Mathematical Cognition*, New York, 157-176.

Saxe, G.: 1988, 'Candy Selling and Math Learning', *Educational Researcher* 17(6), 14-21.

Saxe, G.: 1991, *Culture and Cognitive Development: Studies in Mathematical Understanding*, Erlbaum, Hillsdale.

Schliemann, A.: 1984, 'Mathematics among Carpentry Apprentices: Implications for School Teaching', in P. Damerow, M. Dunkley, B. Nebres and B. Werry (eds.), *Mathematics For All*, UNESCO, Paris, 92-95.

Shan, S. and Bailey, P.: 1991, *Multiple Factors: Classroom Mathematics for Equality and Justice*, Trentham Books, Staffordshire.

Shirley, L.: 1988, *Historical and Ethnomathematical Algorithms for Classroom Use*, paper presented at ICME VI, Budapest (mimeo).

Shirley, L.: 1991, 'Video Games for Math: A Case for "Kid-culture"', *ISGEm-Newsletter* 6(2), 2-3.

Skovsmose, O.: 1994, *Towards a Philosophy of Critical Mathematics Education*, Kluwer, Dordrecht.

Smart, T. and Isaacson, Z.: 1989, "It Was Nice Being Able to Share Ideas', Women Learning Mathematics', in C. Keitel, P. Damerow, A. Bishop and P. Gerdes (eds.), *Mathematics, Education, and Society*, UNESCO, Paris, 116-118.

Soares, D. and Ismael, A.: 1994, 'Popular Counting Methods in Mozambique', in P. Gerdes (ed.), *Explorations in Ethnomathematics and Ethnoscience in Mozambique*, ISP, Maputo, 24-29.

Soto, I.: 1995, 'Stratégies de Résolution des Problèmes de Proportionnalité par des Paysans Chiliens', in *First European Summer University Proceedings: History and Epistemology in Mathematics Education*, IREM, Montpellier, 557-570.

Souviney, R.: 1989, 'The Indigenous Mathematics Project: Mathematics Instruction in Papua New Guinea', in C. Keitel, P. Damerow, A. Bishop and P. Gerdes (eds.), *Mathematics, Education, and Society*, UNESCO, Paris, 106-110.

Stigler, J. and Baranes, R.: 1988, 'Culture and Mathematics Learning', *Review of Research in Education* 15, 253-306

Stott, L. and Lea, H.: 1993, *Common Threads in Botswana*, British Council, Gaberone.

Touré, S.: 1984, 'Preface', in *Mathématiques dans l'Environnement Socio-culturel Africain*, Institut de Recherches Mathématiques d'Abidjan, 1-2

Touré, S. (ed.): 1993, *Collection Inter-Africaine de Mathématiques, 6e*, Nouvelles Éditions Ivoiriennes & Edicef, Abidjan.

Touré, S.(ed.): 1994, *Collection Inter-Africaine de Mathématiques, 5e*, Nouvelles Éditions Ivoiriennes & Edicef, Abidjan.

Tro, G.: 1980, *Étude de Quelques Systèmes de Numération en Côte d'Ivoire*, Abidjan.

Turner, J.: 1992, 'Complementarity, Ethnomathematics, and Primary Education in Bhutan', *Canadian and International Education* 21(1), 20-43.

Watson, H.: 1987, 'Learning to Apply Numbers to Nature', *Educational Studies in Mathematics* 18, 339-357.

Watson, H.: 1989, 'A Wittgensteinian View of Mathematics: Implications for Teachers of Mathematics', in N. Ellerton and M. Clements (eds.), *School Mathematics: The Challenge to Change,* Deakin University, Geelong, 18-30.

White, L.: 1947, 'The Locus of Mathematical Reality: An Anthropological Footnote' (reproduced in J. Newman (ed.), *The World of Mathematics*, New York, 1956, vol. 4, 2348-2364).

Wilder, R.: 1950, 'The Cultural Basis of Mathematics', *Proceedings International Congress of Mathematicians*, Vol.1, 258-271.

Wilder, R.: 1968, *Evolution of Mathematical Concepts*, John Wiley, New York (Transworld Publications, London, 1974).

Wilder, R.: 1981, *Mathematics as a Cultural System*, Pergamon Press, Oxford.

Wilson, B.: 1981, *Cultural Contexts of Science and Mathematics Education*, University of Leeds, Leeds.

Wilson, P.: 1992, *Annotated Bibliography of Multicultural Issues in Mathematics*, University of Georgia, Athens (mimeo).

Zaslavsky, C.: 1973, *Africa Counts: Number and Pattern in African Culture*, Prindle, Weber and Schmidt, Boston (new edition: Lawrence Hill Books, Brooklyn, NY, 1979).

Zaslavsky, C.: 1989, 'Integrating Math with the Study of Cultural Traditions', *ISGEm-Newsletter* 4(2), 5-7.

Zaslavsky, C.: 1992, *Multicultural Mathematics: Interdisciplinary Cooperative Learning Activities*, Weston Walsch, Portland.

Zaslavsky, C.: 1994, ''Africa Counts' and Ethnomathematics', *For the Learning of Mathematics* 14(2), 3-8.

Zaslavsky, C.: 1995, *The Multicultural Math Classroom: Bringing in the World*, Heinemann, Portsmouth.

Zepp, R.: 1983, *L'Apprentissage du Calcul dans les Langues de Côte d'Ivoire*, Institut de Linguistique Appliquée, Université d'Abidjan.

Zepp, R.: 1989, *Language and Mathematics Education*, API Press, Hong Kong.

Chapter 25: Research and Intervention Programs in Mathematics Education: A Gendered Issue[1]

GILAH C. LEDER, HELEN J. FORGASZ AND CLAUDIE SOLAR

La Trobe University, Australia, La Trobe University, Australia and Université de Montréal, Canada

ABSTRACT

Research into gender issues in mathematics education and, in particular, into the effectiveness of related intervention programs is summarised in this chapter. Where possible, international and cultural dimensions are emphasised, and duplication of research summarised in recent reviews has been avoided. The review embraces both traditional approaches to explorations of inequities in educational practice and the growing feminist literature on the gendering of mathematics.

Models of gender equity and the historical progression from empirical research to feminist perspectives are discussed and examined. These analyses are linked with changing emphases in curriculum development and intervention strategies. Various kinds of interventions aimed at attracting and retaining females and minorities in mathematics are considered. The variety of strategies adopted in the intervention programs is emphasised, and consideration is given to the issue of developing appropriate criteria and methods for evaluating the effectiveness of such programs.

> Education is a basic [human] right and an essential tool for achieving goals of equality, development and peace. Non-discriminatory education benefits both girls and boys, and thus ultimately contributes to more equal relationships between women and men. Equality of access to and attainment of educational qualifications [are] necessary if more women are to become agents of change. ... Investing in formal and non-formal education and training for girls and women, with exceptionally high social and economic return, has proved to be one of the best means of achieving sustainable development and economic growth that is both sustained and sustainable.
>
> (United Nations Fourth World Conference on Women: Draft Platform for Action, 1995, p.1)

A.J. Bishop et al. (eds.), International Handbook of Mathematics Education, 945 - 985

1.   INTRODUCTION

Females around the world still face discrimination. The 1995 United Nation's Women's conference in Beijing provided ample testimony of the breadth of issues of concern. These varied widely according to national, ethnic, cultural and religious backgrounds. Education rated highly among the areas requiring attention. The Jomtien Conference on *Education For All* (Haggis, 1991), sponsored by the United Nations Educational, Scientific and Cultural Organisation (UNESCO), also reported that the education of females was a high priority, since 'women constitute half the world's population, [yet] they make up 63 percent of adult illiterates' (p.65). The Jomtien Conference report noted that 'today, some 1,000 million adults, with women as the silent majority, are labelled illiterate. Over 130 million children, almost two-thirds of them girls in the developing countries, have no access to primary education' (Haggis, 1991, p.1).

Educational opportunities are affected by gender, class and ethnicity. The impact of these factors differs across industrialised and developing nations. Completing secondary education is more likely for females from socially advantaged backgrounds than for males from families in poverty. Although recent figures from countries like the USA, France, Canada, Britain and Australia show that a higher proportion of females than males is now completing secondary schooling (see, for example, Ministerial Council on Education, Employment, Training and Youth Affairs, and Curriculum Corporation, 1994), secondary education for females is far less likely than for males in economically poor nations (Graham-Brown, 1991) such as Ethiopia and Papua New Guinea (Kaely, 1995). Furthermore, participation in education by females does not guarantee their access to all disciplines. For example, in Iran, women are denied access to many science-related fields of endeavour (Paivandi, 1994). In this chapter we focus on countries in which women can study mathematics freely, without formal barriers to their participation.

Internationally, mathematics and related occupational fields have been clearly identified as areas in which males predominate. Over twenty years ago, Sells (1973) exposed the extent to which mathematics served to screen entry into a range of higher education and post-school training courses. Limited mathematical backgrounds continue to block many occupational options in Western industrialised nations. Statistics in the USA and elsewhere reveal that women and minorities are underrepresented in the most advanced mathematics courses and in science- and engineering-related occupations. When enrolments in the most demanding mathematics subjects are examined at the school level and in higher education, gender imbalance is evident. In Britain, for example, in 1991/1992 the ratio of males to females studying the physical sciences full-time was 2.5:1, with more than six times as many males as females being enrolled in engineering and technology (Central Statistical Office, 1994).

It should be remembered that statistical data by gender were generally unavailable in developed nations prior to 1975, International Women's Year. Neither governments nor educational institutions compiled data disaggregated by gender, and this omission made the promotion of women's participation in mathematics and related areas seemingly irrelevant. Separate statistics for males and females are still often unavailable in developing countries. In the mid-1980's it was estimated that there were seven males for every female enrolled in African universities, and that women were grossly underrepresented in natural science and engineering courses (Graham-Brown, 1991). A similar pattern of tertiary enrolments was reported more recently for Papua New Guinea by Kaely (1995), for Singapore by Kaur (1995), and for Malawi by Hiddleston (1995).

There has been increasing research activity in the field of gender and mathematics education since the early 1970's. Fennema's (1974) early review of research in the field was based on work from the USA and revealed that research up to that time had been fairly limited, the emphasis having been on performance differences. Leder's (1992) later review, which focused on research from English-speaking Western nations, particularly the USA, showed that the areas under investigation had broadened. Considerable research attention had been paid to the affective domain and to classroom research. When international perspectives are introduced, they are usually limited to large-scale comparative studies such as those of the International Association for the Evaluation of Educational Achievement (IEA).

1.1   Chapter Outline

In this chapter, we discuss an extensive range of work in the field and draw on research from around the world. We have broadened the definition of research on gender and mathematics education to include intervention studies. We have taken mathematics education to cover the teaching and learning of the subject, its curricular aspects as well as contextual issues. In addition to the traditional approach of examining inequities in educational practice, this chapter also incorporates the growing literature, framed within feminist perspectives, on the gendering of mathematics and mathematics education. A wide range of sources is examined, since some leading, mainstream journals have not yet recognised all types and areas of scholarship in the field as appropriate for publication (Fennema and Hart, 1994).

We begin with a discussion of equity issues in mathematics education and follow this with an overview of relevant research. A conscious decision was made not to duplicate recent and extensive reviews of developments in 'gender and mathematics education' (see, for example, Leder, 1992; Fennema and Hart, 1994; Fennema, 1995), but to concentrate on international and cultural dimensions.

The models of equity presented early in the chapter are contextually situated within the research perspectives and intervention strategies subsequently reviewed. This approach highlights the close links between research and interventions and similarities in their respective developments over time.

The historical progression from traditional, empirical research to feminist perspectives is reflected in the changing foci of curriculum initiatives and intervention strategies surveyed. As the equity models presented illustrate, definitions of gender equity followed various paths, across and within time periods.

An extensive review of gender and mathematics intervention programs completes the chapter. Particular emphasis is given to initiatives aimed at attracting and retaining females and members of minority groups in mathematics and related fields. The analysis provides a summary of the types of programs and strategies used. Factors contributing to successful outcomes are synthesised. The chapter concludes with a summary and an overview of critical issues.

2.   ISSUES OF EQUITY

Equity issues, particularly with respect to gender, are an important focus of this chapter. In line with Fennema (1990) and Secada (1989), we believe it is useful to consider equity issues from three specific perspectives, namely equity as equal educational opportunity, equity as equal educational treatment, and equity as equal educational outcome. That is, educational outcomes should not be unreasonably affected by gender, class, or a non-inclusive curriculum. Thus both young women and men should know that mathematics is applicable to their adult lives and occupations.

The substantial literature on gender issues in mathematics education and the continuing focus on this topic confirm that the path to attaining gender equity is not an easy one. Various models for achieving gender equity have been proposed. Despite differences in detail and terminology, many of them fall into one of the following models:

1. The *assimilationist model* has been accepted at different times in different countries. It assumes that males and females have very similar learning characteristics and should strive for similar educational goals. The acceptance and implementation of its underlying principles are an important factor in providing females with access to the same educational programs and curricula as males. Support for co-educational learning settings flows from this model.

2. In the *deficit model* it is also assumed that the goals and outcomes of the educational process should be the same for females and males. Compensatory activities to overcome deficiencies, typically targeted at females, are built into educational programs.

3. In the *pluralistic model* the goals of education are not necessarily assumed to be the same for different groups. An acceptance that learning characteristics may vary across groups is integral to this model, and differences in such characteristics are not considered to be deficits. Instead, it is argued, the educational environment should be structured so that such differences can be taken into account. If this is done then diversity among learners is a likely and expected outcome of the educational process.

4. In the *social justice model*, it is accepted that individuals will differ in some ways but are similar in others. Educational provisions are adjusted so that identical treatment is given where appropriate, but different treatment and actions are offered when that is likely to be most beneficial. Justice and equity, it is implied, can be achieved only if differences are respected and catered for appropriately.

The four models listed above have been applied to education in general as well as to mathematics education in particular. They are inclusive of equity issues with respect to gender, class, race and, particularly for societies with multicultural populations. Research and practice become more complex as each of these perspectives is added.

2.1 Equity Issues and Research

The assimilationist, deficit, and pluralistic models have evolved from, and contributed to, traditional, positivist-empirical research on gender issues. Each of these models has shaped, and has been shaped by, the aims and goals of research endeavours. Links between these models and aspects of feminism are discussed in a later section of this chapter.

Research consistent with the assimilationist paradigm has been especially influential and has led to a multitude of studies concerned with participation and performance data, particularly comparisons between males and females in mathematics and related areas. While sometimes regarded as simplistic and reinforcing of stereotypes, this research was an important foundation for feminist inquiry. Monitoring of (large scale) statistical trends still has a place on the contemporary research agenda. 'We need to continue research that documents the status of gender differences as they exist' (Fennema, 1995, p.35).

Equity issues in mathematics education remain of critical importance and interest internationally. Gender differences in outcomes have persisted in Western nations despite the volume of research undertaken to uncover and understand the contributing factors, and the range of government reports, articulated policies and many intervention strategies adopted to address them. Pursuing equity in mathematics learning has received growing attention in developing countries, despite competing priorities.

Inequities in mathematics/science areas are frequently assumed to reflect gender and cultural inequities in society and in education. This is based on the status attached to pursuing studies and career options in these fields. Females are often, but not invariably, the disadvantaged group. Kaely (1995) pointed out, for example, that in matrilineal communities within Papua New Guinea and some South Pacific Islands, girls are treated with respect in the classroom as well as in society as a whole. And indeed, females exhibit equal, if not better, performance in mathematics compared with males (p.95).

Hanna's (1989) analysis of the IEA's Second International Mathematics Study (SIMS) data confirmed that differences in mathematics performance are influenced not simply by gender, but also by cultural factors. When mathematics learning outcomes are examined by gender within nations having culturally diverse populations, differences may also be apparent. In New Zealand, for example, Forbes' (1995) analysis of the mathematics performance levels of 13-year-old students revealed no gender differences for students of European descent, but Maori girls' performance levels were lower than those for Maori boys. It was concluded that strategies targeting girls' participation and performance in mathematics seemed to be having 'greater impact on girls of European descent, but are failing to meet the needs of Maori girls' (Forbes, 1995, p.115). These between- and within-country differences illustrate that gender issues cannot be divorced from culture, race and class effects. They also highlight the limitations of the deficit model and the usefulness of combining the pluralistic and social justice models to deepen understandings of gender differences in mathematics education outcomes.

In recent years feminist theories have been invoked by mathematics educators to re-examine inequities in mathematics education. Indeed, some of the early work on gender and mathematics has been re-classified to conform with various feminist perspectives. Thus, the assimilationist and deficit models, with their emphasis on females striving for culturally accepted male norms, are perceived as consistent with the tenets of liberal feminism; the pluralistic and social justice models which value 'difference', with radical feminist research.

2.2 Contribution of Feminist Theories

Challenging, new perspectives on unresolved equity issues have been put forward, influenced by the pluralistic and social justice models, as well as by feminist theories in other disciplines (for example, Women's studies and Black studies). The McIntosh (1983) five-stage model for curriculum transformation within educational institutions, which has been adapted by Kaiser and Rogers (1995) to examine mathematics education curriculum development with respect to gender issues, is described below. Where appropriate, a representative selection of research studies, government documents, intervention strategies, and curriculum innovations is presented to illustrate and clarify the stages. The assumptions inherent in the different stages are also reflected in the research on which we draw.

2.3   Kaiser and Rogers' Stages of Curriculum Developments

2.3.1 Stage 1. Womanless mathematics

'Mathematics was what men did'.
(Kaiser and Rogers, 1995, p.4)

The view that mathematics is a 'male domain' characterises this stage. Clear evidence of this is revealed when the history of women's engagement with mathematics is examined and when mathematics text books of the past are compared to more contemporary ones. Beliefs that mathematics and related fields are more appropriate for males than for females persist in many contemporary societies.

Until women had access to education or until they were permitted to study at universities in the late nineteenth century, the mathematics taught to boys and to girls was not the same. Differing gender-role expectations meant that certain parts of mathematics, such as geometry, were only learnt by boys.

Much of the arithmetic taught to females overlapped with what boys had to learn, however. In the preface to his textbook for 'The Use of Young Ladies', Butler (1801) extolled the virtues and achievements of educated women and appeared to question the prevailing view that what young women learned in the area of arithmetic was inferior. The *Ladies' Diary* (Leybourn, 1816), a publication ostensibly for women, published non-routine mathematical questions to which readers were encouraged to send solutions. This seems to imply that women in the early nineteenth century were doing mathematics beyond basic arithmetic. Closer inspection challenges this inference. Consider the following question (No. 1107) taken from the *Ladies' Diary* of 1803-1804 and proposed by the Rev. J. Furnass from Ponteland.

Two persons, A and B, found a square ingot of pure silver, being 40 inches in length, and 8 inches on the side, which they carried home between them, each extremity resting on their shoulders; and then agreed to share it in proportion to the weight or pressure sustained by each, the height of A's shoulder being 5 feet, and that of B's 4 feet; required the value of each man's share, at the rate of five shillings the ounce?

(Leybourn, 1816, p.20)

As well as linking 'persons' exclusively with 'men', the solution printed with the question was submitted by a Mr. O.G. Gregory of Woolwich. It is difficult to sustain an argument that mathematics is an inclusive discipline when all personal references are to males. Until more recent times, females and female contexts were similarly absent from the problems included in widely-used school mathematics text books.

Recent studies have examined the degree of gender stereotyping in mathematics textbooks. Northam (1982) reported marked gender-bias favouring males in British primary-level textbooks published in the 1970's. Similarly, Verhage (1990) found that textbooks in the Netherlands overtly conveyed messages that mathematics was a male pursuit. Although Garcia, Harrison and Torres (1990) reported that there was better gender balance in the 1980's for popular American elementary level textbooks, they nevertheless found that mathematics was portrayed as lacking a human dimension. Typical of early attempts at gender neutrality was a resultant over-emphasis on numerical questions unrelated to human endeavour (Forgasz, 1994). In Canada, current by-laws forbid gender and race stereotyping in school textbooks. In Australia, publication guidelines assist authors in the use of gender-inclusive language (Forgasz, 1994).

2.3.2   Stage 2. Women in Mathematics

'The history of exceptional women in mathematics was injected into our experience'.

(Kaiser and Rogers, 1995, p.4)

Features of this phase include the supplementation of portrayals of male mathematicians with references to a small number of outstanding women (for example, Hypatia, Sonya Kovalevskya, and Emmy Noether) who made significant contributions to the field, and the publication of resource materials for mathematics classrooms and of research into the factors contributing to some women's success in the field of mathematics. Perl's (1978) book of mathematical activities, based on the work of several female mathematicians, whose biographies are also included, is one example. Taylor's (1990) research, which documents the significant influences on a number of successful contemporary female mathematicians, another.

2.3.3   Stage 3. Women as a Problem in Mathematics

'Mathematics is a field in which women have difficulty'.

(Kaiser and Rogers, 1995, p.5)

The assumption that women are mathematically deficient symbolised this period. Much of the research reviewed later in this chapter fits into this phase, though some reflects the transition into Stage 4 described below. Also representative are writings that draw attention to the perpetuation of myths about women's capabilities and achievements in mathematics (see, for example, Tracy and Davis, 1989). It might be inferred from the exclusion of women in celebrated volumes on the history of mathematics – such as Bell's (1937) *Men of Mathematics* – that their contributions to developments in the discipline were deemed to be inconsequential.

Female 'deficits' could also be inferred from recommendations made in earlier government documents aimed at redressing gender inequities in mathematics learning. Representative examples from Australia and the UK are presented below:
- Australia:
  '... research is needed to guide the choice of alternatives: improving mathematical performance among girls, for example,...' (Schools Commission, 1975 p.162)
- United Kingdom:
  '... we suggest a number of strategies which we believe may contribute to improvement in the mathematical performance of girls'. (Cockcroft, 1982, p.64)

The work of Walkerdine (Walden and Walkerdine, 1985; Walkerdine, 1989) challenged the deficit interpretations given to performance differences in mathematics in favour of males.

The idea that girls lack spatial ability or mastery orientation or autonomy or holistic thinking, or whatever the next incapacity turns out to be, is not best served by trying to prove *either* that they have it *or* by trying to find the cause of their deficit. Deficit theories tend to blame the victim.
(Walkerdine, 1989, pp.18-19)

2.3.4 Stage 4. Women as Central to Mathematics

'Women's experience and women's pursuits are made central to the development of mathematics'.
(Kaiser and Rogers, 1995, p.6)

Uncovering privilege and redistributing power is the thrust of stage 4. The emphases are on the need to change pedagogical methods and to reconsider the nature of the discipline of mathematics. Writers within mathematics education who advocate these approaches have relied on the pioneering efforts of feminist thinkers about science (e.g., Harding and O'Barr, 1987; Harding, 1991; Keller, 1992; Shepherd, 1993).

The work of Gilligan (1982) has also affected work in mathematics education, directly and indirectly. For example, Belenky, Clinchy, Goldberger, and Tarule's (1986) explorations of women's ways of knowing drew on the theoretical structure developed by Gilligan. They, in turn, influenced Becker (1995), who discussed the implications of women's ways of knowing on the teaching and learning of mathematics, and posed several challenging research questions. Reflecting on the impact of Gilligan's (1982) notions of connectedness in women's thinking processes, Rogers (1995) described her personal transition from a traditional pedagogical style to a feminist approach in her teaching of university level mathematics. Solar (1995) drew on feminist, liberation, and anti-racist pedagogies in offering guidelines for the design of an inclusive pedagogy.

Noddings (1990) has characterised feminist pedagogy as involving:

> a shift from teacher to students as the centre of attention; openness and dialogue; student-to-student talk; increased participation of students in the choice of questions, topics, and projects; more opportunities for direct contact in the field; variable modes of evaluation; more generous and direct help in learning; and a reluctance to grade on the basis of 'natural' talent or test scores. (p.400)

In line with those who have challenged the epistemological basis of science, Burton (1995) questioned the 'objectivity' of mathematics and argued that mathematics is contextually bound. If knowing mathematics was viewed in this way, Burton claimed that mathematics might be 're-perceived as humane, responsive, negotiable, and creative' (p.222), what and how mathematics is taught would be challenged, and the constituency of learners attracted to the subject might change. Damarin (1995) reflected on the nature of mathematics and the consequential implications for women learning mathematics from two broad feminist theoretical perspectives: feminist empiricism and feminist standpoints. The former basically accepts science and its methods as sound but considers some practices and outcomes to be biased against women.

Feminist empiricists reject the incomplete perspective of masculinist science and wish to replace it with a more objective science that recognises the experiences of women. Feminist standpoints, Damarin claimed, allow 'for a multiplicity of truths, none of them complete, and find most valuable those investigations that begin with the lives of women' (p.248). Arguing from a feminist standpoint, Damarin maintained that in the current climate of high technology, social power is associated with an ability to understand and use mathematics. Therefore, feminist work on women in mathematics is important and marks the shift from adapting women to mathematics to adapting mathematics to women (Goldstein, 1992).

2.3.5 *Stage 5. Mathematics Reconstructed*

'... it will involve a fundamental shift in what we value in mathematics, in how we teach it, in how mathematics is used, and in the relationship of mathematics to the world around us'.

(Kaiser and Rogers, 1995, p.9)

Kaiser and Rogers (1995) argue that this stage, which represents a revolutionary change in views, has not yet been reached. They consider that the evolutionary process in mathematics curriculum has reached a transitional phase between stages 3 and 4, but that stage 5 is the ultimate goal. They point to Shelley's (1995) provocative essay as encapsulating the spirit of the final stage.

Feminist theories are numerous, diverse, and overlapping. Kaiser and Rogers (1995) provide one useful framework for understanding changes in mathematics education and for a critical assessment of gender equity research and related intervention programs. Another perspective is offered by Noddings (1990), whose categorisation in terms of three 'generations of feminism' can also be applied to mathematics education:

a)   women seek equality with men,
b)   women embrace their own special qualities and reject uncritical assimilation into the male world, and
c)   women critique what they sought and accomplished in the first two phases and seek solutions that arise out of a careful synthesis of old and new questions.

Overlap with the four models described in the earlier section on 'issues of equity', and with the Kaiser and Rogers' (1995) stages, is apparent.

3.   RESEARCH ON GENDER AND MATHEMATICS EDUCATION

So far, we have reviewed different approaches to equity issues in mathematics education that provide insights and understandings of the reforms implemented to challenge gender inequities. We now focus on recent research in the field of gender and mathematics education in different cultural settings and begin with a brief overview of research employing traditional empirical-scientific methods.

Much of what we have learnt about gender and mathematics has come from work conceived within the positivist framework. The Fennema-Sherman studies of the late 1970's which exemplified this approach have been widely cited (Walberg and Haertel, 1992), replicated, and used as a basis for further work in many countries. An indication of the strong research activity in the gender area can be gauged from the contents of the *Journal of Research in Mathematics Education* (JRME). During the 1980's about 10 per cent of its articles explored gender issues, but with 'one major research paradigm, an empirical-scientific-positivist approach' (Fennema and Hart, 1994, p.652). In contrast, not a single article with a gender theme has appeared in *Recherches en Didactique des Mathématiques* (RDM), a journal published in France for over 15 years.

Comprehensive reviews of studies drawn mainly from research in English-speaking countries (USA, UK and Australia) are found in several recent publications (see, for example, Joffe and Foxman, 1988; Linn and Hyde, 1989; Fennema and Leder, 1990; Leder, 1992; Forgasz, 1994). Solar, Lafortune, Kayler, Barette, Caron and Pasquis (1992) provide an overview of relevant work reported in French. To include a further international perspective of work undertaken in the field, a representative sample of findings from non-English speaking, non-Western nations is summarised in Table I. Many of these appeared in *Educational Studies in Mathematics* (ESM), a journal published in Europe, with a fair representation of articles reporting on research conducted in developing nations. Also included in the table are published research papers from the proceedings of *Psychology of Mathematics Education* [PME] annual conferences, a further source of research from less-developed countries. Studies are listed in alphabetical order, by author.

Author (date)	Country/ participants	Selected findings
Birenbaum & Kraemer (1992)	Israel: Grade 9: 324 (Jewish & Arabic)	Jewish students: Ms[1] expressed more positive attitudes towards mathematics than did Fs. Not found with Arabic students. Overall, Ms more stereotyped than Fs. For success, Fs listed motivational factors (liking/interest/parent or peer support) more frequently than Ms.
1 M = male, F = female		

Table 1: Selected international research studies on affective variables, gender and mathematics learning outcomes.

956

Author (date)	Country/ participants	Selected findings
Cheung (1988)	Hong Kong: Grade 7: 5644	Compared with Fs, Ms more stereotyped about mathematics and believed they had more natural ability. Students' perceptions of ability, usefulness of mathematics, and extent of creativity in mathematics were related to levels of mathematics achievement.
Clarkson & Leder (1984)	Grade 10: Australia: 85M, 73F New Guinea: 237M, 96F	Fs more likely than Ms to attribute success to effort. Ms and Fs (both countries) success attributions ranked in same order: effort, environment, task, ability. Failure/effort ranked first and failure/environment last by each group.
Kaiser-Messmer (1993)	(West) Germany 357M, 391F Age: 14-19	Compared to the Fs, Ms more interested in mathematics, high attainment is more important for them, and they maintain more traditional gender-role expectations.
Lummis & Stevenson (1990)	USA, Japan & Taiwan: Kindergarten (24x3 groups), Grades: 1 (N=2111) & 5 (N=2155). Smaller target samples for interview	Trends same in the three locations – Grade 1: like maths-F>M; favourite subject: F-English, M-Maths; better at maths – most said Ms and Fs same; Grade 5: like maths - M>F; favourite subject and who better at maths – same as grade 1; expectation of high school performance: M>F. Gender/culture interactions rare. Beliefs about gender differences stronger than performance differences. Mothers less biased about mathematics than reading and rated Ms higher than Fs. Children rated Ms higher in mathematics, Fs higher in reading.
Mukuni (1987)	Kenya: primary and secondary	Studies from the 70's and 80's indicate that Ms have more positive attitudes towards mathematics than Fs
Otten & Kuyper (1988)	Netherlands: 144M, 210F secondary students	Achievement, attitudes towards mathematics and whether preferred vocation required mathematics were significant predictors in choice to study mathematics. Combinations differed for Ms and Fs.
1 M = male, F = female		

Table 1: Selected international research studies on affective variables, gender and mathematics learning outcomes.

Author (date)	Country/ participants	Selected findings
Sayers (1994)	Zambia: 478M, 478F grades 8-12	Compared to Fs, the Ms were more confident, less anxious, enjoyed mathematics more and perceived mathematics to be more useful. Gender gaps widened at higher grade levels.
Skaalvik (1990)	Norway: Grade 6: 117M, 114F 10 classes	No gender differences in achievement, general academic self-esteem, or mathematics self-efficacy. Achievements overestimated by Ms and Fs. Stereotypes might 'affect evaluative math self-concept but not success expectations on specified and familiar problems' (p.596).
Tocci & Engelhard (1991)	USA: 1787M 2059F Thailand: 1828M 1700F Age: 13	Gender differences in attitudes for students from both countries, even after controlling for achievement and parental support. Largest differences were for mathematics as a male domain -- Ms more stereotyped.
Visser (1988)	South Africa: Grade 7: 824 Grade 9: 781 and parents	Grade 7: significant gender differences favouring Ms on some variables: e.g. male domain, usefulness Grade 9: significant gender differences favouring Ms on several attitudinal variables. Intended participation in mathematics was predicted from attitudinal variables for Fs but not for Ms.
1 M = male, F = female		

Table 1: Selected international research studies on affective variables, gender and mathematics learning outcomes.

The research summarised in Table 1 originated in different countries: Australia, Germany, Hong Kong, Israel, Kenya, the Netherlands, Papua New Guinea, Norway, South Africa, Taiwan, Thailand, and Zambia. The findings indicate that:

— Males hold more functional beliefs about themselves as learners of mathematics than do females.
— Gender differences are more prevalent among older students and seem to increase as students progress through school.
— Mathematics continues to be viewed as a male domain, more so by males than by females.
— Confidence is a critical variable and has been linked to mathematics achievement levels and to participation in elective mathematics courses.

— Perceptions of the usefulness of mathematics may not be as strongly implicated in gender-differentiated mathematics learning outcomes as was earlier believed.
— Compared to males, females are less likely to attribute mathematical success to ability and failure to lack of effort, and are more likely to attribute failure to lack of ability.
— External influences can differentially influence students' beliefs: for example, parents, the peer group, socialisation patterns, and the media.

These results corroborate the major trends found in research from English-speaking nations on gender differences with respect to affective variables and make it clear that the impact of affect is not confined to any one country.

References to feminist themes in mathematics education exist but are not yet generally found in traditional mathematics education journals, except in special issues with gender as the dominant focus. Summaries of the articles from special issues of *Zentralblatt für Didaktik der Mathematik* (ZDM), *Educational Studies in Mathematics* (ESM), and the *International Journal of Educational Research* are shown in Table 2. There have also been several collected volumes published recently that feature 'gender and mathematics' (Solar and Lafortune, 1994; Grevholm and Hanna, 1995; Rogers and Kaiser, 1995; Secada, Fennema and Adajian, 1995). Chapter summaries of these books are also included in Table 2. These summaries draw attention to the continued interest in the field of gender issues in mathematics education as well as to the increasing diversity of paradigms and methodologies being used by researchers. The headings, 'empirical' and 'feminist perspectives', have been chosen to reflect the transition from liberal to other feminist perspectives. We believe, together with Fennema and Hart (1994), that research incorporating feminist theory and using feminist research paradigms has the potential to extend understandings of gender issues in mathematics learning.

Table 2: Summary of recent articles on gender and mathematics

1. Special issue ESM (Vol. 28, No. 3, April 1995): *Mathematics and Gender*

Empirical: four articles	*Feminist: three articles*
Tartre and Fennema examined quantitative longitudinal data from American students in grades 6, 8, 10 and 12 for links between affective factors and gender differences in mathematics achievement. The statistical relationships between classroom factors and a range of affective variables among Australian grade 7 students were investigated by Forgasz. Using quantitative and qualitative methods, Boekarts et al. explored the interaction of cognitive and affective variables as Dutch grade 6 students solved mathematical problems. Taole et al. described a program in Botswana arising from classroom interaction data that raised teachers' awareness of inequities in the mathematics classroom and aimed to change attitudes and instructional practices.	In parallel with critical discourses about science, Burton drew on philosophical, pedagogical and feminist writings focusing on mathematics to examine critically traditional views of the nature of mathematics and mathematical knowledge. Within the interpretative qualitative research paradigm, and informed by feminist discourse, Atweh and Cooper observed mathematics classrooms in two Australian girls schools of different socioeconomic background to investigate and compare girls' constructions of mathematics and of themselves as learners. Through an extensive exploration of literature on feminist pedagogy, Solar extracted a set of common characteristics from which guidelines for an inclusive mathematics education pedagogy were derived.

2. Special issues of *ZDM* (Vol. 26(1) and (2), 1994)

Part 1: *Empirical: two articles*	*Feminist: one article*
Menacher examined various explanations for females' continued reluctance to enter mathematical, scientific, and technical fields. Brandon and Jordan discussed the higher performance in both mathematics and language of female students in Hawaii compared with males. Data were examined for immigrant students as well as for indigenous Hawaiian students.	Jacobs argued that women often opt out of mathematics because they reject the way mathematics is currently defined, conceptualised and taught. Rather than accepting that women are at fault, she contented that instructional approaches and mathematical content should capitalise on their preferred learning strategies and interests.

Part 2: *Empirical: two articles*	*Feminist: two articles*
Schwank relied on cognitive science to explain gender-related differences in algorithmic formation in mathematics. In her article (*also in German*) Jungwirth examined gender-related approaches to the use of computers inside the classroom.	The theme of different content for girls (see Jacobs) is continued by Barnes who described a calculus course with content and instructional approach geared to girls' interests and preferences. Niederdrenk-Felgner proposed several changes to the way mathematics is traditionally taught. If implemented, these will `affect classroom interaction, teaching styles, curricula and teachers' behaviour to suit girls.

Table 2: Continued

3. Special issue of *International Journal of Educational Research* (Vol. 21, 1994)

Seven articles in the empirical research tradition

Friedman reported the findings of a meta-analysis of correlations of spatial and mathematical tasks. The results of two meta-analyses examining gender differences in mathematical performance and affect were reported by Frost et al. For high school students enrolled in Algebra II, Fry Bohlin explored the relationships between sex, grades in Algebra I and II and Geometry, mathematics learning styles and interests, and scores on the PSAT-M. Comparisons were made by Druva-Roush of the comprehension skills used in problem-solving for mathematics anxious and non-anxious males and females. Longitudinal gender differences in science achievement and mathematics problem-solving achievement were described by Becker and Forsyth. Using data collected in the Second International Study of Mathematics [SIMS], Hanna examined cross-cultural gender differences in mathematics achievement. Taking several other factors into account, Blithe et al., examined the patterns of gender difference in mathematics performance for students at the secondary-tertiary interface.

---

4. Solar, C., and Lafortune, L. (eds.): 1994, *Des Mathématiques Autrement*, Montréal: Remue-ménage.
The book's six chapters are based on workshops organised by MOIFEM.

Empirical: two chapters

Solar discusses four case studies in which teachers' expectations and treatment of students were gender-differentiated. Included in another chapter are the research findings presented at a colloquium on spatial skills that challenged the existence of gender differences. Summaries are included for each presentation (Mongeau, Pallascio & Allaire; D'Amour; Pallascio & Allaire; and Osta).

Feminist: four chapters

Whether mathematics is experienced differently by male and female mathematicians was the focus of the chapter by Kayler and Caron. In another chapter, the views of four panelists (Morin, Solar, Dumais, and Lafortune) on the roles of feminists in mathematics and in feminist research are presented. A workshop on the mathematical aspects of women's traditional handcrafts is described by Barrette and Lafortune. Mathematics as it relates to the lives of Inuit women is outlined in the chapter by Paquin and Puttayuk.

5. Rogers, P., and Kaiser, G. (eds.): 1995, *Equity in Mathematics Education: Influences of Feminism and Culture*, The Falmer Press, London.

The editors divided this book into three parts. The chapters included in the first section, they claimed, reflected the transition between Phases 3 and 4 of the adapted McIntosh model described earlier in this article. This model evolved from a North American perspective. In the second section, the chapters were grouped to indicate that situations in developing nations might be different from the West. Chapters of the book that have already been discussed or referenced elsewhere in this article are not included in the summary.

Six chapters reflecting the transition between McIntosh's phases 3 and 4

The single-sex 'Summermath' program for females is described by Morrow and Morrow. They outline the background and underlying feminist principles of the program, and discuss the teaching approaches and the learning environment. Based on statistical evidence, Friedman favoured continued efforts to encourage females to enter and complete graduate programs in mathematics. Fullerton discussed a study conducted with women training to become elementary teachers. Factors contributing to low mathematical self-concept were identified and recommendations made. Grevholm discussed the goals of the Swedish Women and Mathematics Network and its origins. The activities of the French-Canadian branch of the International Organisation of Women in Mathematics Education [IOWME] were presented by Solar. Outlined by Niederdrenk-Felgner were the aims and study materials developed by the German Institute for Distance Education's project 'Girls and computers' for the inservice training of teachers using computers in mathematics and other disciplines. The basis for a unique mathematics exhibition, 'Common Threads', displaying only needlework, and its effects on peoples' perceptions of women were discussed by Harris.

Seven chapters incorporating cultural perspectives: traditional empirical research

Brandon et al. suggested factors which may explain why Hawaii females outperform males in mathematics. The subtle ways in which the contents of two major newspapers in Canada and Australia conveyed traditional stereotyped images of males and females were discussed by Leder. Habibullah argued that societal factors in non-Western societies were likely to render the adoption of western strategies to overcome gender inequities in mathematics learning less effective. A review and discussion of Singaporean research on gender issues in mathematics learning were presented by Kaur. Through an examination of the cultural factors influencing girls' education in Papua New Guinea, Sukthankar suggested ways to improve their learning of mathematics. Discussed by Delon were the deleterious consequences on females' studies of mathematics by the move to coeducation in the prestigious French higher education institutions, Écoles Normales Supérieures. The impact of single-sex schooling on the mathematics and science performance of females at university level in Malawi was discussed by Hiddleston.

Six chapters with feminist perspectives The connections between three trends within contemporary feminism – feminism of equality, radical feminism and feminism of difference – and four perspectives on gender imbalance in mathematics – intervention, segregation, discipline, and feminist – are discussed by Mura. A pedagogical approach used to teach mathematics at the college level and its successful outcomes were described by Rogers. Willis argued that appropriate school mathematics curriculum reform would have wider impact on gender formation in schools.	Finding that the interactions between male and female students engaged in mathematical games disadvantaged girls, Higgins proposed classroom strategies and curriculum that were likely to benefit girls. The implications of a group of women's memories of their experiences of mathematisation, as evidenced by their personal stories, were discussed by Johnston. The transmission model that underpins the Dutch approach to mathematics education, Witte argued, serves to inhibit girls' participation in mathematics.

6. Secada, W. G., Fennema, L. B., and Adajian, L. B. (eds.): 1995, *New Directions for Equity in Mathematics Education*, Cambridge University Press, Cambridge.

The editors adopted a broad view of equity in mathematics education. Four chapters were considered to have a specific gender focus by Leder, Campbell, Damarin, and Stanic and Hart. Of the other chapters, gender was not central but was incorporated in the equity perspective (Secada, and Carey et al.), or gender-related data were provided (Keynes), or gender was absent as a variable. Only those chapters in which gender was an important aspect of the view of equity are briefly summarised here.

Three chapters in the empirical research tradition Starting with an historic overview, Leder argued that it was important to consider gender differences in their social context. In-depth, classroom-based studies using alternative research methods to de-emphasise gender differences and explore the effects of contextual factors were advocated. Concerned with the construct of persistence, Stanic and Hart conducted an in-depth study in a multiracial classroom. They emphasised that findings on race differences and gender differences should not be overgeneralised and that the two factors interacted. Carey et al. discussed the implementation of the Cognitively Guided Instruction [CGI] project in one school. They maintained that CGI was one example of the blending of equity concerns with mainstream mathematics education research about children's learning.	*Three chapters with feminist perspectives* In a critical examination of the barriers encountered in moves towards achieving equity, Secada drew attention to the social construction of mathematics education, in particular the norms and beliefs associated with the field. Campbell argued that the previous focus on changing girls in efforts to redress the problem of 'girls and mathematics' had not been entirely successful. Several intervention projects, including extracurricular activities, and suggestions for the classroom aimed at achieving gender equity were discussed. Recent developments in feminist scholarship and their applicability to the fields of mathematics and mathematics education were the focus of Damarin's chapter.

7. Grevholm, B. and Hanna, G. (eds.): 1995, *Gender and Mathematics Education: An ICMI Study*, Lund University Press, Lund, Sweden.

The sections of this book represent the various forums of the ICMI gender study conference. The issues addressed covered the range of key areas outlined by Hanna and Nyhof-Young in their chapter on the rationale for the ICMI study: factors creating gender inequities in mathematics—attitudes, culture, and mathematics as a discipline; manifestations of gender inequities—jobs and careers, girls and technology; foci for change—curriculum, assessment, teachers and the school, and working with parents. Reported research involved traditional empirical research paradigms and feminist perspectives. Studies conducted in both developed and developing nations were included.

Plenary addresses: Fennema spoke of the need for new directions in scholarship. While much had been learnt from research using traditional social science empirical research paradigms, Fennema asserted that research based in cognitive science and feminist perspectives held great promise for future developments in the field. Gray identified a number of strategies and research questions to recruit more women into graduate programs in mathematics. The similarities and differences in gender perspectives on physics and mathematics education were discussed by Beyer.

Panel discussions: The opening panel addressed the range of issues relevant to the conference's rationale (Hanna, Jacobbson, Keitel, Kristjànsdóttir, and Leder). Feminist perspectives were explored by Burton, Damarin, Koblitz and Ruskai. Burton offered five areas defining an epistemological perspective on mathematics based on the writings of mathematicians and feminist philosophers of science. Damarin discussed the feminist writings influencing her work. Koblitz illustrated how theories or explanations suggesting essentialism did not account for culture, race, and class in different nations around the globe; in particular, diverse cultural and historical patterns were revealed when gender and mathematics interacted. Ruskai pointed to the dangers of judgments based on essentialist premises while ignoring individual attributes. Adda, Brandell, Hag and Sadolsky explored the roles of organisations in addressing gender and mathematics education. Various research perspectives were examined by Beyer, Jungwirth, Kimball and Staberg.

Table 2: Continued

Paper presentations: *1. Empirical research tradition.* ***Topics***: statistical data on mathematics education outcomes examined by gender in France (Adda), Sweden (Grevholm), Japan (Senuma), and Prague gymnasia (Kadlezek, Odvárko, & Troják); In New Zealand, gender issues associated with tertiary statistics examination questions (Blithe & Clark), national calculus examinations (Reilly, Morton & Lee), and women in tertiary mathematics (Thornley); anxiety and confidence as determinants of college major selection (Chipman, Krantz, & Silver); means to empower young women in mathematics (Cordeau); mathematics anxiety in boys and girls (Dunkels); difficulties with putting mathematical questions 'in context' (Evans); gender-bias in assessment (Forbes); attitudes of girls in mixed and single-sex mathematics classrooms (Forgasz); women's participation in tertiary mathematics in Australia (Gaffney); gender issues and TIMSS (Grønmo), and in primary classrooms (Haynes); interpretation of teacher-student interactions (Jungwirth); qualitative aspects of mathematics and learning (Keitel); gender, performance factors and multiple-choice formats (Leder & Taylor); gender and mathematics issues in Portugal (Ralha), Kuwait (Saif), Papua New Guinea (Sukthankar), China (Tang), and in American classrooms (Revak); spatial performance and computers (Reiss & Albrecht);	*2. Interventions.* ***Topics:*** gender-inclusive calculus curricula (Barnes); increasing female participation in the University of Minnesota Talented Youth Mathematics program (Cavallo & Bibelnieks); encouraging positive attitudes (Jones & Smart) *3. Feminist perspectives.* ***Topics:*** implications for gender and mathematics derived from feminist science (Damarin); gender-differentiated dealings with mathematics in everyday life (Knight & Thornley); issues associated with an 'inclusive' pedagogy (Solar); construction of gender in the science classroom (Staberg)

NB. Articles and chapters described in these summaries have not been included as separate entries in the reference list.

Major themes and research perspectives found in these publications can be summarised as follows:

— Research in the empirical tradition continues to dominate.
— Quantitative, as against qualitative, studies are more prevalent, irrespective of the country in which the research is located.
— Affective variables continue to attract research attention.
— Increasingly, authors draw on multiple research methods to plan their studies and analyse their data. This is an important development.

- Drawing on publications other than those found in the traditional, mainstream journals yielded a broader perspective. In particular, work exploring feminist theories was identified. However, there was some overlap in the authorship, ideas, and studies found in the collected volumes.
- Authors tended to draw on publications written in their own language. Work written in English has the largest penetration.
- There was considerable interest in gender issues relevant for those engaged in post-compulsory education

The work reviewed in Tables 1 and 2 illustrates the fact that gender issues in mathematics education have been, and continue to be, explored internationally. The contents of Table 2 also reveal an increased diversity in the inquiry methods used to examine and unpack contributing factors. More radical feminist perspectives are being adopted, women are less frequently considered as a homogeneous group, and scholarly evaluations of interventions are becoming more prevalent.

The effects of interventions have been felt by many who otherwise may not have pursued studies in mathematics or related fields. Yet intervention programs and strategies are rarely reported in research journals, even though links with research are often apparent. Some initiatives were described in the edited books mentioned earlier (also see Table 2), others in special reports authored by established researchers, or in publications aimed at practitioners. Consistent with our belief that the gap that often exists between research and practice should be bridged, we now turn to intervention studies. Attaining equity in mathematics education depends on the implementation of research activities through appropriate programs, interventions and initiatives such as those discussed in the next section. The review includes examples of different intervention orientations but cannot claim to be exhaustive.

4.   INTERVENTION PROGRAMS

On December 6, 1989,
at the Ecole polytechnique de Montréal,
a young man entered an engineering classroom.
He ordered women to stand on one side,
men on the other side.
He shot the women.
Then he walked through the school
and shot some other women.[2]

4.1 Introduction

Intervention programs aim to foster change in the sex and race composition of specific fields of study and work in which women and minorities are still underrepresented. Initially promoted by women, they are increasingly becoming national concerns. Men's voices have joined women's in striving for inclusiveness in male-dominated fields such as mathematics. In countries where gender imbalance has been uncovered and where equity values have been absorbed into political philosophy, attempts to attract and retain women in mathematics have taken place over the last two decades.

Research on women and mathematics began in the USA during the 1960's, through projects such as TALENT (Wise, 1985), at a time when the Women's Studies Movement was in its early stages of development (Porter and Eileenchild, 1980). General intervention programs and programs for minorities started in the period 1965-1969. Women's intervention programs began later, 1970-1974, with great expansion during the International Decade of Women, 1975-1984 (Malcolm, 1984).

This part of the chapter deals with intervention programs. An attempt is made to provide a synthesis of the range of activities and of their results. The emphasis is on providing a general overview of the different orientations dealing with the issue, rather than on presenting an exhaustive picture of the various projects conducted throughout the world. To do this, we have built on Malcolm's (1984) extensive research on intervention programs. Subsequent analyses have tended to corroborate the findings of this thorough study.

4.2 A General Overview

Intervention programs are numerous and their multiplicity in some countries is overwhelming. Between 1976 and 1981, the *Women in Science* program of the National Science Foundation, in the United States, funded 136 projects (Malcolm, 1984). By 1980 the American Association for the Advancement of Science had compiled over 300 interventions in *Programs in Science, Mathematics, and Engineering for Women in the United States* (Aldrich and Hall, 1980, cited in Davis and Humphreys, 1985). According to Clewell, Anderson and Thorpe (1992) there were over 160 mathematics and science intervention programs for minority and female students in grades 4 through 8 in 1992. The regular surveys of the *Women in Engineering Programs* (WIEP) showed that the number of intervention activities in that field more than doubled from 395 in 1975 to 859 in 1991 (Wadsworth, 1993). These figures reflect only part of the reality. Indeed it is difficult to estimate the exact number of intervention programs which have been carried out in the United States, and elsewhere, and this is especially true if a broad definition of 'intervention' is used, including individual initiatives as well as efforts within institutions and schools (see, for example, Barnes and Coupland, 1990; Barnes, 1994; Rogers, 1995).

Intervention programs usually combine mathematics with engineering, sciences or computer science, with the last most frequently integrated within other areas. Mathematics was represented in 50 per cent, 70 per cent and 76 per cent respectively of the contents of general, women's and minority mathematics projects listed in Malcolm's (1984) survey. The mix of mathematics with the sciences was also found for Canada in the Nova Scotia Women's Directorate (1994) compilation of programs (Québec was not included in the survey). Of the 92 cited, only 18 included mathematics as a named component, and only five had mathematics in the title. In Québec, the government's efforts have usually been geared towards non-traditional work (see, for example, Berthellot and Mailloux, 1985; Barrette, 1986; Poitras and Berthellot, 1986; Yergeau, 1988).

Mathematics intervention programs, such as *Math Equals* (Perl, 1978) and *Multiplying Options and Subtracting Bias* (Fennema, Becker, Wolleat and Pedro, 1980), are usually promoted by women in mathematics education or by specific mathematics associations such as MOIFEM[3] (the Québec and French-speaking section of Canada's IOWME). Unless intervention programs are described in publications or evaluated in reports, they become inaccessible, sink into oblivion and the ideas and outcomes are lost to future development. In particular, lack of evaluations has been a weakness of many programs (Lantz, 1985; Brainard, 1993; Gray, 1995). More often, if undertaken at all, evaluations are limited to the reactions of participants (see Nova Scotia Women's Directorate, 1994).

The USA has a long history of intervention programs, starting in the 1960's, well ahead of Canada, the UK, other European countries, and Australia. Each of these nations is now known for its activities on equity issues in general, and on the promotion of women in science in particular. It is therefore worth examining some of the trends over the 35-year span in order to build possible analogies for other countries and different cultures.

4.3   Historical and Political Influences on Intervention Programs

The civil rights movement in the USA created a desire for change, fuelling many intervention programs which sought methods to achieve such change (Malcolm, 1984). Initially local, these programs answered specific needs and used local human and financial resources (Malcolm, 1984; Anderson, 1993). Reflecting the ideology of equity, their primary goals were to attract and retain women and girls in mathematics and science. Many programs which started outside schools eventually ended up inside.

Initially, during the 1960's the school levels targeted were mainly precollegial or high school (Anderson, 1993). However, during the 1980's, it was recognised that the problem of the underrepresentation of women started at an earlier age (Berryman, 1983; Anderson, 1993), and the scope of intervention programs broadened to include elementary schools (Miller, 1993; Wadsworth, 1993).

Despite the many local initiatives that had been put in place in earlier years, national recognition for intervention programs for women and minorities did not emerge until the 1980's. At that time, financial support became available for substantial analyses of the effectiveness of intervention programs – see, for example, Malcolm (1984) for details of one undertaken by the American Association for the Advancement of Science. Changes in the demography of the workforce, and in the economic need for scientists to maintain the competitiveness and leadership of the USA, propelled the issue of women and minorities in mathematics-related fields and careers from concerns about equity into the free market ideology. The following quotation is typical of this new perspective:

> If population trends continue as expected and if the participation of minorities in the sciences remains abnormally skewed, then the availability of an educated, scientifically literate workforce needed to meet the challenge of a highly competitive economy will continue to be at risk.
>
> (Matthews, 1990, p.CRS-63).

The attraction and retention of women and minorities in these fields is now considered so economically strategic that the National Science Foundation, with Congress' influence, has established a program to 'encourage improvements in science, mathematics, and engineering education through comprehensive systemic changes in the education systems of the states' (Clarke, 1994, p.1). In 1994, 25 states and Puerto Rico received five-year grants averaging about $9.5 million each. This new orientation in funding is expected to result in institutional change, unlike previous funding that targeted efforts outside institutions, be they government, universities, industry or professions.

While a greater emphasis on women's needs is consistent with feminists' interest in attracting and retaining women in scientific careers, the shift in the rhetoric away from women's issues towards broad economic and governmental concerns is not unproblematic. Unless special efforts are made to change scientific learning and working environments, there is no guarantee of any improvement in gender equity. Mura (1995) noted that 'it is important to keep in mind the distinction between the goal of increasing women's participation and the goal of redressing gender imbalance' (p.160). Governments' goals are usually directed towards the former rather than the latter.

In summary, the history of intervention programs in the USA illustrates a shift from an ideology of equity to a free market ideology, from strategies outside schools and educational institutions to within educational walls, from targeted populations of women at times of career decision-making or learning (precollegial) to younger ages (elementary), from individual initiative to national concern, and from non-institutional changes to systemic changes. In addition, the history also shows that intervention programs are often not widely disseminated or evaluated, rarely deal with mathematics alone, make mathematics one of the basic prerequisites for scientific careers and, to some extent, limit mathematics to a service discipline. Similar trends are evident in other Western countries.

In the next section the different purposes for intervention programs and the various forms they have taken are described.

4.4   Program Types

'Intervention programs are typically implemented to effect some change in the status quo' (Brainard, 1993, p.23), and usually 'employ approaches that differ from those of the traditional school system' (Anderson, 1993, p.32). There is a close relationship between intervention programs for women and research on gender and mathematics and science education – see for example, *Multiplying Options and Subtracting Bias* (Fennema et al., 1980; Fennema, Wolleat, Pedro and Becker, 1981), and the *Scientifines* (Chamberland, Théorêt, Garon and Roy, 1995). That information gathered from research can be translated into action through intervention programs is made explicit in the recommendation suggested for teachers by Leder and Forgasz (1995). The forms of the actual changes desired often shape the type of actions taken.

There are many different ways of classifying intervention programs. One difficulty is that they often contain several components. Hence, different types of classifiers can be used to describe a particular program.

4.5   Classification by Time

A convenient classifier is time. Davis and Humphreys (1985) used this classification to distinguish between short-term and long-term interventions. Short-term programs included activities such as conferences and workshops. 'Many women's projects are one-day workshops designed to impart career information' (Malcolm, 1984, p.10). The *Expanding Your Horizons* conference initiated in 1976 by the Mills Women's College and reproduced by others (Sebrechts, 1993) and *Be a Sumbody* (Burton and Townsend, 1986) are typical examples of short-term interventions on careers. Examples of workshops are presented in *Les Femmes Font des Maths* (Lafortune and Kayler, 1992).

Long-term programs tackle classroom activities and curriculum content. They often combine different approaches, as is illustrated by the *Women in*

970

Engineering Programs (Brainard, 1993), and are usually recognised as the most effective.

4.6 Classification by School Calendar

When discussing middle-school interventions for minority females, Anderson (1993) used Matyas and Malcolm's (1991) five groupings:

1) Programs conducted during the school year, including after school and Saturday programs. (*Example:* the *METRO Achievement Program* – Thompson, 1995)
2) Summer programs. *(Examples:* the non-residential METRO summer program; and the residential *SummerMath Program* at Mount Holyoke (women's) College – Morrow and Morrow, 1995).
3) Career fairs and outreach recruiting programs. These are often paired with college programs in science and engineering.
4) Research apprenticeship programs 'that enable students to engage in research projects with the assistance of scientists and engineers' (Anderson, 1993, p.34). *(Example*: the research internship at Dartmouth University – Muller, 1993).
5) Inservice programs for teachers. *(Example:* teachers are frequent participants in MOIFEM activities in Québec. They were also one of the targeted groups for the *Multiplying Options and Subtracting Bias* intervention program – see Fennema et al., 1981.)

4.7 Classification by Targeted Population

Intervention programs can also be classified in terms of the groups they target. Most intervention programs in mathematics, science and engineering surveyed in this chapter were designed for female students. Many have targeted minority groups or the wider public. Examples include single-sex girls schools, projects in women's colleges (Sebrechts, 1993) and programs such as EUREKA at Brooklyn College (Miller and Silver, 1993).

In some cases programs planned for female students are restricted for some activities but open to male students for others. This often occurs for programs in elementary or secondary schools and, in particular, when media such as videos are used. The videos accompanying *Multiplying Options and Subtracting Bias* (Fennema et al., 1981) targeted several groups involved in the education of girls: students, teachers, counsellors and parents. General publicity campaigns such as *Maths Multiplies Your Choices*, described in Leder and Forgasz (1992), also have wide penetration and reach broad audiences. Targeting teachers, the video *Au Fait les Filles! Filles et Sciences* (1995) provided information collected from an intervention project to Lycées and Collège science teachers. Parents seem to be targeted less often. *Family Math*, developed at the Lawrence Hall of Science (University of California, Berkeley) is one notable exception that has been exported to other states and countries (Vasey, 1989; Rodgers, 1990).

Malcolm's (1984) survey, which gathered data about 167 intervention programs in the USA, including 54 women's projects, 95 minority projects and 18 general projects, revealed that they were mainly run by universities, museums or research centres and that urban populations were generally better served by interventions than were the populations of rural areas.

4.8   Classification by Location: Within or Outside Educational Institutions

Another way of classifying programs is by their location – within schools and institutions, or outside them. Outside programs are often run by professional associations or produced by governments (for example, Canada's video *Rap-O-Matics/Rap-O-Matiques*). Some short-term interventions outside schools and institutions have gained international recognition and have been widely embraced. *Common Threads*, for example, brought traditional women's work into the mathematical arena via an exhibit that travelled internationally (Harris, 1995).

4.9   Program Strategies

To be effective, intervention programs should have attainable goals, appropriately set for a specific population. The selection of strategies should also reflect the needs and interests of the targeted population. Options may vary from distributing flyers to orchestrating a state campaign; from reviewing one's teaching practices to opening a new school; from targeting only women to intervening with all relevant adults and peers; from mentoring to teaching; from changing the teaching approach of subject matter to transforming the subject; or from tackling aspects of the problem to tackling the problem as systemic.

Experience has shown that intervention programs can be effective. In the next section some critical determinants of success are presented.

4.10   Elements of Success

Over a decade ago, Malcolm (1984) had already noted that programs were successful if 'they involve(d) the students in the "doing" of science and mathematics and convey(ed) a sense of their utility' (p.vii). More recently, they have succeeded when, according to Muller (1993),

972

institutions provide early, hands-on research experience, create a network of faculty and student mentors, arrange visits with technical professionals outside academia, and offer financial aid packages that enable science students to spend their time on lab work, rather than on part-time jobs outside the institution. (p.43)

Other writers have reported success through 'direct instruction, academic counselling, advisers and role models, guest speakers, and field trips' (Anderson, 1993, p.34).

Constant, regular evaluation is needed if programs are to adapt to the changing needs of groups. From this perspective, the strategies used to set up the *Women in Engineering* program in Seattle are instructive. From the start, female students were members of a committee mandated with defining the barriers they faced. Initially, the project was small. It involved tutoring, peer mentoring, professional mentoring and support group meetings. The process created its own synergy: 'students exhibit(ed) pride in their programs and in turn receive(d) praise for their accomplishments' (Brainard, 1993, p.25). From an organisational point of view, Brainard (1993) presented a number of prerequisite conditions for successful implementation including:

commitment and support from the top, a designated director of the program, a reasonable and adequate budget, assistance in fund-raising, faculty commitment, a system of accountability, and student involvement in designing and implementing programs. (p.23)

The program now includes: peer mentoring, professional mentoring, faculty mentoring, tutoring, freshman intervention programs, a study centre for women in engineering, a study class for women in engineering, international exchanges, scholarships and fellowships, support groups, seminars, an annual women in engineering conference, summer outreach programs for high school students, publications (newsletter, resource directory, and conference proceedings), and an annual evaluation by the corporate advisory board, the faculty advisory board, the students and the staff.

Evaluation fostered close links between perceived needs and activities organised, and this resulted in the disappearance of some activities and the development of others. The program is recognised as a national model by the National Research Council and the National Science Foundation in the USA. Brainard (1993) attributed much of the success of the program to the students' involvement and ownership. Participation by women increased from 10 per cent at the beginning of the program to 68 per cent in four years.

4.11 Creating New Organisations and Institutions

The previous example illustrated a successful program mounted from within an existing institution. Another strategy is to create a completely new organisation, as happened with the Linden School in Metropolitan Toronto (Canada). It is a 'feminist', private single-sex school which opened in 1993. In 1995 the enrolment was nearly 100 girls (Moore and Goudie, 1995). The teaching staff has experience and knowledge of feminist perspectives on teaching, learning and content. The school has classes from grade 4 through 12, has started developing its own teaching materials, is women-centred (Rich, 1975), and uses pedagogical strategies including collaboration, negotiation, group work, cooperative teaching and learning. This applies to all subjects, including mathematics. The young women in the school are constantly being asked what they think and why; they cannot remain silent and passive. This strategy is rarely used consistently throughout a whole school and promises much potential for researchers and activists.

4.12 Teaching and Learning Strategies

When it comes to the teaching and learning aspects of intervention programs, most reports have highlighted the need for and the effectiveness of group work, cooperative learning and collaborative approaches in contrast to individualised or competitive learning strategies (Becker, 1995, p.170). Emphasis has been placed on providing investigative activities, legitimating women's 'common sense' knowledge, giving them confidence in their ability to learn new mathematics, creating a climate conducive to enjoying work, and on sharing experiences, activities and ideas (Isaacson, 1990, p.21). Much has been achieved – see, for example, chapters in Burton (1990). And yet, practice and theory are often inconsistent: 'there is considerable evidence that mathematics teaching at all levels neither exemplifies connected teaching, nor encourages constructed knowing' (Becker, 1995, p.170).

In summary, the best intervention programs use strategies that are not only effective for females but for all students. They respond to the needs of participants, involve 'hands-on' activities, tutoring, mentoring (or role models), the establishment of some kind of networking among students, between students and teachers, or between students and professionals. That is, a mathematical environment is created in which females are welcome and invited to contribute, a world in which they, and others, believe they can succeed. Active participation is integral to the definition and evaluation of programs. An atmosphere conducive to collaboration, exchange and dialogue is developed.

4.13 Characteristics of Exemplary Programs

Exemplary programs are those worth copying and using as models. In the search for equity and excellence, the following criteria used by Malcolm (1984) to assess programs are still useful:

— achievement of primary goals as measured by staff, participants or external evaluation;
— length of time of the program's operation;
— ease in attracting outside support;
— ratio of applicants to participants (program popularity);
— reputation of program with scientists from relevant fields;
— program 'imitation' or internal expansion;
— cost effectiveness;
— the strength of the academic content; and
— the competence and orientation of teachers for programs with an academic orientation.

Also needed are targeted recruitment strategies, staff who empathise with the target population, parental involvement, and a developed base of community and organisational support. Wherever and whenever it is appropriate, 'mainstreaming' should be considered so that program elements supportive of women and minorities are integrated into institutional programs.

4.14 Common Elements Emerging from the Analysis

Most intervention programs continue to be voluntary. That is, there is no coercion to implement institutional change or to enrol females from targeted groups. Participation is also voluntary. Even the contemporary state initiatives in the USA, described earlier, are not compulsory. Thus the ability to offer intervention programs is still largely dependent on efforts to gain financial support from governments and other sources, and on the enthusiasm of committed individuals.

Another aspect that emerges from the literature on intervention programs is the scarcity of mainstream curriculum change or of innovative practice within educational systems. Mathematics course content is rarely questioned, despite new insights into the epistemology of the discipline (Mura, 1986; Damarin, 1990, 1991, 1994, 1995; Burton, 1995). The degree of freedom in course content and program structures is only evident in intervention programs outside educational systems, such as summer activities, summer camps, and retreats. These programs are often based on women-centred approaches to mathematics education. The transition of long-term programs from outside educational institutions to the inside has the potential to benefit and change mainstream curriculum.

975

Single-sex schooling has been an important feature in some countries, for example, the United Kingdom, Australia, and countries where religious custom favours this educational setting. In Western countries with a long history of single-sex provisions, the benefits to females of such segregation are increasingly being questioned (Gill, 1988). The learning setting, co-educational or single-sex, is but one of many factors influencing women's learning outcomes. The Potsdam College example described by Rogers (1990) is instructive, in that it emphasised the importance of the pedagogical approach adopted. The almost exclusively male staff of that small co-educational college shared a common belief that students could learn the course material. Such an expectation is a criterion included among the list for exemplary academic-based programs.

The following list of commonalities emerged from a careful reading of the descriptions of intervention programs – for more details, see Solar (1995):
- mathematics as a human activity, including contexts that appeal to female learners;
- learners as active participants in the learning process, with group work and cooperative activities;
- a pedagogy that requires the learner to build on mathematical understandings and where the teacher facilitates the construction of knowledge and developing understandings;
- teachers who are unbiased and believe in women's potential;
- a willingness to validate women's mathematical experience and common sense;
- an ideology of gender, class and ethnicity equity;
- safe and enjoyable learning environments;
- a willingness to develop the learner's confidence through success.

Details of many intervention programs have been provided in published materials distributed under the auspices of the International Organisation of Women in Mathematics Education (IOWME) and MOIFEM. The recent ICMI study on 'gender and mathematics' (Grevholm and Hanna, 1995) would not have occurred without the efforts of IOWME members. IOWME has been an important international forum for the exchange of ideas, the initiation of research projects, and the dissemination of findings.

Two major concerns emerge from the overview of intervention programs. First, the language used in some key official documents about equity issues appears to be changing. For example, no mention is made of gender in the statement of equity principles developed by the National Research Council (1993), in the United States of America. Terminology changes – from 'equality for women' to 'sex equity', 'gender equity', then to 'gender and racial equity' and 'gender, race and class equity' – have resulted in the use of the generic term 'equity' which no longer focuses on females. Coincidentally, articles focusing on gender issues have been less prevalent in mainstream mathematics education journals in recent years. Compared to the 10 per cent of articles found in JRME during the 1980's (discussed earlier in the chapter), none was found in the 1990-1994 volumes.

Second, at a quite different level, there seems to be an overwhelming concentration of interventions which use, exploit or claim to rely on the notion of 'connectedness'. This construct, emerging from the work of Gilligan (1982) and Belenky et al. (1986) is becoming a new absolutism. These authors have presented two major perspectives grounded in research on women. The notions of 'separation' and 'connection' on the one hand, and 'women's ways of knowing' on the other are very powerful tools to understand the relationship between gender and mathematics, and to develop strategies for change.

These models have their own limits. They emerged from a socio-cultural context in which a woman's traditional role is one of caring and of cooperation in managing family life. The systematic use of these models might lock women into their traditional roles and could jeopardise the discovery of new perspectives. One of the feminist gains of the last decade is the claim that there is not just 'one' model of 'woman' but that they are many women, from different origins, different cultures, and different religions. When used judiciously, however, research and implementation based on the models can be helpful and insightful.

CONCLUSION

In this chapter, we have attempted to give an overview of research foci and trends by 'reviewing' major journals and collected volumes. A similar attempt was made for intervention programs. However, it must be noted that the languages available to us as authors (English, French, Dutch and Spanish), and the difficulty in accessing work published in many languages other than English, have imposed limits on our analysis. Consequently, we may have missed some very interesting and different reviews, research, and reports of intervention programs that might have extended our understanding of the complexity of the issue and of the changes required.

Participation and performance data have been gathered in many countries. Knowledge about gender and mathematics education is not limited to highly technological societies. However, there is a difference in the range of issues and research perspectives in writings from developed Western countries and developing nations. Where equity has been an issue for more than two decades and active feminist movements exist, male norms are more likely to be challenged. Also, claims for acceptance of difference without value judgements are more likely to be questioned, and feminist critiques which raise new questions on gender and mathematics education are more likely to be used.

Data from intervention programs and from other countries have drawn attention to the role of culture. Women's social, sexual, and family roles are usually considered in a general framework for understanding the status of women in society and the status of mathematics in women's lives. In this context, feminist critiques of the disciplines, and qualitative methods, can play a role in providing renewed insight into equity issues in mathematics education.

Gilligan's (1982) work serves as a good example. She succeeded in reviewing the concept of moral development when it was noticed that women rarely succeeded in reaching the higher levels of Kohlberg's scales (see Golombok and Fivush, 1994). Similarly, after 20 years of research and intervention programs, the interpretation of the consistent pattern of 'lack of confidence' and 'lower self-esteem' found for girls and women is being questioned, for example, by Davis and Steiger (1994). They argue that 'the way in which individuals view success and failure is a highly gendered matter' (p.152) and opens the way to a reconceptualisation of previously accepted concepts. A further example is provided by the approach to the teaching of calculus developed by Barnes (1995) in which females' experiences and interest have explicitly informed the settings of the mathematical problems used in the program.

Looking more closely at women's lives, experience, responsibilities, and work can also be of value in modifying myths about women and mathematics. Experiences like *Common Threads* surprise by their success. But the search for mathematics in women's lives is appealing to females, and Harris (1995) is not alone in bringing new contextualisations of mathematical problems. Dumont and Pasquis (1979) have done the same in France and Barrette and Lafortune (1994) in Québec. Further insights and understandings about gender and mathematics can result from studying adult women. This group is less often targeted in research and intervention programs. This assumes that mathematics learning stops after formal schooling and initial professional training.

Traditional empirical research monitoring females' participation and performance in mathematics and related career activities should continue, as should documenting the effects of intervention programs. Whatever strategies are used to extend our knowledge and understanding of women's mathematics learning, be they informed by more classical approaches or by feminist critiques, within traditional classroom settings or intervention programs, it is worth remembering that these approaches are complementary. Scholars concerned with girls' and women's learning of mathematics now have a solid basis of research, achieved in less than 30 years, on which to build new agendas for the attainment of gender equity in mathematics education.

ENDNOTES

1. We wish to thank Teresa Smart for her helpful comments on an earlier version of this chapter.
2. In this tragic incident, 13 female students and one female staff member were killed. The perpetrator believed that women had usurped his rightful place in engineering and in society.
3. Mouvement International pour les Femmes et l'Enseignement des Mathématiques.

REFERENCES

Anderson, B.T.: 1993, 'Minority Females in the Science Pipeline: Activities to Enhance Readiness, Recruitment, and Retention', *Initiatives* 55(3), 31-38.
Au Fait les Filles! Filles et Sciences: 1995, Video, 13 minutes, UNESCO, Rectorate de Dion, Delegation Droits des Femmes, Centre audio-visual de l'Université de Bourgogne, Dijon. France.
Barnes, M.: 1994, 'Investigating Change: A Gender-inclusive Course in Calculus', *Zentralblatt für Didactik der Mathematik* 25(2), 49-56.
Barnes, M.: 1995, 'Integration: Making Connections', in J. Wakefield and L. Velardi (eds.), *Celebrating Mathematics Learning*, Mathematical Association of Victoria, Melbourne, 210-214.
Barnes, M. and Coupland, M.: 1990, 'Humanizing Calculus: A Case Study in Curriculum Development', in L. Burton (ed.), *Gender and Mathematics: An International Perspective*, Cassell, London, 72-80.
Barrette, D.: 1986, *Accès aux Carrières Technologiques: Guide de la Formatrice*, Ministère de l'Éducation, Québec.
Barette, M. and Lafortune, L.: 1994, 'Dentelle Mathématique', in C. Solar and L. Lafortune (eds.), *Des Mathématiques Autrement*, Remue-ménage, Montréal, 115-169.
Becker, R.J.: 1995, 'Women's Ways of Knowing Mathematics', in P. Rogers and G. Kaiser (eds.), *Equity in Mathematics Education: Influences of Feminism and Culture*, Falmer Press, London, 163-174.
Belenky, M.F., Clinchy, B.M., Goldberger, N.R. and Tarule, J.M.: 1986, *Women's Ways of Knowing: The Development of Self, Voice and Mind*, Basic Books Inc., New York.
Bell, E.T.: 1937, *Men of Mathematics*, Simon and Schuster, New York.
Berryman, S.: 1983, *Who Will Do Science? Trends and their Causes in Minority and Female Representation among Holders of Advanced Degrees in Science and Mathematics*, Rockefeller Foundation, New York.
Berthelot, M. and Mailloux, T.: 1985, *Explorons de Nouveaux Espaces*, Conseil du Statut de la Femme, Ministère de l'Éducation & Ministère de la Science et de la Technologie, Québec.
Birenbaum, M. and Kraemer, R.: 1992, 'Effects of Gender and Ethnicity on Students' Perceptions of Mathematics and Language Study', *Journal of Research and Development in Education* 26(1), 30-37.
Brainard, S.G.: 1993, 'Student Ownership: The Key to Successful Intervention Programs', *Initiatives* 55(3), 23-30.
Burton, L. (ed): 1990, *Gender and Mathematics: An International Perspective*, Cassell, London.

Burton, L.: 1995, 'Moving Towards a Feminist Epistemology of Mathematics', *Educational Studies in Mathematics* 28(3), 275-291.

Burton, L. and Townsend, R.: 1986, 'Girl-friendly Mathematics', in L. Burton (ed.), *Girls into Maths Can Go*, Holt, Rinehart & Winston, London, 187-195.

Butler, W.: 1801, *Arithmetical Questions, on a New Plan: Designed as a Supplement to the Author's Engraved Introduction to Arithmetic; and Intended to Answer the Double Purpose of Arithmetical Instruction and Miscellaneous Information* (3rd ed., enlarged), S. Couchman, Throgmorton-Street, London.

Central Statistical Office.: 1994, *Annual Abstract of Statistics, 1994,* HMSO, London.

Chamberland, C., Théorêt, M., Garon, R. and Roy, D: 1995, *Les Scientifines en Action: Conception, Implantation et Évaluation*, Faculté des Arts et des Science, École de Service Social, Université de Montréal, Montréal.

Cheung, K.C.: 1988, 'Outcomes of Schooling: Mathematics Achievement and Attitudes Towards Mathematics Learning in Hong Kong', *Educational Studies in Mathematics*, 19, 209-219.

Clarke, M.: 1994, *Achieving Equity in Mathematics, Science, and Engineering Education: In Brief*, National Governor's Association, Washington, DC

Clarkson, P.C. and Leder, G.C.: 1984, 'Causal Attributions for Success and Failure in Mathematics: A Cross-cultural Perspective', *Educational Studies in Mathematics* 15, 413-422.

Clewell, B.C., Anderson, B.T. and Thorpe, M.E.: 1992, 'The Prevalence and Nature of Mathematics, Science, and Computer Science Intervention Programs Serving Minority and Female Students in Grades Four Through Eight', *Equity and Excellence* 25, 209-215.

Cockcroft, W.H. (Chair): 1982, *Mathematics Counts*, Her Majesty's Stationery Office, London.

Damarin, S.K.: 1990, 'Teaching Mathematics: A Feminist Perspective', in T.J. Cooney and C.R. Hirsch (eds.), *Teaching and Learning Mathematics in the 1990's*, National Council of Teachers of Mathematics, 1990 Yearbook, 144-151.

Damarin, S.K.: 1991, 'Rethinking Science and Mathematics Curriculum and Instruction: Feminist Perspectives in the Computer Era', *Journal of Education* 173(1), 107-123.

Damarin, S.K.: 1994, April 7, 'Genders, Mathematics, and Feminisms', in Research on Gender and Mathematics Symposium, American Educational Research Association Annual Meeting *Research on Gender and Mathematics: Perspectives and New Directions*, New Orleans, 8-11.

Damarin, S.K.: 1995, 'Gender and Mathematics from a Feminist Standpoint', in W.G. Secada, E. Fennema and L.B. Adajian (eds.), *New Directions for Equity in Mathematics Education*, Cambridge University Press, Cambridge, 242-257.

Davis, B.G. and Humphreys, S.: 1985, *Evaluating Intervention Programs: Application from Women's Programs in Math and Science*, Teachers College, Columbia University, New York, London.

Davis, F. and Steiger, A.: 1994, 'Self-confidence in Women's Education: A Feminist Critique', in P. Bourne, P. Masters, N. Amin, M. Gonick and L. Gribowski (eds.), *Feminism and Education: A Canadian Perspective*, Centre for Women's Studies in Education, Ontario Institute for Studies in Education, Toronto, 143-160.

Dumont, M. and Pasquis, F.: 1979, *Mathématiques Pour la Tête et les Mains*, CEDIC, Paris.

Fennema, E.: 1974, 'Mathematics Learning and the Sexes: A Review', *Journal for Research in Mathematics Education*, 5(3), 126-139.

Fennema, E.: 1990, 'Justice, Equity, and Mathematics Education', in E. Fennema and G.C. Leder (eds.), *Mathematics and Gender*, Teachers College Press, New York, 1-9.

Fennema, E.: 1995, 'Mathematics, Gender and Research', in B. Grevholm and G. Hanna (eds.), *Gender and Mathematics Education*, Lund University Press, Lund, 21-35.

Fennema, E. and Hart, L.: 1994, 'Gender and the JRME', *Journal for Research in Mathematics Education* 25(6), 648-659.

Fennema, E. and Leder, G.C. (eds.): 1990, *Mathematics and Gender,* Teachers' College Press, New York.

Fennema, E., Wolleat, P. and Pedro, J.D.: 1979, 'Mathematics Attribution Scale', *JSAS: Catalog of Selected Documents in Psychology* 9(5), 26 (Ms No. 1837).

Fennema, E., Becker, A. D., Wolleat, P. and Pedro, J.D.: 1980, *Multiplying Options and Subtracting Bias*, Educational Development Corporation, Cambridge, Massachussetts.

Fennema, E., Wolleat, P., Pedro, J.D. and Becker, A.D.: 1981, 'Increasing Women's Participation in Mathematics: An Intervention Study', *Journal for Research in Mathematics Education* 12(1), 3-14.

Forbes, S., 1995, 'Mathematics and New Zealand Maori Girls', in P. Rogers and G. Kaiser (eds.), *Equity in Mathematics Education: Influences of Feminism and Culture*, Falmer Press, London, 109-116.

Forgasz, H.J.: 1994, *Society and Gender Equity in Mathematics Education*, Deakin University Press, Geelong, Victoria.

Garcia, J., Harrison, N.R. and Torres, J.L.: 1990, 'The Portrayal of Females and Minorities in Selected Elementary Mathematics Series', *School Science and Mathematics*, 90(1), 2-12.

Gill, J.: 1988, *Which Way to School? A Review of the Evidence on the Single Sex Versus Coeducation Debate and an Annotated Bibliography of the Research*, Curriculum Development Centre, Canberra.

Gilligan, C.: 1982, *In a Different Voice*, Harvard University Press, Cambridge, Massachussetts.

Goldstein, C.:1992, 'On ne Naît pas Mathématician', *Autrement: Numéro Spécial sur 'Le Sexe des Sciences'*, 6, 143-155.

Golombok, S. and Fivush, R.: 1994, *Gender Development*, Cambridge University Press, Cambridge.

Graham-Brown, S.: 1991, *Education in the Developing World*, Longman Publishing, New York.

Gray, M.W.: 1995, 'Recruiting and Retaining Graduate Students in the Mathematical Sciences and Improving Their Chances for Subsequent Success', in B. Grevholm and G. Hanna (eds.), *Gender and Mathematics Education: An ICMI Study*, Lund University Press, Lund, Sweden, 39-44.

Grevholm, B. and Hanna, G. (eds.): 1995, *Gender and Mathematics Education: An ICMI Study*, Lund University Press, Lund, Sweden.

Haggis, S.M.: 1991, *Education for All I: Purpose and Context*, UNESCO, Paris.

Hanna, G.: 1989, 'Mathematics Achievement of Girls and Boys in Grade 8: Results From Twenty Countries', *Educational Studies in Mathematics* 20, 225-232.

Hanna, G.: 1994, 'Cross-cultural Gender Differences in Mathematics Education', *International Journal of Educational Research* 21, 58-68.

Harding, S.: 1991, *Whose Science? Whose Knowledge?* Open University Press, Milton Keynes.

Harding, S. and O'Barr, J.F.: 1987, *Sex and Scientific Inquiry*, University of Chicago Press, Chicago.

Harris, M.: 1995, 'Common Threads: Perceptions of Mathematics Education and the Traditional Work of Women', in P. Rogers and G. Kaiser (eds.), *Equity in Mathematics Education: Influences of Feminism and Culture*, Falmer Press, London, 77-87.

Hiddleston, P.: 1995, 'The Contribution of Girls-only Schools to Mathematics and Science Education in Malawi', in P. Rogers and G. Kaiser (eds.), *Equity in Mathematics Education: Influences of Feminism and Culture*, Falmer Press, London, 147-152.

Isaacson, Z.: 1990, '"They Look at You in Absolute Horror": Women Writing and Talking about Mathematics', in L. Burton (ed.), *Gender and Mathematics: An International Perspective*, Cassell, London, 20-28.

981

Joffe, L. and Foxman, D.: 1988, *Attitudes and Gender Differences: Mathematics at Age 11 and 15*, NFER-Nelson, Windsor, Berkshire.

Kaely, G.S.: 1995, 'Culture, Gender and Mathematics', in P. Rogers and G. Kaiser (eds.), *Equity in Mathematics Education: Influences of Feminism and Culture*, Falmer Press, London, 91-97.

Kaiser-Messmer, G.: 1993, 'Results of an Empirical Study into Gender Differences in Attitudes Towards Mathematics', *Educational Studies in Mathematics* 25, 209-233.

Kaiser, G. and Rogers, P.: 1995, 'Introduction: Equity in Mathematics Education', in P. Rogers and G. Kaiser (eds.), *Equity in Mathematics Education: Influences of Feminism and Culture*, Falmer Press, London, 1-10.

Kaur, B.:1995, 'Gender and Mathematics: The Singapore Perspective', in P. Rogers and G. Kaiser (eds.), *Equity in Mathematics Education: Influences of Feminism and Culture*, Falmer Press, London, 129-134.

Keller, E.F.: 1992, *Secrets of Life: Secrets of Death*, Routledge, New York.

Lafortune, L. and Kayler, H.: 1992, *Les Femmes Font des Maths*, Remue-ménage, Montréal.

Lantz, A.: 1985, 'Strategies to Increase Mathematics Enrolments', in S.F. Chipman, L.R. Brush and D.M. Wilson (eds.), *Women and Mathematics: Balancing the Equation*, Lawrence Erlbaum Associates, Hillsdale, NJ, 329-354.

Leder, G.C.: 1992, 'Mathematics and Gender: Changing Perspectives', in D.A. Grouws (ed.), *Handbook of Research in Mathematics Education*, Macmillan, New York, 597-622.

Leder, G.C. and Forgasz, H.J.: 1992, 'Gender: A Critical Variable in Mathematics Education', in B. Atweh and J. Watson (eds.), *Research in Mathematics Education in Australasia 1988-1991*, Mathematics Education Research Group of Australasia (MERGA), Brisbane, Australia, 67-95.

Leder, G.C. and Forgasz, H.J.: 1995, 'Girls and Mathematics: Research for Action', in L. Grimison and J. Pegg (eds.), *Teaching Secondary School Mathematics*, Harcourt Brace, Sydney, Australia, 186-207.

Leybourn, T.: 1816, *The Mathematical Questions Proposed in the Ladies' Diary* (four volumes), Mawman, Oxford.

Linn, M.C and Hyde, J.S.: 1989, 'Gender, Mathematics, and Science', *Educational Researcher* 18(8), 17-27.

Lummis, M. and Stevenson, H.W.: 1990, 'Gender Differences in Beliefs and Achievement: A Cross-cultural Study', *Developmental Psychology* 26(2), 254-263.

Malcolm, S.: 1984, *Equity and Excellence: Compatible Goals: An Assessment of Programs that Facilitate Increased Access and Achievement of Females and Minorities in K-12 Mathematics and Science Education*, Office of Opportunities in Science, American Association for the Advancement of Science, Washington, DC.

Matthews, C.M.: 1990, *Underrepresented Minorities and Women in Science, Mathematics, and Engineering: Problems and Issues for the, 1990's*, Library of Congress, Congressional Research Service, Washington, DC.

Matyas, M. and Malcolm, S.: 1991, *Investing in Human Potential: Science and Engineering at the Crossroads*, American Association for the Advancement of Science, Washington, DC.

McIntosh, P.:1983, *Phase Theory of Curriculum Reform*, Centre for Research on Women, Wellesley, MA.

Miller, A.: 1993, 'Introduction', *Initiatives* 55(2), 1-3.

Miller, A. and Silver, C.B.: 1993, 'The Limits of Intervention: Lessons from EUREKA, a Program to Retain Students in Science and Math-Related Majors', *Initiatives* 55(2), 21-29.

Ministerial Council on Education, Employment, Training and Youth Affairs, and Curriculum Corporation: 1994, *National Report on Schooling in Australia: 1993*, Curriculum Corporation, Carlton, Victoria.

Morrow, C. and Morrow, J.: 1995, 'Connecting Women with Mathematics', in P. Rogers and G. Kaiser (eds.), *Equity in Mathematics Education: Influences of Feminism and Culture*, Falmer Press, London, 13-26.

Moore, E. and Goudie, D.: 1995, 'The Linden School': A Women-centred School', in H. MacKinnon (ed.), *Encouraging Gender Equity: Strategies for School Change*, Human Rights Research and Education Centre, Ottawa, 34-39.

Mukuni, E.M.: 1987, 'A Critical Survey of Studies, Done in Kenya, on the Dependence of Attitudes Toward Mathematics and Performance in Mathematics on Sex Differences of the School Pupils', *Proceedings of the Eleventh International Conference for the Psychology of Mathematics Education [PME]*, 147-155.

Muller, C.B.: 1993, 'The Women in Science Project at Dartmouth', *Initiatives* 55(3), 39-47.

Mura, R.: 1986, 'Regards Féministes sur la Mathématique', *Resources for Feminist Research/ Documentation Sur la Recherche Féministe* 15(3), 59-61.

Mura, R.: 1995, 'Feminism and Strategies for Redressing Gender Imbalance in Mathematics', in P. Rogers and G. Kaiser (eds.), *Equity in Mathematics Education: Influences of Feminism and Culture*, Falmer Press, London, 155-162.

National Research Council: 1993, *Measuring What Counts*, National Research Council, Washington.

Noddings, N.: 1990, 'Feminist Critiques in the Professions', in C.B. Cazden (ed.) *Review of Research in Education* 16, American Educational Research Association, Washington DC, 393-424.

Northam, J.: 1982, 'Girls and Boys in Primary Maths Books', in L. Burton (ed.), *Girls into Maths Can Go*, Cassell, London, 110-116.

Nova Scotia Women's Directorate: 1994, *l'Éventail des Choix*, Condition Féminine Canada, Halifax.

Otten, W. and Kuyper, H.: 1988, 'Gender and Mathematics: The Prediction of Choice and Achievement', *Proceedings of the Twelfth International Conference for the Psychology of Mathematics Education [PME]*, 519-527.

Paivandi, S.: 1994, 'L'Alphabétisation des Femmes en Iran: Des Progrès, Mais les Inégalités Persistent', *Convergence* 27(2/3), 68-78.

Perl, T.: 1978, *Math Equals: Biographies of Women Mathematicians and Related Activities*, Addison-Wesley, Menlo Park, California.

Poitras, L. and Berthelot, M.: 1986, *À Chacune Son Métier*, Coordination à la Condition Féminine, Ministère de l'Éducation, Québec.

Porter, N. and Eileenchild, M.: 1980, *The Effectiveness of Women's Studies Teaching*, U.S. Department of Health, Education and Welfare, National Institute of Education, Program on Teaching and Learning, Washington, DC.

Rap-O-Matiques/Rap-O-Matics, video, Distribution: Chromavision International, 1172 Rainbow Street, Ontario, CDN, K1J 6X7.

Rich, A.: 1975, 'Toward a Women-centred University', in H. Florence (ed.), *Women and the Power to Change*, McGraw-Hill, New York, 15-46.

Rodgers, M.: 1990, 'Mathematics: Pleasure or Pain?', in L. Burton (ed.), *Gender and Mathematics: An International Perspective*, Cassell, London, 29-37.

Rogers, P.: 1990, 'Thoughts on Power and Pedagogy', in L. Burton (ed.), *Gender and Mathematics: An International Perspective*, Cassell, London, 38-46.

Rogers, P.: 1995, 'Putting Theory into Practice', in P. Rogers and G. Kaiser (eds.), *Equity in Mathematics Education: Influences of Feminism and Culture*, Falmer Press, London, 175-185.

Rogers, P. and Kaiser, G: 1995, *Equity in Mathematics Education: Influences of Feminism and Culture*, Falmer Press, London.

Sayers, R.: 1994, 'Gender Differences in Mathematics Education in Zambia', *Educational Studies in Mathematics* 26, 389-403.

Schools Commission: 1975, *Girls, Schools and Society*, Schools Commission, Canberra, ACT.

Sebrechts, J.S.: 1993, 'Cultivating Scientists at Women's Colleges', *Initiatives* 55(2), 45-51.

Secada, W.G.: 1989, 'Educational Equity Versus Equality of Education: An Alternative Conception', in W.G. Secada (ed.), *Equity in Education*, Falmer Press, London, 68-88.

Secada, W.G., Fennema, L.B. and Adajian, L.B. (eds.): 1995, *New Directions for Equity in Mathematics Education*, Cambridge University Press, Cambridge.

Sells, L.: 1973, *High School Mathematics as the Critical Filter in the Job Market,* (ERIC No. ED080 351), University of California, Berkeley.

Shelley, N.: 1995, 'Mathematics: Beyond Good and Evil', in P. Rogers and G. Kaiser (eds.), *Equity in Mathematics Education: Influences of Feminism and Culture*, Falmer Press, London, 247-264.

Shepherd, L.J.: 1993, *Lifting the Veil: The Feminine Face of Science*, Shambhala: Boston.

Skaalvik, E.M.: 1990, 'Gender Differences in General Academic Self-esteem and in Success Expectations on Defined Academic Problems', *Journal of Educational Psychology* 82(3), 593-598.

Solar, C.: 1995, 'An Inclusive Pedagogy in Mathematics Education', *Educational Studies in Mathematics* 28, 311-333.

Solar, C. and Lafortune, L.: 1994, *Des Mathématiques Autrement*, Remue-ménage, Montréal.

Solar, C., Lafortune, L., Kayler, L., Barette, M., Caron, R. and Pasquis, L.: 1992, 'Où en Sommes-nous?', In L. Lafortune and H. Kayler (eds.), *Les Femmes Font des Maths*, Remue-ménage, Montréal, 15-39.

Taylor, L.: 1990, 'American Female and Male University Professors' Mathematical Attitudes and Life Histories', in L. Burton (ed.), *Gender and Mathematics: An International Perspective*, Cassell, London, 47-59.

Thompson, D.R.: 1995, 'The METRO Achievement Program: Helping Inner-city Girls Excel', in P. Rogers and G. Kaiser (eds.), *Equity in Mathematics Education: Influences of Feminism and Culture*, Falmer Press, London, 27-36.

Tocci, C.M. and Engelhard G. Jr.: 1991, 'Achievement, Parental Support, and Gender Differences in Attitudes Towards Mathematics', *Journal of Educational Research* 84(5), 280-286.

Tracy, D.M. and Davis, S.M.: 1989, 'Females in Mathematics: Erasing Gender-related Math Myth', *Arithmetic Teacher* 37(4), 8-11.

United Nations Fourth World Conference on Women: Draft Platform for Action: 1995, 'Unequal Access to and Inadequate Educational Opportunities', *Linkages: A Multimedia Resource for Environment and Policy Makers*, available HTTP: http://www.iisd.ca/ linkages/ 4wcw/dpa-021.html, 1-2.

Vasey, J.: 1989, 'The Family Maths Project', in G.C. Leder and S.N. Sampson (eds.), *Educating Girls: Practice and Research*, Allen and Unwin, Sydney, 98-104.

Verhage, H.: 1990, 'Curriculum Development and Gender', in L. Burton (ed.), *Gender and Mathematics: An International Perspective*, Cassell, London, 60-71.

Visser, D.: 1988, 'The Influence of Socialization and Emotional Factors on Mathematics Achievement and Participation', *Proceedings of the Twelfth International Conference for the Psychology of Mathematics Education [PME]*, 633-639.

Wadsworth, E.M.: 1993, 'Women's Activities and Women Engineers: Expansions Over Time', *Initiatives* 55(2), 59-65.

Walberg, H.J. and Haertel, G.D.: 1992, 'Educational Psychology's First Century', *Journal of Educational Psychology* 84(1), 6-19.

Walden, R. and Walkerdine, V.: 1985, *Girls and Mathematics: From Primary to Secondary Schooling*, Institute of Education, University of London, London.

Walkerdine, V.: 1989, *Counting Girls Out*, Virago, London.

Wise, L.L.: 1985, 'Project TALENT: Mathematics Course Application in the, 1960's and its Career Consequences', in S.F. Chipman, L.R. Brush and D.M. Wilson (eds.), *Women and*

Mathematics: Balancing the Equation, Lawrence Erlbaum Associates, Hillsdale, NJ, 25-58.

Yergeau, N.: 1988, *SPRINT: Stratégies Pour Réussir l'Intégration au Non-traditionnel*, Ministère de l'Éducation, Coordination à la Condition Féminine, Québec.

Chapter 26: Language Factors in Mathematics Teaching and Learning

NERIDA F. ELLERTON AND PHILIP C. CLARKSON
Edith Cowan University, Perth, and Australian Catholic University, Melbourne, Australia

ABSTRACT

Although language factors have long been recognised as having an important influence on mathematics learning, possible frameworks for researching the nature and extent of that influence have only been developed relatively recently. In this chapter the authors emphasise one of these frameworks, and summarise pertinent research findings which have implications for mathematics teaching and learning.

Possible reasons for the dearth of research in linking language factors with mathematics education during the 1980's are put forward. The chapter draws attention to a range of factors – including social, cognitive, cultural, linguistic, and affective – which impinge on the development of a wider range of communication patterns in mathematics classrooms. Several areas – including writing in mathematics, bilingualism in mathematics teaching and learning, and language and assessment of mathematics learning – in which there is a danger that potentially false assumptions are likely to influence practice, are identified. Evidence is put forward indicating that carefully designed research studies in these areas are urgently needed.

1. LANGUAGE FACTORS IN MATHEMATICS TEACHING AND LEARNING

1.1 Some Historical Perspectives

Perhaps the first major commentary on the role of language in mathematics education appeared over 40 years ago, in the form of a paper written by Brune (1953). He noted, in particular, that 'words are links in the chain of communication' (p.160), that 'mathematical words often represent mental constructs rather than tangibles' (p.161), that 'spoken words are symbols', and that 'words represent agreements among people' (p.161). Brune referred to different meanings associated with the same word in different cultures, to the ways in which context can clarify the meaning of specific words, and to the importance of semantics (which he described as a young discipline). He also discussed the importance of having pupils work on projects which have been specifically designed to emphasise mathematical concepts. Brune maintained

A.J. Bishop et al. (eds.), International Handbook of Mathematics Education, 987 - 1033

that once students understood concepts through their own experiences, they should have the opportunity of communicating the mathematical principles underlying these concepts to their classmates.

Brune's (1953) paper effectively foreshadowed most of the elements and themes which are currently being taken into account by those who are concerned to investigate relationships between mathematics, mathematics education, and language. Brune made no attempt, however, to link the various factors he identified as important in his consideration of mathematics and language.

The broad term 'language factors in mathematics learning' has been used in recent years to refer to diverse research areas – from psycholinguistics and sociolinguistics to classroom discourse, and to teaching mathematics in bilingual classrooms. A quarter of a century ago, Aiken's (1972) review focused on the crucial role of classroom discourse, for example. In the 1970's and 1980's researchers tended to work in separate camps, largely unaware of what was being studied in closely related fields. At that time, the expression 'language factors in mathematics learning' meant different things to different people.

Historical perspective makes it clear that what was needed was some kind of coordinating framework which not only identified the main components of the field, but also began the task of investigating issues and relationships within and between these components. In their review of language and mathematical education, Austin and Howson (1979) presented a 'framework for discussion' which, they said, would impinge on a range of disciplines, including sociology, psychology and anthropology. As a starting point, they listed three key issues concerned with teachers and learners – do they share

    a)   the same language;

    b)   the same culture; and

    c)   the same logic and reasoning system?

In the light of the comprehensive early reviews by Brune, Aiken, and Austin and Howson, it is somewhat surprising that comparatively little research in the language and mathematics area was published in the early 1980's in the United States. One possible reason for this could be the straitjacketing of research by two influential books which set out to define the research agenda for mathematics education – *Critical Variables in Mathematics Education* (Begle, 1979), and an edited collection of articles, *Research in Mathematics Education* (Shumway, 1980).

Begle identified five key issues for mathematics education research:

    a)   the relationship between teacher knowledge of subject matter and student achievement;

    b)   drill;

    c)   expository teaching of mathematical objects;

d) acceleration; and

e) predictive tests.

These issues seem far removed from the themes that have subsequently emerged within the international mathematics education community.

The listing of these variables, Begle's emphasis on the need for a 'scientific' approach, and the effective endorsement of this stance by the fact that both of these books were published by major discipline associations, would appear to have had a major influence, particularly in the United States. The predetermined major themes chosen for mathematics education research, and the emphasis placed by major funding bodies on supporting theory-driven research in certain well-defined areas, effectively confined language factors to the periphery of the main mathematics education research agendas in the United States.

Research in the language and mathematics area continued in countries outside the United States, however (see, for example, Irons and Jones, 1982; Wheeler, 1982; Clements, 1984). It would appear to be the case that, in the United States, recognition of the importance of the field was revived, at least in part, by special sessions, at the 1988 and 1989 annual meetings of the Mathematical Association of America, on the use of writing to teach mathematics (Sterett, undated). At about that time, a number of articles addressing the language and mathematics area were published in journals such as *The Arithmetic Teacher* and *The Mathematics Teacher* (examples include Burton, 1985; Nahrgang and Petersen, 1986; Kenyon, 1987). There was, however, still a dearth of articles in the major mathematics education research journals, and an absence of any overall coordinating framework.

The Commission on Standards for School Mathematics in the United States, which was established by the National Council of Teachers of Mathematics (NCTM) in 1986, included communication and 'language in mathematics' as major themes to be incorporated by the Commission into the draft (NCTM, 1987) and final (NCTM, 1989) versions of the *Standards*.

The earlier draft version presented a much narrower interpretation of the notion of 'communication' and of 'language' in mathematics classrooms than the final version. The expansion of this section during the period of wide consultation between 1987 and 1989 probably reflected the involvement of mathematics educators and teachers who had not been influenced by the narrow research agenda set for mathematics education research (Begle, 1979; Shumway, 1980).

Nor would most teachers have been significantly influenced by the strong views of radical constructivists, who vehemently denied that 'words convey ideas or knowledge' (von Glasersfeld, 1990, p.36 – but see Ellerton and Clements, 1992a; and Suchting, 1992).

In Australia, language factors in mathematics learning continued to be a major area of research interest throughout the period 1975-1996 (Ellerton and

Clements, 1996a). Its importance was also recognised in all Australian curriculum documents of the period (see, for example, Victorian Ministry of Education, 1988). In the second half of the 1980's several frameworks which attempted to link the various elements of the language and mathematics field were published. For example, a conceptual overview was presented by Gawned (1990), and is summarised in Figure 1. This framework, which she referred to as 'a socio-psycho linguistic model', was based on a model of language learning which had been developed by Wells (1984) and Wood (1988).

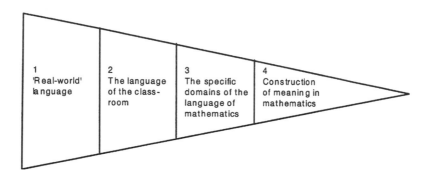

Figure 1. A summary of Gawned's (1990) socio-psycho-linguistic 'model'.

Gawned's (1990) framework derived from the sociolinguistic premise that the origins of all language, including the language of mathematics, are

> rooted in the child's first experiences in the world. The way people communicate with young children, especially the language they use, aids the organisation of the child's own perceptions and concrete experiences. ... Language helps to shape these internal (mental) and external experiences. They are given names and descriptions. Their use begins to fit into predictable pattern. Children develop schema for daily or other regular events on to which new language is then mapped. Simultaneously, the child's own perceptions and experiences serve as a stimulus for him (sic.) to initiate interaction and to communicate with those around him. (p.31)

The framework acknowledged that the language of the classroom has a particularly important formative effect on learners' understandings of mathematics. According to Gawned (1990), each mathematics classroom has a particular culture of its own. Classroom discourse patterns are different from what learners experience out of school. Generally, Gawned stated, these discourse patterns are rule-bound, operate within a fairly tightly defined set of relationships, and are dominated by teachers.

Some educators believed that in order to understand the role of language in mathematics learning it was necessary to look beyond the classroom to develop a broad framework of communication and culture. Yet, according to Corson (1985):

> A school curriculum is a selection of knowledge from the culture: all those things in the culture considered worth passing on through schooling. Since all forms of knowledge are 'filtered' through language, the chief item of knowledge in any culture is its *language*. The chief object of the school is to encourage the complete mastery of the language of the culture, since without this mastery children are denied powers and influence over their own affairs and an opportunity for success in education. (pp.1-2)

Thus any consideration of curriculum in general and of mathematics teaching and learning in particular should not neglect the influence of the cultures of schools, in general, and of classrooms in particular, within their different social milieux.

These notions are especially pertinent for mathematics education. There is an increasing body of research fundings which suggests that many of the difficulties encountered by students in mathematics classrooms can be attributed to mismatched purposes. The serious lack of mutual understanding is evident in the discourses of students, teachers, textbooks, and curriculum materials (see, for example, Ellerton and Clements, 1990; Garaway, 1994).

During the last ten years, a number of books have been published on how language factors influence mathematics learning (Orr, 1987; Pimm, 1987, 1995; Cocking and Mestre, 1988; Hunting, 1988; Zepp, 1989; Bickmore-Brand, 1990; Durkin and Shire, 1991; Ellerton and Clements, 1991; Stephens, Waywood, Clarke and Izard, 1993; Griffiths and Clyne, 1994). Some, though not all, mathematics education researchers interested in how language factors influence mathematics learning, turned away from the fragmentation of earlier studies – which had been carried out in narrow focus areas – and began to adopt a more eclectic approach by which they located their work within larger social and cultural domains.

1.2 A Framework Relating Language, Mathematics and Mathematics Education

The framework put forward by Ellerton (1989), and summarised in Figure 2, represented an initial response to the need to link the different facets of the general field of language factors in mathematics education. The complexity of Figure 2 is consistent with the multifaceted nature of relationships between mathematics, school mathematics, and language. It can be seen that at the centre of Figure 2 there is a section labelled 'Mathematics Classroom and Curriculum Implications'.

The framework can be regarded as a cross-section of a 3-dimensional depiction of relationships. Viewed from a macro level, the framework suggests that culture is all-pervading, and that communication within culture is of fundamental importance. From a micro level, on the other hand, issues related to the teaching and learning of mathematics such as assessment, bilingualism, and writing mathematics, intersect, in fact, with most parts of the framework.

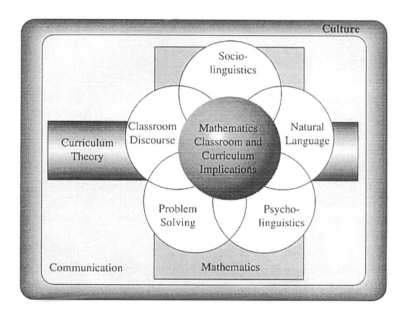

Figure 2. A framework for interpreting language factors in mathematics learning.

Such a framework, of course, should not be set in stone. Its strength, in fact, lies in its ability to respond to changes in thinking and continuing research in the area. Recent research such as that by Lave (1988), McBride (1989), Secada (1988), Voigt (1995), and Walkerdine (1988), suggests that new theoretical bases are emerging in mathematics education, and that a reconstruction of research methodologies is underway. Some of the ongoing research which is enabling us to view what goes on in mathematics classrooms from important new perspectives will be described in the sections which follow.

1.3   Mathematics and Communication

The notion of communication would appear to be an essential ingredient of any human endeavour if the elements of that endeavour are to be passed on to the next generation. If, however, key ideas in mathematics remain enshrined in language which is only accessible to a few chosen academics, then those same ideas will remain inaccessible to the majority of learners. Undoubtedly, the need to bring the findings of mathematics education research and the wisdom of best practice before most teachers of mathematics contributed to the recent reform movements in mathematics education in countries such as the United States (NCTM, 1989), and Australia (Australian Education Council, 1991).

Perhaps it was an awareness of the need to communicate the importance of the role of mathematics in the school curriculum to a wider audience which inspired the chapter 'Mathematics and the Public' (Slaught, 1926), which appeared in the first Yearbook published by the National Council of Teachers of Mathematics (NCTM). The sixth Yearbook, titled *Mathematics in Modern Life,* also attempted to communicate with the stakeholders associated with the teaching and learning of mathematics (Reeve, 1931). In a further attempt to clarify and focus what was described as 'much loose thinking among educators and laymen generally with respect to the importance of mathematics' (Reeve, 1936, p.iii), one of the themes of the chapter 'Attacks on Mathematics and How to Meet Them' was the importance of teaching mathematics in such a way that students would offer the desired testimony to the public (Reeve, 1936).

Thus although Griggs (quoted in Reeve, 1936) commented that mathematics is the 'grammar of science, a language for the statement of all scientific facts and laws' (p.16), his emphasis was on communication being *about* mathematics and its place in education. Some 17 years after Griggs wrote, as noted above, the importance of communicating *mathematics* was more clearly articulated (Brune, 1953).

1.3.1 Communication in Mathematics Classrooms

The term 'communication' in mathematics classrooms in the 1990's can refer to many different aspects of language. The 1996 Yearbook of the National Council of Teachers of Mathematics in the United States, for example, contains 28 articles on 'Communication in Mathematics K-12 and Beyond', each dealing with a different aspect of communication (Elliott and Kenney, 1996). In this present chapter, however, communication will be discussed under four major headings – classroom discourse, language and assessment, semantic structure, and writing.

Superficially, classroom discourse can be viewed as merely the language exchanges which take place in the classroom. When viewed from multiple perspectives – from cognitive, social, and linguistic perspectives (Cobb, 1990) – however, analyses of discourses in mathematics classrooms can help researchers begin to understand how forms of interactions which take place can effectively frame any learning which occurs (Atweh, Cooper and Kanes, 1992).

Atweh (1993), who adopted a 'social critical sociology perspective' (p.61) in his ethnographic studies of mathematics classrooms, and Kanes (1992, 1993), who used the 'later' Wittgensteinian concepts of 'language-game', 'form of life', and 'family resemblance', concluded that for learners, mathematical concepts only have meaning within the linguistic and social contexts from which they were derived. Therefore, they argued, mathematics is mediated through language rather than through thinking. Pimm (1987) used 'talking for oneself' and 'talking for others' to describe two forms of classroom discourse. He drew on the work of Brown (1982) to respond to the question 'What kind of talking is worthwhile in mathematics?'. Brown contrasted two different forms of language – *message-oriented* and *listener-oriented* – and argued that the former needs to be taught explicitly in schools.

During the last decade there has been a burgeoning literature on the role of discourse in mathematics classrooms as the main element underlying the cultures in these classrooms. Many of the concepts have derived from the German interactionist literature (Voigt, 1985, 1994, 1995; Bauersfeld, 1988, 1994, 1995), but other major contributions have been made by Nickson (1992), Mellin-Olsen (1993), and Alrø and Skovsmose (1996). These writers have emphasised that it is the culture of the classroom which effectively determines how meanings are negotiated between learners and teachers.

If a teacher with an absolutist view of mathematics teaches in a way which carries the message that it is the students' task to learn what is transmitted to them, and if the students are concerned about constructing mathematical meaning for themselves, then the meanings constructed will be those that they believe to be in the mind of the teacher and textbook writer. In other words, they will see their task as clarifying someone else's meaning for themselves, and any negotiation of meaning will be towards this end. Alrø and Skovsmose (1996) introduced the notions of 'classroom absolutism' and 'bureaucratic absolutism', and claimed that these determine, for both teachers and students, the philosophy of mathematics and mathematics education from which perspectives and meanings are negotiated in classrooms. They emphasised that communication in the mathematics classroom 'establishes an idea about mathematics and simultaneously produces a verification of this philosophy' (p.5).

In interactionism, the culture of the classroom has a special position. Teachers of mathematics might plan lessons, but they are never able to predict precisely what will be learned by students, or how it will be learned. Indeed the interactions within a classroom community as a whole profoundly affect what is learned, both by the students and by the teacher. Although the interactions are unpredictable, they are nevertheless shaped by reasonably stable classroom cultures. These are certainly not completely static, however, and evolve largely as a result of the qualities and patterns of interactions (Woods, 1992; Lerman, 1996).

For interactionists, then, classroom culture is the most fundamental object of study. Mathematics education researchers working from an interactionist perspective are concerned to investigate not only the mathematical meanings which are interactively constructed, and stabilised, by individuals and by groups within the different cultures of different mathematics classrooms, but also how these meanings relate to distinguishable characteristics and patterns of the classrooms and the interactions within the classrooms. They are particularly concerned with how mathematics classroom cultures emerge and change, and yet are sufficiently stable that they can be observed and described at any given point of time (Cobb, 1990).

Interactionists claim that various assumptions, patterns, routines and constraints on interaction, explain the recurrence of themes of classroom discourse in individual classrooms. Different kinds of classroom interaction — for example 'funnelling', focusing, reciting, and 'concrete-to abstract' tendencies (Voigt, 1985, 1995; Brousseau, 1986; Steinbring, 1994; Bauersfeld, 1995; Krummheuer, 1995; Bruner, 1996) — profoundly affect the quality and extent of what is learned by individuals and by the teacher and students as a whole. However, the often subtle forces associated with channelling, focusing and other forms of interaction are not always consciously recognised by students, or even by teachers.

Studies of classroom discourse are revealing details of the hidden curriculum operating in mathematics classroom (Lampert, 1990; Atweh, 1993). In a microanalysis of a sequence of 24 lessons, Voigt (1985) found that a teacher who had thought he was teaching in a constructivist manner (with a range of open-ended questions), was in fact 'channelling' or 'funnelling' the students towards the correct answer. The teacher achieved this through a series of implicit markers and non-verbal cues.

The following passage from Alrø and Skovsmose (1996) captures the spirit of much of the research on classroom discourse carried out in the last decade.

It is important to realize that the students are brought up within a certain school discourse, which influences their expectations of the teacher's role compared to their own, which again influences the way they think things can be put forward and talked about in the classroom. For example, students often expect the teacher to take the lead, to decide and control what is going to happen, and to present the knowledge which he (sic.) wants them to gain. These students would not insist on their own perspective because they expect that they are going to be evaluated and corrected by the teacher. This means that the students do not need to take full responsibility for their answers – the teacher will always provide the right algorithm or the right result. Such preunderstanding of school discourse naturally prevents all negotiation of meaning. Consequently it is necessary to change the way of communicating in a more general sense of the term in order to be able to negotiate meaning. (p.7)

It is clearly also important to take account of the fact that interpretation of the terms 'communication', 'negotiation' and 'responsibility' will vary depending on the perspective of the reader.

Buerk (1994) stated that as students broaden their conceptions of knowledge they seem to pass through three distinct positions:
1) Seeing all mathematical knowledge as external, fundamental, and black or white;
2) Acknowledging personal thoughts and ideas, often in a subjective way;
3) Integrating known theories and new, carefully developed individual ideas into an internal model and thereby gaining ownership of the mathematics they are learning. (p.46)

Those who have developed theories of mathematics classroom culture, however, argue that progress through these positions is by no means automatic. If rigid absolutist philosophies are reflected in autocratic teacher behaviours, then research indicates that even senior secondary and tertiary students still believe that mathematical knowledge is external to the learner, and that a good teacher or lecturer or textbook is one which transmits this knowledge to them clearly and accurately (Crawford, Gordon, Nicholas and Prosser, 1993).

Brown (1994) discussed radical constructivism in the light of the philosophical traditions of post-structuralism and hermeneutic phenomenology. He suggested that the mathematical understandings developed by students in the classroom 'are not so much 'constructions' in their own right but rather elements in a dialogue between teacher and learner consequential to the teacher framing a certain structure' (p.80). In light of this framing used by teachers, Brown urged caution 'in moving from epistemologies to recommendations for practice' (p.81).

Thus Brown (1994) saw any form of mathematical instruction introduced by a teacher as concealing 'a socially conventional way of making associations between symbolic forms and phenomena seen as mathematical' (p.88). In other words, it is false to claim that a child is responsible for 'controlling the agenda' in an environment which was established by a teacher. It follows, then, that in any discussion about a student's constructions, it needs to be recognised that any constructions by the student must be inextricably and inex-

996

orably linked with the conventions of the language and culture in which the student is working.

Much of the contemporary writing on discourse patterns in mathematics classrooms which focus on allowing children to construct their own understanding of mathematics pays too little attention to the reality that although students are *learning* to communicate mathematics, the teachers are *fluent* in using mathematical language. Pimm (1994) referred to this 'asymmetry of power', and its visibility in discourse structures, and noted how it is necessarily part of education settings.

1.4.1 Establishing New Forms of Discourse

The question arises which mathematics learning environments are most likely to facilitate genuine negotiation, by learners, of meaning and perspective. Some writers have advocated changing the structure and form of questions which frame classroom discourses. Stigler and Baranes (1988), for example, argued that in Japanese classrooms

   a) students expect to become engaged in lengthy, genuine discussions about problems;
   b) the atmosphere is more divergent than convergent; and
   c) errors are seen as starting points for discussion rather than end points.

1.4.2 Open-Ended or Goal-Free Problems/Questions

As part of the move towards reconstructing mathematics classroom discourse patterns, mathematics educators have called for a much wider use of so-called 'open-ended' or 'goal-free' questions which will stimulate rather than stifle students' thinking about the contexts, constraints and meanings of task situations (Shimada, 1977; Nohda, 1995; Pehkonen, 1995; Silver, 1995). Use of open-ended problems in school mathematics has been incorporated into mathematics curricula in several countries – for example, in Germany (see Pehkonen, 1995); in the United States (see NCTM, 1995), and in Australia (see Stacey, 1995).

Currently, however, there is no agreement within the international mathematics education community about what is meant by 'open-ended' or 'open' questions/problems. Pehkonen (1995), in his description of the debate which took place in July, 1993 in the Psychology of Mathematics Education Discussion Group on the use of open-ended problems in mathematics classrooms, commented that the Group adopted the view that 'open-ended' problems are not 'closed' problems. A problem was defined as closed 'if its starting situation and goal situation are closed' (p.55). He went on to describe three types of open problems:

a) problems in which the starting situation is closed, but the goal situation is open;
b) problems in which the starting situation is open but the goal situation is closed, and
c) problems in which both the starting and the goal situations are open.

The NCTM (1989) *Standards* document, on the other hand, emphasised that 'some problems also should be open-ended with no right answer' (p.6), which might be taken as referring to project-type problem situations rather than to the multi-answer type advocated as appropriate for routine classroom work (Sullivan and Clarke 1991). Silver (1995) discussed several possible interpretations of the term 'open problems', and included
a) problems to which no solution had yet been found;
b) problems which are susceptible to different interpretations or to different possible answers;
c) problems which invite different methods of solution; and
d) problems which naturally suggest other problems or generalisations.

Associated with these different terminologies are subtle variations in meaning which can be linked to a number of assumptions. Although this lack of clarity might be expected in a relatively new development in mathematics education, nonetheless the corresponding lack of research evidence to match the claims and suggestions for the use of 'open-ended' questions is disturbing. The most pervading common ground for discussion is, in fact, the emphasis on the expressive use of language on the part of the learner in responding to such questions.

Very few, if any, convincing research studies have, in fact, been carried out into the effectiveness of open-ended problems in stimulating students' learning in mathematics classrooms. Reports in the literature tend to focus on the design and categorisation of problems, and on the possible range of responses and methods of analysing these responses (see, for example, Nohda, 1995; Pehkonen, 1995).

Clarke, Sullivan and Spandel (1992) found that many students in Years 6 through 10 were reluctant to provide more than a single answer to open-ended questions such as 'If a rectangle has a perimeter of 30 units, what might be its area?' Clarke et al. found a similar reluctance in three other areas of the curriculum (English, Social Studies, and Science). When students were explicitly asked to seek and present multiple solutions, a significant increase in the number of multiple responses was observed in all four areas of the curriculum. Clarke et al. (1992) concluded that 'it may not be realistic to expect students of any age to access recently-acquired skills in open-ended or problem-solving situations', and 'substantial additional research is required if we are to understand the meanings constructed by students in responding to open-ended tasks sufficiently well to employ such tasks with success in mathematics classrooms' (p.220)

Such conclusions suggest that the intuitive appeal of open-ended questions, and the apparent flexibility that such questions offer in the mathematics classroom should not exempt the area from intensive and critical research investigations.

Owen and Sweller (1985), arguing from an information-processing perspective, claimed that open-ended or 'goal-free' tasks facilitate learning because the learner is not required to attend to directed goals and therefore has available more processing capacity with which to explore different aspects of the problem tasks. It could be argued, however, that, for learners who lack confidence in working with problems which involve newly acquired concepts, the need to decide between different possible solution paths *and then* process the chosen path would take *more* processing capacity rather than *less*. For a learner, these two acts (deciding and processing) are more likely to be competing actions. They are not necessarily discrete or sequential steps in the problem-solving process.

Sweller (1992) has reiterated his claim that learning is enhanced by goal-free problems, stating that this claim is based on results of studies carried out over the past 10 years 'over many experiments using geometry, trigonometry and kinematics problems' (p.53). However, in a study by Sullivan (1992), no statistically significant difference was found in the gain score of two groups of students – an experimental group of randomly allocated students whose program (of 7 one-hour sessions) consisted of responding to 'good' questions of an open-ended nature, and a control group which was taught the topic in a traditional way using a commonly used textbook. In his analysis of the post-treatment instrument data, Sullivan (1992) reported that very few multiple answers were given. He also analysed data on pre- and post-treatment measures of the attitudes of the students in this study, and found no statistically significant differences in the gain scores of the two groups.

Sullivan, Bourke and Scott (1995) presented three questions involving the perimeter of a rectangle, to 30 students in Year 6. They found that a statistically significantly greater proportion of students responded correctly to an open-ended question (A shape has a perimeter of 16 cm. What might the shape look like?) than to a closed question (What is the perimeter of this shape? – note that a diagram showing a rectangle 10 cm x 4 cm was given but the lengths of the sides were not shown). This result was interpreted by Sullivan et al. as consistent with the findings of Owen and Sweller (1985). However, no interview data were available to clarify whether the closed question was ambiguous to many Year 6 students. For example, would a student who gave the response 'the distance around the shape' be regarded as having responded correctly?

Sullivan et al. (1995) also found that, although many students gave multiple answers to the open-ended question above after the 10-week training program, in a post-test given 3 months later, most students gave only one answer. Thus claims that open-ended questions provide students with an opportunity to give multiple responses, as well as related opportunities in divergent thinking, greater communication with other students, exploring mathematics within given contexts, and assessing their own understanding (see Scott, 1994), need to be carefully evaluated through research.

The increasing importance being attached to more open forms of assessment such as projects and responses to open-ended problems in the assessment of students' mathematical understanding (see, for example, NCTM, 1995) points to the need to reach agreement on the terminology used to describe different aspects of the general area, and to carry out appropriate research into each of these aspects.

1.5 Language and Assessment

1.5.1 Language in Traditional Pencil-and-Paper Tests of Mathematics

During the 1990's, there has been a major emphasis in the mathematics education community on the need to develop more authentic methods for assessing student learning (Ruthven, 1994; Clarke and Jasper, 1995; NCTM, 1995; Silver Burdett Ginn Inc., 1995a). In spite of this thrust, however, pencil-and-paper short-answer and multiple-choice tests continue to be widely used throughout the world for assessing the mathematical performance of school children (Olssen, 1993; Garret and Mills, 1995). In fact, in view of the increased use for accountability purposes of the results of statewide, national, and even international pencil-and-paper tests, it would not be an exaggeration to say that pencil-and-paper tests continue to play a dominant role in mathematics education (Clements and Ellerton, 1995, In press).

Given the public acceptance of pencil-and-paper tests for school mathematics, the language structures used in questions on such tests are obviously important, as are the interactions of students with these structures. Apparently simple questions such as 'Why do learners give correct and incorrect answers to pencil-and-paper items?' need to be answered.

The most important body of evidence pertaining to issues associated with pencil-and-paper tests for school mathematics has been generated by what has become known as 'Newman research', which has been widely used in Australia, Oceania, and SouthEast Asia. Much has been written on the use of the Newman procedure in mathematics education research. According to Newman (1977, 1983), any person confronted with a written mathematics task needs to go through a fixed sequence: Reading (or Decoding), Comprehension, Transformation (or Mathematising), Process Skills, and Encoding. Errors can also be the result of unknown factors, and Newman (1983) assigned these to a composite category, termed 'Careless'.

With the Newman procedure students who have already attempted to solve a mathematics word problem are asked a sequence of questions which are aimed at seeing whether they can

a) Read the question;
b) Comprehend what they have read;
c) Carry out a mental Transformation from the words of the question to the selection of an appropriate mathematical strategy;
d) Apply the Process Skills demanded by the selected strategy; and
e) Encode the answer in an acceptable written form.

Over the past two decades the 'Newman method' has been widely used throughout the Asia-Pacific region – in Australia (e.g., Casey, 1978; Clarkson, 1980; Clements, 1980; Watson, 1980; Tuck, 1983; Clements and Ellerton, 1992; Faulkner, 1992); in Brunei (Mohidin, 1991); in India (Kaushil, Sajjin Singh and Clements, 1985); in Malaysia (Marinas and Clements, 1990; Teoh Sooi Kim, 1991; Ellerton and Clements, 1992b; Kownan, 1992; Sulaiman and Remorin, 1993); in Papua New Guinea (Clements, 1982; Clarkson, 1983, 1991); in Singapore (Kaur, 1995); in the Philippines (Jiminez, 1992); and in Thailand (Singhatat, 1991; Thongtawat, 1992).

Analyses of data based on the Newman procedure have drawn special attention to the influence of language factors on mathematics learning, and by so doing have challenged mathematics educators and teachers to redefine what is 'basic' in school mathematics. Newman research has generated a large amount of evidence pointing to the conclusion that far more children experience difficulty with the semantic structures, the vocabulary, and the symbolism of mathematics than with standard algorithms. Also, Newman research has consistently pointed to the inappropriateness of many 'remedial' mathematics programs in schools in which the revision of standard algorithms is over-emphasised, with hardly any attention being given to difficulties associated with Comprehension and Transformation.

In many Newman studies carried out in schools in Australia, Oceania, and SouthEast Asia, the proportion of errors first occurring at the 'Comprehension' and Transformation' stages has been great (Ellerton and Clements, 1992b). Thus, for example, Marinas and Clements (1990) and Ellerton and Clements (1996b), working with Year 7 students in Australia and Malaysia, and Singhatat (1991), working with Thai students, found that about 70 per cent of errors made on typical Year 7 mathematics questions were in the Comprehension or Transformation categories. These researchers also found that Reading (that is to say, Decoding) errors accounted for less than 5 per cent of initial errors made by students in their samples. The same was true for Process Skills errors (mostly associated with standard numerical operations).

A range of 'alternative' assessment procedures which, it is claimed, can give different perspectives on students' receptive and expressive mathematical understandings, has been widely advocated (see, for example, Clarke, 1992, 1993). An overview of the constraints on authentic classroom assessment (as well as strategies which might minimise these constraints) has been provided in tabular form by Clarke and Jasper (1995). The table includes the following assessment strategies: annotated class lists, practical tests, student constructed test items, student self-assessment, student mathematics journals, student mathematics portfolios, student investigative projects, and student-generated solutions to challenging problems. Six of these eight strategies involve students expressing their mathematical understandings rather than responding to tightly defined questions almost exclusively in a receptive mode. Thus it is being proposed that students' expressive use of language should play a more important role in assessment.

The notion that assessment of mathematical understanding should involve an examination of students' work as they engage in 'real' mathematics has been recognised by education policy makers around the world. Thus, for example, in the United States, the policy brief *Measuring Counts* (National Academy of Sciences, 1993) prefaces its major statement about assessment with the heading 'Mathematics as Language', and a brief discussion on how assessment in writing 'provides a good analogy for assessment in mathematics' (p.8). The *Assessment Standards for School Mathematics* (NCTM, 1995) include examples of how student writing in mathematics can be incorporated into a balanced approach to assessment.

In the early 1990's, in Australia, the Victorian Certificate of Education incorporated a broader range of assessment styles for all mathematics subjects taken by senior secondary students (Years 11 and 12). Two of the four Common Assessment Tasks (CATs) involved the preparation and submission of individual responses – CAT 1 was an 'investigative project' for which a 1500-word written report of a mathematical investigation into a set theme was required, and for CAT 2, students were required to submit an individual response to one of four challenging problems (see Clarkson, 1992a; Stephens, 1993, for further details). From a pedagogical perspective, expressive language factors were being accorded both a more direct and a more important and varied role in mathematics learning at the senior secondary level than had ever been the case before.

With any major change, however, there is likely to be resistance – and as a result of the new assessment schedule in Victoria, some were convinced that mathematical standards of beginning tertiary students had declined sharply (Swedosh, 1995). In 1993, largely as a result of public reaction to such controversies, the CAT 2 problem-solving task was dropped. Waywood (1993) lamented this decision, claiming that 'the connection between writing and learning has motivated many pedagogical practices and movements – writing across the curriculum, writing to learn, and writing in mathematics' (p.162).

Of particular significance is what can be described as the 'ripple effect' felt throughout the secondary school system as a direct consequence of the introduction of these forms of assessment at senior secondary levels. Research has shown that, because of a perceived need to prepare students for future assessment procedures, teachers at more junior levels in Victorian schools gave students opportunities to engage in extended project work and extended problem-solving tasks (Blane, 1992; Clarke, Stephens and Wallbridge, 1993; Stephens, Clarke and Pavlou, 1994).

However, although few would debate the importance of achieving a balanced assessment program, four fundamental research questions in relation to the new forms of assessment need to be addressed (Ellerton and Clements, 1992c):

1) Is the genre of writing expected in these reports fundamentally different from that expected in school mathematics in the past?

2) Do students who satisfactorily complete an investigative report acquire research techniques that were never previously acquired in school mathematics?

3) Is the time spent on researching and writing an investigative report justified, given a criterion of satisfactory performance in subsequent tertiary mathematics courses?

4) Is the time spent on researching and writing an investigative report justified, given a criterion of being able to carry out independent research investigations in later life? (p.157)

Unless research questions such as these are investigated, it is harder to present convincing arguments to critics such as Swedosh (1995) who claim that under the new VCE program, the mathematical skills of beginning tertiary students have declined. Furthermore, in many countries, there are moves to instigate large-scale pencil-and-paper testing programs – apparently for reasons of accountability – in which the emphasis will be on multiple-choice and/or short-answer questions. Thus the United Kingdom has initiated a program of national assessment (Black, 1994), and most states in the United States have statewide or district assessment at two or more year levels (McDonnell, 1995). All but one state in Australia has adopted state-wide testing programs in which the main instrument is the ubiquitous pencil-and-paper test (Clements and Thomas, 1996).

It would appear to be the case, then, that there is an urgent need to examine assessment approaches for school mathematics in order to achieve more valid, balanced, and reliable assessments of students' mathematical learning. Those responsible for carrying this agenda forward should work from a range of perspectives, including the role of receptive and expressive language in mathematics.

1.6 Semantic Structure

In his early paper, Brune (1953) referred to eight 'principles' concerning the effective use of words in mathematics teaching and learning. In the first of these principles, he predicted that semantics is likely to become 'the science explaining how *language affects other behaviour, especially thinking*' (p.170, emphasis in original). Later in the paper, he gave the following example:

> From situations such as: 'John had 15 cents, and he earned 10 cents more. How much money did he then have?' the pupil may associate 'more' with addition. When the same pupil meets the circumstance: 'John has 15 cents, but the movie he desires to see costs 25 cents. How much more does he need?' then the pupil finds the word 'more' in another context; the question, he notes, requires subtraction. (p.171)

Research (Riley, Greeno and Heller, 1983; Lean, Clements and Del Campo, 1990) has demonstrated that Brune's predictions about what might become a major focus in investigations into the language and mathematics interface were accurate.

A recent Newman error analysis study involving 101 Year 7 students in Malaysia and 61 students in Year 7 in Australia included mathematics questions with various semantic structures (Clements and Ellerton, in press), and results indicated that semantic structure is perhaps the most crucial variable affecting understanding. Thus, for example, 74 per cent of the Malaysian sample and 70 per cent of the Australian sample gave incorrect responses to the following question (given in *Bahasa Melayu* for the Malaysian students, with the name 'Radiah' being used instead of 'Roslyn'):

> Roslyn is 12 days older than Mary. If Roslyn's birthday is January 29, on what day is Mary's birthday?

Data from the Newman interviews carried out in this study suggest that, in fact, semantic structure was the main factor contributing to the difficulty of this and many other problems. Semantic structure has a much more important influence on learning and the quality of participation in classroom discourse than other more obvious language variables (such as vocabulary).

There have been two major thrusts in the psycholinguistic literature concerning the effect of semantic structure on word problems which may be regarded as having additive, subtractive or multiplicative structures. Fuson (1992) introduced her summary of recent research on whole number addition and subtraction in the following way:

Children's competence in addition and subtraction of whole numbers has been an exceedingly active and productive area of research. Research has yielded a description of developmental progression of successively more abstract and efficient conceptual structures that children in the U.S. construct for addition and subtraction of numbers up to about 100. We know less about how and why children move through this progression and about how parents and teachers can best help them to do so. A great deal of progress has also been made in understanding the different kinds of addition and subtraction situations that exist in the real world, and there is considerable agreement concerning a categorical system of these situations. (p.269)

Thus Fuson has painted an encouraging picture of the extent and quality of research which has informed those concerned with the teaching and learning of whole number addition and subtraction. The earlier work of Riley, Greeno and Heller (1983), and Carpenter and Moser (1984) laid the foundations to defining the range of possible structures.

However, an important warning needs to be voiced: although some of the research described in the international literature has generated results which are in accord with findings of researchers in the United States, there have been major studies outside the US which have generated results which are not in accord with theories and results of the US studies (see, for example, Del Campo and Clements, 1987; Lean, Clements and Del Campo, 1990). Systematic investigations into whether the findings based on learners from one country can be generalised to children from other countries need to be carried out.

The semantic structures of one-step word problems which might be regarded as having 'multiplication' and 'division' as structures have also been the subject of large-scale research studies (Vergnaud, 1982; Fischbein, Deri, Nello and Merino, 1985; Nesher, 1988; Bell, Greer, Grimison and Mangan, 1989; Mulligan, 1992; Mulligan and Mitchelmore, 1995). Greer (1992) presented a comprehensive summary of research which has focused on multiplicative concepts. A recent classification by Schmidt and Weiser (1995) has produced a comprehensive and differentiated classification, based on German data. Within this classification, Schmidt and Weiser linked and extended the part-part-whole structure of addition and subtraction to the part-whole structure of multiplication and division.

Research which focuses on multicultural mathematics classrooms, and on children who bring with them the experience of working in mathematics with different language structures is urgently needed. For example, the cultural specificity of certain elements of semantic structure such as the polarised comparative terms of 'more than' and 'less than' was pointed out by Christie (1995). According to Galligan (1995), structural differences between the Mandarin and English languages are likely to be responsible for differences observed in the performance of tertiary Australian business studies students on three tests, each in the students' first language, and presented in a one-to-one interview situation. The first test involved pure calculations, the second, context-free word problems, and the third, word problems in context.

The role of semantic structure in solving algebraic word problems has also been investigated (see, for example, MacGregor, 1994; Stacey, 1994; Mac-Gregor and Stacey, 1995). Kieran (1992), in her summary of the learning and teaching of algebra, traced the history of the transition from the use of ordinary language descriptions for the presentation of algebra to the current use of a truly symbolic notation. She stated that, just as algebra developed historically along a procedural-structural cycle, 'there is some strong evidence to support the notion that students pass through the same cycle in their learning of algebra' (p.414). She observed that, although both the teaching and content of algebra emphasise structural considerations, 'research has shown that most students do not reach this goal', and recommended a reconsideration of both the content and the teaching of algebra 'in the light of a procedural-structural dynamic of learning mathematics' (p.414).

Although it is recognised that length, detail and space limitations all restrict what can be included in major curriculum documents, there is little evidence in such documents and textbooks that anything other than superficial applications of the main research results are being incorporated into classroom practices. Thus, for example, in Australia, one might have expected appropriate reference to be made to the importance of semantic structure in the 'Using Mathematical Language' strand of the *Mathematics Profile* (Curriculum Corporation, 1994). Some reference to the group of additive and subtractive word problems was made. For example, Level 3 students were expected to be able to:

- Read and write numerical statements involving the four operations (18 - (24 - 7) = 1).
- Relate alternative everyday language expressions to one arithmetic expression ($45 \div 5 = ?$ may be read 'What is 45 divided by 5?' or 'How many lots of 5 in 45?'). (p.53)

A teacher who is familiar with the implications of incorporating a wide range of semantic structures into the language of the mathematics classroom would try to observe students' use of this range of structures when confronted with outcome statements such as these. However, a teacher who is *not* familiar with these implications would tend to adopt a superficial interpretation of the above outcome statements, and of other similarly generally-worded outcome statements included under the headings of 'Equations', 'Applying Numbers', and 'Written Computation'.

In Standard 7: Concepts of Whole Number Operations of the United States *Curriculum and Evaluation Standards for School Mathematics* (NCTM, 1989), the following statements were made:

In grades K-4, the mathematics curriculum should include concepts of addition, subtraction, multiplication, and division of whole numbers so that students can:

- develop meaning for the operations by modelling and discussing a rich variety of problem situations;
- relate the mathematical language and symbolism of operations to problem situations and informal language;
- recognize that a wide variety of problem structures can be represented by a single operation;
- develop operation sense. (p.41)

However, the discussion of possible additive and multiplicative structures, or of their importance, was confined to: 'Children should encounter the four basic operations in a wide variety of problem structures' (p.41), and the inclusion of two small illustrations with the captions 'Maria has 5 cars. Bill has 8 cars. How many more cars does Bill have?', and 'Anton, Juanita and Booker want to share 6 cookies equally. How many cookies does each one get?' (p.41).

Much more needs to be done to link research and practice. In particular, a concerted effort is needed to help practising teachers not only to become more aware of important research findings in this area, but also to support them as they design appropriate classroom environments.

There have been some major professional development programs which were not only aimed at communicating such research results, but also at actively involving teachers in applying them in their classrooms. An important example is the Cognitively Guided Instruction (CGI) program developed at the University of Wisconsin (see, for example, Fennema, Carpenter and Peterson, 1989). Mulligan and Mitchelmore (1995) in Australia have done much to make teachers aware of semantic difficulties in 'multiplicative' word problems. Also, examples of a broad range of contemporary research-based professional development programs were included in the 1994 NCTM Yearbook (Aichele and Coxford, 1994) titled *Professional Development for Teachers of Mathematics*.

2.   WRITING IN MATHEMATICS CLASSROOMS

The notion of 'writing to learn mathematics' has been used to describe, in broad terms, a range of approaches to the teaching and learning of which have been used increasingly, around the world, during the last decade. In spite of the increased attention paid to such approaches, and in spite of the growing number of articles and books which have been published with titles such as *Using Writing to Teach Mathematics* (Sterrett, undated), *Math Writing: Mak-*

ing the Connection (Rose-Piver and Short, 1995), and *Writing in Math Class* (Burns, 1995), systematic research into the effectiveness of using writing in mathematics classrooms to enhance mathematics learning is lacking.

The following five forms of 'writing mathematics' were identified by Ellerton and Clements (1992c):

a)   process/conference approaches;
b)   problem posing;
c)   journal writing;
d)   interactive monitoring of children's learning of mathematics, and
e)   investigative mathematics project reports.

Other manifestations of 'writing mathematics' include the use of story shells which emerge from children's literature (Griffiths and Clyne, 1993; Williams, 1993), and the use of projective techniques, such as having children write letters to, and devise problems for, classmates who have 'missed' mathematics classes (Ellerton, 1988).

2.1   A Research Agenda for the Writing Mathematics Movement

The following research agenda for the various forms of 'writing in mathematics' was proposed by Ellerton and Clements (1992c):

2.1.1   Research issues relating to students.

If students participate regularly in a particular form of 'writing mathematics', are they likely to

– perform as well as students who do not participate in this form of 'writing mathematics' on standard tests of mathematical skills, concepts and principles?
– link more readily their mathematical understandings with their personal worlds?
– become more efficient and effective at monitoring their own mathematical thinking so that they improve their own problem-solving and problem-posing performances?
– develop more positive affective (for example, liking/disliking, confident) responses to mathematics and mathematical situations? In particular, are students likely to develop feelings of ownership over mathematics they construct or write about?
– become more aware of their own abilities, attitudes and preferences in mathematics, and to be prepared to modify these in response to their own reflections?

2.1.2 Research issues relating to teachers.

At least three issues relate to teachers:
- From a teacher's point of view, is classroom time spent on 'writing mathematics' activities time wasted or time well spent from the point of view of developing students' mathematical understandings and positive attitudes?
- From a cost-benefit point of view, do students' mathematics scripts provide teachers with sufficiently valuable diagnostic and predictive data to justify the time taken for students to produce the scripts, and for teachers to read and comment on them, and to maintain pertinent records?
- Certain ethical questions arise: for example, are teachers entitled to assess a student's journal entries?

2.1.3 A research issue for curriculum developers.

From a curriculum developer's point of view, does the new genre of mathematical writing demanded by extended projects (such as the investigative projects referred to in the 'Language and Assessment' section of this chapter) resemble the kind of writing in which professional mathematicians engage, and if so, is this a strong justification for modifying curricula and assessment?

2.2 The Need For A Stronger Theoretical Base

The intuitive appeal of having students write in mathematics classrooms would appear to have had a major impact on the thinking of mathematics educators and mathematics education researchers during the last decade. Many articles have appeared in which possible ways of involving students in writing activities in mathematics classrooms are discussed; examples of students' writing are often included. Rarely, however, has any attempt been made to link the particular focus on writing in mathematics to any theoretical framework, or to the notion that 'writing' represents one of the expressive modes of communication, as discussed by Del Campo and Clements (1987). Most mathematics educators have failed to address many of the fundamental questions raised in the above research agenda.

In the section which follows, a brief summary will be presented of several studies which represent preliminary steps towards addressing this need to establish a stronger research base.

Problem posing incorporates various expressive modes of language, but at the school level it has been especially associated with the writing-to-learn mathematics movement. Problem posing has been explored from contrasting perspectives for over 50 years. Duncker (1945), for example, saw problem posing as the generation of a new problem or reformulation of a given.

More recently, Shukkwan (1993) interpreted problem posing as the formulation of a sequence of mathematical problems from a given situation; Mamona-Downs (1993) viewed problem posing as the activity which is precipitated when a problem invites the generation of other problems; and problem posing was referred to by Silver (1993, 1995) as involving the creation of a new problem from a situation or experience, or the reformulation of given problems.

The importance of an ability to pose significant questions in science was recognised by Einstein and Infeld (1938), who wrote: 'The formulation of a problem is often more essential than its solution, which may be merely a matter of mathematical or experimental skills. To raise new questions, new possibilities, to regard old questions from a new angle, requires creative imagination and marks real advance in science' (p.92). Mathematics educators, however, have been slow to recognise that developing the ability to pose mathematics problems is at least as important as developing the ability to solve them. Silver, Kilpatrick and Schlesinger (1990), for example, recognised that the incorporation of problem-posing activities into regular classroom situations can be a powerful approach for developing students' mathematical thinking.

More recently, Bruner (1996) has stated that the art of framing challenging questions is undoubtedly as important and as difficult as the art of giving clear answers. He went on to say that the 'art of cultivating such questions, of keeping good questions alive, is as important as either of those' (p.127).

The mathematics curriculum documents of several countries include brief reference to the place of problem posing in the curriculum. In Australia, for example, *A National Statement on Mathematics for Australian Schools* notes that: 'Students should engage in extended mathematical activities which encourage problem posing, divergent thinking, reflection and persistence. They should be expected to pursue alternative strategies, and to pose and attempt to answer their own mathematical questions' (Australian Education Council, 1991, p.39). In the United States*, The Curriculum and Evaluation Standards for School Mathematics*, (NCTM, 1989) stated 'Students in grade 9-12 should also have some experience recognising and formulating their own problems, an activity that is at the heart of doing mathematics' (p.138).

There is a growing interest towards incorporating problem posing-activities into mathematics classroom (see, for example, Brown and Walter, 1990, 1993; Kilpatrick, 1987; Silver and Mamona, 1989; Silver, Kilpatrick and

Schlesinger, 1990; Silver and Cai, 1993; Stoyanova and Ellerton, in press), and researchers have tried to use different frameworks for exploring problem posing. This movement makes it all the more important for researchers to develop appropriate frameworks for exploring problem posing.

The absence of a framework which has identified the different language factors involved in problem posing and has linked problem solving, problem posing and mathematics curricula has hampered research into the impact of problem posing on mathematics teaching and learning. A framework for research on problem posing which draws on Krutetskii's (1976) problem-solving categories was proposed by Stoyanova (1995). This framework adopted the notion that every problem-posing situation can be classified as free, semi-structured or structured.

A problem-posing situation can be described as *free*, when students are asked to generate a problem from a given, contrived or naturalistic situation. Richardson and Williamson (1982), for example, asked children to make up mathematics problems for each other. Kennedy (1985) had students devising mathematical problems about particular topics, and van den Brink (1987) asked Grade 2 children to make up mathematics problems and games for Grade 1 children. Ellerton (1986) asked children to make up mathematics problems that would be difficult for a friend to solve. Ellerton (1988) commented that: 'children's expression of mathematical ideas through the creation of their own mathematics problems demonstrates not only their understanding and level of concept development, but also reflects their perception about the nature of mathematics' (p.281).

According to Stoyanova (1995), a problem-posing situation can be described as *semi-structured* when students are given an open situation and are invited to explore the structure and to complete it by applying knowledge, skills, concepts and relationships from their previous mathematical experiences. Hart (1981), for example, asked children to make up mathematics problems to fit given computations. Winograd (1991) found that children generally composed problems which they themselves had difficulty understanding or solving. In another study, students who wrote problem stories tended to learn to integrate mathematics with other subject areas and to develop creative writing skills (Bush and Fiala, 1986).

A problem-posing situation will be called *structured* when problem-posing activities are based on a specific problem. In order to reveal the structure of students' mathematical abilities Krutetskii (1976) used a research tool involving students in finishing or reconstructing a specific problem structure. In his study he used problems with unstated questions, problems with insufficient and problems with surplus information. Hashimoto (1987) asked students to pose problems similar to a given problem. Stover (1982) investigated the impact of having students make format changes to given mathematics problems. Smilansky (1984) investigated the relationship between being able to solve problems and to pose problems in the same domain. After students had completed a mathematics test, he asked them to create new problems which would be particularly difficult if they were included in a future version of the test.

It is to be hoped that the development and clarification of a suitable research framework for mathematical problem-posing will enable full advantage to be taken of a relatively untapped area of 'writing mathematics' in the classroom. Because of the range of problem posing activities suggested by this framework, problem posing has the potential to challenge and change the approaches used by many mathematics teachers.

2.4   Journal Writing in Mathematics Classrooms

Clarke, Waywood and Stephens (1993) re-analysed data associated with a longitudinal study of journal writing which involved 500 secondary students, and developed a grid to help in the analysis and presentation of data from such studies. The grid contained four columns to describe students' journal entries and provided examples, summaries of questions asked, and applications of the mathematics students used in their journals; it also included six rows, to describe student behaviours in sequence from simple ('Able to regularly copy part or most of the board notes into the journal') to complex ('Able to extrapolate from material presented in class, or in a text, and reshape it in terms of own learning needs').

Waywood (1993) recommended that students should be encouraged to 'tell a story' when they keep journals simultaneously with 'pursuing a study'. His theoretical stance has been drawn from working with students and staff in a school over a number of years, and from his observations that students appear to have difficulty in constructing reports (Waywood, 1992). He concluded that there is a distinction between 'language as lived' and 'language as reflected on', and he suggested that an appropriate heuristic for the mathematics classroom may be to integrate telling a story (a chronicle account, record, or journal) with doing a study (Waywood, 1993).

A study in which several hundred examples of students' expository writing over a two-year period were examined was reported by Shield (1995a), and built on work carried out by Shield (1995b) and Shield and Swinson (1994). The following types of elaborations produced by students were identified, although it was recognised that finding all types in any given presentation would be very unlikely.

— nucleus: definition or general statement of procedure;
— goal: statement identifying the concept or procedure being explained;
— demonstration: worked example of the concept or procedure elaborated with
    a) symbolic representation,
    b) verbal description,

c) diagrammatic representation, and

d) statement of convention;

— justification: statement justifying parts of the procedure in terms of known ideas;

— link: reference to prior knowledge or everyday experience;

— practice: exercises to be attempted by the reader by modelling on the demonstration.

(Shield, 1995a, p.38)

The development and refinement of frameworks such as this should help teachers and researchers begin to understand the complexity of students' writing, and to help them start to see where and how students make links between the mathematical concepts they are learning, the mathematical language they are developing, and the 'real-world' experiences which they bring with them to the classroom.

2.5   Is it Natural for Students to Write in Mathematics Classrooms?

What and how do children communicate in mathematics classrooms? The focusing and channelling modes which have been revealed in interactionist research (Steinbring, 1994; Voigt, 1995) suggest that much of the interaction in classrooms stems from students' reactions to the teacher's agenda. There is a danger that the writing-in-mathematics movement will come to be regarded by mathematicians, students, parents and teachers alike, as a superficial add-on to the mathematics curriculum, the dream-child of mathematics educators remote from the classroom. Yet, hidden within the notion is the very essence of mathematics itself. The challenge, therefore, is to create learning environments in which writing mathematics becomes a natural, regular and creative form of expressive communication. As Burns (1995) has stated:

Over a school year, writing in math class seems to change for students from a tag-on demand to math assignments, to a reasonable extension of what they're doing in class, and finally to a natural and integral part of their math learning. (p.125)

Changes to classroom culture do not take place in a day or a week or by the mere inclusion of a few spasmodic and uncoordinated mathematics writing activities.

When Glen Lean, the Australian mathematics educator, set out to study the indigenous counting systems of Oceania, Polynesia and Melanesia, he found himself confronted with the task of documenting and exploring relationships between about 2000 different systems. His seminal doctoral thesis provides a large body of evidence to support his conclusion that every distinct language had an associated unique counting system. Even when two different counting systems appeared to have the same structure (for instance, some form of base 5) there were always subtle differences. For example, one system might have a generic name for the cardinality of different sets of objects which could be put in one-to-one correspondence, whereas another system might have different names depending on the objects in the sets (Lean, 1992).

Lean (1992, 1995) placed great emphasis on the fundamental idea that counting systems are an integral part of language, and that language is inextricably bound to culture. That is not to say that all who speak the same language automatically share the same culture, for there are many obvious counter-examples to such a proposition. However, those who speak the same first language are likely to have at least some common cultural understandings, and where this is not the case, at least there is a common language with which differences can be identified and discussed.

Bishop (1988) has developed the thesis that all indigenous societies have their own forms of 'small m' mathematics – which differ from the internationalised 'Capital M' Mathematics. Although Bishop recognised the uniqueness and richness of each system of indigenous mathematics, he argued that it is helpful to seek to identify commonalities. In order to do this he argued for six major categories: counting, locating, measuring, designing, playing, and explaining.

Gay and Cole's (1967) research was motivated by a need to understand why the Kpelle children (in Liberia) had difficulty handling the 'new mathematics' in their Westernised schools. Gay and Cole (1967) reported that the problems faced by the Kpelle children included:

– The linguistic potential for classification in the Kpelle language did not guarantee that the process would occur (p.39);
– The Kpelle rarely need to count beyond 30 or 40 (p.42);
– All arithmetic activity is tied to concrete situations (p.50);
– The Kpelle name only those geometrical shapes which are commonly used in their culture (p.61);
– Units of measure are not generalised, but are specific to particular objects being measured (p.75);
– The Kpelle language includes a negative, several conjunctions, both inclusive and exclusive disjunctions, and several linguistic structures for expressing inference. However, equivalence can only be expressed in complicated ways (p.83).

Notice the inseparability of different aspects of indigenous mathematics, language and culture in these points.

Harris (1987), in her provocative analysis of measurement concepts in Aboriginal communities in Australia, reached similar conclusions. Harris had taught Aboriginal students for many years, and was concerned about the great difficulty that most Aboriginal students experienced with prescribed Western mathematics curricula. Her research which involved extensive linguistic analysis of Aboriginal languages, led her to conclude that 'any applied number program which is written for English-speaking white Australian children mainly living in urban situations is likely to be both inappropriate and inadequate for use with vernacular speaking Aboriginal children living in remote tribal communities' (p.75). This was because:

— Many of the concepts presented will be foreign to Aboriginal children, and in conflict with their traditional world views;
— In many instances, it is very difficult to express Western mathematical concepts in the Aboriginal children's first languages. Even if this is possible, the 'translation' will often be semantically awkward and complex, thus causing confusion with vocabulary and terminology;
— In some cases, where concepts are totally foreign to the children's cultures, there will be no concise ways of explaining them in the children's own languages. Thus, the children will be required to learn new vocabulary and new concepts simultaneously, and usually they are expected to do this when the language of instruction is not their first language;
— Many of the concepts introduced will not be reinforced outside school since they are not used in the Aboriginal communities (and often they are in conflict with established custom);
— The concepts presented often assume prior knowledge and experiences that Aboriginal children do not have, yet ignore the sets of knowledge and experiences that Aboriginal children do have;
— The programs fail to take into account the Aboriginal children's different cultures, and therefore do not observe the fundamental pedagogical principle that teaching should start with the known before proceeding to the unknown.

One of Harris's (1987, 1991) main concerns was to attempt to assist teachers of Aboriginal students to link elements of existing mathematics curricula with the personal worlds of the students, including their first languages. Zevenbergen (1995) on the other hand, was not comfortable with the propensity of Westerner educators to describe indigenous activities, objects and relationships in terms of Western mathematics, claiming that this compromises the inherent uniqueness of the indigenous culture. She specifically criticised Harris for drawing attention to sets of concentric circles which appear in Aboriginal Western Desert art, claiming that this 'subjugates the inherent spirit-uality of Aboriginal art' (p.43).

Zevenbergen (1995) also criticised Bishop's (1988) six categories, claim-ing that this was another instance of a Westerner using mathematics to impose structure and meaning on indigenous activities:

> In this way, mathematics as it is defined in Western terms, is an inappropriate classification system for other cultures. For example, the search for hidden mathematics in sacred dances (Lawlor, 1982) seems reasonable since, for Westerners, geometry is a means for organising our world. The movements which are displayed by the women dancers translated into geometric activities where there are distinct, measurable, angles constructed by the body. This translation of the activity is [a] very ethnocentric and Western translation of the activity. For those people whose dance is being investigated, the notions of geometry in dance may be antithetical to the interpretation of the dance, and in fact may be sacrilegious. For such people, the category of geometry may not exist so the geometric interpretation of dance movements is very (Western) mathematico-centric.
>
> (Zevenbergen, 1995, pp.37-38)

Stephen Harris (1990) argued along similar lines, and emphasised the impor-tance of locating education theory and practice within cultural frameworks:

> The nature and degree of the difference between Aboriginal and European culture is so great that the only honest conclusion we can arrive at is that they are largely incompatible. The two cultures are antithetic — consisting of more opposites than similarities. They are warring against each other at their foundations. Recognising and accepting the truth of the term incompatible was for me … the point of theoretical liberation and the starting point for a more effective educational theory to be applied in Aboriginal schools. This degree of difference is so great that it is harder to find what they have in common in cultural terms than it is to see the differences. (p.9)

No doubt, there is some point to Zevenbergen's and Stephen Harris's argu-ments. However, one needs to recognise the reality that, as we approach the year 2000, an increasing number of children from non-Western backgrounds are being required to study Western mathematics for many years. Under these circumstances, if school mathematics is to have any meaning in the context of students' personal worlds, then it is important to explore how appropriate links can be developed.

As Jones, Kershaw and Sparrow (1995) have noted, the process whereby Aboriginal and other non-Western groups will have the right for their children to experience a curriculum which links with their personal worlds rather than being in opposition to it, is underway. Effectively, 'cultural reaffirmation has translated into a decolonising process, particularly with respect to education' (p.2). Western mathematics, together with its associated language and symbol forms, represents a highly specialised way of thinking, and to a certain extent that explains Béchervaise's (1992) description of mathematics as a foreign language.

In a comparative study, Bishop (1992) showed that the cultural perspective challenges in fundamental ways 'the instrumental 'arrow' of intended, to implemented, to attained' curriculum (p.185). According to Bishop (1992):

> The cultural perspective requires us to culturalise the curriculum at each of the levels, and demonstrates that no aspect of mathematics teaching can be culturally neutral. The cultural 'messages' in the educational enterprise are created and manifested by people. People create the national and local curriculum statements, people write the books and computer programs, people bring their cultural histories into the classroom, and people interpret and reconstruct the various messages. (p.185)

For Bishop, this cultural perspective reaffirmed the centrality of people in the educational enterprise, and demonstrated that mathematical knowledge is constructed, interpreted and shaped by people who exercise choices.

One of the most fundamental aspects of all cultures is language, and it should be of serious concern that so many mathematics education researchers appear to have paid little more than lip service to the centrality of language factors in all aspects of mathematics teaching and learning (Mousley, Clements and Ellerton, 1992).

2.6.1 Bilingualism and Mathematics Learning

In many classrooms around the world, particularly those in large cities, children are learning mathematics in their second or third (and sometimes fourth or fifth) language. There are numerous classrooms in which ten or more different first languages are represented among the children present. With increased mobility of families and children — for a wide range of reasons — the issue of bilingualism (or multilingualism) can no longer be pushed to one side. Research by Secada (1988) and by Duran (1988), for example, suggests that there is a relationship between the degree of bilingualism and logical reasoning. In the following passage, Secada asks readers to assume that it is the norm to be bilingual — as, indeed, it is in many parts of the world:

Then, from the beginning, we would have pursued a line of research based on the premise of the cognitive advantages of being bilingual. … In such a world, we would be worrying about the deviant behaviour of monolingual children who seem unable to free themselves from the semantic constraints of the word problems they were encountering. We would be looking for models of comprehension and learning by which their deficit performance would be explained. In such a world we would probably try to understand these children's deficiencies: the lack of dual language competence and limited flexibility in applying strategies to new problems. (p.32)

Secada's (1988) comments underscore the fact that research necessarily reflects the perspective of the researcher.

Many major curriculum documents now include specific comments and recommendations about students from minority language and ethic backgrounds. In New Zealand, for example, the New Zealand Ministry of Education's (1992) *Mathematics in the New Zealand Curriculum* acknowledged that 'factors such as out-of-school experience and language have profound effects on the way students learn mathematics' (p.12). In a statement about catering for individual needs, the New Zealand Ministry of Education argued:

It is important that mathematical learning experiences for Maori students acknowledge the background experiences which have led to the formation of ideas and skills which those students already have. Maori students will be helped to achieve if teachers acknowledge and value those ideas and experiences. (p.12)

A Maori version of the New Zealand national curriculum has been published (Ta Tahuhu o te Matauranga, 1994).

Bilingual programs in New Zealand focus on the Maori language, and a framework for teaching mathematics bilingually to students in Forms 1 and 2 has been developed (Nathan, Trinick, Tobin and Barton, 1993). The aim of this framework is to integrate bilingual education and mathematics education by:
— extracting mathematical ideas from within the Maori culture which support cultural themes;
— providing opportunities for students to connect ideas within and across cultures, and within and outside the mathematics curriculum; and
— emphasising Maori language and Maori structures in the organisation of mathematics programs. (p.296)

There is, however, a wide range of fluency in the Maori language in New Zealand classrooms.

A National Statement on Mathematics for Australian Schools (Australian Education Council, 1991) acknowledged that the 'complex interaction of linguistic and cultural factors on the learning of mathematics is only beginning to be understood' (p.9). The *National Statement* went on to say

> Surface facility with English can often mask the language difficulties of students for whom English is a second language or with non-English speaking backgrounds. Sometimes such students are regarded as lacking in mathematical ability when they are actually experiencing problems with the formal language of the mathematics classroom. (p.9)

The *National Statement* noted that it was another matter to ensure that acknowledging diversity did not become a different name for stereotyping individuals.

In the United States of America, the *Curriculum and Evaluation Standards for School Mathematics* included a section titled 'Learner Characteristics' in its Overview of the Curriculum Standards for Years 5 to 8 (NCTM, 1989). The following statement appears to reflect the view that students' cultural backgrounds and experiences should be respected, and that the teaching and learning of mathematics in multicultural classrooms should differ in subtle ways from that in monolingual/monocultural mathematics classrooms.

> Whenever possible, students' cultural backgrounds should be integrated into the learning experience. Black or Hispanic students, for example, may find the development of mathematical ideas in their cultures of great interest. Teachers must also be sensitive to the fact that students bring very different everyday experiences to the mathematics classroom. The way in which a student from an urban environment and a student from a suburban or rural environment interpret a problem situation can be very different. This is an important reason why communication is one of the overarching goals of these standards. (p.68)

Two serious concerns are:
  a) the lack of a comprehensive research base for such approaches; and
  b) the extent to which findings reported in the literature on the learning of mathematics in bilingual classrooms have not been incorporated into major curriculum documents.

Over the past decade, research into the influence of bilingualism on mathematics education has been strongly influenced by the linguistic theories of Cummins (1979, 1986). Cummins recognised that, for learners who speak two or more languages, the interplay in the learning process between the language codes may either assist or detract from learning. Thus, if it is an accepted part of classroom culture for learners to use more than one language, then learners may have a cognitive advantage if a threshold of competence in the two (or more) languages has been reached. However, if learners are expected to use only the language of instruction (and are made to feel guilty for employing any language other than this), 'then a subtractive environment with deficit cognitive outcome results' (Clarkson and Thomas, 1993, p.265).

A longitudinal study being conducted by Clarkson and Dawe (1994) is examining the mathematical problem-solving processes of 600 Italian, Arabic, or Vietnamese speakers who were in Year 4 in 1994 in schools in Melbourne and Sydney. The levels of competence of the students in their different languages, including English, the extent of code switching used by students during problem solving, and the effect of time and schooling on such code switching, are being investigated.

The effects of monolingualism, bilingualism, and multilingualism on mathematics learning in Papua New Guinea have been investigated by Clarkson (1992b), Clarkson, 1994; and Clarkson and Kaleva (1993). Results from these studies suggest that, in schools where English is predominantly the language of instruction, non-English-speaking background (NESB) learners benefit from receiving mathematics *instruction in their first language,* at the same time as they are learning to speak English. In Queensland, Australia, Berthold (1995) has investigated the notion of 'immersion', with English-speaking-background primary school children learning mathematics in another language.

An important implication of Cummins' (1979) threshold hypothesis is that bilingual students who are not really fluent in either of the two languages that they use tend to experience difficulty in mathematics. Clearly, also, problems are likely to be encountered if teachers in bilingual programs lack fluency in either language (see, for example, MacGregor, 1993; Woo-Hyung Whang, 1996). Thomas (1995) argued that, in the light of the accumulated data on performance patterns of NESB students, language policies for the teaching of mathematics should be revised immediately. Thomas pointed out that many NESB children are proficient in neither their first language nor English. Consistent with Cummins's Threshold hypothesis, these children often experience major learning difficulties in many subjects, including mathematics.

'Glossaries' of mathematical terms in other languages for use by mathematics students are now available commercially. For example, glossaries for Grades K-2, 3-5 and 6-8 have been produced for several languages by the publishers Silver Burdett Ginn Inc. (1995b). One should be concerned, however, that the language used for the definitions given in the glossaries is sometimes quite sophisticated, and technical, and is more likely to make learning mathematics in English *more* difficult rather than support and facilitate it. For example, two 'definitions' given in the K-2 Glossary for Cantonese-English are:

— *Doubles:* Having equal addends in one operation. The sum of two addends is twice one of the addends.

— *Zero:* One minus one. The number that is to the left of one on the number line.

One might ask whether such definitions are likely to help young children aged between about 6 to 8 years in their endeavours to learn mathematics in a language other than their mother tongue.

In summary, then, bilingualism is natural for many children, but it is too often assumed — especially by researchers and educators who can read, write and speak only one language fluently — that it is the norm to be monolingual (Secada, 1988). Also, most of the so-called multicultural materials available take the form of 'Here are some of the number ideas which have come from other countries'. True valuing of approaches used by other countries does not appear to be present — nor is there any research to suggest ways in which the experiences/mathematical understandings of students from other social and cultural backgrounds can be valued/incorporated in normal classroom routines.

CONCLUSION

In keeping with the findings of interactionist research (for example, Voigt, 1985, 1995; Steinbring, 1994; Bauersfeld, 1995; Lerman, 1996), we contend that much of the interaction and communication in mathematics classrooms is still predominantly symbolic and contrived. Mathematics, as presented in many classrooms, does not evolve naturally from the students' own environments, but is dictated by adults' simplification of what they perceive to be appropriate 'mathematics' for the students concerned, and by the students' reactions and expectations to this imposition.

Nickson (1992) described the unique culture of the mathematics classroom as

> the product of what the teacher and pupils bring to it in terms of knowledge, beliefs, and values, and how these affect the social interactions within that context. It is all too easy to assume that these invisibles of the cultural core are shared by all the participants and that there is harmony of views about the goals being pursued and the values related to them. ... There is more possibility for choice and more possibility that those choices will be guided by different beliefs and values. Consequently, there will be greater variation in the cultures of mathematics classrooms. (p.111)

Hand-in-hand with this greater variation is an 'increased potential for lack of consensus' (Nickson, 1992, p.111), and a potential for serious mismatches between the goals and views of teachers and students.

Mathematics educators need to take up the challenge of working within the freedom defined by individual beliefs and values while, at the same time recognising the potential restrictions created by mismatches and a lack of consensus. An essential first step is an awareness of such mismatches; a logical second step is to find ways of avoiding the mismatches, or at least of dealing with them without removing the freedom which created them.

The role of language is pivotal in both steps. As Bruner (1996) concluded: 'What language permits is the construction and elaboration of that 'network of mutual expectations' which is the matrix on which culture is constructed' (p.184). If it is through language forms adopted in mathematics classrooms that mismatches between the goals and views of teachers and students are created, then it is also the case that, by coming to understand these language forms, the mismatches can be identified, observed, and ultimately resolved in ways which facilitate richer modes of communication between all involved in the creation of mathematical meaning.

ACKNOWLEDGMENT

The authors wish to acknowledge the contributions made by Mr. Michael Liau (RECSAM, Malaysia) and Dr. Cathy Anegbi (University of Jos, Nigeria).

REFERENCES

Aichele, D.B. and Coxford, A.F. (eds.): 1994, *Professional Development for Teachers of Mathematics,* National Council of Teachers of Mathematics, Reston, VA.
Aiken, L.R.: 1972, 'Language Factors in Learning Mathematics', *Review of Educational Research* 42, 359-385.
Alro, H. and Skovsmose, O.: 1996, 'On the Right Track', *For the Learning of Mathematics* 16(1), 2-22.
Atweh, B.: 1993, 'A Sociolinguistic Perspective in the Study of the Social Context in Mathematics Education', in B. Atweh, C. Kanes, M. Carss and G. Booker (eds.), *Contexts in Mathematics Education,* Mathematics Education Research Group of Australasia, Brisbane, 57-63.
Atweh, B., Cooper, T., and Kanes, C. (eds.): 1992, 'The Social and Cultural Contexts in Mathematics Education', in *Research in Mathematics Education in Australia,* Mathematics Education Research Group of Australasia, Brisbane, 43-66.
Austin, J.L. and Howson, A.G.: 1979, 'Language and Mathematical Education', *Educational Studies in Mathematics* 10, 161-197.
Australian Education Council: 1991, *A National Statement on Mathematics for Australian Schools,* Curriculum Corporation, Melbourne.
Bauersfeld, H.: 1988, 'Interaction, Construction, and Knowledge: Alternative Perspectives for Mathematics Education', in D.A. Grouws and D. Cooney (eds.), *Effective Mathematics Teaching,* Reston, VA.

Bauersfeld, H.: 1994, 'Theoretical Perspectives on Interaction in the Mathematics Classroom', in R. Biehler, R.W. Scholtz, R. Sträber and B. Winkelmann (eds.), *Didactics of Mathematics as a Scientific Discipline*, Kluwer, Dordrecht.

Bauersfeld, H.: 1995, 'Language Games in the Mathematics Classroom: Their Function and their Effects', in P. Cobb and H. Bauersfeld (eds.), *The Emergence of Mathematical Meaning: Interaction in Classroom Cultures*, Lawrence Erlbaum Associates, Hillsdale, New Jersey.

Béchervaise, N.: 1992, 'Mathematics: A Foreign Language?', *The Australian Mathematics Teacher* 48(2), 4-9.

Begle, E.G.: 1979, *Critical Variables in Mathematics Education*, Mathematical Association of America and the National Council of Teachers of Mathematics, Washington, D.C.

Bell, A., Greer, B., Grimison, L., and Mangan, C.: 1989, 'Children's Performance on Multiplicative Word Problems: Elements of a Descriptive Theory', *Journal for Research in Mathematics Education* 20, 434-449.

Berthold, M.: 1995, *Rising to the Bilingual Challenge: Ten Years of Queensland's Secondary School Immersion*, National Languages and Literacy Institute of Australia, Canberra.

Bickmore-Brand, J. (ed.): 1990, *Language in Mathematics*, Australian Reading Association, Carlton, Vic.

Bishop, A.J.: 1988, *Mathematical Enculturation*, Kluwer, Dordrecht.

Bishop, A.J.: 1992, 'Cultural Issues in the Intended, Implemented and Attained Mathematics Curriculum', in G.C. Leder (ed.), *Assessment and Learning of Mathematics*, Australian Council for Educational Research, Hawthorn, Victoria, 169-189.

Black, P.J.: 1994, 'Performance Assessment and Accountability: The Experience in England and Wales', *Educational Evaluation and Policy Analysis* 16(2), 191-203.

Blane, D.: 1992, 'Curriculum Planning, Assessment and Student Learning in Mathematics: A Top-Down Approach', in G.C. Leder (ed.), *Assessment and Learning of Mathematics*, Australian Council for Educational Research, Hawthorn, Victoria, 290-304.

Brousseau, G.: 1986, 'Fondements et Méthodes de la Didactique des Mathématiques', *Recherches en Didactique des Mathématiques* 7, 33-115.

Brown, G.: 1982, 'The Spoken Language', in R. Carter (ed.), *Linguistics and the Teacher*, Routledge and Kegan Paul, London.

Brown, S. and Walter, M.I.: 1990, *The Art of Problem Posing*, Franklin Institute Press, Philadelphia, USA.

Brown, S. and Walter, M.I. (eds.): 1993, *Problem Posing: Reflections and Applications*, Lawrence Erlbaum, Hillsdale, NJ.

Brown, T.: 1994, 'Creating and Knowing Mathematics Through Language and Experience', *Educational Studies in Mathematics* 27, 79-100.

Brune, I.H.: 1953, 'Language in Mathematics', in H.F. Fehr (ed.), *The Learning of Mathematics: Its Theory and Practice*, National Council of Teachers of Mathematics, Washington, DC, 156-191.

Bruner, J.: 1996, *The Culture of Education*, Harvard University Press, Cambridge.

Buerk, D.: 1994, 'Broadening Students' Conceptions of Mathematics: Theory into Action', in D. Buerk (ed.), *Empowering Students by Promoting Active Learning in Mathematics*, National Council of Teachers of Mathematics, Reston, VA, 45-48.

Burns, M.: 1995, *Writing in Math Class*, Math Solutions Publications, Sausalito, CA.

Burton, G.: 1985, 'Writing as a Way of Knowing in a Mathematics Education Class', *The Arithmetic Teacher* 33, 40-45.

Bush, W. and Fiala, A.: 1986, 'Problem Stories: New Twist on Problem Posing', *The Arithmetic Teacher* 34(4), 6-9.

Carpenter, T.P. and Moser, J.M.: 1984, 'The Acquisition of Addition and Subtraction Concepts in Grades One Through Three', *Journal for Research in Mathematics Education* 15, 179-202.

Casey, D.P.: 1978, 'Failing Students: A Strategy of Error Analysis', in P. Costello (ed.), *Aspects of Motivation,* Mathematical Association of Victoria, Melbourne, 295-306.

Christie, M.: 1995, *The Purloined Pedagogy: Aboriginal Epistemology and Maths Education,* paper presented at the Eighteenth Annual Conference of the Mathematics Education Research Group of Australasia, Darwin, July 1995.

Clarke, D.J.: 1992, 'The Role of Assessment in Determining Mathematics Performance', in G. Leder (ed.), *Assessment and Learning of Mathematics,* Australian Council for Educational Research, Hawthorn, Victoria, 145-168.

Clarke, D.J.: 1993, 'The Language of Assessment', in M. Stephens, A. Waywood, D. Clarke and J. Izard (eds.), *Communicating Mathematics: Perspectives From Classroom Practice and Current Research,* Australian Council for Educational Research, Hawthorn, Victoria, 211-222.

Clarke, D. and Jasper, K.: 1995. 'Reflections on Assessment: A Practical Scheme for Classroom Assessment', *Reflections* 20(2), 5-10.

Clarke. D.J., Stephens, M. and Wallbridge, M.: 1993, 'The Instructional Impact of Changes in Assessment', in B. Atweh, C. Kanes, M. Carss and G. Booker (eds.), *Contexts in Mathematics Education: Proceedings of the Sixteenth Annual Conference of the Mathematics Education Research Group of Australasia,* Mathematics Education Research Group of Australasia, Brisbane, 177-182.

Clarke, D., Sullivan, P., and Spandel, U.: 1992, 'Student Response Characteristics to Open-ended Tasks in Mathematical and Other Academic Contexts', in B. Southwell, B. Perry and K. Owens (eds.), *Proceedings of the Fifteenth Annual Conference of the Mathematics Education Research Group of Australasia,* Mathematics Education Research Group of Australasia, Richmond, New South Wales, 209-221.

Clarke, D.J., Waywood, A., and Stephens, M.: 1993, 'Probing the Structure of Mathematical Writing', *Educational Studies in Mathematics 25,* 235-250.

Clarkson, P.C.: 1980, 'The Newman Error Analysis – Some Extensions', in B.A. Foster (ed.), *Research in Mathematics Education in Australia 1980* (Vol. 1), Mathematics Education Research Group of Australia, Hobart, 11-22.

Clarkson, P.C.: 1983, 'Types of Errors Made by Papua New Guinean Students', in *Report No. 26,* Papua New Guinea University of Technology Mathematics Education Centre, Lae.

Clarkson, P.C.: 1991, 'Language Comprehension Errors: A Further Investigation', *Mathematics Education Research Journal* 3(2), 24-33.

Clarkson, P.C.: 1992a, 'Evaluation: Some Other Perspectives', in T.A. Romberg (ed.), *Mathematics Assessment and Evaluation,* State University of New York Press, Albany, NY, 285-300.

Clarkson, P.C.: 1992b, 'Language and Mathematics: A Comparison of Bilingual and Monolingual Students of Mathematics', *Educational Studies in Mathematics* 23(4), 417-430.

Clarkson, P.C., 1994, 'Mathematics and Language: Culture and Implementation.' *Journal of Science and Mathematics Education in Southeast Asia* 17(1), 25-31.

Clarkson, P.C. and Dawe, L.: 1994, 'Problem Solving in Two Languages: A Longitudinal Study of Bilingual Students in Melbourne and Sydney', in G. Bell, B. Wright, N. Leeson and J. Geake (eds.), *Challenges in Mathematics Education: Constraints on Construction,* (Vol. 1), Mathematics Education Research Group of Australasia, Lismore, New South Wales, 173-178.

Clarkson, P.C. and Kaleva, W.: 1993, 'Mathematics Education in Papua New Guinea', in G. Bell (ed.), *Asian Perspectives on Mathematics Education: Maths x Language = Language x Maths,* Asian Perspectives on Mathematics Education Project, Lismore, NSW, 111-121.

Clarkson, P.C. and Thomas, J.: 1993, 'Communicating Mathematics Bilingually', in M. Stephens, A. Waywood, D. Clarke, and J. Izard (eds.), *Communicating Mathematics: Perspectives from Classroom Practice and Current,* Hawthorn, Victoria, 263-273.

Clements, M.A.: 1980, 'Analysing Children's Errors on Written Mathematical Tasks', *Educational Studies in Mathematics* 11(1), 1-21.

Clements, M.A.: 1982, 'Careless Errors Made By Sixth-Grade Children on Written Mathematical Tasks', *Journal for Research in Mathematics Education* 13(2), 136-144.

Clements, M.A.: 1984, 'Language Factors in School Mathematics', in P. Costello, S. Ferguson, K. Slinn, M. Stephens, D. Trembath, and D. Williams (eds.), *Facets of Australian Mathematics Education*, Australian Association of Mathematics Teachers, Adelaide, South Australia, 137-148.

Clements, M.A. and Ellerton, N.F.: 1992, 'Overemphasising Process Skills in School Mathematics: Newman Analysis Data From Five Countries', in W. Geeslin and K. Graham (eds.), *Proceedings of the Sixteenth International Conference on the Psychology of Mathematics Education* (Vol. 1), International Group for the Psychology of Mathematics Education, Durham, New Hampshire, 145-152.

Clements, M. A. and Ellerton, N. F.: 1995, 'Short-answer and multiple-choice pencil-and-paper tests: Still useful for school mathematics in the 21st century?' *Journal of Science and Mathematics Education in Southeast Asia* 18(2), 10-23.

Clements, M.A. and Ellerton, N.F.: In press, *Mathematics Education Research: Past Present and Future*, UNESCO, Bangkok.

Clements, M.A. and Thomas, J.: 1996, 'Politics of Mathematics Education: Australasian Perspectives', in B. Atweh, K. Owens and P. Sullivan (eds.), *Mathematics Education Research in Australasia 1992-1995*. Mathematics Education Research Group of Australasia, Sydney, 89-117.

Cobb, P.: 1990, 'Multiple Perspectives', in L.P. Steffe and T. Wood (eds.), *Transforming Children's Mathematics Education: International Perspectives*, Lawrence Erlbaum, Hillsdale, NJ, 200-215.

Cocking, R.R. and Mestre, J.P.: 1988, *Linguistic and Cultural Influences on Learning Mathematics*, Lawrence Erlbaum Associates, New Jersey.

Corson, D.: 1985, *The Lexical Bar*, Pergamon Press, Oxford.

Crawford, K., Gordon, S., Nicholas, J., and Prosser, M.: 1993, 'Learning Mathematics at University Level: Initial Conceptions of Mathematics', in B. Atweh, C. Kanes, M. Carss, and G. Booker (eds.), *Contexts in Mathematics Education*, Mathematics Education Research Group of Australasia, Brisbane, 209-214.

Cummins, J.: 1979, 'Linguistic Interdependence and the Educational Development of Bilingual Children', *Review of Educational Research* 49, 222-251.

Cummins, J.: 1986, 'Empowering Minority Students: A Framework of Intervention', *Harvard Educational Review* 56, 18-36.

Curriculum Corporation: 1994, *Mathematics – A Curriculum Profile for Australian Schools*, Curriculum Corporation, Carlton, Victoria.

Del Campo, G. and Clements, M.A.: 1987, 'Elementary Schoolchildren's Processing of 'Change' Arithmetic Word Problems', in J.C. Bergeron, N. Herscovics and C. Kieran (eds.), *Proceedings of the Eleventh International Conference on the Psychology of Mathematics Education*, PME Montréal, Vol. 2, 382-386.

Duncker, K.: 1945, 'On Problem Solving', *Psychological Monographs* 58 (5, Whole No. 270).

Durkin, K. and Shire, B. (eds.): 1990, *Language in Mathematical Education: Research and Practice*, Open University Press, Milton Keynes, UK.

Duran, R.P.: 1988, 'Bilinguals' Logical Reasoning Ability: A Construct Validity Study', in R.R. Cocking and J.P. Mestre (eds.), *Linguistic and Cultural Influences on Learning Mathematics*, Lawrence Erlbaum, Hillsdale, NJ, 241-258.

Einstein, A. and Infeld, L.: 1938, *The Evolution of Physics*, Simon and Schuster, New York.

Ellerton, N.F.: 1986, 'Children's Made-up Problems: A New Perspective on Talented Mathematicians', *Educational Studies in Mathematics*, 17, 261-271.

Ellerton, N.F.: 1988, 'Exploring Children's Perception of Mathematics Through Letters and Problems Written by Children', in A. Borbas (ed.), *Proceedings of the Twelfth International Conference on the Psychology of Mathematics Education,* International Group for the Psychology of Mathematics Education, Oaxtepec, Mexico, Vol. 2, 177-184.

Ellerton, N.F.: 1989, 'The Interface Between Mathematics and Language', *Australian Journal of Reading* 12(2), 92-102.

Ellerton, N.F. and Clements, M.A.: 1990, 'Cognitive Dissonance Versus Success as the Basis for Meaningful Mathematical Learning', in G. Booker, P. Cobb, and T.N. de Mendicuti (eds.), *Proceedings of the Fourteenth International Conference on the Psychology of Mathematics Education,* vol. 2, International Group for the Psychology of Mathematics Education, Oaxtepec, Mexico, 177-84.

Ellerton, N.F. and Clements, M.A.: 1991, *Mathematics in Language: A Review of Language Factors in Mathematics Learning,* Deakin University, Geelong.

Ellerton, N.F. and Clements, M.A.: 1992a, 'Some Pluses and Minuses of Radical Constructivism in Mathematics Education', *Mathematics Education Research Journal* 4(2), 1-22.

Ellerton, N.F. and Clements, M.A.: 1992b, 'Implications of Newman Research for the Issue of 'What is Basic in School Mathematics?'', in B. Southwell, R. Perry and K. Owens (eds.), *Proceedings of the Fifteenth Annual Conference of the Mathematics Education Research Group of Australasia,* Mathematics Education Research Group of Australasia, Sydney, 276-284.

Ellerton, N.F. and Clements, M.A.: 1992c, 'A Research Agenda for the 'Writing Mathematics' Movement', in M. Horne and M. Supple (eds.), *Mathematics: Meeting the Challenge,* Mathematical Association of Victoria, Melbourne, 153-159.

Ellerton, N.F. and Clements, M.A.: 1996a, 'Researching Language Factors in Mathematics Education: The Australasian Contribution', in B. Atweh, K. Owens and P. Sullivan (eds.), *Mathematics Education Research in Australasia 1992-1995,* Mathematics Education Research Group of Australasia, Sydney.

Ellerton, N. F. and Clements, M.A.: 1996b, 'Newman Error Analysis: A Comparative Study Involving Year 7 Students in Malaysia and Australia', in P. Clarkson (ed.), *Proceedings of the Nineteenth Annual Conference of the Mathematics Education Research Group of Australasia,* Mathematics Education Research Group of Australasia, Melbourne.

Elliott, P.C. and Kenney, M.J.: 1996, *Communications in Mathematics, K-12 and Beyond,* National Council of Teachers of Mathematics, Reston, VA.

Faulkner, R.: 1992, *Research on the Number and Type of Calculation Errors Made By Registered Nurses in a Major Melbourne Teaching Hospital,* unpublished M.Ed. research paper, Deakin University, Victoria, Australia.

Fennema, E., Carpenter, T.P., and Peterson, P.: 1989, 'Teachers' Decision Making and Cognitively Guided Instruction: A New Paradigm for Curriculum Development', in N.F. Ellerton and M.A. Clements (eds.), *School Mathematics: The Challenge to Change,* Deakin University Press, Geelong, Victoria, 174-187.

Fischbein, E., Deri, M., Nello, M.S., and Merino, M.S.: 1985, 'The Role of Implicit Models in Solving Verbal Problems in Multiplication and Division', *Journal for Research in Mathematics Education* 16, 3-17.

Fuson, K.C.: 1992, 'Research on Whole Number Addition and Subtraction', in D. A. Grouws (ed.), *Handbook of Research on Mathematics Teaching and Learning,* Macmillan, New York, 243-275.

Galligan, L.: 1995, 'Comparison of Chinese and English Mathematical Word Problems: Consequences for Student Understanding', in R.P. Hunting, G.E. FitzSimons, P.C. Clarkson and A.J. Bishop (eds.), *Regional Collaboration in Mathematics Education 1995,* Monash University, Melbourne, 271-282.

Garaway, G.B.: 1994, 'Language, Culture, and Attitude in Mathematics and Science Learning: A Review of the Literature', *The Journal of Research and Development in Education* 27(2), 102-111.

Garet, M.S. and Mills, V.L.: 1995, 'Changes in Teaching Practices: The Effects of the Curriculum and Evaluation Standards', *The Mathematics Teacher* 88(5), 380-389.

Gawned, S.: 1990, 'An Emerging Model of the Language of Mathematics', in J. Bickmore-Brand (ed.), *Language in Mathematics,* Australian Reading Association, Carlton, Vic., 27-42.

Gay, J. and Cole, M.: 1967, *The New Mathematics in an Old Culture,* Holt, Reinhart and Winston, New York.

Greer, B.: 1992, 'Multiplication and Division as Models of Situations', in D.A. Grouws (ed.), *Handbook of Research on Mathematics Teaching and Learning,* Macmillan, New York, 276-295.

Griffiths, R. and Clyne, M.: 1993, 'Real Books and Real Mathematics', in M. Stephens, A. Waywood, D. Clarke, and J. Izard: 1993, *Communicating Mathematics: Perspectives from Classroom Practice and Current Research,* Australian Council for Educational Research, Hawthorn, Victoria, 90-101.

Griffiths, R. and Clyne, M.: 1994, *Language in the Mathematics Classroom,* Eleanor Curtain Publishing, Armadale, Victoria.

Harris, P.: 1987, *Measurement in Tribal Aboriginal Communities,* 2nd edition, Northern Territory Department of Education, Darwin.

Harris, P.: 1991, *Mathematics in a Cultural Context: Aboriginal Perspectives on Time, Space and Money*, Deakin University, Geelong, Victoria.

Harris, S.: 1990, *Two Way Aboriginal Schooling,* Aboriginal Studies Press, Canberra.

Hart, K. (ed.): 1981, *Children's Understanding of Mathematics: 11-16,* John Murray, London.

Hashimoto, Y.: 1987, 'Classroom Practice of Problem Solving in Japanese Elementary Schools', in J.P. Becker, and T. Miwa, (eds.), *Proceedings of the US-Japan Seminar on Mathematical Problem Solving,* Southern Illinois University, Carbondale, IL, 94-119,

Hunting, R.P. (ed.): 1988, *Language Issues in Learning and Teaching Mathematics,* La Trobe University, Melbourne.

Irons, C. and Jones, G.: 1982, 'A Language Basis for Fostering Arithmetic', in J. Veness (ed.), *Mathematics – A Universal Language*, Australian Association of Mathematics Teachers, Sydney, 68-73.

Jiminez, E.C.: 1992, *A Cross-Lingual Study of Grade 3 and Grade 5 Filipino Children's Processing of Mathematical Word Problems,* SEAMEO-RECSAM, Penang.

Jones, K., Kershaw, L., and Sparrow, L.: 1995, *Aboriginal Children Learning Mathematics,* Mathematics, Science and Technology Education Centre, Edith Cowan University, Perth.

Kanes, C.: 1992, 'Knowing and Meaning in Mathematics', in B. Southwell, B. Perry, and K. Owens, (eds.), *Proceedings of the Fifteenth Annual Conference of the Mathematics Education Research Group of Australasia,* Mathematics Education Research Group of Australasia, Richmond, NSW, 349-361.

Kanes, C.: 1993, 'Language, Speech and Semiosis: Approaches to Postconstructivist Theories of Learning Mathematics', in B. Atweh, C. Kanes, M. Carss and G. Booker, (eds.), *Contexts in Mathematics Education,* Mathematics Education Research Group of Australasia, Brisbane, 361-368.

Kaur, B.: 1995, 'A Window to the Problem Solvers' Difficulties', in A. Richards (ed.), *Forging Links and Integrating Resources*, Australian Association of Mathematics Teachers, Darwin, 228-234.

Kaushil, L.D., Sajjin Singh, and Clements, M.A.: 1985, *Language Factors Influencing the Learning of Mathematics in an English-Medium School in Delhi,* State Institute of Education (Roop Nagar), Delhi.

Kennedy, W.: 1985, 'Writing Letters to Learn Math', *Learning* 13, 59-60.

Kenyon, R.W.: 1987, 'Writing in the Mathematics Classroom', *New England Mathematics Journal* (May), 3-19.

Kieran, C.: 1992, 'The Learning and Teaching of School Algebra', in D.A. Grouws (ed.), *Handbook of Research on Mathematics Teaching and Learning*, Macmillan, New York, 390-419.

Kilpatrick, J.: 1987, 'Problem Formulating: Where Do Good Problems Come From?' in A.H. Schoenfeld (ed.), *Cognitive Science and Mathematics Education*, Erlbaum, Hillsdale, NJ, 123-147.

Kownan, M.B.: 1992, *An Investigation of Malaysian Form 2 Students' Misconceptions of Force and Energy*, SEAMEO-RECSAM, Penang.

Krummheuer, G.: 1995, 'The Ethnography of Argumentation', in P. Cobb and H. Bauersfeld (eds.), *The Emergence of Mathematical Meaning, Interaction in Classroom Cultures*, Lawrence Erlbaum Associates, Hillsdale, New Jersey.

Krutetskii, V.A.: 1976, *The Psychology of Mathematics Abilities in Schoolchildren*, University of Chicago Press, Chicago, USA.

Lampert, M.: 1990, 'Connecting Inventions with Conventions', in L.P. Steffe and T. Wood (eds.), *Transforming Children's Mathematics Education: International Perspectives*, Lawrence Erlbaum, Hillsdale, NJ, 253-265.

Lave, J.: 1988, *Cognition in Practice: Mind, Mathematics and Culture in Everyday Life*, Cambridge University Press, Cambridge, UK.

Lean, G.A.: 1992, *Counting Systems of Papua New Guinea and Oceania*. Unpublished PhD thesis, Papua New Guinea University of Technology, Lae, Papua New Guinea.

Lean, G.A.: 1995, *Counting Systems of Papua New Guinea and Oceania* (3rd ed., Vols. 1-24), Papua New Guinea University of Technology, Lae, Papua New Guinea.

Lean, G.A., Clements, M.A., and Del Campo, G.: 1990, 'Linguistic and Pedagogical Factors Affecting Children's Understanding of Arithmetic Word Problems: A Comparative Study', *Educational Studies in Mathematics* 21, 161-191.

Lerman, S.: 1996, 'Intersubjectivity in Mathematics Learning: A Challenge to the Radical Constructivist Paradigm?' *Journal for Research in Mathematics Education* 27(2), 133-150.

Marinas, B. and Clements, M.A.: 1990, 'Understanding the Problem: A Prerequisite to Problem Solving in Mathematics', *Journal for Research in Science and Mathematics Education in Southeast Asia* 13(1), 14-20.

McBride, M.: 1989, 'A Foucauldian Analysis of Mathematical Discourse', *For the Learning of Mathematics* 9(1), 40-46.

McDonnell, L.M.: 1995, September, 'Defining Curriculum Standards: The Promise and the Limitations of Performance Assessment in Schooling', in *Papers Presented at a Conference on 'Efficiency and Equity in Education Policy'*, Canberra: National Board of Employment, Education and Training, 231-296.

MacGregor, M.: 1993, 'Teaching Mathematics in English to Students of Non-English-Speaking Background', *Multicultural Teaching* 11(3), 31-34.

MacGregor, M.: 1994, 'Metalinguistic Awareness and Algebra Learning', in J.P. da Ponte and J.F. Matos (eds.), *Proceedings of the Eighteenth International Conference for the Psychology of Mathematics Education*, PME Lisbon, Portugal, 200-205.

MacGregor, M. and Stacey, K.: 1995, 'The Effect of Different Approaches to Algebra on Students' Perceptions of Functional Relationships', *Mathematics Education Research Journal* 7(1), 69-85.

Mamona-Downs, J.: 1993, 'On Analysing Problem Posing', in I. Hirabayashi, N. Nohda, K. Shigematsu, and F.L. Lin (eds.), *Proceedings of the Seventeenth International Conference for the Psychology of Mathematics Education* (vol. III), PME, Tsukuba, Japan, 41-47.

Mellin-Olsen, S.: 1993, *Dialogue as a Tool to Handle Various Forms of Knowledge*, Paper presented at the Political Dimensions of Mathematics Education Conference, Johannesburg.

Mohidin, R.: 1991, *An Investigation Into the Difficulties Faced by the Students of Form 4 SMJA Secondary School in Transforming Short Mathematics Problems Into Algebraic Form,* SEAMEO-RECSAM, Penang.

Mousley, J.A., Clements, M.A., and Ellerton, N.F.: 1992, 'Teachers' Interpretations of Their Roles in Mathematics Classrooms', in G.C. Leder (ed.), *Assessment and Learning of Mathematics,* Australian Council for Educational Research, Hawthorn, Victoria, 107-144.

Mulligan, J.: 1992, 'Children's Solutions to Multiplication and Division Word Problems: A Longitudinal Study', *Mathematics Education Research Journal* 4, 24-42.

Mulligan, J. and Mitchelmore, M.: 1995, 'Children's Intuitive Models of Multiplication and Division', in B. Atweh and S. Flavel (eds.), *Galtha,* Mathematics Education Research Group of Australasia, Darwin, 427-433.

Nahrgang, C. and Petersen, B.: 1986, 'Using Writing to Learn', *Mathematics Teacher* 79, 461-465.

Nathan, G., Trinick, T., Tobin, E., and Barton, B.: 1993, 'Tahi, Rua, Yoru, Wha: Mathematics Counts in Maori Renaissance. In M. Stephens, A. Waywood, D. Clarke, and J. Izard (eds.), *Communicating Mathematics: Perspectives from Classroom Practice and Current Research,* Hawthorn, Victoria: Australian Council for Educational Research, 291-300.

National Academy of Sciences: 1993, *Measuring Counts: A Policy Brief,* National Academy Press, Washington DC.

National Council of Teachers of Mathematics (NCTM): 1987, *Curriculum and Evaluation Standards for School Mathematics (Draft),* National Council of Teachers of Mathematics, Reston, VA.

National Council of Teachers of Mathematics (NCTM): 1989, *Curriculum and Evaluation Standards for School Mathematics,* National Council of Teachers of Mathematics, Reston, VA.

National Council of Teachers of Mathematics (NCTM): 1995, *Assessment Standards for School Mathematics,* National Council of Teachers of Mathematics, Reston, VA.

Nesher, P.: 1988, 'Multiplicative School Word Problems: Theoretical Approaches and Empirical Findings', in J. Hiebert and M. Behr (eds.), *Number Concepts and Operations in the Middle Grades,* vol. 2, National Council of Teachers of Mathematics, Reston, VA, 19-40.

Newman, M.A.: 1977, 'An Analysis of Sixth-Grade Pupils' Errors on Written Mathematical Tasks', *Victorian Institute for Educational Research Bulletin* 39, 31-43.

Newman, M.A.: 1983, *Strategies for Diagnosis and Remediation,* Harcourt, Brace Jovanovich, Sydney.

New Zealand Ministry of Education.: 1992, *Mathematics in the New Zealand Curriculum,* New Zealand Ministry of Education, Wellington.

Nickson, M.: 1992, 'The Culture of the Mathematics Classroom: An Unknown Quantity?', in D.A. Grouws (ed.), *Handbook of Research on Mathematics Teaching and Learning,* Macmillan, New York, 101-114.

Nohda, N.: 1995, 'Teaching and Evaluating Using 'Open-ended Problems' in Classroom', *Zentralblatt für Didaktik der Mathematik* 27(2), 57-60.

Olssen, K.: 1993, *Assessment and Reporting Practices in Mathematics,* Department of Employment, Education and Training, Canberra.

Orr, E.W.: 1987, *Twice as Less: Black English and the Performance of Black Students in Mathematics and Science,* Norton, New York.

Owen, E. and Sweller, J.: 1985, 'What Do Students Learn While Solving Mathematical Problems?' *Journal of Educational Psychology* 77(3), 272-284.

Pehkonen, E.: 1995, 'Use of Open-ended Problems', *Zentralblatt für Didaktik der Mathematik* 27(2), 55-57.

Pimm, D.: 1987, *Speaking Mathematically: Communication in Mathematics Classrooms,* Routledge and Kegan Paul, London.

Pimm, D.: 1994, 'Spoken Mathematical Classroom Culture: Artifice and Artificiality', *Cultural Perspectives on the Mathematics Classroom,* in S. Lerman (ed.), Kluwer, Dordrecht, 133-147.

Pimm, D.: 1995, *Symbols and Meanings in School Mathematics,* Routledge, London

Reeve, W.D. (ed.): 1931, *Mathematics in Modern Life,* National Council of Teachers of Mathematics, New York.

Reeve, W.D. (ed.): 1936, *The Place of Mathematics in Modern Education,* National Council of Teachers of Mathematics, New York.

Richardson, J. and Williamson, P.: 1982, 'Towards Autonomy in Infant Mathematics', *Research in Mathematics Education in Australia,* 109-136.

Riley, M.S., Greeno, J., and Heller, J.I.: 1983, 'Development of Children's Problem-solving Ability in Arithmetic', in H.P. Ginsburg (ed.), *The Development of Mathematical Thinking,* Academic Press, New York, 153-196.

Rose-Piver, V. and Short, S.: 1995, *Math and Writing: Making the Connection,* Teaching Resource Centre, San Leandro, CA.

Ruthven, K.: 1994, 'Better Judgement: Rethinking Assessment in Mathematics Education', *Educational Studies in Mathematics* 27, 433-450.

Schmidt, S. and Weiser, W.: 1995, 'Semantic Structures of One-step Word Problems Involving Multiplication or Division', *Education Studies in Mathematics* 28(1), 55-72.

Scott, A.: 1994, 'Another Look at Open-ended Tasks', in C. Beesey and D. Rasmussen (eds.), *Mathematics Without Limits,* Mathematical Association of Victoria, Melbourne, 353-355.

Secada, W.G.: 1988, 'Diversity, Equity, and Cognitivist Research', in E. Fennema, T.P. Carpenter, and S.J. Lamon, (eds.), *Integrating Research on Teaching and Learning Mathematics,* University of Wisconsin, Madison, 20-58.

Shield, M.: 1995a, 'Interpreting Student Mathematical Writing', *Australian Mathematics Teacher* 51(4), 36-39.

Shield, M.: 1995b, 'Describing Student Expository Writing in Mathematics', in B. Atweh and S. Flavel (eds.), *Galtha,* Mathematics Education Research Group of Australasia, Darwin, 471-476.

Shield, M., and Swinson, K.V.: 1994, 'Stimulating Student Elaboration of Mathematical Ideas Through Writing', in *Proceedings of the Eighteenth International Conference for the Psychology of Mathematics*, vol. 4, International Group for the Psychology of Mathematics Education, Lisbon, 273-280.

Shimada, S. (ed.): 1977, *Open-end Approach in Arithmetic and Mathematics: A New Proposal Toward Teaching Improvement,* Mizumishibi, Tokyo, Japan.

Shukkwan, S.L.: 1993, 'Mathematical Problem Posing: The Influence of Task Formats, Mathematics Knowledge, and Creative Thinking', in I. Hirabayashi, N. Nohda, K. Shigematsu, and F.L. Lin (eds.), *Proceedings of the Seventeenth International Conference for the Psychology of Mathematics Education* (vol. III), PME, Tsukuba, Japan, 33-40.

Shumway, R.J. (ed.): 1980, *Research in Mathematics Education,* National Association of Teachers of Mathematics, Reston, VA.

Silver Burdett Ginn Inc.: 1995a, *Authentic Assessment* (A Series for Grades K Through 8), Silver Burdett Ginn Inc., Morristown, NJ.

Silver Burdett Ginn Inc.: 1995b, *Glossary: English-Cantonese, Cantonese-English, Grade K-2, Grade 3-5 and Grade 6-8.* (3 volumes), Silver Burdett Inc., Morristown, NJ.

Silver, E.A.: 1993, 'On Mathematical Problem Posing', in I. Hirabayashi, N. Nohda, K. Shigematsu, and F.L. Lin (eds.), *Proceedings of the Seventeenth International Conference for the Psychology of Mathematics Education* (vol. I), PME, Tsukuba, Japan, 66-85.

Silver, E.A.: 1995, 'The Nature and Use of Open Problems in Mathematics Education: Mathematical and Pedagogical Perspectives', *Zentralblatt für Didaktik der Mathematik* 27(2), 67-72.

Silver, E.A. and Cai, J.: 1993, 'Mathematical Problem Posing and Problem Solving by Middle School Students', in C.A. Maher, G.A. Goldin and R.B. Davis (eds.), *Proceedings of PME-NA 11*, vol. 1, Rutgers University, New Brunswick, NJ, 263-269.

Silver, E.A., Kilpatrick, J., and Schlesinger, B.: 1990, *Thinking Through Mathematics: Fostering Inquiry and Communication in Mathematics Classrooms,* College Entrance Examination Board, New York.

Silver, E.A. and Mamona, J.: 1989, 'Problem Posing by Middle School Teachers' in C.A. Maher, G.A. Goldin and R.B. Davis (eds.), *Proceedings of the Eleventh Annual Meeting of the North American Chapter of the International Group for the Psychology of Mathematics Education,* PME-NA, New Brunswick, 263-269.

Singhatat, N.: 1991, *Analysis of Mathematics Errors of Lower Secondary Pupils in Solving Word Problems,* SEAMEO-RECSAM, Penang.

Slaught, H.E.: 1926, 'Mathematics and the Public', in R. Schorling (ed.), *A General Survey of Progress in the Last Twenty-five Years,* National Council of Teachers of Mathematics, New York.

Smilansky, J.: 1984, 'Problem Solving in the Quality of Invention', *Journal of Educational Psychology,* 76, 377-386.

Stacey, K.: 1994, 'Challenges and Constraints for Constructing Curriculum', in G. Bell, B. Wright, N. Leeson and J. Geake (eds.), *Challenges in Mathematics Education: Constraints on Construction* (vol. 1), Mathematics Education Research Group of Australasia, Lismore, NSW, 1-8.

Stacey, K.: 1995, 'The Challenges of Keeping Open Problem-Solving Open in School Mathematics', *Zentralblatt für Didaktik der Mathematik* 27(2), 62-67.

Steinbring, H.: 1994, 'Dialogue between Theory and Practice in Mathematics Education', in R. Biehler, R. W. Scholtz, R. Sträßer, and B. Winkelmann (eds.), *Didactics of Mathematics as a Scientific Discipline,* Kluwer Academic Publishers, Dordrecht.

Stephens, M.: 1993, 'Valuing and Fostering Writing in the Victorian Certificate of Education', in M. Stephens, A. Waywood, D. Clarke and J. Izard (eds), *Communicating Mathematics: Perspectives from Classroom Practice and Current Research,* Australian Council for Educational Research, Hawthorn, Victoria, 164-176.

Stephens, M., Clarke, D.J. and Pavlou, M.: 1994, 'Policy to Practice: High Stakes Assessment as a Catalyst for Classroom Change', in G. Bell, B. Wright, N. Leeson and J. Geake (eds.), *Challenges in Mathematics Education: Constraints on Construction* (vol. 2), Mathematics Education Research Group of Australasia, Lismore, NSW, 571-580.

Stephens, M., Waywood, A., Clarke, D., and Izard, J. (eds.): 1993, *Communicating Mathematics: Perspectives from Classroom Practice and Current Research,* Australian Council for Educational Research, Hawthorn, Victoria.

Sterret, A. (ed.): undated, *Using Writing to Teach Mathematics,* Mathematical Association of America, USA.

Stigler, J.W. and Baranes, R.: 1988, 'Culture and Mathematics Learning', in E.Z. Rothkopf (ed.), *Review of Research in Education 15, 1988-89,* American Educational Research Association, Washington DC, 253-306.

Stover, G.B., 1982, *Structural Variables Affecting Mathematical Word Problem Difficulty in 6th-Graders.* Unpublished doctoral dissertation, University of San Francisco. (*Dissertation Abstracts International, 42,* 5050A).

Stoyanova, E.: 1995, *Developing a Framework for Research into Students' Problem Posing in School Mathematics,* Paper presented at the Eighteenth Annual Conference of the Mathematics Education Research Group of Australasia, Darwin, July, 1995.

Stoyanova, E., and Ellerton, N.F.: in press, 'Problem Posing in Mathematics Classrooms', in N.F. Ellerton (ed.), *Research in Mathematics Education: Some Current Trends*, Australian Institute for Research in Primary Mathematics Education, Perth.

Suchting, W.A.: 1992, 'Constructivism Deconstructed', *Science & Education* 1, 223-254.

1031

Sulaiman, S. and Remorin, P.R. (eds.): 1993, *Science- and Mathematics-related Project Work Abstracts of SEAMEO-RECSAM Participants* (April-June 1993), RECSAM, Penang.

Sullivan, P.: 1992, 'Using Open Questions for Teaching: A Classroom Experiment', in B. Southwell, B. Perry and K. Owens (eds.), *Proceedings of the Fifteenth Annual Conference of the Mathematics Education Research Group of Australasia,* Mathematics Education Research Group of Australasia, Richmond, NSW, 510-520.

Sullivan, P., Bourke, D., and Scott, A.: 1995, 'Open-ended Tasks as Stimuli for Learning Mathematics', in B. Atweh and S. Flavel (eds.), *Galtha,* Mathematics Education Research Group of Australasia, Darwin, 484-492.

Sullivan, P. and Clarke, D.: 1991, *Communication in the Classroom: The Importance of Good Questioning,* Deakin University, Geelong, Victoria.

Swedosh, P.: 1995, *Evaluating the New Victorian Certificate of Education Mathematics Subjects,* unpublished PhD Thesis, Deakin University.

Sweller, J.: 1992, 'Cognitive Theories and Their Implications for Mathematics Instruction', in G.C. Leder (ed.), *Assessment and Learning of Mathematics*, Australian Council for Educational Research, Hawthorn, Victoria, 46-62.

Ta Tahuhu o te Matauranga.: 1994, *Pangarau te tauaki Marautanga: He Tauira,* Te Pou Tahi Korero, Whanganui a Tara.

Teoh Sooi Kim: 1991, *An Investigation into Three Aspects of Numeracy Among Pupils Studying in Year Three and Year Six in Two Primary Schools in Malaysia.* SEAMEO-RECSAM, Penang.

Thomas, J.: 1995, 'Bilingual Students and Their Participation in Tertiary Mathematics', in R.P. Hunting, G.E. FitzSimons, P.C. Clarkson and A.J. Bishop (eds.), *Regional Collaboration in Mathematics Education 1995,* Monash University, Melbourne, 703-712.

Thongtawat, N.: 1992, *Comparing the Effectiveness of Multiple-choice and Short-answer Paper-and-pencil Tests,* SEAMEO-RECSAM, Penang.

Tuck, S.: 1983, *An Investigation of the Effectiveness of the Newman Language Mathematics Kit,* unpublished M.Ed thesis, Monash University.

van den Brink, J.: 1987, 'Children as Arithmetic Book Authors', *For the Learning of Mathematics* 7, 44-48.

Vergnaud, G.: 1982, 'A Classification of Cognitive Tasks and Operations of Thought Involved in Addition and Subtraction Problems', in T.P. Carpenter, J.M. Moser and T.A. Romberg (eds.), *Addition and Subtraction: A Cognitive Perspective,* Lawrence Erlbaum, Hillsdale, NJ, 39-59.

Victorian Ministry of Education: 1988, *The Mathematics Framework: P-10*, Victorian Ministry of Education, Melbourne.

Voigt, J.: 1985, 'Patterns and Routines in Classroom Interaction', *Récherches en Didactique des Mathématiques* 6, 69-118.

Voigt, J.: 1994, 'Negotiation of Mathematical Meaning and Learning Mathematics' 26, 275-298.

Voigt, J.: 1995, 'Thematic Patterns of Interaction and Sociomathematical Norms', in P. Cobb and H. Bauersfeld (eds.), *The Emergence of Mathematical Meaning: Interaction in Classroom Cultures,* Lawrence Erlbaum, Hillsdale, NJ.

von Glasersfeld, E.: 1990, 'Environment and Communication', in L.P. Steffe and T. Wood (eds.), *Transforming Children's Mathematics Education: International Perspectives,* Lawrence Erlbaum, Hillsdale, NJ, 30-38.

Walkerdine, V.: 1988, *The Mastery of Reason: Cognitive Development and the Production of Rationality,* Routledge, London.

Watson, I.: 1980, 'Investigating Errors of Beginning Mathematicians', *Educational Studies in Mathematics* 11(3), 319-329.

Waywood, A.: 1992, 'Journal Writing and Learning Mathematics. *For the Learning of Mathematics* 12(2), 34-43.

Waywood, A.: 1993, 'A Phenomenology of Report Writing: From "I Am" to "I Think" Through Writing', in M. Stephens, A. Waywood, D. Clarke and J. Izard (eds.), *Communicating Mathematics: Perspectives from Classroom Practice and Current Research,* Australian Council for Educational Research, Hawthorn, Victoria, 153-163.

Wells, G.: 1984, *Learning Through Interaction: The Study of Language Development,* Cambridge University Press, Cambridge.

Wheeler, D.: 1982, 'Mathematics and Language: Aspects of their Interaction', in J. Veness (ed.), *Mathematics – A Universal Language,* Australian Association of Mathematics Teachers, Sydney, 30.

Williams, D.: 1993, 'Linking Language and Mathematics', in M. Stephens, A. Waywood, D. Clarke, and J. Izard (eds.): 1993, *Communicating Mathematics: Perspectives from Classroom Practice and Current Research,* Australian Council for Educational Research, Hawthorn, Victoria, 102-118.

Winograd, K.: 1991, *Writing, Solving and Sharing Original Math Story Problems: Case Studies of Fifth Grade Children's Cognitive Behaviour,* University of Northern Colorado, unpublished doctoral thesis.

Wood, D.: 1988, *How Children Think and Learn,* Basil Blackwell, Oxford.

Woods, P.: 1992, 'Symbolic Interactionism: Theory and Method', in M.D. LeCompte, W.L. Millroy, and J. Preissle (eds.), *The Handbook of Qualitative Research in Education,* Academic Press, San Diego.

Woo-Hyung Whang: 1996, 'The Influence of English-Korean Bilingualism in Solving Mathematics Word Problems', *Educational Studies in Mathematics* 30, 289-312.

Zepp, R.: 1989, *Language and Mathematics Education,* API Press, Hong Kong.

Zevenbergen, R.:1995, *The Construction of Social Difference in Mathematics Education.* Unpublished PhD thesis, Deakin University.

Chapter 27: Anthropological Perspectives on Mathematics and Mathematics Education

BILL BARTON

The University of Auckland, New Zealand

ABSTRACT

Viewed from a European knowledge perspective, much of the writing about mathematics and mathematics education might be regarded as instances of several different genres: including, for example, mathematical, philosophical, historical, sociological, educational, psychological, and a diverse corpus of writings concerned with mathematics and culture. This present chapter is specifically concerned with summarising and critiquing the literature pertaining to anthropological perspectives on mathematics and mathematics education,

Numerous articles and books were written during the 1980's and 1990's on what has come to be known as the field of 'ethnomathematics'. The first part of this chapter presents a framework for discussion of ethnomathematical concepts and issues from anthropological perspectives. The question of which activities, and investigations might profitably be classified as 'anthropological' is raised. In the second part of the chapter emphasis is placed on recurring themes, on problems, on recent developments, and on likely future directions for the study of mathematics education from anthropological perspectives.

The final part of the chapter offers an overview of anthropological writings on mathematics education which link with the growing body of literature calling for a radical rethinking of the educational task with respect to mathematics.

1. AN EXPLANATORY FRAMEWORK

1.1 Definitions

At the outset it will be useful to discuss the terms 'culture' and 'anthropology'. Bishop (1988, pp. 4-19) has provided an extensive discussion of the concept of culture, and how this has been, is being, and might be, used in mathematics and mathematics education settings. Following Stenhouse (1967), Bishop defined culture as a set of shared understandings. He also used

A.J. Bishop et al. (eds.), International Handbook of Mathematics Education, 1035 - 1053

White's (1956) four categories of culture – ideological (beliefs), sociological (customs), sentimental (attitudes), and technological (tools).

D'Ambrosio (1984) is another mathematics educator who has given much attention to the concept of culture. His definition, which has been used by many mathematics education writers around the world, is specific to mathematics: a cultural group is a group which has developed practices, knowledge, jargons and codes (in particular to encompass the way they mathematise) (D'Ambrosio, 1984).

Both Bishop's and D'Ambrosio's definitions allow us to refer to the cultures of mathematics, to national and ethnic cultures, and to the cultures of smaller social groups (such as, for example, carpenters).

Lerman (1994) referred to the reflexive possibility that culture is defined by how the word is used. This can give rise to a functional definition of culture, as the amalgam of those characteristics which are useful to refer to when describing the practices and products of a distinctive group of people.

Pinxten (1994) noted that anthropology 'used to be the study of exotic, or at the least non-Western cultures' (p.85), and Stigler and Baranes (1988) described the way this had led to a pre-occupation with the concept of 'primitive'. However an increasing awareness of subjectivity and the complexity of social context has resulted in there being an increasing awareness of, and investigations into, a wide variety of cultural groupings within humankind. In particular, there has been an ever-increasing tendency to study the cultures of special groupings (like, for example, occupational groups), and the qualities and characteristics of relationships between those within and outside given cultural groups.

Traditionally those who focus on the study of cultures are called 'anthropologists', and the past two decades have seen an increasing interest in anthropological investigations in the field of mathematics education. Those carrying out such investigations may or may not have been themselves members of the international mathematics education community. In particular, anthropologist researchers have studied educational institutions, and in particular, mathematics education practices within these institutions, for the characteristics they exhibit as a result of intentional and unintentional – or conscious or unconscious – decisions by individuals or groups of individuals.

Anthropologists typically assume the existence of broad social constructs (like, for example, cultural reproduction, or linguistic behaviour), which can provide frameworks for their observations, investigations and reflections on some aspect of a cultural group. Pinxten (1994) identified four foci for anthropological research within the domain of mathematics education – types of learning, cognitive content, language structure, and institutional aspects.

The perennial challenge for those involved in anthropological investigations in mathematics education settings is to describe and analyse cultural characteristics in an authentic manner. This is particularly difficult when mathematics is being considered, because mathematics is a subject for which there are long-standing connotations of universality and ultimate truth. It is hard to describe mathematical aspects of a culture using the knowledge categories of that culture without imposing the 'realities' of the 'capital-M' Mathematics which has been developed, and is largely accepted, as an international, academic discipline (Bishop, 1988). Nevertheless, the development of genuinely anthropological perspectives on mathematics must involve a willingness to redefine the working concepts (in this case 'mathematics') in response to the perspectives of the culture(s) being considered.

1.2 A Framework for Discussion

It will help the discussion to construct a continuum (see Figure 1) on which writing (and other modes of commentary) on or about mathematics and culture can be located. Although such a device might oversimplify the diversity of the corpus, in that it would locate the writing along a linear scale, it is likely that it would be worthwhile as a preliminary organiser. The continuum chosen represents the extent to which the subject of the writing is *inside* or *removed from* the internationalised version of 'capital-M' Mathematics. Thus at one end is 'Pure Mathematics' itself, and as we move along the continuum the subject of the writing becomes more and more *about* mathematics. Note that there is no value-judgement implied or expected so far as location on the continuum is concerned.

With respect to Figure 1, the following 'working definitions' for categories of mathematical writings are put forward

1) *Pure Mathematics:* pure mathematicians tend to record their work in formally approved ways in mathematical journals and conference proceedings.

2) *Applied Mathematics:* this form of writing uses mathematics explicitly, in the form of mathematical models which are intended to assist analysis and to enable predictions to be made within other subjects (like, for example, theoretical physics, econometrics, engineering). Writings are also formal, and appear in journals or conference proceedings of subjects or disciplines.

3) *Mathematical Studies:* forms of writing in this category might be described as mathematical, but are not usually identified as such (as in, for example, articles on design or navigation).

4) *Mathematics in Cultural Settings*: descriptions of activities which are particular to a cultural grouping, but which might be described as 'mathematical' (like, for example, weaving systems, counting procedures, sporting statistics).

5) *Descriptions of the Culture of Mathematics*: writing which has mathematics as the subject but which is in another mode (like, for

example, history of mathematics, sociology of mathematics, anthropology of mathematics).

6) *The Cultural System of Mathematics:* writing which describes the way in which mathematics is itself a system or a culture, and which describes its cultural characteristics (see, for example, Wilder, 1981).

7) *Mathematics as a Cultural Phenomenon*: writing which describes mathematics as a way of knowing, or places it in relation to other cultural forms such as art or religion (like, for example, the historiography of mathematics – how we write about the development of mathematics).

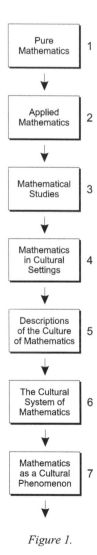

Figure 1.

On this continuum there is an indistinct dividing line at about position 4 which has "writing mathematics" before it and "writing about mathematics" after it.

It is possible to construct parallel continua for the history, philosophy and sociology of mathematics, thereby creating a theoretical matrix for all writing about mathematics (Barton, 1996).

With regard to anthropology, which is the focus of this chapter, the continuum can help to distinguish between the anthropology of mathematics and an anthropological perspective on mathematics. The former is located around positions 4 and 5, and is a particular field which studies mathematics as a feature of cultural groups. It is concerned with questions such as: how does mathematics develop within various cultures, and how does it relate to other aspects of specific cultures. Such studies will usually consider mathematics within one particular cultural context. An example is the work of Pinxten and his colleagues on Navajo mathematics (Pinxten, van Dooren and Soberon, 1987). Another example is the joint work of an anthropologist and a mathematician – Marcia and Robert Ascher – as can be found in *The Code of the Quipu* (Ascher and Ascher, 1981). This is, explicitly, both an anthropological and a mathematical study. The experience of working jointly in these two modes is graphically described in D'Ambrosio and Ascher (1994).

An anthropological perspective, however, describes a more 'removed' body of work, and is to be located at positions 6 and 7 on the continuum above. In this work mathematics is the secondary subject of attention, and the construct of culture is the first subject. At position 6, mathematics is regarded as a cultural system itself, and the object of attention is how it functions as a system – *not* what mathematics is like *qua* mathematics. The secondary subject could just as well be science, or literature, or art. Wilder's (1981) work in this mode was the result of another notable anthropologist/mathematician pairing (this is described in more detail later in this chapter). The writing at position 6 has developed into a debate – the Crowe-Daubin debate (see Gillies, 1993) – on whether revolutions in the Kuhnian sense occur in the development of mathematics.

At position 7, mathematics is also a secondary subject, but here the attention is on how mathematics exists as a part of *any* culture. No one particular culture is being considered, rather it is a description of the role of this knowledge form within the way in which humans organise their societies. Again it need not be mathematics which is singled out – it could be religion, or art, or language.

1.3   Ethnomathematics

There is considerable confusion over the nature of ethnomathematics (Barton, in press). D'Ambrosio's recent writing seems to be around position 7

(D'Ambrosio and Ascher, 1994), but most of the other material is around position 4: it describes cultural practices which can be called mathematical. The main works in ethnomathematics (like, for example, Ascher, 1991; Gerdes, 1995) draw attention to the idea that perspective is important. On the one hand a practice may be regarded as mathematical only by the observer (in which case it may bear a different, non-mathematical relationship to the culture in which it resides); on the other hand, a practice is situated within a cultural context and relates to the problems and resources in that context (in which case it creates a unique relationship between the practitioner and mathematics as a subject). Thus the focus of ethnomathematical study becomes how these practices are seen by those who carry them out.

2. THEMES IN ANTHROPOLOGICAL WRITING

Much of the writing fits uneasily within the boundaries which have been theoretically created by the above continuum. The following account of development in the area first looks at studies of mathematical features of particular cultures, and then examines the wider concepts of mathematics as a culture and mathematics as a general cultural phenomenon.

2.1 Directions in the Anthropology of Mathematics

In the eighteenth and nineteenth centuries, as Africa and other territories were being explored and colonised by Europeans, there was a considerable amount of work done by anthropologists who investigated and described 'primitive' cultures. The anthropological theorising of societies in Africa, for example, saw these societies as early forms of civilisation, and the various counting systems provided evidence for judgement on how far a particular society had developed. Thus anthropological studies contained descriptive accounts of the numeracy and design characteristics of different people.

Stigler and Baranes (1988) reviewed this fascination with the theme of 'primitive' in anthropology and cross-cultural psychology, describing how this developed into an appreciation of the culturally constituted nature of our own thought, and of mathematical thought in particular. Writing on mathematics in different cultures today deals more with whole structures of thought: for example Pinxten on the Navajo, or Cooke (1990) on Australian Aborigines. The stated intent of such writing is to encourage reflection on the cultural nature of mathematics, and thereby to challenge the idea that mathematics is universal. Bishop's (1988) book entitled *Mathematical Enculturation* included a section where this distinction was elaborated by discussing pan-cultural activities which are significant for the development of mathematical aspects of any culture.

Bishop maintained that one amalgam of these has developed into the Mathematics (with a capital M) which is commonly regarded as universal. His explanation makes it clear that the intellectual sphere has been dominated by those increasingly technological cultures which have together developed Mathematics. It was only to be expected, then, that other culturally constituted forms of mathematical thinking would be either subsumed as part of the imperialism of such a widely recognised body of knowledge, or be sidelined, even trivialised, by a definition of mathematics which legitimates only Mathematics.

Given such a situation, there is a tendency for those working from a Position 1 or Position 2 perspective to interpret other cultures' counting systems or design as inferior (or, at best, limited) versions of Mathematics. The acceptance of (mathematical) systems of thought in different cultures as meaningful and potentially equivalent systems has had to wait for a change in anthropological orientation – from an orientation which saw one form of mathematics as, in some way, more 'advanced' than another, to one in which other cultures could be recognised as containing different conceptual structures rather than earlier forms of a universal structure.

The result of this has not been to halt studies on, for example, the counting systems of other cultures. Indeed a comprehensive account of 1800 counting systems of Papua New Guinea and Oceania has been the subject of a recent PhD thesis (Lean, 1992). But these are now regarded as studies of counting systems, not of mathematical thought (see Crump, 1989). The anthropology of mathematics (small m) encompasses much wider perspectives, and draws parallels with Mathematics at the level of integrated systems of cognition, rather than at the level of mathematical practices.

The transition has been a slow one. In retrospect we can look back at Zaslavsky's (1973) book on African mathematical practices as the first in a series of empathetic descriptions of other cultures' mathematics. Harris' (1991) work on Australian Aboriginal conceptions of time, space and money provided another example of a study written from a wider perspective which categorised aspects of perception and cultural practice as mathematical.

Cooke's (1990) description of Yolgnu genealogy went the next step by claiming this cultural mode as a 'mathematics' in the general sense. He discussed three definitions of mathematics. One definition arose 'from its characteristics and prominence as a basis for the schema of European culture' (p.4). Any search for such mathematics in other cultures is doomed to failure. A second definition assumed that 'mathematical activity is a human characteristic and thus pan-cultural ... and the prominence of mathematical thinking varies widely from culture to culture' (p.4). A search for this type of mathematics in other cultures will be successful, but does not help to shed light on the culture itself because the description is in Western terms. Finally, as Cooke (1990) argued:

Thus a third and far broader way of defining mathematics is to view it as society's system for encoding, interpreting and organising the patterns and relationships emerging from the human experience of physical and social phenomena. The emergence of a cultural schema is then a manifestation of the continual negotiation and refinement within a society of a framework for discerning patterns and for describing/ defining their governing rules and interrelationships as a coherent, ordered system of meaning. Whilst this process is common to all cultures the resulting schemata can be fundamentally different. (p.5)

This interpretation of the nature of mathematics confronts, directly, more formal, traditional interpretations which held that 'mathematical thinking' was confined, almost exclusively, to those consciously using or reflecting on aspects of the internationalised version of Mathematics.

2.2   The Problem of Identification

One of the difficulties experienced by readers of mathematical/anthropological studies is recognising and defining other cultural systems. It is not surprising that systems of mathematics currently being investigated and written about are part of cultures which are based on ways of thinking and epistemologies of knowledge which are most removed from internationally recognised knowledge forms. For example, the Inca society described by the Aschers was remote in time, and the contemporary Navajo (North America) and Yolgnu (Australia) systems described by Pinxten and Cooke are from recognisably different cultures.

If distinct mathematical systems exist in contemporary developed societies, then they are likely to be intertwined with Mathematics. Not only will they be difficult to isolate for study, but they will also be difficult to recognise as mathematics. For example, imagine the difficulty of describing the differences between the mathematical practices in, say, Japan and Italy without school Mathematics becoming a dominant theme.

In the case of cultures remote from international academia another problem arises. The structure being described is incomprehensible in its totality to any observer from outside that culture, but its importance as a description of mathematical thought may be unknown to participants inside that culture. Hence finding the appropriate mathematical anthropologist is a serious problem. What is worse is that, having achieved a description, the extent to which the system is presented as mathematical is also the extent to which it is removed from its context and thus corrupted as a true description.

These problems do not make the anthropology of mathematics pointless, however. It seems likely that future studies will explore increasingly complex culturally specific systems of relationships, and that the mathematical nature of these relationships will be increasingly recognised. The value of such work is that it widens the concept 'mathematics' so that it is less ethnocentric, and distinguishes it from the techno-subject 'Mathematics'.

2.3   Exposing Mathematics

Another way in which the concept of mathematics is being widened is to be found in the work of George Joseph (1991), and others (see, for example, Berggren, 1986), who are challenging the validity of historical accounts which view mathematics as having developed in so-called 'Western' societies alongside Western science. In doing this, fundamental characteristics of mathematics are being questioned and the construction of mathematics as a European science is seen as limiting. As Joseph, (1994) has pointed out:

> The non-recognition of the foundational conceptions and methodologies of non-European mathematical traditions has restricted our understanding of the nature and potentialities of mathematics. Can we seriously believe that we come to grips with the foundational tensions in modern mathematics without recognizing the deeper culturally determined ideological differences that went into the creation of this mathematics: stress on becoming (dynamic) versus stress on being (static), constructibility versus indirect proof, empiricism versus idealism ... the polarities are many and hardly ever discussed. (pp.201-202)

Joseph is not only questioning the origins and nature of mathematics, but also the culturally determined ways in which we think about it.

2.4   Situated Cognition

The anthropological studies so far described are related to the parallel areas of situated cognition and mathematics and language, which come mainly from a psychological tradition. A research synthesis of these areas is given in Nesher and Kilpatrick (1990).

Situated cognition takes a smaller social unit than the ethnic or national cultures so far mentioned. Lave (1988) explored cognition in a cultural context and described some of the difficulties in this area. She rejected a functionalist conception of culture as a completed entity shaped in socialisation, and sought a model which assumed cultures were evolving entities. What she called a social anthropology of cognition is a theory of individual practice. She chose arithmetic as a vehicle for this study for methodological reasons, and argued that the source of mathematical practice is found in everyday settings rather than in school classrooms.

Lave (1988) argued that it is unhelpful to analyse arithmetical thinking using the pre-judged, scholastic view of arithmetic as an exemplar of rationality. With the scholastic view, algorithmic processing is the model, and arithmetic is identified as technique. However, mathematics is not a mental exercise except in its pedagogical guise. Allowing oneself to be constrained by such scientific 'myths', Lave asserted, rendered the socio-cultural aspects of mathematics invisible. Research on everyday mathematics practice challenged the idea of rationality in arithmetic. Rather arithmetic is seen as a quantitative activity taking different forms in different situations.

Saxe (1991) used candy sellers' mathematics to illustrate out-of -school learning, as did other work coming out of South America on street vendors and peasant farmers (see Nunes (1992) for an overview). Such investigations focus our attention on the way in which goals and functions affect the form of mathematical practice. The main purpose is in the domain of sociology, rather than in studying the anthropology of mathematics. As such, the studies illuminate the relationship of individuals with the society in which they live, rather than the actions of individuals as examples of cultural norms.

Situated cognition focuses on mathematical activities and practices rather than on the written corpus of mathematics as a cultural construct.

2.5 Language and Mathematics

Chapter 26 in this volume on language factors surveys many aspects of the way in which language affects mathematical thought, as well as how such thought is developed. Given the recent attention to encompassing cultural modes of thought (rather than particular cultural practices), the role of language will become more important than ever.

Most of the work linking mathematics and language is in mathematics education (see below). Pinxten (1994) noted that a weak version of the Whorfian hypothesis (that is to say, the hypothesis that language and thought co-determine each other) is now generally accepted by linguistic anthropologists. He discussed the implications of this for the development of mathematical ideas in young children, notably that the "world view" of the child must be linked to the "world view" embedded in the language of mathematics before successful learning can take place.

More and more practitioners in mathematics and mathematics education are working at cultural interfaces, and therefore are having to deal with language issues. For example, consider:

a) the increased migration of Chinese, Koreans, and Malaysians to Pacific Rim countries;
b) the leap in mathematical exchange through Internet; and
c) the renaissance of indigenous peoples through educational initiatives.

These are three situations which have drawn attention to the role of language in mathematics. They have challenged the general perception of this subject as the one most free of linguistic influence. More communication will show up problems at a deeper level, and linguistic anthropology is likely to become more relevant for the mathematical arena.

2.6 Directions in Anthropological Perspectives on Mathematics

There is a growing awareness of mathematics as a differentiated feature of all cultures, although it is now recognised that calling this feature 'mathematics' is part of an ethnocentric tradition of knowledge. Perhaps the first writer who acknowledged this explicitly and who attempted to describe mathematics in relation to culture was Oswald Spengler.

Spengler's grand conception was that a mathematic (singular) was a feature of each cultural era (like art or architecture), and that all features grow, flourish and decline contemporaneously in every culture. The chapter entitled 'Meaning of Numbers', in his two-volume tome (Spengler, 1926; but see Spengler, 1956 for an abridged version of this chapter), elaborated this idea with particular reference to the mathematics of the Classical era (c600BC-250BC) and that of the Western era (c1600-1900).

Spengler focused on the conception of number as a representation of thought, of a conception of the world. The difference between the Classical and the Western forms of mathematics is the conception of number as measurement in the former, and number as relation in the latter. The important point made by Spengler was that this is not a development, there is a destruction of the concept of number of the previous cultural era. It is interesting that, 80 years after Spengler, a modern version of this idea is part of the debate over whether mathematics exhibits Kuhnian revolutions (see Gillies, 1993).

The Decline of the West (Spengler, 1926) is primarily about history. The chapter on mathematics was an example of Spengler's general thesis about cyclical cultural development. He argued that mathematics is a part of culture, and is demonstrating the dependence of culture on all its parts – including on mathematics. Each culture's mathematic is a reflection of the underlying nature of that culture.

Such a stance was a radical departure from the thought of Spengler's day. Spengler was not claiming that mathematics stagnates, nor was he debating the nature of mathematical truths. He was arguing that the understanding of mathematical concepts is reflected in the culture of the time. That is to say, everyone comprehends mathematics according to their cultural understandings, and the members of one culture cannot understand the basic ideas of another. Spengler was discussing our understanding of mathematics, not mathematics itself. He was not adopting a relativistic stance on the existence of mathematical objects – he was avoiding such a debate altogether. This concentration on cultural perception and avoidance of philosophical debate has become a feature of much later writing.

In the period from 1930 to 1970 the idea developed that mathematics grew in response to the cultural make-up of each era. Notable was Hardy's (1941) *A Mathematician's Apology*, and a book of essays edited by Schaaf (1948) on the nature and cultural significance of mathematics. This writing has diverged into related threads, of which four can be usefully identified.

One of these threads focuses on the way Mathematics as an academic subject has affected, and has been affected by, different aspects of society. This sociology of mathematics was identified as an important area for study by the historian Struik (1948), and has gained renewed impetus from the writings of Restivo, Fischer and others (see Restivo, 1983, 1992; Restivo, Van Bendegem and Fischer, 1993). This corpus can no longer be considered anthropological as it increasingly draws on sociology, particularly the sociology of knowledge, as its theoretical base (cf., the work on situated cognition).

A second thread is that which seeks to maintain the place of mathematics as an Art in the sense of the word used in academia – that is to say, as within the Humanities. This tradition has a long history (writers such as Plato, D'Alembert, and Bacon have been associated with it), but is undergoing a renaissance guided by Alvin White under the banner Humanistic Mathematics (White, 1993). This movement represents a compromise between the relativistic basis of the sociology of mathematics, and the realism of those who remain in the tradition of G.H. Hardy.

A third thread concerns mathematics as part of the culture of humankind – as a feature of the way humans come to know. In 1949 Leslie White wrote 'The Locus of Mathematical Reality: An Anthropological Footnote' (later republished in Newman's (1956) collection), which took up Spengler's theme of mathematics as having only a cultural existence. White, however, wished to make a different point, namely, that while mathematics is outside of any one human mind it can be entirely contained within a cultural collective of human minds.

Kline's *Mathematics in Western Culture* (1953) and Bronowski's *The Ascent of Man* (1973) can be viewed in the same light. Both works seek to describe mathematics as a feature of cultural organisation, and to place it in relation to other cultural features such as architecture, fine art, and music, although both are written from a Western cultural viewpoint.

The use of the term 'mathematics' to describe a way of human understanding has been taken up by D'Ambrosio in a much more pro-active way. The elaboration of what he means by 'ethnomathematics' has taken him away from particular cultural practices to the encompassing concept of a research program in history and philosophy 'not just of mathematics, but of everything' (D'Ambrosio and Ascher, 1994, p.43). D'Ambrosio says that every human activity brings with it mathematical aspects, and that these, collectively, form the way in which we come to understand our world. The reason for recognising this is to stop capital-M Mathematics (the techno-subject) exercising a 'social terrorism' over different groups of people (D'Ambrosio, 1990, p.23).

Thus the study of mathematics as knowledge has moved from an anthropological task, to a more political one. This comes from an increasing awareness of the importance of who it is who is defining (and thus creating this knowledge), and of who is gaining from mathematics defined in this way. One manifestation of this is the formation of the group known as the Political Dimensions of Mathematics Education (PDME). The future direction of writing in the area is therefore likely to be ideological rather than descriptive. This will bring problems of definition and competing historiographies rather than archaeological difficulties of tracing previous mathematical practice.

The fourth thread is mathematics as a culture itself. Leslie White's work, mentioned above, clearly affected a colleague of his at the University of Michigan. Just one year after White's first major work (1949), his friend Wilder (1950) published his first paper on a theme which was to become a lifelong research interest, and which he variously described as the culturological history of mathematics, or as the subculture of mathematics from the standpoint of the anthropologist.

Each man reviewed and cited the other's work, and this collaboration culminated in Wilder's (1981) definitive work *Mathematics as a Cultural System*, published a year before his death. In this book Wilder examined cultural systems in general as a prelude to examining mathematics as a cultural system. He described this strategy as a theoretical device for understanding the development of mathematics, and used it to state 'Laws' governing the evolution of the subject.

Wilder was not the first to refer to 'Laws' of mathematical development. Crowe (1975a,b) postulated sets of laws of historical and conceptual change in mathematics. One of these in particular (Law 10) denied the possibility that mathematics was subject to 'revolutionary' change in the sense of Kuhnian revolutions in science. Wilder modified this law, but it has since been the subject of intense argument, being at the heart of the Crowe/Daubin debate (see Gillies (1993) for a collection of papers). The discussion has become increasingly metaphysical, although the language-game nature of the interchanges is acknowledged by most writers. The ongoing debate is part of the process of defining the way in which terms (such as 'mathematics', revolutionary change' and 'law') may be used.

2.7   Summary

There are several quite different ways in which mathematics is related to culture. The distinctions partly rest in the way in which the term 'mathematics' is used: whether it refers to the academic techno-subject Mathematics, or to wider ways of human knowing. Another aspect of the distinction is the way in which the term 'culture' is used: whether it is a particular culture in the ethnic sense, or an expression of the totality of human interaction and endeavour, or a term for the characteristics of mathematics itself.

Not all of the writings in these areas are anthropological. Theoretical foundations from sociology and psychology, for example, inform some contemporary work. The emerging field of ethnomathematics is developing its own theory and methodology (Gerdes, 1995). However valuable contributions have been forthcoming from conjunctions between anthropology and mathematics, and as noted earlier, in two documented cases this has been represented by the collaboration of particular individuals. Among all the new directions emerging from these works it is possible to identify a general trend towards characterising mathematics as a product of human minds, and therefore as an instrument which can be directed to serve all humans.

3.   ANTHROPOLOGICAL PERSPECTIVES ON MATHEMATICS EDUCATION

When we turn our attention to mathematics education the focus shifts more directly to the ways in which mathematics might serve humankind. Six directions in which anthropological perspectives are contributing to mathematics education can be identified.

3.1   A Cultural View of Mathematics

Much writing which seems to be about culture and mathematics education is actually about culture and mathematics – that is to say, it is about the education of a cultural view of mathematics. For example, that is part of the aim of the Humanistic Mathematics movement mentioned above (White, 1993), and of the Ethnomathematics movement (D'Ambrosio, 1984). Examples of the latter can be found in the work of Gerdes (see, for example, 1986, 1988a,b) in Mozambique and Zaslavsky (1993) in the United States of America. Gerdes uses culturally relevant examples of mathematics as inspiration for Mozambican students to enter the field and to become able to utilise its technological advantages. Zaslavsky (1993, 1994), in a similar fashion, seeks to improve access to mathematics for cultural groups who have been alienated from the subject in school. She also intends to broaden the view of mathematics for all students as a contribution to intercultural understanding.

3.2 Mathematics Learning as Enculturation

Another direction is in the theoretical work of Bishop (1988, 1990). His aim is to elaborate a more appropriate way to conceive of mathematics education and, since mathematics is a cultural phenomenon, he uses anthropological constructs. In Chapter 1 of his book (Bishop, 1988) he detailed these constructs, and then used them to suggest ways in which it was possible to relate people (specifically children) with their mathematical culture. In doing this he focused on the culture of mathematics and how it might be taught or acquired.

3.3 Comparative Mathematics Education

Stigler, pursuing another direction, sought to use anthropological concepts to illuminate the way mathematics education takes place in different cultures (in the ethnic sense). His early work with Baranes (Stigler and Baranes, 1988) provided details of these foundations and described research into mathematical learning (both in and out of school) in different cultures. He argued that the benefit of cross-cultural studies in mathematics education is that cultural practices appear implicit to those who participate in them. Thus, recognition of certain aspects of our own mathematics education practice will only become apparent when seen in the light of those of other cultures.

As cultural differences in mathematics education become more apparent, there is likely to be more attention paid to the role of mathematics in different cultures. IEA surveys and the Mathematics Olympiad operate on assumptions of equivalence regarding the importance and purpose of mathematics education across nations. The broader view of mathematics emerging from anthropological studies will generate a reaction against quantitative measurement of a supposed universal mathematical skill. There are likely to be studies on the way mathematical systems are reproduced within cultures, and cross-cultural comparisons on the values and functions which go with these systems.

3.4 Anthropological Perspectives on the Mathematics Classroom

Lerman (1994) used anthropological constructs to examine the culture of the mathematics classroom. His book is a collection of contributions on this theme. In particular, Pinxten (1994) identified four anthropological foci: types of learning, cognitive contents, language structure, and institutional aspects. The term 'culture' has only recently been used to describe the context of the mathematics classroom. There is a merging of the terms 'social' and 'cultural' which signals the dual approach to the problems of mathematics education.

3.5   Language and Mathematics Education

Language issues affect all parts of mathematics education (see Ellerton and Clarkson's chapter in this volume; Cocking and Mestre, 1988; Zepp, 1989; Laborde, 1990; Lerman, 1994; Stephens, Waywood, Clarke and Izard, 1994). From an anthropological point of view the importance of language is in bilingual and indigenous language mathematics teaching. Both of these are taken up in the above references.

Interest will continue to grow in these areas as a consequence of the political imperatives of the late 20th century. National and cultural groups want to know how they have been disadvantaged, and how they can re-establish their cultural heritage. This involves far more than just land and customs, but includes an intellectual heritage carried in language. The way people mathematise is part of that heritage, and enculturation depends on the use of first languages.

3.6   Political Issues

The late twentieth century renaissance of indigenous peoples provides another context for the development of anthropological perspectives on mathematics education. People from indigenous cultures are increasingly using education as the mechanism to gain economic resources and personal equity. As such, education becomes a political issue. Capital-M Mathematics is a key gatekeeper in most societies, and therefore it also is political. For example 'Mathematics and Indigenous People' was the subject of a Theme Group for ICME-7 in Quebec in 1992. The way in which Mathematics has colonised mathematical knowledge (see Bishop, 1990; Fasheh, 1991) is being exposed, and the use of mathematical knowledge in culturally specific and appropriate ways is being described as part of the political process of reclamation of educational power.

There are several critical dilemmas in the politics of mathematics education. For example Barton and Fairhall (1995) describe the fear of the Maori people in New Zealand that, in the search for a contemporary technical education, their cultural values will be overridden. Is it necessary to choose between their own view of the world and the powerful knowledge of modern society?

Mathematics – or mathematical thought – is critical for all cultures. It is therefore important to know the role it plays in the functioning and development of every culture, and how each of us comes to understand and participate in that role. Anthropological perspectives have contributed, and are increasingly contributing to our understanding of mathematics education.

ACKNOWLEDGMENT

I wish to acknowledge the support and scholarly advice given to me by Alan Bishop and George Joseph, during the period when I was preparing the manuscript for this chapter.

REFERENCES

Ascher, M. and Ascher, R.: 1981, *Code of the Quipu: A Study in Media, Mathematics and Culture*, University of Michigan Press, Ann Arbor.

Ascher, M.: 1991, *Ethnomathematics: A Multicultural View of Mathematical Ideas*, Brooks/Cole Publishing Co., New York.

Barton, B.: in press, 'Making Sense of Ethnomathematics: Ethnomathematics is Making Sense', to be published in *Educational Studies in Mathematics*.

Barton, B.: 1996, *Ethnomathematics: Exploring Cultural Diversity in Mathematics*, Unpublished PhD Dissertation, The University of Auckland.

Barton, B. and Fairhall, U.: 1995, 'Is Mathematics A Trojan Horse? Mathematics and Maori Education', Paper presented at the History and Pedagogy of Mathematics Conference, Cairns, July, 1995

Berggren, J.L.: 1986, *Episodes in the Mathematics of Medieval Islam*, Springer-Verlag, Frankfurt.

Bishop, A.J.: 1988, *Mathematical Enculturation: A Cultural Perspective on Mathematics Education*, Kluwer Academic Publishers, Dordrecht.

Bishop, A.J.: 1990, 'Western Mathematics: The Secret Weapon of Cultural Imperialism', *Race & Class* 32(2), 51-65

Bronowski, J.: 1973, *The Ascent of Man*, Science Horizons Inc., London.

Cocking, R.R. and Mestre, J.P. (eds.): 1988, *Linguistic and Cultural Influences on Learning Mathematics*, Lawrence Erlbaum, Hillsdale, New Jersey.

Cooke, M.: 1990, *Seeing Yolngu, Seeing Mathematics*, Batchelor College, Northern Territory, Australia.

Crowe, M.J.: 1975a, 'Ten "Laws" Concerning Patterns of Change in the History of Mathematics', *Historia Mathematica* 2, 161-166

Crowe, M.J.: 1975b, 'Ten "Laws" Concerning Conceptual Change in Mathematics', *Historia Mathematica* 2, 469-470

Crump, T.: 1989, *The Anthropology of Number*, Cambridge University Press, Cambridge, UK.

D'Ambrosio, U.: 1984, 'The Socio-cultural Bases for Mathematical Education'. In *Proceedings of ICME-5*, Adelaide.

D'Ambrosio, U.: 1990, 'The Role of Mathematics Education in Building a Democratic and Just Society' *For the Learning of Mathematics* 10(3), 20-23.

D'Ambrosio, U. and Ascher, M.: 1994, 'Ethnomathematics: A Dialogue', *For the Learning of Mathematics* 14(2), 36-43.

Fasheh, M.: 1991, 'Mathematics in a Social Context: Math Within Education as Praxis Versus Math Within Education as Hegemony'. In M. Harris (ed.), *Schools, Mathematics and Work*, The Falmer Press, Basingstoke, UK.

Gerdes, P.: 1986, 'How to Recognise Hidden Geometrical Thinking? A Contribution to the Development of Anthropological Mathematics' *For the Learning of Mathematics* 6(2), 10-12, 17.

Gerdes, P.: 1988a, 'A Widespread Decorative Motif and the Pythagorean Theorem', *For the Learning of Mathematics* 8(1), 35-39.

Gerdes, P.: 1988b, 'On Possible Uses of Traditional Angolan Sand Drawings in the Mathematics Classroom'. *Educational Studies in Mathematics* 19(1) 3-22.

Gerdes, P.: 1995, *Ethnomathematics and Education in Africa,* Institute of International Education, University of Stockholm.

Gillies, D. (ed.): 1993, *Revolutions in Mathematics,* Clarendon Press, Oxford. UK.

Hardy, G.H.: 1941, *A Mathematician's Apology,* Cambridge University Press, Cambridge, UK.

Harris, P.: 1991, *Mathematics in a Cultural Context: Aboriginal Perspectives on Space, Time and Money,* Deakin University, Geelong, Australia.

Joseph, G.G.: 1991, *The Crest of the Peacock: Non-European Roots of Mathematics*, Tauris, London.

Joseph, G.G.: 1994, 'Different Ways of Knowing: Contrasting Styles of Argument in Indian and Greek Mathematical Knowledge', in P. Ernest (ed.), *Mathematics, Education and Philosophy: An International Perspective*, The Falmer Press, London.

Kline, M.: 1953, *Mathematics in Western Culture,* Oxford University Press, Oxford, UK.

Laborde, C.: 1990, 'Language and Mathematics', in P. Nesher and J. Kilpatrick (eds.) *Mathematics and Cognition*, ICMI Study Series, Cambridge University Press, Cambridge, UK.

Lave, J.: 1988, *Cognition in Practice: Mind, Mathematics and Culture in Everyday Life,* Cambridge University Press, New York.

Lean, G.A.: 1992, *Counting Systems of Papua New Guinea and Oceania,* Unpublished PhD Thesis, Papua New Guinea University of Technology, Lae.

Lerman, S.: 1994, 'Changing Focus in the Mathematics Classroom', in S. Lerman (ed.), *Cultural Perspectives on the Mathematics Classroom*, Mathematics Education Library, Vol. 14, Kluwer Academic Publishers, Dordrecht, 191-213.

Nesher, P. and Kilpatrick, J. (eds.): 1990, *Mathematics and Cognition: A Research Synthesis by the International Group for the Psychology of Mathematics Education*, ICME Study Series, Cambridge University Press, Cambridge, UK.

Nunes, T.: 1992, 'Ethnomathematics and Everyday Cognition', in D.A. Grouws (ed.), *Handbook of Research on Mathematics Teaching and Learning*, MacMillan, New York, 557-574.

Pinxten, R.: 1994, 'Anthropology in the Mathematics Classroom?', in S. Lerman (ed.), *Cultural Perspectives on the Mathematics Classroom*, Mathematics Education Library, Vol. 14, Kluwer Academic Publishers, Dordrecht.

Pinxten, R., van Dooren, I. and Soberon, E.: 1987, *Towards a Navajo Indian Geometry*, K.K.I. Books, Gent.

Restivo, S.: 1983, *The Social Relations of Physics, Mysticism, and Mathematics*, D. Reidel, Dordrecht.

Restivo, S.: 1992, *Mathematics in Society and History: Sociological Enquiries*, Kluwer Academic Publishers, Dordrecht.

Restivo, S., Van Bendegem, J. P. and Fischer, R. (eds.): 1993, *Math Worlds: Philosophical and Social Studies of Mathematics and Mathematics Education,* State University of New York Press, Albany, New York.

Saxe, G. B.: 1991, *Culture and Cognitive Development: Studies in Mathematical Understanding*, Lawrence Erlbaum Press, Hillsdale, NJ.

Schaaf, W. L. (ed.): 1948, *Mathematics Our Great Heritage: Essays on the Nature and Cultural Significance of Mathematics*, Harper, New York.

Spengler, O.: 1926, *The Decline of the West: Form and Actuality* (trans. C. F. Atkinson), London

Spengler, O.: 1956, 'Meaning of Numbers', in J.R. Newman (ed.) *The World of Mathematics,* vol. IV, George Allen & Unwin Ltd., London, 2315-2347

Stephens, M., Waywood, A., Clarke, D. and Izard, J.: 1994, *Communicating Mathematics: Perspectives from Classroom Practice and Current Research*, Australian Council for Educational Research, Hawthorn, Australia.

Stenhouse, L.: 1967, *Culture and Education,* Weybright and Talley, New York.

Stigler, J. W. and Baranes, R.: 1988, 'Culture and Mathematics Learning' in E.Z. Rothkopf (ed.), *Review of Research in Education 15, 1988-89*, American Education Research Association, Washington, DC, 253-306

Struik, D. J.: 1948, *A Concise History of Mathematics (2 vols.)*. New York: Dover Publications

White, A.M. (ed.): 1993, *Essays in Humanistic Mathematics*, Mathematical Association of America, Washington DC.

White, L.A.: 1949, *The Science of Culture,* Grove Press Inc., New York.

White, L.A.: 1956, 'The Locus of Mathematical Reality: An Anthropological Footnote', in J.R. Newman (ed.), *The World of Mathematics* vol. IV, George Allen & Unwin Ltd., London, 2348-2364.

Wilder, R.L.: 1950, 'The Cultural Basis of Mathematics', in *Proceedings of the International Congress of Mathematicians*, Vol. 1, Cambridge, MA, 258-271

Wilder, R. L.: 1981, *Mathematics as a Cultural System*, Pergamon, Oxford, UK.

Zaslavsky, C.: 1973, *Africa Counts: Number and Pattern in African Culture,* Prindle, Weber & Schmidt, Boston, USA.

Zaslavsky, C.: 1993, *Multicultural Mathematics: Interdisciplinary Cooperative Learning Activities*, J. Weston Walch, Portland.

Zaslavsky, C.: 1994, '"Africa Counts" and Ethnomathematics', *For the Learning of Mathematics* 14(2), 3-8.

Zepp, R.: 1989, *Language and Mathematics Education*, API Press, Hong Kong.

Chapter 28: The Role of Theory in Mathematics Education and Research

JOHN MASON AND ANDREW WAYWOOD
Open University, United Kingdom and Australian Catholic University, Australia.

ABSTRACT

Theory is seen as playing both a foreground role, in the sense that the enterprise of research in mathematics education is to develop theory, and a background role, since all observation is theory laden. After considering different theoretical stances towards observation, data, and analysis, three broad approaches to research in mathematics education are identified and the role played by theory in each of these is discussed. The chapter concludes with some speculations concerning possible directions for development, moving from language as core domain of problematicity, to images, icons, and the impact of electronic media on interpretation in the future.

1.   INTRODUCTION

Research is comprised of many different aspects. Among these one can distinguish, as Bishop (1992) does, enquiry, evidence, and theory as three essential components. Our concern in this chapter is with theory, but theory cannot be kept separate from the other aspects of research practice, and so in section 1 these will be developed in the context of theory as a world-view.

Theory is a value-laden term with a long and convoluted history. Its roots are in the Greek meaning *seeing*, with derivatives such as *contemplation* and *speculation* as well as the mathematical term *theorem*. In research terms it can be used with a number of senses, such as

— an organised system of accepted knowledge that applies in a variety of circumstances to explain a specific set of phenomena, as in 'true in fact and theory';

— an hypothesis, or possibility such as a concept that is not yet verified but that if true would explain certain facts or phenomena, as in 'he proposed a fresh theory of alkalis that later was accepted in chemical practices';

— a belief that can guide behaviour, as in 'the architect has a theory that more is less', or 'they killed him on the theory that dead men tell no tales'.

A.J. Bishop et al. (eds.), International Handbook of Mathematics Education, 1055 - 1089

What is common in the use of the word 'theory' is the human enterprise of making sense, in providing answers to people's questions about why, how, what. How that sense-making arises is itself the subject of theorising.

To understand the role of theory in a research program is to understand what are taken to be the things that can be questioned and what counts as an answer to that questioning. The process of asking and answering questions gives rise to explicit theorising in the second sense of hypothesising. We will call this sense *foreground theory* because the foreground aim of most mathematics education research is to locate, precise, and refine theories *in* mathematics education about what does and can happen within and without educational institutions. The second sense of theory, when it is implicit, and the third sense, we refer to as *background theory* because every act of teaching and of research can be seen as based on a theory *of* or *about* mathematics education. Theory serves as a backdrop to teaching and/or research, and often remains in the background. As René Thom (1973) put it at the first International Congress on Mathematical Education, 'all mathematical pedagogy, even if scarcely coherent, rests on a philosophy of mathematics' (p.205)

It is a matter of (theoretical) discussion just how firmly one espouses the 'based on' of Thom's remark, a point which will be taken up in more detail in section 3. In discussing theories and theory building, this chapter is an example of metatheorising (Royce, 1978, p.267).

The notions of background and foreground theory do not exhaust the sources that inform mathematics education and research. All senses of 'theory' are in part defined through contrast with practice. The dialectic between theory and practice reflects a tension between life as lived and life as understood or construed. This tension is encountered by researchers within themselves, and in any research to do with teaching. All individuals, in and through their research activity, manifest a synthesis and integration (however partial) of that dialectic. Personal positions are particularly visible in the choice of methodology for any particular project. One way to recognise alternative paradigms in mathematics education is to look at the products of research in relation to practitioners. Some have practitioners in mind, some are oriented to the institutional and socio-political, some are oriented towards other researchers, and some are focused on the researcher's personal development. Mason (1994) argued that often the most significant product of any research is the transformation of the being of the researcher.

Mathematics education tends to embrace theories which come to hand insofar as those theories provide a language or a perspective for drawing distinctions, addressing issues, and startling colleagues. But invoking a theory entails ontological commitment to the objects created in, by, and for that theory. Behaviourism entails commitment to a relatively unproblematic existence of identifiable behaviours, and eschews commitment to states or thoughts; constructivism entails commitment to individuals making sense for themselves on the basis of perceived sense impressions; social constructivism entails commitment to language practices as enduring entities and for some at least, eschews Platonic forms or archetypes; taxonomies entail commitment to what is classified; analysis of transcripts and recordings of events entails commitment to the relatively objective existence of events, and so on. In overlooking such ontological commitment, pragmatic adoption of handy theories is prone to instability, which might account for the increasingly rapid swings of fashion between different theoretical stances, from behaviourism, through stage and levels theories, to psycho-constructivism, social constructivism, post-modernism, and post-post-modernism, as well as the eclectic use of ethnographic, hermeneutic, phenomenological, action-based, and reflective self-research methods.

This chapter looks at both roles of theory in mathematics education as background and as foreground. The first section considers effects of different theoretical stances on the notion of observation, data, and analysis, then elaborates aspects of research which are influenced by theory. They can be seen as struggles between cause-and-effect and systemic-causation or mutual-co-evolution as mechanisms on the one hand, and between stressing particularly the social or the psychological on the other. They can also be compared by attending to the emphasis placed on objects of study as things, and as experience.

In the second section we have chosen to distinguish three broad approaches to research in mathematics education on the basis of the role which theory plays in them. The final section offers descriptions of possible trends in the development of theory both in, and for, mathematics education, highlighting a current fixation on language, but suggesting that images and icons might be topics for concentration in the future.

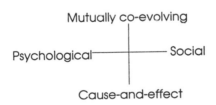

2.   THEORIES

This section looks both at theories of mathematics education, and theories within mathematics education research. The ways in which theory influences and frames different aspects of research practice, providing a world-view are elaborated.

Background theories encompass an *object* (aims and goals of the research, including what constitutes a researchable question, a problematique), *objects* (what sorts of things are studied, even if they are not perceived as 'things' in any material sense (Waywood, 1993)), *methods* (how research is carried out, validated and applied), and *situation* (as perceived by the researcher), and provide a language for discussing these. The *situation* necessarily assumes, manifests, encompasses, and is constituted through a philosophic stance manifested in the discourse and in other practices. Language describes, but it also frames. When a question is asked, we act as if it can therefore be answered, and answered in terms relevant to the questioner, yet often in education this is simply not the case.

Theory plays an important role in discerning and defining what objects are to be studied, indeed, theoretical constructs act to bring those objects into being. Considering the extent to which the objects constructed are adequate or appropriate to the situation you want to study (itself only identifiable through ontological commitment of theory) produces an ethical dimension in theorising, since restricting research to psychological constructs, to social constructs, to political constructs, or to mathematical constructs can seriously impoverish applicability and generalisability.

A modern way of distinguishing natural and social sciences is to see the objects studied by science as material objects ('nature'), and the objects studied by social science as signs. We seem to be able to experience material objects directly, whereas social sciences deal with constructs which can only be approached through signs and indicators. But even this distinction grows fuzzy as physicists 'observe' quarks through signs in bubble chambers.

Some phenomenologists argue that their object of study is lived experience, and that accepting signs already forces research to be *about* rather than *of* phenomena. Marton (1981, 1988) and Mason (1996) have argued that it is possible to make experience the object of research rather than at best using experience to research something else. It is interesting to note that the words 'experience' and 'experiment' have the same root: *per-io* meaning 'to go through', whence as in a trial, or taking a risk, and so *ex-perio* means 'to learn from going through trials and risks'.

Where the objects of investigation are conceived of as material 'things' then it is appropriate to offer explanations in terms of chains of logical cause-and-effect. Where the objects are conceived of as signs, it is appropriate to offer informative descriptions and interpretations of histories. This distinction underlies the split between quantitative and qualitative methodologies and their appropriateness in different enquiries. Lincoln and Guba (1985) developed the distinction in reference to the background theories which informed them, by looking at the nature of reality, the relationship between knower and known, the possibilities for generalisation and causal links, and the role of values in the two sciences. Bakhtin put the distinction strongly:

> The exact sciences are a monological form of knowledge: the intellect contemplates a 'thing' and speaks of it. Here, there is only one subject, the subject that knows (contemplates) and speaks (utters). In front of him there is only a voiceless thing. But [in the social sciences] the subject as such cannot be perceived or studied as if it were a thing, since it cannot remain a subject if it is voiceless; consequently, there is no knowledge of the subject but dialogical.
>
> (Quoted by Todorov, 1984, p.18)

The presence of background theory, and its role in defining questions, objects, methods, products, and validation means that research is not only a matter of framing a question and then searching around for a method, not simply a matter of collecting data and then looking for analytic tools, not merely a matter of looking at results and evaluating their validity. These activities are all framed and constructed by the discourse of the background theory.

There is a welter of theoretical positions – what Mason and Davis (1989) called episte-methodologies (on the grounds that methodology is inextricably intertwined with epistemological positioning) – and these can be related to a tension between the subjectively-personal and the objectively-material. At one extreme, 'experience-of' is all that matters. At another extreme, 'experimenting-on' others is the only reliable path to knowledge. But the apparently objective can turn out to be subjective, and the apparently subjective can be seen to apply widely. Study and observation, or *spection*, (the root of inspection, perspective, etc.) can be strictly from the outside *(extraspective),* can involve elements from the inside by the researcher *(intraspective),* and can involve varying degrees of negotiation and interaction with others *(interspection)* (Mason, in press). Results can be taken to influence through spontaneously informing choices in the moment, and as declarations of what must be true in given circumstances.

Subject – Person		Object – Thing
Experience-of		Experiment-on
Inter- & Intra-spective	———————	Extra-spective
Interpretative		Extra-pretative
Informative		Declaritive

For example, critical theory (Adorno and Habermas) can be seen as predominantly social and interpretative, though like all writing, caught up in making assertions with nouns and predicates which are hard to contradict within the discourse itself. Post-modern concerns with experiencing and construal as 'textual interpretation', and denying the possibility of global all-encompassing theory (Derrida, Levinas, Lyotard) can be seen as stressing the social but calling upon the personal. Phenomenological investigation (Husserl, Heidegger, Gadamer) can be seen as stressing the subjectively interpretative. Introspection and Gestalt methods can be seen as stressing experience but trying to study it through more objective methods. Pragmatists (Dewey, Peirce, James) can be seen as more balanced between the social and the psychological, the material and the experienced. Vygotsky and Piaget can be seen as both stressing the extraspective while disagreeing about where to place stress in the social-psychological dimension.

2.2   Theories Within Mathematics Education Research

Theories generated by research *in* mathematics education usually have one or more functions (Nagel, 1961; Royce, 1978,). They can have a *descriptive* function, providing a language to frame a way of seeing, and in this sense they effect an ideology. They may offer an *explanation* of how or why something happened, thus relating what has been observed to the past, whether through statistical correlation, cause-and-effect analysis, influence, or co-evolving mutuality (Varela, Thompson, & Rosch, 1991). They may attempt to *predict* what will happen in similar situations through stating necessary or appropriate conditions (and for this they need to specify what constitutes 'similar' and 'situation'). They may serve to *inform* practice by sharpening or heightening sensitivity to notice and act in the future.

Whichever of these functions a theory contributes to, it comes from, belongs to, even constitutes, a *weltenschauung*, and communication between different world-views is at best problematic (Orton 1988).

Edwards asked masters-level students who were all experienced teachers, what they thought a theory was, and to give an example. They saw theory as explanatory, testable, and as abstraction.

Predictive ↑ Informative
Descriptive
|
Explanatory

2.3   A Reflective Aside

There is, potentially, an opportunity for you to notice freshly the ubiquitous presence of theoretical positioning, by attending to your reaction to the three diagrammatic structures displayed above (a pair of orthogonal axes, a single axis, and an arrow) and to the attempts to describe various stances according to a particular scheme. Some people react by asking 'why this structure?' and adding other elements. Others want to know the source or justification for the structure (the background theory and context). Others react against the very making of distinctions. Many people find that someone else's diagram says nothing to them. Each reaction can be read as indicative of a theoretical stance challenged by or resonant with what is taken-as being offered.

The theoretical construct manifested by the display of four elements of theory comes from a structuralist approach in which the quality of fourness is activity and activity is seen as having an essential four-foldness (Bennett, 1993). This framework can be used as a reminder in any particular situation to look for balance and correspondence among the four components. Both axes (direction and resource) require appropriate contributions from the other. The second diagram was chosen to indicate a connection with development in time, since explanation is about the past and prediction about the future. They provide an opportunity to experience afresh the difference between someone else's apparently random structure and one's own sense of principled structure.

3.   THEORIES AS WORLD-VIEWS

Theory integrates methodology and *Weltenschauung*, philosophy and practice. Foremost, theories provide a language in which to frame and describe and, hence, through which to discern. Any research paradigm uses language to
- formulate questions and enquiry;
- specify a methodology for pursuing enquiry;
- delineate a coherent and consistent view of the objects of study;

- specify a coherent and consistent view of the nature and role of data collection and analysis;
- support a means for validating findings;
- format reporting of findings in a consistent manner to others.

Different goals are appropriate in different worlds.
- A world of external facts supports repeatable experiments, and is typical of research in the natural sciences;
- A world of opinion and belief supports surveys of representative population samples, and is typical of sociological research;
- A world of other's experience supports vivid description from a participant observer, and is typical of ethnographic research;
- A world of involvement in action and decision making supports description and prediction, and is typical of action research;
- A world of personal experience of reflective practice supports sensitising, noticing, and resonance seeking, and is typical of phenomenological, phenomenographic, experiential research.

Each of these worlds involves its own psychology, sociology, ideology, culture, and political perspective. The theory provides
- a view of epistemology, of what it means to know, and to come to know, within that paradigm, and a self-consistent view of the role of theory and its interaction with practice;
- ontological commitment, through the use of technical terms which bring into existence described phenomena and attributes;
- a value system indicating what types of questions are researchable, worth asking, and resolvable within that paradigm;
- a view of the psychology of being a researcher and of being the subject of research;
- a view of how the individual (researcher and subject) is influenced by the environment (including people and institutions), how the environment is influenced by individuals, and how the fact of participating in research as researcher or subject influences the enquiry, even whether distinctions between individual and group are discernible.

Integral to research is the placing of current concerns in historical and cultural context, through locating sources of similar ideas in the past, as expressed by current and earlier authors. This includes trying to be explicit about one's own implicit and background theories

Most research methods involve some sort of data. Something becomes a datum only when it is constructed as such by someone taking a research stance, with the intention to analyse it in relation to other data. Some approaches admit that observations can be turned into data, while others require that data has to be intentionally collected *as* data in order to be useable as data. Data might include

— descriptions of experiments, and publication of their outcomes, as in the natural science paradigm;
— descriptions of surveys and presentation of responses and their analysis, as in the sociological paradigm;
— descriptions of events and experiences, and comments on those, by the researcher and others, as in the ethnographic paradigm;
— descriptions of significant incidents and constructed exercises which highlight informative distinctions and alternative actions, as in the noticing paradigm.

Descriptions may consist of instructions (of how to carry out experiments), instruments (for conducting surveys), transcripts, recordings, notes-in-the-moment, and reconstructions of events. In experiments scientists take the initiative and construct the situation for their own purposes; in surveys researchers take the initiative to probe an existing situation but do not generate the situation itself; in describing events and experiences ethnographers influence the situation by their presence, but their presence is not the primary focus; in action research the initiative taken is the object of research; and in describing incidents and constructing exercises for others researchers are using the presence of an audience to make deeper contact with their own experience.

For example, it is becoming common to collect audio and video recordings of interviews and other interactions, and then to analyse these. But what sense can be made of them, and what is appropriate to do with them in the way of selection, analysis, and presentation to others, depends on theoretical assumptions about the nature of recorded events. If you assume that there is or was a specific event, and that a recording provides a closer approximation to what really happened than, for example, notes taken at or after the time, then it makes sense to construct an elaborate framework of analytic tools to process the data and draw conclusions relating to that incident. A concomitant assumption is that what people say and do when being taped in some way displays what they are thinking or experiencing.

But it is not unusual for a pupil to remain silent and still throughout a taping session and then to report completely and fully about what the others were doing once the taping finishes. As Lave (1988) pointed out, silence is not evidence for anything except silence. Indeed, more generally, absence of evidence cannot be taken as evidence of absence. When children do not perform, all we know is that they did not perform. To generalise to 'will not' on another occasion, or to 'cannot', is to overstep the bounds. It is possible to participate fully and appear to be on the periphery, just as it is possible to appear to participate centrally, but to be only superficially engaged in actual thinking or reflection.

A common device for pilot studies is to ask people to fill in questionnaires. But questionnaires are peculiar instruments. When designing one, you are deeply in touch with what you want to know, and you cast around for probes that you think will release or expose what you are thinking of. But when you are faced with a questionnaire, you are in a completely different state. Even if you are eager to be of assistance, interested to probe the same domain yourself, you will not interpret the questions in the same way as the designer. Questions often start genuinely but are interpreted as 'guess what is in my mind'.

Just as teachers discover that often when they ask students a question it is only when the response comes back that they realise explicitly what they were expecting and why they asked the question, so questionnaire designers and interviewers often only appreciate what they were trying to accomplish when they receive a response. Pilot studies are necessary in order to generate contact with the world of the respondent. The popularity of informal interview-discussions rather than tight and precise questions conceived as *instruments* is largely due to the flexibility that appears to be available. However, it is much harder to be disciplined and systematic when responding in free-flow.

3.2 Products and Validity of Research

The overt product of research usually consists of conjectured generalities, such as concepts, definitions, distinctions, and connections arising as a result of analysing data, and these constitute the emerging theory associated with the research. Data can be used as a source of insight or pattern spotting, and also to illustrate generalisations. In the former, it is used to move from the particular to the general; in the latter, from the general to the particular in order to appreciate the general.

A covert product is a transformation in the perspective and thinking of the researcher, a reconstruction of their world and world-view. The effect on the researcher of collecting data varies according to the paradigm being used, but the most common experience of researching in any paradigm is that the researcher develops or changes in their sensitivities to issues and details associated with their domain of interest. Paradigms differ in the extent to which such changes are even recorded, much less expressed or offered in some practical way to others.

Offering a conjectured generality as the product or result of research activity requires clarity in delineating the scope of the domain in which some things are changeable while others remain invariant. If conjectures are idiosyncratic, then the scope is necessarily very narrow, and if conjectures can be tested by anyone under any circumstance, the scope can be very broad. Generalities of course have to be justified, by a combination of logical argument in the analysis of data and theory-spinning or conjecture formulating. Paradigms may call upon a variety of forms of justification, but tend to emphasise particular ones:

— inference and significance in experiments;
— significance and correlation in surveys;
— triangulation (seeking consistency or consonance of observations by matching descriptions from several different sources such as from different people in the same role, or from the people in different roles), distinction recognition (training several people to make certain distinctions and then get them all to analyse the same data and see if they agree; what is being tested is the training as much as the conclusions from the data, but is essential if a framework is being put forward for the analysis of qualitative data);
— evidence of resonance found in and by colleagues, and experience of informed choices in practice, in the case of experiential research such as noticing;
— replicability, whether by direct repetition experimentally or in practice, or indirectly through informing recognition of relevance to act in practice.

For many educational researchers the role of theory is down-played in favour of practice. But practice requires different questions to be answered and to answer these questions also requires a theoretical perspective, as Cobb (1995) says in respect of constructivism (*qua* theory),

> (constructivism) is of value only to the extent that it constitutes a useful framework within which to cast issues, interpret events, and develop courses of action that contribute to the improvement of students' mathematics education. (p.250)

Emphasis on the practical, which was formed as a philosophy in the writings of James, Dewey, and Peirce, employs a criterion of performance (Lyotard, 1984, 1991) rather than of theoretical logic and argument. Performance can be seen as a product (how the research shows you can behave) which then has to be adhered to strictly and systematically so that predictions will in fact be observed. This view is consistent with an objective, cause-and-effect stance. Performance can also be seen as creative and responsive, generated by informed choice of action in the moment, and evaluated through a sense of flow and appropriateness. This view is consistent with a perspective of co-evolving mutuality.

Theory is implicit not only in any research, but even in this exposition, which is founded in structural distinction-making but cognisant of maintaining post-modern complexity.

3.3 Issues in Observing

All research, no matter how theoretical or philosophical, is based on observation, whether of incidents and things in the material world, or metaphorically, of reconstructed experience and abstract form. No matter what approach is taken to research in mathematics education, no matter what kinds of questions are addressed, no matter what the audience, there are some theoretical notions which are universally accepted, although even those are interpreted differently in different paradigms. For example, the principle that observation is theory laden is certainly widely accepted, having been put forward explicitly many times from different perspectives, with roots traceable in many cultures and over many generations.

Hanson (1958) argued that 'facts are theory-laden', and Goodman (1978) balanced it with the statement that 'Facts are theory laden as we hope our theories are fact-laden ... facts are small theories, and theories are big facts (pp.96-97).

Schwab (1962), made a similar point in outlining the directions of research in education:

> For the purposes of science, facts can no longer be treated as self-existing givens. They are matters contingent on the knower ... A fresh line of scientific research has its origin, not in objective facts alone, but in a conception, a construction of the mind. And on this conception all else depends. It tells us what facts to look for in the research. It tells us what meaning to assign these facts. (p.12)

Freudenthal used to say 'Observe, observe, observe', in an attempt to divert academics from rapid theorising; others have promoted approaches which might be summarised as 'analyse-plan-act-evaluate' (action research), 'try-listen-notice' (practitioner research), 'experiment-experiment' (scientific educationalists), and 'interrogate your experience as a baby' (Gattegno, 1970).

Even if observation is theory laden, there are many different stances with respect to the ontology of observation. What is observation, what is observed, and where is it located?

Some people go so far as to say that there is no way to demonstrate the independent existence of an objective world to which observations and descriptions approximate, and so they apply Ockham's razor and refuse to assume such an existence; others hover around accepting that there is a phenomenon to be observed, but that all observations are ultimately idiosyncratic or socially enculturated; others use the conceit of *taken-as-shared* so that they can remain agnostic as to whether there is any 'thing' which is in fact shared and focus instead on the language employed; and still others take the material world and the world of human actions for granted as relatively unproblematic.

Taking events and people as material and objective means that attention can be focused on ever more precise approximation to the whole. From notes made from memory or during the event, researchers have moved to transcripts of speech, with increasingly sophisticated devices for indicating tone, overlap, and hesitancy. With CD-Rom it becomes feasible to present hypertext linked to audio and video recording itself. It is possible that multimedia developments will enable juxtaposition of multiple cameras and perhaps even other sensory modes like temperature and smell, developing a generalised Alexandria Quartet of multiple perspectives. But providing rich recordings only defers observation. The richer the sensory recording, the more analysis that may be required in order that the user can make sense of what is provided.

Tapes of children working after the teacher leaves them can be informative about the effects of interventions; tapes can be reviewed numerous times and in slow motion to discern detail in the rapid and complex profusion of gestures and actions which take place in the moment (Schoenfeld, Smith & Arcavi, 1993). But each act of recording captures only some aspect of what it was like to be in the event, because it necessarily selects and attenuates according to its physics. The act of selecting which episodes to analyse or to show to others is a further level of selectivity. Assertions made on the basis of recordings need to be related to the underlying theoretical constructs which support the observations and contextualise the assertions.

Taking all observation as idiosyncratic and socially constituted if not driven leads some researchers to move away from details of transcripts and incidents, and to engage in more global social commentary and critique of institutionalisation and political forces which inevitably frame the educational enterprise. It has also provoked detailed study of the *situation didactique* (Brousseau 1984), of ways of making detailed sense of pupil-pupil and pupil-teacher interaction based on symbolic-interactionism (Bauersfeld, 1991), and pedagogic positions such as situated-cognition and cognitive apprenticeship (Lave, 1988; Brown, Collins, & Duguid, 1989).

Denying or doubting external, shared, objective reality means that incidents and events do not exist in and of themselves, but only through the presence and description of the observer. Events then consist of reports and memories of those who participated, and subsequently, of the reports and constructions of those who read and talk about those reports. Piaget and Freudenthal, like many researchers, gave brief-but-vivid accounts of incidents with children, particularly their own relatives. Some of these reports have become generic exemplars of technical terms, being repeatedly referred to and interwoven in the fabric of people's sense of the author's constructs. In this perspective, what is being studied is not that which is described overtly, but the description itself, the describer, and an awareness, sensitivity, or distinction-making which generates the description and which is being exemplified.

If a description resonates with experience, seems to fit with the past or helps inform future acts, then it becomes an 'it'. An ontological movement takes place. But the ontological reality is perceptual rather than material. When someone describes an incident or comments on someone else's description, the semiotic distinction between signifier and signified applies, extended into three terms. The description can be taken as referent (the object of study, the signified), as reference (referring to some event, the signifier), or as referee (in the sense of indicating the sensitivity and orientation of the describer, the author who signifies).

To appreciate research reports in mathematics education, it is necessary to bear in mind the cultural heritage of the investigation, data collection, and analysis being undertaken. It can be taken at any or all of three levels: as saying something about the world (of experience, of material, of education, etc.), saying something about the paradigm being employed, and saying something about the author. These are revealed by looking through the text to experience, at the text for patterns of discourse, and via the text at what is not said as well as said to reveal the author's sensitivities.

Most researchers are located somewhere on a spectrum from description as referent (as describing some event whether actual, taken-as-shared, or mythologised), through description as reference (as object of study as in transcript or recording), to description as referee (as indicator of what the describer is stressing and hence ignoring). In the last section we argue that the spectrum is more usefully seen as a tension than a location; that just as the discourses in which light is most usefully seen as wave or as particle depend on the context and problem, so the nature and role of description encompasses a whole spectrum.

It seems important for many people to employ the metaphor of space and position to 'locate' ideas and constructs. For example, some people want to find a place for mathematical ideas. For many, the notion of a mathematical world is sufficient, but for others the metaphor implies the necessity for logical consistency, in which Euclidean and non-Euclidean geometries cannot sit side-by-side.

Some people argue that our dependence on language locates all of our perceived phenomena in language, so that mathematics, mathematics teaching, and mathematics education research are all to be seen as discourses, as residing in the language practices of various communities. Others stress individual insight, imagery, and intuition, and see public mathematics as an attempt to communicate cognitively, affectively, and enactively. It is also possible to encompass the implied exclusivity of assertions by seeing language as at best an impoverished expression of experience, and to juxtapose the individual and the group, the psychological and the social, just as mathematicians juxtapose the Platonic world of mathematical forms with the personally constructed or invented world of new mathematics.

There are curious resonances between social-constructivist post-modernist emphases on the syntactics of discourse, and the formalist position in mathematics attributed to Hilbert and associated with structuralist views of mathematics based on axioms and strong foundations (Frege, Russell & Whitehead, Bourbaki). Both stress language and appear to ignore or de-emphasise semantics. Similarly there are curious resonances between psycho-constructivist structuralist emphasis on semantics, and mathematical empiricism (Lakatos, 1976; Kitcher 1984). Both stress meaning as a personal, psychological experience.

4.   THREE BROAD PRACTICES

It is tempting to speak of 'traditions' of research practice in mathematics education, but extremely difficult to delineate these, because different researchers treat theory and practice differently, even when they are following similar paradigms. The following three practices (pragmatic empiricism, philosophical well-foundedness, and results-focused) are intended to be broadly defined, with no intention of squeezing even any single researcher into just one of them. Many research programs have a pragmatic orientation, are well-founded philosophically, and are results-focused in their research reporting. The three practices do represent distinguishable responses to concerns about theoretical underpinnings of research activity, and consequently may be useful for raising awareness of other possibilities. Having distinguished our three practices, we found that they correspond closely to three principle research traditions described by Bishop (1992):

- *Pedagogue* tradition with goal of direct improvement of teaching, providing exemplary children's behaviour as evidence, and theory comprising accumulating shareable wisdom of expert teachers;
- *Scholastic-philosopher* tradition whose goal is a rigorously argued theoretical position, with evidence presumed already collected, and theory focused on idealised situations to which educational reality should aim;
- *Empirical scientist* tradition whose goal is explanation of educational reality, through offering facts to be explained, and seeking explanatory theory to be tested against data.

These in turn correspond to distinctions made by Howson et al. (1981), and more recently by Woodrow (1995), who noted a drive to doing things, a drive to understanding things, and a drive to knowing things. Once such distinctions are drawn, everyone relates to all three, but for outsiders, one aspect often seems to dominate.

5.   PRAGMATIC EMPIRICISM

Often identified with anglo-saxon cultures, practitioners in many different situations find themselves faced with having to act. The situation as perceived is of children, students, or teacher performing less well than hoped for, or not enjoying their activities. Practitioners ponder deeply, draw upon their experience, and try something. Then they make modifications according to how they judge the effects. Their aim is to inform practice in the future, in order to enhance the learning of their children. They may have no interest in generalising or theorising, may even deny the appropriateness of trying to go beyond their own classroom or beyond the present moment because they lay great store by the importance of situatedness, context, and milieu. Their theories are embedded in their practices (Elbaz, 1983); their methods are eclectic. The objects of study tend to be materials, apparatus and software, particular children, and acts of teaching. They tend to agree that their actions can be interpreted as consistent with a theory, but they do not usually recognise being driven *by* theory, to basing actions *upon* theory as suggested by the Thom remark quoted in the introduction.

The work of Maria Montessori had a strong element of pragmatism, of seeing what seemed to work, and allowing theories to account for what worked to emerge in their own time. Explorations in England of implications of Piagetian research, and the rise in England of mathematical investigations in school in the work of the Association of Teachers of Mathematics (which began as an association devoted to the use of apparatus in teaching mathematics) were similarly intensely pragmatic. What mattered was whether children engaged effectively in mathematics. Many of the constructs employed by pragmatists can be traced to Dewey and his focus on the importance of action and activity by the learner, and through him, connected to Plato's effusive praise of Egyptian educational practices (Laws VII 819, see Hamilton & Cairns, 1961, pp.1388-1389).

Another example of pragmatic empiricism at work can be seen in the way technology was introduced into mathematics teaching in England, by teachers getting hold of machines and seeing what happened. There was a sudden burst of creativity as teachers and researchers developed software for use with children. Teacher journals began to publish a variety of articles with suggestions of tasks that could be given to children, and indications of what sorts of things might happen. At the same time, researchers took up particular software and used it as a context in which to investigate collaboration between children in a computational environment, as a means to enhance children's experience of different topics in algebra, geometry, and data-handling, or to explore ways of introducing children to the use of the software itself. As more and more research was carried out, new specialist journals, aimed first at teachers, then at other researchers, were initiated.

A pragmatic approach underlies the action-research movement which acts as a broad umbrella for a variety of practices. At one end of the spectrum of directiveness, some researchers engage teachers or other practitioners in questioning their practice and trying things out; they guide and direct the investigation, supporting the practitioners in evaluating outcomes and modifying their plans for the future. It has become common to employ the cycle of *analyse-plan-act-evaluate* repeated over and over, sometimes rigidly in sequence, sometimes flexibly and in whatever order arises, as the underlying methodology. Along the spectrum of directedness, some researchers provoke teachers into, and support teachers in posing and exploring their own issues. The researcher acts less as director and more as a facilitator or experienced colleague. Further along the spectrum teachers work on their own practice with varying degrees of systematicity, attention to methodology, reading of literature, and reflection on the theoretical basis of their activities.

A line of research undertaken by Carraher, Carraher, and Schliemann (1985), Lave (1988), Frankenstein (1989), and others, summarised in Nunes (1992), which studies the mathematical competencies of people engaged in 'authentic' life activity in contrast to institutionalised settings can also be seen as pragmatic in basis and intention. It reveals a distinct gap between social practices inside and outside schools, reveals unexpected competencies that often fail to appear under formal testing, and leads to a revival of apprenticeship (Brown et al., 1989) and real-problem solving (Open University, 1980). How to validate authentic knowledge and know-how derived from non-institutionalised sources is a major area of concern, and not just in mathematics.

Many researchers in mathematics education started as teachers, moved into initial teacher education either via management or professional development or directly. They found themselves required by funding conditions to do research, and naturally turned to the most available subjects. They turned to their own practice as teachers or to their novice teachers as subjects. The mathematics education research community is fractionated by what different people are willing to accept as bonafide research, rather analogously to the professionalisation of sport. Some see research as the province of people employed to do research who are properly trained as professionals; some admit systematic and methodical investigation under the guidance of researchers or by people employed to teach as well as to research; some see research as a state of mind, and admit principled investigation by anyone, even where there is no tangible outcome.

Pragmatic empiricists often end up with a great deal of data, such as videotape, audio tape, and transcripts of lessons to analyse. Consistently with their pragmatism, they then set about locating ways to analyse that material. Their aim as always is to sensitise themselves to aspects they had not previously been aware of, so as to improve their students' experience.

With the aim of researching experience rather than researching through experience, Marton (1981, 1988) brought to expression what he calls phenomenography, in which utterances and behaviour are analysed by noting the ways in which primitive terms and stock expressions are used, rather as Wittgenstein located meaning in use. The aim is to appreciate the intentionality of the subject through abduction, based on resonance with oneself and with the practitioner and research community generally. The effect is to assume that what people say and do is meaningful in their terms, and to try to find perspectives from which such utterances would be used in a similar way, as an approach to what it might be like for the individual. Verification is then often statistical, gauging prediction against further observation, much as a computer-based model for a novice or expert in a specific domain is validated by the confluence of predictions with observations. The 'Discipline of Noticing', or 'Researching from the Inside' (Mason, 1994) is a similarly oriented approach which focuses attention on the moment by moment decisions made by teachers (and students), and which develops devices for becoming increasingly sensitive to the experience of others through awareness of one's own experience. Research products are informative theoretical constructs (labels for noticing) presented through task-exercises for others to engage in order to get a taste of what the researcher has noticed, to see if they too can notice something similar.

In a pragmatic empiricist approach, theoretical constructs tend to emerge over time as researchers try to make sense of the practical investigations and to formulate research proposals that might get funded. Of course from a theory-based perspective, the actions and observations are all theory-laden and theory-based, and the absence of clarity about these contributes to the sense of unfoundedness which is strongly felt by researchers with other perspectives. Researchers in other traditions are sometimes astonished that researchers working pragmatically do not appear to appreciate the fact of the theoretical underpinnings through which they are construing their practice (Carr, 1986, p.178). Evident eclecticism is often seen as opportunism and eccentricity rather than as bonafide research.

6.　PHILOSOPHICAL WELL-FOUNDEDNESS

By way of contrast with the pragmatic, some researchers, particularly in continental Europe, stress the importance of background theory in any investigation and are at pains to delineate those foundations before proceeding to conjecture, observe, and modify. Thom's remark quoted in the introduction is typical of this position. They see every action, every utterance, as generated by or based upon a (usually largely implicit) theory. Research is therefore directed towards exposing those theories. In order to justify altering practice, they have to make their own theories explicit and articulated before engaging in observation and experiment. It only makes sense to observe and experiment if the background is relatively stable. Then experiments can be precisely and systematically constructed in order to distinguish between competing hypotheses, and results can be interpreted in terms of that theory, or used to modify it.

Piaget's epistemological investigations provided a foundation for research in mathematics education for many years (Vergnaud, 1981). Vergnaud himself (1990) developed Piaget's epistemological perspective in the study of specific mathematical topics, using the notion of a scheme as a functional dynamic totality which drives competencies and yields concepts-in-action and theories-in-action. Others pursued the notion of epistemological obstacles (Bachelard, 1938) and epistemological analysis of mental structures corresponding to mathematical structures as the basis for instructional design. Boero (1990) uses an historical-cultural orientation to the same ends: the design of epistemologically well founded teaching materials, and among others, Hart (1993) and Carpenter and Fenema (1992), have led projects to develop curriculum materials based on research findings.

As the notion of Piagetian stages became more and more rigid in the work of authors trying to apply it to curriculum development, other researchers were able to demonstrate that it is very difficult to maintain clear distinctions between stages. Similar difficulties were experienced with van Hiele levels (Usiskin, 1982). Questions were also raised about the robustness of findings under perturbations of language (Donaldson, 1978). Despite the richness of Piaget's investigations, it takes only a slight lack of confidence to stimulate people to go in search of something fresh. Vygotsky's Russian school of activity theory, accessed at first through Bruner (1986), then Wertsch (1985), and latterly Davydov (1990) and Confrey (1995) among many others, offered an alternative formulation. At the heart of the differences between Piaget and Vygotsky is the issue of where 'higher order psychological functioning' originates: in the individual or in the social, but perhaps neither is justified in claiming exclusive rights.

Radical constructivists, building on von Glasersfeld (1984) and Steffe and Cobb (1983) but tracing roots back at least to Vico (1744 trans.) and St. Augustine (389 trans. Howie, 1969) (see also von Glasersfeld (1995) for historical roots) have endeavoured to remain epistemologically and philosophically well-founded and consistent, and are trying to maintain that consistency in making sense of teaching, and in locating teaching which can be justified on constructivist grounds (Simon, 1995).

A school of researchers in France have developed a perspective based on the *situation didactique* of Brousseau and colleagues (Douady and Mercier, 1992), and when used to generate curricula, becomes *didactic engineering* (Artigue and Perrin-Glorian, 1991). Reflecting on the roots of this foundational approach, Laborde (1989a, p.31) adumbrates the following three criteria for the theoretical framework known in France as *didactique des mathématiques* (even in France the term 'didactique' is interpreted variously, and although the word is found in most other Indo-European languages, there are subtle differences of usage in different cultures):

1) relevance in relation to observable phenomena;
2) exhaustivity in relation to all relevant phenomena;
3) consistency of the concepts involved within the theoretical framework.

To accomplish this requires systematic identification of all possible pupil reactions as predicted by theory, followed by detailed observation, and then modification of theory as required. Theory and experiment are seen as dialectically interacting and co-evolving. Researchers in this paradigm have worked on the relation between teaching and learning, raising such questions as

— What is the meaning of the knowledge we want the pupils to acquire?
— What is the meaning of the concepts constructed by the learner during the teaching process? (Laborde, 1989a, p.32)

Locating choices at the level of content, interactions between learners and knowledge, and teacher interventions, they discerned a variety of choices in each domain. They noticed that 'everything the teacher attempts to do in order to make the pupil produce the reaction expected, tends to deprive the pupil of the conditions necessary for the understanding and learning of the notion aimed at' (Brousseau, 1984, quoted in Laborde, 1989, p.34). Brousseau (1981) identified three forms of functioning of knowledge corresponding to variations in the organisation of the milieu:

1) implicit use (action situations);

2) explicit use (formulation situations);
3) justification (validation situations).

The aim of *didactic engineering* is to produce situations which promote precise and unambiguous formulations in response to a problem (Laborde, 1989a, p.35)

Mathematics educators at Bielefeld have developed the influential sociological notion of symbolic interactionism (Bauersfeld, 1990) for the purpose of studying in careful detail the nature of classroom interactions as social practices. Notions such as reflexivity and indexicality (Bauersfeld, 1991), and taken-as-shared (Cobb, 1990) emerged from this theoretical perspective. Also at Bielefeld, Steinbring (1989) and colleagues have developed the semiotic distinction between signifier and signified, to build an *epistemological triad* (object or context of reference, sign or symbol, and concept) as a theoretical underpinning for studying the interaction between pupils and between pupils and teachers and appreciation of how students come to construe mathematical ideas meaningfully.

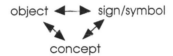

The importance of the triad is in the co-evolutionary development of each of the components as meaning is made.

The Freudenthal Institute bases its work on the principled design of exemplary materials (Gravemeijer, 1994). By repeatedly and thoroughly testing teaching materials in practice, they produce examples for other authors to follow in the design of curricula. The intention is not just curriculum development as such, but effecting change in teaching practices. Pre-service, in-service teacher training, counselling, text development, and opinion shaping in the community are all considered to be integral. Freudenthal (1971) emphasised that mathematics is to be seen not as a dry collection of printed pages, but as a human activity. Highly pragmatic in its aims and products, the Institute is nevertheless theory-guided.

Researchers in a philosophically well-founded tradition may collect videotape, audio-tape, or transcripts of lessons to analyse, but they know in advance what they are looking for and what they are going to do with what they find. There may be surprises which were not predicted from the theories, and these are used to modify the theory or to extend their predictive capabilities. Their aim is to validate for themselves the inclusiveness of their theory.

From a well-foundedness position, pragmatic enquiry looks unprincipled, undisciplined, ungeneralisable, and chaotic. From a pragmatic position, well-foundedness can generate useful ideas to pursue in practice, but often seems caught up in an intricate and almost impenetrable technical discourse. It seems to take forever to get going. In order to understand assertions you have not only to be familiar with the theoretical basis, but to some extent, accepting of it.

Pragmatism and post-modern philosophy are congenial partners in their conclusion that there is no grand-narrative, no theory that encompasses the condition of being human. In this respect there can only be practice, and as such no genuinely philosophical well-foundedness. It is no wonder that cross-perspective critique and integration is so difficult.

7.   RESULTS FOCUSED

An approach to research which is particularly prominent in North America is to base current research on recent findings and writings of colleagues. This is consistent with an image of a growing *body of knowledge* whose constant expansion signals progress in the field. It provides a ready base for funding agencies to gauge proposals: funding depends on adding a new piece to extant knowledge. The theoretical justification for one project is founded on the accumulation of results from other recent projects, to the extent that Kilpatrick (1981) complained about a lack of home-grown theories not borrowed from other disciplines. Methods and topics are varied to greater or lesser extent in each succeeding project, but the variations at each step tend to be small. Although superficially similar to philosophical well-foundedness in drawing upon a developing practice and theoretical stance, the difference is in adherence to background theory. In the case of results-focused-research, reference to previous work is not so much theory-driven as results-incorporating. Previous work from different traditions is cited, but it is the results which are important. Research is carried out according to the researcher's preferred paradigm.

In a results-focused orientation, energy is often devoted to building and validating tests (both quantitative and qualitative) which are designed to provide evidence or indication of subtle and otherwise inaccessible constructs, such as attitude, interest, affectivity, gender-sensitivity, intelligence, orientation, personal propensity etc. (Cohen, 1976). These tests can then be used by subsequent researchers to build a literature of studies which can be summarised, compared, and surveyed because they share a common base.

Originating in a strongly positivist behavioural perspective which tried to transfer scientific methods, certainty, and the efficiency of the production line to studying and employing people, historical consistency as an ethos has been applied to qualitative research as well as to quantitative. Just as those who tried to initiate qualitative research found that to be accepted in journals they had to refer to previous quantitative studies, those continuing to espouse statistical studies find themselves suddenly in a minority, and having to quote and build upon qualitative studies (Stallings, 1995).

From a results-focused perspective, research that is from a philosophically well-founded tradition uses a plethora of technical terms which appear meaningless unless you already appreciate the background. Alternatively it can appear over-abstract because results are buried under extensive theoretical exposition. Pragmatic enquiry is seen as constantly starting afresh. It appears not to build on established knowledge and fails to develop systematically and progressively. From other perspectives, historical consistency seems narrowly focused almost to the extent of superficiality: to gain acceptance you have to quote the right sources. Because of the interpenetration of theory in all aspects of enquiry and research, it is inappropriate to mix and match. In order to make substantive use of an approach it takes some years of apprenticeship to learn the vocabulary of a world view, (e.g. to appreciate *dasein* in phenomenology), and the implicit distinctions and contrasts they invoke.

The principle results in a results-focused paper are presented and referenced and so seem unproblematic, but to researchers from other traditions they often seem to miss the point, being driven by the available 'tool' rather than the research question being pursued. From a pragmatic perspective, papers in a results-oriented perspective appear either to demonstrate the obvious or to wander off into some arcane world in which measurements are made of what can be measured and sight seems lost of what the original research was supposed to explore.

8.   INTEGRATION

In a climate of exponential growth in researchers and research reporting, it is impossible to keep abreast of what used to appear as very focused domains, such as the teaching and learning of ratio and proportion, algebra in primary schools, geometry in secondary schools, or early number learning by visually impaired students, much less in more theoretical or broadly applicable domains. The result is a profusion of journals, physical and electronic, to provide a forum for every voice. It is virtually impossible now to build on what has been done before, even to know about recognisably similar investigations in other domains much less from other perspectives. Reviews of the literature in doctoral theses reflect the reading of the supervising panel and of the candidate.

All researchers draw on ideas they encounter. Some are more eclectic than others, and in drawing on multiple sources, may not do full justice to the origins of the notions they employ. For example, those drawing on both Piaget and Vygotsky, on both James and Skemp, on both Skinner and Husserl, are seeking to integrate what on the surface is mutually contradictory. They are criticised by proponents of one or other source, pointing out where the integrator has gone astray. But in the final analysis, each researcher is an integration of their re-construction of the sources which have struck them as significant. They represent a theoretical stance, with local meanings and uses of terms taken-as-shared in a wider community. Bauersfeld (1992) provides an excellent example of a precise and insightful researcher pursuing a particular path but seeking to integrate the best of a multitude of sources.

9.   TRENDS IN THEORY EVOLUTION

This section is rather speculative. It tries to turn experience of a succession of dominating theories into an extrapolation based on experience of that succession. Kant is supposed to have said that a succession of experience does not add up to experience of that succession. Something else is required, such as reflection and standing back. The principal observation is that whatever theories individuals and groups employ now, they are bound to be overturned by the advent of electronic text (words, images, and sounds).

9.1   The Primacy of Language

The significance of language (verbal, gestural, and diagrammatic) is currently being re-examined in most disciplines, including mathematics education. Language has always been a topic of philosophical investigation, as far as we know, and most thoughtful writers address the question of how thought and language are related.

The hermeneutic tradition which developed from the interpretation of sacred texts into the semiotics of text 'reading' has been extended to take almost any thing or act as 'text'. Language is like the air we breath or the water that surrounds a fish. It is very hard to exist for long in an intellectual pursuit without recourse to language. But the patterns of language use, the discourse, already presupposes and formats what can be said. Hermeneutics has come back into vogue as people tussle with the origins of thought (does it require language or does language emerge through thought?). Although the Sapir-Whorf hypothesis (Mühäusler & Harré, 1990; Koerner, 1992) that language structures, even determines what is thinkable, has been largely discounted as being too simple, it seems self-evident that immersed as we are in language, what we can express must influence what we can experience as we try to make sense of what other people say.

The *logos* has always been of deep and fundamental importance to human beings, as is evidenced in the opening passages in many religious texts, where the *word* is associated with creation (and hence with ontological commitment). We are re-experiencing the fascination of creation-by-text in the explosion of mind-polluting images which serve a similar ontological process. They infect the mind with supplanted images (Salomon, 1979). Maturana and Varela (1988) see language as the means for going beyond the consensual coordination of action observed amongst co-operating animals who seem to cooperate like two actors following each other's lead in an improvisation. Language is the consensual co-ordination of the consensual co-ordination of action. Language makes it possible to pre-arrange and to modify in the moment the co-ordination of action, which otherwise has to be achieved by careful observation and harmonious interaction.

The advent of writing drew attention to the contrast between an ephemeral oral tradition and the effect of permanent text, not just through crystallising language, but in the transformation of internalised god-voice into authoritarian priesthood (Jaynes, 1976) and the interpretation of signs (augury) into the interpretation of text (hermeneutics). Starting as records of oral authority (e.g., Babylonian tablets), text became argument (e.g., Plato's dialogues, Euclid's elements, etc.). The invention of printing widened access to original text, but thereby produced a profusion of commentary and argument. Unicity of meaning as controlled by a centralised church could be challenged by reformers with access to texts. The people could be reached by translations into the vernacular, but with all the problems of interpretation that translation brings. The printed word facilitated mass education and industrialisation, but also multiple interpretation.

We are now experiencing electronic text where presence and sequence are removed from communication, and where access is vastly enhanced. Audio and video images are almost as easy to produce as words. But the hope that more (visual, aural) detail would make events less problematic and text less ambiguous, is ill-founded. Every act of recording is caught in a web of selection and editing. Every image has a past as well as a present and a future. Every text, in the widest sense, requires interpretation, and where words are not present, are likely to be imported and imposed. The lessons of the encyclopaedists of the enlightenment are about to be learned all over again: there is no single truth to be captured on a CD Rom.

As words and images proliferate, their significance decreases. It becomes easier and easier to pick holes in, to re-interpret, or even deliberately to misconstrue, what others have written or displayed. Thus in the midst of proliferation we find multiplicity of theorising and of technical terms in which to cast theorising, but not general enlightenment. The tower of Babel is amongst us. Perplexed and disenchanted by the perfidy and profusion of text, directions of development span a broad spectrum beyond the notion of text as communicating meaning or of revealing (in the case of transcripts and audio-video tapes) behaviour and meaning, towards text as:

- speaking about the author's awareness (phenomenography);
- indicating the social discourse in which the author is embedded and through which they are constituted (social constructivism);
- a well-lit mirror of the reader's sensitivities and world-view (research from the inside);

How these can be integrated, if indeed they can or are, or chosen for emphasis by socio-political forces, remains to be seen.

Bakhtin (1986a, b) took the novel as his object of study and influenced the post-modern view of the relation between thought and language (see also Holquist 1981; Todorov, 1984). He sees the word as essentially dialogical. For there to be a word there has to be a speaker and a hearer. The terms *speaker* and *hearer* are already language structures which need not be mapped uniquely to biologically distinct organisms, since for example, inner speech is almost unstoppable when you are not speaking to others. For Bakhtin, there can be no consciousness without the 'other' that is needed for language.

Another influential post-modernist, Lacan (1977), takes an opposite view, that awareness of 'other' requires language. Although it can seem strange that self is an amorphous entity poised between the social and the psychological, requiring language to come into existence and producing language through existing, there are analogies with the physical body as extending beyond the confines of the skin, and of societies in which self appears to have incorporated more than just the individual, sometimes even being the community itself. The commune ideal, which revolutionised the Russian culture of Bakhtin, Vygotsky and others, may have influenced their views. The Indian doctrine of universal Will with a tiny fragment trapped inside each of our personalities but trying to escape to its rightful place, provides a supportive image. There is resonance also with the Piaget-Vygotsky debate as to whether the source of inner speech is from within the individual, permitting them to contact others, or from others in the culture, permitting the individual to recognise otherness. Winnicot (1971) identified the recognition of self, as opposed to other, as one of the early potential traumas for an emerging psyche, Baron-Cook (1995) points to autistic children lacking awareness of others as capable of mental actions, and Patrick Casement is supposed to have summed it up in the memorable assertion that 'every word is a step away from mother' (Tahta 1991, p.26).

The eternal recurrence of deep questions has brought us back again to Socrates' advice: *know thyself*. Who or where is the self? Who is the subject? For some it is a psychological construct, for others it resides in language. For both Piaget and Vygotsky, the subject is the centre of action in the world. For post-moderns, the very notion of 'centre' has evaporated. Lyotard (1984, 1992, 1994) goes so far as to speak of selves as 'nodes for the transmission of discourse'. The post-modern is now a culture, and in respect of this culture, what was said by Bakhtin of medieval man, applies to the life of senior school students:

> It can be said, with some restrictions to be sure, that medieval man in a way led two lives: one official, monolithically serious and sombre; beholden to strict hierarchical order; filled with fear, dogmatism, devotion, and piety; the other, of carnival and the public place, free; full of ambivalent laughter, sacrileges, profanations of all things sacred, disparagement and unseemly behaviour, familiar contact with everybody and everything.
>
> (Todorov, 1984, p.132)

Separation comes with distinctions. A part of us yearns for connectedness, for unity. Even post-modernists experience a pull in this direction, for if that were not the case they would be content with their idiosyncratic perceptions and not feel so moved to expound their point of view to others. Eastern philosophy has much more to say on movement towards wholeness, while Western philosophy seems bound towards dissolution in the many. Plato and Heraclitus are alive and well in new garb.

It is not surprising therefore that interpretation is of major concern in mathematics education at the present, whether in the form of interpretation of children's behaviour in the midst of an event, assessment, or interpretation of recordings of events. Mathematics educators have turned from psychology and cognitive science, through social sciences, to literary criticism in the search for theoretical base for interpretation. Psychoanalysis offers a further domain of experience and expertise to exploit. The pervasive presence of electronic screens covered in icons and images suggests that electronic words may give way to increasingly sophisticated use of icons and images, with implications at all levels from mathematics itself to mathematics learning, teaching, and researching.

9.2   Unicity

Is there a theory of mathematics education? Does mathematics education comprise any theories? What does a theory look like? Different people respond to these questions with widely varying answers. Some researchers feel that they are contributing to a developing theory, others take a post-modernist stance and deny the possibility of any comprehensive theory. A simple view of theory sees any general principles or validated distinctions as components of an emerging theory. Theoretical constructs can act as condensations of experience, and as guiding principles to inform future practice.

Mathematics education has traditionally drawn its methods and theories from other domains, psychological, sociological, statistical, qualitative, literary criticism, and psychoanalysis. Yet mathematics seems to be different from all other domains in its tensions between abstraction and modelling, between discovery and invention, between objectivity and subjectivity, between axiomatic formality and intuitive informality. This makes the mathematics classroom a unique environment, and although it is important and useful to draw on approaches and methods of other disciplines, any theory, whether background or foreground, in order to be convincing as explanation and effective in prediction or informing in practice must integrate the qualities of mathematics and mathematical experience with the process of education.

The positivist legacy and the success of science-engineering in modifying the designed world have meant that the notion of remediation, of misconceptions, of altering treatments in order to see altered effects, of evaluating outcomes in order to judge success, continues to pervade the research community. But this requires the assumption of a relatively stagnant background against which to detect change, as well as a commitment to cause-and-effect as the principle mechanism. An alternative perspective sees mutual co-evolution in which teacher and student together comprise an evolving discourse and community of practice with each influencing the other. Teacher professionalism is seen as a process of transformation that starts afresh in each generation with each individual, rather than as a process of accumulating wisdom which can be handed on to the next generation. But this is the direction in which research seems to be taking us as a community.

9.3   Multiplicity

Mathematics education is certainly infused with the problématique of clashing paradigms, and may be in the process of a further paradigm shift as the disquiet of and disaffection of and with the post-modern seeps into the consciousness of researchers. Originally mathematics education grew out of educational psychology and curriculum development, so its roots were in the design of agricultural-like experiments in which different treatments or different conditions were applied to selected samples, and the effects observed. Educational research, and with it mathematics education research specifically, was originally set in a behaviourist, positivist perspective. Mathematics education has been maturing during a time when the belief in the role of natural science as the epitome of success and rigour to the emerging disciplines concerned with studying human beings has begun to be questioned. Piaget and Vygotsky in their, at the time, separate worlds, opened up the experiential domain, seeing children as epistemologists and as social beings enculturated into and forming practices. Philosophical sources and inspiration were located, and what we see now is a proliferation of methodologies and paradigms as individuals seek to locate and ground their concerns in a compatible discourse.

As positions, perspectives, and theoretical stances are elaborated, it becomes clear that no one perspective is 'correct'. Multiplicity seems to be the direction of movement. Physicists have for generations been able to use the contradictory discourses of wave and of particle in theorising about light. We make sense of the abstract by basing it metaphorically on physical experience, and so instead of using *light* as a primitive term, we use *wave* and *particle* which are more easily theorised because of our experience. The same is likely to be true in theories in and about mathematics education. Instead of asserting exclusivity, people will increasingly acknowledge that each discourse provides a way of seeing and speaking which may or may not seem appropriate to the context, issue, and participants, which may or may not prove to be informative in the future. But multiplicity is not easy to accept or attain. Perry's monumental elucidation of different epistemological positionings of undergraduates at Harvard (Perry, 1968) includes descriptions of struggles to come to terms with multiplicity thus reflexively demonstrating how hard multiplicity is to come to terms with.

Pedagogic movements similarly tend to be based on one or at most a few fundamental positions. To be heard, it is necessary to be extreme, and since 'to express is to over stress' anyway, the result is that instead of eclectic merging of disparate perspectives in different contexts, pedagogical proposals tend to be univocal. Examples include *Real Problem Solving* (Mellin-Olsen, 1987; Open University, 1980) with almost complete emphasis on the importance of the practical and the personal for relevance, motivation and meaning; *discovery learning* stressing individual construal and putting almost exclusive emphasis on children discovering for themselves the accumulated wisdom of the ages; *fill & drill* stressing formalism and instruction and almost exclusively emphasising repetitive rehearsal in order to produce performance. Finding a balanced approach which integrates several different pedagogies is not easy (Mason 1979).

Steiner (1985) in an article written for the first meeting of the TME (Theory of Mathematics Education) group, promoted a systemic perspective, integrating theories-in-the-small (*micro-models* as called-for by Skemp, 1983), theories-in-the-large (*macro-models*, as sought by Romberg, 1983), and meta-theories about the overall process.

It is popular to distinguish form and content, process and object, and in mathematics education these distinctions have been the basis of theories about transitions between them (Sfard, 1991; Gray & Tall 1994). Another view might be that as distinctions they help us to discern detail, but like waves and particles, they have to be reunited in order to appreciate light. So too form and content have to be integrated in order to appreciate utterance, and process and object have to be integrated in order to understand mathematics. The weakness of proposed theories such as various forms of constructivism lies in implicit or explicit assertions of uniqueness and all-encompassing utility.

Orton (1988) employed two theories of theory in mathematics education, based on the epistemological enquiries of Kuhn (1970) and Lakatos (1976) respectively, to raise the question of how to choose between competing theories, whether they are theories *in* mathematics education, or theories *about* mathematics education. His article nicely models the content and resonates with Perry (1968), for he ends on a note of hopefulness that somehow there can be a rational basis, but that the roots of that rationality may lie in deep commitment to particular values. He ends by hoping for a dualist approach in which Kuhn and Lakatos are both involved as seems appropriate in different circumstances.

One major trap for theorists is to get caught up in category errors by analysing some words in detail using other words as primitives which might just as readily be probed and rendered problematic. Another trap is arguing logically about multiple perceptions which are not compatible when formalised, yet which can be collectively lived. Logic is not usually appropriate when considering worlds accessed through imagination. Complexity is just that, complex, and while analysis can be helpful, simplistic reduction often obscures as much as it reveals. Holding on to multiple perspectives and working at holding apparently irreconcilable tensions seems to be what the post-industrial world is about.

9.4   Self Reflection

Having theorised about theories in mathematics education, and emphasised the ontological, methodological, and philosophical implications of background and foreground theories, we should say a little bit about where we see ourselves standing. We have proposed distinctions, tried to relate distinctions together, and in so doing, the chapter reflects structuralist-constructivist tendencies. We have emphasised multiplicity, and while not espousing specifically the post-modernist slogan that 'there are no general theories' (including that one!), we have tried to apply a broad brush and to respect different perspectives.

Of considerable interest in the social appreciation of mathematics education as a community endeavour, and the role of theory in particular, is the overlapping waves of enthusiasms which seem to capture portions of the community. Some articulation, often drawn from another discipline, suddenly seems to provide a different way of making sense of experience. A resonance, such as 'I've been thinking that', or 'I've been trying to say that' often initiates take-up of a particular discourse. A strong discourse and a close-linked community often attract commitment and exploration, then some members fall away and are attracted to some new perspective. Holding it all together in a complex whole is not easy!

What is perhaps most important for researchers is to attempt to reveal and expose their underlying philosophical positions (not just by trotting out labels like socio-cultural-constructivism, or post-modernism) so that others can locate and relate themselves to the perspective being taken. Theses and dissertations are expected to do this. It is probably good for everyone to work on the role of theory in their research, and to attempt to clarify the particular theories being called upon.

ACKNOWLEDGMENT

The authors would like to thank Prof. Hans-Georg Steiner for his many helpful comments and suggestions, and Mary Spence for her useful questions.

REFERENCES

Artigue, M. and Perrin-Glorian, M-J.: 1991, 'Didactic Engineering Research and Development: Some Theoretical Problems Linked to this Duality', *For the Learning of Mathematics* 11(1),13-17.

Bachelard, D.: 1938 (republished 1983), *La Formation de l'Esprit Scientifique*, Presse Universitaire de France, Paris.

Bakhtin, M.: (1986a), 'Extracts from "Notes" (1970-1971)', in G.S. Morson (ed.) *Bakhtin: Essays and Dialogues on his Work*, The University of Chicago Press, Chicago.

Bakhtin, M.: (1986b). 'Extracts from "The Problem of Speech Genres"', in G.S. Morson (ed.) *Bakhtin: Essays and Dialogues on his Work*, The University of Chicago Press, Chicago.

Balacheff, N.: 1990, 'Towards a *Problématique* for Research on Mathematics Teaching', *Journal for Research in Mathematics Education* 21(4), 258-272.

Baron-Cook, S.: 1995, *Mindblindness*, MIT Press, Cambridge, Boston

Bauersfeld, H.: 1990, 'Activity Theory and Radical Constructivism: What do they have in Common?' in F. Steier (ed.) *Ecological Understanding*, Annual Conference of the American Society for Cybernetics, Oslo.

Bauersfeld, H.: 1991, 'Structuring the Structures', in L. Steffe (ed.) *Constructivism and Education*, Lawrence Erlbaum, Hillsdale, NJ.

Bauersfeld, H.: 1992, 'Integrating Theories for Mathematics Education', *For the Learning of Mathematics* 12(2), 19-28.

Bennett, J.: 1993, *Elementary Systematics: A Tool for Understanding Wholes*, Bennett Books, Santa Fe.

Bishop, A.: 1992, 'International Perspectives on Research in Mathematics Education', in D. Grouws, (ed.) *Handbook of Research on Mathematics Teaching and learning*, MacMillan, Oxford, 710-723.

Boero, P.: 1990, 'On Long Term Development of Some General Skills in Problem-solving: A Longitudinal Comparative Study', in G. Booker, P. Cobb, and T.N. Mendicuti (eds.) *Proceedings of the Fourteenth PME Conference*, International Group for the Psychology of Mathematics Education, Mexico, vol. 2, 169-176.

Brousseau, G.: 1981, 'Problèmes de Didactique des Décimaux', *Recherches en Didactique des Mathématiques* 2(1), 37-125.

Brousseau, G.: 1984, 'The Crucial Role of the Didactical Contract in the Analysis and Construction of Situations in Teaching and Learning Mathematics', in H-G Steiner (ed.) *Theory of Mathematics Education*, Paper 54, Institut fur Didaktik der Mathematik der Universitat Bielefeld.

Brown S., Collins A. and Duguid P.: 1989, 'Situated Cognition and the Culture of Learning', *Educational Researcher* 18(1), 32-41.

Bruner, J.: 1986, *Actual Minds, Possible Worlds*, Harvard University Press, Cambridge.

Carpenter, T. and Fennema, E.: 1992, 'Cognitively Guided Instruction: Building on the Knowledge of Students and Teachers', in W. Secada (ed.) *Curriculum Reform: The Case of Mathematics Education in the US*.

Carraher, T. Carraher, D. and Schliemann, A.: 1985, 'Mathematics in the Streets and in Schools', *British Journal of Developmental Psychology* 3, 21-29.

Carr, W.: 1986, 'Theories of Theory and Practice', *Journal of Philosophy of Education* 20(2), 177-186.

Cobb, P.: 1990, 'A Constructivist Perspective on Information-processing: Theories of Mathematical Activity', *International Journal of Educational Research* 14, 67-92.

Cobb, P.: 1995, 'Cultural Tools and Mathematical Learning: A Case Study', *Journal for Research in Mathematics Education* 26(4), 362-385.

Cohen, L.: 1976, *Educational Research in Classrooms and Schools: A Manual of Materials and Methods*, Harper & Row, London.

Confrey, J.: 1995, 'A Theory of Intellectual Development' (in three parts), *For The Learning of Mathematics* 15(1) pp.2-8, 15(2), pp.38-47, 15(3) pp.36-47.

Davydov, V.: 1990, *Soviet Studies in Mathematics Education: Types of Generalization in Instruction*, vol. 2, National Council of Teachers of Mathematics, Reston, VA.

Dawood, J. (trans): 1956, *The Koran*, Penguin Classics, Harmondsworth.

Donaldson, M.: 1978, *Children's Minds*, Norton, New York.

Douady, R., and Mercier, A.: 1992 (eds.), *Research in Didactique of Mathematics*, La Pensée Sauvage, Grenoble.

Elbez, F.: 1983, *Teachers' Thinking: A Study of Practical Knowledge*, Nichols, New York.

Frankenstein, M.: 1989, *Relearning Mathematics: A Different Third R – Radical Mathematics*, Free Association Press, London.

Freudenthal, H.: 1971, 'Geometry Between the Devil and the Deep Blue See', *Educational Studies in Mathematics* 5, 413-435.

Freudenthal, H.: 1991, *Revisiting Mathematics Education*, Kluwer, Dordrecht.

Gattegno, C.: 1970, *What We Owe Children: The Subordination of Teaching to Learning*, Routledge & Kegan Paul, London.

Goodman, N.: 1978, *Ways of World Making*, Harvester press, Hassocks.

Gravemeijer, K.: 1994, 'Educational Development and Developmental Research in Mathematics Education', *Journal for Research in Mathematics Education* 25(5), 443-471.

Gray, E. and Tall, D.: 1994, 'Duality, Ambiguity, and Flexibility: A 'Proceptual' View of Simple Arithmetic', *Journal for Research in Mathematics Education* 25(2), 116-140.

Hamilton, E. and Cairns, H. (eds.): (1961, reprinted 1985) *Plato: The Collected Dialogues*, Bollingen Series LXXI, Princeton University Press, Princeton.

Hanson, N.: 1958, *Patterns of Discovery*, Cambridge University Press, Cambridge, UK.

Hart, K.: 1993, 'Confidence in Success', in I. Hirabayashi, N. Nohda, K. Shigematsu and Fou-Lai Liu (eds.) *Proceedings of the Seventeenth International PME Conference*, vol. 1, Tsukuba, Ibaraki, Japan, 1-17.

Holquist, M. (ed.): 1981, *The Dialogic Imagination*, University of Texas Press, Austin.

Howie, G.: 1969, *St. Augustine on Education*, Henry Regnery Co., Chicago.

Howson, G., Keitel, C. and Kilpatrick, J.: 1981, *Curriculum Development in Mathematics*, Cambridge University Press, Cambridge, UK.

Jaynes, J.: 1976, *The Origins of Consciousness in the Breakdown of the Bicameral Mind*, University of Toronto, Toronto.

Kilpatrick, J.: 1981, 'Research on Mathematical Learning and Thinking in the United States', *Proceedings of PME I*, vol. 2, 18-29.

Kitcher, P.: 1984, *The Nature of Mathematical Knowledge*, Oxford University Press, Oxford.

Koerner, K.: 1992, 'The Sapir-Whorf Hypothesis: Leibniz to Lucy', *Journal of Linguistic Anthropology* 2(2).

Kuhn, T.: 1970, *The Structure of Scientific Revolutions*, University of Chicago, Chicago.

Laborde, C.: 1989a, 'Audacity and Reason: French Research in Mathematics Education', *For the Learning of Mathematics* 9(3), 31-36.

Laborde, C.: 1989b, 'Hardiesse et Raison des Recherches Françaises en Didactique des Mathématiques', in G. Vergnaud, J. Rogalski and M. Artigue (eds.) *Actes de la 13e Conférence Internationale PME*, vol. 1, 46-61.

Lacan, J.: 1977, 'The Mirror Stage', in A. Sheridan (trans.), *Écrits: A Selection*, Tavistock, London.

Lakatos, I.: 1976, *Proofs and Refutations*, Cambridge University Press, Cambridge.

Lave, J.: 1988, *Cognition in Practice: Mind, Mathematics, and Culture in Everyday Life*, Cambridge University Press, Boston.

Lincoln, Y. and Guba, E.: 1985, *Naturalistic Enquiry*, Sage, Beverly Hills.

Lyotard, J.-F.: 1984, *The Postmodern Condition: A Report on Knowledge, Theory and History of Literature* V10, Manchester University Press, Manchester.

Lyotard, J.-F.: 1991, *Phenomenology*, (trans. B. Beakley), State University of New York Press, Albany.

Lyotard, J.-F.: 1992. 'From the Postmodern Condition: A Report on Knowledge', in D. Ingram, and J. Ingram (eds.) *Critical Theory: The Essential Readings*, Paragon House, New York.

Lyotard, J.-F.: 1994, 'Bureaucracy: Resistance, Witnessing, Writing', *L'Esprit Creative* 34(1), 101-108.

Marton, F.: 1981, 'Phenomenography: Describing Conceptions of the World Around Us', *Instructional Science* 10, 177-200.

Marton, F.: 1988, 'Phenomenography: A Research Approach to Investigating Different Understandings of Reality', in J. Sherman and N. Webb (eds.) *Qualitative Research in Education: Focus and Methods*, Falmer press, London, 141-161.

Mason, J. and Davis, J.: 1989, 'Notes on a Radical Constructivist Epistemethodology Applied to Didactic Situations', *Journal of Structural Learning* 10, 157-176.

Mason, J.: 1979, 'Which Medium, Which Message?' *Visual Education*, Feb. 1979, 29-33.

Mason, J.: 1994, 'Researching from the Inside in Mathematics Education: Locating an I-You Relationship', in J.P. da Ponte and J.F. Matos (eds.) *Proceedings of the Eighteenth Conference for the Psychology of Mathematics Education*, vol. 1, PME, Lisbon, 176-190.

Mason, J.: 1996, *Personal Enquiry: Moving from Concern Towards Research*, Open University, Milton Keynes.

Mason, J.: in press, 'Researching from the Inside in Mathematics Education', in A. Sierpinska and J. Kilpatrick (eds.) *ICMI Study: What is Research in Mathematics Education and What are its Results?* Kluwer, Dordrecht.

Maturana, H. and Varela, F.: 1988, *The Tree of Knowledge: The Biological Roots of Human Understanding*, Shambala, Boston.

Mellin-Olsen, S.: 1987, *The Politics of Mathematics Education*, Reidel, Dordrecht.

Mühäusler, P. and Harré, R.: 1990, *Pronouns and People: The Linguistic Construction of Personal Identity*, Basil Blackwell, Oxford.

Nagel, E.: 1961, *The Structure of Science*, Routledge & Kegan Paul, London.

Nunes, T.: 1992, 'Ethnomathematics and Everyday Cognition', in D. Grouws (ed.) *Handbook of Research on Mathematics Teaching and Learning*, Macmillan, New York, 557-574.

Orton, R.: 1988, 'Two Theories of 'Theory' in Mathematics Education: Using Kuhn and Lakatos to Examine Four Fundamental Issues', *For the Learning of Mathematics* 8(2), 36-43.

1087

Open University: 1980, *PME233 Mathematics Across the Curriculum*, Open University, Milton Keynes.

Perry, W.: 1968, *Forms of Intellectual and Ethical Development in the College Years: A Scheme*, Holt, Rinehart & Winston, New York.

Romberg, T.: 1983, 'Toward 'Normal Science' in Some Mathematics Education Research', *Zentralblatt fur Didaktik der Mathematik* 15(8), 89-92.

Royce, J.: 1978, 'How Can We Best Advance the Construction of a Theory in Psychology? *Canadian Psychological Review* 19(4), 259-276.

Salomon, G.: 1979, *Interaction of Media, Cognition and Learning*, Jossey-Bass, London.

Schaeffer, J.D.: 1990, *Senus Communis: Vico, Rhetoric, and the Limits of Relativism*, Duke University Press, London.

Schoenfeld, A. Smith, J. and Arcavi, A.: 1993, 'The Microgenetic Analysis of One Student's Evolving Understanding of Complex Subject Matter Domain', in R. Glaser (ed.) *Advances in Instructional Psychology*, vol. 4, Lawrence Erlbaum, Hillsdale, NJ.

Schwab, J.: 1962, 'The Teaching of Science as Enquiry', in J. Schwab and P. Brandwein (eds.) *The Teaching of Science*, Harvard University Press, Cambridge.

Sfard, A.: 1991, 'On the Dual Nature of Mathematical Conceptions: Reflections on Processes and Objects as Different Sides of the Same Coin', *Educational Studies in Mathematics* 22, 1-36.

Simon, M.: 1995, 'Reconstructing Mathematics Pedagogy from a Constructivist Point of View', *Journal for Research in Mathematics Education* 26(2), 114-145.

Skemp, R.: 1983, 'The International Group for the Psychology of Mathematics Education: Past, Present and Future', *Zentralblatt fur Didaktik der Mathematik* 15, 112-117.

Stallings, W.: 1995, 'Confessions of a Quantitative Educational Researcher Trying to Teach Qualitative Research', *Educational Researcher* 24(3), 31-32.

Steffe, L. and Cobb, P.: 1983, *Construction of Arithmetical Meanings and Strategies*, Springer-Verlag, New York.

Steinbring, H.: 1989, 'Routine and Meaning in the Mathematics Classroom', *For the Learning of Mathematics* 9(1), 24-33.

Steiner, H-G.: 1985, 'Theory of Mathematics Education (TME): An Introduction', *For the Learning of Mathematics* 5(2), 11-17.

Tahta, D.: 1991, 'Three Apples Fell From Heaven ...', in ... *Reflections on a Day ... '*, IF 2, Centre for Mathematics Education, Open University, Milton Keynes, 25-30.

Thom, R.: 1973, 'Modern Mathematics: Does It Exist?' in G. Howson (ed) *Developments in Mathematical Education*, Cambridge University Press, Cambridge.

Todorov, T.: 1984, *Mikhail Bakhtin: The Dialogical Principle* (trans. W. Godzich), University of Minnesota Press, Minneapolis.

Usiskin, Z.: 1982, *Van Hiele Levels and Achievement in Secondary School Geometry*, University of Chicago, Chicago.

Varela, F., Thompson, E. and Rosch, E.: 1991, *The Embodied Mind: Cognitive Science and Human Experience*, MIT press, Cambridge.

Vergnaud, G.: 1981, 'Quelques Orientations Théoriques et Méthodlogiques des Recherches Françaises en Didactique des Mathématiques', in *Actes du Vième Colloque de* PME, Grenoble, Edition IMAG, vol. 2, 7-17.

Vergnaud, G.: 1990, 'La Théorie des Champs Conceptuels', *Recherches en Didactique des Mathématiques* 10(2-3), 133-170.

Vico, G-B.:1744, *Principi di Scienza Nuova*, Republished as Bergin & Fisch (trans.) 1961, Anchor Books, Garden City.

von Glasersfeld, E.: 1984, 'An Introduction to Radical Constructivism', in P. Watzlawick (ed.), *The Invented Reality*, Norton, London, 17-40.

von Glasersfeld, E.: 1995, *Radical Constructivism*, Falmer Press, London.

Vygotsky L.: 1978, *Mind in Society: The Development of the Higher Psychological Processes,* Harvard University Press, London.

Watzlawick P.: 1984, *The Invented Reality: How do we Know what we Believe we Know? — Contributions to Constructivism,* Norton, London.

Waywood, A.: 1993, 'Looking for an Appropriate Object of Educational Research: A Reflection on Three Presentations', *Mathematics Education Research Journal* 2(5), 83-89.

Wertsch, J.: 1985, *Culture, Communication and Cognition: Vygotskian Perspectives,* Cambridge University Press, Cambridge, UK.

Winnicot, D.: 1971, *Playing and Reality,* Tavistock, London

Woodrow, D.: 1995, 'The Quest for Multiple Beliefs in Learning Theories: Its Frustration by Single Faiths', *Chreods* 9, 10-14.

Section 4

Social Conditions & Perspectives on Professional Development
Christine Keitel – Section Editor

Introduction to Section 4

CHRISTINE KEITEL

Freie Universität, Berlin, Germany

Research in mathematics education can become effective in two ways: by implementing its results through the development of curricula, guidelines, and recommendations or material and assessment modes by various media – the technological model of innovation – and by having an impact on improving of professional education of mathematics teachers at all levels and in multifarious forms. The question then is how to evaluate, to synthesize and to suitably transform the knowledge gained in research so it can serve as an aid to the re-orientation of teacher preservice and inservice education, and to determine what models can be most appropriate and can best provide future oriented social perspectives. In this section, the social conditions of this transformation of knowledge gained in research into professional knowledge of teachers will be explored, and examples of successful models for reorganisation and changing in teachers' education and professional development are discussed and evaluated.

Mathematics education is a socially dependent field, and there are many professionals playing a strong role in its development. It will be shown how the increasing international and regional collaboration contribute to the professionalisation of people working in the field in general and in non-industrialised or poor countries in particular. The role of the different social and professional groups which are shaping the interdisciplinary field for the future is reflected, and some more recent social perspectives for mathematics education are outlined which will have – if adopted – a strong impact on the topics and methods of research in mathematics education as well as on the practical teaching of mathematics on all levels.

In chapter 29, 'Mathematical Didactics and the Professional Knowledge of Teachers', Paolo Boero, Carlo Dapueto and Laura Parenti from Italy are concerned with the professional knowledge development of mathematics teachers by transforming results of research in the didactics of mathematics into tools and theories guiding practice. Didactics of mathematics, a term which is common in German and French speaking countries, and which has become increasingly adopted by other European colleagues in mathematics education research, refers to the fairly young scientific discipline dedicated to research into the processes of teaching and learning mathematics, and to the development of models and materials for the improvements of these processes (Biehler et al., 1994). The chapter deals with the relationships between didactics of mathematics and the professional knowledge of mathematics teachers as an individual and social construction. Through examples of systematic contact

A.J. Bishop et al. (eds.), International Handbook of Mathematics Education, 1093 - 1095

between researchers and educators in teachers' pre-service and in-service education, the authors discuss the present difficulties in establishing this relationship as a productive one and relate the problem to the different strands of research in the didactics of mathematics, and different perspectives about how to realise such a productive relationship.

In chapter 30, 'Preservice mathematics teacher education. Preparing Teachers To Teach Mathematics: A Comparative Perspective' Claude Comiti, France, and Deborah Loewenberg Ball, U.S.A., provide an international examination of current approaches to the preparation of mathematics teachers. After situating the theme in the evolution of mathematics education – both practice and research – over the past, they offer an overview of mathematics teacher education in four countries – England, France, Germany, and the United States, focusing both on the structure and contexts of teacher preparation in each country, and on characteristic features of each country's system. In particular cases of France and the United States the authors probe a discussion of issues embedded in each setting, and a comparative look at their similarities and differences.

Chapter 31, 'Inservice mathematics teacher education' by Thomas Cooney, U.S.A., and Konrad Krainer, Austria, addresses issues related to practice and research in inservice teacher education programs. Through the eyes of an experienced teacher, who participates in an inservice program and who struggles to improve her teaching of mathematics, the personal goals for teaching, her expectations for inservice programs, and her perceptions about self as teacher researcher are considered. The literature related to both practice and research in teacher education, expectations for inservice programs, and conceptualizing inservice as a context for integrating theory and practice is carefully analysed to design this case, and the importance of listening for the creation and realisation of inservice programs is emphasized.

Chapter 32, 'Mathematics teachers as researchers' by Kathryn Crawford and Jill Adler explores the ways in which teaching, learning and research are conceptualised by various members of the mathematics education community and makes an argument for research-like activities by teachers as a means to professional development. Examples from Australia and South Africa are used to illustrate the need for change and the importance of active participation of teachers in research activities associated with their professional practice.

In chapter 33, 'Mathematics teachers and curriculum development', Barbara Clarke, Doug Clarke and Peter Sullivan, Australia see the teacher as playing a crucial role in creating worthwhile mathematical experiences for children in any meaningful curriculum; and argue for a better recognition that teachers need to be supplied with appropriate resources and time. They discuss factors which constrain the teacher's role in mathematics curriculum development, as well as a range of curriculum projects and approaches to curriculum policy.

Chapter 34, 'Mathematics education in the global village. International co-operation in mathematics education' by Edward Jacobsen, examines the change in policy from education for developing high-level manpower only to universal primary education and its global implications for mathematics education. In order to evaluate what international collaboration in mathematics education has achieved, its role is described, and a perspective on the future of world wide collaboration in mathematics education is outlined.

In chapter 35, 'Critical mathematics education', Ole Skovsmose and Lene Nielsen define, analyse and examine the term 'Critical Mathematics Education' by referring to crucial issues of concern about:

a)   citizenship and an active participation in political life,
b)   mathematics as a tool for identifying and analysing crucial issues in society,
c)   pupils' interest in terms of competence and autonomy in acting and judging,
d)   culture and social conflicts,
e)   reflection on power relationships including those between teachers and pupils in the classroom.

The final chapter 36, 'Towards humanistic mathematics education' by Stephen Brown, USA, explores the forces and assumptions that have influenced conceptions of humanistic mathematics education. The author refers to recent developments in the philosophy of mathematics and emphasizes the need to re-consider the meaning of reason-giving and reason-seeking, the possibility of a reconstructed conception of personhood, a desire for a more robust conception of problem and its educational uses, and the need to locate appropriate contexts within mathematics education.

REFERENCES

Biehler, R., Scholz, R.W., Strässer, R. and Winkelmann, B.: 1994, *Didactics of Mathematics as a Scientific Discipline*, Kluwer, Dordrecht.

Chapter 29: Didactics of Mathematics and the Professional Knowledge of Teachers

PAOLO BOERO, CARLO DAPUETO, AND LAURA PARENTI
Department of Mathematics, University of Genoa, Italy

ABSTRACT

This chapter will deal with the problem of the relationships between didactics of mathematics as a rapidly developing field of investigation and the professional knowledge of mathematics teachers as an individual and social construction. We will focus on teachers' pre-service and in-service education as the situations where systematic contacts may be established between research in didactics of mathematics and the construction of teachers' professional knowledge.

We will discuss present difficulties in establishing a productive relationship between teachers' education and different strands of research in didactics of mathematics, and different perspectives about how to establish such a relationship.

1. INTRODUCTION

In less than one century, mathematics changed from a set of elementary tools needed in everyday life and a specialised domain of investigation, to a pervasive component of today's culture: mathematics is deeply embedded in technology and in many aspects of today's manner of viewing natural and social phenomena. Mathematics became a general language to represent reality and a powerful, flexible simulation tool. This increasing need for mathematics education developed in parallel with another, rather contrasting orientation: in many countries mathematics took the place of Latin (or Greek) as the subject matter responsible for school orientation and selection.

After the Second World War mathematics teacher education became more and more complex for other, different reasons: the increasing number of students for each age group made the profession of teaching more difficult (if the teacher wants to or is required to ensure efficiency in his activity) – especially in the case of mathematics because of its specific difficulties. In the field of mathematics, like in other fields, the impact of new technologics has changed some priorities within the educational aims (making the previous curriculum partly obsolete); it has also brought on the need for new competencies on the teacher's part, in order to take advantage of the new educational opportunities

A.J. Bishop et al. (eds.), International Handbook of Mathematics Education, 1097 - 1121
© 1996 Kluwer Academic Publishers, Printed in the Netherlands

offered by new technologies and better understand their cultural and social impact (see: Ciosek, 1990; Keitel, 1986; NCTM, 1991; Boero, 1992, 1993).

The speed of changes (in mathematics, and in the school system) in itself provoked a crisis in the old manner of conceiving the profession of the teacher as an art, personally developed through apprenticeship in the school environment and based on a good knowledge of mathematics. Another reason for crisis depends on the fact that in many countries some teachers become teachers for reasons which are very far from a genuine vocation to teach mathematics. Their apprenticeship as mathematics teachers may be strongly influenced by this lack of specific motivation to teach mathematics.

A crucial point of our chapter will concern the need for research in didactics of mathematics in relationship with today's situation of mathematics education and the profession of mathematics teaching, and the related need that pre-service and in-service teacher education introduce teachers to and involve them in research methods and results.

Present research in didactics of mathematics (a rapidly developing field with different trends and schools) may offer some tools in order to increase the effectiveness of pre-service and in-service mathematics teacher education and provide support to the profession (see: Arzarello & Bartolini, 1994; Boero & Szendrei, 1994; Cobb, Wood & Yackel, 1990; Cooney, 1994, 1994 b; Krainer, 1994; Wittman, 1991).

In this chapter we will consider the relationships between didactics of mathematics as a domain of investigation and the professional knowledge of mathematics teachers as an individual construction, socially situated (in the school system and society contexts) and a social construction (performed inside formal or informal groups of teachers).

We will try to move from our personal experiences and points of view towards a more general perspective, including other points of view. Some examples will be taken from our direct experiences of cooperative work with teachers, concerning research and innovation in the teaching of mathematics, other examples will derive from the Italian situation. The aim of these examples is to provide concrete references for general statements and perspectives; the reader may find similar examples in the reality of other countries (and some references will be provided in this direction).

The subject matter of this chapter will be organized according to two criteria:
- a classification of different strands of research in didactics of mathematics, based on the different nature of research results. This criterion was chosen because we think that both the involvement of teachers in research and the exploitation of research results in the school system strongly depend on the characteristics of the different strands of research (especially for what concerns the nature of their results);
- the idea that the relationships between didactics of mathematics and the professional knowledge of mathematics teachers especially concern pre-

service and in-service teacher education. This criterion was chosen in order to show some direct implications of our general analysis about the different types of research results on the teaching profession; indeed, in many countries teacher education is the most important occasion for teachers to encounter research perspectives and results.

The relationships between research in didactics of mathematics and mathematics teacher education may be considered under different points of view, according to the ideas people have of both research in didactics of mathematics and mathematics teacher education. In this chapter we will try to give a general outline of the problems. First of all, we will focus on some current ideas of mathematics teacher education, trying to point out some historical perspectives and present motivations. Then, we will discuss what kind of tools and results which research in didactics of mathematics offers today may be introduced into mathematics teacher education, comparing present needs with actual offers and pointing out some possible directions in order to improve the present situation. Finally, we will try to explain some specific methodological issues, concerning the introduction of results and tools of research in didactics of mathematics into mathematics teacher education, relatively independent of the choice of a peculiar orientation in the field of research in didactics of mathematics.

2. THREE EXTREME ORIENTATIONS IN MATHEMATICS TEACHER EDUCATION

We will consider different ideas people have of mathematics teacher education. We will describe only 'extreme' positions, although intermediate ones are possible, in order to make different orientations clearer which explicitly or implicitly have contrasting influences on political decisions and their practical implementation (see: Barra & al., 1992; Boero, 1993; Bottino & Furinghetti, 1994, 1994b; Furinghetti, 1994; Houston, 1990; Hoyles, 1992; Ponte & al., 1994).

2.1 The teacher must become more and more competent in mathematics: 'He who knows mathematics, knows how to teach it'.

This traditional idea in its rough version is not popular amongst mathematics educators, but it is still very common amongst mathematicians and mathematics teachers (especially in high schools), with possible misunderstandings about mathematics ('school mathematics' or 'mathematician mathematics'?). We think that the reasons for the widespread permanence of this idea might be an interesting subject for research in didactics of mathematics. Does it depend on the need to protect some specific 'competence' and related 'criteria of quality' pertaining to the domain of mathematics; or on the difficulties of mathematicians and mathematics teachers in evaluating and taking advantage of contributions deriving from scientific domains which are very far from mathematics (like sociology of education, psychology etc.); or on the presumption of being able to cover all the needs concerning the 'transmission' of mathematical knowledge with a sufficiently deep mastery of the subject field (mathematics) and some professional expertise obtained through ongoing professional experience?

As to the exclusive focus on 'knowing mathematics' as a requisite to become a teacher, we think that is it important to consider a possible, more sophisticated (and not so popular) version of this conception: 'knowing mathematics' might include knowledge of history of mathematics, epistemology of mathematics, philosophy of mathematics. Different perspectives in these fields are given by books and articles such as: Davis & Hersh (1980); Kline (1980); Lakatos (1967); Steen (1978); Goodman (1980); Mac Lane (1981); Swart (1980); Dapueto & Ferrari (1983). This broad competence might allow teachers to understand both the relationships between concept construction, formalization and theoretical framing in the domain of mathematics, and the relationships between mathematics and other cultural domains (physics, philosophy, etc.). According to this sophisticated conception, some strands of research in didactics of mathematics might have something to say about teacher education (see: 'epistemological obstacles', in Brousseau, 1983 and Sierpinska, 1985, 1987; 'didactical transposition', in Chevallard, 1991, etc.). In some countries (e.g.: France, Germany, Italy) there are still traditions or new experiences developed, in which 'knowing mathematics' in a broad, cultural sense is considered as a crucial aspect of mathematics teacher education, and some researchers in didactics of mathematics are involved in it. Unfortunately, in those cases there is a dramatic contradiction between ordinary, technical education in mathematics (ensured through traditional, non-interactive technical lectures and exercises concerning isolated and specialized fields of today's mathematics) and some courses or seminars where prospective teachers (or in-service teachers) get to know different historical and epistemological perspectives. In short, this contradiction results in a 'cultural varnishing', with no practical, deep influence on professional choices and classroom activities.

2.2 The teacher must develop his/her professional competence like an artisan (if possible, an artist)

We will use the words 'artisan', 'artist' to evoke the idea of a teacher who is able to face professional problems in a flexible way ('artisan') or to create substantial innovations ('artist').

This conception, too, is very popular amongst mathematics teachers and mathematicians. Its implications for mathematics teacher education may include the preceding conception, with a special emphasis on apprenticeship, usually at the end of the mathematics preparation or while taking up teaching: *'he who knows mathematics, knows how to teach it'* is replaced by *'a good mathematics teacher must master mathematics and be acquainted with the art of teaching'*. This conception can be better understood under a historical perspective, and recognized as one of the sources of present research in didactics of mathematics (although many researchers in mathematics education today refuse it).

Up to the 70's, this conception was shared by many 'mathematics educators'. At that time, 'innovation' was considered the most valuable and useful outcome of 'investigation', so 'artists' (those who produced new brilliant ideas about teaching specific subject matters, or new methodologies) had a place in mathematics teacher education (especially in the in-service mathematics teacher education). Besides 'innovations', 'artists' frequently produced general ideas about teaching of mathematics as an 'art', in the form of 'principles', or 'general orientations', or 'comments about experiments'. Such ideas usually involved a wide range of considerations with different levels of deepening, depending on competence, background and traditions from rather deep epistemological or historical analysis about mathematics in general and specific mathematical subjects, to rather naive (and not well framed) considerations about learning of mathematics, assessment, sociology of mathematics education. In many countries, research in didactics of mathematics (as we nowadays know it) has developed sometimes (Hungary is an example) in continuity with, sometimes (France) in opposition to these 'general ideas' about teaching of mathematics as an 'art'.

Despite the importance attributed in the field of sciences of education to 'apprenticeship', today few researchers in didactics of mathematics agree with the idea of teaching as an 'art' learned through a suitable apprenticeship, an idea which excludes (or reduces) the importance of scientific knowledge about didactics of mathematics in pre-service and in-service teacher education. But sometimes mathematics teachers recognised as 'artists' seem to have a very strong influence on teaching of mathematics (...stronger than the community of researchers in M.E.). Is this true? Are those influences beneficial to mathematics education? Another interesting research topic for research in didactics of mathematics! We should distinguish the different levels at which the influence of 'artists' works today. If we take into consideration the environment of teachers involved in innovation, comparison of ideas, etc. (very few teachers who join in associations of mathematics teachers, take part in regional or national or, some of them, international meetings, etc.), the influence of 'artists' is important and beneficial. But today many mathematics teachers in the world do not take part in 'movements', do not read specialized reviews for mathematics teachers, are not involved (as volunteers) in innovations. In this case, the 'artists' contributions are taken as an alibi not to change anything: *'they do it, but I am not so involved as they are, so well trained as they are, etc., so I cannot do it'*. Actually, important changes occurred in the 80's all over the world. With some exceptions (e.g. Hungary and U.K.), in most countries the teaching of mathematics became less and less important socially, and more and more people took it up as a second (or third) choice job. For instance, in Italy now we may estimate that only few young teachers have chosen this profession because they like teaching mathematics (frequently, they like neither teaching, nor mathematics!).

Another issue is related to 'how to become a good artisan': in the case of mathematics teachers, strong personality requirements seem to be necessary. In other words, it is not sufficient (although it is necessary!) to like mathematics and teaching in order to become an efficient 'artisan' (or, especially, an 'artist'). In our experience of mathematics teacher education (especially, in-service education) we have frequently met motivated people, frustrated because they are not able to manage classroom work as they would like, or to quickly penetrate the student's thinking process in order to interact productively with him/her, or to make real time connections between different subjects, in order to increase the learning opportunities offered to students during a discussion.... More likely, an efficient 'artisan' (especially, an 'artist') is supported by important psychological resources (a strong personality, open-mindedness towards introspection, quickness in real time interacting and making cultural connections,...). However, if the model of the good teacher is that of an 'efficient' artisan, the lack of these attributes may result in an increasing de-motivation towards the profession of teacher.

Can present research in didactics of mathematics offer opportunities for increasing professional performances and satisfaction to all teachers (including those who do not succeed as artisans or artists, even though devoted to their work; and those who choose the profession of teacher as a second or third choice job)? Today this is a good challenge for research in didactics of mathematics, whose outcomes may result in an important motivation for future development of research in didactics of mathematics – or in a big failure of it. In this sense, it is very important to follow what will happen in the future in countries such as France or Canada, where important groups of researchers in didactics of mathematics may reach a large number of teachers in their pre-service and in-service vocational education.

2.3 The teacher's professional competence must be grounded in different scientific domains (mathematics, sciences of education, didactics of mathematics)

Teacher education must enable prospective teachers to widen their knowledge connected to the relevant field (mathematics) providing a well-balanced mixture of different subjects related to the different school levels, different sciences of education (from psychology of learning to sociology of education) and mathematics education (as a specific field of professional competence and/or as a specific field of research).

Since the Second World War, this conception has been more and more extensively represented and realized at political and academic level, particularly after the 60's. Mathematics educators and many teachers (especially at the level of compulsory education) share this conception; but behind their general agreement we can recognize very different orientations, concerning:

— the institutional environment where knowledge and skills can be developed: pre-service and/or in-service mathematics teacher education? In case of pre-service mathematics teacher education, through 'in series' or 'in parallel' subjects? And what about the academic environment for pre-service mathematics teacher education: the department of mathematics of the 'faculty' (or 'institute') of sciences of education, the department of mathematics of the 'faculty' (or 'institute') of exact sciences, or an ad-hoc academic environment for teacher education? Each of these solutions is experienced (or has been experienced, or is scheduled) in some countries of the world! Sometimes the solution consists in a cooperative, parallel process, including courses of mathematics and mathematics education offered by the department of mathematics and courses of general education, psychology, etc. offered by the 'faculty' (or 'institute') of sciences of education. Sometimes an 'in series' process takes place in different academic environments starting with mathematics education followed by vocational education. Sometimes different solutions are carried out in the same country (Hungary is an example), according to different levels of schools and education;

— the proportion of the different subjects in pre-service and in-service mathematics teacher education, depending on traditions, school levels, academic environments for mathematics teacher education, academic power of the different scientific groups;

— the methodology, especially as far as it concerns professional competence. As to this issue, different options may be considered (and different options are concretely practised in the world): from lectures to interactive courses, from individual problem-solving sessions, to working groups reflecting on students' behaviour. We will develop this point in the fourth section. We must point out that unfortunately few experiences concern effective methodologies to teach mathematics to future teachers (Canada, Hungary and U.K. offer some interesting examples). In many other countries, mathematics courses in pre-service mathematics teacher education follow the model of traditional university courses in mathematics (sometimes at a lower level than required to become a mathematician). And this may have deep, negative influences on future professional orientations (very often, university students of

1103

today will reproduce tomorrow, as school teachers, the model of their university course!)

— the content of education in didactics of mathematics. We will develop this point in the following section. Here we remark that there are two extreme positions in the academic environment. Those (mathematicians or mathematics educators, or researchers in the domain of sciences of education) who do not recognize the value of mathematics didactics research results and tools in mathematics teacher education press for including in it only professional techniques (frequently identifying vocational education with apprenticeship). On the contrary, those who recognize the value of mathematics didactics research results and tools in mathematics teacher education tend to emphasize (both for pre-service and in-service mathematics teacher education) those specific results and tools and submit the reflection on apprenticeship to criteria of analysis for research in didactics of mathematics.

3.   DIFFERENT MODELS OF RESEARCH IN DIDACTICS OF MATHEMATICS AND
      THEIR IMPLICATIONS FOR MATHEMATICS TEACHER EDUCATION: WHY IS
      IT SO HARD TO CREATE A PRODUCTIVE DIALOGUE BETWEEN RESEARCH
      IN DIDACTICS OF MATHEMATICS AND MATHEMATICS TEACHER
      EDUCATION? HOW TO IMPROVE THE SITUATION?

This part of the chapter deals with the contributions that present research in didactics of mathematics may give to mathematics teacher education. Nowadays, research in didactics of mathematics is not a homogeneous reality in the world. There are different traditions and schools, sometimes in the same country, depending on local and general factors concerning the history of both the community of mathematicians and the community of researchers in sciences of education, and the history of mathematics education in that country (for some different perspectives, see: Artigue, 1990; Arzarello & Bartolini, 1994; Balacheff, 1990; Barra & al., 1992 Boero, 1993; Chevallard, 1992; Kilpatrick,1992; Steiner, 1984)

   In our opinion, a good way to classify the different kinds of research in didactics of mathematics now existing in the world, establishing a close relationship with their possible implications in mathematics teacher education, is to consider the nature of their possible outcomes; following Boero & Szendrei (1994), we may consider different kinds of results in research in didactics of mathematics:

   i)   'innovative patterns' to teach a specific subject (old or new for school
         mathematics), or to develop some mathematical skills; or, more
         generally, innovative methodologies, curricula, projects, etc. Results
         may consist in innovative educational material, 'proposals', or reports
         about innovations or projects that have been experimented. Frequently,

teachers take part in the production of these results as researchers or researchers' partners who perform teaching experiments. An important variable is the dimension of innovation (both in terms of time: a short sequence, an innovative five year curriculum; and in the terms of content: a specific subject, or an integrated system of topics and methodologies). Other variables depend on philosophical grounding and purposes of innovation, theory-practice relationships, etc.;

ii) *'quantitative information'* about the results of: educational choices related to the teaching of a specific mathematical subject; general methodologies; curricular choices (including comparative and quantitative studies). Or quantitative information about general or specific difficulties regarding learning of mathematics, and their possible correlations with factors influencing the learning process. Information is based on quantitative data, collected and analyzed according to standard or ad hoc statistical methods; the level of statistical treatment may be elementary (only percentages and histograms) or quite sophisticated. Usually, research is performed by researchers who are not school teachers;

iii) *'qualitative information'* about the results of some innovations as to methodology or content, or some general or specific difficulties concerning mathematics, etc. In this case, information is based on careful consideration of students' papers, of recorded teacher-student interactions, of recorded group or class discussions, etc.; frequently, these analyses implicitly or explicitly refer to general educational or psychological or didactical theories. Frequently, teachers take part in the production of these results as 'participant observers' (Eisenhart, 1988), sometimes as researchers.

iv) *'theoretical perspectives'* regarding the relationship between 'teacher', 'students' and 'mathematical knowledge' in the class; the role of the mathematics teacher in the class; the relationships between school mathematics and mathematicians' mathematics; topics to be taught; the relationships between research results and classroom practice in mathematics education, etc. These results may involve descriptions and classifications of 'phenomena', interpretations of 'phenomena', 'models', historical or epistemological analysis (oriented towards educational aims) of a topic, etc. In most cases, teachers have a marginal role in the production of these results.

3.1 Our general orientation

We agree with Boero & Szendrei (1994) that results of the 'qualitative information' and 'theoretical perspectives' types are important not only in themselves, but also because they allow teachers and researchers to keep other results under control, while results of the 'innovative patterns' and 'quantitative information' types immediately provide teachers with working tools. We may add that all these different results should be provided to teachers during both pre-service and in-service education, in order to help them accomplish their professional choices constructively and critically.

3.2 The present situation

Nowadays, this ideal orientation is very far from reality both as to the relative popularity of different kinds of results amongst teachers, and as to the results of different kinds actually offered by researchers. In particular, teachers tend to neglect some results which might be very useful for them, and researchers offer results which frequently do not fit teachers' needs. We will try to explain this mutual 'incomprehension' and point out some possible directions in order to improve the present situation.

3.2.1 The lack of a common vocabulary and a common background

At present, the results of the 'innovative patterns' and 'quantitative information' types are the most accessible and known for mathematics teachers, especially secondary school teachers, although their application at schools may often result in frequent malfunctions and failures. Several reasons may explain this fact; in our opinion, one of them lies in the teachers' background. Most secondary school mathematics teachers have only a background in mathematics and, possibly, experimental sciences. On the other hand, the research and related results of the 'qualitative information' and 'theoretical perspectives' types need a specific 'human sciences' vocabulary, and are necessarily more overtly grounded on philosophical assumptions.

3.2.2 Failure of promising innovations

Innovations are demanded as products of research in didactics of mathematics, even though their diffusion has not always been successful and in spite of the attack by some mathematics educators on the idea of 'change through innovation' (see the paper by J. Robinson, in Clements & Ellerton, 1989).

Useful and successful innovations (i. e. results of the 'innovative patterns' type) might be very important to justify (in mathematicians and teachers' eyes) systematic connections between research in didactics of mathematics and mathematics teacher education. Why did many promising 'innovations' result in a failure when they had been so widespread?

As to this issue, some phenomena should be quoted. We will consider only some examples of innovations concerning specific mathematical subjects. In the past twenty years, mathematics educators have been concerned with the distance between proposals and prototypical innovation, and widespread innovation about subjects like the 'set' approach to natural numbers, or 'ratio, proportion and linear functions'. A comprehensive research perspective is lacking, and few research papers tackling this subject can be offered to teachers during mathematics teacher education in order to help them understand what happened (Brousseau, 1980, 1981, 1986).

Other phenomena refer to 'popular' and 'not popular' innovations: in Italy, the introduction of substantial topics of elementary probability in the comprehensive school (even if many prototypes are available) meets with many obstacles (Belcastro, Guala & Parenti, 1986); on the other hand, the introduction of elements of analytic geometry in the comprehensive school has taken only few years to succeed. Concerning probability, the situation in U.K. and U.S.A. is quite different! It is not easy to tackle these differences (which might be very interesting to deal with in mathematics teacher education) in a research perspective in didactics of mathematics.

In general, we must face the problem of the conversion of proposals and prototypes (typical of a research environment) into widespread innovations; it is well known that it is very difficult to reproduce innovations on a large scale without substantial degeneration and loss of effectiveness (cf. Arsac, Balacheff & Mante, 1991; Artigue, 1990).

As researchers, we think that intercultural differences should be taken into account, because frequently the situation is not the same in different countries; other aspects should also be considered: in-service teacher education; the institutional aspects (official programs, relationships with the preceding and following levels of school, structure and content of final examinations); specific 'didactical transposition' (Chevallard, 1991) problems; difficulties in integrating new subjects in the old curriculum and/or changing some parts of this in the perspective of new subjects (Dapueto & C, 1994); the incidence of textbooks; the distance between the community of researchers and the school system (a good integration is realized only in few countries). But there are few research articles and surveys available on these issues!

Generally, teachers should understand what 'variables' may cause innovations to succeed (or to fail or degenerate) and to be reproduced on a large scale in the field of mathematics education. Research in didactics of mathematics should provide teachers' tutors and teachers with the opportunity of developing and/or exploiting careful and comprehensive descriptions and analysis of:
— class teaching-learning processes, and (possibly) their interpretations and models;
— students' long term learning processes, in order to better understand many aspects of the development of their mathematical knowledge,

which depends on individual and social factors, cultural influences and emotional constraints, etc.;

— teachers' conceptions in different countries.

The results of the 'qualitative information' and 'theoretical perspectives' types are needed, in order to go beyond the present, very limited knowledge of some of these aspects on teachers and teachers' tutors' part. In particular, teachers' conceptions and students' mathematical experiences in everyday life should be carefully investigated because they can deeply affect class teaching-learning of mathematics (see Jaworski, 1994); we would also like to point out that this is the reason why, frequently, 'quantitative' information provided by international comparative studies is biased because of the lack of knowledge about these aspects.

3.2.3 The decreasing involvement of leading research schools in didactics of mathematics in carrying out innovations

If we agree that teachers need the results of the 'innovative patterns' type and that research in didactics of mathematics must produce them, then these results must be spread and compared through international journals and meetings of mathematics educators; but if we actually read outstanding journals and take part in specialized international meetings we find fewer and fewer 'didactical proposals' or reports about innovations.

For instance, we estimate that from 1970 to 1974 over 60 per cent of the papers published in Educational Studies in Mathematics dealt with the results of 'innovative patterns' type, while from 1987 to 1992 less than 15 per cent of the papers dealt with these. The situation of other outstanding journals is similar. Fewer and fewer results of the 'innovative patterns' type are considered as outstanding 'research outcomes', worth publishing by important journals. And even in many rather specialized international meetings of researchers (like the conferences of the International Group for the Psychology of Mathematics Education) the introduction of 'innovations' takes place especially in the poster session.

Actually nationally circulated journals continue publishing a good number of papers of that kind, but they are not considered (in most countries) to be 'research' journals. On the other hand, if we consider most of the results of the 'innovative patterns' type presented at congresses or in local journals, we see that they are limited to educational material and/or descriptions of proposed (or experimental) short or long educational sequences, and do not try to go through the related educational, epistemological or psychological problems. The consequence of this fact is that the conditions under which innovations can be reproduced, variables which affect effectiveness, etc., are not known.

Taking into account all these remarks, a stronger involvement of research in didactics of mathematics in innovation and a proper style of presentation of results of the 'innovative patterns' type is needed for mathematics teacher education; as to this issue, we think that the presentation should be supported and framed by already existing results of the other types (especially of the 'qualitative information' and 'theoretical perspectives' type), in order to make them valuable as research results.

In particular, if the innovation turned out to be a successful experiment, a careful consideration of the conditions which allowed such success (for instance: teachers' motivation, teachers and students' cultural background, school traditions, etc.) should be provided, trying also to point out possible limitations of the 'reproducibility' of the innovation. In an experimental program concerning innovation, phenomena such as 'obsolescence of innovation' (with consequent effects on the teaching-learning process) should be taken into account.

Here is another example: the epistemological analysis of a mathematical topic, as well as the analysis of the relationships between current and historical points of view in mathematics and in school mathematics concerning it, seem to be necessary in order to make an educational proposal concerning that topic from the cultural point of view: a teacher must therefore be encouraged to take some distance from his/her cultural background; and possible 'epistemological obstacles' inherent in that topic must be anticipated.

3.2.4 *Paradigmatic mathematical topics or topics which might be interesting for teachers?*

If we agree that research in mathematics education must keep in contact with present mathematics and thus help teachers teach topics which are relevant to modern views about mathematics, or take into account the opportunities offered by new technologies, research should then create connections with these modern views and opportunities. But, if we read articles published by leading international M.E. journals, we will find out that most of them deal with 'paradigmatic' topics and problems (i.e. topics and problems which allow the comparison of new research results and perspectives with previous ones), regardless of the importance of the content or problems in mathematics education (while many traditional and new fields are not covered). And results of the 'innovative patterns' type also focus on only a few directions (regardless of the importance and difficulty of the subject).

Here is an example about this issue: today 'rational numbers, decimal numbers and approximations of numbers in a calculator or computer environment' form a very important field for everyday choices in mathematics classes which is, however, almost neglected by the main journals. And here is another example: with the exception of spreadsheet, there are few research studies in didactics of mathematics dealing with the educational opportunities offered by professional software in the field of mathematics education and the new educational needs which depend on their diffusion out of the school system.

3.2.5 *The results of 'quantitative information'*

Some results of the 'quantitative information' type (especially those presenting 'objective', easy to read comparative data) are very popular amongst school teachers and administrators; some mathematicians consider them as the only 'scientific' results in didactics of mathematics. We think that the dissemination of those results must be seriously considered by researchers in didactics of mathematics because they provide teachers as well as parents, school administrators, etc. with information which often seems to be 'objective' and 'scientific'. Taking this aspect into account, the quantitative evaluation of students, teachers, school systems, projects and innovations needs special attention, as it may cause serious damage (for instance, it may orient the teachers' work only towards preparing students to be successful in assessment tests).

This is one of the main reasons why we think that teacher education must provide teachers with the results of both the 'qualitative information' and 'theoretical perspectives' types: they need them in order to keep the methodologies and the results of the 'quantitative information' type under control. For instance, in our opinion it is crucial that teachers be acquainted with the following problem: is it really possible to keep variables 'constant' in order to create effective control groups? In fact, such a problem deeply affects the comparison of results among different classes, different teachers, different methodologies.....The nature of tests is another important problem: the debate about different kinds of tests (multiple choice, open questions, etc.) is very important for mathematics education, because each kind of test provides information about specific skills and knowledge. Teachers should become familiar with this problem; indeed, their choices may deeply affect the evaluation of students' performances and class work.

It would also be important to explain in mathematics teacher education why some 'laboratory' results of the 'quantitative information' type, which may be interesting from a psychological or sociological point of view, may be scarcely relevant to mathematics education and, in any case, must be critically considered. Actually, correlations are often interpreted as cause/effect relationships and some effects of educational choices are confused with epistemological difficulties!

In short, results of the 'qualitative information' and 'theoretical perspectives' types are useful for teachers in order to make use, in the field of mathematics education, of experimental and statistical methodologies borrowed from sciences of education in a critical way. Unfortunately, research in didactics of mathematics today provides few understandable, critical materials in this domain, that are suitable to be used in current pre-service and in-service mathematics teacher education

4.   DIFFERENT METHODOLOGICAL PERSPECTIVES CONCERNING TOOLS AND RESULTS OF RESEARCH IN DIDACTICS OF MATHEMATICS IN MATHEMATICS TEACHER EDUCATION

Prospective and in-service mathematics teachers learn about tools and results of research in didactics of mathematics according to different methodologies such as the following:

4.1   Involvement of future teachers and/or in-service teachers in research in didactics of mathematics, which frequently implies a model of teacher as researcher (although not in the sense of a full time job)

As to pre-service teacher education, it takes place in a research environment: students take part in classroom experiments (as observers or as 'participant observers', Eisenhart, 1988), frequently they take part in planning experiments and working out data. Usually students must prepare a thesis or a report on their research experience, sometimes they cooperate in writing reports or articles with experienced researchers. Evidently, students are more oriented towards profession and change when they are directly involved and innovation and innovative experiments take place.

During the 70's, about one hundred students at Genoa University took their first level mathematics degree discussing a thesis about their one-year voluntary experience in a secondary school classroom. The mathematics teacher and the student were involved in long-term innovations planned in a large, cooperative groups of university researchers and teachers.

The long-term effects of that experience are generally considered positive by all partners involved (researchers, classroom teachers, prospective teachers). Some of those students became teachers-researchers and are cooperating in the research activities of our group. Similar experiences were performed in other Italian universities.

Unfortunately, those experiences had no consistent development in the 80's and 90's for different reasons which partly depend on the specific Italian situation. Actually, no 'reform' of the pre-service secondary school teacher education was carried out at University level, and the inertia of the university system became stronger and stronger and discouraged volunteer professional experiences in the classroom. Some other reasons seem to be more general and interesting to compare with other realities: when the research work was relatively simple and strictly connected with classroom innovations, it was possible to involve in it mathematics students with no specific background in mathematics education or in general education. Now the situation is completely different: research activities include relatively deep epistemological reflections about mathematics, teaching experiments are quite sophisticated, the effective observation and analysis of what happens in the classroom needs a relatively important explicit or implicit background in the field of mathematics education. Students, when starting work for their degree thesis in mathematics education, need a wide and deep specific background. The 144 hours of university courses available today at Genoa University in the field of mathematics education for prospective mathematics teachers are not sufficient to provide students with that preparation.

As to in-service mathematics teacher education through involvement in research in didactics of mathematics, very interesting experiences are performed in some countries (Australia, Austria, Canada, U.K., etc.). Also the Italian experience seems to be advanced and qualitatively interesting in the world scene, although involving only few teachers (Arzarello & Bartolini Bussi, 1994; Barra & al., 1992; Boero, 1993). Most Italian research groups in didactics of mathematics involve primary and/or secondary school teachers in a long term, deep experience of cooperative work which includes planning of teaching experiments, 'participant observer' experiences in the classroom, and analysis of what happened in the classroom according to different theoretical frameworks. These experiences show very interesting outcomes for in-service mathematics teacher education: teachers overcome the individualistic, 'isolationist' idea of their profession and learn to cooperate with one another. They learn to use both research tools and results to plan, observe and evaluate their classroom work. They learn to take some distance from their classroom experience and to profit from other people's experience.

Unfortunately, these in-service education experiences involve only very few teachers on a voluntary basis, and their influence on the whole school system is still very weak. On the other hand, sometimes these teachers-researchers have a strong influence in their own school environment because they try to introduce methods of cooperative discussion with their colleagues, elementary research tools useful to interpret classroom phenomena, up-to-date views about mathematics and mathematics teaching. Teachers may discover that their profession can functionally include stimulating cultural activities (posing problems, explaining phenomena, etc.) Finally, the ability to make good use of teachers-researchers' skills seems to depend on the school policy (the head of the school plays an important role in it!).

4.2 Introduction of research topics in didactics of mathematics in more or less traditional 'courses'

Nowadays, mathematics educators do not like traditional, non interactive (we will call them 'frontal') lectures, where a teacher presents his topics to a public of 'listeners'. This system of 'transmission' of knowledge normally has a rather low level of effectiveness in every cultural domain, especially in primary and lower-secondary education.

In pre-service and in-service mathematics teacher education, sometimes 'frontal' lectures may be very useful – if the audience is sufficiently motivated and 'frontal' lectures are part of a comprehensive program which includes other activities (small study groups, working groups, general discussions, brain storming sessions, practical experiences...); actually they can provide:
- introduction and/or framing of problems, to be dealt with in working group sessions;
- presentation of a theory in the field of didactics of mathematics (especially when theory meets the need of interpretation of important phenomena);
- presentation of a new perspective about mathematical issues already known, or cultural connections between school mathematics and mathematician mathematics (producing a critical revision of school mathematics);
- synthesis of general discussions or working group experiences.

In these cases, prospective (or in-service) teachers may appreciate (in consideration of their professional future) using 'frontal' lectures in a functional way (which obviously is not the only one). Actually the only experience of 'frontal' lectures most of teachers usually have is their own experience as students – where frontal lectures, followed by 'practical exercises' and 'evaluation tests', represented the standard organization of the 'transmission' of mathematical knowledge. If teachers experience an efficient teaching system where 'frontal' lectures are functionally included in a wider educational program, they may change their attitude towards 'frontal' lectures in their teaching activities.

4.3 By carrying out problem-solving activities prospective teachers directly experience what constructive learning means and what kind of difficulties it may involve

Here, we mean 'problem solving' in a broad sense, including: construction of conjectures and mathematical proofs, construction of definitions, formulation of an original survey about a topic, etc.

Nowadays, problem-solving experiences are very common in teachers' pre-service and in-service mathematics teacher education. Many articles have been published in the last fifteen years on this subject, which show the potentialities of these activities from different points of view. Problem-solving activities for adults properly carried out (i.e., directed by a competent 'tutor') may help prospective or in-service teachers:

— to experience and discuss difficulties similar to those met by students in the class;
— to understand the importance of evaluating, in mathematical activities, the 'process' instead of the 'result';
— to discover the cultural importance and working value of mathematical topics previously learned as specialized objects with no cultural perspective and retained as inert knowledge;
— to understand what mathematical tools are not really mastered (quite often, prospective and in-service teachers believe they master some subjects only because they passed some examinations on them; this does not imply working mastery of those subjects as requested in problem-solving activities);
— to find out where to apply epistemological, cognitive, 'didactical' tools — or where to experience the need of them.

The tools and results of research in didactics of mathematics that the methodology we are considering allows to introduce in mathematics teacher education, especially the 'qualitative information' and 'theoretical perspective' type results, can be focused under the guide of a competent tutor. Being personally involved in problem solving makes concepts like 'didactical contract', or 'epistemological obstacle', or 'didactical transposition' easier to understand. If the tutor carries out a cross analysis of problem solving strategies and solutions amongst the teachers, it is also possible to train them in the psychological and didactical analysis of the problem solving process.

The general favour gained by the methodology we are dealing with, generally shared by mathematics educators, may hide some of its deficiencies and limits:

— reasoning, motivations, relationships with the teacher may be different in adults and in young students;
— the occasional application of some tools and results of research in didactics of mathematics during the analysis of problem solving strategies and difficulties met by adults does not allow a general view about theoretical framing and the relative importance of those tools and results in the field of research in didactics of mathematics;
— the success of the education through this methodology heavily depends on the tutor's personal qualities: the ability to choose suitable problem situations (according to teachers' previous experience in the domain of mathematics), great facility in interacting and quickness in connecting

different domains of knowledge in research in didactics of mathematics are needed.

Besides these deficiencies and limits, some institutional and cultural aspects may prevent the methodology we are dealing with from working properly: if the evaluation system of pre-service mathematics teacher education does not distinguish clearly the assessment of mathematical competence and the assessment of competence in the field of didactics of mathematics, it is very difficult to involve pre-service teachers in a constructive problem-solving activity and to get their cooperation in providing genuine materials concerning their problem-solving process. In-service mathematics teacher education experiences another kind of difficulties, when problem-solving activities are proposed to teachers: they may fear to compromise their image of 'competent' people – who never fail! And sometimes this fear does not concern only other people's estimation, but their own self-consideration, in the sense that they could not cope with failure. In this case, the tutor's role is very important and difficult: he/she should encourage teachers to run the risk of failing, carefully consider their difficulties, and suggest that their students might profit from a situation where a positive 'solution' is not ensured as the final, unavoidable consequence of a process driven by stereotyped models.

4.4   Discussing professional problems personally met in the class (during pre-service apprenticeship, or normal teaching experience)

This methodology is widely practiced in the world as a crucial aspect of self-training of groups of school teachers; sometimes it takes place under the supervision of a coordinator (a school teacher with special competence in teacher education, a professional teachers' tutor or an university teacher). In any case, this methodology seems to be very useful to show the potentialities of planning of teaching, overcoming teaching difficulties and learning from experience as a collective task.

Traditionally, the teacher (especially the mathematics teacher, whose subject frequently is not connected with the other subjects taught to the same class) acts under his personal responsibility as an 'isolated' entity in the school and may end up finding himself in a difficult personal situation, due to the special hardness of his subject and its value as a way to perform selection. In this perspective, discussing with colleagues about what happens in the class is a good opportunity to escape isolation and share responsibilities.

Unfortunately, in many cases the lack of specific knowledge in mathematics education as a field of scientific investigation prevents from taking advantage of the potentialities of these peers' discussions. Especially when pre-service teacher education in the domain of mathematics education is not proper, the discussion is nothing more than an 'episode'; at first this may be useful from a psychological point of view (in any case it gives the impression of sharing with others some heavy professional responsibilities!), but in the long run it becomes very difficult to share common problems and interpret them within a common frame, working out solutions together. Frustrations may come out from it, and the final idea of a 'waste of time' too. This is the reason why we think that teachers' working group concerning their professional problems must be supported by M.E. researchers in many ways (according to traditions, material and economic constraints, etc.): videotapes, booklets, education of tutors, direct involvement in the teachers' working groups.

Taking into account our experiences, we think that the best solution is a direct (though not continuous) involvement of researchers in teachers' working concerning the problems they meet in their classrooms: this helps teachers make immediately contact with research tools and results, and offers researchers the opportunity to know teachers' problems and learn how to make their own language and perspectives understandable. This choice results in a mutual trust climate and a common language.

In our experience, especially the results of the 'qualitative information' and 'theoretical perspective' types need researchers and teachers to be directly in contact in a working group to discuss teachers' professional problems. Other kinds of results, useful to support these teachers' group discussions, may be easily provided through booklets, articles, etc.

4.5 Discussing selected materials, videotapes, quantitative results, etc. resulting from research work or from other teachers' class experiences.

Videotape facilities and extensive research reports now available make this methodology of teacher education very popular all over the world. Distance teacher education is commonly based on that: the education of the tutor who coordinates peripheral group discussions seems to be relatively easy, due to the fact that discussions concern a pre-established set of written or video materials.

This methodology should provide teachers with a quick, concrete, understandable access to tools and results of research in didactics of mathematics, especially of the 'innovative pattern' and 'qualitative information' types.

However, the implementation of the Italian regional programs of compulsory in-service primary school teacher education at the beginning of the 90's shows some intrinsic limitations of this methodology. Our group was directly involved in the program for our region (both in making some videos, and tutor education). We tried to make videos showing class experiences, and provide some general guidelines to frame and interpret them from the point of view of research in didactics of mathematics (both as comments about what had happened in the class, and as lectures based on examples and students' class materials). Some teachers belonging to the Genoa Research Group in Mathematics Education directly took part in the peripheral tutoring program.

The main education problem was to help in-service teachers get to know a complex field like research in didactics of mathematics through this methodology in order to get tools and results useful for their profession. In our experiences, two facts emerged: on one side, teachers tended to get, from other people's experience, 'recipes' (regarding how to behave in the class on a specific subject, or innovative methodologies) rather than 'criteria of analysis' for what happened in the class. On the other side, teachers thought that some experiences did not concern them: *'I am able to prevent that problem from emerging', 'My students do not behave in such a way', 'Those students are great, I never met such a class', 'I do not understand why to waste so much time in analyzing a thinking process that resulted in a failure'.* Similar things were reported about similar education experiences carried out in other Italian regions by local research group in mathematics education. In the U.K. the Open University has done a lot of research on these beliefs.

In conclusion, we think that the methodology we are dealing with may be very profitable (from the point of view of teacher education and inexpensive dissemination of tools and results of research in didactics of mathematics) when the methodologies considered at 4.3 and 4.4. are adopted as well, providing teachers with a preliminary, direct access to educational perspectives through the discussion of their professional problems and personal experiences.

4.6   As a conclusion concerning methodologies

In our opinion, each of methodologies described above gives some opportunities and has some intrinsic limitations in mathematics teacher education; a well balanced mixture of them is needed (according to different kinds of results of research in didactics of mathematics to be made available to teachers as well). And we think that such a mixture might also suggest that teachers should be flexible in organizing their own teaching activities!

(as to our experiences, cfr. Belcastro, Guala & Parenti, 1986; Chiappini & Parenti, 1991; Chiappini, Laviosa & Parenti, 1990; for other countries, cfr. Borasi & al., 1994; Carpenter & Fennema, 1989; Cooney, 1994; Krainer, 1994; NCTM, 1994; Silver, 1994; for general discussion, see Cobb & al., 1990; Cooney, 1994; Houston, 1990; Hoyles, 1992; Lerman, 1990; Simon, 1994; Wittman, 1989, 1991).

CONCLUSION

In our opinion, results and tools of research in didactics of mathematics are needed both to study phenomena concerning mathematics teacher education (teachers' conceptions about their cultural and professional needs, failures and success of specific mathematics teacher education experiences, and so on: see 2. and 4.), and to increase teachers' professional performances (see 3.). Unfortunately, not always today research in didactics of mathematics is able to provide teacher education with the necessary tools (see 3.), and not always mathematics teacher education is sufficiently open towards research in didactics of mathematics – or conveniently organized from the methodological point of view (see 4.).

As a consequence of this situation, we see that many opportunities are lost in both directions: the increase of the level of teacher vocational education, and the further development of research in didactics of mathematics. Local institutional and cultural aspects and traditions may create additional difficulties in some countries: as a result, tools and results of research in didactics of mathematics frequently remain outside the 'core' of mathematics teacher education, with a considerable waste of skills and energies.

REFERENCES

Arsac, J., Balacheff, N. & Mante, M.: 1991, 'The teachers' role and the reproducibility of didactical situations', *Educational Studies in Mathematics,* 23, 5-29

Artigue, M.:1990, 'Ingénierie didactique', *Recherches en didactique des mathématiques,* 9, 281-308

Arzarello, F., Bartolini Bussi, M.G.: 1994, *Italian trends of research in mathematics education: elements for a case study,* paper presented at the ICMI Study Conference on 'What is research in mathematics education and what are its results', University of Maryland

Balacheff, N., 1990, 'Future Perspectives for Research in the Psychology of Mathematics Education', in Nesher, P. & Kilpatrick, J. (eds.), *Mathematics and Cognition,* Cambridge University Press, 135-147

Barra, M.; Ferrari, M.; Furinghetti, F.; Malara, N.; Speranza, F.(eds.), 1992, *The Italian Research in Mathematics Education: Common Roots and Present Trends,* T.I.D. - C.N.R., Quad. 12

Bartolini Bussi, M.G.: 1991, 'Social Interaction and Mathematical Knowledge', in Boero, P. et al. (eds) *Proceedings of PME-XV,* Assisi, vol.I, 1-16

Bartolini Bussi, M.G.: 1994, 'Theoretical and empirical approaches to classroom interaction', in Biehler et al. (eds.), *Didactics of mathematics as a scientific discipline,* Kluwer, Dordrecht, 121-132

Belcastro, A.; Guala, E.; Parenti, L.: 1986, 'Un'esperienza di aggiornamento su probabilità e statistica rivolta a insegnanti di scuola media...', *L'ins. della mat. e delle sc. int.,* vol.9, 5-70

Bishop, A.: 1988, *Mathematical Enculturation,* Kluwer Academic Publishers, Dordrecht

Boero, P.: 1989 a, 'Semantic fields suggested by history: their function in the acquisition of mathematical concepts', *Zentralblatt fur Didaktik der Mathematik,* 20, 128-133

Boero, P.: 1989 b, 'Mathematical Literacy for All: Experiences and Problems', Vergnaud, G. et al. (eds.), *Proceedings of PME-XIII,* Paris, vol. I, 62-76

Boero, P.: 1993, 'Situations didactiques et problèmes d'apprentissage: convergences et divergences dans les perspectives de recherche', in Artigue, M.; Gras, R.; Laborde, C.; Tavignot, P. (eds.), *Vingt ans de didactique des mathématiques en France,* La Pensée Sauvage, Grenoble, 17-50

Boero, P.; Szendrei, J.: 1992, 'The problem of motivating pupils to learn mathematics', Weinzweig, I. et al. (eds.), *Students confronted to Mathematics -Proceedings of CIEAEM- 42,* Chicago, 226-240

Boero, P.; Szendrei, J.: 1994, *'Research and results in mathematics education: some contradictory aspects',* paper presented at the ICMI Study Conference on 'What is research in mathematics education and what are its results', University of Maryland

Borasi, R.: 1992, *Learning Mathematics Through Inquiry,* Heinemann, Portsmouth, NH

Borasi, R.; Fonzi, J.; Rose, B.: 1994, 'Teaching mathematics in inclusive classrooms: a project integrating theory and practice for researchers, teachers and students in the USA', in Bazzini, L. (ed.), *Proceedings SCTP-V,* Grado, 47-55

Bottino, R. M., Furinghetti F.: 1992, *The emerging of teacher's conception on new topics inserted in mathematics programs: the case of computer science,* paper presented at the ICME 7 Conference, WG 17, Quebec

Bottino R. M., Furinghetti F., 1994, 'Teacher education, problems in mathematics teaching and the use of didactic packages', in Tilson, J., Warson, D. (eds), *Proceedings of IFIP Working Group 3.1* (Barcelona) (in press).

Bottino R. M., Furinghetti F.: 1994b, 'Teaching mathematics and using computers: links between teachers' beliefs in two different domains', in Ponte J. P., Matos J. F. (eds), *Proceedings of PME XVIII,* Lisboa, vol. 2, 112-119

Brousseau, G.: 1980, 'Problèmes de l'enseignement des décimaux', *Recherches en didactique des mathématiques* 1, 11-59

Brousseau, G.:1981, 'Problèmes de didactique des décimaux', *Recherches en didactique des mathématiques* 2, 37-127

Brousseau, G.: 1983, 'Les obstacles épistémologiques et les problèmes en mathématiques', *Recherches en didactique des mathématiques* 4, 165-198

Brousseau, G.: 1986, *Théorisation des phénomenes d'enseignement des mathématiques,* thése d'Etat, Université de Bordeaux I

Brown, S. I.; Cooney, T.J. & Jones, D.: 1990, 'Mathematics teacher education', in Houston, W. R. (ed.): *Handbook of research on teacher education,* MacMillan, New York, 639-656

Carpenter, T.P. & Fennema, E.: 1989, 'Building of knowledge of students and teachers', Vergnaud, G. et al. (eds.), *Proceedings of PME-XIII,* Paris, vol. I, 34-45

Carraher, T., 1988: 'Street mathematics and school mathematics', Borbas, A. et al. (eds) *Proc. of PME-XII, OOK-* Vezsprem, vol. 1, 1-23

Chevallard, Y.:1991, *La transposition didactique,* La pensée sauvage, Grenoble (II Ed.)

Chevallard, Y.: 1992, 'Concepts fondamentaux de la didactique: perspectives apportées par une approche anthropologique', *Recherches en didactique des mathématiques* 12, 73-112

Chiappini, G.P.; Parenti, L.: 1991, 'Insegnanti, Didattica, Calcolatore: analisi di una esperienza di aggiornamento rivolta ad insegnanti di matematica della scuola media', *L'ins. della mat. e delle sc. int.,* 14, 337-354

Chiappini, G.P.; Laviosa, L.; Parenti, L.:1990, 'Enseignants et formateurs d'enseignants face au defi informatique: analyse d'une experience de formation en service', in Ciosek, M. (ed.), *The teacher of mathematics in the changing world - Proceedings CIEAEM-42,* Szczyrk, 71-78

Ciosek, M. (ed.): 1990, *The teacher of mathematics in the changing world - Proceedings CIEAEM-42,* Szczyrk, Poland

Clements, M.A.; Ellerton, N. (eds.): 1989, *School Mathematics: The Challenge to Change,* Geelong Deakin University

Cobb, P.; Wood, T. & Yackel, E.: 1990, 'Classrooms as learning environments for teachers and researchers', *Journal for Research in Mathematics Education,* Monograph No. 4, 125-146

Cooney, T. J.: 1994, On the application of science to teaching and teacher education, in Biehler & al.(eds.), *Didactics of mathematics as a scientific discipline,* Kluwer, Dordrecht, 103-116

Cooney, T. J.: 1994, 'Teacher education as a crucible for systematic cooperation between theory and practice', in Bazzini, L. (editor) *Proceedings of SCTP-V,* Grado, 67-80

Dapueto, C., Ghio S., Pesce G.: 1994, Statistica e Probabilità nel biennio: nodi culturali e didattici da affrontare, parte 1ª e parte 2ª, *L'insegnamento della matematica e delle scienze integrate,* 17 B, 309-316, 357-384

Dapueto, C. & Ferrari, P.L.: 1983, 'On some recent contributions on the philosophy of mathematics', *Proceedings 7th International Congress of Logica, Methodology and Philosophy of Mathematics,* Salzburg, vol. 6, 55-56

Davis, P. J. & Hersh, R.: 1980, *The mathematical experience,* Birkhauser

Douady, R.: 1984, *Jeux de cadres et dialectique outil-objet,* thèse d'Etat, Université Paris VII

Even R.: 1990, Subject matter knowledge for teaching and the case of functions, *Educational Studies in Mathematics,* 21, 521-544

Freudenthal, H.: 1978, *Weeding and Sowing,* D.Reidel, Dordrecht.

Eisenhart, M.A.:1988, 'The Etnographic Research Tradition and the Mathematics Education Research', *Journal for Research in Mathematics Education* 19, 99-114

Furinghetti, F.:1994, 'Ghosts in the classroom: beliefs, prejudices and fears', in Bazzini, L. (ed.) *Proceedings of SCTP-V,* Grado, 81-91

Goodman, N.D.: 1980, 'Mathematics as an objective science', *Am. Math. Monthly,* 86, 540-551

Houston, W. R.(ed.): 1990, *Handbook of research on teacher education,* New York, MacMillan

Hoyles, C.: 1992, 'Illuminations and reflections: teachers, methodologies and mathematics', Geeslin, W., Graham, K. (eds.) *Proceedings PME-XVI,* Durham, N.H.,vol. III, 263-286

Jaworski, B.: 1994, *Investigating Mathematics Teaching,* Falmer Press

Keitel, C.: 1986, 'Social needs in secondary mathematics education', Bowie, P. (ed.) *Mathematics for those between 14 and 17, is it really necessary?-Proceedings CIEAEM-38,* Southampton, 52-64

Kilpatrick, J.: 1992, 'A history of research in mathematics education', in D. A. Grows (Ed.), *Handbook of Research on Mathematics Teaching and Learning,* Macmillan, New York.

Kline, M.: 1980, *Mathematics. The loss of certainty,* Oxford University Press

Krainer, K.:1994, 'Integrating research and teacher in-service education as a means of mediating theory and practice in mathematica education', in Bazzini, L. (ed.) *Proceedings of SCTP-V,* Grado, 121-132

Laborde, C.: 1988, 'L'enseignement de la géométrie en tant que terrain d'exploration de phénomènes didactiques', *Recherches en didactique des mathématiques* 9, 337-364

Lakatos, I. (ed.): 1967, *Problems in the philosophy of mathematics,* North Holland, Amsterdam

Lerman, S.: 1990, 'The role of research in the practice of mathematics education', *For the Learning of Mathematics,* 10, 25-28

Mac Lane, S.: 1981, Mathematical models: a sketch for the philosophy of mathematics, *Am. Math. Monthly,* 88, 462-472

NCTM (National Council of Teachers of Mathematics), 1991: *Professional Standards for Teaching Mathematics,* NCTM, Reston, VA

Ponte, J.P.; Matos, J.P.; Guimaraes, H.M.; Leal, L.C. & Canavaro, A.P.: 1994, Teachers' and students' views and attitudes towards a new mathematics curriculum: a case study, *Educational Studies in Mathematics,* 26, 347-366

Robert, A.: 1992, 'Problèmes méthodologiques en didactique des mathématiques', *Recherches en didactique des mathématiques* 12, 33-58

Sierpinska, A.: 1985, 'Obstacles épistémologiques relatifs à la notion de limite', *Recherches en didactique des mathématiques* 6, 5-67

Sierpinska, A.: 1987, 'Humanities students and epistemological obstacles relative to limits', *Educational Studies in Mathematics* 18, 371-397

Silver, E. A.: 1994, 'Mathematical thinking and reasoning for all students: moving from rhetoric to reality', in Robitaille, D.F.; Wheeler, D.H.; Kieran, C.(eds.), *Selected Lectures from the 7th Congress on Mathematics Education,* 311-326

Simon, M.A., Schifter, D.: 'Towards a constructivist perspective: the impact of a mathematics teacher inservice program on students' *Educational Studies in Mathematics,* 25, 331-340

Simon, M.A.: 1994, 'Learning mathematics and learning to teach: learning cycles in mathematics teacher education', *Educational Studies in Mathematics,* 26, 71-94

Steen, L.A. (ed.): 1978, *Mathematics today: twelve informal essays,* Springer, New York

Steiner, H.G.: 1984, *Theory of Mathematics Education,* Occasional Paper 54, I.D.M. Bielefeld

Swart, E.R.: 1980, 'The philosophical implications of the four-color problem', Am. Math. Monthly, 87, 697-787

Wittman, E.C.: 1989, 'The mathematical training of teachers from the point of view of education', *Zentralblatt fur Didaktik der Mathematik,* 10, 291-308

Wittman, E.C.: 1991, 'From inservice-courses to systematic cooperation between teachers and researchers', *Zentralblatt fur Didaktik der Mathematik,* 23, 158-160

Chapter 30: Preparing Teachers to Teach Mathematics: A Comparative Perspective

CLAUDE COMITI AND DEBORAH LOEWENBERG BALL

Université Joseph Fourier, Grenoble, France and Michigan State University, East Lansing, U.S.A.

ABSTRACT

This chapter provides an international examination of current approaches to the preparation of mathematics teachers. The authors, one French and one American, begin by situating the chapter in the evolution of mathematics education – both practice and research – over the past 40 years. The second section of the chapter offers a bird's-eye-view of mathematics teacher education in four countries – England, France, Germany, and the United States, focusing both on the structure and contexts of teacher preparation in each country, and on characteristic features of each country's system. In the third section, the authors probe the particular cases of France (as a European case) and the United States. Three elements of teacher education frame the descriptions of each country's approach to the preparation of primary and secondary teachers to teach mathematics – teacher education students, teacher educators themselves, and the curriculum of teacher education. The chapter concludes with a discussion of issues embedded in each setting, and a comparative look at their similarities and differences.

1. INTRODUCTION: THE PERSISTENT CALL FOR IMPROVEMENTS IN MATHEMATICS TEACHING AND LEARNING

Over the past four decades, societal needs for scientific and technical knowledge have led to increased concern for the teaching of scientific subjects in school. Although this has played out differently across countries, one common objective has been not only to increase the number and quality of scientists but also to broaden the scientific understanding common to the whole population in order to improve the possibilities of collaboration, circulation, use, and creation of technical material. However, despite repeated efforts to reform instruction and curriculum, observers in many countries agree that difficulties are not being overcome.[1]

Beginning in the late 1950's, many Western countries undertook ambitious reforms aimed at the improvement of mathematics (and science) education. In European countries, this meant making instruction more pupil-centered,

A.J. Bishop et al. (eds.), International Handbook of Mathematics Education, 1123 - 1153 while also focusing on a more general and more organised vision of the subject matter. In the United States, the parallel Sputnik-era reforms were centered mostly on reorienting the curriculum around formalist disciplinary content structures, and emphasised the needs of college-bound and college students.[2] However, in neither context did these reforms succeed in bringing about the desired improvements in practice. Analyses of these reforms later revealed weaknesses in some of their fundamental assumptions.

One such widespread assumption was that university mathematicians and scientists were best equipped to shape the improvement of elementary and secondary instruction.[3] It soon became apparent, however, that being a good scientist or mathematician was not sufficient to ensure good teaching of that subject. The next best solution seemed to take scientific discourse, make it accessible to students using a set of pedagogical principles, and to develop and refine the actual pedagogy of that content over time, based on experience. Teaching was considered a personal and artistic implementation of principles and theories, not something to be developed more systematically. Pedagogy was also seen as generic, not as something that was deeply interwoven with the particulars of the content itself. Experts in the human sciences offered a stream of ideas for developing teaching: Behavioural objectives, classroom management, teacher decision making, motivation theory – the sources of suggestions to teachers multiplied. However, responsibility for the selection and organisation of knowledge was still left to the disciplinary experts, reifying a traditional separation of content from pedagogy.

In the 1970's, new fields of research began to develop that challenged this divide between disciplinary knowledge and pedagogy, as well as the concomitantly idiosyncratic view of teaching. In France, the IREM (Instituts de Recherches sur l'Enseignement des Mathematiques) were created, and a community of researchers emerged whose focus was mathematical didactics. In the United States, during this period, teaching effects arose as a new field of inquiry. Researchers studied teachers' behaviours and sought patterns between particular teacher actions and students' learning. Teacher thinking and decision making also attracted researchers' attention.

In the 1980's, cognitive science, a new branch of psychology, explored how human beings process information; researchers explored students' thinking about scientific phenomena, students' learning, and teachers' thinking. Research on teaching reopened investigations of the relations between what teachers know and believe and what they do in their practice.

In France, didactics of mathematics emerged[4] – *'la science des conditions spécifiques de la diffusion et de l'acquisition provoquée des connaissances mathématiques utiles au fonctionnement des institutions humaines'*[5]. This line of work investigated the ways in which knowledge was structured in the thinking of scientists, of students, and within particular situations. Theories of didactics sought to discern and articulate patterns in the ways these structures overlapped and influenced one another. Some studies focused on 'didactical transposition'[6], others on pupil's scientific knowledge within particular conceptual fields[7], and others on 'didactical situations'[8]. The first looked at knowledge from an anthropological perspective[9], the second was rooted more in psychology[10], and the third examined interplay of these perspectives in the context of different forms of knowledge, experience, and instruction[11]. Linked, these theories complemented, and often overlapped one another.

In the mid-1980's other new areas of inquiry developed. Some researchers began to probe the subject-specific nature of learning and teaching. What elements of learning seem to hold true across subject matters, or within subject matters, across topics? How does the subject matter influence teaching? These fields of research were simultaneously theoretical, experimental, and technical. International communities worked at synthesising understandings of the learning and teaching processes across subject fields, within particular subject matters, and comparatively. Their divide breaking down, disciplinary knowledge and pedagogy were increasingly seen as more tightly interwoven – in curriculum design and in teaching.

The late 1980's saw another large wave of reform aimed at school mathematics, this time based on new conceptions of the relations between disciplines and school subjects, between content and pedagogy, and rooted in the big theoretical shifts in theories of learning and cognition.

2.   THE IMPROVEMENT OF MATHEMATICS TEACHER PREPARATION: A NEW
      CHALLENGE

As a consequence of new views of mathematics teaching and of the teacher's role, crucial questions emerged for the development of new curricula and teaching methods, and for the preparation of teachers, both elementary and secondary. What did teachers need to know to teach mathematics well? How could they be prepared to draw both on deep understandings of content and of how pupils learn that content? How might teachers be equipped to teach maths in ways appropriate for particular students, and in ways that helped the wide range of their students learn?

Although widespread and common, issues of what counts as appropriate teacher education are different across contexts. For example, the preparation of elementary teachers, who usually are not content specialists, raises different issues than does the preparation of secondary teachers who do major studies in mathematics at the university. The structures of the broader educational system, and the political and social context make a difference as well. Hence, the challenges of preservice teacher preparation can vary across countries.

In order to gain a broader view of how these challenges are addressed in different countries, our chapter begins with an examination of new trends for teacher preparation in European countries and the United States, and, in the second section, focuses more closely on a comparison of a set of specific problems related to elementary and secondary teacher education in France and the U.S.. We conclude with a discussion of four issues central to preparing mathematics teachers: time pressures concomitant with the recognition of the constructive process of teacher learning; the balancing act of pedagogy and subject matter in teacher education; preparing teachers for a 'new' approaches to teaching mathematics with which they have had scant experience; and connections across contexts and program components.

3.   PART I: A BRIEF OVERVIEW OF CONTEMPORARY TEACHER PREPARATION
      IN EUROPE[12] AND THE U.S.

In this first section, we make some brief (and necessarily general) remarks about the variety of teacher education systems in Europe, and then we take a bird's-eye view of mathematics teacher preparation in three European countries − Germany, The United Kingdom and France − and the United States. This overview offers a glimpse of the different issues that have been in the foreground in each country and how the structures and issues compare across the different systems.

In Scandinavia and the Netherlands, teacher education is integrated into departments of education in universities or polytechnic institutes; students generally choose teaching as a career, and professional aspects of teaching are integrated into the course from the start. Research methods are included, usually in some special projects, and typically a secondary mathematics teacher would be qualified at masters level. Belgium has the diversity of the French and Flemish speaking areas with separate curricula, and currently five qualifications for teaching at different levels. The courses tend to be 'consecutive' with academic study preceding any pedagogical studies.

In Spain and Portugal reforms in the teacher education system are in progress. Teachers Colleges and Educational Institutions now come within the university system, although the instructional model is still generally one of 'information - transmission'. However, there are some excellent centres for higher qualification and research in mathematics education in some universities.

In Italy, there have been no fundamental changes to the system since 1923. Compulsory schooling finishes at age 14, and prospective primary teachers then attend a four year course at a 'Scuola Magistrale'. Secondary teachers must have a university degree, and whether they receive any pedagogical training depends on the enthusiasm and persistence of individual members of university mathematics departments. Didactics of mathematics is virtually unrecognised by Italian universities as a course contributing to a students final degree. In contrast to this, the Italian government has sponsored a number of curriculum research groups which already provide significant contributions to research in didactics of mathematics.

Greece fares no better. Primary teachers study a variety of subjects at a university department of pedagogy for four or five years, while secondary teachers need to obtain a degree in the subject they choose to teach. Secondary teachers may get some pedagogical training if they happen to be in a mathematics department where an individual teacher has some expertise or interest. At the time of writing prospective teachers have to wait ten years or more for a place in a state school once they are qualified. Hence, the only way they can gain teaching experience is by taking on private students, or working in a 'Frontesteria', a school for coaching students to pass examinations.

3.1 The educational system in Germany: Two phase training and subject matter specialisation [13]

Mathematics teacher education in Germany has undergone several periods of reform and revision, focusing alternately on either academic or pedagogical preparation. Attempts to create a comprehensive system of teacher education, integrating both academic and professional studies, began in the 1970's but have never been fully realised. One main goal has been to try to raise the standards for teacher education and the teacher training institutions themselves. Toward that end, policies were developed to reorganise the institutions, integrating pedagogical academies into universities. However, according to analysts, 'this integration of pedagogical academies into universities did not solve the biggest and most urgent problems of the new design for teacher education: to produce an expert who was both scientifically educated as well pedagogically skilled. The single courses of study remained separated and it was left to the student to integrate them from himself.' [14] We note also that Germany consists of 16 'Lander'; regional bodies in charge of the organisation, structure, content and methods of teacher education so that considerable differences exist among the Lander in all aspects of teacher education.

'The teacher as subject matter specialist' has remained a central goal in Germany, and in order to prepare teachers who could be seen as such, teacher education for all levels is organised into two phases: the academic studies at the university, providing a more theoretical and more scientific component, and a practical phase at the Haupt- and Fach-seminaries, relating general didactics and subject matter didactics to practical teaching under the supervision of the school administration and the direction of experienced teachers.

Characteristic of the German teacher education system is the second, or practical, phase after the first state examination. Teacher candidates are required to teach in a school for two years with a reduced number of hours. They attend three weekly seminars run by experienced teachers. The common seminar provides an opportunity to study general professional issues for all teachers. The two subject matter-specific seminars, where expert teachers address practical problems in connection with teaching a particular subject. Experienced mathematics teachers working in this phase develop prospective teachers' understandings of mathematics teaching by generalising successful practice and creating theories of that practice. This phase places a greater emphasis on learning from the actual practice of mathematics instruction than on findings from research in didactics of mathematics or education.

3.2 The recent reform of the educational system in England and Wales: School-based training[15]

In England, the 1980's saw an important growth of research in mathematics education, the acknowledgment of which can be found in the commissioning of reviews of research[16] at the time of the Cockcroft Committee: its current state can be seen in the Handbook of Research on Mathematics Teaching and Learning[17].

Since the 1990's, the reform of the educational system in England and Wales, driven by an outdated 'apprenticeship' model put emphasis more on 'competencies,' and on creating different relations and partnerships between the university and the schools. According to the Ministry Circulars, new qualified teachers should be able to 'produce coherent lesson plans, ensure continuity and progression within and between classes and in subjects, set appropriately demanding expectations for pupils.' They should be able to 'employ a range of teaching strategies appropriate to the age, ability and attainment level of pupils, present subject content in clear language and in a stimulating manner.' They should also be able to 'contribute to the development of pupils' language and communication skills, and demonstrate the ability to select and use appropriate resources, including technology.'

These emphases are clearly reflected in the accreditation criteria issued in 1992. Schools are to play a much larger part in preservice teacher education, and accreditation should be based on whether schools focus on competencies of teaching. The government heavily prescribes the syllabus for teacher education (now called teacher training), in terms of the hours to be given to specialist subject content, teaching methods and class control, teaching of specialist subjects and practical teaching.

The government controlled Teacher Training Agency determines the regulations for the development of accreditation criteria, arrangements for partnerships between higher education institutions and schools, and procedures for institutional accreditation. Three basic requirements are specified:
- *prerequisite study:* Students applying for any initial teacher training course should have attained a standard equivalent to GCSE mathematics Grade C before entering a course. (The GCSE is the public examination

taken at age 16, and this means that many prospective teachers have not studied mathematics for at least two years before they enter a course.)

— *standards for the extent of particular components of teacher preparation:* The minimum time students are to spend in schools in full-time primary and secondary PGCE courses should be 24 weeks. (The PGCE is a 36 week course taken by students who already have a university degree.) For part-time courses the minimum time is 18 weeks; in two- and three-year primary and secondary undergraduate courses 24 weeks, and in four year primary and secondary undergraduate courses, 32 weeks;

— *relationship between TTA and individual programs:* The statement of the competencies expected of newly qualified teachers are necessary but not sufficient to provide a complete syllabus for initial teacher training. Individual institutions are required to develop their own competence-based approaches to the training and assessment of students according to the syllabus referred to above.

Several aims of preservice teacher preparation are specified. First, all newly qualified teachers entering state schools should have achieved the levels of knowledge and standards of professional competence necessary to maintain and improve standards in schools. Second, partner schools and higher education institutions will share responsibility equally for the planning and management of courses and the selection, training and assessment of students. Schools have the primary responsibility for training students to teach their specialist subjects (e.g., mathematics), to assess pupils, and to manage classes, as well as for supervising students and assessing their competence in these respects. Higher education institutions are responsible for ensuring that courses meet the requirements for academic validation, presenting courses for accreditation, awarding qualifications to successful students, and arranging student placements in more than one school. Higher education institutions, schools, and prospective teachers should all focus on the competences of teaching throughout the whole period of initial teacher training.

Future teachers with a bachelor's degree are given a one-year professional training (PGCE) course in a higher education institution associated by means of a agreement with partner schools which have the lead responsibility for training students to teach their area of specialisation, to assess pupils and manage classes; and for supervising students and assessing their competence in these areas students should be given opportunities to observe good teachers at work, to participate with experienced practitioners in teaching their area of specialisation and to undertake periods of continuous whole class teaching[18].

K. Ruthven[19] underscores the opportunities and threats of this school based approach which 'allows students to be accepted within a school community, to feel valued and to have some stake in that community... Students gain immeasurably from the opportunity to learn and develop through working closely and collaboratively with talented mentors...; at its best, the approach provides opportunities for school staff to learn and develop through encountering the need to articulate, demonstrate, justify and reconsider their practice; and for university staff, to develop ideas with schools on a broader front, linking initial training and professional renewal.' But 'inadequate funding is the major threat to the success of the school-based approach... Initial training may become a marginal part of the work of both university and school staff, with the consequent problems of lack of concern for quality and renewal... Teaching may become less attractive ... as it appears to distance itself from the universities and the analytic tradition that they represent.'

It should be noted that the present system of teacher education in the UK must be seen in the context of the 1988 Education Act where sweeping changes were made to the whole of the state system in England and Wales. Not only was a National Curriculum introduced, but also a national system of testing pupils, both of which are monitored by a newly privatised system of inspectors. It is inevitable that these changes have a significant effect on the content and approach to teacher education. For example, universities have to pay schools to allow their students to practice teaching, good role models for prospective mathematics teachers are difficult to find, curriculum development as a cooperative enterprise between schools, local authorities and universities is virtually non-existent, and educational research has practically no effect on the system at present.

3.3 The recent reform of the educational system in France: Integrating subject matter and professional training.

The social demands of the last decade have brought increasing attention to, and pressure on, teacher education in France[20]. A new mandate that 80 per cent of each age class must reach the top of secondary schools, to complete the French *baccalauréat*, resulted in a rapid expansion of secondary schooling over the past decade and an urgent teacher shortage. Taking account of these increasing demands, coupled with predictions of coming retirements, an estimated 25,000 teachers must be recruited in France each year over the next several years: This includes about 10,000 elementary teachers and 2,000 secondary mathematics teachers. This demand can be best understood by setting the numbers in context: France, with a population of 56 millions, has a primary and secondary teaching force of approximately 680,000, of who 320,000 teach at the elementary level.

An answer to these demands prepared in 1988-89 was the Bancel Report[21], which provided the basis for defining the new approach to teacher education. It listed the professional skills and content, organised under three categories: '*connaissances liées à l'identité des disciplines*' (knowledge of the disciplines), '*connaissances relatives à la gestion des apprentissages*' (child development), and '*connaissances relatives au système éducatif*' (the educational system). In this report, disciplinary knowledge is considered insufficient for teaching. Teachers must have 'achieved an understanding of the ways in which scholarly knowledge is developed and constructed in such a way that they can link curricular content at different levels of schooling to academic knowledge. …This kind of understanding requires careful attention to pupils' conceptions of knowledge and the epistemological and didactical challenges that might arise in the course of learning…' In a chapter entitled, 'How to articulate the practical and theoretical knowledge necessary to develop professional competence,' the Bancel Report explains: 'In the course of his or her professional education, the future teacher must transform the knowledge that he or she has acquired in the course of academic studies into competencies to work up in schools. This demands a harmonious and ongoing interaction between the practical and theoretical components of the professional training. These different experiences must be carried out in simultaneous ways.' There is therefore a dialectic in the acquisition of different kinds of knowledge, including equally disciplinary knowledge, knowledge of didactics, and knowledge of how to put these ideas into practice in the field. For the author of this report, this entails helping future teachers completely transform their understandings. Little, however, is specified as to *how* to accomplish this transformation.

A new Education Law was adopted in July 1989, requiring the development and improvement of teacher education. In September 1990, three pilot *Instituts Universitaires de Formation des Maîtres*[22], or *I.U.F.M.* were founded. One year later, institutes were established in the remaining 25 districts. The aims of the reforms in teacher education took into account the Bancel report's conclusions and included much more coherence between elementary and secondary education, a shift to a five-year teacher education process, better coordination between scientific training and professional training, as well as between theory and practice, and also better links between educational research and teacher education.

Each of the current IUFM (29 in all) is a free-standing institution, unaffiliated with a university; yet they are clearly institutions of higher education. No easy analogue exists in European or American system; indeed, even the name, '*Instituts Universitaires de Formation des Maîtres,*' defies direct translation into English, revealing the special and different structure of the current French system.[23]

3.4 The American system: Standards-based reform in an uncentralised system

In the United States, considerable press exists to reform the teaching and learning of mathematics and specially elementary mathematics. Over the past 15 years, reformers have promoted a shift to a greater emphasis on problem solving, meaning, and applications. Since 1989, the National Council of Teachers of Mathematics has published three volumes of 'standards,' or guidelines for the mathematics curriculum, instruction, professional development, and assessment of both students and teachers.[24] These standards documents have been widely distributed and have played a role in recent revisions of curriculum materials and goals.They frame a set of curricular goals and articulate a vision of teaching significantly different from modal practice in U.S. schools. The new visions promote a shift from an emphasis on speed and accuracy to an emphasis on reasoning, from an emphasis on memorisation and procedures to an emphasis on conceptual understanding. Classrooms are to be structured in ways that promote group interaction, cooperative learning and group discussion. Moreover, threaded throughout is a clear commitment to the idea that learning is a constructive process. These ideas represent a major shift from traditional practice in U.S. elementary classrooms where teachers usually do most of the talking, presenting content and asking convergent questions. Arithmetic has long dominated the elementary curriculum, with an emphasis on skill and speed. Other mathematical topics such as geometry or probability get little attention, and learning is primarily individual and oriented to getting right answers more than reasoning about, constructing, or applying mathematical ideas.

Mathematics reform shapes the milieu of U.S. teacher education in three important ways.[25] First, it means that many teacher educators seek to prepare new teachers who are current with these reforms, who know about the directions in which mathematics education is headed, and who are positioned to work on developing such teaching. This adds to the challenge for teacher educators, for prospective teachers lack exposure to or experience with this kind of mathematics teaching (see below where we discuss teacher candidates). Second, teacher educators, too, lack experience with these approaches. They are in the uncomfortable position of trying to teach their teacher candidates about a kind of teaching they do not know well and may never have tried to do. Third, it puts teacher educators in the difficult position of trying to find good field placements. Since the reforms aim to change typical practice, many classrooms into which teacher candidates might be placed show little evidence of these new ideas. This leaves teacher educators often lacking images of this kind of teaching which they might show their students.

In contrast with the European systems which we have examined, the American system is fragmented and lacks the centralised authority of the French system. Control of schools is distributed among the Federal government, state departments of education, districts, and individual schools. Teacher education is still less-regulated than are elementary and secondary schools, with no national control, and a great deal of autonomy for teacher educators. Judge, Lemosse, Paine, and Sedlak[26] refer to U.S. teacher education as a 'non-system.' A European observer would find 'the lack of order, scheme, or plan at the regional.... [or] the national level' striking (p. 123). Teachers are prepared in a wide variety of public and private institutions: research universities, large comprehensive universities, four-year colleges grown from old normal schools, and small independent and religious-affiliated liberal arts colleges. In all, almost 1300 public and private institutions prepare teachers.

As in Germany, France and the UK, questions about the desirable balance and relationship between academic and professional studies have figured prominently. In some cases, the questions are structural (i.e., four year program or post-B.A.?) and in others more curricular (i.e., how should academic departments and schools of education share in teacher education?). Certification is granted by states, and while many states have reciprocal agreements, there is no Federal oversight of teacher education. Currently under development is a new system of national professional certification, under the auspices of a new professional organisation, the National Board of Professional Teaching Standards (NBPTS). However, it is voluntary, and designed to mark distinctions among practising teachers by creating a special certification status for 'accomplished' teachers. States, under this plan, would continue to grant basic licenses to teach. Close on the heels of the NBPTS efforts is a multistate initiative to design initial teacher performance assessment. INTASC, the Interstate New Teacher Assessment and Support Consortium, is developing a portfolio assessment that states would use to evaluate beginning teachers for licensure, continuation, or, in some cases, focused professional development. Approximately 28 states are currently participating in this developmental effort.

In the 1990's, as always in the U.S., the messages about public education are mixed. On one hand, criticism of schools abounds, and report after report reveals poor achievement by many students. Still, Americans when surveyed, report being pleased with their own schools. Mathematics education is riddled with conflicting aims. Reformers press for changes in content, to make mathematics both more intellectually rigorous and more usably connected to everyday life. And the public seems to want students prepared for the 21st century. Yet many are also reluctant to let go of any of the content of the traditional mathematics curriculum. In addition to political debates about ends and means of schooling, the rapidly increasing diversity of the already heterogeneous American population presses on public education. In the midst of a changing demographic picture, and conflicting signals about what schools should try to do, teachers are both objects of criticism and those charged with making change and improvement. All this combines to place pressure on teacher education, itself the regular target of criticism.[27]

Evident in these brief overviews is the fact the several factors shape what is expected of teacher education and what it tries to do. Moreover, several areas of similarity can be seen across countries. First, in each country there is a history of efforts to define the relations between academic and professional preparation, as well as between the university or teacher training institution and the schools. Second, concern for teachers' subject matter understandings is common, and yet no country seems entirely satisfied with its solution. The fact remains that many primary teachers are really not at all prepared in mathematics, and the means to change this fundamentally are elusive. Finally, teacher education is and continues to be seen as a linchpin in countries' larger aims for the improvement of schools and of school learning.

4.   PART II. PREPARING ELEMENTARY AND SECONDARY TEACHERS TO
      TEACH MATHEMATICS: A COMPARATIVE EXAMINATION OF TEACHER
      EDUCATION IN FRANCE AND THE U.S.

In this section, we take a closer look at the systems for preparing elementary and secondary mathematics teachers specifically in France and the United States. This comparative examination offers a perspective on how the challenges of preparing mathematics teachers, at both levels of schooling, are met and managed in the two different countries. We organize our discussion in three parts:

   1) Prospective teachers in France and the United States: What kinds of
       students enrol in elementary or secondary mathematics teacher
       education programs in the two countries?
   2) Who are 'teacher educators' responsible for the professional studies
       component of the program in France and the U.S.? What are their
       experiences?
   3) Curriculum in France and the United States: What comprises teacher
       education for future mathematics elementary and secondary teachers,
       and under what arrangements, in the two countries?
   4) What problems are faced in preparing mathematics teachers in France
       and the United States? What are the areas of similarity and where are
       the distinct differences?

4.1   Who are the prospective teachers in France and the United States?

Much has been written about the importance of paying attention to who the learner is and to what learners bring. Most often applied in the context of children's learning, it is nonetheless equally appropriate in teacher education. What teachers bring to their professional preparation influences their expectations, their notions of what they need to learn, their images of teaching and of learning, their ideas about children, and about who can learn what, and what helps children learn.

The situation differs for elementary and secondary teaching. Prospective secondary teachers who intend to teach mathematics have completed a solid major in the discipline. In France, some intending teachers have even completed a master's degree in mathematics.

For elementary teachers, the story is completely different. Mathematics is a field whose pursuit they have, for the most part, abandoned years ago. And because mathematics is not part of the wider culture, or valued as part of general literacy, people's mathematical learning is confined to their academic studies. Thus, it is not surprising that prospective teachers' mathematical understandings are based primarily on memories from their own primary schooling. This is not the case for other subjects that elementary teachers must know – music, history, literature, for example – fields which they encounter in the wider culture and that they typically continue to study as well.

Although some research has been done on what prospective elementary teachers bring to their professional preparation[28], we know nothing about how different this may be cross-culturally. Below we provide some short sketches of the teacher education population in each country.

In France, now about 60 per cent of the people entering elementary teaching are under 25 and over 80 per cent under 30, and two-thirds are female. Elementary teacher certification follows the undergraduate degree; seventy-five percent have a bachelor's degree and the remaining entrants have advanced degrees. The increasing value placed on teaching and the establishment of the IUFM have accomplished the goal of increasing the number and quality of those intending to become teachers. Teacher education programmes currently attract on average five times as many applicants as there are places; in some attractive geographic locations, this number can be as high as tenfold.

Moreover, these candidates usually have good application materials: good academic records at the university, often accompanied by a preliminary examination of methods of instruction completed as part of some 'paraprofessional' work on teaching pursued as a complement to their other university studies. The coherence of this work is taken into account in evaluating applications to the IUFM.

Still, very few intending elementary teachers have studied mathematics at the university: While all prospective elementary teachers have majored in a university field prior to entering teaching, less than 10 per cent of the people entering the IUFM have had any specialised training in mathematics, statistics, physics or chemistry, or technological sciences, while specialisation in human and social science, language, and art account for over two thirds of the candidates. Nearly half of them have not had any contact with mathematics or science since the ninth grade.

In the United States, approximately 145,000 new teachers graduate from teacher education programmes per year. The extant U.S. teaching force numbers 2.6 million, approximately equally divided between elementary and secondary. Of secondary teachers, 24 per cent teach mathematics as their main assignment.[29]

Unlike teacher education students in France, prospective U.S. elementary teachers most often (about 78 per cent) major in education as part of their undergraduate programs, or an education-related speciality such as physical education, reading, or English as a second language. Fewer than 0.05 per cent have a specialisation in mathematics as preparation to teach. An overwhelming percentage – 88 per cent – are female.[30] Although criticisms abound that education draws disproportionately from among the least successful college students, this has been challenged, and has also been changing. The academic records of newly qualified teachers are better now than they were ten years ago.[31]

In both countries, women hold the clear majority among elementary teacher candidates, although more dramatically so in the United States. In both countries, only a tiny fraction of intending elementary teachers have focused on mathematics for the disciplinary majors. The major apparent difference between the two groups seems to be that the French teacher candidates have already completed their undergraduate studies, while the vast majority of U.S. students earn their teaching credentials as part of their undergraduate program. But in neither France nor in the United States do we see prospective elementary teachers bringing depth or strength with mathematics.

In the United States, that women so overwhelmingly comprise prospective elementary teachers is significant, given the striking differences among males and females in school mathematics.[32] Moreover, they must do this in a milieu where the kind of teaching that is being advocated for classrooms is substantially different from what they themselves have experienced or seen. This places considerable burdens on professional education to prepare prospective elementary teachers to teach mathematics.

4.2 Who are the teacher educators in each country?

In France, the reforms of the 1990's have placed emphasis on the need to develop coordination between scientific training and professional training, between theory and practice, and between research on education and education. Those responsible for teacher training are chosen precisely to foster the development of these interactions.

Those who work with future mathematics teachers are housed within a department of mathematics, whose members comprise instructors of different expertise and experience. Some are lecturers or professors (university status), who devote half their time to instruction, and the other half to research. Others are mathematics teachers (secondary status), who devote all their time to instruction. However, both kinds of instructors direct action research about elementary or secondary school teaching and learning. Both give courses, conduct workshops and visit student teachers in their field classrooms.

In the case of primary teacher preparation the staff includes also elementary school teachers who have been trained in analysing practice, who have passed a special examination, and are called Instituteurs Maîtres Formateurs. These instructors have six hours a week reserved for the supervision of students during their school experience, as well as sometimes leading the Analysis of Practice Session, or giving courses at the Institute.

In the case of secondary teacher preparation, mathematics staff are of three categories who work in cooperation: University and IUFM mathematics professors and teachers, and mathematics teachers serving in secondary schools. Those colleagues who teach at the IUFM may hold positions in a university or in the IUFM. Similarly, the clinical instructors may hold a post at an IUFM or may be in a school full time and part-time at the IUFM.

In the United States, that teacher education is university-based and part of prospective teachers' undergraduate education creates some special issues around the notion of who is – or should be – a 'teacher educator.' Conceived broadly, teacher educators are university and college lecturers, holding master's degrees or doctorates, and whose courses enrol prospective teachers. Since prospective teachers take the overwhelming majority of their required studies in the academic departments (e.g., history, English, sociology, physical science, communication, psychology), the members of these departments are indeed preparing teachers. However, as members of specialist subject departments, they typically spend little time thinking of their role as educators of future teachers, despite the fact that how they teach plays a significant role in the images of good teaching and the understandings of content, culture, and people that prospective teachers develop.[33]

'Teacher educators' might be seen as those staff who are affiliated with 'education' departments in higher education (e.g., educational psychology, curriculum and instruction). However, they argue, many of these members of staff identify more with their disciplines (sociology, psychology, history, philosophy) than they do with teaching. Those who do identify with this label are staff within colleges of education who teach courses about methods of instruction. Some supervise student teachers in the schools, lead analysis sessions in schools, and maintain communication between the schools and the university. Of these, many have taught in school, later earning a doctorate and becoming a university-based education faculty member.

Mathematics teacher education sits in a puzzling position when viewed from the perspective of who function as the teachers of teachers. Too often those working with prospective elementary teachers in schools have no specialisation in mathematics – perhaps not even in elementary education. At larger institutions, those who supervise secondary teacher education students are more likely to be specialised in mathematics teaching, but at small teacher education institutions, this is impossible. In the case of secondary teacher education, small institutions may offer no special course in 'mathematics methods,' offering instead a 'general secondary methods' course. In this case, the teacher educator with whom they work may be someone without expertise in mathematics teaching and learning. In general, at larger institutions, those who work with prospective secondary mathematics teachers are likely to be mathematics educators, with secondary school teaching experience themselves. Quite often, they also have studied advanced mathematics as part of their graduate work. In addition to university instructors, practising teachers in schools spend considerable time working with prospective teachers who are assigned to their classrooms for fieldwork. They are thus also functioning as 'teacher educators.' Many of the new reforms in the U.S. are focused on expanding the partnerships between universities and schools, hence expanding the roles played by experienced teachers in the education of future teachers.

4.3   What is the curriculum of teacher education in each country?

With a sketch of the broader context, and views of the kind of teaching for which prospective teachers are being prepared, who teaches teachers, who goes into teaching, we turn now to the curriculum of teacher education. What are teachers taught in each country to prepare them for teaching elementary or secondary mathematics? How is the curriculum organised and where is it situated?

4.3.1   *Teacher education curriculum in France*

We begin with the French program for elementary teacher preparation. The program for teacher preparation is made up of three components: courses at the IUFM *(Institut Universitaire de Formation des Maîtres),* school experience, and a professional project. These are interrelated in order to help them develop knowledge, skills, methods, attitudes and habits. The aims of the program are to help teacher education students:
  — rethink and change their view of and approach to mathematics;
  — become familiar with methods, reasoning, and structures of maths;
  — understand mathematical knowledge, concepts and skills and the place of particular mathematical topics in the school curriculum
  — learn how logical thought develops in pupils' minds and how to teach maths while taking pupils' levels into account;
  — design learning situations which give meaning to mathematical subjects;

- develop their own ability to learn – e.g., reflecting on their actions and transforming them, being open to change, thinking about what they wanted to do and what they actually did, observing and analysing their own teaching, learning to search for aids (e.g., books, computer environments or programs).

We examine each of these components in turn, using the programme at the I.U.F.M. de Grenoble[34] as an example:

In the first year, elementary teacher candidates at Grenoble take 392 hours in subject matter study - following the outline for the competitive examination- of which the 100 hours of mathematics represents slightly more than one fourth. They also take 168 hours in pedagogical studies: psychology, information and communication, management of the classroom. They thereby complete seven weeks of classes, distributed across the year.

In the second year, they take 170 hours of coursework in French, mathematics, psychology, and methods for teaching at the different levels of elementary school, 134 hours in the teaching of the other elementary subjects (science, history and geography, music and art). 20 hours in analysis of practice, and a 39-hour professional project workshop. They choose over 100 additional hours from among a set of options (e.g., children with special problems, communication techniques, creative expression for young children, citizenship for young children, or deepening a particular aspect of their practice). They complete 14 weeks of coursework – four courses, each two to five weeks in length, distributed across the year.

During the first year courses, student teachers begin by observing classes and then do some closely supervised teaching. They spend seven weeks at different levels of the elementary school. During the second year, they continue to practice teaching – first for three weeks under supervision, then for three weeks with another teacher, and then for eight weeks alone. The eight-week teaching constitutes an assessment of their teaching proficiency.

In the field, student teachers in the first year elaborate specific projects for two subject areas – for example mathematics and music. During the second year, student teachers must complete a professional project report (*un mémoire professionnel*). This professional project report is actually the central structuring element of the curriculum. To complete it, student teachers must elaborate rationales and questions emerging from teaching practice, carry out a teaching experiment in their classrooms, and analyse it. In Grenoble, about 20 per cent of them choose to do it about mathematics teaching. Each student must present and defend this professional project in front a board of three examiners including an inservice teacher and an educational researcher. The aims of the professional project are to promote students' reflections on their experiences and the development of their ability to articulate professional practice. Further down the road, the goal is that they would be interested in educational research, and want to both read and participate in it.

We turn to look more closely at their training in mathematics and mathematics pedagogy. Traditionally, subject matter and didactics were studied separately from actual teaching. Much of what was studied was merely an updating of mathematics taught in elementary school and methods for teaching mathematics. In the field, teacher education students encountered real-life teaching and learning of mathematics, but engaged in little analysis of the contents or methods of what they saw. Research in the didactics of mathematics began to convince French teacher education faculty that this separate approach was quite pointless when the ultimate aim is to prepare to teach a subject as complex and elaborate as mathematics, and, furthermore to do so in ways that differ from standard practice. This led to organising French teacher preparation in ways that associate both mathematical and professional training in order to facilitate the acquisition of patterns of practice that help them to manage properly the teaching of particular mathematical notions.

Two mathematics-related courses are required of all elementary teacher education students. In the first year, teacher education students take a minimum of 80 hours of mathematics and can take an additional 20 hours. The additional mathematics course is intended to help students to think about the contents and objectives of mathematics teaching and to allow them to understand meaning by practising mathematical activities themselves. This course was at first reserved for those who did not have sufficient background in mathematics; this option is in fact now chosen by 70 per cent of students.

These two required courses use multiple pedagogical approaches – didactic as well as more discovery-oriented. The mathematical content includes problem-solving, numeration, multiplicative area, natural numbers, decimal, rational and real numbers, elementary whole number arithmetic, multiplication computation, long division, prime numbers, divisibility; geometry, and proportionality. In addition to the mathematical content, student teachers are encouraged to develop their own methods to construct specific pedagogical knowledge and learning such as ways to identify and solve teaching and learning problems; analyse children's problem-solving strategies; analyse curriculum material; work with children, assess pupils' work, organize their activities according to their specific needs; manage a classroom; analyse the method chosen and its consequences; develop long-term planning; design modes of assessment; and provide individual assistance to pupils.

In the second year, the 40-hour mathematics course is one component of the 170 hours of coursework, and focuses on mathematics at different levels. In this course, student teachers also continue their investigation of mathematical topics that are strongly related to analysing pupils' work: natural numbers, additive area and measures of length and area related to decimal numbers, and geometrical activities for school. In addition, those student teachers who choose to do their professional projects focused on mathematics participate in a mathematics workshop for 39 hours. This workshop allows small groups of students to enhance a common project theme and promotes social interaction among student teachers while encouraging them to discuss and try to solve together problems they have encountered.

We turn now to the preparation of secondary teachers in France. Since 1990, and the birth of the IUFM, secondary school teacher preparation has been organised in five years. Intending teachers complete first either a three-year (*licence*) or four-year (*maîtrise*) course in mathematics at University, followed by two years in a IUFM. This initial training is to be continued through further education for teachers. The IUFM's ensure initial training for teachers on the basis of the combination of university and professional studies, across the two last years. The entire responsibility for secondary teachers' professional studies rests with the IUFM.

In the first training year students prepare for the national competitive examination which admits them to the second year of the program (nearly 250 hours of mathematical studies and 100 hours preparing formally for the examination), and are assisted in their first attempts at teaching (36 hours of direct contact time, plus 18 hours of analysis seminar meetings). They also gain skill with regard to class management, planning, observation, and analysis (nearly 90 hours of pedagogy and didactics). In the second training year, future maths teachers progressively develop professional competency on the basis of what they have learned in university and in the first training year. Along with their professional studies, they continue to study mathematics.

Their second year educational program is organised along three main strands:

1) Placement in a secondary school with responsibility for a class (6 hours each week). During this placement, 'trainees' have the opportunity to build their professional practice with the help of IUFM teachers and mentors, the latter being school teachers associated with the IUFM.

2) The *mémoire professionnel*[35] (professional project report) deals with a problem encountered in the teaching and/or learning of mathematics in relation with professional practice. Its aim is to give coherence to and unify the various training strands. It also provides initiation to a research process, a process which in itself is also an element of training. The writing of such a dissertation is a step towards the prospective teacher's professionalisation because it fosters interaction between theory and practice[36]. Teacher trainees are encouraged to develop their own positions, working in methodologically disciplined ways to consider, interpret, and develop their ideas through analytic use of their experiences.

3) Training modules (nearly 220 hours)[37]: One module is subject matter didactics and mathematics pedagogy and assists teacher candidates in progressively developing their professional practice. It is aimed at enabling them to work out the concepts, methods and tools necessary to the development and analysis of well-thought-out professional practice. Another module is centered on reflection on practice: Its aim

is to pool the various problems encountered by trainees in their placements; to work on class management in relation with subject issues; and to link practice and training through common analysis of the actual unfolding of a lesson. Additional mathematical study is another module, organised in co-operation with the university to help prospective teachers strengthen their knowledge in the subject they will have to teach in secondary school, particularly concentrating on topics that have not or hardly been dealt with during their previous years in university (for instance probability, or history of mathematics). Specific modules in social and human sciences can include subjects dealing with adolescent clinical and cognitive psychology, information about the education system and training. This latter is done together with future elementary school teachers to make all intending teachers aware of the common characteristics of issues at stake throughout the education system and to situate their work within a elementary-secondary school continuum). Teacher trainees engage also, for 20 hours, in a 'analysis of practice seminar.' The aim of this seminar is to provide opportunity for reflection and exchange in order to enable trainees to examine problems they are likely to encounter in class and which are not specific to the teaching of a given subject; it is also meant to favour work in multidisciplinary teams.

Three principles guide the work. First, a detached standpoint is seen as crucial to developing the analytic skills needed to teach well. Professional training depends on a prior awareness of what a classroom is and what teaching means. In order to help students develop their practice, they are helped to learn to observe and analyse the teaching process by themselves in a method-ical and rationalised way. For example, one way in which this is developed is by means of a systematic approach to conferencing about observed lessons taught by teacher education students. Instructors meet with students before-hand and ask them what is planned for class, and why and how it will be done, and what has influenced their choices and decisions. They ask them what they anticipate will happen. Then, after class, they analyse together what actually happened, how it compared with what the student had planned, and what might explain certain unanticipated events?

Second, strong links are made between practice and theory. In order to make students aware that there is a possibility of choice, in the practice of their profession and that their professional preparation is meant to help them make these choices, students are induced first to analyse their practice in the light of the theoretical elements given during training. Then, conversely, they are encouraged to question these theoretical elements in the light of their practice. This is achieved in close cooperation with mentors in schools. More-over, the courses in social and human sciences as well as in didactical and mathematics methods are based on material drawn from students' own practice work in schools.

Third is the strengthening of scientific knowledge. Prospective teachers continue to study additional mathematics in order to enrich and deepen the knowledge acquired during their university years. These principles and elements are seen as essential to equipping beginning teachers with the knowledge and skill that they need to teach secondary school mathematics.

In short, mathematics teacher education in France can be summarised as follows: the first year is focused on mathematics as a subject, in connection with preparing for the competitive examination, while also beginning to reflect on methods of teaching mathematics – especially learning to observe teaching more closely. The second year is focused on professional issues, based on a purposive link between theory and practice intended to help students understand that it is necessary to reorganise, process, sometimes even deepen their knowledge in order to be able to teach it, develop their capacity to analyse and plan learning situations, take into account pupils' ideas and representations as regards notions to be taught, choose a pedagogical approach according to their aims, conceive, carry out and assess learning sequences, set their practice in a broader theoretical and professional frame, and vary their teaching patterns.

4.4   Teacher education curriculum in the U.S.

Characterising teacher education in the United States is less clear than in France, for it is so much less standardised and coordinated. U.S. teacher education programmes, as we have mentioned, exist in almost 1300 diverse institutions. Some certify teachers as part of a four-year undergraduate programme, while others place teacher certification in a five-year or a fifth-year programme. In addition, 39 states provide alternate routes to licensure, where people can become certified quickly without entering a standard teacher education programme. Some of these programmes are affiliated with universities and others with school districts.[38] However, although programme structure and sequence is often the focus of heated debate, Feiman-Nemser argues that the structure is not the main issue. She argues that 'we know relatively little about what goes on inside these different programme structures.'[39]

On one hand, despite the lack of centralisation and regulation, and despite much variation in surface features, language, and structure, teacher education programmes in the U.S. nonetheless share many similarities. On the other, the contents of what appears to be a similar course pattern and structure of programme components across diverse U.S. programmes, may be substantively quite different. Based on her examination of a sample of teacher education programmes, Feiman-Nemser identifies five distinct conceptual orientations to the preparation of teachers: critical/social, personal, technological, practical, and academic:[40]

> An orientation refers to a set of ideas about the goals of teacher preparation and the means for achieving them. Ideally, a conceptual orientation includes a view of teaching and learning, and a theory about learning to teach. Such ideas should give direction to the activities of teacher preparation such as programme planning, course development, instruction, supervision, and evaluation. Unlike structural alternatives, conceptual orientations are not tied to particular forms of teacher preparation. They can shape a single component or an entire professional sequence and apply to undergraduate or graduate programmes.

Thus, although structures may differ, what really shapes the content and pedagogy of the teacher education programme are the conceptual orientations of those designing and teaching it. Attempting to capture this sort of variation is beyond the scope of this chapter, although significant differences do exist in conceptual orientations among the many teacher education programmes in the U.S.

Three basic components typically comprise the teacher preparation sequence for both elementary and secondary teachers in the United States.[41] First is the candidates' liberal arts studies. Unlike in France, in the U.S. teacher candidates are completing their undergraduate subject matter studies parallel to their professional studies. Consequently, the majority of teacher education students' credits are earned outside the college of education, as they complete general studies requirements. Although there has been debate about whether elementary teacher candidates should have a single subject matter major or continue to study a little of many different subject areas, the latter has persisted in most cases. Secondary teacher candidates, in contrast, major in one subject area, and minor in another.

The second component is the pedagogical studies, including courses in learning, society, child development, and methods of instruction. For education majors (78 per cent of those intending to prepare for elementary teaching major in educational studies rather than in a subject field), the education coursework comprises about 50 out of 125 credits (40 per cent). For secondary teacher candidates, the professional courses total about 20 per cent of their university degree.[42] Usually this includes a subject-specific methods of teaching course, one course in learning theory, and one in foundations of education (e.g., philosophy, history, sociology, politics), but the exact contents of these courses vary significantly.

Third, teacher education students have field experiences. Beginning with directed observation and teacher assistance, the students in some programs spend a day or two per week in schools throughout the program, culminating with an extended student teaching experience, during which they assume elementary responsibility for instruction for several weeks. In other programs, prospective teachers may have little field work other than student teaching. This varies widely, and no good data exist on the distributions of format and content of field experiences. States govern the requirements for specific courses (e.g., the history of that state, reading methods), a certain number of hours' worth of particular topics (e.g., reading in the content areas; special education pedagogy and laws); the number of hours required for student teaching.

Secondary teachers in the U.S. take a major in mathematics. However, no comprehensive information exists about what mathematics they must study, and it can vary. In some institutions, prospective secondary teachers (if they so identify themselves) have some different requirements from the regular mathematics majors. For example, whereas other mathematics majors may choose to take advanced algebra *or* geometry, prospective teachers may be required to take both. In some institutions, some of the major content requirements may be met by mathematics education, rather than mathematics, courses. In general, however, intending secondary teachers most often take the same major as do those not preparing to teach.

The amount of mathematical study that U.S. prospective elementary teachers get varies, but is most often no more than one course in the mathematics department, 'mathematics for elementary teachers,' and one course in the education department, a methods course in mathematics. Compared with the French system, these two courses together comprise a little less than 90 hours, although, like everything else, this varies considerably. What each course includes and whether and how they are linked also varies. In some cases, the course in the mathematics department focuses on pedagogy explicitly, while in other cases, it emphasises content that elementary teachers would teach but does not take up pedagogical considerations. Rather, students engage the course as learners of mathematics. Some instructors use the time to concentrate on 'new' content with which prospective teachers are likely to be unfamiliar (e.g., probability, discrete mathematics). Others use the time to help prospective teachers develop more meaningful understandings of conventional content (e.g., fractions, numeration). With little time, and students whose mathematics background is typically thin, instructors face hard choices about depth and breadth, and make them differently. In some cases, with special programmes, or with outside funding, programmes offer longer mathematics content and pedagogy sequences. Many programmes require a methods course in each of the 'core' elementary school subjects. Mathematics methods courses vary as much as do the mathematics content courses, but usually include components on interviewing children, planning and teaching lessons, and units on assessing children's learning. Many programmes include a heavy component in reflection and analysis, although detailed information about what this means is lacking. In some programs, students take only a single general methods course that covers all school subjects and deals with generic issues of planning, classroom management, and assessment. In these course, students get little, if any, mathematics-specific pedagogy.

Still, these descriptions do little to illuminate the specifics of what mathematics or mathematics pedagogy teacher education students actually have opportunities to learn. In their field settings, their experience varies as well. Most teach math as part of their field work, and as part of student teaching, but most practice relatively traditional approaches to mathematics. Some are placed with teachers who are themselves involved with reforming their mathematics teaching, and some have field supervisors whose area of concentration is mathematics education. In such cases, prospective teachers have opportunities to explore and develop alternative approaches to the teaching and learning of mathematics. But more often, the teaching of reading and writing is focal, and prospective teachers' opportunities to develop their mathematics understandings and pedagogy are limited.

According to Darling-Hammond, 'loose linkages' often exist between the three components of the teacher education program – liberal arts, professional study, and practical experience.[43] Consequently, connections among subject matter content, theory, and practice are relatively less orchestrated. Just as the content of any of the components varies across programs, so too does the integration: that is, what the experiences and emphases of the elements of the program add up to. Judge and his colleagues, contemplating the 'non-system' of U.S. teacher education, comment that the 'apparent chaos' and lack of order evident to the European observer may be seen by another as 'the reflection of a reality which, by its very nature, is always complex, diverse and polymorphic,'[44] given the enormous and uncentralised system of American public schooling.

4.5 What issues are common in preparing teachers to teach mathematics in France and the United States? What issues are unique to one country or the other?

In this concluding section, we look back on our examination of French and U.S. teacher preparation, and consider challenges faced in the preparation of elementary and secondary teachers in each country. How differently does the enterprise play out in France or the United States? What seem to be common challenges?

Teacher educators who seek to prepare teachers to teach mathematics face tough questions about how to make significant changes; and on so many fronts. Teacher educators in both settings seek to:
- help prospective elementary teachers become familiar with the methods, reasoning and structures of mathematics and help them deepen their understandings and skills of mathematics and the place of math in the school curriculum;

- challenge all prospective teachers' (elementary and secondary) approach to mathematics and their views of how mathematics is taught and learned;
- help them to learn about children's and adolescent's mathematical thinking, and how to teach mathematics while taking into account the pupils' level; constructing learning situations which give meaning to mathematical subjects;
- coach them in developing their capacity to learn, thinking about their actions and transforming it, becoming able to change, thinking about what they wanted to do and what they actually did, thinking about their practice, doing self-observation and self-analysis, and becoming able to search for and use resources.

Most teacher educators in both countries would agree with some form of these principles. The difficult challenges arise in finding out *how* to do this, especially in the limited time and space of preservice teacher education. Preservice mathematics teacher education has simultaneously to help preservice teachers develop knowledge, know-how, methods, attitudes and habits. Teacher education must recognise teacher education students as learners, and realise that they, too, need time to reconstruct their ideas, and to construct new ones. While they may feel pressed by the shortage of time, they confront the limits of what teacher-learners can 'take in' all at once. Much of the learning entailed demands reconsideration, re-examination, and reconstruction. It cannot be speeded up. Still, worries can propel teacher educators to work much as classroom teachers do when they feel they have things to cover, trying to get through as much material as possible. Wrestling with constructivist ideas about learning is not easy for teacher educators, eager to transform their students.

The U.S. structure, which most often conducts professional studies alongside the university, must negotiate both elementary and secondary teacher education with the academic departments, something the French with their consecutive approach do not. French teacher educators control the two years of professional studies, and as we have shown, can therefore have exclusive control over the distribution of the sequence and extent of the curriculum.

A second major challenge faced by both French and U.S. teacher educators is to enhance and increase prospective teachers' pedagogical understandings of mathematics. In both countries, the problems of elementary and secondary teacher education are different.

Elementary teachers come with little post secondary study of mathematics, and yet must prepare to teach it. Neither the French nor the U.S. programmes are organised to offer a major section of mathematical study to prospective elementary teachers. In both cases, only approximately 100 or 140 hours are available to help teacher-students develop their own mathematical understandings of new content, to revise and deepen their understandings of familiar content, and to learn about children's mathematics and about ways to help children learn mathematics. A tall order. The French example illustrates a use of the 140 hours that 'covers' much ground. U.S. teacher educators vary – some do much less and do it with more depth, sacrificing breadth for depth. The consequence of this is to leave untouched much that is crucial for teachers to understand. Many U.S. teacher educators try to cover a wide range of mathematical and pedagogical topics, moving along at a greater rate of speed, taking more risks with what their students are able to learn. In either case, however, preservice elementary teacher education is poorly structured to address prospective teachers' needs in preparing to teach mathematics. Worth further inquiry is the comparative development of French and U.S. elementary teachers over time, in their practice, and as a function of continuing opportunities for learning in and outside of their own practice.

The case of secondary teachers' subject knowledge is different. In both countries, teacher candidates come having studied mathematics intensively at the university level. The French organize teacher education to provide ongoing opportunities for teacher trainees to deepen their study of mathematics intertwined with their developing understandings of practice. For U.S. teacher candidates, rarely are there such opportunities. The subject specialism is usually pursued separately from the educational studies, and although they are more or less concurrent, the two strands are often not interconnected.

A third crucial issue is how to prepare beginning teachers who can teach in ways with which they have had little experience, and that is not widely practiced in schools. This is currently a great challenge for U.S. teacher educators, who themselves lack knowledge and experience with the kind of teaching advocated by reformers. Faced with a strong demand to aim for deeper and more complex learning for children, teachers must develop new ways of teaching for which there are few available models. With little time to spare, and a great deal of content to cover, the challenge for teacher education is enormous. The risks are that, with so little time, teacher education can manage to convince teacher education students that the 'old' ways of teaching did not consistently help all children learn worthwhile things, but may fail to equip them with what they need to develop effective ways of learning to develop their teaching.

A fourth crucial issue is connections – among the components of the teacher education programme, and across institutions. What can best be learned through coursework, and what in schools? How can the two be related conceptually? In France, the relatively structured setting for teacher education makes possible a degree of coordination that is often elusive in the U.S. The professional project required of all teacher candidate is one illustration of this. While U.S. teacher educators, too, design and carry out projects like this, the obstacles are greater simply because 'programmes' are often merely courses and field experiences, unbound.

In France, teacher education students' science or liberal arts studies are completed before they enter the teacher education programme. The IUFM are not part of the universities, nor are they part of schools. In this divided system, energy is not absorbed to collaborate across contexts. Still, efforts to link pedagogy, didactics and content are evident within courses (e.g. the links between didactics and content within the mathematics courses, and the professional practice project report).

In the U.S., although the programmes exist much more wholly within universities and colleges, the traditional separation of education professors from other faculty creates intra-institutional divides. With the teacher education programme spread over three contexts, and yet occurring concurrently, the challenges to support connections in the U.S. are considerable. The current professional development school movement is but one new example of continued efforts to shift the settings of teacher education, and to forge tighter bonds across the settings. Beyond structures and intention, whether prospective teachers can taken the different experiences they encounter in their professional preparation and begin to teach mathematics thoughtfully to all their students is a question about which we know far too little.

Cross-national comparisons of teacher preparation in mathematics can help to illuminate common problems, and to identify issues specific to features of the cultural and social contexts of particular countries. Worth considerably more investigation and research would be comparative examination of the learning of French and U.S. elementary and secondary teachers over time. How do the differences in their initial preparation affect the results of training? What opportunities for continued preparation to teach do teachers in each country have? What other factors affect the development of mathematics teachers?

ENDNOTES

1. See Johsua et Dupin (1993) *'Introduction à la Didactique des Sciences et des Mathématiques'*
2. See Romberg. (1992) 'The New Math: Was It Really a Failure?'
3. See, for example, Sarason, *The Culture of the School and the Problem of Change (1982).*
4. See Brousseau 1994) 'Perspectives pour la didactique des mathématiques', in *Vingt Ans de Didactique des Mathématiques en France.*
5. A science of the conditions of the spread and teaching of mathematical knowledge useful for human institutions.
6. See Chevallard (1985) *La Transposition Didactique, Du Savoir Savant au Savoir Enseigné.*
7. See Vergnaud (1990): 'La Théorie des Champs Conceptuels', *Recherches en Didactique des Mathématiques*, vol.10-2/3.

8. See Brousseau (1986) 'Fondements et Méthodes de la Didactique des Mathématiques' *Recherches en Didactique des Mathématiques*, vol.7-2.
9. Information exchange from one institution to the other implies modifications (called didactical transpositions): each institution hands over part of the design and control tasks by using algorithms or materials designed somewhere else, transmitted and then memorised. This induces various relations to knowledge and ultimately various 'cultures.' The legitimacy of any teaching institution derives in part from its promise to represent faithfully the knowledge that it claims to teach.
10. The pupils' scientific knowledge, even in mathematics, is not final and cannot be so. The knowledge acquired at the beginning of their learning process is necessarily incomplete and is correct only within a limited area and according to limited conditions. Each acquisition of knowledge is the result of a different learning process for pupils as well as for all people. Therefore it cannot be duplicated by simply designing and implementing a standard approach to the presentation and inculcation of knowledge.
11. Theoretical models for the study of teaching situations: Whether you want to understand the difficulty to teach a notion or to invent learning ways, you will have to go through a theoretical reformulation which will make it possible to reorganise - around the content - all the other aspects according to your own point of view (social, psycho-cognitive, relational and language-related aspects).
12. See SIGMA EUROPEAN UNIVERSITIES' NETWORK, 1995, Actes de la Conférence Européenne La Formation des Enseignants en Europe, Universität Osnabrück.
13. According to Keitel, 1992, Mathematician or pedagogue? On the education of teachers in Germany, *The curriculum Journal*, Vol.3 N° 3.
14. Keitel, ibid.
15. See the Circular N° 9/92 and 35/92 from Ministry of Education.
16. Bell, Küchemann and Costello (1983) *A Review of Research in Mathematical Education: Research on Teaching and Learning.* Bishop and Nickson (1983), *A Review of Research in Mathematical Education: Research on the Social Context of Mathematics Education.* Howson (1983) *Curriculum Development and Curriculum Research.*
17. Grouws (1992) *Handbook of Research on Mathematics Teaching and Learning.*
18. According to the Circular N° 9/92 and 35/92 from Ministry of Education.
19. Ruthven (1994) The school-based training of secondary maths teachers: a Cambridge perspective, *Teaching maths and its applications*, vol. 13, N° 3.
20. Comiti (1992) New trends in French Teacher Education, in *Proceedings of the Working Group Preservice and Inservice Teacher Education*, ICME 7, Québec, Dossey J. A. (ed.).

21. Source: Rapport Bancel, (1989) *Créer une nouvelle dynamique de la formation des maîtres*, Ministère de l'éducation nationale.

22. The term *institut* may not present difficulties for an English observer. But *universitaire* cannot be translated as there is simply no English adjective derived from the word university. Something is either a university or it is not; it cannot be universitarian or universityish. *Formation* cannot be adequately translated as training, while *maître* defies exegesis. H. Judge and al. 1994 (p. 89)

23. Judge & al., *The University and the Teachers: France, the United States, and England. Oxford Studies in Comparative Education*, (Vol. 4(\f(1,2)).

24. Source: National Council of Teachers of Mathematics. *Curriculum and Evaluation Standards for School Mathematics* (1989); *Professional Standards for Teaching Mathematics* (1991); *Assessment Standards for School Mathematics* (1995). (Reston, VA.).

25. See Ball 'Teacher Learning and the Mathematics Reforms: What Do We Think We Know and What Do We Need to Learn?' *Phi Delta Kappan*. (forthcoming).

26. Judge, et al., ibid.

27. See Conant, (1963) *The Education of American Teachers*.; Koerner, *The Miseducation of American Teachers*.; G. Clifford & J. Guthrie, (1988) *Ed School*.

28. See, for example, on U.S. elementary and secondary teachers: Ball. *Knowledge and Reasoning in Mathematical Pedagogy: Examining What Prospective Teachers Bring to Teacher Education*. Unpublished doctoral dissertation.

29. Source: National Center for Education Statistics. *America's Teachers: Profile of a Profession*. (NCES 93-025) (Washington, D.C.: 1993).

30. Source: National Center for Education Statistics. *America's Teachers: Profile of a Profession*. (NCES 93-025) (Washington, D.C.: 1993).

31. See Lanier and Little, (1986) 'Research on Teacher Education.' In M. Wittrock, (Ed.), *Handbook of Research on Teaching*. Darling-Hammond & Cobb (1995) 'The Changing Context of Teacher Education.' In F. Murray (Ed.), *The Teacher Educator's Handbook*.

32. See Feiman-Nemser & Remillard. (1995) 'Perspectives on Learning to Teach.' In F. Murray (Ed.), *The Teacher Educator's Handbook*.

33. Lanier & Little, ibid., p. 529.

34. Source: Plan de Formation, Projet d'Etablissement 1995-1999, IUFM de l'Académie de Grenoble, *La Passion d'Apprendre*

35. See Comiti & Nadot, (1994) 'Identification et analyse des effets du mémoire professionnel dans la formation des enseignants du second degré', *Recherche et Développement Professionnel* n°17.

36. See Comiti, (1995) 'Rôle du mémoire professionnel dans la formation des enseignants en France', in *Didactique des Disciplines Scientifiques et Formation des Enseignants*

37. As the content of these modules varies among the IUFM, the examples given here are taken from the program at the Grenoble IUFM.
38. See Darling-Hammond (1995) 'The Changing Context of Teacher Education.' In F. Murray (Ed.), *The Teacher Educator's Handbook.*
39. Feiman-Nemser., (1990) 'Teacher Preparation: Structural and Conceptual Alternatives.' In W. R. Houston (Ed.), *Handbook for Research on Teacher Education.*
40. Feiman-Nemser, ibid., p. 220.
41. Darling-Hammond, ibid., pp. 36 - 37.
42. L. Darling-Hammond, ibid., p. 36.
43. Darling-Hammond, ibid., p. 37.
44. Judge, Lemosse, Paine, & Sedlak, ibid., p. 125.

REFERENCES

Ball, D.L., 'Teacher Learning and the Mathematics Reforms: What Do We Think We Know and What Do We Need to Learn?' *Phi Delta Kappan.* (forthcoming)
Ball, D.L., 1990, 'Prospective elementary and secondary teachers' understandings of division'. *Journal for Research in Mathematics Education,* 21,132-144
Ball, D.L., 1990, 'The mathematical understandings that prospective teachers bring to teacher education'. *Elementary School Journal,* 90, 449-466
Bell, A., Küchemann, D., Costello, J., 1983, *A Review of Research in Mathematical Education: Research on Teaching and Learning,* Windsor, NFER-Nelson
Bishop A., Nickson, M., 1983, *A Review of Research in Mathematical Education: Research on the Social Context of Mathematics Education.* Windsor: NFER-Nelson
Brousseau, G., 1986, 'Fondements et Méthodes de la Didactique des Mathématiques', *Recherches en Didactique des Mathématiques,* 72, Grenoble, La Pensée Sauvage, 33-115
Brousseau, G., 1994, 'Perspectives pour la Didactique des Mathématiques', in Artigue, M. et al.(eds.)*Vingt Ans de Didactique des Mathématiques en France,* Grenoble, La Pensée Sauvage, 51-66
Chevallard, Y., 1985, *La Transposition Didactique, Du Savoir Savant au Savoir Enseigné,* 2° édition, Grenoble, La Pensée Sauvage
Clifford, G., Guthrie, M., 1988, *Ed School.* Chicago, University of chicago Press
Comiti, C., 1992, 'New trends in French Teacher Education', in Dossey, J.A. (ed.)*Proceedings of the ICME 7 Working Group: Preservice and Inservice Teacher Education,* Illinois State University
Comiti, C., Nadot, S., 1994, 'Identification et analyse des effets du mémoire professionnel dans la formation des enseignants du second degré', *Recherche et Développement Professionnel* n°17, Paris, INRP, 116-122.
Comiti, C., 1995, 'Rôle du Mémoire Professionnel dans la Formation des Enseignants en France' in Comiti, C., Ngo, A.T. (eds.) *Didactique des Disciplines Scientifiques et Formation des Enseignants,* Actes du Premier Colloque Régional des Pays Francophones du Sud-Est Asiatique, Grenoble, IUFM de Grenoble et Hanoï, Maison d'Édition de l'Éducation, 98-104
Conant, J., 1963, *The Education of American Teachers.* New York, McGraw Hill
Darling-Hammond, L., Cobb, V., 1995, 'The Changing Context of Teacher Education.' In F. Murray (ed.), *The Teacher Educator's Handbook,* San Francisco, Jossey-Bass, 14-62

Feiman-Nemser, S., Remillard, J., 1995, 'Perspectives on Learning to Teach' In F. Murray (ed.), *The Teacher Educator's Handbook,* San Francisco, Jossey-Bass, 63-91

Feiman-Nemser, S., 1990, 'Teacher Preparation: Structural and Conceptual Alternatives.' In Houston, W. R. (ed.), *Handbook for Research on Teacher Education,* New York, McGraw Hill, 212-233

Grouws, D. (ed), 1992, *Handbook of Research on Mathematics Teaching and Learning.* New York, Macmillan

Howson, G., 1983, *Curriculum Development and Curriculum Research.* Windsor, NFER-Nelson

Johsua, S., Dupin, J.J., 1993, *Introduction à la Didactique des Sciences et des Mathématiques,* Paris, P.U.F.

Judge, H., M. Lemosse, L. Paine, Sedlak, M., 1994, *The University and the Teachers: France, the United States, and England.* Oxford Studies in Comparative Education, (Vol. 4.) Oxfordshire

Keitel, C., 1992, 'Mathematician or Pedagogue? On the education of teachers in Germany', *The Curriculum Journal,* 3, 3, 290-309

Koerner, J., 1988, *The Miseducation of American Teachers.* Boston, Houghton Mifflin

Lanier, J., Little, J. W., 1986, 'Research on Teacher Education.' In Wittrock, M., (ed.), *Handbook of Research on Teaching,* New York, McGraw Hill, 527-569

Romberg, T., 1992, 'The New Math: Was It Really a Failure?' in: *UME Trends,* 2, 6, 1,3.

Ruthven, K., 1994, 'The School-based Training of Secondary Mathematics Teachers: a Cambridge Perspective', *Teaching mathematics and its applications,* 13, 3, 116-119

Sarason, S., 1982, *The Culture of the School and the Problem of Change.* 2nd edition, Boston, Allyn and Bacon

Vergnaud, G., 1990, 'La Théorie des Champs Conceptuels' *Recherches en Didactique des Mathématiques,* 10, 2-3, Grenoble, La Pensée Sauvage, 133-170.

OTHER SOURCES

Ministry of Education (eds), 1992, *Circular n. 9/92; Circular n.35/92,* London

IUFM de l'Académie de Grenoble, Plan de Formation, Projet d'Etablissement 1995-1999, *La Passion d'Apprendre*

National Center for Education Statistics, 1993, *America's Teachers: Profile of a Profession.,* NCES 93-025, Washington, D.C.

National Council of Teachers of Mathematics (eds.), 1989, *Curriculum and Evaluation Standards for School Mathematics;* 1991, *Professional Standards for Teaching Mathematics;* 1995, *Assessment Standards for School Mathematics,* Reston, VA.

Rapport Bancel, 1989, *Créer une Nouvelle Dynamique de la Formation des Maîtres,* Paris, Ministère de l'éducation nationale

SIGMA European Universities' Networks, (eds.), 1995, *Conférence Européenne 'La Formation des Enseignants en Europe',* Osnabrück, Universität Osnabrück

Chapter 31: Inservice Mathematics Teacher Education: The Importance of Listening

THOMAS J. COONEY AND KONRAD KRAINER

University of Georgia, Athens, U.S.A. and University of Klagenfurt/IFF, Klagenfurt, Austria

ABSTRACT

This chapter addresses issues related to practice and research in inservice teacher education programs. Some issues are addressed through the eyes of Maria, an experienced teacher, who participates in an inservice program and who struggles to improve her teaching of mathematics. Considered are Maria's personal goals for teaching, her expectations for inservice programs, and her perceptions about self as a teacher researcher as she strives to understand the research literature. The chapter draws upon literature related to both practice and research in teacher education, expectations for inservice programs, and conceptualizing inservice as a context for integrating theory and practice. Fundamental to the chapter is the importance of listening for the creation and conduct of inservice programs.

1. MEETING MARIA THE TEACHER

It was a rainy Saturday afternoon as Maria was preparing for Monday's lesson on stochastics for her class of 15 year olds. She was frustrated as she was feeling uncomfortable with the materials she had developed; she couldn't find the 'right' activity. Her desk was covered with textbooks, copies of journals, previous lesson plans, and materials about stochastics from her last inservice course. Her feeling of insecurity was not new. She had felt this way before when teaching a subject in which her background knowledge was, in her mind, shaky. Her last inservice course, which happened to be on stochastics, was not a satisfying experience. The instructor communicated more with the chalkboard and himself than with the teachers. Many problems were presented that were over the heads of the teachers. He did communicate a certain love of stochastics, something that was contagious and sparked Maria's interest in the subject. Still, she felt ill prepared in designing activities for her students and that inservice course wasn't helping any. 'I could give a good lecture on stochastics,' thought Maria. But she had been down that road before and it was not a pleasant one.

A.J. Bishop et al. (eds.), International Handbook of Mathematics Education, 1155 - 1185
© 1996 Kluwer Academic Publishers, Printed in the Netherlands

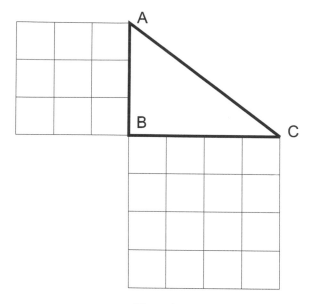

Figure 1.

Her mind drifted back to her beginning days of being a mathematics teacher. She recalled vividly an activity she had used when teaching a lesson on the Pythagorean Theorem to a class of 13 year olds. She had provided students with small tiles and right triangles on which they were to create squares on the legs and then rearrange the tiles to form a square on the hypotenuse. Following these activities she had the students develop a statement of the Pythagorean Theorem. She then followed this statement by asking, 'What does this say about the following triangle?'

The students dutifully responded that $a^2 + b^2 = c^2$. She suspected that they knew this relationship before the activity. This was a lesson she had learned from her former days as a preservice teacher. She felt comfortable with it.

She recalled anticipating either the correct response or 'I'm not sure.' She was not prepared for Paul's response, 'The theorem won't work for that triangle.' Subsequent questions revealed that Paul was confused in two ways. First, he didn't consider the angle to be a right angle since it wasn't pointing to the right and hence the theorem didn't apply. Second, Paul thought the theorem only worked when the 'c' side was opposite the right angle.

That episode was etched in Maria's mind forever. It so clearly demonstrated to her how students unexpectedly generalize from the examples used and how they latch onto the symbolism of mathematics without developing an underlying understanding of what those symbols mean. She felt fortunate that

Paul had responded as he did and that she had listened to him enough to pose additional questions. It was a defining moment in her teaching career.

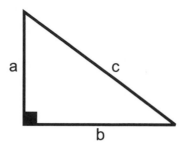

Figure 2.

On this particular day, she had posed an additional question – one she had never asked before, 'And what does this say about the following triangle?'

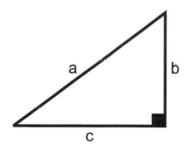

Figure 3.

Yes, she knew that a lecture on stochastics would not be productive with her 15 year olds who tended to be unusually immature. But what activities would likely engage her students in a productive way? Again, Maria remembered her last inservice course and its emphasis on learning vocabulary. She didn't see the connections that she was sure the instructor wanted the teachers to make. It was not the kind of shining example of mathematical education that she had been reading about in her journals. She queried, 'Do my students have the same feeling with regard to my lessons? Do they see my lessons as exercises in memorizing definitions and theorems?' She hoped not. But, to be truthful, she wasn't sure.

Later that evening when the children were in bed, she took out the application form for another inservice course. She had received a letter from the course organizer who had probably received Maria's name because of her participation in previous inservice courses. One of the guiding principles of the course was on teachers reflecting on their teaching and the professional communication that the director hoped to create among the teachers. Although cautious, this sounded interesting to Maria. She wondered if other teachers had their 'Pauls' and how they might have reacted to her Paul. Her oldest son, now a middle schooler, needed the kind of teaching she wanted to provide. He was bright and inquisitive. Having three children had certainly provided Maria with a different orientation toward teaching as she recognized the need for students to think for themselves. She could not turn away from the challenge of improving her teaching of mathematics. At the bottom of the application form she wrote a note to the organizer: 'I am looking forward to the course and to exploring ways of improving my teaching.' Maria only hoped that what she wrote was truthful when the time came to attend that first session.

2.   THE NATURE OF INSERVICE PROGRAMS

The education of teachers occurs in many contexts depending on the needs of society, schools and teachers. Nebres (1988) identified two problems in mathematics education which he termed micro problems and macro problems that are related to teacher education. To Nebres (1988) micro problems are those internal to mathematics education which involve curricula or teacher training. In contrast, macro problems are those emanating from society itself, e.g., the economy, politics, culture, or language. Nebres argues that the most pressing problems in developing countries are macro in nature. For example, Nebres (1988) notes that in Mexico only 60 per cent of children in the first grade continue their education beyond the first year and only 3 per cent eventually complete their secondary education. In contrast, 95 per cent of the Japanese children are in school until the age of 18. Yet, the curricula of these two countries are remarkably similar. To further illustrate diversity across countries, Howson (1994) observed that class size varies dramatically from country to country with some countries averaging more than 100 students per class while others average about 22 per class. Too, the amount of resources spent on education varies even more dramatically with a magnitude of 300:1 for some western countries compared to some developing countries (Howson, 1994). In light of these diverse circumstances, it is not surprising that teacher education assumes many forms.

One could argue that inservice programs are necessarily micro in orientation in that every teacher deals with the constraints unique to his/her situation. The severity of those constraints may be extensive, of course, depending on the context in which schooling occurs. We will concentrate here on the more micro problems in teacher education rather than address issues related to the larger contexts in which teacher education occurs. In doing so, we are mindful of the fact that these more global concerns significantly affect the means and substance of inservice education. But it is also the case that teachers are concerned about improving their 'local' conditions and hence are more likely to be interested in addressing issues perceived relevant to their particular situation. Such is the case with Maria who teaches in a relatively isolated school but one marked by stability in both the student population and among the staff and which has reasonable resources for her disposal.

2.1 The Practice of Inservice Education

Given the various contexts for teacher education and the fact that no single overarching theoretical orientation drives teacher education, it seems safe to conclude that no single approach to either preservice or inservice teacher education is on the horizon. Kilpatrick (1982) provided the following analysis over a decade ago:

> If many of the preservice programs are reminiscent of medical school training – with their emphasis on an internship experience and their conscious building-up of group cohesiveness and loyalty – then the in-service programs seem more like medical training clinics in developing countries, where native practitioners are brought in for intensive instruction in new techniques and sent back home to spread the good word. (p. 87)

Although the field of mathematics education is a more sophisticated field now than 15 years ago, Kilpatrick's analysis has merit even today.

One factor related to this apparent eclecticism is the question of who should assume primary responsibility for teacher education. In England and Wales, for example, there is a question of whether teacher education should be housed in schools or in universities. In varying degrees, this question persists in North America as well. In contrast, France tends to house teacher education at the university level involving both mathematics educators and mathematicians in the process. In 1990 the French initiated three Instituts Universitaires de Formation des Maitres (I.U.F.M.) at Grenoble, Lille, and Reims for the training of teachers.

Various elements of constructivism pervade many teacher education programs in North America, United Kingdom, parts of Western Europe, Australia, and many other countries as well. Consequently, teacher education programs are becoming less technically oriented and more process or constructivist oriented with an emphasis on reflection and self analysis. Brown, Cooney, and Jones (1990) note how the so-called 'competency' based movement in the United States during the 1970's has given way to a more constructivist orientation in the late 1980's. Perhaps as part of this shift, teacher education programs began to pay attention to what teachers believe about mathematics and teaching mathematics and how those beliefs could be addressed in a teacher education context. (See Brown, Cooney, & Jones, 1990; Thompson, 1992.) Similarly, the state of teacher education centers in Spain has shifted from a 'technical rationality model' to one marked by a more reflective/rational approach (Blanco, 1994).

A prominent factor that affects educational systems in developing countries is their colonial histories. Gerdes (1985, 1988) noted that nations with a colonial history have had to alter their educational system when the inherited system is based on an elitist approach reflecting the western-European cultures of the 19th century. While the inherited system may have been appropriate for colonial capitalism, it is inappropriate for a developing country which is trying to educate the masses and to embed mathematics education in the specific cultural contexts of that country. In these situations macro problems shape mathematics education in general and teacher education in particular.

In the United States it makes little sense to talk about teacher education in absence of the standards on curriculum, teaching, and assessment developed by the National Council of Teachers of Mathematics (NCTM). (See NCTM, 1989; 1991; 1995). These standards suggest a more process-oriented approach to teaching and teacher education in which problem solving, communication, and reasoning are emphasized. Reform movements in other countries include standards being developed in The Netherlands and various efforts in England to introduce constructivism in teaching and teacher education. While the reform movements vary in intensity, scope, and intent, they generally share the common theme that mathematics is a humanistic endeavour with an emphasis on the processes of doing mathematics.

Unfortunately, a considerable gulf exists between preservice and inservice education. Even more damaging is the situation where schools perpetuate a climate contrary to reform thus dissipating or eliminating whatever dispositions a beginning teacher might have toward reform. Even in schools where reform is encouraged, teacher isolation represents a formidable obstacle to reform. In some countries or school districts, beginning teachers are paired with mentor teachers who can help break down this isolation. The notion of 'co-reform' provides one kind of linkage between university preservice programs and schools (Frasier, 1993). The concept entails creating contexts in which preservice and inservice teachers work together to enhance the professional lives of each and to enrich students' learning of mathematics. Co-reform could emphasize many different themes, e.g., infusing technology into the teaching of mathematics. Krainer (1994a) describes a program in which teachers share various classroom problems as they engage in group problem solving focused on teaching situations. Such an approach helps overcome the isolation that many teachers feel in their professional lives.

A variety of perspectives on the public images of mathematics and mathematicians was presented at the 1992 International Congress of Mathematical

Education. These images have relevance for teacher education. For example, university mathematicians tend to communicate a formalistic view of mathematics (Mura, 1992) which may carry with it a more formalistic approach to teaching. Lin, Huang, and Chu (1992) describe 'exam math' a condition in Taiwan where examinations dictate a limited view of mathematics. This circumstance may pervade many societies that emphasize high stake examinations. It seems reasonable to assume that high stake examinations would influence the nature of inservice programs as well given that teachers are expected to 'deliver' good test scores from their students. As perhaps a counterpoint to this formalistic orientation, a more intuitive approach is taken by the Math Trails project in Australia. (See Blane, 1992.) In this approach students are provided contexts for connecting mathematics to the real world. Teacher education is then a matter of helping teachers envision these connections and design materials for their students. Parental expectations also influence the role of the teacher in the classroom (Fujii, 1992). While there may not be a direct linkage to teacher education, it seems likely that inservice programs will reflect parental and societal expectations. Some inservice programs address explicitly the image parents have of mathematics. For example, Family Math (see De la Cruz & Thompson, 1992) is a program in which parents and children work together in cooperative settings to solve problems and engage in mathematical explorations.

The use of technology is an issue in most countries in terms of defining what role technology should play in the teaching of mathematics and how teachers should be educated for using technology. In western countries, technology is generally available and calculators, even graphing calculators, are prevalent. But the use of computer software for either algebra or geometry is still infrequent in most classrooms although there are increasing efforts of ministeries and educational institutions to promote their use. Some schools do not have the resources to purchase either computers or the software. Too, many teachers lack the expertise to use such technologies. In countries where technology is less apparent, inservice programs focus more on acquainting teachers about technology and its potential for both society and schools.

2.2   Research Related to Inservice Education

It seems fair to say that research in mathematics teacher education is sparse. This makes linkages between what we have learned about children's learning and about mathematics teaching tenuous. The Cognitively-Guided-Instruction (CGI) Project (Fennema & Franke, 1992) is one attempt to bridge the gap between what we know about young children's learning and the way teachers can use this knowledge to inform their own teaching. But similar projects, especially at the higher grades, are virtually nonexistent. What research on teachers or teacher education does exist is concentrated more at the elementary level and tends to focus on individual teachers and what they know or believe about mathematics rather than programs per se. For example, Wheeler and Feghali (1983) found that preservice elementary teachers have an inadequate concept of zero given that 75 per cent of them could not respond correctly to the question, 'What is 0 divided by 0?' Graeber, Tirosh, and Glover (1986) concluded that preservice elementary teachers have difficulty selecting an appropriate operation for solving arithmetic story problems. Fisher (1988) found that many teachers do not understand proportions and direct and inverse variations. At the secondary level there is a particular paucity of research on what teachers know about mathematics although there is research on what secondary teachers believe about mathematics. (See Thompson, 1992; Brown, Cooney, & Jones, 1990). Weiss, Boyd, and Hessling (1990) observed that inservice programs intending to teach teachers mathematics do indeed increase teachers' knowledge of mathematics. Yet, the relationship between teachers' knowledge of mathematics and their ability to effectively teach mathematics does not seem to be educationally significant (Eisenberg, 1977). Despite the fact that evidence has yet to emerge that suggests a strong relationship exists between a teacher's knowledge of mathematics and student achievement, few would argue that a teacher's knowledge of mathematics is irrelevant to the quality of mathematics students learn.

Inservice education is far more complex than simply increasing teachers' knowledge of mathematics. One aspect of this complexity is the consistency or lack thereof between the substance of what is taught and the medium by which it is taught. Often teachers gravitate toward the medium rather than the message. This suggests a need for emphasizing a reflective component of inservice programs in which teachers explicitly consider the implications of their own learning experiences for their teaching and for creating contexts in which pedagogy and content are intertwined in a reform minded way. In short, teachers need to learn mathematics as they are expected to teach it. The notions of teacher change and of teachers being reflective practitioners (Schön, 1983, 1987) is predicated on the assumption that the teacher is a rational, thinking being and not the 'object' of an inservice program. Brown and Borko's (1992) review of the literature on the processes of becoming a mathematics teacher focuses on this rationality. Their effort to understand teachers' acquisition of knowledge systems or schemata, and cognitive skills such as pedagogical problem solving and decision-making led them to conclude, 'To understand learning to teach, one must study how these systems – and the relationships among them – develop and change with experience, as well as identify the factors that influence this change process' (p. 211). It follows that research of this type necessitates an emphasis on understanding teachers' thought processes.

Fortunately, the number of studies about the teaching of mathematics and the enveloping complexity of issues has increased. For example, at the 1992 International Congress of Mathematical Education in Quebec there were a number of lectures, working groups, and topic groups that focused explicitly on teachers and their teaching. Hoyles (1992) analyzed lectures and working groups at PME conferences and observed, 'A quantitative increase in re- search incorporating the teacher as an integral and crucial facet of learning mathematics, and a series of qualitative shifts as to how the teacher and the teacher's role are conceptual' (p. 283). A similar trend has been observed by Krainer (1994b) at recent conferences in mathematics education among Ger- man speaking countries. The list of international publications tell a similar story including chapters in this volume.

In general, teacher education is moving toward a more process orientation in which teachers are encouraged to be reflective beings. Research methodol- ogies also reflect this change. For example, Schifter (1990) maintains that journal writing is an effective way of demonstrating teacher change. As Cooney (1994a) observed, research on teaching has moved from a reduction- ist orientation toward a constructivist one. The realization that teachers con- struct their realities much as students construct their realities suggests a quite different orientation toward teacher education than one marked by receiving. Accordingly, research has moved into an era of telling stories about teachers and their experiences as they struggle to make sense of their professional lives. This research is often grounded in anthropologically based methodolo- gies in which sense making is at the core of the investigation.

3.   MEETING MARIA THE STUDENT

It was a beautiful autumn morning as Maria drove along headed for the first day of a three day inservice course. She enjoyed being a student again, even more so as a teacher taking an inservice course. She recalled the agenda that had been mailed to her by Liz Crainey, the course organizer. She particularly recalled one of the sessions entitled 'The Importance of Listening.' Maria was interested in this topic despite the fact that her last inservice experience that supposedly had something to do with listening was rather boring. Nay, it was aggravating. The instructors had presented a video from their research which illustrated teachers' reactions to various students' statements. The in- tended purpose was to focus on students' mathematical thinking. Maria found it curious that the instructors failed to listen to her and the other teachers' Paul-like stories which surely involved students' thinking about mathematics. After short presentations by various groups of teachers, the staff members gave their explanation to the situations, according to their theory. To Maria, it smacked of the instructors telling the teachers the 'right' answers. Though the topic was to emphasize listening to students, listening to the participants didn't seem to play an important role to the course instructors.

Maria was looking forward to the day despite the fact that she had reserva- tions when she registered for the program. She questioned whether she had the time or the energy to participate in a three day program. Maria considered herself a humble person but nevertheless relished the fact that students, administrators, and parents heaped considerable praise on her teaching. Parents held her in high esteem, students considered her demanding yet fair, and her principal often pointed her out as a model teacher. 'So why am I taking this course?' she asked herself as she drove along. She allowed her students to use calculators when solving word problems but the articles she had read were emphasizing a far more sophisticated use of calculators such as using graphing calculators to investigate various properties of functions and to model real world phenomena. Indeed, part of this inservice program was to focus on learning how to use the graphing calculator. In a way, she was thankful that her principal said budget cutbacks precluded purchasing such calculators. After all, if she didn't have them, she couldn't be expected to use them. Still she was concerned that her teaching didn't take advantage of recent advances in technology.

Suddenly, she got lucky as a car was pulling out of a parking space close to the building where the first meeting was to be held. She breathed a temporary sigh of relief. As Maria parked her car and trotted off to the meeting place, she continued her self-debate on why she had decided to take another inservice course. Maybe it had something to do with her insecurity in using technology. She wasn't sure. When she finally found the room, she encountered Liz Crainey, the course instructor. She was gracious in welcoming Maria. Maria was flattered and surprised that Dr. Crainey knew who she was. She found an empty chair which wasn't so easy as about 25 other teachers had already arrived. Her trepidations increased. Some were playing with those graphing calculators. Others seemed to be sharing ideas about teaching. She noted that Dr. Crainey was conversing with some of them in a friendly way. Obviously she knew these teachers from other contexts. This did not quiet Maria's fears. She felt isolated. In part she wanted to leave and in part she felt a responsibility to stay. She decided to stay for at least the first day, perhaps slither away early, and then decide whether or not to return for the remaining sessions.

'What do you teach?' The question, asked by the teacher next to her, shocked Maria out of her semi-state of withdrawal. 'Oh, I teach in a small rural school. This year I am teaching grade 8 and 10 mathematics. What about you?' Andrea formally introduced herself and indicated that she taught in a large urban school. This year she was teaching students in grades 9 and 10. 'I really don't know what to do sometimes. I hope this program gives me some good activities to use with my kids. I took another course two years ago. It wasn't very good. None of the ideas worked. I need answers!' It was a brief, but relaxing conversation for Maria. Although she hated to see a colleague experience difficulty, it was comforting to know that she wasn't the only one who didn't have answers for her problems in teaching. Maybe this course was going to work out after all.

On her way home that evening, Maria reflected on the first meeting. She felt lucky to have met Andrea and to learn that Andrea had her Pauls as well. Despite the fact that they taught in quite different circumstances, they shared many common beliefs about teaching. Both had ambivalent feelings about the program's first day. The graphing calculator session started with a lecture aimed at showing the advantages of using graphing calculators. But the talk was too theoretical and the few examples that were provided seemed far removed from the reality of the classroom. The lecture was followed by a discussion dominated by 'calculator fans' who seemed more intent on showing off than engaging in a discussion on when and how graphing calculators could be used. The group work after the discussion was better, however, as Andrea and Maria shared their experiences and concerns with the other teachers. Here, they obtained valuable insights from those who used graphing calculators. Maria realized how much she enjoyed talking with other teachers about professional matters. She guessed it was the student in her that made the discussions interesting.

As the rain settled in and Maria had to slow down, she further reflected on the program's first day and her own teaching. The first session helped her feel more secure – she reasoned that her ideas were as good as any others'. She also appreciated the fact that she had learned two or three interesting activities to use with her students. Yet, there was still that feeling of doubt about the program. Maybe it had something to do with the agenda. Dr. Crainey had advertised what the program was about and, indeed, the outline she provided at the beginning of the morning session seemed faithful to what was advertised. So why was she feeling that the program wasn't quite on target for what she needed? Maybe it was because she wanted to talk about that agenda. She felt a need to put her 'twist' on the agenda so that it would address issues of concern to her. She guessed that other teachers felt the same way. Surely Andrea did as they had talked briefly before they departed. Maria recalled reading about the dangers of teaching 'prefabricated mathematics' but this seemed like 'prefabricated didactics.' Maybe it was like that book she had read long ago about the consistency between the medium and the message. 'Why don't inservice programs teach us like they want us to teach our students? Why do inservice instructors so often start from what we don't know rather than from what we do know?' Maria asked herself. 'Ok. So what if I had to design the program. What would I do differently?' She wasn't sure but she speculated that the agenda would have something to do with the following questions.

- How can we enable students to become mathematical thinkers and problem solvers?
- What kinds of activities can help students see connections between mathematics and real life?
- How can I create better activities for my students without driving myself crazy trying to find resource materials?

Finally, Maria saw the signpost signifying her home town. It had been a hectic day but, in many ways, a rewarding one. If nothing else, her self esteem had been raised considerably. She began to realize just how complex her role as a teacher was and how many issues she had to address in the classroom — almost instantaneously. Maybe this is what those various authors she had read meant when they talked about professionalism in the teaching of mathematics.

4.   REFLECTING ON EXPECTATIONS FOR INSERVICE PROGRAMS

We can see much of Maria in the expectations and concerns many teachers express about inservice programs. Perhaps Maria could profit from learning more mathematics, e.g., stochastics, albeit her concern for teaching stochastics was focused more on finding the 'right' activities than on content per se. In a project involving one of the authors, teachers were interviewed about their reactions to an inservice program designed to increase their mathematical competence and to provide an array of activities for classroom use. In the main, teachers spoke fondly of the activities but remained essentially mute with respect to their increased mathematical competence. As Weiss, et al. (1990) observed, teachers' mathematical competence can be improved through inservice programs but the question remains whether teachers see such gain as a basis for improving their teaching. Suffice it to say that a teacher's orientation is largely practical, as is Maria's.

When teachers focus on collecting activities, they may fail to see themselves and their professional development in a broader context — one in which they see mathematics less as a matter of accumulating knowledge and more as a process of developing quantitative thinking. But such a shift in orientation is a scary one for teachers — especially teachers who come under the scrutiny of parents or administrators concerned about test scores and entrance examinations. Maria, as we see her now, tends to be 'activity' oriented, a not unreasonable position for a classroom teacher. Consequently, her propensity to be reflective is entangled in a web of polarities. For example, she tends to judge activities as good or bad rather than reflecting on the contexts which might account for students' reactions to the activities. Still, it would be a disservice to ask Maria to abandon her ways, ways that have been certified acceptable, even exceptional, by administrators, parents, and students alike. The challenge of working with teachers like Maria is to provide a means by which they can become self-evaluative and expansive in their thinking without denigrating what made them worthy professionals in the first place.

While it is generally the case that inservice education deals more explicitly with what Nebres (1988) calls micro problems, macro problems often shape the design of the programs. In western countries, inservice programs often focus on such issues as technology, assessment, and how mathematics can be related to the real world. Inservice education is predicated on the assumption that the educational system constitutes a relatively stable environment with reasonable resources. But where macro problems are extensive, inservice often focuses on more fundamental problems such as providing teachers with usable materials and helping them develop a reasonable mathematical background. Given the complexity of interactions between micro and macro problems and the fact that no overarching theory exists for teacher education (arguably there never will or should be), the direction for inservice programs is not universally clear. This raises the question of what we can expect from inservice programs.

4.1   Thesis 1: We expect too much from inservice programs.

Schools are often seen as the vehicle by which societal problems can be addressed if not resolved. While schools can do much to address many problems, they, like any institution, are limited in their ability to impact society as a whole. By implication, inservice education holds the key for educating teachers to address whatever concerns society deems important. As schools are asked to deal with more and more societal issues, the demands placed on teachers become greater and more complex. Consequently, the expected outcomes of inservice programs may become unrealistic. We forget that there is considerable slippage between the intent of an inservice program and the means by which teachers translate what they learn into their own, localized interpretations. From another perspective, we have a tendency to inflate our expectations when inservice is based on research which certifies that a particular teaching strategy or a particular curricular approach positively affects students' achievement or attitudes toward mathematics. The question remains, however, as to how the teacher translates that knowledge into teaching strategies for her students.

The ever increasing complexity of classroom teaching and the increasing demands placed on schools (e.g., see Posch, in press) make it necessary for teachers not only to have a command of the state of the art content-related and didactical principles but also to be adaptive regarding the ever changing conditions of schools and society. Teachers who express 'burn out' are sometimes alluding to the perceived expectations of change within classrooms regarding, e.g., new technologies and teaching methods and, at the same time, the demands placed on them by societal changes. Indeed, some teachers participate in inservice programs that are not directly related to mathematics education per se, e.g., training in group dynamics and communication, as they are expected to address concerns in the classroom beyond mathematical ones. We expect much from teachers! In light of the complexity of linking inservice programs to the betterment of society in general and the mathematics achievement of students in particular, we should be cautious in what we expect from our inservice programs.

4.2 Thesis 2: We expect too little from inservice programs.

Traditionally inservice programs in all fields rely on experts to share their expertise with the 'consumers' of the program. What makes education different is the considerable diversity of circumstances that influence either the delivery or the interpretation of the program. As opposed to more clearly defined disciplines, e.g., engineering or even medicine, the existing circumstances within education are all too often ignored. When contexts are provided for teachers to engage in professional dialogues about problems they deem important, inservice programs are generally well received. It is also important for teachers to have mathematical experiences similar in kind to what we would like their students to experience (Cooney, 1994b). This is not a trivial point for it argues that mathematics and pedagogy must be integrated if we expect reasonable translations into the classroom. Cooney, Brown, Dossey, Schrage, and Wittmann (1996) have developed curricular materials to address this integration between content and pedagogy. In a symposium on 'Inservice teacher training – an international comparison' a conference participant commended to one of the authors that it is increasingly necessary to practice a process-oriented approach in specific contexts in order to make it possible for teachers to experience new methods themselves and to develop similar activities for their students. It is this sort of orientation that seems best suited for improving the teaching of mathematics. To do otherwise, is to accept a very limited view of the potential of inservice programs to affect change.

Unfortunately, inservice programs often take a limited view. Zeichner and Gore (1990) maintain that most inservice programs fail to challenge teachers beliefs about what or how they should teach. As a consequence the inertia that teachers bring into their preservice education program continues and may deepen when they become inservice teachers. A sort of self fulfilling prophecy exists. When inservice programs fail to consider the circumstances and beliefs of teachers, they ensure that their effect will be essentially random, significantly diminishing any potential impact. Such an approach underestimates the potential of inservice programs to affect change and, in a sense, dishonors the potential teachers have for realizing reform.

5. THINKING OF INSERVICE AS A CRUCIBLE FOR THEORY AND PRACTICE

Inservice education places a twofold demand on mathematics educators. Firstly, it requires attention to the state-of-the-art developments in the field

1168

such as considering mathematics learning as a social, constructive process. Secondly, these developments must be seen as relevant to teachers' practical concerns for otherwise their rejection is virtually assured. The linkage of these two demands requires that barriers between theory and practice be dissolved if inservice is to provide a context for meaningful reform. For example, Wittmann (1991) emphasizes the need for teachers' self-reliant thinking and decision-making (which he integrated as a fundamental aspect of an inservice course) given the realization that didactical knowledge cannot be transmitted from researchers to teachers. Wittmann maintains that didactical knowledge must be reconstructed and made meaningful by teachers themselves. In contrast, Jaji, Nyagura, and Robson (1985), described a teacher education course in Zimbabwe in which a teacher educator was quoted as saying, 'Now what I am about to say is very important. It will almost certainly come up in the examinations, so I suggest that you write it down. (The group took out their pens...) In the new, modern approach to teaching... (They wrote it down as she spoke...) we no longer dictate notes to children. Instead we arrange resources in such a way as to enable children to discover things for themselves' (p. 153). As did Jaji, et al. (1985), one can only imagine that the impact of such an approach was counter to the instructor's intent as theory and practice had remained isolated.

Krainer (1994c) points out that most examples of successful cooperation between researchers and practitioners share at least three crucial characteristics:

1) A balance between the researcher's interest in research and the practitioner's interest in improving practice,
2) A constructive assessment of each other's work, and
3) An atmosphere in which research methods, modes of teaching, views on mathematics, and views on teacher education are explored in an open-minded way.

The interplay of all three characteristics creates a 'culture of cooperation' in which mutual respect is a crucial element. Too, it seems clear that the act of reflection (see Steffe and D'Ambrosio, 1995) is an integral part of this culture and is necessary for the integration of theory and research as the researcher develops an appreciation for the practice of teaching and the teacher develops a research orientation to her teaching.

But what of the multitude of demands placed on teachers? Bromme (1992) points out that teaching is primarily a matter of making 'situation-appropriate' decisions based on available knowledge rather than generating additional perspectives for solving newly presented problems. It seems clear, then, that the focus of teachers' work in the classroom primarily calls for a holistic and integrated view of knowledge rather than the existence of separate solutions to discrete problems. This perspective is supported by Berliner, et al. (1988) who found that expert teachers are able to process a greater array of information about students and classroom situations than are novice teachers and can therefore demonstrate a greater range of techniques for dealing with individual students. The conception of teachers' professional knowledge cannot be adequately described using the singular category of 'knowledge' for their knowledge is a product of many types of knowledge created in quite diverse settings and often rooted in 'local theories' (Brown and Cooney, 1991) specific to their classroom situation. As suggested by Fennema and Franke (1992) and Thompson (1992), the translation of teachers' mathematical knowledge into viable teaching strategies is mediated by the way that that knowledge is held. That is, one's philosophy of mathematics and of the teaching of mathematics influences how one's knowledge of mathematics per se gets translated into classroom activities. Shulman's (1986) notion of pedagogical content knowledge is, in part, a function of these translations.

Many preservice secondary teacher education programs place a heavy emphasis on mathematical knowledge. Yet, there is evidence (Owens, 1987) that this domain of knowledge may impede the development of a teacher's pedagogical content knowledge – the latter being the more relevant for teaching school mathematics. Wittmann's (1992) argument that the formalistic nature of mathematics carries the hidden message that formalism has a formalistic pedagogical counterpart has merit. From a formalistic perspective, the student is relegated to a passive role. Reliance on formalistic ways of teaching is often perpetuated by a lack of cooperation among academics, a situation that leads to a separation between content and pedagogy. Consequently, many teachers see teacher education as irrelevant to their professional development. Noddings (1992) proposes the interesting hypothesis that the pervasive lack of genuine cooperation between professors of education and academic mathematicians further weakens the professional status of mathematics teachers. Indeed, many teachers, especially secondary teachers, strive to model the characteristics of the university mathematicians they have had and learned to respect as academics. When one of the authors interviewed a number of preservice teachers regarding what they considered to be good teaching by the academic mathematicians, there was considerable convergence of their views: The mathematicians had clear lectures with reasonable pace and excellent examples. Never did they mention the less traditional modes of teaching – ones they often encountered during their courses on the teaching of mathematics.

Cooney (1994b) emphasized the need for teacher education programs to exhibit the following goals:
- Enable teachers to develop a knowledge of mathematics that permits the teaching of mathematics from a constructivist perspective;
- Offer occasions for teachers to reflect on their own experiences as learners of mathematics;

- Provide contexts in which teachers develop expertise in identifying and analyzing the constraints they face in teaching and how they can deal with those constraints;
- Furnish content in which teachers gain experience in assessing a student's understanding of mathematics;
- Afford opportunities for teachers to translate their knowledge of mathematics into viable teaching strategies. (p. 16)

Cooney's premise is that teacher education should be predicated on the notion of adaptation which has as a basic tenet the ability to recognize constraints as contextual and the knowledge to be flexible in dealing with those constraints. Such a perspective requires the integration of many types of knowledge rather than a compartmentalized notion of mathematics on the one hand and pedagogy on the other.

Another dichotomy that restricts the kind of integrated knowledge of which we speak is that between the orientations of researchers and teachers. Respective work conditions and agendas differ as one culture emphasizes reflecting, analyzing, and writing and the other culture emphasizes quickly perceiving and acting. In science communities we speak about 'publish or perish'; with regard to teaching we might use the slogan 'act or perish' (see Krainer 1994b, p. 221). Bishop (1992) provides the following analysis: 'Yet, in reality, it seems as if researchers are not talking directly to the other people who are key aspects of the educational system, but are increasingly talking to each other. Research journals are edited by researchers, with editorial boards of researchers, and they are increasingly read only by researchers. Books on research are expensive because the publishers know they only have a very limited market - only researchers buy them. Researchers are concentrating on communicating with other researchers and it is becoming increasingly difficult for anyone else to hear what is being said, let alone to understand it' (p. 719). The danger of this difference with respect to cooperation lies in possible one-sided distributions of interests, in forcing one culture on the other. The difference of cultures is less a counter-argument against cooperation and more a pro-argument for it because of the opportunities to learn from each other and to build a bridge between the two cultures of theory and practice. There is a certain symmetry, often unrecognized, between the goals of both the researcher and the teacher. The teacher is interested in student learning; the researcher is interested in teacher learning. Both, then, are interested in how humans construct knowledge. The principles of constructivism have no age limitations.

A basic issue is how one construes science and what it means to conduct research. If research is conceived as objective, the search for absolutes, then it seems likely the gulf between research and teacher will persist. While the researcher can afford to position him/herself as separated from the object being studied, the act of teaching requires just the opposite. On the other hand,

1171

if research is conducted from a humanistic perspective (Mitroff & Killmann, 1978), then the researcher necessarily strives to minimize the 'distance' between him/herself and the informant. This perspective is more consistent with the way teachers position themselves when working with students. It is from this perspective that common ground exists between the researcher and the practitioner as both are interested in the meanings people create. Although the methodology of the researcher is more structured and the questions asked more focused, both are involved in the process of communication and exploring the sense-making of others. Too, each is interested in telling stories. Recent thrusts in the research literature indicate that stories, often in the form of case studies, are becoming increasing important in communicating findings about research – witness the nature of research about teachers or teacher education presented at recent research conferences. Similarly, one doesn't have to talk with teachers very long before one encounters stories about classrooms and students.

Potentially productive organizing themes for inservice programs are those of 'particularizing' and 'generalizing'. Elbaz's (1983) study of Sarah can be thought of as searching for linkages between particularizing and generalizing as Elbaz tried to unpack the particular principles that guided Sarah's teaching and create 'practical knowledge' that had more theoretical overtones. Similarly, Cooney's (1985) story about Fred describes a particular teacher but it speaks more generally, in the sense of forming 'naturalistic generalizatons' (Stake, 1978), about many preservice teachers who encounter turmoil in their first year of teaching. Inservice programs need to find ways of honoring both the teachers' world of practicality and the researchers penchant for generality, the recognized sine qua non of scientific inquiry. It is this interplay between the particular and the general, seeing them as intertwining and not as polarities, that offers a crucible for theory and practice and a context for meaningful exchanges between researchers and teachers.

What we are calling for is a vision of the teacher as a researcher rather than as a recipient of research. The identification of a problem, recognizing the constraints in dealing with the problem, generating alternative ways of addressing the problem (some of which may originate from the research literature), implementing one or more of the alternatives, observing the impact of the implementation, and deciding which one(s) seem to work best and why are key elements of being a teacher researcher. In some sense, many teachers do this intuitively as they struggle with new or different ways of teaching. With respect to inservice programs, the contrast is between thinking of the teacher as a receiver of inservice versus thinking of the teacher as a co-designer of inservice.

Krainer (1994a) describes an example of a process-oriented inservice program, called 'Pedagogy and Subject-Specific Methodology for Teachers' (PFL), in which pedagogical and didactical aspects of teaching are interconnected. The program calls for three years of intensive theoretical and practical work. The activities of the team members are seen not only as a contribution to the further education of teachers but also as an experience in interdisciplinary cooperation.

The guiding principles of the PFL program include:
- Stressing the importance and interconnectedness of pedagogical and didactic aspects of teaching and learning,
- Identifying teachers' strengths rather than their weaknesses as building blocks for the program,
- Conducting action research which emphasizes the systematic reflection of practitioners,
- Promoting professional communication among teachers,
- Connecting individual and social learning experiences,
- Encouraging close cooperation between researchers and teachers, and
- Promoting a sense of self directed education and professional development among teachers that is self sustaining.

One of the more notable outcomes of the PFL program is the creation of a self-organized group of teachers who carry out joint projects, observe mathematics lessons in non-traditional schools, write booklets for other mathematics teachers, and organize inservice education courses for themselves and for other teachers. In a report about their work, one group of participating teachers provided the following explanations of their intentions: 'We want to express on the one hand our mutual interest in action research for which we have been inspired within the PFL course. On the other hand, we want to express our interest in actions, in activities in the field of teacher inservice education. Thereby we start from the assumption that teachers have, or can acquire, enough competence to realize teacher inservice education by themselves, that nobody knows as much about school and learning as they themselves, that nobody knows their needs as well as they themselves. And we are not only interested in our own further education but also in putting the idea of 'teachers train teachers' into practice...'

Internationally seen, there are many examples of groups of mathematics teachers who participate in organized groups in which they share their professional expertise. The German teacher group MUED (Storing Mathematics Teaching Units) has about 600 members and organizes regular regional and national meetings to discuss problems of their daily teaching. MUED is well-known for its collection of teaching units for all levels of mathematics instruction which can be ordered, modified and supplemented. The main focus is to emphasize problems from daily life and environmental situations aimed at empowering students to act and judge competently and autonomously in their future life. (See Keitel, 1989; 1992.) The MINERVA Project in Portugal generated a nationwide community of teachers, trainers, and researchers with varied backgrounds including technology that took as their task the 'formation of teacher teams and the assertion of a project culture in schools' (Ponte, 1994, p. 161).

One challenging aspect of inservice education is dealing with the phenomenon that the instructors may want to initiate active learning by the participants but the teachers remain in a receiving mode in which they see themselves as consumers who will take with them specific activities for specific situations. Von Harten and Steinbring (1991) expressed it this way, 'The best offers and materials for teachers would seem to be those which can be directly copied and handed out to pupils, that is materials which can 'bypass' the teacher' (p. 169). It is tempting to meet this demand in such a way that researchers confine themselves to presenting research results, with the argument that there are no general recipes and that it is the task of teachers to put theory into practice. These two attitudes strengthen each other and inhibit a closer cooperation within the course. There probably is no alternative but to oppose this consumer attitude, to make the seeming conflict of interests visible and discussible, and to initiate active learning processes. Kreith (1993), in describing a summer institute in the United States, explicitly addresses the 'consumer mentality' by informing teachers that the program is not about providing specific activities but rather about helping them design a program that enables students to connect mathematics to environmental issues. The evaluation of an Austrian teacher inservice education course suggests that making participants' consumer attitude problematic initially causes resistance but in the long run releases profound learning processes. One teacher writes: 'The disappointment at the first seminar... was very great for all of us.... for many of us the way the seminar was conducted was totally new and we had come with other expectations... however, it was this very disappointment which caused the change.' (Krainz-Dürr, 1990, p.16).

Teachers' systematic reflections on their own practice can not only improve their teaching but can also have consequences for discussing issues related to teacher education (see, e.g., Krainer & Posch, in press) as well as issues related to mathematics education more generally (see, e.g., Fischer & Malle (1985)). An important component of the reflective process is recording and analyzing experiences via the written word. But writing something intended for one's own consumption is quite different than writing something intended for public display and scrutiny. The latter is generally not part of a teachers' normal practice as it requires them to do at least three things that are different from their usual practice. They have to:
— gather data, analyze and reflect on the data, and take action,
— write down their findings (and not just communicate them orally), and
— formulate these results for other people (and not just practice something in their own classrooms).

That this is more difficult for teachers than for us who live in a 'culture of publishing' should be taken into consideration. However, the benefit derived

1174

from such activity includes the creation of knowledge that can positively influence their teaching. Further, the public sharing of ideas expressed in written form increases the opportunities for communication and cooperation among one's peers and with others who play different roles in the schooling process, e.g., teacher educators or administrators.

There is a subtle difference between thinking of teacher education as being based on research and thinking of teacher education as a research process. In the former, teacher education is informed by the research literature – interpreting, modifying, adapting, and adopting what is read in an intelligent way to address classroom problems. In the latter, the process of teacher education is formulated in a research paradigm acceptable to the participants. It is here that teachers and researchers are essentially on an equal footing, each an expert in his/her own particular domain. These two perspectives need not constitute polarities, however. In the latter case, the issue of what literature is considered relevant stems from the problem being addressed; in the former case the literature is determined a priori. Some medical schools and business schools use what is called the 'case study method' of teaching. In this approach the problem is identified and the search begins for a literature base that would help address the problem. Applied to education, the researcher is more of a resource person as the teacher helps describe the nature of the problem. What should be realized is that the teacher may not recognize the problem as seen by the researcher. Perhaps the researcher lacks familiarity with the classroom situation. But, on the other hand, the teacher may suffer from what Scheffler (1965) calls 'motivated blindness,' a form of denial that potentially masks real problems. This is a delicate situation for both the researcher and the teacher. The use of videotapes is sometimes helpful for both parties to appreciate each other's interpretation of the problem.

In thinking of teacher education as a research process, a very important component is that of a 'critical friend.' (See Altrichter, Posch, & Somekh, 1993.) A critical friend can be a researcher or a dedicated colleague who can help design an investigation or help collect and analyze data. Critical friends can encourage a teacher to record and analyze his/her experiences in such a way that they can be shared and discussed by others.

As mentioned earlier, the notion of co-reform (Frasier, 1993) is an emerging construct for reforming both teacher education and the teaching of mathematics in schools. It requires a certain harmony between teacher educators or researchers and teachers as they share a vision of reform deemed relevant to their own particular situation. The notion of co-reform embodies most of the principles previously described. One of the authors is involved in such a program and has observed that reform is an emerging construct, not one readily agreed to or perceived in the same way by teacher and teacher educator alike. The glue to the program is one of recognizing and honoring the venturing into the unknown, the enactment of an educational experiment. This context alone accounts for a considerable amount of professional growth and

1175

self-esteem on the part of teachers and university personnel as well as they begin to see what aspects of theory and research have real meaning for teachers. It also provides a context for teachers to engage in research activities as they consider how their teaching can be modified while working with preservice teachers from a university. There are many techniques that can be used, including analyses of videotapes and transcripts.

We close this section by posing the following questions to be considered by those who are willing to embrace teacher education as a process of inquiry.

— To what extent do we incorporate teachers into the planning and defining of goals for the program?

— To what extent do we provide a context for teachers to engage in a research process wherein they pose their own questions, collect and analyze data, and reflect on what their findings suggest about their teaching?

— To what extent do we engage teachers in a process whereby they develop the ability to critique their own teaching?

— To what extent do we enable teachers to see themselves as developing professionals?

— To what extent do we enable ourselves to develop a deeper appreciation for the complexity of teaching and to honor that complexity as we engage in our research and teacher education activities?

6. MEETING MARIA THE RESEARCHER

As Maria reflected on her inservice program, she was surprised how much she had come to appreciate the relevance of research to her own professional development. At first she agreed with Verstappen (1991) who opined that teachers are often skeptical about the benefits of research to teaching given that research is often seen as abstract and teachers have to deal with the practicalities of dealing with students, some of whom are not motivated to learn mathematics. But Dr. Crainey had helped her see research not as something abstract and inapplicable to her teaching but as an activity that informed teaching. She was impressed with the series of books published by the National Council of Teachers of Mathematics entitled Research Ideas for the Classroom. She had also developed a knack for seeing how research was relevant to her teaching. She began to see research not as an accumulation of abstract findings but as a process of searching for viable alternatives for teaching mathematics. In this context, she could think of herself as a researcher. She was becoming a more reflective teacher and less one who was interested only in accumulating activities for students. She was also beginning to appreciate that the contexts of the classroom and what students believe about mathematics are mitigating circumstances for determining whether students are interested in or can profit from the activities she used. She had never thought about teaching from this perspective.

She found the notion of storytelling an interesting way of thinking about research. She thought of all the stories she could tell about her teaching, the anecdote with Paul being one. She recognized the distinction between the common sense notion of telling stories about the classroom and the more sophisticated notion of storytelling that researchers used. Brown and Cooney's (1991) claim that we can find theory in practice and practice in theory was particularly intriguing to her. She mused that she probably did have 'local theories' about how to handle certain situations but she had never thought of herself as having theories. She would have to think more about this. But she also appreciated the sense in which stories were means of communicating the meanings people hold. In this broader sense, Maria could envision research as a way of informing and energizing her teaching. She was beginning to feel comfortable with the notion that she was a teacher and a researcher.

For her own research she decided to investigate various ways of teaching functions. She wanted to teach part of the material using cooperative learning groups and the other part of the material in a more traditional style by covering homework, presenting new material in a lecture/discussion format, and then assigning problems to be solved. She also wanted to vary her approach from a mathematical perspective. She planned on using two different conceptions of functions; one would focus on the algebra of functions and the other would emphasize functions as a vehicle for modeling real world phenomena. She was interested in which students would gravitate to which conception.

She realized that the study wouldn't be as 'scientific' as some of the studies she had read, but she was really interested in how her students would react. She was particularly interested in the quality of interaction among students when they engaged the different approaches to functions. She wondered how she might react to the anticipated increase in noise level when students were busily discussing mathematical ideas in their respective groups. She wanted to see how students would respond and react to some of the open-ended items she had created and what conditions seemed to promote quality responses and which ones didn't. She thought she would interview some of her students to better understand how they were constructing the concept of function. This was really new to Maria. She had never before thought about how her students were constructing mathematical knowledge; she had just considered whether or not they could do the mathematics, that is, get it right. She planned on having her students keep a diary which she would use as a data source and as a means of communicating with them. She planned to keep a diary herself so that she could assess the students' reactions on a daily basis and promote her own reflection on teaching. The entire study would take several months but she was excited about getting started. She knew it would be a lot of extra work but she was sure it would be worth it. It made her feel professional.

She recalled one of her personal diary entrees that she had written last year that, in retrospect, seemed to capture what she believed about teaching mathematics.

'It is no longer my intention to teach year in, year out in the same manner. I want to sort out methods which have been successful from those which are not. I need to find out which activities give me the kinds of results I want.'

Now, she had a sense of how she could consider the effectiveness of her teaching. She realized that the conceptions of functions she wanted her students to learn were complex but the research she had read would be helpful in understanding that complexity. She still believed in finding the 'right' activities but she realized that 'good' comes in many different forms. She saw research as a process that could enlighten her notion of what was good and what was not. In truth, she sensed that the terms 'good' and 'bad' really made little sense. She could see that research could inform many aspects of her teaching. She wondered how she could have been happy before just going through the routine of finding or creating activities – albeit she had felt comfortable with that routine. She recognized the change in herself. There was no returning to the 'old' ways. She was sure of that!

At first Maria hypothesized that some of her fellow teachers would scoff at her research. How wrong she was. Her fellow teachers were very supportive; many offered to be 'critical friends.' This, alone, was very rewarding to Maria. She was truly impressed with how her colleagues had also become interested in research and the articles that had influenced their projects. One teacher cited Doyle (1986) who described the demands of teaching with the characteristics 'multidimensionality', 'simultaneity', 'immediacy', 'unpredictability', 'publicness' and 'history' (accumulation of joint experiences). These constructs made sense as she thought about her own teaching experiences. Maria realized that recently more and more books, articles and discussions dealt with topics like 'teachers as experts', as 'professionals' and 'researchers.' These writings enabled her to feel a part of the larger profession referred to as 'mathematics education.'

Andrea was curious about the notion that 'theory dominates practice' which she encountered when reading Schön's (1983) book. She recalled Schön talking about the interplay between theory and practice and his concept of 'technical rationality', a concept that potentially separates the teacher from the researcher. Andrea shared the following quote from Schön's book and invited other teachers to react to it.

Within the conceptual framework of technical rationality, they are working on a low level of theoretical knowledge and are merely applying what has been predefined in the academic and administrative power-structure above them.

(Schön, 1983, p. 202)

Maria felt uncomfortable with the notion of 'technical rationality' as it seemed to depict research as an abstract entity – something she had come to reject. She expressed her viewpoint to the class.

Hans enjoyed reading about research on teachers' professional knowledge, the complexity of teachers' tasks, and the richness of their knowledge as described by Bromme (1992). Hans indicated that he began to think of himself differently as he read about the professional knowledge of teachers which could not be described by other professional knowledge, e.g., mathematical knowledge. Hearing Hans talk led Maria to see teachers' professional knowledge as both an integration of different disciplines and as a new creation fitting the particular demands of the profession.

Thomas expressed an appreciation he had developed for the complexity of teaching when he encountered a study by Clark and Peterson (1986) who reported that teacher statements were classified as belonging to 'subject-matter', to 'students' or to 'instructional process.' Yet, statements like 'I was thinking that they don't understand what they're doing' (being classified to belong to 'students') seemed to involve all three categories. This was interesting to Thomas. He was pleased that some researchers seemed to understand the complexity of a teacher's professional life. Thomas indicated that he had developed a new found respect for researchers who were trying to grapple with the complexities in classrooms like his and yet were cautious when generalizing to other classroom situations.

Another teacher, Monica, identified with Schwab (1983) as she felt his position was consistent with her thinking about teachers and teaching. She shared the following quote she had taken from his article.

Teachers practice an art. Moments of choice of what to do, how to do it, with whom and at what pace, arise hundreds of times a school day, and arise differently every day and with every group of students. No command or instruction can be so formulated as to control that kind of artistic judgment and behaviour, with its demand for frequent, instant choices of ways to meet an ever varying situation. Therefore, teachers must be involved in debate, deliberation, and decision about what and how to teach.

(Schwab, 1983, p. 245-246)

This quote was particularly meaningful to Monica for it honored her artistry as a teacher. She could sense a rise in her own self-esteem as she shared with other teachers some of the things she did with her students and the new found respect she had for her own artistry. She had never articulated this feeling before.

Elizabeth expressed particular interest in something she had read by Altrichter, Posch, and Somekh (1993). She described how the authors had identified the following assumptions regarding educational problems.

— Complex practical problems demand specific solutions.
— These solutions can be developed only inside the context in which the problem arises and in which the practitioner is a crucial and determining element.
— The solutions cannot be successfully applied to other contexts but they can be made accessible to other practitioners as hypotheses to be tested.

These assumptions helped Elizabeth think about the action research she was planning for her own teaching.

As Maria listened to her colleagues, she could see many elements of professionalism that were consistent with Altrichter and Krainer's (in press) dimensions of 'action', 'reflection', 'autonomy' and 'networking.' She could appreciate that in order to understand the nature of teacher change an adequate description of teachers' beliefs and ways of conceptualizing teaching are needed. She, as had her friend Andrea, identified with Schön's (1983) notion of 'reflective practice' which formulated different relationships between professional knowledge and professional action such as 'tacit knowing-in-action' (professional practice flows smoothly and appears simple to an onlooker), 'reflection-in-action' (new and complete situations have to be dealt with or disturbances and problems disrupt the smooth flow of routinized action), and 'reflection-on-action' (it is necessary to formulate knowledge explicitly and verbally, to distance ourselves from action for some time and to reflect on it).

Many of the teachers had resonated with Burton (1991) who had written,

I wish to conclude by reaffirming my purpose in doing research through which is to make clearer the processes through which mathematics is learnt and taught. With this aim I cannot find myself occupying a distinctly different role as researcher than that which I occupy as a teacher although it is clear that role demands and imperatives do vary. If that is valid for me, I cannot do other than recognize its validity for all teachers and researchers (p. 120-121).

Research conceived in this way seemed consistent with what Maria had read by Eisner (1993) who views research as an art, as an interpretive process. Although Maria had difficulty understanding some of the authors, she could see that researchers were looking at teaching in a sort of 'meta-way.' She was struck by the fact that various scholars were conducting analyses that enabled them to describe events in a language that went beyond the events themselves. This was exciting for Maria. For example, she had read how Belenky, Clinchy, Goldberger, and Tarule (1986) used the metaphor of voice to characterize the different ways that women construct their own knowledge. She could see the potential of this work for developing a set of lenses for how she and other teachers come to know and, perhaps, how some of her students come to know. She hoped to uncover other models that might help her reflect on her own understanding.

Perhaps foremost in Maria's mind was a saying she remembered by R. Feynman, winner of the Nobel prize in physics, who emphasized that the most fundamental principle for conducting research was that of not cheating oneself or others. For Maria, it was a challenge she was excited about accepting. From now on, it would be part of her professional persona.

CONCLUSION

In writing this chapter, the authors sought common ground among our notions of inservice education, preservice education, what it means to do mathematics, what it means to teach mathematics, and what it means to do research. In presenting the case of Maria, we were faced with how the many teachers we have worked with over the years made sense of these ideas and what it meant for them to grow professionally, as we felt we had grown professionally from working with them. For us that commonality was rooted in the humanistic side of teaching, leading us to think of Maria as she struggled to make sense of her world often failing to give credit to her own practitioner's wisdom. We suspect that there are many Marias in many different lands. In a sense, Maria represents a resultant vector of our beliefs, different from our individual beliefs, but we hope not orthogonal to the experiences of other teachers and researchers. Fundamentally, we are committed to the notion that research and practice ought not to be separate and discrete entities when related to teacher education.

The title of this chapter emphasizes the importance of listening as we see listening as the foundation from which teacher education should be conducted. Listening honors teachers and provides a context in which inservice education can be based on what teachers know rather than on what they don't know. Listening to others and to ourselves as well promotes reflection which can lead to a conception of teaching grounded in adaptation, a condition necessary for professional development. So conceived, listening creates an atmosphere of understanding and mutual respect between researcher and teacher. Inservice education provides us the opportunity to promote this kind of understanding and respect and, concomitantly, the professional development of all.

REFERENCES

Altrichter, H., Krainer, K.: (in press) 'Wandel von Lehrerarbeit und Lehrerfortbildung', In K. Krainer, Posch, P. (eds.). *Lehrerfortbildung zwischen Prozessen und Produkten.* Klagenfurt, Interuniversitäres Institut für interdisziplinäre Forschung und Fortbildung (IFF)

Altrichter, H., Posch, P., Somekh, B.: 1993, *Teachers Investigate Their Work: An Introduction to the Methods of Action Research,* London, Routledge

Belenky, M., Clinchy, B., Goldberger, N., Tarule, J.: 1986, *Women's Ways of Knowing: The Development of Self, Voice, and Mind,* New York, Basic Books

Berliner, D., Stein, P., Sabers, D., Clarridge, P., Cushing, K., Pinnegar, S.: 1988, *Implications of Research on Pedagogical Expertise and Experience for Mathematics Teaching.* In D. Grouws, Cooney, T. (eds.) *Effective Mathematics Teaching,* Erlbaum Associates and National Council of Teachers of Mathematics, 67-95.

Bishop, A.: 1992, 'International Perspectives on Research in Mathematics Education'. In D. Grouws (ed.) *Handbook of Research on Mathematics Teaching and Learning.* Macmillan, New York. 710-723.

Blanco, L.: 1994, 'The Problem of Inservice Teacher Training'. In Malara, N., Rico, L. (eds.): *Proceedings of the First Italian-Spanish Research Symposium in Mathematics Education.* Dipartimento di Matematica. Modena, Universita di Modena, 149-156.

Blane, D.: 1992, 'Changing the Image of Mathematics Through Using the Environment. ' Paper presented at ICME 7, Quebec, Canada. (Also cited in C. Gaulin, B. Hodgson, D. Wheeler, Egsgard, J. (eds.), 1994, *Proceedings of the Seventh International Congress of Mathematical Education.* Sainte-Foy (Quebec), Les Presses de l'Universite Laval, 223.)

Bromme, R.: 1992, *Der Lehrer als Experte. Zur Psychologie des professionellen Wissens.* Bern, Huber.

Brown, C., Borko, H.: 1992, 'Becoming a Mathematics Teacher.' In Grouws, D. (ed.) *Handbook of Research on Mathematics Teaching and Learning.* New York, Macmillan, 209-239

Brown, S., Cooney, T.: 1991, 'Stalking the Dualism Between Theory and Practice' *Zentralblatt für Didaktik der Mathematik,* 23, 4, 112-117

Brown, S., Cooney, T., Jones, D.: 1990, 'Mathematics Teacher Education' In Houston, W. (ed.) *Handbook of Research on Teacher Education.* Macmillan, New York, 639-656.

Burton, L., 1991, 'Models of Systematic Cooperation Between Theory and Practice' *Zentralblatt für Didaktik der Mathematik,* 23, 4, 118-121

Clark, C., Peterson, P.: 1986, 'Teachers' Thought Processes' In Wittrock, M. (ed.) *Third Handbook of Research on Teaching.* New York, Macmillan, 255-296.

Cooney, T.: 1985, 'A Beginning Teacher's View of Problem Solving' *Journal of Research in Mathematics Education,* 16, 324-336

Cooney, T.: 1994a, 'Research and Teacher Education: In Search of Common Ground' *Journal for Research in Mathematics Education,* 25, 608-636

Cooney, T.: 1994b, 'Teacher Education as an Exercise in Adaptation' In Aichele, D. (ed.), *Professional Development of Teachers of Mathematics,* Reston, VA, National Council of Teachers of Mathematics, 9-22.

Cooney, T., Brown, S., Dossey, J., Schrage, G., Wittmann, E.: 1996, *Mathematics, Pedagogy, and Secondary Teacher Education: Reweaving the Frayed Braid.* Portsmouth, Heinemann Publishing Company

De la Cruz, Y., Thompson, V.: 1992, 'Influencing Views of Mathematics Through Family Math Programs.' Paper presented at ICME 7, Quebec, Canada. (Also cited in C. Gaulin, B. Hodgson, D. Wheeler, Egsgard, J. (eds.), 1994, *Proceedings of the Seventh International Congress of Mathematical Education.* Sainte-Foy (Quebec), Les Presses de l'Universite Laval, 223.)

Doyle, W.: 1986, 'Classroom Organization and Management'. In Wittrock, M. (ed.) *Third Handbook of Research on Teaching.* Macmillan, New York, 392-431.

Eisenberg, T.: 1977, 'Begle Revisited: Teacher Knowledge and Student Achievement in Algebra.' *Journal for Research in Mathematics Education* 8, 216-222

Eisner, E.: 1993, 'Forms of Understanding and the Future of Educational Research' *Educational Researcher* 22, 5, 5-11

Elbaz, F., 1983, Teacher Thinking: A Study of Practical Knowledge. New York, Nichols

Fennema, E., Franke, M. L.: 1992, 'Teacher's Knowledge and Its Impact' In Grouws, D. (ed.), *Handbook of Research on Mathematics Teaching and Learning*. New York, Macmillan, 147-164.

Fisher, L.: 1988, 'Strategies Used by Secondary Mathematics Teachers to Solve Proportion Problems' *Journal for Research in Mathematics Education* 19, 157-168

Fischer, R., Malle, G.: 1985, Mensch und Mathematik. Eine Einführung in didaktisches Denken und Handeln. Mannheim, Bibliographisches Institut

Frasier, C.: 1993, *A Shared Vision: Policy Recommendations for Linking Teacher Education to School Reform*. Denver, Education Commission of the States

Fujii, T.: 1992, 'Images of Mathematics Held by Japanese Parents'. Paper presented at ICME 7, Quebec, Canada. (Also cited in C. Gaulin, B. Hodgson, D. Wheeler, Egsgard, J. (eds.), 1994, *Proceedings of the Seventh International Congress of Mathematical Education*. Sainte-Foy (Quebec), Les Presses de l'Universite Laval, 221.)

Gerdes, P.: 1985, 'Conditions and Strategies for Emancipatory Mathematics Education.' *For the Learning of Mathematics* 5, 1, 15-20

Gerdes, P.: 1988, 'Developing Countries', Cited in Hirst, A., Hirst, K. (eds.) *Proceedings of the Sixth International Congress on Mathematical Education*, Budapest, Bolyai Mathematical Society, 196.

Graeber, A., Tirosh, D., Glover, R.: 1986, 'Preservice Teachers' Beliefs and Performance on Measurement and Partitive Division Problems' In G. Lappan, Even, R. (eds.) *Proceedings of the Eighth Annual Meeting of the North American Chapter of the International Group for the Psychology of Mathematics Education* East Lansing, MI, Michigan State University, 262-267.

Howson, G.: 1994, 'Teachers of Mathematics' In C. Gaulin, B. Hodgson, D. Wheeler, Egsgard, J. (eds.) *Proceedings of the Seventh International Congress of Mathematical Education*. Les Presses de l'Universite Laval, Sainte-Foy, Quebec, 9-26.

Hoyles, C.: 1992, 'Illuminations and Reflections: Teachers, Methodologies and Mathematics'. In Geeslin, W., Graham, K. (eds.) *Proceedings of the 16th Psychology in Mathematics Education Annual Meeting*. Durham, University of New Hampshire, NH, V. III, 263-283.

Jaji, G., Nyagura, L., Robson, M.: 1985, 'Zimbabwe: Support for Tutors Utilising Video and Printed Modules' In Morris, R. (ed.) *Studies in Mathematics Education Volume 4: The Education of Secondary School Teachers of Mathematics*, Paris, UNESCO, 153-158.

Keitel, C.: 1989, 'Mathematics Education and Technology' *For the Learning of Mathematics*. 9, 7-13

Keitel, C.: 1992, 'The Education of Teachers of Mathematics: An Overview' Zentralblatt für Didaktik der Mathematik, 24, 265-273

Kilpatrick, J.: 1982, 'Casing the Case Studies: Concluding Remarks' *Journal of Research and Development in Education,* 15, 4, 87-88

Krainer, K.: 1994a, 'PFL-Mathematics: A Teacher Inservice Education Course as a Contribution to the Improvement of Professional Practice in Mathematics Instruction' In J. Ponte, Matos, J. (eds.): *Proceedings of the 18th Psychology in Mathematics Education Annual Meeting*. Lisboa, University of Lisboa, v. III, 104-111.

Krainer, K.: 1994b, 'Zum Wandel von Lehrerfortbildung im Bereich Mathematik' In Schönbeck, J., Struve, H., Volkert, H. (eds.): *Der Wandel im Lehren und Lernen von Mathematik und Naturwissenschaften. Band I: Mathematik,* Weinheim, Deutscher Studienverlag, 203-225.

Krainer, K.: 1994c, 'Integrating Research and Teacher Inservice Education as a Means of Mediating Theory and Practice in Mathematics Education' In Bazzini, L. (ed.) *Theory and Practice in Mathematics Education.* Pavia, ISDAF

Krainer, K., Posch, P.: (in press), *Lehrerfortbildung zwischen Prozessen und Produkten.* Klagenfurt, Interuniversitäres Institut für interdisziplinäre Forschung und Fortbildung (IFF)

Krainz-Dürr, M.: 1990, *Auswertung von schriftlichen Rückmeldungen von TeilnehmerInnen zu den PFL-Lehrgängen 1982-84 und 1985-87. Endbericht.* Klagenfurt, Interuniversitäres Institut für interdisziplinäre Forschung und Fortbildung (IFF)

Kreith, K.: 1993, *Report on 1993 Northern Carolina Mathematics Project Summer Institute,* Davis, University of California

Lin, F., Huang, M., Chu, T.: 1992, 'The Influence of Examinations in Shaping Students' Images of Mathematics' Paper presented at ICME 7, Quebec, Canada. (Also cited in C. Gaulin, B. Hodgson, D. Wheeler, Egsgard, J. (eds.): 1994, *Proceedings of the Seventh International Congress of Mathematical Education.* Sainte-Foy (Quebec), Les Presses de l'Universite Laval, 220.)

Mitroff, I., Kilmann, R.: 1978, *Methodological Approaches to Social Sciences.* San Francisco, Jossey-Bass.

Mura, R.: 1992, 'Images of Mathematics Held by Mathematicians' Paper presented at ICME 7, Quebec, Canada. (Also cited in C. Gaulin, B. Hodgson, D. Wheeler, Egsgard, J. (eds.): 1994, *Proceedings of the Seventh International Congress of Mathematical Education.* Sainte-Foy (Quebec), Les Presses de l'Université Laval, 220

National Council of Teachers of Mathematics (NCTM) (ed): 1989, *Curriculum and Evaluation Standards for School Mathematics.* Reston, VA, NCTM

National Council of Teachers of Mathematics (NCTM) (ed): 1991, *Professional Standards for the Teaching of School Mathematics.* Reston, VA, NCTM

National Council of Teachers of Mathematics (NCTM) (ed): 1995, *Assessment Standards for School Mathematics.* Reston, VA, NCTM

Nebres, B.: 1988, 'School Mathematics in the 1990's: The Challenge of Change Especially for Developing Countries' In Hirst, A., Hirst, K. (eds.) *Proceedings of the Sixth International Congress on Mathematical Education,* Budapest, Bolyai Mathematical Society, 11-28.

Noddings, N.: 1992, 'Professionalism and Mathematics Teaching' In Grouws, D. (ed.) *Handbook of Research on Mathematics Teaching and Learning,* New York, Macmillan, 197-208.

Owens, J.: 1987, *A Study of Four Preservice Secondary Mathematics Teachers' Constructs of Mathematics and Mathematics Teaching.* Unpublished doctoral dissertation, Athens, University of Georgia

Ponte, J.: 1994, *MINERVA Project. Introducing NIT in Education Portugal.* Lisboa, Ministry of Education

Posch, P.:(in press) *Teachers and Curriculum Reform in Basic Education. Report for OECD/CERI.* Klagenfurt, University of Klagenfurt

Scheffler, I.: 1965, *Conditions of Knowledge: An Introduction to Epistemology and Education,* Glenville, Scott Foresman

Schifter, D.: 1990, 'Mathematics Process as Mathematics Content: A Course for Teachers. ' In Booker, G., Cobb, P., de Mendicuti, T. (eds.): *Proceedings of the 14th Psychology in Mathematics Education Annual Meeting,* Mexico City, V. 1, 191-198.

Schön, D.: 1983, *The Reflective Practitioner: How Professionals Think in Action.* New York, Basic Books

Schön, D.: 1987, *Educating the Reflective Practitioner.* San Francisco, Jossey-Bass

Schwab, J.: 1983, 'The Practical 4: Something for Curriculum Professors to Do.' *Curriculum Inquiry,* 13, 3, 239-265

Shulman, L.: 1986, 'Those Who Understand: Knowledge Growth in Teaching.' *Educational Researcher,* 15, 4-14.

Stake, R.: 1978, 'The Case Study Method in Social Inquiry.' Educational Researcher 7, 7, 5-8

Steffe, L. P., D'Ambrosio, B. S.: 1995, 'Toward a Working Model of Constructivist Teaching: A Reaction to Simon.' *Journal for Research in Mathematics Education,* 26, 146-159.

Thompson, A.: 1992, 'Teachers' Beliefs and Conceptions: A Synthesis of the Research.' In Grouws, D. (ed.): *Handbook of Research on Mathematics Teaching and Learning,* New York, Macmillan, 127-146.

Verstappen, P.: 1991, 'Ten Major Issues Concerning Systematic Cooperation Between Theory and Practice in Mathematics Education' *Zentralblatt für Didaktik der Mathematik,* 23, 4, 122-127.

Von Harten, G., Steinbring, H.: 1991, 'Lesson Transcripts and Their role in the Inservice Training of Mathematics Teachers.' *Zentralblatt für Didaktik der Mathematik,* 23, 5, 169-177.

Weiss, I., Boyd, S., Hessling, P.: 1990, *A Look at Exemplary NSF Teacher Enhancement Projects,* Chapel Hill, NC, Horizon Research, Inc.

Wheeler, M., Feghali, I.: 1983, 'Much Ado About Nothing: Preservice Elementary School Teachers' Concept of Zero.' *Journal for Research in Mathematics Education,* 14, 147-155.

Wittmann, E.: 1991, 'From Inservice Courses to Systematic Cooperation Between Teachers and Researchers.' *Zentralblatt für Didaktik der Mathematik,* 23, 158-160

Wittmann, E.: 1992, One Source of the Broadcast Metaphor: Mathematical Formalism. In F. Seeger, H. Steinbring (eds.): *The Dialogue Between Theory and Practice in Mathematics Education: Overcoming the Broadcast Metaphor,* Bielefeld, Institut für Didaktik der Mathematik der Universitat Bielefeld, 111-120.

Zeichner, K., Gore, J.: 1990, 'Teacher Socialization.' In Houston, R. (ed.) *Handbook of Research on Teacher Education.* Macmillan, New York, 329-348.

Chapter 32: Teachers as Researchers in Mathematics Education

KATHRYN CRAWFORD AND JILL ADLER

University of Sydney, Australia and The University of Witwatersrand, South Africa

ABSTRACT

This paper explores the ways in which teaching, learning and research are conceptualised by various members of the mathematics education community and makes an argument for research-like activities by teachers as a means to professional development. Such development is viewed as a prerequisite for changes in the processes and quality of mathematics education for school students. Examples from Australia and South Africa, two different ex-colonial contexts undergoing rapid social change, are used to illustrate the need for change and the importance of active participation of teachers in research activities associated with their professional practice.

1. INTRODUCTION

Mathematics teachers are involved in the practice of the construction of knowledge. Their knowledge is generated through their participation in the established educational practices of which they are both products and participants; and, through their efforts to support, in their chosen role of 'teacher', the knowledge of their students. Through their activity, mathematics teachers form and are formed by the educational institutions in which they work. Traditionally, learning by means of activities such as questioning, problem definition, reflection and systematic investigation of chosen aspects of education and mathematics has been the province of university academics. There is little evidence that much of the knowledge generated by research at universities is embodied in the teaching and learning practices in schools. It seems possible that if teachers and student-teachers act in generative, research-like ways, they may learn about the teaching/learning process, and about mathematics, in ways that empower them to better meet the needs of their students.

A.J. Bishop et al. (eds.), International Handbook of Mathematics Education, 1187 - 1205

2.   RELATING TEACHING, RESEARCH, LEARNING AND MATHEMATICS: A
      NEO-VYGOTSKIAN PERSPECTIVE

In a systemic and dialectical view of human learning and development (Vygotsky 1978; Valsiner 1994; Crawford, Gordon, Nicholas & Prosser 1994)
the actions of people and the meanings and purposes that they attach to an activity, the relationships between people and the arena in which they think, feel
and act, and the presence of culturally significant artefacts, all become important as determinants of multiple consciousnesses. The subjective and personal
views of individuals, their location in a context, and their conceptions derived
from past experience all shape their conceptions of needs and their interpretations of the goals of an activity. They also determine individual interpretations of the 'reality' of the experience and their choices about thought and
action. Thus the terms 'teaching' and 'research' have meanings that are experienced and formed through social activity.[1] Similarly, 'learning' is another
closely related phenomenon that is understood at a personal level through cultural experience – usually in relation to teachers. However, researchers also
'learn' through systematic investigation, inquiry and reflection in a socio-cultural context.

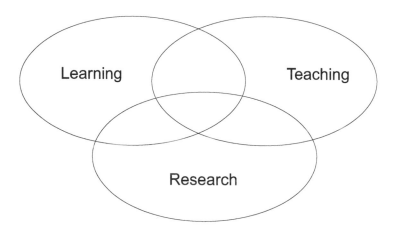

Figure 1. Learning, Teaching and Research

As shown in Figure 1 above, the three activities are related in complex ways.
Learning is an expected outcome of both teaching and research activities.

   The work of Brousseau and others (Douady & Mercier 1992) provides an
account of the ways in which scholarly knowledge is transformed through didactical transposition in institutionalised educational contexts. As Brousseau
(1992, p.22) says:

The effort made in order to obtain knowledge independently of situations where it works (decontextualisation) has as a price the loss of meaning and performance at the time of teaching. The restoration of intelligible situations (recontextualisation) has as a price the shift in meaning (didactical transposition).

The above researchers take an anthropological view of the ways in which the social context of teaching and learning and the nature of institutional settings in which education occurs shape the meaning of knowledge. In the case of mathematics, they stress the qualitative differences between knowledge that enables people to do mathematics and knowledge about mathematics derived from teaching in traditional forms.

From the perspective of neo-Vygotskian researchers all knowledge and consciousness has a social ontogeny. The nature of awareness or knowledge – the developing consciousness of people – is formed and reformed through action in a social context. For them, scholarly knowledge is the form of knowledge derived from scholarly activities. Different scholarly activities such as reflection or empirical research result in different forms of knowledge. Similarly, teachers' knowledge of both their specialist discipline and of educational processes is a result of their experience of learning and teaching activities. For students also, the nature of their knowledge reflects the nature of their learning activity within a socio-cultural context. From such a perspective knowledge or meaning is not so much transposed as constituted through activity within a socio-cultural context.

Learning may be experienced through investigation and inquiry, through reading about someone else's research, or through being taught. In each case the quality of the resulting knowledge will be different (Rogoff 1994). That is, the quality of the social context in which learning occurs – including the relationship between the learners and the social context in which they act and the ways in which they relate to the subject that is the focus of their attention – shapes the quality of their activity – the ways in which they think, feel and act – and the resulting knowledge. Knowledge is constituted in the relationship between the knower and the subject and mediated through action in a social context.

Students taught and assessed in traditional ways, learn to demonstrate that they have encoded the culturally approved knowledge and can reproduce it. Those who learn about teaching through reading about educational research develop knowledge of a similar kind. In neither case is the knowledge necessarily a basis for further action or a changing personal view of reality. Systematic investigation and reflection undertaken with the aim of resolving a dilemma or answering a personally meaningful question – research activity – results in knowledge of a different kind. Knowledge derived from research activity is necessarily personal. That is, a researcher takes action to research stimulated by an interest or perceived need that is based on personal awareness and goals. Even when the research activity is carried out using culturally approved techniques, the researcher defines a problem from a personal perspective, hypothesises about possible outcomes, selects strategies to test hypotheses and possibilities, gains insights and evaluates the outcomes of the research activity with reference to a selected and thus also personal view of the world. In forms of research that investigate ways to make a change, such as action research, there is a potential for knowledge about how to act so that change occurs. The resulting knowledge of the researcher forms the basis for capabilities of problem solving and acting to produce change. This form of knowledge seems particularly important for teachers who are, after all, professionally responsible for change and development through learning.

In the field of mathematics education a fourth socially constructed concept must be considered – mathematics.

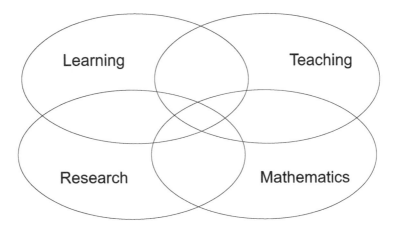

Figure 2. Teaching, Learning and Mathematics

In this paper we explore the possibility of mathematics teachers learning about teaching and mathematics through research activities. Thus the focus of the paper is on the possibilities of the intersection sets, in Figure 2 above, and the extent that conceptions of teaching, learning, mathematics and research – beliefs and expectations about power relationships, qualifications to carry out these activities and have access to resulting knowledge – constrain or enhance possibilities for research by practising teachers of mathematics. We have used two different contexts to exemplify the social nature of experience and resulting knowledge. Examples from Australia and South Africa also highlight educational and political tensions that occur as teachers seek to meet the needs of their students for mathematical knowledge in rapidly changing societies.

3. LEARNING ABOUT TEACHING AND CHANGING CONTEXTS

3.1 Student teachers learning about mathematics and education.

Mathematics teachers are widely viewed as those who 'know mathematics'. In traditional teaching they play the role of 'the one who knows' – the 'expert' in mathematics. Implicit in teacher education and school organisation, particularly at the secondary level, is a transmission model of learning and teaching whereby approved mathematical knowledge is passed from the expert to the novice. At university, student-teachers receive and memorise mathematical knowledge and demonstrate to experts through tests and examinations that they have successfully encoded the culturally approved axioms, rules and techniques. For the vast majority, these capabilities constitute scholarly mathematical knowledge – they have no other experience.

In most teacher education courses, education theories, including recent theories of learning, are taught by lectures and assessed in traditional ways through essay-writing and examination. Little attention is paid to providing experiences designed to ensure that student-teachers develop a working rationale for educational decision making and are able to apply educational theories in their professional practice. Even during practical experience in schools, in most cases, student-teachers play the role of apprentices – they are required to 'fit in' and show that they can 'teach' in the ways in which it has always been done. Therefore, it is hardly surprising that most 'qualified' teachers teach mathematics in the same way as they were taught.

3.2 Australian mathematics teachers' professional experience.

The quality and appropriateness of mathematics education in Australia has been widely questioned. In the report of The Discipline Review of Teacher Education in Mathematics and Science, Speedy (1989, p.16) suggested that:

> Mathematics on the whole, as a school subject, or as a higher education course, is not sufficiently related to the developing needs of our society which is being driven to respond to, and interact with, more technologically advanced countries.

The report recommended a shift away from 'chalk and talk' methods towards providing experience of application of mathematical knowledge to 'real life' situations. Since that time, government policy and most curriculum documents have advocated increased attention to problem solving, investigation and inquiry in mathematics education, where problems include those outside and inside of mathematics. These changes are similar to mathematics curriculum reform initiatives elsewhere (e.g. the Curriculum and Evaluation Standards in the USA, (NCTM 1989)), and are echoed in new aims for school mathematics in South Africa.

Public criticism and pressure for change create tensions and contradiction in the professional lives of teachers. Many primary teachers, and a large number of secondary teachers, have little understanding of mathematics or capability for mathematical modelling, application of mathematics to solve problems and evaluation of the results of research, investigation or inquiry. They have no experience of these activities. Even those with experience of mathematical research have often been constrained to carrying out approved techniques to test the idea of the leader of the research team. Many of those with undergraduate qualifications in mathematics have merely survived the examination system at some time by demonstrating their capacity to carry out mathematical techniques in culturally approved ways. Further, the quality of their mathematical knowledge, at the level at which they are expected to teach, is strongly influenced by their own experience of schooling. As Ball (1988) says teachers need to unlearn old conceptions of mathematics derived from schooling experiences. They need to have learning experiences in mathematics similar to those we expect them to foster as teachers before we can expect them to act in different ways.

In large Australian school systems, the limitations of teachers' knowledge is recognised, though little attempt has been made in universities to make appropriate changes in pre-service learning experiences in mathematics or education. The usual response of educational administrators tends to consolidate the situation and makes change more difficult to achieve. Externally set curricula, set text books and other teaching aids are made mandatory as a means to maintain standards and support teachers. In many cases, teaching in schools is practically defined as merely supervising culturally approved educational activities because they are in the curriculum. In an age of quality management, and hierarchical administrative structures, teaching activities are increasingly circumscribed by requirements for planning, documentation and measurable outcomes. In such a strongly regulated environment teachers play an educationally powerless and unprofessional role. They are not supposed to make decisions about how best to meet the changing needs of their students, even in cases when they have developed the professional knowledge to do so. As one teacher remarked poignantly during a post-graduate professional development course:

What I have learned here merely widens the gap between what I would like to do, and now am able to do, and what I know must be done in my school.

3.3　Embracing Change?

In the information era, mathematical techniques are increasingly used in research in all fields, from archaeology to astro-physics, as computerised information becomes most prevalent. The paper and pencil techniques that still dominate mathematics education in schools are now widely carried out by machines at all levels of our highly technologically oriented society. As Willis (1990, pp. 12-13) suggests:

> Computing technology has changed the way mathematics is produced and also the way it is applied at all levels of mathematical sophistication. Some things will now be done differently than they were in the past, some things will be done that previously were not possible or at least not practicable, and some things done in the past may no longer be necessary. This is as true of everyday arithmetic as it is true of the mathematics of tradespeople, technicians, and technologists; shop assistants accountants and economists; social, physical and biological scientists; and professional mathematicians.

The rapid change poses problems for experts educated in the past. First, there are indications that learning in traditional ways at school results, even for the most successful students entering mathematics courses at university, in a fragmented conception of mathematics for most students (>80 per cent) and little capability or inclination to apply mathematical knowledge in problem solving, interpret mathematical information, develop mathematical models or evaluate solutions (Crawford, Gordon, Nicholas & Prosser, 1993, 1994). Second, teachers' conceptions of mathematics and their experience as learners of mathematics lead them to expect that students will learn mathematics through copying and practising with an intent to reproduce approved techniques in assessment tasks. Again, as has been argued above, their learning about teaching through experience as students and through observing teachers in schools, reinforces a transmission model of learning. During practical experiences as apprentices in schools, they learn to act in an expert role that assumes power relations with respect to students that are inconsistent with collaboration and the tentative and uncertain processes of seeking new knowledge, investigation, and creative problem posing and solving. Although many have intellectually espoused recent theories of learning and the need for problem solving and inquiry, after reading set texts and completing assignments, most have no experiences through which they could learn how a teacher acts to create a learning environment in which such activities are fostered.

In short, for a large majority, mathematics teachers' conceptions of mathematics, teaching and learning, learned from their educational experiences, make it difficult or impossible for them to act in new ways to foster a different quality of mathematics learning for students. Their low status and lack of

1193

power in most education systems further reduce their capacity to act as agents of change.

4. A WAY FORWARD: MATHEMATICS TEACHERS LEARNING THROUGH RESEARCH

From the perspective of new theories of learning and teaching (Vygotsky 1978; Lave 1988, Lave and Wenger 1990, Valsiner 1994, Rogoff 1994; Wertsch 1994) knowledge has a social ontogeny and is inextricably related to experience. From such a view teaching and learning are parts of an interactive process and both result in the formation of knowledge of particular kinds.

Research is another activity through which people learn. Research also occurs in a social setting according to culturally approved rules that govern who should do research and how it should be done. Traditionally, research has been a learning activity restricted to university staff and others with approved qualifications. The positivist conception of a researcher as an objective and impartial seeker of the truth through systematic investigation according to approved techniques remains widely accepted – particularly in scientific fields, and despite significant developments informed by interpretivist conceptions. Positivist research seeks to provide a description and an explanation for 'what is'. Facts are reported by the media as 'scientifically proven'. With the advent of systems analysis and advanced modelling techniques, more dynamic theoretical models of educational processes are now tested by purposefully changing variables. Moreover, in most educational research, participation in the intellectual activities of systematic investigation, reflection, analysis and reporting about conclusions – learning – are restricted to a 'researcher' apart from the educational settings, people and processes under investigation. Although much educational research makes recommendations for change, the 'subjects' of research usually remain unaware of the conclusions and recommendations.

The notion of 'teacher as researcher' can be traced back to Stenhouse (1975, p.42) and the curriculum debates of the time between the objectives and the process models. The latter was considered to entail a reconceptualisation of curriculum development as belonging to the teacher.

The term *action research* is now widely used to describe investigation and inquiry processes undertaken with an intent to change professional practice or social institutions through the active and transformative participation of those working within a particular setting in the research processes. A major aim of most action research projects is the generation of knowledge among people in organisational or institutional settings that is actionable – can be used as a basis for conscious action. In action research the traditional lines between researchers and the subjects of their investigation are blurred. The resulting knowledge is constituted in the changed practice and awareness of the

1194

researcher/practitioners. This form of research seems particularly appropriate for teachers who are professionally responsible for change through learning.

To elaborate, inquiry, investigation, reflection, interpretation and creative application are appropriate activities for both teachers of mathematics and their students. As Duckworth (1983, p.173) states: 'Action and point of view are central in the development of knowledge'. Action research activities present possibilities for teacher learning and professional development in relation to mathematics, the processes of teaching and learning and the more particular cultural views, needs and goals of their students. Action research processes can be designed to facilitate reconceptualisation and the development of an actionable and accountable rationale for practitioners. This is possible only when traditional cultural rules about authority and qualifications to carry out research activities are set aside – when clear shared goals are negotiated within a research team, and opportunities are provided for an inclusive, systematic, cyclical and evolutionary process in which ideas and theories are tested, and results are analysed and reflected on.

The International Group for the Psychology of Mathematics Education (PME) has provided a forum for research reports by teachers and teacher educators working in the field (e.g. Geeslin & Graham 1992; Hirabayashi, Noheda, Shigematsu & Lin 1993; De Ponte & Matos 1994). Many contributions describe innovations in teacher education and run counter to Bennett's (1993, p. 4) charge that:

In an era when teacher educators and researchers have been exhorting teachers to engage in action research on their own practice, they have singly failed to heed their own prescriptions.

As in any area of social change and knowledge production, particularly in the socio-political arena of education, there is conflict and contestation. At this time, control of the research agenda tends to remain in academic hands. Differential access to training, skills, experience, time and institutional support account for the differences in activity and awareness. Nevertheless academic hegemony runs counter to the goal of teacher ownership of the research agenda and of the knowledge generated as they learn through research activity.

Teacher research has been reported in the United Kingdom, United States, Australia and South Africa (Elliot 1988; Lerman 1990; Crawford 1992; Mousley 1992; Adler 1992; Walker 1993). However, from a South African perspective, teacher-based curriculum development and research have developed organically from teacher cultures receptive to notions of innovation, reflection and curriculum theorising where teachers viewed themselves as autonomous professionals. As Walker (1993) points out when writing about the situation in South Africa,

...far from there being an existing culture on which to build such research and development endeavours in township schools, the dominant teaching culture... has been shaped by the legacy of Bantu education, authoritarian practices and working relations.

Thus for an inclusive and generalised argument for research activity by mathematics teachers, our exploration needs to extend to mathematics teaching and learning activity in the South African context where rapid political change and democratic ideals are juxtaposed by historical inequalities and significantly limited human, material and financial resources, the latter a condition in education in much of the world.

4.1 Inservice Mathematics Teacher Development in South Africa

South Africa is a special case which illustrates powerfully the impact of political and social forces on learning and teaching in mathematics (ANC 1994; Edusource 1994; Adler 1995). Over and above the pervasive racial inequality which historically allocated four times as much per capita to 'white' as to 'black' children, apartheid education has left in its wake serious teacher shortages in mathematics, onerous and demoralising work conditions for the majority of teachers, authoritarian practices, and a system of teaching and learning lamentably deficient in its quantitative and qualitative practices.

Under apartheid, teacher education was institutionally fragmented in universities, technikons and colleges of education broadly organised along ethnic lines. The majority of South Africa's teachers have been trained in racially segregated colleges of education most of which are academically isolated, small, poorly equipped and ineffective in the provision of quality teacher education (NEPI 1993, p.237). The dominant ideology in these colleges is Fundamental Pedagogics, where a particular brand of pervasive authoritarianism in social relations and knowledge production disguises itself by positing education as a 'science' separate from politics and human values (Enslin 1990). This particularly perverse form of positivism in teacher education is not dissimilar from those described earlier. This qualitative dimension is coupled with a quantitative one through a system which has produced enormous variation in teacher qualifications. Whereas 'white' secondary mathematics teachers have a degree with some tertiary mathematics, the vast majority of 'black' secondary mathematics teachers have a three year post school teaching diploma – often with very little post secondary mathematics. Overcrowding in schools and classrooms is common, particularly in rural areas where primary classes can have as many as 100 pupils. Facing over 50 pupils, with a debilitating lack of confidence in subject knowledge (induced by little or no tertiary mathematics experience) is the living reality for large numbers of secondary teachers in African schools. In order to reach the targeted average teacher-pupil ratio of 1:35, the projected overall need is to train an additional 135000 primary and 95000 secondary teachers over the next ten years.

While apartheid produced this inexcusable picture of quantitative and qualitative educational neglect, it simultaneously stimulated a great deal of oppositional and developmental educational activity, including inservice professional development of mathematics teachers and action research projects. South African literature about teachers and their research ranges from debates about general initiatives in action research projects (Flanagan 1991; Walker 1993; Davidoff 1993), reports on small, individual mathematics teachers' action research projects (Adler 1992; 1993), reports on primary and secondary teachers' reflective practice (Coombe et al. 1995; Orpen et al. 1995) and to project facilitator reports on supporting mathematics teacher development (Breen and Coombe 1992, Goldstein et al. 1994, Davis 1995).

'Teachers' Voices' (Orpen et al. 1995) is a collection of reflective journal writings from primary teachers who attend the intensive primary mathematics inservice course run by the Mathematics Education Project (MEP) in Cape Town in 1994. In Teachers' Voices we are introduced to teachers' struggles and astonishing enthusiasm in thinking about and working on their practice in seriously overcrowded and under resourced classrooms in squatter areas and black townships in Cape Town. As an example, Tshego Senamelo is a primary school teacher in the vast squatter area of Khayelitsha in Cape Town. Tshego trained in one of apartheid's impoverished black colleges of education and has 6 years teaching experience. She has 53 pupils in her grade 3 class. Writing of her frustration while teaching in Khayelitsha, where aside from severe lack of resources, impermanence, violence and instability are defining characteristics of the community, Tshego says:

I never deal with the same children year after year. This is because many people in Khayelitsha come from rural areas and often the children go back there, and new children come into the school. Some children go and come back twice in the same year. There are very few people who live in this area for a long time.

This in turn affects my ability to use teaching aids. Often children don't know how to handle the teaching aids, one finds that they get broken or destroyed. I feel that if I had the same children every year this might not happen as I will be able to build up a relationship with them....the school has no funds it does not provide us with technical aids...So it is up to the teacher herself to buy these things, and this is very difficult for us...

Sometimes one feels this is a hopeless situation and it is difficult not to become demotivated. Teaching aids help our teaching a lot, they certainly help the children to remember and understand what they are being taught. However, we try to make use of what we already have such as bottle tops for counting adding and subtracting. We also use pieces of fruit to demonstrate halves, quarters and other fractions....(in Orpen et al. 1995)

In terms of the university-based definitions of research these writings reflect on practice but lack the usual requirements for intentional and systematic inquiry. There is also little, if any, explicit use of evidence or building of a theory (Bishop 1992, p. 711). However, reflection on problems and issues within a context is one aspect of research. The point of Tshego's story is not to pathologise nor patronise squatter communities, nor Tshego as teacher, but to pose and consider this question: If research is arguably a means for teachers' learning and professional development, then how can teachers like Tshego, and large numbers like her throughout the world, be included in research and inquiry about mathematics education?

In her writing about her project, Walker (1993) confronts the fact that her collaboration with teachers focussed on curriculum development. She undertook research on her own practices in the project. The teachers did not. She had research skills. There was no explicit attempt to impart these to the teachers beyond discussions about reflection and while their reflective ability grew their research skills did not. In her own reflection on this experience, Walker states that it was over-ambitious to have expected both teacher-based curriculum development and research activity in the same time frame of the project. Davidoff reiterates the importance of realistic expectations in the conditions that pertain to many teachers:

...when basic skills and materials are often not part of teachers' daily repertoires, how much less would be their ability to reflect upon their practice, and then within the broader social concerns of equality, justice and freedom?

Davidoff suggests that such a situation requires people to 'think big and start small'. Both authors argue for a continuum of activity by teachers from reflection to research as it is defined by university academics. Tshego has had an introduction to reflective practice through supportive and encouraging experiences with the Mathematics Education Project. She has benefited from the inquiry towards her own teaching, for this is how learning about teaching occurs. And, as a result, she has made changes in her own practice, however limited these steps may appear. In Davidoff's terms, Tshego has taken some real steps. She, and others like her, would benefit from further participation in communities of inquiry into teaching, from ongoing learning about teaching and mathematics which over time become more extensive, building reflective capacity and research skills.

Tshego's story is one of many diverse teacher research stories in South Africa. Teachers fortunate enough to work in different conditions have different experiences of professionalism. Small action research projects for post graduate mathematics teachers offer very different possibilities from those available to Tshego (Adler 1992). But it is this instance of teacher inquiry in the South African context that forces a contextual awareness for any activity — there is no one form of research-like activity suited to all teachers in all situations and contexts. Simultaneously, however, it supports the argument developing in this paper that inquiry into teaching is appropriate learning activity for all teachers.

To consolidate our argument, we now explore an Australian example that examines research-like activity among student teachers, that is, in pre-service education. The belief that practicing teachers and student teachers have different histories and experiences of teaching and learning is often accompanied by notions that student teachers do not have sufficient teaching experience to reflect on, that they do not yet have burning questions, and hence research-like activity is less appropriate in preservice education.

4.2   Student Teachers Learning to Act Through Research

At the University of Sydney, final year student-teachers work in groups to construct an educational environment in which children from local primary schools take part as active and reflective learners of mathematics (Crawford & Deer 1993, Crawford 1992). The program supports the student-teachers as they create, implement, adapt and evaluate a program of work on a mathematical topic in which the focus shifts from solely teacher-directed reproduction of existing knowledge and techniques to a context in which children participate actively and creatively in meaningful investigation, inquiry and reflection — for the children, the generation of mathematical knowledge.

The student-teachers also become active learners in the role of action researchers of applied education. They work in small groups and each group has a responsibility to make decisions, try out new ideas, explain strategies and choices in educational terms, review their practice and reflect on and evaluate their solutions. Later they use their own experiences as a basis for further analysis, reflection, theory building and theory testing. The experience initially confronts student-teachers with their own deep seated beliefs about:

- The nature of mathematics
- The roles of a teachers and learners
- The power relationships within a classroom
- The capabilities of young children
- The ways in which children learn
- The nature of mathematical knowledge.

Learning through action research is a new experience for all of them. Their skills in encoding and reproducing the content of a course, which have been a mainstay in their school and university careers, are less useful in a context where they are asked to demonstrate new capabilities for defining problems, decision making about strategies for inquiry, gathering of evidence and explanation, creatively changing habits of practice, reflection and self evaluation. Since the course was initiated in 1991, none of the students have reported prior experiences as active and independent learners of mathematics or of active and independent decision making about educational matters.

They are generally confronted by tensions and inconsistencies between the recent theories of learning that they have been told about, and that most have espoused intellectually, and the transmission model of learning that is implied in their habits and inclination to act as 'teacher'. They know about learning through investigation and inquiry, by reading set texts and research articles, but few have experienced it either in mathematics or in their education courses. These experiences of other peoples knowledge have not prepared them for the very personally challenging activity of learning through creating and investigating their own practice. At a deep level, they still conceptualise learning in terms of their own experience of being told. Most initially feel a need to tell children about the mathematics before asking them to solve problems or investigate. All are initially focussed on their own teaching behaviours, needs and goals with little attention to or awareness of the students' learning processes and outcomes. All are accustomed to working professionally as individuals in isolation. They find collaboration and group planning difficult. Most importantly, all have internalised the usual power relationships in the classroom. They begin by being in charge, setting clearly defined tasks, demonstrating how they should be completed and ensuring that all the students are compliant and follow the standard techniques. In such a setting there is little evidence of learning through inquiry among their students as a basis for observation, reflection and evaluation.

Over several weeks each group works in a different school context and develops a program of mathematical activity that reflects the interests and needs of the children in their care. Most choose aspects of mathematics that are interesting or challenging to them such as probability or ratio. They learn a great deal about mathematics as they work with their students to define and refine mathematical ideas and use them actively as a means to inquiry. Each group research project is carried out in a different educational setting. However, experiences are shared within and between groups. This process is critical in the development of a more abstract and generalised rationale for educational processes. Advice and support from an experienced tutor are available on request. For all student-teachers the project requires them to change existing classroom practice and create a learning environment and demonstrate professional behaviours that they have not seen in local Australian schools. Then they are asked to reflect upon the processes occurring and continuously evaluate them and review their plans, goals and strategies in the light of observations of the students' learning of mathematics.

The process of actively and transformatively participating in change is a powerful learning experience for student-teachers. In all cases the experience results in:

- Widening of attention from a focus on teaching to include learning processes and the learners' needs, goals and emerging mathematical awareness.
- Awareness of the distinction between teachers' needs and goals and those of the students.
- An appreciation of the dialectic nature of teaching and learning.
- Awareness of the importance of trust and a capability to share authority and power as well as responsibility.
- A heightened awareness of the extent of individual differences.
- A view of mathematical knowledge which includes capabilities for problem posing, problem definition, modelling, investigation inquiry and self evaluation.
- Demonstrated capabilities for educational decision making, explanation, creative development of a new learning context and effective assessment of the learning of mathematics that occurs within it.

In a situation where it is very difficult to provide professional images of teachers applying recent theories of learning in schools, the action research approach is effective in widening student awareness of the practical implications of educational theory (and the wider possibilities for teaching and learning in mathematics) and in supporting them in the development of their own professional rationale for decision making about the teaching and learning processes in mathematics in various school contexts. In addition, after such experiences, they have the confidence that comes from experiences of effective practical action using mathematics.

CONCLUSION

If teachers are to learn about their profession in the active ways that are now known to be empowering and recommended in curriculum documents, then they will need opportunities to explore, investigate, create, reflect and solve problems and answer research questions for themselves. Only through active engagement with problems and questions that are personally meaningful to them will they develop a rationale for action. Only through understanding their own learning through research, inquiry, investigation, and analysis will they come to understand such processes among students in their care. As Vygotsky describes it:

Thought itself is engendered by motivation, i.e. by our desires and needs, our interests and emotions. Behind every thought there is an affective volitional tendency, which holds the last answer to why in the analysis of thinking. A true and full understanding of another's thought is only possible when we understand its affective-volitional basis.

(Vygotsky 1962, p. 150).

The gap between research knowledge and teaching practice has long been recognised (e.g. Stenhouse 1975; Speedy 1989, p.6). Clearly, research carried out by academics and from their point of view does not of itself enhance teachers' capabilities in schools. The knowledge generated by researchers generally rests with the researchers. Reading and talking about published accounts of other people's research does not necessarily provide a rationale for personal action. Rather, traditional educational processes have produced static forms of knowledge and capabilities for routine techniques and procedures that are now the province of new information technologies and unsuited to the learning needs of people.

Unlike traditional forms of teacher education in preservice or inservice courses, learning through research results in knowledge that is actionable – a basis for professional action. Further, in an era of rapid change in the nature and uses of information that challenges traditional education practice, learning through research provides a means for:

- less authoritarian experiences of learning through investigation, collaboration and inquiry among peers as a basis for facilitating similar experiences for their students.
- an opportunity to review and extend their knowledge of mathematics – in particular of the practical applications of mathematics in society.
- professional empowerment through the development of a practical understanding of the dynamic social interactions that mediate knowledge generation in educational settings as a basis for educational decision making.
- opportunities for continuous learning throughout a professional career and a basis for responsive adaptation to the changing educational needs of students in changing societies.

In the information era many of the paper and pencil mathematical activities that have dominated the curriculum in the past now seem less appropriate. For teachers the pressures for a change to more active and reflective forms of learning mathematics through processes of investigation and problem solving present a challenge. Action research has the potential to both support change in professional practice and provide appropriate active learning opportunities for teachers.

South Africa and Australia are both countries in which there are large social, cultural and vocational changes in progress. In times of change new forms of learning are needed that allow for the reflection, problem definition, experimentation and problem resolution that is a necessary part of human adaptation. For the survival of democratic forms of social organisation in the twenty first century, it is imperative that the cultural constructions of teaching and learning are changed to include a range of more active, flexible and meaningful activities for many more people. The intellectual processes associated with research of various kinds need to be more widely practiced outside the university system. In an era when information technologies have mathematised all forms of activity, including structures determining social opportunity, more active, reflective and meaningful mathematical activity by more people is particularly important. A key element in achieving such changes will be changes in the learning experiences of teachers through their active involvement in a process of research-based change in educational institutions.

ENDNOTES

1. Some contemporary theory uses the term social 'practices' in order to include sets of discourses which also shape and are shaped by persons thinking, feeling and acting (Evans & Tsartsaroni, 1994). Foregrounding discourses as opposed to activities is not unsimilar to the agency-structure debate. Our view is that these are mutually constitutive, and that either term can and should imply persons acting both with intentionality, and within sets of social constraints.

REFERENCES

Adler, J.: 1992, 'Mathematics Teachers in the South African Transition', *Mathematics Education Research Journal* 6, 2, 101-112.
Adler, J.: 1993, 'Activity Theory as a Tool for a Mathematics Teacher-as-Researcher'. in V. Reddy (ed.), *Proceedings of the First Annual Meeting of SAARMSE.* Grahamstown,, Rhodes University, 53-57.
Adler, J.: 1992, 'Action Research and the Theory-Practice Dialectic: Insights from a Small Post Graduate Study Inspired by Activity Theory'. in Geeslin, W., Graham, K. (eds.) *Proceedings of the 16th Psychology of Mathematics Education Conference, (PME-16) Vol 1,* Durham, University of New Hampshire, 41-48.
African, National Congress (ANC): 1994, *A Policy Framework for Education and Training: Discussion Document.* Johannesburg, ANC Education Dept.
Ball, D.: 1987, 'Unlearning to Teach Mathematics', *For the Learning of Mathematics,* 8, 1, 40-47.
Bennett, N.: 1993, Knowledge Bases for Learning to Teach. in: Bennett, N., Carre, C. (eds.), *Learning to Teach.* London, Routledge, 1-17.
Bishop, A.: 1992, 'International Perspectives on Research in Mathematics Education.' in: Grouws,D.A. (ed.), *Handbook of Research on Mathematics Teaching and Learning.* Macmillan, New York, 710-734.

Breen, C., Coombe, J. (eds.): 1992, *Transformations: The First Years of the Mathematics Education Project (MEP)*. Cape Town, MEP, University of Cape Town

Brousseau, G.: 1992, ''Didactique: What It Can Do for the Teacher'. in R. Douady, Mercier, A. (eds.) *Research in Didactique of Mathematics*. Grenoble, La Pensee Sauvage, 7-39.

Coombe, J., Galant, J., Ncube, C, Parsraman, A. (eds.): 1995, *The Atlantic Proceedings*, MEP, University of Cape Town, Cape Town.

Crawford, K.: 1992, 'Applying Theory in Teacher Education: Changing Practice in Mathematics Education'. in: Geeslin, W., Graham, K. (eds.), *Proceedings of the 16th Psychology of Mathematics Education Conference, (PME- 16) Vol II*, Durham, University of New Hampshire, 161-168.

Crawford, K. P., Deer, C. E.: 1993, 'Do We Practice What we Preach: Putting Policy into Practice in Teacher Education', *Journal of South Pacific Association of Teacher Education*, 21, 2, 111-121

Crawford, K.P., Gordon, S., Nicholas, J. Prosser, M.: 1993, 'Learning Mathematics at University Level'. in W. Atweh (ed.): *Contexts in Mathematics Education, The Proceedings of the 16th Annual conference of the Mathematics Education Research Group of Australasia*, Brisbane, 209-214.

Crawford, K., Gordon, S., Nicholas, J., Prosser, M.: 1994, 'Conceptions of Mathematics and How It Is Learned: The Perspectives of Students Entering University', *Learning and Instruction* 4, 331-345.

Davidoff, S.: 1993, 'Emancipatory Action Research in South Africa: Fanning the Fires of Theory and Practice.' in: Davidoff, S., Julie, C., Meerkotter, D., Robinson, M. (eds.): *Emancipatory Education and Action Research*. Pretoria, Human Sciences Research Council, 75-83.

Davis, Z. (ed.): 1995, *Exploring Mathematics Teaching and Teacher Education*, MEP, Cape Town, University of Cape Town

Douady, R., Mercier, A. (eds.): 1992, *Research in Didactique of Mathematics*. La Pensee Sauvage, Grenoble.

Duckworth, E.: 1983, 'Teachers as Learners', *Archives de Psychologie*, 51, 171-175.

Edusource: 1994, 'A Brief Overview of Education, 1993'. in *Data News*, 5, 3, Johannesburg, The Education Foundation

Elliot, J.: 1988, *Teachers as Researchers: Implications for Supervision and Teacher Education*, Address to the American Educational Research Association, New Orleans

Enslin, P.: 1990, 'Science and Doctrine: Theoretical Discourse in South African Teacher Education'. in Nkomo, M. (ed.) *Pedagogy of Domination*, New Jersey, African World Press

Flanagan, W. (ed.),: 1991, *Teachers and their Work: Case Studies of In-service Education in African Primary Schools*, Cape Town, Primary Education Project, University of Cape Town

Geeslin, W., Graham, K. (eds.): 1992, *Proceedings of the 16th Psychology of Mathematics Education Conference (PME 16)* Vol. 1, Durham, University of New Hampshire

Goldstein, C., Mnisi, P., Rodwell, P.: 1994, 'Working Together for Change.' in: J. da Ponte, J. Matos (eds.): *Proceedings of the Eighteenth International Conference for the Psychology of Mathematics Education*. Vol. III, Lisbon, Lisbon University, 9-16.

Hirabayashi, I., Nohda, N., Shigematsu, K., Lin, F. (eds.): 1993, *Proceedings of the 17th International conference of the Psychology of Mathematics Education (PME 17)* Vol. 1, Tsubuka, University of Tsubuka, 228-235.

Lave, J.: 1988, *Cognition in Practice*, Cambridge, Cambridge University Press.

Lave, J., Wenger, E.: 1990, *Situated Learning: Legitimate Peripheral Participation*, Palo Alto, CA, Institute for Research on Learning, Report No. IRL 90-0013

Lerman, S.: 1990, 'The Role of Research in the Practice of Mathematics Education', *For the Learning of Mathematics*, 10, 2, 25-28.

Mousley, J.A.: 1992, 'Teachers as Researchers: Dialectics of Action and Reflection'. in: Geeslin, W., Graham, K. (eds.): *Proceedings of the 16th Psychology of Mathematics Education Conference, (PME-16)* Vol II, Durham, University of New Hampshire, 334-341.

National Council of Teachers of Mathematics (NCTM): 1989, *Curriculum and Evaluation Standards for School Mathematics,* Reston, VI, NCTM

National Education Policy Investigation (NEPI): 1993, *The Framework Report and Final Report Summaries,* Cape Town, Oxford/NECC

Orpen, B., Colyn, W., Wilson-Thompson, B.(eds.): 1995, *Teachers' Voices,* Mathematics Education Project (MEP), Cape Town, University of Cape Town

Rogoff, B.: 1994, 'Developing an Understanding of the Idea of Communities of Learners', *Mind, Culture and Activity,* 1,4, 209-229.

Stenhouse, L.: 1975, *An Introduction to Curriculum Research and Development,* London, Heinemann

Speedy, G.: 1989, *The Discipline Review of Teacher Education in Mathematics and Science,* Canberra, Government Printing Office.

Valsiner, J.: 1994, 'Irreversability of Time and the Construction of Historical Developmental Psychology', *Mind Culture and Activity,* 1, 1, 25-42.

Vygotsky, L.S.: 1962, *Thought and Language,* Cambridge, MIT Press

Vygotsky, L.S.: 1978, *Mind in Society,* Cambridge, Harvard University Press

Walker, M.: 1993, 'Developing the Theory and Practice of Action Research: A South African Case', *Educational Action Research* 1, 1, 95-109

Wertsch, J.: 1994, 'The Primary of Mediated Action in Socio-cultural Studies', *Mind Culture and Activity,* 1, 4, 202-208.

Willis, S.: 1990, 'Numeracy in Society: the Shifting Ground.' in S. Willis (ed.), *Being Numerate: What Counts?* Hawthorne, Victoria, Australia, ACER, 1-23.

Chapter 33: The Mathematics Teacher and Curriculum Development

BARBARA CLARKE, DOUG CLARKE AND PETER SULLIVAN
Monash University and University of Melbourne, Australia

ABSTRACT

The teacher is the key to worthwhile mathematical experiences for children. In this chapter, we offer an appreciation of the crucial role played by teachers in any meaningful curriculum; a recognition that teachers need to be supplied with appropriate resources (text or student materials, teacher support material, relevant technology, and an appropriate physical environment); and an acknowledgment that teachers need time: Time to plan, time to meet together, time to assimilate new content and pedagogy into their repertoire, and sufficient hours timetabled for mathematics. The views of teachers as either irrelevant or merely agents of change are examined, and these are contrasted with a view of the teacher as curriculum maker. Some factors which constrain the teacher's role in mathematics curriculum development are considered, and a range of curriculum projects and approaches to curriculum policy are discussed. During the discussion, reference will be made to experiences in a variety of countries and contexts, illustrative of the points we are making. We also report in greater detail on three specific examples of curriculum development (in Papua New Guinea, a Dutch/U.S. joint initiative, and Australia), and reflect on the implications of these examples for those seeking to maximise the role of the teacher in curriculum development.

1. INTRODUCTION

We take the mathematics curriculum to be the experiences, whether intended or not, which occur within the mathematics classroom, and we see curriculum as an account of teachers' and students' lives, both together and separately (Clandinin and Connelly, 1992). We acknowledge that this does not include all learning opportunities in mathematics, but it clarifies the emphasis in this discussion of the influences on the curriculum, and allows us to give due emphasis to the centrality of the teacher in the curriculum enterprise.

Many writers have distinguished between the *intended* curriculum, the *implemented* curriculum, and the *attained* curriculum (e.g. Robitaille et al., 1993). The intended curriculum is the mathematics content as defined at the national or educational system level. The implemented curriculum is the mathematics content as it is interpreted by teachers and made available to stu-

A.J. Bishop et al. (eds.), International Handbook of Mathematics Education, 1207 - 1233
© *1996 Kluwer Academic Publishers, Printed in the Netherlands*

dents. The attained curriculum is taken to be the concepts, processes, and attitudes towards mathematics that students acquire in the course of schooling. Our discussion will focus largely on the first two of these.

We first examine some trends, influences and constraints which affect the classroom curriculum, including those which relate to the culture of teaching mathematics, those which are imposed by political influences, and those which are the result of specific projects or initiatives. We then explore the critical and central role of the teacher in the creation of the curriculum and some attempts to support teachers in this task. Finally, we examine in some detail the role of the teacher in curriculum development in three different contexts, within the framework of the previous sections.

2. TRENDS, INFLUENCES, AND CONSTRAINTS AFFECTING CURRICULUM

Education is seen worldwide as a vehicle for the transmission of culture and identity. Community leaders, including politicians, examine society and often seek to effect some desired change in the behaviour of citizens. Schools are usually a focus of attention for such reformers. As Cuban (1992) put it, 'If society itches, the schools scratch' (p. 216). These on-going, and usually competing, pressures for change are often accompanied by a perception that schools and teaching practices are resistant to change, and that teachers are reluctant to endorse the programs of reformers. As a result, many initiatives or school reforms are accompanied by a strategy to enlist the support of teachers. The fine line between the genuine involvement of teachers and token consultation is a recurring theme in this chapter.

Our view of curriculum development places teachers and students very much in the foreground. However, despite our emphasis on curriculum as being largely the story of the work of teachers and students in classrooms, a whole range of trends, influences, and constraints impact on this work.

2.1   A Commonality of Trends in Mathematics Curricula Over Thirty Years

In most countries, syllabus documents are prepared centrally for the respective school systems. Yet the mathematics curriculum across the countries of the world has a similarity which does not reflect the diversity of the cultures and contexts. It seems there is a culture of mathematics education which gives rise to a natural commonality of content.

Two broad areas of influences on commonality of mathematics curriculum are evident. One is the 'natural' commonality of content that arises from the culture of mathematics education, the other is the commonality of external influence from beyond the school system. Throughout this century, there has been almost universal adoption of what Howson and Wilson (1986) called a

1208

school mathematics 'canonical curriculum', developed in Western Europe in the aftermath of the Industrial Revolution, and adopted practically everywhere during the 1900's. They comment on the 'extraordinary uniformity of syllabuses across the world' (p. 19), even in countries which differ massively in, for example, resources, retention rates, and cultural contexts. They describe a basic 'core' curriculum consisting of arithmetic, algebra and measurement, 'to which other content is added partly on the whim of the nation, partly on that of the teacher' (p. 40).

This sense of commonality is even more amazing given that across the countries of the world, mathematics is timetabled for anything from one-tenth of the school week to almost half (Howson and Wilson, 1986). In Japan and Mexico, where approximately 95 per cent and 3 per cent respectively of the populations complete secondary school, there is remarkable similarity in year-by-year syllabuses. We endorse the call of the authors for less adherence to the content derived from the culture of mathematics and for more attention to local needs and context:

> Every nation wants the best for its children, and things are unlikely to improve country by country in isolation. What is necessary, however, is that those responsible for the development of school mathematics should become much more critical of experience derived from elsewhere, and pay more attention to their own actual circumstances and needs than to considerations of international 'standards' and issues of comparability.
>
> (Howson and Wilson, p. 21)

In considering trends in curriculum development in the past thirty years, an amazing commonality also emerges in external influences from beyond schools and school systems. 'New Mathematics' or 'Modern Mathematics' in the 60's and early 70's, for example, became the dominant movement around the world. Despite the original source of the changes (the flurry of mathematical and scientific activity in the United States, in response to the success of the U.S.S.R. space programs) having little apparent relevance to a small country in another part of the world, many such countries attempted to embrace similar syllabus documents and teaching methods, sometimes with greater fervour than the original initiators of the movement (Howson and Wilson, 1986). As Wilson (1992) later commented in discussing the African situation:

> What did it matter that the chapters on stocks and shares, and rates and taxes were meaningless to an African pupil? Such relevance was simply not a criterion.... Any deviation would have been regarded by well-educated Africans as having their children fobbed off with a second-best or watered-down education. (p. 127)

These attempts to 'mimic' the curriculum of more highly-developed nations are understandable when the cost and necessary expertise required to create relevant local curriculum support materials are considered, but it would appear that community perceptions of what constituted 'real mathematics' were also a major determinant, with reality being seen as what the rest of the developed world was doing.

The modern mathematics era was followed in many places by a 'back to basics' push in the late 70's and early 80's, which in turn was followed by a trend (still current) towards a greater emphasis on problem solving, extended investigations, and recognising and encouraging the reality of students 'constructing' their own understanding of mathematical concepts and ideas, in a collaborative rather than authoritarian/competitive setting.

Niss (1992) summarises this more recent trend in his description of mathematics teaching in Denmark:

> The focus is on pupils as individuals, on their personal development and needs, as well as on their social interaction. Mathematical processes are emphasised more than the product.... Children, working independently as well as in groups, are encouraged to experiment, to measure, to guess, to feel their way, to conjecture, to refute, and to play, so as to gain mathematical knowledge. (p. 69)

This statement or very similar ones could have been found in curriculum documents in any number of other countries.

2.2   Influence of National Assessment Schemes

While these trends influence the content of mathematics, national assessment schemes are significant determinants of both content and teaching method. Attempts to develop the use of innovative curriculum support materials in schools have increasingly been impeded by the imposition of national assessment structures, the goals of which often conflict with the goals of the national curriculum statements of those countries. From time to time, in various places, and in different ways, communities become concerned about schooling 'standards', and seek to measure outcomes of schooling in some way. This often takes the form of external tests of children, and mathematics, which is seen as the easiest subject to test objectively, features as a prominent component of such assessment. This has some potential to affect teachers' choice of content, but more explicitly it must impact on the ways teachers teach. While this impact presents itself in different ways in different contexts, it seems that external assessment schemes do have an influence on both content and teaching methods in different countries.

The professional association of mathematics teachers in the United States (the National Council of Teachers of Mathematics, NCTM), recently produced national curriculum guidelines supportive of a different view of mathematics and mathematics learning than has traditionally been the case in that country (NCTM, 1989, 1991). These documents, being in reasonable harmony with constructivist views of learning, lead to immediate conflict with the reality of standardised testing, which has been a considerable force on curriculum and curriculum change in the United States for a number of years.

Two of the present authors (Clarke and Clarke) worked with teachers in a curriculum development project in the United States, but were asked by teachers and administrators to 'leave the teachers alone' for the month of April, which was solely devoted to preparation for the standardised testing that was to occur in May. Of course tests, of themselves, are not necessarily detrimental to learning. They do however, have a major impact on what is taught and the way it is taught. Since problem solving or analytical items are usually under-represented in tests, they will also be under-represented in curriculum driven by standardised assessment. As Apple and Teitelbaum (1986) stated:

> With control over content, teaching, and evaluation shifting outside the classroom, the focus is more and more only on those elements that can be easily measured on standardized tests. Knowledge 'that' and occasionally low-level knowledge 'how' are the primary foci. Anything else is increasingly considered inconsequential. That is bad enough, of course, but in the process even the knowledge 'that' that is taught is made 'safer', less controversial, less critical.
>
> (Apple and Teitelbaum, 1986, p. 181)

Requirements of educational systems for accountability therefore continue to be a major determinants of the mathematics curriculum. In Hong Kong, for example, frequent public examinations dominate classroom practice. Morris (1988) argued that lessons in most Hong Kong classrooms are structured as one continuous practice session for the public examination and hence students seem to fall into a pattern of rote learning and excessive drilling in skills. Interestingly, the order of curriculum development is the development of examination syllabuses first, followed by notes on teaching, written according to these syllabuses. Wong (1993) claimed that most mathematics teachers teach in accordance with three things: the text book, the examination syllabus, and past papers in public examinations. Innovations of the kind that are being advocated presently in much of the world, and more recently in Hong Kong itself (Curriculum Development Council, 1995) must be considered in the context of average class sizes of around 43 and the highest student/teacher ratio in the Second International Mathematics Study (Brimer and Griffin, 1985).

Gillespie (1992), commenting on the United Kingdom assessment program, argued that there was little professional support for the scheme from teachers, educators, or Her Majesty's Inspector of Schools, and therefore 'the present testing proposals in the new curriculum seem certain to change' (p. 100). Based on the experience of testing schemes in other countries, such confidence may not be justified.

Arfwedson (1976), in discussing the Swedish setting, identified a range of external constraints, including assessment, which impact on the work of teachers and students. He contrasted the written system of goals (pedagogical methods and attitudes based on humanistic and democratic ideology) with the written system of rules including the fragmentation of the timetable, rules about government approval of textbooks, and appropriate forms of assessment. He commented that

> The system of rules ties up the teaching situation to an extent that makes the 'open' areas — e.g., that of teaching methods — in practice very much dependent on the rest of the closed system.... The teacher lands in conflict with either the system of rule (the 'progressive' teacher), or with the system of goals (the 'conservative' teacher) or with both (the 'ordinary' teacher). (pp. 140-142)

This conflict between goals and rules may account partially for the canonical curriculum, where even though teachers are given freedom within 'guidelines' to develop their own curriculum, the imposition of external rules or required outcomes from students has the effect of focusing the teacher's curriculum decisions in a way much like a prescribed curriculum.

2.3   Large-Scale Curriculum Development Projects

Another significant influence on school curriculum derives from externally initiated projects. Of particular interest here is the way that such projects perceive the role of the teacher.

The style of curriculum documents developed for classroom teachers by outsiders often says much about the writers' views of the role of the teacher in curriculum development. Where teachers are viewed as essential 'players' in the process, curriculum documents take the form of 'guidelines', with the assumption that a given teacher will draw upon their experiences and the knowledge of colleagues in 'fleshing out' the material to meet the needs of their students.

Where curriculum developers see little role for teachers' adaptions, they tend to produce what have come to be called 'teacher proof' materials, with extensive and detailed instructions of the form 'use these words, hand these out'. If teachers lack qualifications and/or experience in teaching mathematics, this can create a pressure on curriculum developers to produce such 'teacher proof' materials, because they are claimed to be capable of use by any teachers, with minimal risk of 'misinterpretation'. Such materials generally take the form of worksheets or text materials which focus almost exclusively on drill and practice of a large number of small, (allegedly) sequentially developed skills. The term 'teacher-proof' however ignores the impact of context and culture on the way in which any curriculum materials are implemented in a classroom. As Howson, Keitel, and Kilpatrick (1981) argued, while the teacher who is allowed some freedom in determining the curriculum faces a far from easy task, a teacher using such teacher-proof materials must still be aware of the weaknesses in the materials she or he is using, how to compensate for these, and how to take advantage of their strengths.

Many writers caution that the use of teacher proof materials demeans the role of the teacher. Apple and Teitelbaum (1986) argue that when individuals (teachers in this case) cease to plan and control a large portion of their own work, the skills essential to doing these tasks self-reflectively are forgotten. 'The very things that make teaching a professional activity – the control of one's expertise and time – are also dissipated' (p. 180). While most involved in education would value 'professionalism' as an ideal worth striving for, our later discussion of the Papua New Guinean situation brings the many constraints on this process into focus.

Any international survey of the literature on the teacher's role in curriculum development is likely to reveal many examples reflective of a continuum of perspectives from teacher proofing to teachers as essential players. At the same time, the multiplicity of curriculum development projects and the short life span and perceived lack of success of the majority of these (Weissglass, 1994) indicate the presence of a multitude of inhibitors to curriculum change and professional growth.

The terms 'intended curriculum', 'implemented curriculum', and 'achieved/attained curriculum' (mentioned earlier) are often used to distinguish the original intentions of curriculum developers from the realities of the classroom. Often these terms are used to imply that any differences (and there are always differences) are attributable to the inadequacies of teachers, thereby failing to recognise the desirability of both adaption to the local setting, and the many factors which inhibit teachers from teaching as they would like.

The 60's and 70's were marked by large scale, well funded central curriculum projects, particularly in the United States and the United Kingdom. Despite the quality of the materials produced by many of these, few, if any, of these projects achieved their stated aims. In the past twenty years, there has been a major growth in research into the professional development of teachers, and this research emphasises that professional growth is a gradual, difficult, and often painful process (Clarke, 1994), and must maximise teacher involvement at every possible stage of the process:

One of the great mistakes over the last 30 years has been the naive assumption that involving some teachers on curriculum committees or in program development would facilitate implementation, because it would increase acceptance by other teachers. Of course, it was such an automatic assumption that people did not use the words 'some' and 'other'. It was just assumed that 'teachers' were involved because 'teachers' were on major committees or project teams. Well, they were not involved, as the vast majority of classroom teachers know. Once again, there was a failure to distinguish between 'the change' and 'the change process'. As far as most teachers were concerned, when the change was produced by fellow teachers, it was just as much externally experienced as if it had come from the university or the government.

(Fullan and Stiegelbauer, 1991, p. 127)

There is considerable financial cost attached to genuine involvement of teachers in curriculum development projects, but there are many other costs associated with failing to do so, including a failure to draw upon the wisdom of practice, and a feeling of lack of ownership and therefore commitment among practitioners.

2.4 Numbers, Qualifications, and Status of Mathematics Teachers

In a later section, we outline the advantages of viewing the teacher as 'curriculum maker', and the importance of recognising the wisdom of practice in any new curriculum initiatives. However, we also recognise that there are many factors which act to constrain the opportunities for involvement of teachers, including shortage of qualified teachers and related issues of status.

Although there are still many countries where few students continue on to any form of secondary school mathematics, the past thirty years has seen considerable worldwide growth in the percentage of students continuing their studies. This growth has not generally been matched by an equivalent growth in the number of qualified mathematics teachers. For example, twenty-five years ago, when many African countries were gaining independence, teaching as a profession in Africa generally enjoyed a high status. Wilson (1992) described how the ranks of the teaching force were 'plundered' to fill the roles of civil servants, leading to a decline in numbers of people presenting for teaching. As a result, Zimbabwe and Nigeria put thousands of untrained teachers into schools, attempting to provide inservice support, as they developed the art of teaching.

Similar stories of decline in status and qualifications are evident in many other countries (see, e.g., Drake, 1990; Zawadowski, 1992; and Montaldo, 1992, for a discussion of trends in the United Kingdom, Poland and Italy respectively). In the second IEA Mathematics Study, only 1 of the 19 systems reported 75 per cent or more 'fully qualified' teachers (defined locally as having attained appropriate mathematical background and teacher training) among the ranks of teachers of students up to the age of 13. However, this percentage varied for older students from 80 per cent to 100 per cent (Werry, 1989). In Denmark, for example, upper-secondary teachers in Denmark study on average for 7.5 years, with a minimum of 5.5 required (Niss, 1992).

The lack of qualified teachers raises the issue of the effect of inadequate mathematical content knowledge on the ability of teachers to move into new mathematical or pedagogical territory. With the different, arguably more demanding style of teaching approaches seen to be in harmony with constructivist learning theories, lack of knowledge comes even more clearly into focus.

Shulman (1986) claimed that thinking properly about content knowledge 'requires understanding the variety of ways in which the basic concepts and principles of the discipline are organised to incorporate its facts' (p. 9). This organisation is important, for as Brophy (1991) indicated:

Where (teachers') knowledge is more explicit, better connected, and more integrated, they will tend to teach the subject more dynamically, represent it in more varied ways, and encourage and respond fully to student comments and questions. Where their knowledge is limited, they will tend to depend on the text for content, de-emphasize interactive discourse in favor of seatwork assignments, and in general, portray the subject as a collection of static, factual knowledge. (p. 352)

It seems essential that teachers be thoroughly prepared for their work, in order that their involvement in curriculum development and implementation demonstrate the kind of dynamism described by Brophy.

2.5   Lack of Resources

Teachers in many developing countries lack the resources which are necessary to make effective use of many curriculum materials. A lack of appropriate furniture for large classes, lack of paper and pens or pencils, lack of appropriate text materials, and lack of equipment such as basic calculators, make it unrealistic to attempt to transplant curriculum materials from, say, France or the United Kingdom into a small developing country, as well as all the other cultural factors that should influence such a decision.

In a study of grade eight mathematics in the Dominican Republic, for example, teachers reported that although the textbook was their main resource in teaching mathematics, only 25 per cent of students had their own textbook (Luna, Gonzalez, and Wolfe, 1990).

Many curriculum development projects are based on the assumption of provision of 'basic' equipment, and schools and teachers which are lacking these are clearly handicapped in curriculum implementation.

As well as the provision of material requirements for teachers, the resourcing of appropriate professional development programs is also essential. There is also considerable value in the support and resources that curriculum advisers or consultants in school districts or regions can offer, serving the role of critical friends to teachers who are struggling with innovation or even maintenance of the status quo (Owen, Johnson, Clarke, Lovitt, and Morony, 1988).

In summary, the involvement of mathematics teachers in curriculum development depends to a large extent on external influences (assessment schemes, resources, the focus of large-scale curriculum development projects), but also upon the provision of material resources and ongoing professional development support. These constraints and influences are not presented in any sense of either excusing or criticising teachers, but rather to establish the context in which teachers interact with external influences on the curriculum. In the next section we focus on the teacher and their role in the curriculum, recognising the importance of the teacher as a central figure in curriculum as it is implemented in the classroom and discussing the value of using the 'wisdom of practice' in the development of curriculum materials and curriculum support documents.

3.   THE TEACHER AS CURRICULUM MAKER

Clandinin and Connelly (1992) argued that most models of curriculum reform either see the teacher as irrelevant and therefore to be circumvented through teacher-proofing the curriculum, as an inhibitor of change and therefore requiring re-education as a prerequisite to successful curriculum implementation, or as an agent of the change and therefore to be wooed and inducted into the project.

In proposing that teachers should be viewed as 'curriculum makers', Clandinin and Connelly (1992) challenged their readers to reflect on what would happen if some outside body engaged them in a project with the intention of changing *their* practices through some imposed reform process. The inference is that the professionalism and wisdom of teachers should be acknowledged and built upon in any consideration of the classroom curriculum.

Clandinin and Connelly (1992) reviewed literature on curriculum within the United States and identified few recent references to teachers as having the central role in making the curriculum. They noted that this century had seen swings in the pendulum from centralised to decentralised curriculum. Citing support from John Dewey, they suggested that the central issue should be the 'mutual making of curriculum with teachers and other practitioners' (p. 369). They inferred that Dewey clearly valued collaboration between teachers and children to reconstruct wisdom through inquiry, and saw the development of curriculum as a negotiated process between the teacher, pupils, administrators and parents in which they participated and grew together.

Given problems in many countries regarding qualified mathematics teachers, the reluctance to 'hand over' greater responsibility for curriculum development to teachers is not surprising, and yet there are many settings in which teachers are given significant responsibility. Many European countries have had long traditions of teachers being given considerable freedom to develop syllabuses and classroom experiences from broad, skeletal frameworks or guidelines.

'Didaktik', broadly defined as 'the art or study of teaching' (Hopman and Riquarts, 1995, p. 3), underpins much of the thinking about teaching and teacher education in central and northern Europe. The 'Didaktic triangle' – the content, the learner, and the teacher – structures the field of didaktic research and theory. The didaktical tradition assumes that teachers are given 'substantial leeway to develop their own intentions, interpretations and critiques of both the objectives and content of the state syllabi' (Keitel and Hopman, 1995, p. 1).

Klafki (1995) emphasised the crucial role of the teacher in re-enacting the pedagogical decisions made by syllabus designers and embedded in the curriculum content. Klafki claimed that teachers could only fulfil their task adequately if they represent the content which is to be acquired by education or instruction, and if they themselves personify it and credibly reflect it.

Klafki stressed the need for teachers to study carefully 'wherein the general substance of specific content of education lies' ('didaktic analysis') (p. 22) prior to determining appropriate teaching methods. It is clear that the didaktic tradition places considerable emphasis on the key role of the teacher in curriculum development, and there is no sense of the teacher as 'conduit' for the state curriculum.

In Denmark, teachers are given considerable freedom concerning didaktical and pedagogical decisions, working with textbooks and other materials that have been developed by experienced teachers (Niss, 1992). Over the past thirty years, there has been a move 'from a rigid, centrally controlled curriculum to a curriculum consisting of a limited number of categories described only in general terms; interpretation in detail is left to the individual teacher, with written examination papers [in the Gymnasium] as the main instrument of control at the disposal of central authorities' (p. 74).

The primacy of teachers was a key component of the Cognitively Guided Instruction project (CGI) in the U.S.A. which provided junior primary teachers with access to research-based knowledge about young children's learning of addition and subtraction concepts through four weeks (full-time) of professional development workshops, and then monitored their efforts to use this knowledge in the classroom, as they attempted to build on the rich knowledge base that children bring to the learning situation (Carpenter, Fennema, Peterson, and Carey, 1988; Fennema, Carpenter, and Peterson, 1989).

CGI was not offering teachers a curriculum *per se*, but rather giving them access to research about children's learning, and encouraging them to draw curriculum implications for themselves. It was argued that not only would teachers be better translators of knowledge about children's thinking into practice than the project staff would, but having the opportunity to make the translation would enable them to assume ownership of CGI ideas (Fennema, Franke, Carpenter, and Carey, 1993).

The value that the CGI project placed on the key role of teachers in curriculum development provides a model for the teacher as curriculum maker, where using knowledge of research and their own children's thinking was the basis of curriculum decisions.

Clandinin and Connelly (1992) suggested that some curriculum developers view the recognition of adaption of materials by teachers more as a trade-off than a desirable process. However, if the teacher is viewed as a key figure in the curriculum process, this adaption is an appropriate response. Romberg and Pitman (1990), when reporting on a study of 20 teachers' adaptions of grade one mathematics materials, found that only one of these teachers expressed support for the notion of following the materials faithfully. Most felt that the adaption was part of their role:

> Teachers made conscious decisions about what to teach, how to teach, the amount of time allocated to topics and activities, and the use of time during instruction. They did this knowing the content of the teacher manuals and, in general, the intentions of the authors of the materials. These decisions were made based on their views of the importance and difficulty of the conceptual content of a unit of work, on their beliefs about the degree of homogeneity in their class and the levels of the pupils, and on their assessment of the appropriateness of the content and the complexity of the recommended activities for a particular class. (p. 205)

Although misinterpretation is a concern, it is important that greater acknowledgment is given to the need for teachers to make adaptions to curriculum materials as they draw upon their experience and the perceived needs and level of understanding of their students.

In the next section we discuss ways in which some countries have acknowledged and incorporated the experiences of teachers (the wisdom of practice) in the curriculum development process.

In China, each of the approximately 90,000 secondary schools has its own mathematics teaching research group (Wang, 1992). As part of the activities of these groups, individuals prepare experimental lessons developed around new ideas or new methods. These experimental lessons are observed in classrooms by fellow teachers, followed by seminars, in which what has been observed is discussed in considerable detail, with the teacher providing appropriate background to what has just been presented. As a further activity, teachers are encouraged by the National Ministry of Education to document particular lessons ('Excellent Lessons'). These are shared among other teachers, and an authoritative group of researchers evaluates these according to agreed criteria, awarding prizes in some cases.

Similar status is accorded excellent lessons in Japanese mathematics education (Stigler and Stevenson, 1991). There is a systematic effort to pass on the accumulated wisdom of teaching practice to each new generation of teachers. Senior staff in schools organise meetings to discuss teaching techniques and to devise lesson plans and handouts. Stigler and Stevenson estimated that Japanese elementary school teachers were in charge of classes for only 60 per cent of the time they were at school, providing a considerable amount of time for joint planning and sharing. The authors contrasted this to the U.S. setting, where less than one hour was typically available for such joint planning. This opportunity for joint planning clearly enables teachers to take a substantial role in curriculum development.

In Australia, the Mathematics Curriculum and Teaching Program (Lovitt and Clarke, 1988; 1989) was a national professional development program, the stated aim of which was to 'capture and share the wisdom of practice of classroom teachers'. This was achieved by carefully documenting promising classroom lessons offered by teachers, across a range of themes (mathematical and pedagogical), which were then provided to professional development networks for trialling and enhancement. After four years, 114 exemplary lessons or investigations were documented in four to eight pages each, using photos and teacher commentary to give the reader a 'window' on the classroom. These materials, offering as they did a frame-by-frame description of an 'amalgam' of excellent teaching episodes, were never intended as a script for teachers to follow, but were rather a 'snapshot' of an innovative lesson or lessons, with a view to encouraging teachers to experiment with a new approach to teaching and learning (e.g., small cooperative group work, mathematical modelling), adapting the exemplary lessons as they saw fit. These materials are now being used in professional development settings in several countries.

The Nuffield Mathematics Project in the United Kingdom (Nuffield Foundation, 1972) was a major attempt to involve teachers in curriculum development. Large numbers of teachers throughout the country were involved in preparing teachers' guides, which were discussed in 92 local networks of teachers' centres. These centres then became the locations for inservice programs, where trialling pilot materials was the focus. Interestingly, the decision was made not to produce student materials, leaving this to the discretion of the teachers.

The Scottish *National Guidelines Mathematics 5-14* (Scottish Office Education Department, 1991) acknowledge in their rationale that teachers should use the Guidelines as a lens to examine critically their current practice, but that the Guidelines themselves were based on existing good practice. There is a sense that current practice was valued, and that teachers were encouraged to explore ways to develop this practice further.

3.2   Curriculum Development Takes Time

Any discussion of the meaningful and substantial involvement of teachers in curriculum development invariably moves to a discussion about the need for time. Teachers need time to plan, time to share their experiences with interested colleagues, time to come to grips with new curriculum and new technology, and time to reflect. This notion of reflection emerges from the research literature as crucial in enabling teachers to examine their current practice and beliefs, and hopefully to reconcile the two, at least to the extent that they have control over their own situation (Clarke, 1994; Thompson, 1992). In the second IEA Study of Mathematics in 20 education systems around the world, face-to-face teaching loads varied from means of 13 and 22 hours (Werry, 1989), with consequent variation in time for preparation, administration and reflection.

A common feature of successful curriculum development projects which involve major shifts in content, pedagogy, or both, is the importance placed upon the provision of time for teachers. de Lange (1987) described the Hewet experiment in the upper secondary curriculum in The Netherlands, which commenced in 1985. This experiment was conducted with curriculum for students who were university-bound, but not expected to study higher-level mathematics at tertiary level. It is clear that the strategy was to involve just a small number of teachers initially, and then slowly expand this *over many years*. The project commenced with 2 schools over 2 years, expanded to 12 schools over the next 2 years, and to all schools 2 years later. A similar project started for non-university bound students in 1987, expanding to all schools by 1990. Interestingly, de Lange commented that even this pace of introduction was hasty, and involved risk for successful implementation. A six-year time span was subsequently allowed for the introduction of new curricula for ages 12-16. de Lange and his colleagues were adamant that introducing significantly new curriculum programs was unlikely to be successful without considerable time and resources being given to the process. This suggests that rather than the vast majority of resources being directed towards development of the curriculum materials or documents, that significant funding be allocated to the piloting, subsequent adaption and implementation process. This is supported by Berman and McLaughlin (1976) who concluded after a study of four large projects in the United States, that successful implementation was characterised by the process of *mutual adaptation*, a process whereby adjustments to a curriculum are made by curriculum developers and those who actually use it in the school or classroom context.

Acknowledging the time frame needed in curriculum implementation, Nemetz (1992) claimed that the then current approach to primary mathematics in Hungary was initiated in 1960, and was first taught experimentally in two classes by two teachers, being extended gradually to 200 classes over ten years, 'in a slow, patient endeavour'. The process was sped up subsequently due to political and social pressures, and a 'milder' version was introduced in the early 1980's.

Wilson (1992), in reviewing curriculum development across Africa, noted that the most successful projects went through the test-revise process three or four times before final publication. Yet he notes that the time and money for such a developmental process may not generally be made available by the politicians. 'Africa is in a hurry – not least in education' (p. 130).

In summary, teachers have a central role in implementing the curriculum, whether of their own making or the adaption of externally developed documents or materials. As professionals, they should be given time and the authority to adapt and supplement any external materials in a way that suits their students' needs. We go further in suggesting that teachers have a role in contributing to the development of curriculum policy and materials. Any model of curriculum development should recognise and value the experience of teachers.

4.   CURRICULUM IN PRACTICE: THREE STORIES

We have argued that teachers should be seen as the makers of the curriculum. Given that there are significant external influences and constraints on schools, teachers and school programs, it is clear that teachers do not make their curriculum in isolation. Indeed the differences between an educational environment which results from a teacher predominantly responding to external factors and one where the teacher's curriculum mainly results from their own active intervention and control are subtle. It is possible that the main way in which the teacher as curriculum maker ethos would be manifest is in the language used to describe the work which teachers do, and in the form of professional development which they undertake.

The following are three stories about curriculum, each illustrating the relevance of context and each raising its own issues about the extent to which teachers make their own curriculum.

4.1 A Centrally Developed Curriculum: Community School Mathematics – Papua New Guinea

Papua New Guinea (PNG) is a developing country with a firm commitment to national development through education. PNG represents an example of a centralised approach to development of syllabus documents. The scope of the content is stipulated within broad parameters, within the constraints imposed by scarce resources and limited local support. There is also a centralised approach to the provision of text resources, with most texts being produced on contract rather than as commercial risk ventures. The story illustrates that the provision of text and other support is one thing, but the classroom curriculum is ultimately the responsibility of the teacher.

Papua New Guinea achieved independence in 1975. The nation is made up of over 10,000 tribes and 740 different languages, more than one sixth of the languages in the world (Wurm, 1979). English is the official language, but many Papua New Guineans speak *Tok Pisin* as a lingua franca. The country was formerly administered by Australia from about 1920 to 1975. Since then, although there have still been expatriates working in significant roles, there is an active process of localisation which aims to educate Papua New Guineans to perform all planning and policy roles.

A significant proportion of the population attends the six years of community schooling but only 40 per cent of these continue to secondary school due to the lack of available places. The country also has a system of national high schools (Years 11 and 12), entry to which is highly competitive. Children start school at age seven. Teacher education courses are usually post-year 10, although some current teachers have only themselves completed year 8 or even year 6.

School facilities are generally basic and the responsibility is placed on the local communities to provide both buildings and teacher housing. There is a system of school inspectors who maintain both a monitoring and a support role, and there are regional offices in most provinces in the country.

The history of the development of mathematics curriculum documents in PNG has been one of reform (Britt, 1978; Roberts, 1980). The process is managed by syllabus committees which have virtually all Papua New Guinean members, most of whom are Provincial Education Office personnel and Regional Inspectors. It should be noted though that all have been classroom teachers and their main focus and activity is classroom work. There is also a National Curriculum Unit. A number of senior staff are expatriates, but all have Papua New Guinean associates.

After many years of providing classroom texts which were written for different audiences, predominantly Australian, PNG has systematically sought to develop texts written for PNG students using culturally appropriate mathematical contexts.

The secondary syllabus has undergone development from an Australian syllabus to one specifically designed for students in Papua New Guinea. One secondary text series (Britt, 1978) written specifically for PNG, was an activity based program with emphasis on the use of concrete representations.

A significant development for Community Schools was the Indigenous Mathematics Program (Souviney, 1981). This was a project funded by the World Bank which focused on all aspects of curriculum development, including the establishment of a factory for the production of materials for use in schools. This led directly to a project to prepare a text series for primary schools starting at Grade 4 (Roberts, 1982) which was developed, trialled and published within Papua New Guinea.

More recently, a set of texts for use with grades 1, 2 and 3 in the Community Schools, was produced. This project was internationally tendered and the contract won by Oxford University Press who used an Australian authorship team with previous PNG experience. Directions on content and method were given to the authors by the Mathematics Syllabus Committee. The content of the program was based on activities relevant for Papua New Guinean students, both from the rural areas and from the cities. The program was intended to be flexible in its delivery, and placed emphasis on the use of manipulative materials. Materials used included such items as seeds, shells, sticks, and stones from the environment, and less traditional items such as bottle tops and cardboard boxes.

An interesting feature of the series is that it was designed to be 'language neutral'. The intention for the first book was that teachers would use the language of the children in the school as a language of instruction, although the direction from the Syllabus Committee was that where a mathematical word existed in English but not in the local language, then the English word should be used. An example of this was 'triangle', which in some Papua New Guinean languages would be explained by circumlocution.

This provides an interesting context against which the issue of teacher as curriculum maker can be set. There is no suggestion that teachers in PNG should develop their own syllabus documents or text resources. Teachers expect text and other resources to be produced centrally, and they seek documented syllabuses on which they can base their own teaching. PNG does not have the infrastructure to be able to supply ongoing support for individual teachers and culturally it seems oriented towards providing a centrally determined syllabus. It seems that the authorities have used limited resources to produce quality curriculum support given the limited budget.

Within this context, the implemented curriculum is quite explicitly the responsibility of the teacher. Even though the inspectorial system has a monitoring role, the isolation of most schools sees teachers as professionally autonomous. This then leads to a somewhat paradoxical situation within what appears to be a highly structured regime. Even though the syllabus and texts are produced centrally, and include detailed structured information, what goes on in the classroom is ultimately the responsibility of the teacher. The same limit on resources which requires central curriculum determination also prohibits the imposition of controls. There are few sanctions. If the teachers do not make their own curriculum, no-one else will. Yet the teacher is not seen as the curriculum maker by educational planners. It is in this context that the image of teacher as curriculum maker becomes helpful. If such an image were adopted by educational planners, it would have the potential to change the language used in the curriculum process, the types of professional development offered, and they way that teachers are viewed by the community.

4.2 Mathematics in Context: A Dutch-American Collaboration

This is a story which illustrates the tensions arising from a project motivated by a desire to support reform of teaching practices and curriculum. While recognising that the stimulus for the project was external to the schools involved, a key element was the acknowledgment of teachers as essential players in making their own curriculum.

The project arose from the reforms of school mathematics which are currently underway in the United States, which in turn were motivated by concerns expressed by teachers, the community, and a number of educational commissions (National Research Council, 1989, 1990). The publication of the Curriculum *and Evaluations Standards for School Mathematics* and *The Professional Standards for the Teaching of Mathematics* by the National Council for Teachers of Mathematics (NCTM, 1989, 1991) represented a teacher's voice (or at least the voice of a professional association of teachers) in suggested directions for reform. The *Curriculum and Evaluation Standards* (NCTM, 1989) presented general goals for all students, the implementation of which required a different classroom from that typically evident in the United States (see, e.g., Stigler and Stevenson, 1991). The *Professional Standards for Teaching Mathematics* (NCTM, 1991) painted a picture of this new classroom environment as it described a shift:
  - toward classrooms as mathematics communities – away from classrooms as simply a collection of individuals;
  - toward logic and mathematical evidence as verification – away from the teacher as the sole authority for right answers;
  - toward mathematical reasoning – away from merely memorising procedures;
  - toward conjecturing, inventing, and problem solving – away from an emphasis on mechanistic answer-finding;

1224

— toward connecting mathematics, its ideas, and its applications — away from treating mathematics as a body of isolated concepts and procedures. (p. 3)

Given the move towards a very different kind of mathematics classroom, a different kind of support for teachers was needed. For this reason, the National Science Foundation in the United States funded a series of major development initiatives. One of these, *Mathematics in Context* (Romberg et al., 1991) involved a collaboration between The Netherlands and the United States.

The Netherlands was seen as an ideal country with which to collaborate because of their experience with developing curriculum built around problem solving. The approach in The Netherlands has come to be called 'Realistic Mathematics'. Some background on Realistic Mathematics provides insight into the features of the project.

A significant reform began in The Netherlands in the 1960's and 1970's about the time of the 'New Math' movement in many other parts of the world. It had quite a different basis from the structuralist reforms of that time. In elementary schools, the Wiskobas project was designed to encourage the recreation of mathematical concepts and structures on the basis of intuitive notions (Treffers, 1987). It reflected a view that mathematics instruction should not begin with the formal system (as in rules and procedures) but rather students were encouraged to re-invent key ideas in mathematics for themselves. One of the features of instruction was that the way concepts appear in reality should be the source of concept formation.

Mathematics learning was seen by the Dutch to involve individual construction mediated by discussion with fellow students and the teacher, and through the provision of appropriately structured curriculum materials. Realistic Mathematics drew its basis from both the view of mathematics as a process of invention as well as a social constructivist view of learning. Designers of curriculum support resources did not tend to have clear objectives or specific skills in mind and saw the classroom trialling of materials as a vital component of the development process:

> There is no place for a pre-programmed teaching-learning process, since the whole process would depend on the individual contributions of students and had to be interactively constituted between teacher and students.
>
> (Gravemeijer, 1994, p. 22)

Mathematics in Context was a program for school grades 5-8, and developed around 40 three to five week units of work. The units were initially developed by staff at the Freudenthal Institute. These first drafts were then 'Americanised' by project staff members to adapt the materials to the contexts, needs and interests of U.S. students. Units were trialled with a small number of classrooms, with input from both researchers and classroom teachers on the revision process.

The following quotes from one of the pilot teachers illustrate the changing role teachers had to deal with when using these materials:

> Many of the strategies we had used to help our students master manipulative skills were useless in this new environment.... The possibility that several points of view and, consequently, several answers, were reasonable is difficult to accept, especially when you have spent an average of fifteen years rewarding thought processes that were identical to yours....

> Our role was shifting from that of one who directs the thought processes of the students to one who reacts and guides their reasoning; it was not easy to resist telling students what to do or showing them how, but instead to ask leading questions.

> We had to listen to students, examine their work, and try to learn what they were thinking as they solved a problem....Communication became an integral part of the classroom dynamics.
>
> (de Lange, van Reeuwijk, Burrill, and Romberg, 1993, pp. 190-192)

While the project is still in progress, early data indicate that this international collaboration has been a worthwhile enterprise, in that 'the wisdom of practice' from many years in The Netherlands has been used as a starting point for curriculum development in the United States (see, e.g., Clarke, 1993; de Lange, 1994), while (importantly) valuing the local context in necessary adaptions at national and classroom level.

This then highlights the dilemma. From the perspective of the teacher, *Mathematics in Context* represents an externally imposed course of study. This reflects the tradition in the United States where teachers have relied heavily on textbooks or prepared material. There was some debate during development of materials as to the appropriate extent of adaption by teachers. Concern was expressed that teachers who were not comfortable with aspects of recommended content or pedagogy may adapt the materials back into 'their comfort zone' to such an extent that the spirit of the intended innovation be compromised. Yet the essence of the project was to emphasise the central role of the teacher in stimulating the student control of learning and therefore the need for ongoing adaption of the planned experience during the teaching. So, on one hand, the project was imposed, yet on the other the project gave more prominence to the autonomy of teachers as the makers of the curriculum. In the trialling phase, this tension was resolved by providing frequent opportunities for dialogue between project staff (including two of the present authors) and classroom teachers, so that the kind of mutual adaption mentioned earlier in this chapter could be facilitated to the satisfaction of all involved.

4.3 From School Based Curriculum To Centrally Imposed Structures: The State of Victoria, Australia

The State of Victoria, Australia, provides the context for this third story. It is an example of a move from an educational environment which acknowledged the primacy of teachers and the school community in making the curriculum, towards a model which sought to impose a pre-determined structure on what is taught. For a significant period in Victoria, the teacher was genuinely seen as the curriculum maker, and this was reflected in the style and quality of support provided.

In the mid 1970's, in each curriculum area, Victorian schools, both primary (ages 5 to 11) and secondary/technical (ages 12-17) were given responsibility for their own curriculum. No central syllabus was prescribed, and support for teachers took the form of curriculum guides (e.g., Technical Schools Mathematics Standing Committee, 1977). This move was accompanied by a transfer of significant responsibilities for overall school planning and curriculum to locally structured school councils and school curriculum committees.

Over the next ten to fifteen years support for primary mathematics teachers consisted of the production of curriculum guides (e.g. Ministry of Education, 1985) which were primarily suggestions of classroom activities which could be used to address aspects of mathematics teaching. The main support document for secondary mathematics teachers also consisted of a compilation of suggested teaching activities organised by topic (e.g., Lowe, 1978). More structured guidelines for secondary mathematics were subsequently published (Education Department of Victoria, 1982), although a significant feature of this was a listing of steps which schools could follow in the process of determining their own syllabus and planning processes.

Even after a decade, documented curriculum support was in the form of a book of readings about aspects of mathematics teaching, with particular focus on pedagogy. While this *Mathematics Framework* (Ministry of Education, 1988) did have a scope and sequence chart, it was broad and served only as an overall guide for schools.

As expected, this process was not without its tensions. Some regional groups at the primary level did publish their own syllabus statements in response to the insecurity experienced by some teachers. Those teachers expressed a desire for more detailed guidelines. It must be acknowledged that school-based curriculum development was often more difficult for primary school teachers who, being generalist, needed to develop curricula in all subjects areas. Secondary teachers usually only had to participate in the development of one or two subjects.

A number of interesting developments accompanied the overall process. First, the teachers' association, the Mathematical Association of Victoria, grew from a small organisation into an influential professional group. This association now holds annual conferences attracting over 2000 teachers in a state with a population of approximately 4 million, an ongoing professional development series, and provides support for teachers through resource development.

Second, a unique form of support materials emerged, starting with the *Reality In Mathematics Education* (RIME) program (Lowe and Lovitt, 1984), and followed by the *Mathematics Curriculum and Teaching Program* (MCTP) (Lovitt and Clarke, 1988, 1989), a national project mentioned earlier in this chapter. MCTP produced draft materials in the form of potentially exemplary lessons. Each lesson or set of lessons was selected because it exemplified innovative practices, including cooperative group work and mathematical modelling. These draft lessons were then extensively trialled by teachers participating in a variety of professional development networks around Australia, and then published, using pictures and annotations of teachers' comments, to give a sense of how the activities 'played out' in classrooms. The documentation included comprehensive suggestions for teachers and possible extension activities. The intention was to empower teachers by sharing the wisdom of best practice and to facilitate the construction of further rich classroom experiences based on the structure of the published lessons, which hopefully served as models for this process. This is different from involving teachers in planning and developing a curriculum support project before its implementation. In this, the wisdom of practice served explicitly as the base on which a teacher might choose to build.

Third, a model of teacher development emerged which acknowledged the on-going nature of professional development. For example, one program, 'Exploring Mathematics In Classrooms' (Robinson, 1987), developed ten one-and-a-half hour inservice sessions conducted after school hours, spread over 20 weeks, with trained tutors. The program included readings, classroom activities, and sharing of favourite ideas between teachers. The intention was that groups of teachers from a school would participate. After four years, approximately 50 per cent of schools in the state had been involved in the program.

This was the first of a number of professional development approaches which became aggressively school based. For example, a project Mathematics in Schools (Montgomery, 1995) which was funded by the federal government, involved schools engaging in an extended process of school based development with the support of a facilitator who was usually a university based curriculum researcher. At each school, the staff nominated one aspect of their mathematics program (content, pedagogy, resources, etc.) on which they wished to focus in the following year, and they were supported by the facilitator in that process. This approach to teacher development reflects the culture where the teacher was seen as the curriculum maker, and the school as the appropriate site for planning the curriculum.

Concurrent with the latter stages of this process, educational administrators became attached to the processes of total quality management, which they interpreted to mean there should be an emphasis on education competences and outcome based education (see Ellerton and Clements, 1994, for a stunning critique of this movement). This was a politician led process which was stimulated by carefully targeted funded programs. First the national government produced a statement of detailed outcomes of schooling in all curriculum areas including mathematics (Australian Education Council, 1990). This was interpreted by each state in developing their own curriculum documents.

In Victoria, a *Curriculum and Standards Framework* (CSF) (Board of Studies, 1995) was produced which derived from the national document and was an explicit statement of outcomes. This was accompanied by a further teacher support document which contained collections of classroom activities cross referenced to the CSF outcomes (Directorate of School Education, in press). These two documents reflect both the previous and current regimes. On one hand the current government seeks to specify educational outcomes, and on the other hand, teachers have become accustomed to an activity-based model of curriculum planning which has given them considerable autonomy. Clearly teachers who plan from activities as a first step find it inappropriate to limit their teaching and assessment to predetermined outcomes. Yet teachers who plan from outcomes find it difficult to find focused classroom activities which engage the students in higher level educational experiences.

Jackson (1992) noted that the history of curriculum is periodic; the pendulum swings. Here is a story of a state which chose to acknowledge the expertise of teachers by giving them responsibility for their own curriculum. Within the framework, there were some outstanding initiatives and both the type of support materials and the structure of professional development programs were designed to empower teachers. Some teachers felt insecure, and certainly the government felt insecure. The next stage was the development of beliefs among educational administrators that explicit statements of outcomes would result in a better education for the citizens. Many teachers however, having enjoyed the autonomy that school-based curriculum development offered and having responded by developing curricula for their students which brought national respect, are concerned that a lack of such freedom in the future (coupled with the introduction of standardised testing), may lead to a narrowing of curriculum for their students.

This movement toward more central prescription of curriculum content was in response to perceived community expectations. This suggests that teachers and educators need to ensure that the community is involved in an ongoing dialogue about education so that government policies are the result of meaningful consideration and not simply a reaction to a previous approach.

CONCLUSION

We are suggesting that it is productive for schooling, learning and teaching if dialogue about curriculum development incorporates the perspective which sees the teacher as the curriculum maker. It is recognised that there are important influences on curriculum content from within the mathematics education community, and from the influence on both content and method arising from the imposition of testing regimes. The issue is that teachers do not so much need to be seen as autonomous but more as central to the curriculum process. Irrespective of the degree of imposition or interference on the teacher, the teacher still remains the curriculum maker. However, the influences can be severe enough to affect adversely the teachers' achievement of their own goals. An acceptance of the 'teacher as the maker of the curriculum' view will result in greater acknowledgment of the wisdom of practice in the development of support resources, and in the focus of teacher development programs. We are confident that this will lead to more effective learning for students as a result of better curricula in classrooms and improved professional recognition for teachers.

REFERENCES

Apple, M. W., Teitelbaum, K.: 1986, 'Are Teachers Losing Control of Their Skills and the Curriculum?' *Journal of Curriculum Studies,* 18(2), 177-184.
Arfwedson, G.: 1976, 'Ideals and Reality of Schooling' in *Relating Theory to Practice in Educational Research: A Report on an International Conference* Bielefeld, Institüt für Didaktik der Mathematik der Universität Bielefeld.
Australian Education Council.: 1990, *A National Statement on Mathematics for Australian Schools,* Melbourne, Curriculum Corporation.
Berman, P., McLaughlin, M.: 1976, 'Implementation of Educational Innovation,' *Educational Forum,* 40, 3, 345-370.
Board of Studies.: 1995, *Curriculum and Standards Framework,* Melbourne, Australia, Author.
Brimer, A., Griffin, P.: 1985, *Mathematics Achievement in Hong Kong Secondary Schools. Hong Kong,* Centre of Asian Studies, University of Hong Kong, Hong Kong.
Britt, M.:1978, *Mathematics Our Way (Trial Units),* Department of Education, Port Moresby, PNG.
Brophy, J. E.: 1991, 'Conclusion to advances in research on teaching, Vol. II: Teachers' knowledge of subject matter as it relates to teaching practice', in J. E. Brophy (ed.), *Advances in Research on Teaching: Teachers' Subject-matter Knowledge and Classroom Instruction Volume 2,* JAI Press, Greenwich CT, 347-362.
Carpenter, T. A., Fennema, E., Peterson, P. L., Carey, D. A.: 1988, 'Teacher's Pedagogical Content Knowledge of Students', *Journal For Research in Mathematics Education* 19, 5, 385-401.

Clandinin, D. J., Connelly, F. M.: 1992, 'Teacher as Curriculum Maker', in P. W. Jackson (ed.), *Handbook of Research on Curriculum*, Macmillan, New York, 363-401.

Clarke, D. M.: 1993, *Influences on the Changing Role of the Mathematics Teacher*. Unpublished doctoral dissertation, University of Wisconsin – Madison.

Clarke, D. M.: 1994, 'Ten Key Principles for the Professional Development of Mathematics Teachers', in D. B. Aichele, Coxford, A. F. (eds.), *Professional Development of Mathematics Teachers (1994 Yearbook)*, National Council of Teachers of Mathematics, Reston, VA 37-48.

Cuban, L.: 1992, 'Curriculum Stability and Change', in P. W. Jackson (ed.), *Handbook of Research on Curriculum*, Macmillan, New York, 216-247.

Curriculum Development Council.: 1995, *Target Oriented Curriculum Programme of Study for Mathematics*, Education Department, Hong Kong.

de Lange, J.: 1987, *Mathematics, Insight and Meaning*, Utrecht, The Netherlands, Vakgroep Onderzoek Wiskundeonderwijs en Onderwijscomputerentrum, Rijksuniversiteit Utrecht.

de Lange, J., van Reeuwijk, M., Burrill, G., Romberg, T. A.: 1993, *Learning and Testing in Context: The Case of Data Visualization*, New York: SUNY.

de Lange, J.: 1994, 'Curriculum Change: An American-Dutch Perspective', in D. F. Robitaille, D. H. Wheeler, Kieran, C. (eds.), *Selected Lectures from the 7th International Congress on Mathematics Education*, Sainte-Foy, Quebec, Les Presses De L'Universite Laval.

Drake, P.: 1990, 'Training Teachers in Crisis: A Case Study of a Part-Time Postgraduate Certificate in Education', in P. Dowling and R. Noss (eds.), *Mathematics Versus the National Curriculum*, The Falmer Press, Hampshire, 1990, 216-233.

Education Department of Victoria.: 1982, *Curriculum Development Guidelines*, Melbourne, Author.

Ellerton, N. F., Clements, M. A.: 1994, *The National Curriculum Debacle*, Perth, Meridian Press.

Fennema, E., Carpenter, T. P., Peterson, P.: 1989, 'Teachers' Decision Making and Cognitively Guided Instruction: A New Paradigm for Curriculum Development. In N. F. Ellerton and M. A. Clements (eds.), *School Mathematics: The Challenge to Change*, Deakin University Press, Geelong, Australia, 174-187.

Fennema, E., Franke, M.L., Carpenter, T.P., Carey, D. A.:1993, 'Using Children's Mathematical Knowledge in Instruction'. *American Education Research Journal*, 30, 3, 555-584.

Fullan, M., Stiegelbauer, S.: 1991, *The New Meaning of Educational Change* Teachers College Press, New York.

Gillespie, J.: 1992, 'Trends in Secondary-School Mathematics in the United Kingdom', in R. Morris and M. S. Arora (eds.), *Studies in Mathematics Education*, UNESCO, Paris, 1992, 90-101.

Gravemeijer, K.: 1994, *Developing Realistic Mathematics Education*. Vakgroep Onderzoek Wiskundeonderwijs en Onderwijscomputerentrum, Rijksuniversiteit Utrecht, Utrecht, The Netherlands.

Hopman, S., Riquarts, K.: 1995, 'Starting a Dialogue: Issues in a Beginning Conversation Between Didaktik and the Curriculum Traditions', *Journal of Curriculum Studies* 27, 1, 3-12.

Howson, G. Keitel, C., Kilpatrick, J.: 1981, *Curriculum Development in Mathematics*. Cambridge University Press, Cambridge.

Howson, G., Wilson, B.: 1986, *School Mathematics in the 1990's*, Cambridge University Press, Cambridge.

Jackson, P. W.: 1992, 'Conceptions of Curriculum and Curriculum Specialists', in P. W. Jackson (ed.), *Handbook of Research on Curriculum*, Macmillan, New York, 3-40.

Keitel, C., Hoppmann.: 1995, 'Editorial', *Journal of Curriculum Studies* 27, 1, 1-2.

Klafki, W.: 1995, 'Didactic Analysis as the Core of Preparation of Instruction', *Journal of Curriculum Studies* 27, 1, 13-30.

Lovitt, C. J., Clarke, D. M.: 1988, 1989, *Mathematics Curriculum and Teaching Program Activity Bank (Vols. 1 and 2).* Curriculum Corporation, Carlton, Victoria, Australia.

Lowe, I.: 1978, 'School Based Curriculum Planning in Maths. (GLIMA)', in Costello, P. (ed.), *Aspects of Motivation,* Mathematical Association of Victoria. Melbourne, Australia, 331-334.

Lowe, I., Lovitt, C.: 1984, *RIME Activity Bank,* Ministry of Education, Melbourne.

Luna, E., Gonzalez, S., Wolfe, R.: 1990, 'The Underdevelopment of Educational Achievement: Mathematics Achievement in the Dominican Republic Eighth Grade. *Journal of Curriculum Studies,* 22, 3, 361-376.

Ministry of Education.: 1985, *Guidelines in Number,* Author, Melbourne, Australia.

Ministry of Education.: 1988, *The Mathematics Framework: P-10,* Author, Melbourne, Australia.

Montaldo, O.: 1992, 'Teaching Mathematics in Italy: Yesterday, Today and Tomorrow', in R. Morris and M. S. Arora (eds.), *Studies in Mathematics Education,* UNESCO, Paris, 55-62.

Montgomery, P.: 1995, *Mathematics in Schools,* Mathematical Association of Victoria, Melbourne, Australia.

Morriss, P.: 1988, 'Teachers' Attitudes Towards a Curriculum Innovation: An East Asian Study', *Research in Education,* 40, 75-87.

National Council for the Teachers of Mathematics.: 1989, *Curriculum and Evaluation Standards.* Author, Reston, VA.

National Council of Teachers of Mathematics.: 1991, *Professional Standards for Teaching Mathematics.* Author, Reston, VA.

National Research Council.: 1989, *Everybody Counts: A Report to the Nation on the Future of Mathematics Education.,* National Academy Press, Washington, DC.

National Research Council.: 1990, *Reshaping School Mathematics: A Philosophy and Framework for Curriculum,* National Academy Press, Washington, DC.

Nemetz, T.: 1992, 'Mathematics Education in Hungary', in R. Morris and M. S. Arora (eds.), *Studies in Mathematics Education,* UNESCO, Paris, 105-112.

Niss, M.: 1992, 'The State of and Trends in Scandinavian School Mathematics, as Reflected by the Case of Denmark', in R. Morris and M. S. Arora (eds.), *Studies in Mathematics Education,* UNESCO, Paris, 63-76.

Nuffield Foundation.: 1972, *Nuffield Mathematics Project: Teachers' Guides,* Murray/Chambers, London/Edinburgh.

Owen, J., Johnson, N., Clarke, D. M., Lovitt, C., Morony, W.: 1988, *Guidelines for Consultants and Curriculum Leaders,* Curriculum Corporation, Carlton, Victoria, Australia.

Roberts, B.: 1982, *Curriculum Development and the Quality of Education in Developing Countries,* Paper presented at the Second Mathematics Education Conference, Lae, PNG.

Roberts, R.E., Kada, V.:1979, 'The Primary Mathematics Classroom', *Papua New Guinea Journal of Education,* 15 (Special Issue), 174-201.

Robinson, I.:1987, 'Exploring Mathematics in Classrooms', In W. Caughey (ed.), *From Now to the Future,* Mathematical Association of Victoria, Melbourne, Australia, 13-19.

Robitaille, D. F., Schmidt, W. H., Raizen, S., McKnight, C., Britton, E., Nicol, C.: 1993, *Curriculum Frameworks for Mathematics and Science (TIMMS Monograph No. 1),* Pacific Educational Press, Vancouver, Canada.

Romberg, T. A., Pitman, A. J.: 1991, 'Curricular Materials and Pedagogical Reform: Teachers' Use of Time in Teaching Mathematics', in M. Ben-Peretz and R. Bromme (eds.), *The Nature of Time in Schools: Theoretical Concepts, Practitioner Perceptions,* Teachers College Press, Columbia University, New York, 189-226.

Romberg, T. A., Allison, J., Clarke, B. A., Clarke, D. M., Pedro, J. D., Spence, M.: 1991, *A Blueprint for Maths in Context: A Connected Curriculum for Grades 5-8.* Wisconsin Center for Educational Research, Madison, WI.

Shulman, L. S.: 1986, 'Those Who Understand: Knowledge Growth in Teaching', *Educational Researcher,* 15, 4-14.

Scottish Office Education Department.: 1991, *Curriculum and Assessment in Scotland: National Guidelines Mathematics 5-14,* Scotland, Author

Souviney, R.: 1981, *Teaching and Learning Mathematics in the Community Schools of Papua New Guinea. Indigenous Mathematics Project Working Paper 20,* Port Moresby, PNG.

Stigler, J. W. and Stevenson, H. W.: 1991, 'How Asian Teachers Polish Each Lesson to Perfection. *American Educator,* 15(1), 12-47.

Technical Schools Mathematics Standing Committee.: 1977, *A Suggested Approach to a Continuing Mathematics Program,* Publications Branch- Education Department of Victoria, Melbourne, Australia.

Thompson, A. G.: 1992, 'Teachers' Beliefs and Conceptions: A Synthesis of Research, In D. A. Grouws (ed.), *Handbook of Research on Mathematics Teaching and Learning,* Macmillan, New York, 127-146.

Treffers, A.:1987, *Three Dimensions: A Model of Goal and Theory Description in Mathematics Instruction. The Wiskobas Project* (H. Vonk et al., Trans.), D Reidel Publishing Company (original work published in 1978), Dordrecht, The Netherlands.

Wang Lin Quan.: 1992, 'Chinese Advancements in Mathematics Education', *Educational Studies in Mathematics* 23, 287-298.

Weissglass, J.: 1994, 'Changing Mathematics Teaching Means Changing Ourselves: Implications for Professional Development', In D. B. Aichele, Coxford, A. F. (eds.), *Professional Development of Mathematics Teachers (1994 Yearbook)* National Council of Teachers of Mathematics, Reston, VA, 67-78.

Werry, B.: 1989, 'The Teachers of Mathematics', in D. F. Robitaille and R. A. Garden (eds.), *The IEA Study of Mathematics II: Contexts and Outcomes of School Mathematics,* Pergamon Press, Oxford, 39-62.

Wilson, B. J.: 1992, 'Mathematics Education in Africa', in R. Morris and M. S. Arora (eds.), *Studies in Mathematics Education,* UNESCO, Paris, 125-147.

Wong, N.: 1993, *Mathematics Education in Hong Kong: Developments in the Last Decade,* Northern Rivers Mathematical Association, Lismore, Australia.

Wurm, S.A.: 1979, *New Guinea and Neighbouring Areas, A Sociolinguistic Laboratory,* Mouton, The Hague.

Zawadowski, W. M.: 1992, 'Mathematics Education in Poland: The Changing Scene, 1970-1990', in R. Morris and M. S. Arora (eds.), *Studies in Mathematics Education,* UNESCO, Paris, 113-121.

Chapter 34: International Co-operation in Mathematics Education

EDWARD JACOBSEN
Wisconsin, U.S.A.

ABSTRACT

This chapter examines the change from education for developing high-level manpower, to universal primary education; what have been the implications for mathematics education; and what international co-operation in mathematics education has achieved. Decolonization changed the lives of most of the world's inhabitants, allowing them to demand education. The comparative small percentage of students studying school mathematics, changed to the majority of school-aged children being in school. The mathematics programmes were no longer adequate and needed to be improved. The work in mathematics education of UNESCO, ICMI and its affiliates, and other mathematics education groups and institutions is examined. Their role in international co-operation is examined, giving an example of the interactions of this co-operation in one country in Africa. Finally an opinion is given of the likely future of world wide cooperation in mathematics education.

1. INTRODUCTION

Providing Universal Primary Education is probably the biggest educational challenge facing the majority of nations. Many children never start school because either there is no school within a few miles' walk, or they are not allowed or do not want to attend, or they do not have sufficient money to pay for the school fees imposed. Once in school many drop out before reaching the end of available education; this is the case for the majority of children in many countries. Figure 1 shows the rates by regions of students who remain in schooling.

A.J. Bishop et al. (eds.), International Handbook of Mathematics Education, 1235 - 1256
© *1996 Kluwer Academic Publishers, Printed in the Netherlands*

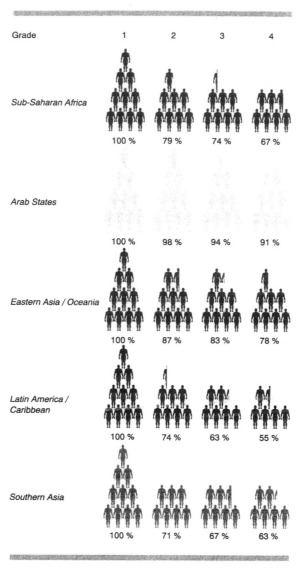

Estimated survival rates of the 1988 entering cohort in first level education in developing countries, by region

Figure 1. Survival rates of students, by region. Reprinted from the World Education Report, by permission from UNESCO.

It is known that quality of education and cost of education are not directly proportional. Poor schools can, up to a point, have acceptable results by suit-

ably motivated students, and that rich schools do have many badly performing students. That this is true in mathematics was shown in both the First and
the Second International Mathematics Studies. The amounts which countries
spend per pupil differ widely, as can be see from Figure 2.

*Public recurrent expenditure per pupil
in pre-primary, first and second level
education in 1988 (US dollars)*

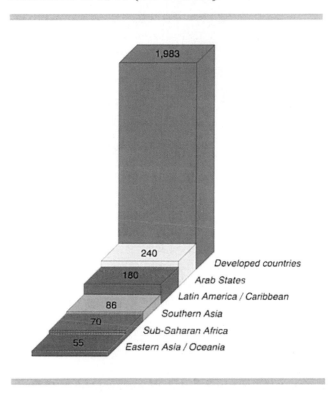

*Figure 2. Expenditure per pupil comparisons, by region. From the World Education
Report.*

The number of school aged-students not in school is large, but even larger are
the numbers of illiterate adults. Most of these adults continue to be deprived
of the education they were denied as children, as can be seen from Figure 3.

The ten countries with the largest number of illiterate adults in 1990 (millions)

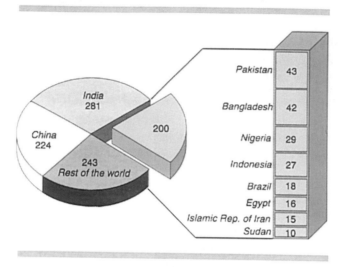

Figure 3. The ten countries with the largest number of illiterate adults in 1990. From the World Education Report.

These educational problems call out for help. This chapter will examine how through international co-operation, countries are being assisted to improve education for all, and mathematics education in particular.

2.   UNIVERSAL PRIMARY EDUCATION

Isn't universal primary education a Third-World problem, outside the responsibility of likely readers of this Handbook? Arguably no! Almost every country has groups that are not being adequately served by its national school system; religious and ethnic minorities, migrant or foreign workers, the poor, the handicapped, and the biggest group, women and girls that are underserved educationally in the majority of nations. Yet for governments, education is already one of the largest budget items, after that of the military, of course. Nevertheless, most countries are reducing educational spending, either because of shrinking national budgets, or in efforts to redirect funds to other social needs such as health, nutrition, water, roads and housing. How then can they offer more educational opportunities?

To respond to this, the World Conference on Education for All met in Jomtien (Thailand) in 1990, organized jointly by the United Nations Development Programme (UNDP), United Nations Educational, Scientific and Cultural Organization (UNESCO), the United Nations Children's Fund (UNICEF) and the World Bank. The resulting Jomtien Declaration and Framework for Action calls on governments around the world to put education at the top of the agenda, to provide Basic Education for All - to ensure that everyone has the opportunity to expand personal horizons while contributing to the general well-being. This comes forty two years after the nations of the world affirmed in the Universal Declaration of Human Rights, that 'everyone has a right to education'. Before examining how this new emphasis on basic education will affect mathematics education, let us see what preceded it.

3.   EDUCATION FOR MANPOWER AND FOR NATION BUILDING – THE 1960'S AND 70'S

During the decade of decolonization in the 1960's, the United Nations nearly tripled in membership. The newly independent countries lacked sufficient skilled manpower for running their governments and emergent economies, and there was intense political pressure to show the fruits of the struggle for independence by establishing schools, especially primary schools. The UN was asked to help, and UNESCO[1], the UN agency having responsibility for education, was given this task. With their own funds and those of the UNDP and the World Bank, hundreds of projects were initiated, involving most developing countries. The focus was on institution building, such as establishing curriculum development centres, educational statistics departments, and faculties of education. Within these projects there was usually a mathematics education component. For example, the author was for seven years a member of two projects, to establish faculties of education; one at the University of Nairobi, and one at the University of Botswana, Lesotho and Swaziland. We will examine in a later section how Swaziland was assisted by international and bilateral aid, and how they complemented each other. With severely limited funds for education, how best should the system be organized for developing a future cadre for the emerging governments' bureaucracies and economies?

The desired outcome would be for students to be educated through the university level, each level educating for the next stage. Thus, primary schools would concentrate on studies for preparation for secondary school, which in turn would focus on university preparation. What kind of mathematics would be taught for nation building? The African Commission on Mathematics Education prepared for UNESCO in 1983 a survey on the officially stated goals of mathematics teaching in 10 African countries. The major goal of teaching primary school mathematics in two-thirds of these countries was to prepare pupils for secondary school, and for half of these countries, the main goal of teaching secondary mathematics was to prepare students for university[2]. Figure 1 above questions the validity of such a programme for those students who remained in school for only a few years. Similar goals were found in the majority of the world's countries. Political pressure was increasing, by those who had been excluded from schooling, to provide primary schools for their children.

In the 1980's, the elimination of illiteracy became a major goal of UNESCO, leading to the declaration of 1990 as International Literacy Year. UNESCO's mathematics education programme also changed, emphasizing numeracy. This is reflected in their documents Mathematics for All (Damerow, et al. 1986) and Mathematics, Education, and Society (Keitel, et al. 1989) and Volume 2, The Goals of Teaching Mathematics in the series Studies in Mathematics Education.

4.   IMPLICATIONS OF UNIVERSAL PRIMARY EDUCATION FOR
       MATHEMATICS EDUCATION

For most countries in the world, Universal Primary Education means that every child goes to primary school, and that these schools are not streamed by ability. Thus the offering in mathematics must be such that every student receives the tools for survival, for work, for participating in community affairs and for being a responsible citizen politically. National and international surveys have shown again and again that this is not happening, that the majority of adults do not function mathematically; that even their arithmetic skills are poor. Citizens are literate but not numerate! An extensive discussion of this point can be found in the two UNESCO documents mentioned just above, the results of full discussions at two international meetings. The late Stieg Mellin-Olsen, after writing Politics of Mathematical Education (1987), was instrumental in gathering a group calling itself the Political Dimensions of Mathematics Education, which held conferences in London in 1991, Johannesburg in 1993, and Bergen in 1995. A discussion of this topic requires a separate chapter, and will be found elsewhere in this volume. Suffice it to say that the mathematics education community cannot continue the 'business as usual' attitude toward this global change in education.

5.   MATHEMATICS EDUCATION IN THE GLOBAL VILLAGE: INTERNATIONAL
       CO-OPERATION

A country's mathematics programme is a national effort; the curriculum is set, textbooks written, teachers educated, schools paid for, and examinations given. It would seem that each country's syllabus would be unique, yet the homogenity of the world's mathematics programmes must indicate much cross-border influence. However, of late there has been more attention to mathematics programmes which are based upon the needs and cultures of the ethnic mixes found in most countries. You will find a discussion of this trend in the chapter on ethnomathematics in this volume. There has been fruitful international co-operation amongst the mathematics education community, which we will now examine, first looking at UNESCO. Most of UNESCO's work is directly with the governments of its Member States, and the mathematics education programme is no exception. Upon request, the mathematics education specialist from UNESCO works with the ministry of education, advising and providing information. UNESCO's principal emphases in mathematics education has been to promote the exchange of information, to work nationally, and to co-operate with regional and international groups. The International Commission on Mathematical Instruction (ICMI) and UNESCO have enjoyed long, fruitful collaboration[3]. UNESCO's mathematics programme co-operates with other Non-Governmental Organizations besides ICMI; the International Statistics Institute (in convening the International Conference on the Teaching of Statistics), The International Federation for Information Processing (its World Conferences on Computers in Education), and the IEA (for their International Mathematics Studies).

6.   ICMI AND REGIONAL ORGANIZATIONS

ICMI, is the teaching commission of the International Union of Mathematicians (IMU), which in turn is a member of the International Council of Scientific Unions (ICSU) based in Paris. The IMU selects the President of ICMI and then approves the selection of officers nominated by the ICMI Executive Board. ICMI is probably best known from its International Congresses on Mathematical Education, (ICME's[4]), four-yearly gatherings now attracting 2500 mathematics educators from over 100 countries. After congresses in France (Lyons), England (Exeter), Germany (Karlsruhe), participation has greatly widened with ICMI's decision to also convene congresses outside of Western Europe. Hence U.S.A. (Berkeley), Australia (Adelaide), Hungary (Budapest), Canada (Quebec City), and soon Spain (Seville) have hosted large congresses. The Congresses are a veritable mathematics education smorgasbord and undoubtedly our best opportunity for an international exchange of information and for forging professional ties. The number attending from developing countries is still depressingly low, accurately reflecting today's economic realities. Extending the benefits beyond the privilege of attending remains a problem, as the proceedings have been expensive and not easy for third-world mathematics educators to obtain. IMCI's decision to allow the various congress interest groups to produce proceedings of their discussions has widened the availability of information. Probably the most widespread of these has been through collaboration with UNESCO. Mathematics for All (Damerow et al. 1986) came out of ICME 5, and Mathematics, Education, and Society (Keitel et al. 1989) summarized one day at ICME 6 which had been devoted to discussions on the political dimension of mathematics education. Both these titles have appeared in English and Spanish and are available free of charge from UNESCO.

More accessible than ICME are the regional conferences organized by ICMI's regional groups, as funds for professionals in Third World Countries are more readily available for organizing and participating in meetings closer to home. The Inter-American Committee on Mathematics Education (IACME), the Southeast Asian Mathematical Society (SEAMS), the African Mathematical Union Commission on Mathematics Education (AMU-CME) all organize regional conferences.

Marshall Stone, the first president of ICMI, organized the first IACME Conference, at which the Inter-American Committee was formed. IACME celebrated its 35th year in 1995 by convening its ninth Conference in Santiago, Chile. Most of its 2000 participants had never attended an International Congress on Mathematical Education (they have all been far from Latin America), yet they comprise the leaders of mathematics education in Latin America. IACME's tend to examine worldwide trends in mathematics education, then discuss what directions are appropriate for Latin America. IACME-9 had panels and discussions on political influences in mathematics education; curriculum and evaluation; informatics and mathematics education; and research. The proceedings will be published by UNESCO, as have those from earlier conferences: Bahia Blanca, Argentina (1972), Caracas, Venezuela (1975), Campinas, Brazil (1979), Santo Domingo, Dominican Republic (1987) and Miami, U.S.A. (1991). Each is published under the title Educación Matemática en las Américas, all in Spanish but with some papers in English, French, and Portuguese. The last two volumes are still available, free of charge, from UNESCO. The conferences in Bogotá, Colombia (1961), Lima, Peru (1966) were edited by Howard Fehr and published by Teachers College of Columbia University (IACME 6 in Guadalajara, Mexico (1985) did not publish proceedings.) IACME represents all of the Americas, but the meetings are largely in Spanish and Portuguese, which tends to discourage mono-English speakers from the Caribbean and North America, even though English is sometimes used and some translation is provided. A close fraternity of mathematics educators has developed from these meetings, and each country's activities are known by all. The group's presidents, Marshall Stone (USA), Luis Santaló (Argentina), Ubiratán D'Ambrosio (Brazil) and Eduardo Luna (Dominican Republic) have, over 35 years, ably led IACME to assume an increasingly influential role in shaping Latin America's mathematics education. IACME's Bulletin is edited and sent by its past-president[5].

Cross-fertilization between Latin American, Spanish, and Portuguese mathematics educators is provided through the Ibero-American Congresses of Mathematics Education (CIBEM). The first CIBEM, convened in Seville,

Spain by THALES, the mathematics education group in Seville, attracted participants from almost every country in the Americas. The Proceedings were published by UNESCO under the title Reuniones del primer Congreso Iberoamericano de Educación Matemática. CIBEM II was held in Blumineau, S.P., Brazil in 1994, organized by the Brazilian Society of Mathematics Education and the Universidade Regional de Blumenau, and attended by nearly 1000 participants from all Brazilian states, and 18 other countries. The proceedings (II CIBEM, 1995). were edited by the conference organizers, Maria Salett Biembengut and Nelson Hein. The IACME and CIBEM conferences both emphasize the social factor in mathematics education. At CIBEM II a panel examined the inclusion of environmental education in mathematics classes[6]. Eight Latin American countries are co-operating in an IACME Project, Calculators in Mathematics Education (PLACEM), which is examining curriculum at all school levels to see how calculators can improve problem solving.

The Southeast Asian Mathematical Society (SEAMS) started as a part of the Association of Southeast Asian Institutes of Higher Learning, an association of presidents of universities in the region. SEAMS was formalized at a meeting at Nanyang University (now the National University of Singapore) in 1972. The aims of the society were to generate activities in Hong Kong and the ASEAN countries, which until 1975 also included Vietnam (which recently rejoined), Laos and Cambodia (now Kampuchea), and to promote mathematics education among the general public and in their governments in order to secure support. Early activities were exclusively at university level: a summer institute on graph theory in Manila, the Philippines, in 1975, and a regional workshop in numerical analysis and computer science at Penang, Malaysia in 1977. An average of two workshops and conferences were held each year. The first Southeast Asian Conference on Mathematical Education (SEACME) was in Manila in 1978, organized with the aims listed above and including papers and discussions on the training of mathematics teachers. The results of this first conference were important, for it was the first time that university level mathematicians had met to discuss school curriculum. The discussion of a survey of the secondary school curriculum led to new textbooks being published based on the content recommended by the conference. In addition, the Mathematics Teachers Association of the Philippines was organized (there were 1300 Filipino participants to the conference), as well as the founding of a quarterly mathematics journal, the Matimyas-Matematika. Both the Association and the journal are still very active.

SEACME 2 was convened in 1981 in Kuala Lumpur, Malaysia, to consider the mathematical education of students 16 years old and above. Three workshops were organized for the 300 participants. Calculators were carefully discussed, and it was agreed that they should be used in secondary schools and universities. Hong Kong presented evidence that calculators were useful aids in learning concepts, and for problem solving. But studies were called for before considering recommending micro-computers in secondary schools. A second workshop was devoted to examining how mathematics teaching could be enriched through the arts. Specific recommendations were made, reflecting the experience of the 20 countries' participants, e.g. that more geometry should be taught, but in an intuitive (not axiomatic) approach; and that the main objective of the syllabus should be to meet the needs of the majority of the children and not merely to meet the requirements of entry to universities which involves only a minority of children[7].

The Third SEACME was held in Hat Yai, Thailand, in 1984, with the theme of undergraduate mathematics education in the computer age. Twelve countries were represented by 150 participants. A panel discussion was based on the issues raised in the ICMI Study on the Influence of Computers and Informatics on Mathematics and Its Teaching. Another panel discussed the most pressing problems of mathematical education in their respective countries [personal communication]. The Fourth SEACME was held in Singapore, with a theme that was the main research interest of the people in Singapore at the time; primary school mathematics. SEACME 5 was entitled 'Enchantment of Mathematics' and was held at the University of Brunei Darussalem, Brunei, in 1990. The Sultan opened the conference and declared the Year of Mathematics in Brunei. The Brunei Mathematical Society was founded, and every one of the country's secondary schools took part in an exhibition. SEACME 6, held in Surabaya, Indonesia in 1993, had 443 participants including 380 from Indonesia, with the rest from 17 other countries. The conference theme, Facing the Challenge of Future Mathematics Education, had subthemes of mathematics and education: for mathematicians, for scientists and engineers, for social scientists, and for mathematics teachers. Hanoi, Vietnam is the host for SEACME 7 in June 1996, which will have two themes: mathematics education in upper secondary schools; and mathematics education for mathematicians, scientists and engineers, social scientists, and mathematics teachers.

SEACME proceedings are not readily available, hence outside southeast Asia, less is known about their activities. SEACME's differ from IACME's in that they emphasize more university and secondary level mathematics education with little attention on the primary level, due to the difficulty of involving primary teachers in national and regional conferences in South East Asia. More than half of the participants at any IACME conference will be primary and secondary teachers. Their participation is encouraged by holding concurrently a workshop for these teachers, often meeting late into the night. Another difference between mathematics education in Asia and in Latin America is that in South East Asia every country except Thailand has an active mathematical society, and Thailand and Singapore each have an association of mathematics teachers. In the early years it was SEAMS which proposed and organized the regional activities, but later the national societies played the central role. These societies are the strength of SEAMS, whereas in Latin America, since it was difficult for mathematics teachers to organize in the days of the generals as heads of state, IACME was made up of individual mathematic teachers rather than associations. This has thankfully changed in Latin America, and some countries now have active mathematics teachers associations.

Africa has been less fortunate in its organization of mathematics education, in part due to the ever more stressing economic realities on the continent. Mathematics has been well served, but mathematics education much less so. The African Mathematical Union (AMU), a subset of the IMU, was founded during the First Pan-African Congress of Mathematicians (PACM), in Rabat, Morocco in 1976. Henri Hogbe-Nlend, from the Universities of Bordeau and Cameroun, was elected the first President, a post he held until 1986. The AMU was able to secure funds through the International Center for Pure and Applied Mathematics (CIMPA) in Nice, France, of which Hogbe-Nlend was also the head. He was good at raising funds, so for a decade, twice-yearly mathematics workshops were jointly organized by the AMU and CIMPA. The Second PACM was held in Nairobi in 1989. Both of these Congresses were devoted almost exclusively to university level, partly because university level teachers could find funds for travelling to professional meetings, while the salaries of education college tutors and school teachers precluded their attending.

To better serve school teachers, an African Commission on Mathematics Education was organized, but it had no funds and hence, little scope. In 1986 it was replaced by the AMU Commission on Mathematics Education, along with AMU Commissions on the History of Mathematics in Africa, on Women in Mathematics in Africa, and on Mathematics Olympiads[8]. The AMU Symposium on Mathematics Education in Africa for the 21st Century (Cairo, Egypt, 1992) was devoted mainly to school mathematics. The discussion groups were as follows: Mathematical learning in the early childhood years in Africa; Mathematics teaching in elementary schools in Africa; Secondary school mathematics programmes; and Mathematics education at tertiary level. The latest AMU activity has been the Fourth Pan-African Congress of Mathematicians, meeting in Morocco in September 1995. The theme of the conference was 'Mathematics sciences and the development of Africa: What challenges for the 21st Century?'

Mathematics educators in the countries of Botswana, Lesotho, Malawi, Mozambique, Swaziland and Zimbabwe formed the Southern African Mathematical Sciences Association (SAMSA), which now also includes South Africa. They have organized regional Olympiads and a regional meeting. They have also published a booklet Who is Who in Mathematics and Mathematics Education in Southern Africa edited by the Association's secretary Gerdes (1992).

There are two regions we haven't mentioned, Europe and the Arab States. There do not exist ICMI regional commissions for either. Since most ICME's are held in Europe, as well as with many other mathematics education groups, there is not a need for a European ICMI group. The International Commission for the Study and Improvement of Mathematics Education (Commission Internationale pour l'Etude et l'Amélioration de l'Enseignement des Mathématiques (CIEAEM)) began as an European organisation, but has now become a more international group. CIEAEM holds its annual meetings in European countries as well as in North America and strictly respects the two conference languages English and French, with the 47th meeting organized by Keitel and held in Berlin in 1995, subtitled 'Mathematics (Education) and Common Sense: The challenge of social change and technological development'. CIEAEM meetings are known for their careful and full discussions on specific and relevant themes, and do not attempt to 'cover' the field of mathematics education as does an ICME. The work of this group is too extensive, 47 years, to be included in this chapter; the meetings are well documented in the proceedings of CIEAEM.

The first large-scale UNESCO project in mathematics education was begun in the Arab States. In 1966 UNESCO was requested to assist the Arab Region in improving mathematics education. Seminars, syllabus determination, textbook writing sessions, and training sessions for teachers were held, which resulted in a new mathematics course for secondary schools which was implemented in most schools in the Arab States. The date of the project should indicate that 'modern mathematics' was at the heart of the programme. The Arab League Education, Culture and Science Organization (ALECSO) extended the reform to intermediate level students, aged 13-15, and revised the UNESCO project books. These books are still the source of adapted versions used in most of the Arab States. The Arab Bureau for Education in the Gulf States (Saudi Arabia), and its Gulf Arab States Educational Research Center (Kuwait) has in turn unified the mathematics curriculum for the first nine grades for seven of the Gulf States. Oman, which has had a phenomenal expansion of its education system in the past decade, held a workshop in September 1995 to discuss changing from the Gulf textbooks to producing their own, but first called for a study of their teaching of geometry, and studies to determine at what level calculators and microcomputers should be introduced into the curriculum. At a recent meeting in Beirut ('The Future of Science and Mathematics and the Needs of an Arab Society', organized in 1993 by the Arab Development Institute and the American University of Beirut) the following features of the above-mentioned unified curriculum were proposed:

i)   a balance between skills and concepts,
ii) emphasis on problem solving,
iii) introduction of computers in the secondary schools,
iv) integration within mathematics and co-ordination with other school subjects,
v)   increased attention to affective objectives,

vi) encouragement of self-learning, and

vii) extensive support for the teacher.

Another paper on an evaluation of the secondary mathematics curricula in three North African Arab countries (Tunis, Algeria and Morocco) concluded that:

i) abstract, as compared to concrete, presentation of mathematical concepts was predominant (86-100 per cent abstract),

ii) the deductive, as compared to inductive, approach was predominant (72-100 per cent deductive), and

iii) the majority of exercises were one-step problems[9].

7.   OTHER ICMI ACTIVITIES

One might think from the above that ICMI and its regional groups organize meetings as their only activity, but they also conduct studies. ICMI Studies each begin with the writing of a discussion paper and then circulating it for comments. Following the revision, an invitational meeting is held to discuss the topic in detail, and finally a publication is prepared. In the Studies, key problems are identified in the subject area, up-to-date accounts are made of relevant research and practice, and finally a framework is provided to facilitate further study and development. Studies' publication titles are:

- The Influence of Computers and Informatics on Mathematics and its Teaching;
- School Mathematics in the 1990's;
- The Popularization of Mathematics;
- Mathematics as a Service Subject;
- Mathematics and Cognition;
- Assessment in Mathematics Education;
- Gender and Mathematics Education (in press); and
- Perspectives on the Teaching of Geometry for the 21st Century (in progress).

The outgoing President of ICMI, Jean-Pierre Kahane, wrote in his farewell message in 1990 that the Studies have not been entirely satisfactory: the discussion papers have had too few comments, partly due to their limited circulation and partly because of too few translations; and the impact of the Study as a function of the distribution of its publication has been poor. Earlier Studies were published by Cambridge University Press, and the later ones by Kluwer Academic Press, all in English, but there have been a number of translations published elsewhere of the various studies.

Several special interest groups have been formed within the ICMI framework. They are sanctioned by ICMI, and must report their activities every year. Undoubtedly the most active of these is the International Study Group for the Psychology of Mathematics Education (PME). Since their founding by Professor Fischbein in 1976, they have met every year in professional meetings. Their annual Proceedings sometimes comprise three volumes, usually published in the country where the meeting is organized. They have met on every continent, giving opportunity to many third-world mathematics educators to attend. The group's premise is that PME serves as a forum for researchers in mathematics education. The group reported at ICME-6 that PME has shifted its focus in three ways:

i)   from the individual child to pupil interactions in the classroom;
ii) from the search for universals in individual learning to specific characteristics in different social situations;
iii) from the psychology of mathematics education to the social psychology of mathematics education, focusing on social aspects of the psychology of learning and teaching.

There is a parallel North-American group that also meets annually, and which also publishes proceedings as well as a newsletter.

The International Group for the Relations Between the History and Pedagogy of Mathematics (HPM), another ICMI Study Group, has also been very active. Their meetings are always linked with other mathematics education meetings. Their newsletter, which has world-wide circulation assured by correspondents in all regions, includes book reviews, articles, notification of meetings; all directed to the incorporation of the history of mathematics within mathematics teaching.

The International Organization of Women and Mathematics Education (IOWME), was added in 1987 and whose main activities have been in organizing a meeting in Höör, Sweden in 1993 whose outcome was the Gender and Mathematics Education Study mentioned above. The meeting Proceedings has been published by Lund University and the Study will be published by Kluwer. IOWME is publishing a Newsletter which is distributed by the National Coordinators in each country.

The World Federation of National Mathematical Competitions (WFN-MC), became an ICMI Study Group in 1994, but their activities began many years ago. It was organized, guided and assured financial support by the late Peter O'Halloran and the Australian Mathematics Trust that he put together. Its members are mainly drawn from the ranks of mathematicians - those leading the nearly 250 national, regional and international mathematics competitions and Olympiads. Mathematics Competitions, its journal, was begun in 1988 and is still published at the University of Canberra in Australia. Anyone involved in mathematics competitions would be much assisted by being associated with WFNMC. Those who still think that mathematics competitions are only for the elite students should know the Australian Mathematics Competition which is given in every school in Australia, as well as in 49 other

1248

countries, and taken by half a million students, while MATHCOUNTS, a four-level competition, is taken by 750,000 junior high school students in the USA. If only there were that many gifted students in mathematics!

The International Study Group on Ethnomathematics (ISGEm), was initiated by Ubiratan D'Ambrosio (1985), whose work links the mathematics to be learned in school with the mathematical experiences the student has outside school. He coined this concept Ethnomathematics. Often discounted by mathematics educators in Europe, many third-world educators have acted upon D'Ambrosio's writings in planning their own mathematics programmes.

8. INTERNATIONAL GROUPS RELATED TO MATHEMATICS EDUCATION

Acting upon a resolution in 1949 in the United Nations, urging UNESCO and the International Statistical Institute (ISI) to take appropriate steps to further the improvement of education in statistics on an international scale, the ISI's Committee on Statistical Education was founded. With financial support from UNESCO, the Committee provided statistical information, trained statisticians at training centres, notably the International Statistical Education Centre in Calcutta and organized Round Table Conferences on statistics teaching aids, methods and curricula which were reported in the Review of the ISI. A Taskforce on the Teaching of Statistics at the School Level founded the journal Teaching Statistics with the aim to

> 'help teachers of geography, biology, the sciences, social science, economics, etc. to see how statistical ideas can illuminate their work and to make proper use of statistics in their teaching. It also seeks to help those who are teaching statistics and mathematics with statistics courses. The emphasis of the articles is on teaching and the classroom. The aim is to inform, entertain, encourage and enlighten all who use statistics in their teaching or who teach statistics.'

The journal, with Peter Holmes as editor for the first eight years, was highly successful in achieving these goals.

Another Task Force has organized three International Conferences On Teaching Statistics (ICOTS), in Sheffield, UK, in 1982, Victoria, British Columbia in 1986, each with about 500 participants, and Dunedin, New Zealand in 1990. The meetings' Proceedings (Gray, et al., 1983, Davidson and Swift, 1987, and Vere-Jones 1991) are prime sources of information about statistics teaching world wide.

The Committee was transformed into the International Association for Statistical Education (IASE), in 1992, with a brief to foster the development of better and more effective means of instruction in statistical theory and methods at all levels of school, as well as the university and the general public. They organized their first meeting in Perugia, Italy, whose proceedings are available free of charge (Brunelli and Cicchitelli, eds., by writing statli@ipguniv.unipg.it). This was followed by the Fourth ICOTS in Marrakech, Morocco in 1994. IASE is ahead of the other mathematics education organizations in that they have begun an electronic journal Journal of Statistics Education and other resources for teaching statistics[10].

Little has been said in this chapter about assessment of mathematics education programmes. The major influence in the field is undoubtedly the International Association for Assessment of Educational Achievement (IEA), founded in 1959 for the purpose of comparing the educational performance of school students in various countries and systems of education around the world. It looks at achievement as a function of school, home, student, and societal factors and thus uses the world as an educational laboratory. This grouping of national institutions for assessment is in the process of completing its third international survey of mathematics curriculum, teaching, and learning. Its first survey included eleven national systems completed in 1964, and was headed by Sweden's Torsten Husén. It showed that a cross-national comparison could be made that was not just a 'horse race' competition. By using some of the first survey, the Second International Mathematics Study, SIMS, could show not only the status of mathematics education in the 1980's, but also the change over time of mathematics teaching and learning. You will appreciate that this period of time was one of intense change in mathematics curricula. SIMS was based on the Intended Curriculum, the Implemented Curriculum, and the Attained Curriculum, i.e., what the governments said their system was teaching, what the teachers said they were teaching, and lastly what the students learned.

The IEA excels at experimental design and statistical analysis, and the mathematics studies had access to the best talent. Ken Travers of the University of Illinois headed SIMS. Almost any question that can be asked about what factors affect mathematics learning can be answered in part by a careful statistical analysis of how differing national systems' results differ as a function of that factor. This is evident when the within country differences are less than the between country differences. Most national assessments of students focus only on what students know, and only on that day. The IEA studies examine data on student achievement within the context of the content of the curriculum and whether or not that content was actually taught to those tested. Fortunately the results are widely reported in journals, as the publications themselves are very expensive, too much so for third-world mathematics educators and libraries[11].

The Third International Mathematics and Science Study, TIMSS, has completed an extensive collection of curricula, and is now making a comparison between them. Most of the classroom testing has been completed, but at the time of this writing, no results are yet known. A persistent problem with the

IEA Studies has been the mass media generally reporting only country rankings, the 'horse race' aspect, ignoring the richness of relevant factors found to affect mathematical learning.

9.   PUTTING IT ALL TOGETHER: AN EXAMPLE IN ONE COUNTRY

In Africa, where I worked for seven years, it was possible to see the influence of the various international and regional groups and bilateral aid. I would like to take one country, Swaziland, and detail this co-operation. It was equally true of most other newly independent countries in Africa and Asia, often by different players. We will see the influence in mathematics education by UNESCO, UNDP, Unicef, British Council/ODA, USAID, SIDA, volunteers from Norway, Sweden, Denmark, the United Kingdom, USA, and others.

The Faculty of Education of the University of Botswana, Lesotho and Swaziland was being set up by UNESCO, using funds from the United Nations Development Programme, and I was responsible for mathematics education at the Swaziland campus. Besides lecturing at the University, I was the external examiner for all mathematics teachers, the Chief examiner for the school certificate examination, and heavily involved in a project of workcards for teaching mathematics. Unicef (the UN Children's Fund) had a project; for upgrading all the uncertified primary teachers in the country, for writing mathematics curriculum materials, for organizing month-long residential courses, for supplying schools with equipment, and for frequently visiting every school. Their international staff all came from different countries, including Australia, New Zealand, Lebanon, Sweden and Ireland.

The head of the mathematics department at William Pitcher College, the principal teacher training college, was recruited by the Overseas Development of the U.K. Only one Swazi was in that department, with the rest Peace Corps Volunteers from the USA, DANAID volunteers from Denmark, and other mathematics educators from SIDA (Sweden) and CIDA (Canada). One of the two other teacher training institutions; this one for two-year primary training, was funded and partially staffed by an American mission.

The Swazi Government set up a curriculum development institution which was partially funded and staffed by USAID for the primary school curriculum, and by the British Council for the secondary. The primary books were extensively rewritten books based on the USAID Entebbe African Mathematics Project, and the secondary books were adaptations from the UK School Mathematics Project textbooks. (I was once told by an African Minister of Education that curriculum development was popular with bilateral aid donors for cultural impact as well as commercial considerations - to sell textbooks.) A large national secondary school was established to help lead the country with educational reforms. The mathematics and science departments were supplied by UNESCO by funds from Sweden, with the staff coming from

Sweden, as well as British and American volunteers, and a couple of Swazi teachers. The sole mathematics inspector came via the British Council. Funds were found so that the Swazi leading the primary curriculum group could participate in an ICME. The Commonwealth Secretariat, at a crucial time for curriculum reform in mathematics, convened a meeting in the Caribbean for heads of mathematics in the Ministries of Education of Commonwealth countries. Swazi mathematics teachers were in universities in the USA and the UK on scholarships. The mathematics exams were administered by the Regional Testing Centre which was a project of USAID. Could you doubt that there was international co-operation in mathematics education? A large percentage of secondary mathematics teachers were volunteers and missionaries from many European and North American countries.

10.   NATIONAL INSTITUTIONS WITH INTERNATIONAL INFLUENCE

In the 1980's, I was gathering from many countries their stated goals for mathematics teaching for a UNESCO meeting. In a large number of these Ministry of Education reports, the National (USA) Council of Teachers of Mathematics (NCTM) Agenda for Action was mentioned in regards to their own goals. Also frequently appearing were such statements as, 'According to the Cockcroft Report...' I won't discuss the appropriateness of this, but mention it only to show how the work of some national institutions extends far beyond what was intended. There are many such institutions and I know that to list a few will bring wrath down on me for those omitted.

We might look at universities that have welcomed many foreign graduate students in mathematics education, especially from developing countries where facilities might not exist for their specific training, helping them to improve their nations' programmes when they return. The Universities of Georgia, of Nottingham, of Campinas, of Bordeau, of Ohio State, of Cambridge, of Paris VII, of Monash, of London, and the Academy of Pedagogical Sciences in Moscow, are a few.

Research Institutes like the Institute for Didactics of Mathematics (IDM) in Bielefeld, the IOWO/Freudenthal Institute in Utrecht, the National Institute for Educational Research in Tokyo, the many Institutes of Research in Mathematics Education (IREM's) in France, the Regional Centre for Education in Science and Mathematics (RECSAM) in Malaysia, have given mathematics educators time to pursue and publish research from which other countries can profit, or offer regional mathematics education workshops for neighbouring countries.

Bibliographical databases in mathematics education, like ERIC at Ohio State, and the International Reviews on Mathematical Education (ZDM) in Karlsruhe, which besides serving their own countries, make (at a cost) their data available to the world. Their holdings, besides the printed reviews, are now on CD-ROM as well as available for on-line searches, a boon for those far from the USA and Germany, as an on-line search very quickly becomes expensive, especially with the additional telephone charges. Latin America is served by the Red Latinoamericana de Documentación en Educación (RE-DUC), and through the Internet by the server 'Educación Matemática' in the direction http://ued.uniandes.edu.co, thanks to the organization 'una empresa docente' at the University of the Andes in Bogota.

11. FUTURE OF INTERNATIONAL CO-OPERATION IN MATHEMATICS
     EDUCATION

Most of my career has centred around international co-operation in mathematics education.

We are experiencing a growing political conservatism in governments. There is less inclination to assist their less fortunate, and certainly not those in countries far away. The rich nations are becoming richer, and the poor poorer. The institutions set up to provide world co-operation, the United Nations and its education agency UNESCO, the World Bank, there are many, are being starved of funds and their activities have had to be curtailed. What gains are made in third-world countries, are negated by the relentless population expansion which stays ahead of the governments provisions of schools, teachers, hospitals, water,...

All this to say that it is becoming more difficult to look to governments for improved international co-operation in mathematics education. I come to the same conclusion as did Miguel de Guzmán, President of ICMI, when he opened ICME-7 with a call for solidarity in mathematics education (Guzmán, 1994), that it was up to professional mathematics educators and their associations to work to improve mathematics teaching worldwide. He has called for a Solidarity Fund, for individuals to give time and funds to help less fortunate mathematics educators in all the nations, and for ICMI to have a fund to help individuals come to ICME and to strengthen their regional associations. ICME-9 in 2000 will coincide with the World Mathematical Year 2000. UNESCO has endorsed the World Mathematics Year, and we might make a concerted effort for funding for international mathematics education from intergovernmental and governmental organizations. National mathematics education associations should seek international co-operation, providing funds for participants from the third-world to join their conferences, and to provide free copies of their journals to at least other associations.

UNESCO has begun Project 2000+, to foster scientific literacy and technological literacy for all, in all countries. ICMI was asked to co-operate with Project 2000+, to 'enter into partnership with, and make their knowledge and experience available to the United Nations and other intergovernmental bodies as well as to establish innovative programmes in a common effort to achieve the goal of scientific literacy and technological literacy for all; and participate in national, regional and international programmes for the enhancement of scientific literacy and technological literacy for the improvement of the quality of life in all societies and for the achievement of sustainable development.' (UNESCO 1993, p.4-5)

Working together through consensus, shared aspirations, and accepting cultural differences, we may provide a mathematics programme that has both cultural relevance and mathematical consistency[12].

ENDNOTES

1. 'The purpose of UNESCO is to contribute to peace and security by promoting collaboration among the nations through education, science and culture in order to further universal respect for justice, for the rule of law and for the human rights and fundamental freedoms which are affirmed for the peoples of the world, without distinction of race, sex, language or religion, by the Charter of the United Nations.' (UNESCO Constitution, Article 1)

2. A discussion on the need for changing the goals of mathematics teaching in Africa may be found in Jacobsen (1984).

3. A fuller description of ICMI-UNESCO co-operation is given in two ICMI Bulletins, No. 10 in an article by Bent Christiansen, who was programme specialist at UNESCO and later Vice-President of ICMI, and in No. 34 in an article by this writer.

4. Note the distinction between ICMI and ICME; the first C stands for Commission, the organization, and the second C is for Congress.

5. Like ICMI, the address of IACME changes with its officers. The current president is Fidel Oteiza, Chile (foteiza@euclides.usachy.cl). The Bulletin is prepared by Past President Eduardo Luna, Dominican Republic, now lecturing at Barry University in Florida, (luna@dominic.barry.edu).

6. The environmental education factor has been conspicuously lacking in mathematics education programmes. The CIBEM II conclusions, and other references have been gathered in Environmental education opportunities in mathematics education: UNESCO's documents as a source, prepared for a special environmental education issue of ZDM's International Reviews on Mathematical Education, 94/6 and 95/1 (December 1994 and February 1995).

7. Chee (1981) for the conference proceedings.

8. Details about the structure of the AMU and its commissions may be found in Kuku, 1991. Paulus Gerdes (Mozambique) is chairing the Commission on the History of Mathematics in Africa, which produces a well distributed newsletter. Grace Alele-Williams (Nigeria) chairs the

Commission on Women in Mathematics in Africa (AMUCWMA) which compiled a list of women in mathematics in Africa, and organized a symposium entitled 'Mathematics Education of Women in Africa - Problems and Prospects' in Benin City, Nigeria, 1990.

9. See Arab Development Institute (1995) for the proceedings of the Beirut Conference. In that, one will find Arab Center for Educational Research in the Gulf States (1993) for the Unified Curriculum, Zaghwan (1993) for the North African Arab Countries mathematics curriculum evaluation. Mathematics education in the Arab States has been described in detail in two works, Ebeid (1992) and Jurdak and Jacobsen (1981). One can trace the influence of the UNESCO project, either directly as to content, or through the many Arab mathematics educators who were first involved in the project and later made important contributions through other institutions.

10. Send an e-mail message to archive@jse.stat.ncsu.edu, without any other information than the exact text given below:
    send index
    send iase/index
    send access.methods

11. Travers, K. and Westbury, I, 1989, Robitaille, D. and Garden, R., 1989, Burstein, L., 1992. The three reports are rich with details that would be invaluable for anyone responsible for curriculum and systems and, for researchers, a source of problems of factors which influence learning.

12. I would like to thank my reviewers, Ben Nebres, and Nigel Langdon, for their helpful suggestions for the manuscript.

REFERENCES

D'Ambrosio, U.: 1985, 'Ethnomathematics and its place in the history and pedagogy of mathematics', For the Learning of Mathematics, 3, 1, 44-48.

Arab Development Institute: (1995), Proceedings of the Conference Future of Science and Mathematics and the Needs of an Arab Society (Beirut, 1993), ADI, Beirut. (A)

Bishop, et al. (eds.): 1993, Significant Influences on Children's Learning of Mathematics, STEDS 47, UNESCO, Paris.

Burstein, L., 1992.: The IEA Study of Mathematics III: Student Growth and Classroom Processes, Pergamon Press.

Chee, P.S. (ed.): 1981, Proceedings of the 2nd Southwest Asian Conference on Mathematical Education (Kuala Lumpur 1981), University of Malaya, Kuala Lumpur.

Congresso Ibero-Americano de Educação Matemática (II CIBEM), 1995, II Congresso Ibero-Americano de Educaço Mathemática, Universidade Regional de Blumenau, Blumenau, S.C., Brazil.

Cornu, B., Ralston, A. (eds.): 1992, The Influence of Computers and Informatics on Mathematics and its Teaching, STEDS 44, UNESCO, Paris.

Damerow, P, et al. (eds.): 1986, Mathematics for All, STEDS 20, UNESCO, Paris. (E,F)

Davidson, R., Swift, J. (eds.): 1987 Proceedings of the Second International Conference on Teaching Statistics, University of Victoria, Canada.

Ebeid, W.: 1992, 'Mathematics Education in the Arab States', in R. Morris (ed.) Studies in Mathematics Education, Vol. 8: Moving into the twenty-first century, UNESCO, Paris. (E,S)

Gerdes, P.: 1992, Who is Who in Mathematics and Mathematics Education in Southern Africa, Southern African Mathematical Sciences Association (SAMSA). ISP, Maputo, Mozambique.

Gray, D, et al. (eds.): 1983, Proceedings of the First International Conference on Teaching Statistics, University of Sheffield, Sheffield, UK.

de Guzmán, M.: 1994, 'Presidential Address', in C. Gaulin, et al. (eds.) Proceedings of the 7th International Congress on Mathematical Education. Québec, University of Laval, Sante-Foy, Canada.

Jacobsen, E.: 1984, 'What goals for mathematics teaching in African Schools?', Educafrica: Bulletin of the UNESCO Regional Office for Education in Africa, 10, 118-134. (E, F)

Jacobsen, E.: 1991, 'Adapting Mathematics Education for the Next Century', Impact of Science on Society 41, 4, 297-303. (E,F,S,A,C,R)

Jacobsen, E.: 1995, 'Environmental Education Opportunities in Mathematics Education: UNESCO's Documents as a Source', International Reviews on Mathematical Education, 94, 6, 176-179.

Jurdak, M., Jacobsen, E.: 1981, 'The Evolution of Mathematics Curriculum in the Arab States', in Studies in Mathematics Education, Vol. 2, UNESCO, Paris. (E,F,S,A)

Keitel, C., et al. (eds.): 1989, Mathematics, Education, and Society, UNESCO, Paris.

Kuku, A.O.: 1991, Presidential address presented at the 3rd Pan-African Congress of Mathematicians, African Mathematical Union, Ibadan.

Luna, E., González, S. (eds.): 1987, Educación Matematica en las Americás VII (IACME 7 Conference, Santo Domingo, Dominican Republic, 1987), STEDS 37, UNESCO, Paris.

Mellin-Olsen, S.: 1987, The Politics of Mathematical Education, Kluwer, Dordrecht.

Morris, R. (ed.): 1989, Studies in Mathematics Education, Vol. 7: The teaching of statistics, UNESCO, Paris. [E,F,S. C (in press)]

Morris, R., Arora, M. (eds.): 1992, Studies in Mathematics Education, Vol. 8: Moving into the Twenty-first Century, UNESCO, Paris. (E,S)

Robitaille, D. and Garden, R., 1989.: The IEA Study of Mathematics II: Contexts and Outcomes of School Mathematics, Pergamon Press.

Robitaille, D.: 1989, Evaluation and Assessment in Mathematics Education, STEDS 32, UNESCO, Paris.

Sanchez, G., Blanco, M. (eds.): 1990, Renuiones del primer Congreso Iberoamericano de Educación Matemática, STEDS 42, UNESCO, Paris.

Scott, P. (ed.): 1992, Educación Matematica en las Americás VIII, (IACME 8 Conference, Miami 1991). STEDS 43, UNESCO, Paris.

Travers, K. and Westbury, I, 1989.: The IEA Study of Mathematics I: Analysis of Mathematics Curricula, Pergamon Press.

UNESCO: 1993, 'Project 2000+ Declaration', ICMI Bulletin, 35.

UNESCO: 1989, INISTE Directory of the International Network for Information in Science and Technology Education, UNESCO, Paris.

UNESCO: 1991, World Education Report 1991, UNESCO, Paris. (A,C,E,F,R,S)

Vere-Jones, D. (ed.): 1991, Proceedings of the Third International Conference on Teaching Statistics, ISI, Voorburg, The Netherlands.

N.B. Publications which exist in several language versions, or whose non-English title is given here in English, are marked by E=English, F=French, S=Spanish, A=Arabic, C=Chinese, R=Russian. STEDS indicates the title is in UNESCO's Science and Technology Education Document Series and available free of charge.

1256

Chapter 35: Critical Mathematics Education

OLE SKOVSMOSE AND LENE NIELSEN

The Royal Danish School of Educational Studies and Aalborg University, Denmark

ABSTRACT

Critical Mathematics education is described in terms of 'concerns' which cover the following issues:
  a) Citizenship identifies schooling as including the preparation of students to be an active part of political life.
  b) Mathematics may serve as a tool for identifying and analysing critical features of society, which may be global as well as having to do with the local environment of students.
  c) The students' interest emphasises that the main focus of education cannot be the transformation of (pure) knowledge; instead educational practice must be understood in terms of acting persons.
  d) Culture and conflicts raise basic questions about discrimination. Does mathematics education reproduce inequalities which might be established by factors outside education but, nevertheless, are reinforced by educational practice?
  e) Mathematics itself might be problematic because of the function of mathematics as part of modern technology, which no longer can be reviewed with optimism. Mathematics is not only a tool for critique but also an object of critique.
  f) Critical mathematics education concentrates on life in the classroom to the extent that the communication between teacher and students can reflect power relations.

1. INTRODUCTION

What is the point of talking about 'critical mathematics education'? In order to clarify this question we take a look at the relationships between conceptions of critique and of mathematics from a historical perspective.

According to what could be called the Euclidean paradigm, mathematical knowledge is built up by careful logical deduction starting from axioms, whose truths can be grasped by intuition. As part of rationalism, the structure of mathematics became the blueprint for all science. By relying on logic and clear reasoning, dogmatism could be eliminated. According to René Descartes the power of human reason ensured that all truths could be grasped, if we proceeded from an 'axiom' which could not be eliminated by universal

A.J. Bishop et al. (eds.), International Handbook of Mathematics Education, 1257 - 1288

doubt. Critical thinking, logical reasoning and mathematics were united and became a pattern for other sciences. So, where were one to find a more critical thinking than mathematical thinking? Self-critique seems to constitute the very nature of mathematical thinking.

This also suggests the possibility of the existence of a once-and-for-all critique. In order to develop science, all uncertain, biased and doubtful perceptions have to be eliminated. True knowledge needs a safe and stable ground. The task of philosophy is to clear the ground, and when this is done, science can start building up knowledge. Immanuel Kant's work, *Critique of Pure Reason*, can also be interpreted as an attempt to provide a once-and-for-all critique. The title reflects the idea that a critique of reason must be made by reason itself. By means of pure reason we are able to prepare the ground for knowledge development.

As a consequence, critical activity becomes a task for philosophy. Critique and construction become separated. While the construction of knowledge is an ongoing activity to be carried out by the individual sciences, critique becomes a once-and-for-all activity carried out by philosophy.

An important attempt to re-work a once-and-for-all critique was launched by logical positivism. A fundamental critique of the individual disciplines, eliminating metaphysical assumptions, was carried out in order to develop a unified science – characterised by being neutral and objective. However, logic and mathematics still had a unique position by representing the 'language of science' and the medium in which critical thinking could be carried out. According to logical positivism, critique still meant 'logical clarification' and, by its very nature, mathematics incorporated critique as a cornerstone in its construction. To develop mathematics, and to develop mathematics as a critical enterprise, was the same thing.

During this century education has become a global enterprise. It is no longer 'elitist'. This global perspective is emphasised by John Dewey[1] who connects the discussion of education with a discussion of democracy. It seems unproblematic to integrate school mathematics, incorporating critical activities, as part of a general education with a democratic concern. Mathematics, as such, appears to ensure that mathematics education becomes anti-authoritarian, since sound reasoning is its main characteristic.

However, this apparent harmony is disturbed by two paradoxes. The first concerns technology. Previously, technological development was described in optimistic terms: Technology provides humankind with a tool which can save us from the difficulties caused by being surrounded by nature which constitutes only 'raw material'. The development of technology and the improvement of the 'quality of life' become closely connected. Technology is interpreted as the ultimate expression of human ingenuity in the struggle for improvement of life. However, this technological optimism is impossible to maintain any longer.

In 'Cultural Framing of Mathematics Teaching and Learning', Ubiratan D'Ambrosio states the paradox of technology in the following way:

'In the last 100 years, we have seen enormous advances on our knowledge of nature and in the development of new technologies... And yet, this same century has shown us a despicable human behaviour. Unprecedented means of mass destruction, of insecurity, new terrible diseases, unjustified famine... are matched only by an irreversible destruction of the environment. Much of this paradox has to do with an absence of reflections and considerations of values in academics, particularly in the scientific disciplines, both in research and in education. Most of the means to achieve these wonders and also these horrors of science and technology have to do with advances in mathematics.'

(D'Ambrosio, 1993, p. 443)

Mathematics appears in the centre of the paradox. In fact, it seems impossible to grasp the paradox without trying to grasp the social role of mathematics. The questions which can be raised in relation to technology and to the problematic development of technology, can also be raised in relation to mathematics. A critique of technology, including a critique of mathematics, becomes important. And the paradox emphasises that this critique does not simply concern logical reasoning. Mathematics obtains a different role when applied in technology, in modelling processes, and in giving a foundation for making decisions of political nature.

Mathematics cannot sustain its role as the 'eminence grise' of critique. Mathematics has in fact served to limit the notion of critique and encapsulated critique in a cage of logic. The historical founded conception of mathematics has cleared the way in providing a 'symbolic power' to also applied mathematics.[2] This has to be combatted and mathematics itself becomes the object of critique. This calls for a concept of critique much broader in its scope than 'logical reasoning'.

A paradox of general education can also be stated. While mathematics was proposed to be a subject structured purely by reason, the teaching of mathematics as a global concern developed rigourous structures far removed from any critical enterprise. Instead of being a discipline reflecting critical thinking, mathematics education became associated with domination, control, tests, and rigid forms of communication. The 'new math' movement emphasised the global and universal nature of mathematics education by projecting the universal architecture of mathematics into a worldwide programme for mathematics education. The actual consequence was that students were again faced with mathematics in a rigourous form. Educators (not only from the Third World) protested against the 'imperialism' which implicitly was connected to the globalising of mathematics education. As mathematics education developed as a worldwide concern, the subject mingled with routines which did not represent a general concern for education as a democratic development. The globality and universality of mathematics education became a barrier for the students in seeing the relevance of mathematics in relation to their daily life and their society.

The paradox of technology and the paradox of general education show that the notion of a once-and-for-all critique and the notion of critique as a sort of logical reasoning appear to be insufficient. Critique cannot develop solely as a philosophical task but must also be developed as an ongoing educational task. Critique cannot be associated with (only) logical reasoning but must refer to broader content matter questions and to social issues as well. By adding 'critical' to 'mathematics education' we emphasise that both mathematics and mathematics education are placed in the middle of a critical development.

The whole point of talking of critical mathematics education is to acknowledge that mathematics plays a crucial role in social and technological development, that mathematics education maintains a critical role in the distribution of power and welfare and that, if a discussion of mathematics education is reduced to questions of content, then mathematics and mathematics education act blindly together.

2.   CONCERNS OF CRITICAL MATHEMATICS EDUCATION

It is not possible to outline a set of rules and, by following these, realise a critical mathematics education. Critical mathematics education cannot be summarised by a particular recipe of actions and content. It is not a sort of methodological principle. 'Critical mathematics education' is an open and incomplete concept like, for instance, 'democracy'. A democracy is not simply sustained by the establishment of free elections. Democracy is a 'way of living', and to realise democracy is an on-going concern.

If 'mathematics education' refers to a certain subject, and 'critical' presupposes interdisciplinarity, then the term 'critical mathematics education' might be perceived as containing a conceptual contradiction. However, by 'critical mathematics education' we do not refer to a certain form of mathematics education, but to a perspective on an educational landscape which includes mathematics. This perspective includes the commitments that influence the choices teachers make concerning curriculum and methodology.

We shall try to describe critical mathematics education in terms of 'concerns'. 'Critical mathematics education' refers to educational practices as well as to research on this practice. A distinction between concerns having to do with practice and concerns having to do with research is not a fundamental one, as research related to critical mathematics education often takes the form of action research. In what follows we think in terms of both practice and research.

1260

The concerns cover the following issues:

a) Citizenship identifies schooling as including the preparation of students to be an active part of a political life.

b) Mathematics may serve as a tool for identifying and analysing critical features of society, which may be global as well as having to do with the local environment of students.

c) The students' interest emphasises that the main focus of education cannot be the transformation of (pure) knowledge; instead educational practice must be understood in terms of acting persons.

d) Culture and conflicts raise basic questions about discrimination. Does mathematics education reproduce inequalities which might be established by factors outside education but, nevertheless, are reinforced by educational practice?

e) Mathematics itself might be problematic because of the function of mathematics as part of modern technology, which no longer can be reviewed with optimism. Mathematics is not only a tool for critique but also an object of critique.

f) Critical mathematics education concentrates on life in the classroom to the extent that the communication between teacher and students can reflect power relations.

These concerns are not 'consequences' of the paradox of technology and the paradox of general education. However, the concerns try to express the importance of recognising the critical position of both mathematics and mathematics education, and to acknowledge the importance of developing critique as an ongoing educational task with a broad cultural and political scope.

Many forms of research and educational practice take (some of) these concerns into consideration. We are, though, not interested in demarcating between critical mathematics education and other forms of mathematics education. In fact, many examples of educational practice as well as research reveal critical features without the teachers or the researchers ever claiming to do critical mathematics education. Thus, the 'public educator', as described by Paul Ernest (1991), belongs to the family of critical educators.[3] External factors may also obstruct the possibilities of realising an intended practice, e.g. lack of resources or lack of political and economic freedom. However, critical mathematics education can still be the underlying concern.

3. CITIZENSHIP

In mathematics education the aim has been to develop mathematical knowledge: to provide as much mathematical understanding to as many students as possible in the best possible way (the students should enjoy their education, etc.). This is, however, a gross simplification when the concern is with developing 'citizenship'.

The idea of interpreting education as a critical concern is a relatively recent one. In 1966, Theodor W. Adorno published the paper 'Erziehung nach Auschwitz'.[4] It was introduced by the following statement:

'The claim that a new Auschwitz shall never happen again, is principal to education.'

(Adorno, 1971, p. 88, our translation)

This statement can be taken quite literally, but can also be read as a metaphor for expressing the idea that education has a general political and sociological significance. Adorno wants an education which can prevent a new Auschwitz, an education with a critical potential, an education for *Mündigkeit*. The German word *Mündigkeit* refers to the legal rights which a person obtains when reaching the age of consent but, more importantly, it also refers to a person who is able to 'speak for herself', and who is able to act according to her own decisions. Education for *Mündigkeit* is the opposite of an education which produces 'followers'. The problem of the follower is dogmatism and the belief in authority. In order to identify the content of education, we have to study society from a political point of view. Adorno stresses an interpretation of education, which includes a reference to the catastrophes caused by the Nazi movement. In this sense critical education appears as a reaction to the Second World War.

In order to understand how Adorno interpreted education, it is important to refer to Critical Theory as developed by Max Horkheimer, Herbert Marcuse and Adorno himself as well as others belonging to the Frankfurt School. Critical Theory made a serious attempt to reinterpret sociology. Instead of building sociology along the pattern of natural sciences, as suggested by logical positivism, it was thought that sociology should develop as an interdisciplinary study guided by an emancipatory interest. The claim of 'neutrality' in the social sciences was interpreted simply as a way of disguising an interest in preserving the status quo. Instead, sociology should struggle with all forms of suppression. From this reinterpretation of sociology as being critical in nature, a different notion of education was established.[5]

The concept of 'sociological imagination' was developed by the sociologist C. Wright Mills (1959) to describe the capacity of identifying alternatives to a given social situation. A sociological imagination questions the appearance of sociological facts. These might appear as unavoidable, but a sociological imagination might reveal a 'necessity' to be merely an ideological illusion. The 'fact' might be historically determined and possible to change. In *Sociology: A Brief but Critical Introduction*, Anthony Giddens states that 'the exercise of the sociological imagination makes it possible to break free from the straitjacket of thinking only in terms of the type of society we know in the here and now'

(Giddens, 1986, p. 22).

In his interpretation of sociology, Giddens re-introduces the notion of 'sociological imagination'.

Oskar Negt's work, *Soziologische Phantasie und exemplarisches Lernen* from 1964, has played an important role in the development of critical education in Europe. Negt, being interested in adult vocational education, combines the notions of 'sociological imagination' and 'exemplarity'.[6] According to the principle of exemplarity, a particular phenomenon can mirror a total complexity. This idea has a sociological interpretation meaning that an individual socio-political event (for instance, an incident at a place of work) can reflect a political totality. Thus, it becomes possible to understand a social complexity by concentrating on a particular event. This makes good sense in relation to vocational education, which might help the workers to come to know and understand their own political situation. To achieve this, it is not necessary to teach the workers a series of basic facts. Instead, an education with such an aim can start from the particular and begin a discussion of an actual situation at the workplace. This does not mean limiting the possibilities of coming to know the basic features of society. This reveals why Negt relates 'exemplarity' and 'social imagination'. Here we find an epistemological root of the idea of concentrating on the situation of the learners as a source of what to learn. It is obvious that Paulo Freire has based his approach on a similar idea, although without using the terminology of exemplarity (Fréire, 1972, 1974).

Negt's radicalisation of 'exemplarity' can be generalised not just to vocational education and adults, but to education in general. It is not difficult to locate this generalisation in catchwords like 'problem orientation', 'project work' and 'thematisation'. A specific problem can become the point of entry to a complexity; a totality can be made comprehensible by an intensive study of a central problem. Project work becomes a possibility when the curriculum is not bound by a sequence of logically identified pieces of information.

As the notion of critical education developed, 'literacy' was seen as a competency which enabled students to see and reinterpret part of (their) reality and to react to this reality. People were supposed to be not spectators, but participants. The essential question for critical mathematics education, then, is whether or not it is possible to develop a competency, *mathemacy*, which has a potential similar to that of literacy and which may help students to reinterpret their reality and to pursue a different reality. Could mathemacy help students to become critical citizens and to develop a *Mündigkeit*?

In Germany and Scandinavia, critical mathematics education opposed to the 'new math' movement which, first of all, had focused on the internal architecture of mathematics. *Elementarmathematik: Lernen für die Praksis* was published in 1974, and this book by P. Damerow, U. Elwitz, C. Keitel and J. Zimmer makes an attempt to analyse mathematics used in economics in order not only to explicate the simple but far reaching mathematical model of calculations in bookkeeping, but also to analyse the impact of its use for decisions in managing and production. Furthermore, it suggests that mathematics education should contribute to the development of competent and autonomous judgements and actions of people concerned or affected by the use of the mathematical model in daily and professional life.

In 1975 Dieter Volk published the article 'Plädoyer für einen problemorientierten Mathematikunterricht in emanzipatorischer Absicht' in which he tried to conceptualise a mathematics education aiming at emancipation. In this way he tried to elaborate on the general claim of critical education which, inspired by Critical Theory, suggests that education must be guided by an interest of emancipation. Later Volk, drawing on a constructive perspective on mathematics, elaborated his notion of mathematics education in such a way as to provide a basis for action (Volk, 1977, 1979, 1980). The book *Kritische Stichwörter zum Mathematikunterrich* (Volk (ed.), 1979) summarises some of the issues of critical mathematics education as expressed in Germany and the Scandinavian countries during the 1970's.[7] It contains papers about the ideology of mathematics education (Peter Damerow), about the importance of relating mathematics education to authentic applications of mathematics (Mogens Niss), about project work in mathematics education (Wolfgang Münzinger[8]), and about many other topics.[9]

In a series of articles Mogens Niss emphasised not only the importance of investigating real applications of mathematics from a critical stance but also the importance of investigating the fundamental social functions of mathematics, both as a scientific discipline and as a school subject.[10] Stieg Mellin-Olsen published the book *Indlæring som social proces* in 1977, in which he broadened the analysis of mathematical learning processes. Such activities could not be investigated in terms focussing on cognitive aspects but had to be investigated from a perspective which also includes the students as part of a community, as citizens and as political agents.[11] In this book Mellin-Olsen anticipated a fundamental critique of the narrow perspective on the learner and the subject which during the 1980's was expressed, for instance, by that constructivistic perspective which focuses merely on how the learner can develop his or her *mathematical* conceptions further. The broad conceptions of the learner and of what learning is about were further developed in his book *The Politics of Mathematics Education* in 1987. Ole Skovsmose has published three books (Skovsmose, 1980, 1981a, 1981b) which discussed the notion of critical mathematics education and related topics.[12]

The development of critical mathematics education was, however, far from only a European concern. In 1983, Marilyn Frankenstein published an article entitled: 'Critical Mathematics Education: An Application of Paulo Fréire's Epistemology'. Here Frankenstein developed a perspective to guide and illuminate classroom practice inspired by Fréire's 'pedagogy of the oppressed' to the very different economic, political and social institutional structures of the US. The work of Frankenstein also depicts the development a mathemacy with a potential similar to that of literacy.[13] Her book *Relearning Mathematics. A different Third R - Radical Maths* is a textbook meant not only for learning mathematics, but

> 'to help you understand mathematics in a way that will enable you to use that knowledge to cut through the 'taken-for-granted' assumptions about how our society is structured, and to act from more informed choices about those structures and processes'
>
> (Frankenstein, 1989, p. 2).

By means of this book, Frankenstein wants to provide a way to develop competencies to understand not only mathematics, but also society.

The book is constructed so that the reader (student) is taken through a process from 'math anxiety' to achieving a mathemacy, or 'a critical maths literacy', in Frankenstein's term. The process (or book) goes through the stage of clarifying misunderstandings about mathematics education which could act as blocks to the student's inclination to become involved in the activities. These are misconceptions such as: 'I will never be able to learn mathematics' or 'I'm stupid if I make a mistake or ask a question'. Another step is making the students realise that mathematics can be used for something which is of interest to them. So, the first part of learning mathematics is not to do mathematics, but getting ready to learn by creating an understanding of the subject. Mathematical concepts and operations are then presented within problems. Real-life data is the basis for problem-creating (asking questions) and problem-solving activities. One example discusses ways of 'counting' the unemployed. The number of unemployed can vary according to the variables which are taken into consideration. For instance, people who are forced to take underpaid jobs to survive could be included in the statistics or people who are only working halftime, because it is the only job available. Many other examples involve analysing the assumptions behind statistical material used in newspapers, political statements, etc. Throughout the book it is constantly explained why specific sections are included and what the purpose of each section is. The learning process is explained to make clear the purpose, not only of learning mathematics, but of learning it in this particular way, and to see that it is important to be able to use mathematics in an empowering way.

During the 1980's the development of critical mathematics education became a world wide concern. Most unfortunately the German and Scandinavian tradition was ignored in the English speaking world. Instead we witnessed an example of 'parallel developments'. However, from the beginning of the 1990's the multiplicity of critical mathematics education was realised.[14]

1265

In Marilyn Frankenstein's approach, students are not 'located' as students of mathematics, but first of all as citizens. This presupposes that mathematics is grasped not only as a tool for illustrating questions, problems and information, but also as a tool which can distort questions, problems and information. However, mathematics can still become a useful tool which, in combination with other tools, can draw our attention to specific topics of social relevance. We shall briefly describe an example of this.

The project 'Energy' was carried out in a Danish secondary school.[15] It concentrated on the following questions: How much energy is contained in a certain meal, and how much is used by performing a specific task (cycling)?[16] How much energy is used in order to produce barley in a field the size of one hectare, and how much energy can be expected to be reclaimed from the harvested barley? How does the input-output figure for energy look like when the barley is used for food in pig breeding?

The first morning the students had to go to school without having eaten breakfast at home. At school each student had to weigh carefully how much breakfast he or she was eating: bread, butter, cheese, etc. Then, based on a variety of statistics, the students calculated how much 'energy supply' the breakfast contained. After this they were all going on a bike trip of known length. The formulas which were going to be used to determine their use of energy for the bike trip contained the parameters 'frontal area of the cyclist', 'speed', and 'time'. Based on those formulas and individual data, they calculated how much energy they had used during a specific cycling trip. This was compared to the energy supply provided by the breakfast. In this way they got an idea of what input-output figures for energy supply could mean.

The next sub-theme, use of energy in farming, was introduced as a variant of this input-output question. The task was to compare, on the one hand, the energy supply the farmer had to provide in order to prepare and harvest a field (use of petrol when ploughing, etc.) and, on the other hand, the energy supply which is contained in the harvested barley. The very detailed calculations showed that the farmer obtained an energy-output six times the energy input. The next step in the project was to find out what the input-output figures look like when the harvested barley is used as food for pig breeding. These calculations showed that the energy-output was approximately a fifth of the energy input.

These results were put into more general terms, but were the calculations reliable? Were the results inaccurate (meaning that more accurate information of the type already gathered would improve the results) or had some essential parameters been forgotten, meaning that no conclusions could be drawn? This part of the project took place as a general classroom discussion. Put into a global perspective, the students learned about the basic conditions for the production of vegetables and of meat. The possibility of improving the input-output figure for pork production was also discussed, and as a result the space in the pigsty was debated. Another point touched upon was: What does the energy account look like in different parts of the world?

'Exemplarity' refers to the idea that a specific example can illustrate a general phenomenon of cultural and political relevance. In 'Energy' the students concentrated their investigations on a specific farm. Nevertheless, they obtained an insight of global relevance. They raised questions about the world's production of food. This also supported a sociological imagination, i.e. the capacity to see that a given situation is not a necessary state of affairs but can be changed. The identification of the 'costs' of producing meat suggests the possibility that we can choose a different sort of food production. Naturally, this does not imply that the individual person has the possibility to choose, but conditions are created for observing that things can be different.

As the project is only described briefly here, nothing is stated about the extent to what the exemplarity of the project was in fact linked with a sociological imagination. To make such a claim would presuppose a careful investigation of the students' actual conceptions. What is stated here is only that it is possible to organise a project which tries to combine exemplary reasoning and sociological imagination. In this sense, a concern of mathematics education can be to provide a tool for identifying and investigating critical features of society.

One element of critical mathematics education is to develop a critical attitude towards all sorts of authority, including different kinds of 'authoritative information'. This must also include information based on mathematics or information expressed by means of mathematics. As part of the project 'Energy', some formulas (about bike resistance, for instance) were provided for the students. But what was the attitude of students towards these formulas? Did they accept them? Were the formulas used for bike-resistance reliable? What about the input-output calculations themselves? Do the calculations really express basic features of farming? Such questions must be raised as part of critical mathematics education. Such an education cannot be defined in terms of one concern only. To use mathematics as a tool for critique also presupposes that the tool itself is considered critically. Critique presupposes self-critique.

5.   STUDENTS' INTEREST

Critical mathematics education is concerned with the development of citizens who are able to take part in discussions and are able to make their own decisions. We therefore have to take into consideration the fact that students will also want, and should be given the opportunity, to 'evaluate' what happens in the classroom. This turns the focus on students' interest.

The notion of students' interest can be interpreted in a simple and direct way. Educational theory in mathematics, especially with reference to structuralism, has emphasised that already established mathematical structures provide the basic guidelines for identifying the content of the curriculum. Following this basic assumption, structuralism has embarked upon the project of making the route to these mathematical structures as pleasant as possible, and much charming material has been developed. In this sense, structuralism has also acknowledged the students' interest, as a phenomenon which has to do with the motivation of students. When we refer to students' interest in the present context, it is, however, to be understood in a more basic epistemological and political sense.

Marcelo Borba (1991, 1995) has discussed how children, who had difficulty in being accepted at school or accepting school, engaged in educational projects involving mathematical activities in a Brazilian slum, a *favela*. Most parents of these children were forced to move from the countryside due to a lack of jobs. They were attracted to the cities with the dream of better working conditions, but ended up living in the slums since the jobs which were offered to them could not pay for housing. The slums, which are usually located at the edge of town, also put children at the edge of social life. These children are known in schools as being the 'slum kids', *favelados*.

These conditions can lead to a lot of 'dropping out'. Children soon see themselves as incapable and either leave school completely or just do not attend very often. The parents of these children are usually hard working people but are often seen as socially dangerous and criminals. The parents are concerned that their children will actually become criminals as they do not go to school but spend the whole day wandering about. In this Brazilian community, parents were able to put pressure on the local government to organise an educational programme to take their children off the streets. This programme, which first of all was aimed at just 'taking the children off the streets' was influenced by educators with a Freirean perspective.

Borba became accepted by the children by acting as referee in their soccer games. As they became involved more and more with playing teams from nearby slums or schools, a problem emerged: How could they get money to buy new uniforms for their soccer team? The children decided to plant a vegetable garden and to sell the produce. This activity of course involved book-keeping to keep account of expenses and earnings. To keep track of what was planted and where, they made a model of paper, which also involved different mathematical activities, for example, scale drawing. In the development of this project over several months, children were engaged in a dialogical relationship with Borba in which each one of the participants would speak from the perspectives of their own 'ethnomathematics'. Borba explains the success of the project in engaging the pupils by pointing to the content:

'What is important from these examples... is that these children, from the slums in Brazil, could also produce mathematics if they were involved with problems which were relevant for them, problems which are an expression of their culture.'

(Borba, 1991, p. 3)

Children in a dialogical relationship with a teacher/researcher were able to learn mathematics, to come to know their social reality better - and to buy a used set of soccer uniforms.

The brief description of this project indicates that paying attention to students' interest can support mathematical learning. The project, however, also indicates that the notion of students' interest is complex. With reference to ethnomathematics, this term has been interpreted as giving considerations to the *background* of students. It seems plausible to suggest that the learning process should relate to the background of the students and to what the students already know and are familiar with. This interpretation can, however, be too simplistic.

When learning is seen a part of a critical activity, it cannot be a forced activity. This is what Fréire states when he refuses 'banking' as a suitable metaphor for the teaching-learning process. To see learning as related to acting, and conditions for learning as similar to the conditions for acting, is to provide a perspective on learning which belongs to critical education. The learning person should also be considered an acting person. In order to describe action, the notion of intention plays an essential role. An action is not an activity performed, for instance, out of blind habit. Acting involves intentions. The intentions of a person relate both to the background and what can be called the *foreground* or 'what is in front' of the person.[17] We intend something because of certain features of our background, but our intentions are also formed because of certain features of our future - not the 'objective' future but our personal interpretation of our future. The foreground, seen in this way, is just as influential as the background when the person forms intentions. Therefore, the intentions of the person should be understood in terms of both background and foreground. This has implications for understanding learning as an activity which also relates to the students' interest.

Borba (1990, 1993) has also emphasised the relevance of having the students engage in the choice of the problem. Of course, teachers are engaged in this choice too, since the notion of dialogue is central to ethnomathematics. However, it should be emphasised that Borba recognises that taking cultural background into account does not guarantee that projects like the one organised in the *favela* will succeed.

Students' interest not only refers to both foreground and background of the students but also to the notions of citizenship, *Mündigkeit* and empowerment. Students do not have some simple and immediate preferences. We cannot assume that the students are able simply to express their interest. However, the conclusion to be drawn is not that some detailed external analysis is able to identify this interest. We find that it only makes sense to think of students' interest as an idea which can be negotiated and expressed in a dialogue. Given the 'right' situation, teacher and students in a shared effort might express what might be of interest to the students. This point is also illustrated by the *favela* project.

An essential task, still left, is to develop an epistemology in which the interest of the students plays a constitutive role. Stieg Mellin-Olsen has worked in many areas of critical mathematics education, and in *The Politics of Education* he has developed 'Activity Theory' to take into consideration the content of education and its relation to the students' situation. Mellin-Olsen distinguishes between 'Activity', which is defined as activities owned by the student, and 'activity' for learning which is organized by the teacher. Mellin-Olsen does not limit Activity to classroom activities but looks at the totality of activities, inside or outside the classroom. He sees Activity as

'a way of describing the complete life of the individual'
(Mellin-Olsen, 1987, p. 30).

Mellin-Olsen's work can be interpreted in different ways. One way is to see it as an attempt to build the notion of Activity, as both an epistemological and a political concept. When students are involved in Activity, they simultaneously become politically involved. The establishment of a theoretical perspective from which the notion of students' interest becomes part of an epistemology and in which the 'politics of knowing' also becomes a constitutive element is crucial for the further development of critical mathematics education.

A further point to remember is that when talking about education, we easily come to focus on school education. The example taking place in the Brazilian *favela*, suggests that educational theory can also refer to out of school practices. If critical mathematics education is to develop as an anti-authoritarian education, it must consider situations in which the very school structure has become an obstruction to learning. A direct example of the necessity to establish critical education as an out of school practice can be seen in South Africa. Here the school system has, in the past, incorporated the whole conception and practice of apartheid education. It is not possible to throw away this institutional structure overnight. As a consequence, much inspiration for new thinking in education including mathematics education must come from out of school settings. This has been a principal idea in the work of Mzwandile Kibi (1993), who studies the 'math clubs' as a forum for the development of a critical mathematics education. Also this indicates that the notion of students' interest refers to both epistemological elements and a 'politics of knowing'.

Bantu Education was introduced by Hendrick Verwoerd to cement apartheid education in South Africa: Education should be organised in accordance with the students' background and their opportunities in life, and because black people have no opportunities beyond routine work, their education should be adjusted to this. Education should reflect the fact that the jobs of black people in all respects should be subservient to the needs of 'white industry' and 'white culture'.

In Bantu Education the differences in opportunities were stated by law and by reference to differences of colour of skin. This is explicit racism. This is an extreme case but we do find similar differences in opportunities in education, not legalised *de jure* but realised *de facto*. This is implicit racism. Throughout the history of education we find examples of *de jure* as well as *de facto* discriminations. We find examples of discrimination concerning 'race', 'class', 'talent' and 'gender'. Critical mathematics education must combat these differences; in research by drawing attention to the differences; in practice by trying to change the differences.[18] Critical mathematics education must strive to provide equal opportunities and outcomes for all.

This can be emphasised by interpreting critique as a reaction to a critical situation. If education takes place in a situation which includes conflicts and contradictions, then a critical education must try to include these as part of education itself. A critical education must try to reflect upon the critical nature of the social reality in which it takes place. To ignore critical situations is to designate education as conformist.[19]

This makes it obvious that critique has different roots. One of these is expressed in the notion of 'critique of ideology' which reflects a connection with philosophy. A different root of critique emerges from 'protest' which reflects the importance of action. A reaction against domination and authority may express itself in protest. This was exemplified by the Soweto uprising in 1976 when students protested against education imposed by the apartheid regime, and also by the student movements in Europe and the US in the late 1960's. A balanced description of critical education must elaborate on both these origins.

References to conflicts and social contradictions can be made in different ways. An explicit interpretation is found in *Multiple Factors: Classroom Mathematics for Equality and Justice*, where Sharan-Jeet Shan and Peter Bailey offer new ways of teaching which can challenge oppression.

'It is about enabling our pupils to understand how the imbalance of economic power is created, so challenges racism directly. Statistics can be used to reflect the social reality of our world and can be a tool for the students to explore inequality and injustice.'

(Shan and Bailey, 1991, p. 16)

The method they use is to raise matters of discrimination directly, or to use statistics from which racism or inequalities can be inferred. Thereby they want to create an awareness of injustice through the use of mathematics.

Shan and Bailey analyse the existing (English) school system to identify features of a social and cultural kind which could influence teaching and learning. Their reasons for doing this arise from their experiences in the English school system with its cultural diversity. They point to aspects such as the language of the mathematics classroom, the teacher's perception of 'race' and 'achievement', classroom techniques, and bias in mathematics books. Most of their book, though, is dedicated to illustrating how mathematics education can be changed. Their educational examples are divided into two different categories: the multicultural approach and the anti-racist approach.

The first approach involves emphasising the inclusion of material from various cultural backgrounds to create an awareness by the students of the universality of mathematics, and thereby challenging a European bias in the history of mathematics. Shan and Bailey especially point at the problems of multicultural societies where many children from ethnic minority groups fail in education. One of the reasons for this, Shan and Bailey suggest, is that the children from these cultures have no confidence in doing mathematics - a key reason underlying this being institutional racism. In trying to rebuild this confidence they suggest providing these children with role-models. They introduce to the children mathematics and mathematicians from different cultures, and try to show them that mathematics is not only a European invention. They suggest looking at the mathematics of famous mathematicians of different nationalities, such as Shakula Devi of India and Chu Shihchieh of China, or to look at different culturebound ways of counting. This approach challenges the traditional conceptions of what could be defined as mathematics, and what subjects belong in the mathematics classroom. This seems inspired by the ethnomathematical perspective, which broadens the definitions of mathematics to incorporate other cultures' mathematical ideas.

The second approach, introduced by Shan and Bailey, is to challenge racism directly in the classroom. They want teachers to allow discussion of sensitive matters and to use mathematics as a tool for analysing matters of discrimination and reasons behind them. This could be carried out in short discussions or in longer projects. A chart of infant mortality in different countries can be the starting point of a discussion (Shan and Bailey, 1991, p. 167). Themes for longer projects could for example be found in the area of energy and famine, for example looking at cash-crops such as tea, following its path from producer to consumer, and perhaps looking at the conditions of the worker (Shan and Bailey, 1991, p. 246). This could give the students an awareness of how wealth is distributed unequally.

Critical mathematics education reacts to the disciplining and suppressive features of mathematics education (in its traditional forms and with traditional content) coming from 'inside' the highly technological societies. Ethnomathematics constitutes a similar reaction, but coming from 'outside'.[20] It is a reaction from Third World countries. This reaction also includes a reaction to the 'colonialism' which is built into the educational systems and linked to the curriculum. In the article 'Western Mathematics: The Secret Weapon of Cultural Imperialism', Alan Bishop substantiates the idea that mathematics has been used in a cultural invasion of the colonies. One of the ways this was done was through education, where the Western ways of doing mathematics secured the superiority of the colonialists.

D'Ambrosio is one of the founders of the ethnomathematical approach.[21] He and the ethnomathematicians focus on the connection between mathematics and culture and on the idea that different cultures have different conceptions of mathematics.[22] These mathematical conceptions are adopted by children growing up in a specific culture, and the clash between this spontaneous mathemacy and the (formal) mathematics presented in school creates a 'psychological blockage'. A method of preventing this is to incorporate the mathematical traditions - ethnomathematics - into the curriculum; that is, finding the foundation for the mathematics education in the students' own world and experiences, and creating mathematical ideas from this. This means, using the reality of the student, their already existing mathemacy, as a material for developing mathematical knowledge.

Gelsa Knijnik relates some of her work to the Movimento dos Sem-Terra, the movement of the landless people. The interesting thing is that Knijnik introduces the potential for self-critique in ethnomathematics:

> 'I have been using the expression ethnomathematical approach in order to refer to the research into the conceptions, traditions and mathematical practices of the specific subordinated social group and pedagogical work developed with the group so that they can interpret and codify their knowledge; acquire academic knowledge and establish comparisons between these two different types of knowledge in order to choose the most suitable one, when they have real problems to solve.'
>
> (Knijnik, 1993, p. 150)

The cultural background cannot be taken for granted.

7. MATHEMATICS AS A PROBLEMATIC TECHNOLOGY

If 'mathemacy' is to be developed as a broader competency, it cannot be defined simply in terms of mathematical skills. It must be related to other competencies as well. Reflection becomes important when related to the notion of critique. Just as it is important to interpret critique in a broad way, it is important to provide reflection with many aspects. Reflection cannot be limited to a focus on mathematical concepts themselves but must also concern the reliability of applying mathematics in a certain context. What is the actual function of using, or not using, mathematics in order to solve, discuss or to identify certain problems?

The paradox of technology, referred to previously, is essential to critical mathematics education. On the one hand, mathematics provides a vehicle for the development of technology. On the other hand, this development as such is highly problematic. Reflection is needed. The scope for such reflection is indicated in *Descartes Dream: The World According to Mathematics*, where Philip Davis and Rueben Hersh talk about, not only descriptive and predictive uses of mathematics, but also about a prescriptive use. A descriptive use can be more or less accurate. But quite different questions can be raised about a prescriptive use which provides a basis for technological design. We re-arrange reality according to mathematics. A prescriptive use can be more or less acceptable, reliable, useful, problematic, etc.

Davis and Hersh describe the prescriptive use of mathematics in the following way:

'We are born into a world with so many instances of prescriptive mathematics in place that we are hardly aware of them, and, once they are pointed out, we can hardly imagine the world working without them. Our measurements of space and mass, our clocks and calendars, our plans for buildings and machines, our monetary system, are prescriptive mathematisations of great antiquity. To focus on more recent instances... think of the income tax. This is an enormous mathematical structure superposed on an enormous pre-existing mathematical financial structure... In American society, there are plentiful examples of recent and recently reinstated prescriptive mathematisation: exam grades, IQ's, life insurance, taking a number in a bake shop, lotteries, traffic lights... telephone switching systems, credit cards, zip codes, proportional representation voting... We have prescribed these systems, often for reasons known only to a few; they regulate and alter our lives and characterise our civilisation. They create a description before the pattern itself exists.'

(Davis and Hersh, 1988, pp. 120-121)

Put in more general terms, we can state that mathematics has a *formatting power*. It is the problems related to the formatting power of mathematics which cause not only the wonders but also the catastrophes, which constitute the paradox of technology.[23] How then do we cope with this in mathematics education?

As part of the German and Scandinavian tradition in critical mathematics education, the importance of making critical investigations of real applications of mathematics and of mathematical modelling has been emphasised.[24] Because applications of mathematics become part of technology, they are as problematic as all other sorts of technology, and they must be evaluated and criticised as such. Therefore, the pragmatic trend in mathematics education causes difficulties. By emphasising the general usefulness of applications of mathematics in all sorts of human affairs, it comes to serve as an ideology: the simplified optimism of technology.

This calls for a study of authentic mathematical modelling. An example of such a study is made by Kirsten Hermann and Mogens Niss (1982). They investigate the 'Simulation Model of the Economic Council' (SMEC) used by Danish economists when advising the government and politicians on economic policy and its possible consequences. This investigation introduces real mathematical modelling of social significance. The description made by Hermann and Niss makes it possible for upper secondary school students to identify some of the assumptions which are included in the construction of the model, and of which it is important to be aware when evaluating output of the model. In SMEC the Cobb-Douglas Function of Production plays a crucial role. It determines the Gross National Product as a function of two variables, namely capital investment and the labour force. This specification is a consequence of encompassing the development of the model by neoclassical economic theory. The next step in the modelling process is to specify additional mathematical conditions which the function has to fulfil, for instance concerning its differentiability and the properties of its partial derivatives. Such specifications are expressed in the form of equations, and by solving these, more is learned about the Function of Production. Then, with this function as the point of reference, the model is elaborated into a great number of equations, making the model useful for performing economic forecasts. Simultaneously, the key-assumptions made during the modelling process become disguised: for instance, the neoclassical origin is hidden - and forgotten.

Clearly, the point is not to indicate that the use of mathematical models is by necessity a dubious affair. In some cases it is possible to solve a problem, which it is difficult or impossible to manage in any other way than by using mathematics. But sometimes the output of a modelling process is highly problematic. An evaluation cannot, however, be made in any *a priori* way. Instead a careful analysis of the modelling process has to be carried out. The evaluation of a mathematical modelling process must be *a posteriori*. It must include a variety of perspectives, including also a mathematical perspective. To carry out a critique of a modelling process *a posteriori,* thus, becomes a concern of critical mathematics education.

This approach, however, easily runs into difficulties. To include real applications of mathematics as an object for critique can become very demanding. In fact it can invite a teacher-guided trip into the modelling process and students can get lost and lose interest. In her studies of examples of mathematical modelling in upper secondary school, Iben Maj Christiansen (1994) has noticed an interesting phenomenon. Even if the example of mathematical modelling raises important questions about the use of mathematics (meaning that critical discussion of the modelling process could be part of the classroom practice) and even if the teachers are well aware of the importance of such reflections, still the school structure may act as an obstruction. Christiansen observed that the students as part of their group work raised questions about the modelling process. Many of these questions were, however, dealt with in 'informal talks' which, as it were, make up a subculture of the classroom. This informal talk may contain essential critical points. But the informal talk was not considered by the students as essential to the 'real' tasks of the classroom, set in exercises and mathematical questions. Therefore, many critical comments remained as incidental remarks. The critical considerations were exiled by the very fact that the activities took place in school. This again emphasises that the school setting is an essential factor to consider, and that many routines developed in mathematics educations can obstruct exactly those reflections which might be essential in order to deal with mathematics as a problematic tool.

Mathematical ways of thinking are also more direct part of everyday life. Newspapers contain lots of information which refers to mathematics. We come to know about unemployment. We read about the stockmarket. We see advertising: The price of a bike is such and such, but we only have to pay a little amount of money each month and it will be ours! Some of this information may be the output of advanced mathematical modelling but some may be the output of much more simple calculations. In both situations such information makes up part of our everyday life. Therefore, it also becomes a task for critical mathematics education to prepare students for a critical interpretation of such everyday mathematics (a point made earlier in the discussion of citizenship).

For most children the first place they face mathematics explicitly is in school. It is just as important to prepare a critical attitude towards exactly those calculations which are part of school practice as it is to begin to develop a critical attitude towards the uses of mathematics which confronts the students outside school.

Whether we have to do with the application of a complex mathematical formalism hidden in some social practice, or we have to do with some everyday use of mathematics, maybe in our own practice, mathematics must itself be an object for critique.

8.   CLASSROOM COMMUNICATION

Much research in critical mathematics education can be labelled 'ethnographic research' or 'action research'. That is, being in the classroom the researcher tries to interpret what is happening and to explain or change the situation. Everything is done in cooperation with teacher and students.

In the paper 'The Culture of the Mathematics Classroom: An Unknown Quantity?' Marilyn Nickson describes how a study of the 'culture' of the classroom can reveal how the context of, and the communication in, the classroom can be an obstacle to a critical mathematics education. Certain views of mathematics held by the teacher can influence the role of the student and become mediated to the students as meta-knowledge. The point is that the 'culture' of the classroom, the values and meanings which the students and the teacher do not explicitly express, can be inferred from their actions and interactions in the classroom. Thus the inference by students of what the teacher expects of them mathematically can deter students from engaging in mathematics in a critical way.

Communication between teacher and students can take different forms: Is the dialogue dominated by the teacher in the way that he or she is doing most of the talking? Can the dialogue be characterised as a real discussion between teacher and students? Do all discussions end with a decision taken by the teacher? etc. Analysing the dialogue can reveal problems important to critical mathematics education, even though a description of the topics and the intentions of the teacher seems in accordance with concerns of critical mathematics education.

Many obstructions to dialogical interactions and the consideration of students' interest, etc., are caused by routines in the classroom. In a microethnographical study of the patterns and routines in classroom interaction Jörg Voigt (1985) has found, that a seemingly very complex interaction between teacher and students can be categorised into specific routines which the teacher uses repeatedly. For example, Voigt found several instances of what he termed 'the elicitation pattern' in a four lessons introduction to probability calculus. The phenomenon that students can answer questions, which for outstanders seem impossible to answer can be explained by this observation. Voigt points at the consequences for the students' learning of letting interaction patterns develop into routines in the classroom. The interaction patterns serves as a mean for treating mathematical tasks smoothly, but does not ensure a shared understanding.

If students' interest is to be considered, students themselves must naturally have a say in the classroom. Education for *Mündigkeit* presupposes that students are treated as participants in the educational process. The routines which dictate that the task of the teacher is to eliminate the students' mistakes can however obstruct this concern. But mistakes *must* be eliminated. This seems an immediate consequence of the fact that mathematics education is also a preparation for tests which first of all focus on the number of mistakes made by the students. Achievement is simply measured by the number of mistakes.

In a study made by Helle Alrø and Ole Skovsmose (1996) the phenomenon of *bureaucratic absolutism* is identified. This absolutism refers to corrections of students' mistakes. The study concerns mathematics teaching in a form which is common in Denmark, i.e. teaching which is closely related to a text-book (although this is not the only form observed). The main task of students is to solve exercises formulated in a textbook.

And the students make mistakes. Some mistakes simply have to do with the mathematical content of the exercise. The students make wrong calculation and the teacher suggests that the students work though the calculations once again. Other mistakes are, however, of a pragmatic nature. Students may write an algorithm in an unusual way. The result may still be correct, but if a student does not apply the standard algorithm, it becomes more difficult for the teacher to help the student memorise what to do. So this mistake is also corrected. Finally, some corrections are based on conventions about how mathematical exercises are set up, the simplest case being that the students have to put a double line beneath the final result. This convention also is a source of the teacher's corrections.

Corrections in the mathematical classroom thus have quite different sources: some refer to mathematical properties, others to pragmatic rules, and some to conventions about how to present an exercise. The observations of Alrø and Skovsmose indicate that corrections, different as they might be, are communicated to the students in a uniform way. Mistakes are simply corrected, independent of the nature of the mistake. This phenomenon of not specifying the reasons for the different corrections is called *bureaucratic absolutism*, and this is what faces many students in the (traditional) mathematics classroom. This absolutism is at the same time the basis for a meta-conception of mathematics: doing mathematics means rule-following, and if the rules are followed properly, then no mistakes are made. The results are correct.

The students may have several 'good reasons' for suggesting a solution. But if the students' good reasons are ignored during the classroom communication due to bureaucratic absolutism, then students' ways of thinking and presumptions do not become part of the communication in the classroom. The elimination of the students' good reasons from classroom discourse leads to the obstruction of critical thinking. The fact that no reasons are stated and no explanations given for the corrections (being mathematical, pragmatic or conventional) supports a general ideology which serves to protect mathematics and the output of mathematics from critical scrutiny.

Even though the chosen topic may have exemplary value and make it possible to discuss mathematics as a problematic tool, still classroom practice in itself need not have much to do with critical mathematics education. If communication in the classroom is carried out in a way that is controlled and dominated by the teacher, the students' 'good reasons' and other sources for potential critical scrutiny might be ignored. Critical thinking has to find a basis in communication practice in the classroom; it cannot be imposed on students. Critical thinking must start at the source of the argumentation. The concern for critical mathematics education must therefore also include a concern for the form of communication in the classroom.

The Criticalmathematics Educators Group, initiated by Marilyn Frankenstein, Arthur Powell and John Volmink, arose from a conference at Cornell
University in October 1990.[26] However, the Criticalmathematics Educators
Group has other organisational and intellectual roots which extend back several decades and across several continents. We know of three international
groupings of mathematicians and mathematics educators whose proceedings
have influenced concerns with social and cultural issues: the Interamerican
Congress on Mathematics Education (CIAEM), the International Congress
on Mathematical Education (ICME), and African Mathematical Union
(AMU).

According to D'Ambrosio, discussions in both CIAEM and ICME experienced a qualitative shift in and around the middle to late 1970's. At first, concerns in those organisations focused largely on the structure and content of
different curricular innovations and preoccupation with conditions of programme implementations. D'Ambrosio describes how in CIAEM by 1975 in
Caracas, Venezuela

'[e]ven though considerable space continued to be dedicated to
discussion of programs, the more crowded sessions, with more
discussions and wider presence and repercussion, were those dedicated
to discussions of a social and, even, of a political nature such as
'mathematics and development''
(D'Ambrosio, 1990, p. 11, translation by Arthur Powell).

Similarly, by ICME3 in 1976 profound inquiry began into the 'position of
mathematics in education systems' and the

'negative that can result from a mathematics education poorly adapted
to the distinct socio-cultural conditions, be it in Third World countries
or, be it in countries with large industrial development'
(D'Ambrosio, 1990, p. 11, translation by Arthur Powell).

Such discussions continue to influence proceedings of CIAEM and ICME.

In Africa, leaders in political, scientific, and educational spheres expressed
concern about the devastating impact of colonial educational structures, textbooks and the colonial disruption of the scientific development. As they began to search for solutions, the African Mathematical Union, through its
Commission on the History of Mathematics in Africa (AMUCHMA) and its
newsletter, disseminated information on research on the history of mathematics in Africa, in part, so that such information would be included in school-
books.[27] Also, the AMUCHMA publishes information on research into
ethnomathematics educational uses. This interest of mathematicians and

mathematics educators from Africa and Europe, as well as South and North America, in the intersection of issues concerning culture and society with mathematics and mathematical education, eventually led to the insistence that these issues occupy more substantive space at ICME.

At the meeting of ICME 6 in Budapest 1988, what became known as the Fifth Day Special Programme on 'Mathematics, Education, and Society' was organised. During this special conference within a conference, presentations and discussion from individuals representing all continents focused not only on social but also cultural influences both on and of mathematics education.[28] As significant and successful as the Fifth Day Special Programme conference was, it was not immune to criticism. Many found that to have had a separate day instead of presentations and discussions being an integral part of ICME 6, implied a marginalisation or ghettoisation of individuals and issues. Others expressed dissatisfaction with the somewhat elitist structure of the sessions themselves. Furthermore and importantly, many agreed with Richard Noss' evaluation that

'while discussion of social and cultural issues was an important break with the dominant psychological paradigm of mathematics education, there was a clear role for a more explicit political focus'

(Noss et al., 1990, p. vii).

In reaction to the Fifth Day Special Programme, a conference entitled 'Political Dimensions of Mathematics Education: Action and Critique' (which later became known as PDME1) was held in London in 1990. Addressing the opening of PDME1, Mellin-Olsen suggested that the conference be a forum for those 'doing research on the political nature of education'; that it 'strengthen the political aspects of our work'; and that it 'foster collectivism' (Noss et al., 1990, p. 1). He went further to insist that the conference be a support system for political action and critique directed against governments, especially those governments which in extreme ways exercise educational politics which denies its citizens access to knowledge. Not only majority groups of certain populations but also other groups, because of colour of skin, religion or other stigmas, are prevented democratic access to mathematical knowledge. An important debate that occupied participants concerned the political implications of, and relationships between, multicultural and anti-racist perspectives in the teaching and learning of school mathematics. Nonetheless, some participants criticised the conference for its emphasis on critique over action. PDME1 was followed by PDME2 in Broederstroom in 1993 (Julie, Angelis, and Davis (eds.), 1993), and PDME3 in Bergen in 1995.

In October 1990, the conference 'Critical Mathematics Education: Towards a Plan of Action for Cultural Power and Social Change' was organised at Cornell University. It can be viewed both as a reaction to and an extension of PDME1. Two aspects of the PDME conference were not followed: presentation of papers were not the currency of the conference and invitations went out to several individuals who had not been invited to PDME1. Also, at this conference, a real attempt was made to develop action plans that would have a life beyond the conference itself. One such action was the development of an international organisation, with a newsletter. The title of the conference points directly to the organisers concern to move academic work outside the academy and to grapple with the issues of how to actually be involved in changing the world. Therefore, the title draws attention to the fact that the notion of critique needs to be scrutinised further. In particular: critique cannot consist of only reflections but must also include action.

Many other initiatives around the world can be described as examples of critical mathematics education.[29] It is not essential, however, that the persons involved do describe their activities in such terms. The concerns are what matters, not the terminology. In Brazil a strong initiative in mathematics education is concentrated at the State University of Sao Paulo (UNESP) at Rio Claro. Here the Graduate Programme of Mathematics Education coordinates several research projects with reference to ethnomathematics and with a concern for cultural conflicts and diversities.

Mathematics education, as the rest of education in South Africa, has been structured by the apartheid policy. This has influenced not only the actual structure of education but also the priorities of research in education. 'White research' in mathematics did not touch upon political issues. This research, thereby, resulted in a caricature of educational research. Not only did it adopt an ostrich-like policy, it also came to support what was the actual apartheid policy. People's Mathematics for People's Power expresses an anti-apartheid and democratic concern in education.[30] Therefore, it also provides an important input to the further development of critical mathematics education. The Ph.D. programme in mathematics education organised by The Centre for the Advancement of Science and Mathematics Education (CASME) in Durban also focuses on the idea that mathematics education must become an education for a critical citizenship.[31]

The project 'Connecting Corners of Europe' is organised as a Greek-Danish cooperative project trying to establish communication between mathematics teachers in both countries. The aim is to share ideas about how to organise mathematics education that is guided by the interests of critical mathematics education.[32] This project is one of several offshoots of the project 'Mathematics Education for Democracy' organised by the Danish Research Council for the Humanities during the period 1988-1993.[33]

This wide range of initiatives are united by the idea that mathematics education must serve as an invitation to participate in democratic life in society, in which conditions for democracy may be hampered by exactly the technological development which mathematics education serves as a preparation. This challenge reflects the two paradoxes and signifies the importance of critical mathematics education.

A LIMITATION

Many educators who certainly belong to the movement of critical mathematics education have been left out in our review. Others might be commented on all too briefly. The cause for this is primarily our choice of perspective which, among other things, has highlighted the German and Scandinavian roots of critical education. Other perspectives will show that critical mathematics education is stronger and more pervasive than our description reveals.

ACKNOWLEDGMENTS

We want to thank Alan Bishop, Marcelo Borba, Benedito Rodrigues Brazil, Iben Maj Christiansen, Anna Chronaki, Fabio Dutra, Henriette Damm Fiske, Marilyn Frankenstein, Rita de Cássia Pedno N. Jardin, Christine Keitel, José Ronaldo Melo, Abigail Fregni Lins, Marilyn Nickson, Arthur Powell, Helena Alessandra Seavazzo, Viviane de Silva, José Eduardo Fezzeira de Silva, Miriam Godoy Penteado da Silva, and Mónica Ester Villarreal for comments and suggestions.

ENDNOTES

1. See Dewey (1966).
2. See also Keitel (1989, 1993); Keitel, Kotzmann and Skovsmose (1993).
3. See also Abraham and Bibby (1988), who are discussing a 'Mathematics and Society Curriculum' with reference to both ethnomathematics and the public educator.
4. 'Erziehung nach Auschwitz' is reprinted in Adorno (1971).
5. This line of development of critical education is outlined in Hoffmann (1978) and Paffrath (1987). See also Mollenhauer (1973), Anzinger and Rauch (eds.) (1972), Raith (ed.) (1973), and Tybl and Walter (eds.) (1973).
6. The notion of 'exemplarity' has been discussed by Martin Wagenschein (1965, 1970). This idea opposed structuralism in curriculum thinking. It developed into the idea of project work, see for instance Vithal, Christiansen and Skovsmose (1995).
7. See also Riess (ed.) (1977).
8. See also Münzinger (ed.) (1977).
9. During this period two universities in Denmark, Roskilde (1972) and Aalborg (1974), were established to include project work as a basic principle, also in mathematics education. See Vithal, Christiansen and Skovsmose (1995).
10. Important statements are found in Niss (1977, 1979, 1983, 1989, 1994).

11. Of special importance is the notion of instrumentalism, which is discussed in Mellin-Olsen (1981).
12. See also Skovsmose (1985, 1990, 1992, 1994).
13. Important sources of inspiration are Fréire (1972, 1974). Related works are Zaslavsky (1979), Apple (1982) and Giroux (1989). See also Frankenstein (1993), Frankenstein and Powell (1992, 1994), and Hoffman and Powell (1989, 1990).
14. For an overview of important literature in English, see Gaddis and Volmink (1993).
15. The project took place at Klarup Skole, and the teacher who planned and carried out the project was Henning Bødtkjer. The students were about 15 years old. The example is described in greater detail in Skovsmose (1994).
16. We talk about 'use of energy' as usually spoken of in everyday language. Physics states that energy does not disappear but changes from one form to another. Naturally, it is this phenomenon of changing which is referred to by the expression of 'use of energy'.
17. For a discussion of the notion of 'foreground', see Skovsmose (1994).
18. See for instance Frankenstein (1990).
19. For a further discussion of 'critique' and 'critical situation', see Skovsmose (1994).
20. For a further discussion of this, see Frankenstein and Powell (1994).
21. See D'Ambrosio (1980, 1981, 1985a, 1985b, 1990, 1994).
22. Culture is to be understood very wide, as a national society, a labour group, children of a certain age bracket, etc. (D'Ambrosio, 1985a).
23. See also Booss-Bavnbek (1991) and Fischer (1993).
24. For an early formulation in English see Niss (1977). See also Christiansen (1994).
25. Much of the following description is based on a text provided by Arthur Powell.
26. The group has a newsletter, which circulates to subscribers around the world.
27. The AMUCHMA Newsletter is published in Arabic, English, French, and Portuguese versions.
28. Papers and discussions from the Fifth Day Special Programme are collected in Keitel et al. (eds.) (1989).
29. See for instance Fasheh (1993), Noddings (1993), Nunes et al. (1993), Volk (1989) and Volmink (1994).
30. See Julie (1993) and also Julie et al. (eds.) (1993).
31. Persons involved in this initiative are Mathume Bopape, Mzwandile Kibi, Herbert Khuzwayo, Cassius Lubisi, Manikam Moodley, Irshad Motala, Anandhavelli Naidoo, Nomsa Sibisi, Ole Skovsmose, Renuka Vithal and John Volmink.

32. This project is organised by Tasos Patronis, University of Patras and Lene Nielsen and Ole Skovsmose, The Royal Danish School of Educational Studies.
33. For an overview of 'Mathematics Education and Democracy' see Nissen and Blomhøj (eds.) (1994). Both editors participated in the project, Gunhild Nissen as chairperson and Morten Blomhøj as academic secretary.

REFERENCES

The following list of references is biased. We have only mentioned a few pieces of Scandinavian, German and Brazilian literature, focussing largely on what is available in English. In this way we support the wrong impression that critical mathematics education had developed mainly in the English speaking world.

Abraham, J. and Bibby, N.: 1988, 'Mathematics and Society: Ethnomathematics and the Public Educator Curriculum', *For the Learning of Mathematics* 8, 2, 2-11.

Adorno, T. W.: 1971, *Erziehung zur Mündigkeit,* Suhrkamp, Frankfurt am Main.

Alrø, H. and Skovsmose, O.: 1996, 'On the Right Track', *For the Learning of Mathematics* 16, 1, 2-8.

Anzinger, W. and Rauch, E. (eds.): 1972, *Wörterbuch Kritische Erziehung,* Raith, Starnberg.

Apple, M. W.: 1982, *Education and Power,* Routledge and Kegan, London.

Bishop, A.J.: 1990, 'Western Mathematics: The Secret Weapon of Cultural Imperialism', *Race and Class* 32, 2, 51-65.

Booss-Bavnbek, B.: 1991, 'Against Ill-founded, Irresponsible Modelling', in Niss, M., Blum, W. and Huntley, I. (eds.): *Teaching of Mathematical Modelling and Applications,* Ellis Horwood, Chichester, 70-82.

Borba, M. C.: 1990, 'Ethnomathematics in Education', *For the Learning of Mathematics* 10, 1, 39-43.

Borba, M. C.: 1991, 'Freire and Ethnomathematics: An Application of Ethnomathematics: Teaching Math in a Brazilian Favela', presented in the panel 'Critical Math in the Classroom', on the Institute in Honor of Paulo Freire's 70th Birthday: Challenging Education, Creating Education, New York.

Borba, M.C.: 1993, 'Etnomatematica e a Cultura da Sala de Aula', *Educacao Matematica em Revista,* 1, Blumenau, Brazil, 43-60.

Borba, M. C.: 1995, *Um estudo de etnomátematica: sua incorporação na elaboração de uma proposta pedagógica para o 'Núcleo-Escola' da Vila Nogueira-Sao Quirino,* Associação de Professores de Matemática, Lisbon.

Christiansen, I. M.: 1994, *Classroom Interactions in Applied Mathematics Courses I-II,* R-94-2045a and R-94-2045b, Department of Mathematics and Computer Science, Aalborg University.

D'Ambrosio, U.: 1980, 'Mathematics and Society: Some historical considerations pedagogical implications', *International Journal of Mathematical Education in Science and Technology* 11, 4, 479-488.

D'Ambrosio, U.: 1981, 'Uniting Reality and Action: A Holistic approach to mathematics education', in Steen, L. A. and Albers, D. J. (eds.): *Teaching Teachers, Teaching Students,* Birkhäuser, Boston, 33-42.

D'Ambrosio, U.: 1985a, 'Ethnomathematics and its Place in the History and Pedagogy of Mathematics', *For the Learning of Mathematics* 5, 1, 44-48.

D'Ambrosio, U.: 1985b, 'Mathematics Education in a Cultural Setting', *International Journal of Mathematical Education in Science and Technology* 16, 469-477.

D'Ambrosio, U., 1990, *Etnomatematica: Arte ou tecnica de explicar e conhecer,* Editora Artica, Sao Paulo.

D'Ambrosio, U., 1994), 'Cultural Framing of Mathematics Teaching and Learning', in Biehler, R. et al. (eds.): *Didactics of Mathematics as a Scientific Discipline,* Kluwer, Dordrecht, 443-455.

Damerow, P., Elwitz, U., Keitel, C., Zimmer, J.: 1974, *Elementarmathematik: Lernen für die Praxis? Ein Versuch der Bestimmung fachüberschreitender Curriculumziele,* Klett, Stuttgart.

Davis, P. J. and Hersh, R.: 1988, *Descartes' Dream: The World According to Mathematics,* Penguin Books, London.

Dewey, J.: 1966, *Democracy and Education,* The Free Press, New York. (First edition 1916.)

Ernest, P.: 1991, *The Philosophy of Mathematics Education,* The Falmer Press, London.

Fasheh, M.: 1993, 'From a Dogmatic, Ready-Answer Approach of Teaching Mathematics Towards a Community-Building, process Orientated approach, in Julie et al. (eds.), 1993, 15-19.

Fischer, R.: 1993, 'Mathematics and Social Change', in Restivo, S. et al. (eds.): *Math Worlds: Philosophical and Social Studies of Mathematics and Mathematics Education,* State University of New York Press, Albany, N.Y., 197-218.

Frankenstein, M.: 1983, 'Critical Mathematics Education: An Application of Paulo Freire's Epistemology', *Journal of Education* 165, 4, 315-339. (Reprinted in Shor, I. (ed.): *Freire for the Classroom,* Boyton and Cook Publishers, Porthmouth, New Hampshire, 1987, 180-210.)

Frankenstein, M.: 1989, *Relearning Mathematics: A Different Third R - Radical Maths,* Free Association Books, London.

Frankenstein, M.: 1990, 'Incorporating Race, Gender, and Class Issues into a Critical Mathematical Literacy Curriculum', *Journal of Negro Education* 59, 3, 336-347.

Frankenstein, M.: 1993, 'Teaching for Empowerment: Raising Class Consciousness in a Business/Consumer Mathematics Curriculum', in Julie, C., Angelis, D. and Davis, Z. (eds.), 1993, *Political Dimensions of Mathematics Education 2: Curriculum Reconstruction for Society in Transition,* Maskew Miller Longman, Cape Town, 274-285.

Frankenstein, M. and Powell, A. B.: 1992, 'Empowering Non-traditional College Students: On Social Ideology and Mathematics Education', in B. Johnston (ed.): *Reclaiming Mathematics,* Canberra, Australia: Department of Employment, Education & Training, 188-195. (Originally published in 1989, *Science and Nature,* 9/10.)

Frankenstein, M. and Powell, A. B.: 1994, 'Towards Liberatory Mathematics: Paulo Freire's Epistemology and Ethnomathematics', in McLaren, P. and Lankshear, C. (eds.): *The Politics of Liberation: Paths from Freire,* Routledge, London, 74-99.

Freire, P.: 1972, *Pedagogy of the Oppressed,* Herder and Herder, New York.

Freire, P.: 1974, *Cultural Action for Freedom,* Penguin Books, London.

Gaddis, K. and Volmink, J. D.: 1993, *Social, Cultural, and Political Issues in Mathematics Education: An Annotated Bibliography of Selected Writings, 1980-1990,* CASME, Durban.

Giddens, A.: 1986, *Sociology: A Brief but Critical Introduction,* 2. Edition, MacMillan, London.

Giroux, II. A.: 1989, *Schooling for Democracy: Critical Pedagogy in the Modern Age,* Routledge, London.

Hermann, K. and Niss, M.: 1982, *Beskæftigelsesmodellen i SMEC III,* Nyt Nordisk Forlag Arnold Busck, Copenhagen.

Hoffman, M. R. and Powell, A. B.; 1989, 'Mathematics and Commentary Writing: Vehicles for Student Reflection and Empowerment', in Keitel, C. et al. (eds.): *Mathematics, Education, and Society*, UNESCO, Division of Science, Technical and Environmental Education, Paris, 131-133.

Hoffman, M. R. and Powell A. B.: 1990, 'Gattegno and Freire: A Model for Teaching Mathematically Unprepared, Working-Class Students', in Noss, R. et al. (eds.): *Political Dimensions of Mathematics Education: Action and Critique: Proceedings of the First International Conference*, 1-4 April 1990, Revised Edition, University of London, London, 205-215.

Hoffmann, D.:1978, *Kritische Erziehungswissenschaft*, Kohlhammer, Stuttgart.

Julie, C., 1993, 'Peoples Mathematics and the Application of Mathematics', in Lange, J. de et al. (eds.): *Innovations in Maths Education by Modelling and Applications*, Ellis Horwood, Chichester, 31-40.

Julie, C., Angelis, D. and Davis, Z. (eds.): 1993, *Political Dimensions of Mathematics Education 2: Curriculum Reconstruction for Society in Transition*, Maskew Miller Longman, Cape Town.

Kant, I.: 1929, *Critique of Pure Reason*, Translated by Norman Kemp Smith, MacMillan, London. (First German edition 1781.)

Keitel, C.: 1989, 'Mathematics and Technology', *For the Learning of Mathematics* 9, 1, 7-13.

Keitel, C.: 1993, 'Implicit Mathematical Models in Social Practice and Explicit Mathematics Teaching by Applications', in de Lange, J. et al. (eds.): *Innovations in Maths Education by Modelling and Applications*, Ellis Horwood, Chichester, 19-30.

Keitel, C. et al. (eds.): 1989, *Mathematics, Education and Society*, UNESCO, Division of Science, Technical and Environmental Education, Paris.

Keitel, C., Kotzmann, E. and Skovsmose, O.: 1993, 'Beyond the Tunnel-Vision: Analysing the Relationship between Mathematics, Society and Technology', in Keitel, C. and Ruthven, K. (eds.): *Learning from Computers: Mathematics Education and Technology*, Springer, Berlin, 243-279.

Kibi, M.: 1993, 'For People's Power', in Julie, C., Angelis, D. and Davis, Z. (eds.): *Political Dimensions of Mathematics Education 2: Curriculum Reconstruction for Society in Transition*, Maskew Miller Longman, Cape Town, 57-67.

Knijnik, G., 1993, 'Culture, Mathematics, Education and the Landless of Southern Brazil', in Julie, C., Angelis, D. and Davis, Z. (eds.): *Political Dimensions of Mathematics Education 2: Curriculum Reconstruction for Society in Transition*, Maskew Miller Longman, Cape Town, 149-153.

Mellin-Olsen, S.: 1977, *Indlæring som social process*, Rhodos, Copenhagen.

Mellin-Olsen, S.: 1981, 'Instrumentalism as an Educational Concept', *Educational Studies in Mathematics* 12, 351-367.

Mellin-Olsen, S.: 1987, *The Politics of Mathematics Education*, Reidel, Dordrecht.

Mellin-Olsen, S.: 1991, *Hvordan tenker lærere om matematikkundervisning?*, Bergen Lærerhøgskole, Landås, Norway.

Mills, C. W.: 1959, *The Sociological Imagination*, Oxford University Press, New York.

Mollenhauer, K.: 1973, *Erziehung und Emanzipation*, Juventa Verlag, München.

Münzinger, W. (ed.): 1977, *Projektorientierter Mathematikunterricht*, Urban und Schwarzenberg, München.

Negt, O.: 1964, *Soziologische Phantasie und exemplarisches Lernen*, Europäische Verlagsanstalt, Frankfurt am Main.

Nickson, M.: 1992, 'The Culture of the Mathematics Classroom: An Unknown Quantity?', in Grouws, D.W. (ed.): *Handbook of Research on Mathematics Teaching and Learning*, MacMillan Publishing Company, New York, 101-114.

Niss, M.: 1977, 'The 'Crises' in Mathematics Instruction and a new Teacher Education at Grammar School Level', *International Journal of Mathematical Education in Science and Technology* 8, 303-321.

Niss, M.: 1979, 'Mathematische Erziehung', in Volk, D. (ed.), *Kritische Stichwörter zum Mathematikunterricht,* Wilhelm Fink, München, 150-158.

Niss, M.: 1983, 'Considerations and Experiences Concerning Integrated Courses in Mathematics and Other Subjects', in Zweng M., et al. (eds.): *Proceedings of the Fourth International Congress on Mathematical Education,* Birkhäuser, Boston, 247-249.

Niss, M.: 1989, 'Aims and Scope of Applications and Modelling in Mathematics Curricula', in Blum, W. et al. (eds.): *Applications and Modelling in Learning and Teaching Mathematics,* Ellis Horwood, Chichester, 22-31.

Niss, M.: 1994, 'Mathematics and Society', in Biehler, R. et al. (eds.): *Didactics of Mathematics as a Scientific Discipline,* Kluwer, Dordrecht, 367-378.

Nissen, G. and Blomhøj, M. (eds.): 1994, *Hul i kulturen,* Spektrum, Copenhagen.

Noddings, N.: 1993, 'Politicizing the Mathematics Classroom', in Restivo, S. et al. (eds.): *Math Worlds: Philosophical and Social Studies of Mathematics and Mathematics Education,* State University of New York Press, Albany, N.Y., 150-161.

Noss, R. et al. (eds.): 1990, *Political Dimensions of Mathematics Education: Action and Critique: Proceedings of the First International Conference,* 1-4 April 1990, Revised Edition, University of London, London.

Nunes, T., Schliemann, A.D. and Carraher, D.W.: 1993, *Street Mathematics and School Mathematics,* Cambridge University Press, Cambridge.

Paffrath, F. H. (ed.): 1987, *Kritische Theorie und Pädagogik der Gegenwart,* Deutscher Studien Verlag, Weinheim.

Raith, W. (ed.): 1973, *Handbuch zum Unterricht: Modelle emanzipatorischer Praxis, Hauptschule,* Raith, Starnberg.

Riess, F. (ed.): 1977, *Kritik des mathematisch naturwissenschaftlichen Unterrichts,* Päd- Extra Buchverlag, Frankfurt am Main.

Shan, S.-J. and Bailey, P.: 1991, *Multiple Factors: Classroom Mathematics for Equality and Justice,* Trentham Books, Stoke-on-Trent.

Skovsmose, O.: 1980, *Forandringer i matematikundervisningen,* Gyldendal, Copenhagen.

Skovsmose, O.: 1981a, *Matematikundervisning og kritisk pædagogik,* Gyldendal, Copenhagen.

Skovsmose, O.: 1981b, *Alternativer og matematikundervisning,* Gyldendal, Copenhagen.

Skovsmose, O.: 1985, 'Mathematical Education versus Critical Education', *Educational Studies in Mathematics* 16, 337-354.

Skovsmose, O.: 1990, 'Mathematical Education and Democracy', *Educational Studies in Mathematics* 21, 109-128.

Skovsmose, O.: 1992, 'Democratic Competence and Reflective Knowing in Mathematics', *For the Learning of Mathematics* 2, 2, 2-11.

Skovsmose, O.: 1994, *Towards a Philosophy of Critical Mathematics Education,* Kluwer, Dordrecht.

Tybl, R. and Walter, H. (eds.): 1973, *Handbuch zum Unterricht: Modelle emanzipatorischer Praxis, Grundschule,* Raith, Starnberg.

Vithal, R., Christiansen, I.M., and Skovsmose, O.: 1995, 'Project Work in University Mathematics Education: A Danish Experience: Aalborg University', *Educational Studies in Mathematics* 29, 199-223.

Voigt, J.: 1985, 'Patterns and Routines in Classroom Interaction', *Recherches en Didactique des Mathématiques* 6, 1, 69-118.

Volk, D.: 1975, 'Plädoyer für einen problemorientierten Mathematikunterricht in emanzipatorischer Absicht', in Ewers, M. (ed.): *Naturwissenschaftliche Didaktik zwischen Kritik und Konstruktion,* Belz, Weinheim

Volk, D.: 1977, 'Entscheidungsfreiraum in den Lehrplänen machen! Wissenschaftstheo-retische Probleme der Mathematik in der Ausbildung der Mathematiklehrer aufnehmen', in Riess, F. (ed.): *Kritik des mathematisch naturwissenschaftlichen Unterrichts,* Päd- Extra Buchverlag, Frankfurt am Main, 347-392.

Volk, D.: 1979, *Handlungsorientierende Unterrichtslehre am Beispiel des Mathematikunter-richts, Band A,* Päd Extra Buchverlag, Bensheim.

Volk, D. (ed.): 1979, *Kritische Stichwörter zum Mathematikunterricht,* Wilhelm Fink, München.

Volk, D.: 1980, *Zur Wissenschaftstheorie der Mathematik: Handlungsorientierende Unter-richtslehre, Band B,* Päd Extra Buchverlag, Bensheim.

Volk, D.: 1989, 'Mathematics Classes and Enlightenment', in Blum, W. et al. (eds.): *Applica-tions and Modelling in Learning and Teaching Mathematics,* Ellis Horwood, Chichester, 187-191.

Volmink, J., 1994, 'Mathematics by All', in Lerman, S. (ed.): *Cultural Perspectives on the Mathematics Classroom,* Kluwer, Dordrecht, 51-68.

Wagenschein, M., 1965, 1970, *Ursprüngliches Verstehen und exaktes Denken I-II,* Klett, Stutt-gart.

Zaslavsky, C.: 1979, *Africa Counts: Number and Pattern in African Culture,* Lawrence Hill Books, New York.

Chapter 36: Towards Humanistic Mathematics Education

STEPHEN I. BROWN

State University of New York at Buffalo, Amherst, U.S.A.

ABSTRACT

An exploration of forces and assumptions that influence the movement of humanistic mathematics education. Particular attention is paid to the limiting perspective of logic as a defining quality of mathematics; to recent developments in philosophy of mathematics; to the irony of the computer as an instrument for encouraging a sharper view of the concept of humanistic mathematics education; to the influence of the progressive education movement (especially on its student-centered focus); and to the Humanistic Mathematics Network as an example of a movement committed to that theme. The essay ends with an exploration of problematic issues – both hidden and made explicit by the movement. Among the topics explored are the need to re-consider the meaning of reason-giving and reason-seeking, the possibility of a reconstructed conception of personhood as it is defined in the humanistic movement, the desire for a more robust conception of problem and its educational uses, and the need to locate appropriate contexts within which mathematics education as both historical and personal drama might flourish.

1.   INTRODUCTION

Those who have experienced mathematics as a depersonalized, uncontextualized, non-controversial and asocial form of knowledge might very well consider the expression *humanistic mathematics education* to be the epitome of an oxymoron. While the concept of humanistic mathematics education can better be understood as a collection of *family resemblances* – to use a Wittgenstein construct – than as a sharply defined concept, it is best appreciated as a reaction to the world view suggested above.

The concept of *humanistic mathematics education* represents an internationally evolving major paradigm shift in its view of mathematics and of education. There have however been harbingers of the shift in various forms in different countries for over half a century.

What are the disciplines and perspectives that one might include in an effort to understand the concept of *humanistic mathematics education*? In fact that question requires considerable reconstruction before it can be under-

A.J. Bishop et al. (eds.), International Handbook of Mathematics Education, 1289 - 1321

stood, no less answered. It requires an awareness of the concept of humanism and human nature and their long history; an understanding of what is meant by education and how that concept has evolved as well; and of course an appreciation of what we mean by mathematics itself.

As a task that falls within the purview of many disciplines – including general philosophy; philosophy of education, of mathematics and science; cognitive and social psychology; linguistics; sociology; history of science and mathematics; anthropology; literature and many others – we are inclined to wonder what disciplines might reasonably be *excluded* rather than what might be *included*. To understand it properly not only requires participation in the fiery theoretical debates of these distinct disciplines, but necessitates an appreciation of forms of praxis that both inform and are informed by their intertwine (See Seeger & Steinbring (1992)). One needs to be aware of the ways in which curriculum and texts influence each other; how teachers define themselves professionally and personally; how students and their image of themselves are affected by the culture of school and society; what concepts of application are both used and ignored in an effort to 'apply' a discipline like mathematics to the real world; what constitutes legitimate research in education; how teachers are 'trained'; how authority in religion and other forms of dogma compare with authority of reason.

Interested in theoretical and practical issues that contribute to a conception of humanistic mathematics education, we shall chart a course that borrows from both domains. We shall make occasional use of anecdotes in order to portray in non-technical terms many of the issues that might otherwise require considerable elaboration. It is important to appreciate that in being illustrative we are trying to sketch the terrain of humanistic mathematics education in broad strokes and are thus leaving out many details that are part of the debate.

The following several sections will be essentially descriptive. They will lay out the terrain in a relatively non-problematic manner. In the sections following 'Extensions and Problematics of Humanistic Mathematics Education', we shall draw upon many of the earlier distinctions and claims – some of which may appear benign – and will locate contradictions and problems that require attention.

One small indication of the enormity of the task – one that supports the argument that there may be precious little to exclude from the effort to understand the concept of humanistic mathematics education – is captured by Wheeler's (1982) insightful claim about the nature of mathematics itself. He asserts that by virtue of the fact that anyone speaks a language, that person automatically has a deep appreciation of mathematics. That claim is undergirded by many beliefs – among them that we need to distinguish between mathematics as a body of knowledge and a way of thinking in and about the world. To the extent that we use language with some degree of consistency and that language both depicts and separates objects within and between classes, we are exhibiting some of the most fundamental mathematical concepts – ones that so deeply pervade every form of inquiry that we barely even notice the fact.

2.   MATHEMATICS AND LIBERAL EDUCATION: THE FORCE OF LOGIC

We begin by situating the practice of humanistic mathematics education in reaction to a popular conception of mathematics that derives from a view of liberal education – one that claims to choose its disciplines based largely upon distinguishing characteristics among the many different fields of human inquiry. Though the particular fields have changed over time, the characteristics that have been picked out for over two thousand years are ones that separate a field from others by virtue of special qualities of the field – qualities that have minimal overlap with others. Though such a program seems both reasonable and benign enough as a way of selecting disciplines, we shall show that its practice is responsible for much mischief.

The British philosopher, Paul Hirst (1974), has a particularly interesting rationale for including the various fields that constitute a liberal education – one that transcends the ancient Greek rationale that the achievement of such knowledge satisfies the mind by virtue of its inherent desire to pursue such knowledge (as for example in Kimball (1986), Phenix (1964)). He argues forcefully not that these different orientations have to be passed down because they expand upon an already existing human quality or that they strengthen or satisfy the mind. Rather, he claims that an ability to think along such lines is in fact what we *mean* by the claim that one *has a mind in* the first place.

Most documents that justify the inclusion of mathematics as one of those special fields, identify the quality of deductive logic – logic in which arguments are derived from sets of axioms – as its distinguishing feature.

Though conceptions of logic have changed over time, and though there have been co-temporaneous conflicting schools of thought that attempt to locate the precise nature of the influence of logic on mathematics, it has been not only an important ingredient but rather a defining characteristic of the discipline.

In order to see how such a point of view with regard to the discipline itself becomes translated (perhaps even unintentionally) into pedagogical experience, we offer the following two student reactions.

The first is by an articulate woman who participated in a study conducted by Buerk (1982). These women were outstanding in some intellectual field but had inordinate fear of mathematics at any level.

And on the eighth day, God created mathematics. He took stainless steel, and he rolled it out thin, and he made it into a fence forty cubits high,

1291

and infinite cubits long. And on the fence, in fair capitals, he did print rules, theorems axioms and pointed reminders. 'Invert and multiply'. 'The square on the hypotenuse is three decibels louder than one hand clapping'. 'Always do what's in the parentheses first'. And when he finished, he said 'On one side of the fence will reside those who are bad at math, and woe unto them, for they shall weep and gnash their teeth'.

Math does make me think of a stainless steel wall — hard, cold, smooth, offering no handhold; all it does is glint back at me. Edge up to it, put your nose against it; it doesn't give anything back; you can't put a dent in it; it doesn't take your shape; it doesn't have any smell; all it does is make your nose cold. I like the shine of it — it does look smart, intelligent in an icy way. But I resent its cold impenetrability, its supercilious glare. (p. 19).

The second is by a college student who eventually majored in mathematics but who was influenced by the de-humanizing effect of a teaching regimen that derived its pedagogy directly from its conception of mathematics exclusively as a logical, deductive field.

In my junior year at college, I took my first graduate level mathematics course — finite dimensional vector spaces. It was offered by a professor who had an international reputation. The first day, he told us that the only things that count in proving anything are axioms, definitions, rules of logic and previously established theorems. Any other crutch was to be interpreted as a bastardization of the discipline. He proceeded to list the axioms of a vector space, and as sometimes happens under such circumstances, he got stuck. He stood before us, mumbled a few inaudible words, and then turning his back to the class, and blocking the blackboard with a stomach that was adequate for the purpose, he sketched a tiny diagram that looked something like:

Attempting to be consistent with his original advice, he quickly erased his sketch and proceeded to list a few more axioms and to prove a few 'baby theorems' based solely upon 'axioms, definitions, and rules of logic'.[1]

What do these anecdotes portray? They can be milked at length, but let us focus upon a few of their qualities in order to establish the backdrop that will be eroded by a humanistic orientation.

For one thing, the axioms were perceived to be handed down in an authoritarian and non-controversial way. This has both pedagogical and logical consequences. We are led to believe that they were created in a way that involved no labor pains and in particular no negotiation between what was considered worth proving and what was to be taken for granted. Consequently we were to *receive* these axioms as if they were devoid of human agency.

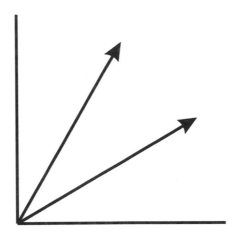

What is one to make of the erased sketches? By hiding how he really thought about these axioms and in particular how he remembered them, one is led to believe that they held essentially no connection with other ways of thinking. If they were to be excluded for the purpose of proof, and if he was somewhat embarrassed by his need to resort to their use, we are lead to believe that it is a weakness to have to engage one's mind in creating a kind of imagery that is a fundamental human impulse in all other fields of inquiry. Reference to a picture, even for the purpose of recalling something to be abstracted at a later point, is an admission of frailty.

While the professor was not trying to define mathematics through this example, consistent efforts to hide one's inner thoughts (while displaying only the rarefied fruits of such thought) leads to the belief that there is very little meaning associated with the games being played.

In fact such an extreme view of meaning has been touted by Bertrand Russell as a defining quality of mathematics. In a remark that is only slightly tongue in cheek, he defined mathematics as follows:

> Mathematics is the subject in which no one ever knows what he is talking about nor whether what he is saying is true.

What does Russell's somewhat tongue-in-cheek definition of mathematics pick out? It is an attempt to come to grips with a conception of (1) *meaning* and (2) *truth* in mathematical inquiry. Briefly, it asserts that the value of mathematics is in its essential *meaninglessness* and its transcendence of truth by virtue of its focus upon *implication* and proof. While most of us would be skeptical of a field that touted meaninglessness as its *raison d'être* – especially if we view human beings as meaning seeking people – Russell had a quite specialized notion of the concept of meaninglessness that had powerful consequences by virtue of applicability to a wide variety of instantiations.

It is one thing to be aware of the limitations and pretences involved in viewing mathematics as only a logical enterprise. It is of course another to seek alternatives. An interest in rectifying this view and in supplementing it with a more robust conception of experiencing mathematics represents a first approximation among people who affiliate with the humanistic camp.

3.   THE FRAILTY OF LOGIC: A FIRST APPROXIMATION OF HUMANISTIC
       MATHEMATICS

From a humanistic point of view, it is not that deductive logic is irrelevant or that it is not a critical component of mathematical thought, but rather that its role requires qualification and that its logical and depersonalized status is more fragile than we are lead to believe by most accounts of the sort depicted above. In the next two sections we will explore a crumbling of this perspective from a philosophical point of view and from the perspective of the computer as well. In sections 7 and 8, we turn to pedagogical challenges *per se.*

3.1   The Philosophy of Mathematics

The field of philosophy of mathematics has begun to redefine its scope. For years, its long-standing inquiry focused upon foundational interests associated with competing 'isms', like logic*ism,* intuition*ism* and formal*ism.* These various philosophical schools attempted to establish the bedrock of mathematical certainty in different ways.

These various schools mirrored for mathematics what philosophy up through the nineteenth century had done in general. If only we could become clear on 'first principles' regarding how the world is put together and how we come to perceive that world, then we would be able to derive how and what education (for example) ought to be without having to attend in a careful way to the meanings and conflicts of educational concepts such as teaching, indoctrination, learning and education itself. For many reasons this program came under attack in general philosophy and in philosophy of education in particular. (See Scheffler (1958)).

For a number of practical and theoretical reasons, the program in mathematics has also undergone some major transformations. One of the most stunning demonstrations in the foundations of mathematics itself – a little over a half a century ago – called into question the optimistic view that logic had the potential to conquer all of its challenges. It was done in response to David Hilbert's program in mathematical formalism. Hilbert set himself the task of demonstrating that mathematics was not inconsistent. He also hoped to establish that we could create descriptions of mathematical systems that were complete in the sense that one would eventually be able to prove or disprove any well formed mathematical statements that were of the order of interest and complexity of arithmetic. He intended thus to show that if any statement could not be proven to be true or false at any particular time by use of well established axioms, then this was merely an indication of momentary frailty.

Gödel, in his groundbreaking 1931 paper, 'Uber formal unentscheidbare Sätze der Principia Mathematica und verwandter Systeme' ('On Formally Undecidable Propositions of Principia Mathematica and Related Systems') demonstrated with Hilbertian rigor that both of these agendas were impossible to achieve. Not only was the longing for a demonstration of absolute consistency found to be a pipe dream, but he also showed that in any area of mathematics that has a modicum of interest, it is impossible to create a formal system that would enable one to prove or disprove all statements belonging to it. That is, there must exist 'undecidable' statements in any interesting system.

How to interpret his findings and exactly what it might mean for a formal view of mathematics is a problem that has been grappled with by philosophers of mathematics ever since. It is clear, as Nagel & Newman (1958) and Hofstadter (1979) argue in popularized accounts of Gödel's work, that Gödel has in some sense hoisted rigor and hung its most optimistic dreams on its own petard.

While Gödel's legacy does not destroy the centrality of deductive logic in mathematical thought, it does provide an initial crack in the façade of the unbounded potential of logic to do its job.

More recently, there have been deeper threats to a view of the growth of mathematics as essentially a logically deductive progression. Lakatos (1976), in his famous *Proofs and Refutations*, demonstrates the virtual impossibility of even stating relatively easy conjectures with any degree of accuracy, no less proving them. He shows that it is not the logical proofs of alleged theorems which advance the discipline of mathematics, but rather the eventual production of counter-examples which move the field ahead. He has argued for how it is that mathematical thought borrows significantly from a modified form of empirical scientific inquiry. Not only what constitutes knowledge and proof, but how they are codified and how they are passed along in the education of mathematicians are now emerging as elements of inquiry within which philosophical issues on the nature of mathematics are explored (See Kitcher (1988); Tymoczko (1985, 1986, 1992, 1993)).

Rather than trying to locate the bedrock upon which all of mathematics can be based (logic vs. set theory for example), there is an increasing inclination to seek out the social factors that account for a fallibilistic view of the subject.

The Belgian philosopher and mathematician Van Bendegem (1993) describes how this newly emerging perspective on the nature of mathematics compares with the earlier schools of philosophy of mathematics.

Philosophers of mathematics can be roughly divided into two types. Type I is particularly fond of questions such as: What are *the* foundations of mathematics? What are numbers? What is a set?... What is mathematical truth? These questions are all situated within mathematics proper. Formalists, logicists, intuitionists,... are in this sense Type I. Type II, however, wants answers to questions such as: How is mathematics done? What is a *real* mathematical proof?... How is it possible that an accepted proof turns out to be wrong? Type II is still a rare species, but happily enough... this is changing. (p. 21).

Bloor (1991), a British sociologist, argues that it is not only philosophers of mathematics but sociologists as well who are in a position to contribute to the philosophical underpinnings of this newly emerging epistemological view. In presenting his *strong programme*, he claims that sociology of knowledge can contribute not only to an understanding of how cultures and sub-cultures of scientific communities communicate with and influence each other, but to the logical sub-strata of the disciplines of mathematics and science. In a particularly revealing example, he explores how it is that what was once taken to be a totally illogical conception (the Euclidean legacy that it is impossible for the whole to be equal in some way to a proper subset of itself) is revived as the central component in the definition of a concept (what it means for a set to have a countably infinite number of elements).

Pedagogical derivatives of the new philosophy of mathematics have had reverberations in the emerging field of philosophy of mathematics education. Borrowing heavily from Lakatos' view of mathematics as a quasi - empirical field (neither based upon imagination alone nor exclusively upon sensory data evidence in the real world), Ernest (1991, 1994, 1994a) is among those who see the fallibilistic nature of mathematics as derived from the sense in which knowledge, truth and canons of proof are inextricably connected with our use of language and with social constructions of reality.[2]

We turn now to a fundamental irony of the computer that has further challenged our view of logic as *the* guiding light in mathematical thought.

3.2 The Irony of the Computer

A popular conception of the computer is that it is a technical device that has the power to replace what heretofore required considerable human effort. It is frequently touted for its ability to outperform complicated logical analysis of human beings. The irony is that the more successful the computer has been in competing with human acts, the more we come to appreciate the importance of extra-logical dimensions of human agency.

To see what is at stake here, imagine what kinds of activities we might associate with proof in mathematics. Not only do we want to

1) *create a proof* for a conjecture (showing it to be true or false), but we would want to be able to

2) *verify* that an alleged proof in fact is legitimate. Furthermore, in order to have anything to prove in the first place, it is necessary for one to

3) *come up with a statement* that is worth proving or disproving.

Consider issue 3): *coming up with* conjectures. Kolata (1989) describes a computer program known as Graffitti, a program in graph theory which is capable of creating three to eight thousand conjectures for any collection of graphs it is handed! That is quite impressive. It is an understatement to say that Graffiti surpasses what we might expect from any human being who is handed the same information.

What is the problem then? If one is handed this morass of data, one has no idea what is worth pursing since the conjectures come with no associated 'tag' that conveys their significance. The creator of the program, Fajtlowicz, found that what was needed was the establishment of criteria for determining what was 'interesting' and he ended up with characteristics that of course require human judgment.

The same kind of problem comes up with both 1) creation and 2) verification of proof. Davis and Hersh (1986) comment on a program called AUTOMATH that was devised in the 1970's for the purpose of *checking* alleged proofs. They comment,

> [T]he Automath project has been virtually abandoned. There are several reasons for this.... Even if these translations into Automath were available in great abundance, how would one verify that they were correct, that the Automath program is itself correct, that the machine program has been correctly written, that it all has been run correctly? (p. 68).

Back to human agency! Forward not only to the need for judgment – for a decision about what is worthwhile and significant – but for the intense realization that we cannot avoid being guided by criteria of an *aesthetic* nature that transcends logic alone when we decide what to prove, why to prove it and whether or not it is a proof at all.

4.   TOWARDS PEDAGOGICAL COMPONENTS OF HUMANISTIC MATHEMATICS
      EDUCATION

In this section, we shall review several pedagogical programs that expand upon, challenge and introduce other categories of personhood than those that are
narrowly associated with logic as an ingredient of the mathematical experience. The purpose here is two-fold: first, to be illustrate and not to exhaust the
many realizations of humanistic mathematics education; secondly, to locate
enough essential ingredients of the paradigm to justify the critical commentary in the next section. We shall explore (1) an historically relevant movement in education (originally primary education), (2) an international re-
orientation of mathematics education (focused upon primary and secondary
education), (3) a newly formed organization in the United States that expresses in a rather self-contained way a movement that has international roots and
reverberations.

4.1   The Voice of Progressive Education

A movement focused primarily focused upon elementary education known as
progressive education emerged with vigor in the first third of this century.

The movement had programs and proponents throughout the world (Dengler (1927), Ensor (1924), Gilbert (1933), Hylla (1927), Kilpatrick (1928),
Roman (1924), Switzer (1932)). Though there were numerous intellectual
leaders and practitioners who advocated and implemented these programs,
the movement is often associated with the American pragmatic philosophy of
John Dewey whose philosophical orientation placed practice in a broad theoretical perspective that focused not only upon classroom experience but upon
democratic ideals as well. Dewey's call for the application of intelligence and
experience to every endeavor of human existence transformed not only the
way we view education but our conception of ethics, aesthetics, epistemology
and mind. He eschewed dualistic thinking – separation of mind and body, action and thinking, the religious as distinct from the secular.

It is helpful in gaining a first approximation of the present movement in humanistic mathematics education to see how he characterized the progressive
education movement. In an address to the Progressive Education Association,
Dewey (1928), reminds his audience of essential elements (some of which
appear today to be platitudes, though they were not seen as such at the time)
of the progressive mode:
  – respect for individual capacities, interests and experiences;
  – enough external freedom and informality at least to enable teachers to
    become acquainted with children as they really are;
  – respect for self - initiated and self - conducted learning;
  – respect for activity as the stimulus and centre of learning;

— perhaps above all, belief in social contact, communication and co-operation upon a normal human plane as an all enveloping medium. (p. 161)

Here we see the expression of a point of view that taps into what are essential elements of many modern programs in mathematics education – especially the varieties of a constructivist outlook in creating knowledge and experiencing the world, and the centrality of the social context of the classroom.[3]

In this brief summary, Dewey says little about the nature of subject matter, though he speaks in general terms about the manner in which it is to be acquired – self initiated and through an environment of co-operation and communication. He does however, clarify what he means by 'interest and experience' in a way that makes it clear that he does not identify himself with a starry-eyed romantic vision of the student – one which mindlessly assumes that setting the child free to explore whatever interests him/her is the cornerstone of progressive education. Dewey (1928, reprinted 1988) comments:

[Individuality] is something developing and to be continuously attained, not something given all at once and ready-made. ...A child's individuality cannot be found in what [a child] does or in what he consciously likes at a given moment. It can be found only in the connected course of his actions (164–5).

What Dewey provides us with is an appreciation for certain pre-conditions that are necessary for the student to connect eventually with the logic of subject matter. Though the teacher may need to be aware of the end product – some body of knowledge and its logical connections (even if interpreted in more liberal terms than Russell's) – the student is differently engaged. The process of *coming to know* as opposed to *having achieved knowledge* requires an engaged and messy interaction with the world, a point of view that is appreciated once again by the constructivist orientation in many of the present calls for curriculum reform. We turn now to some of those considerations.

4.2   Present Day Curriculum Reform Movement: Problem Solving and Applications

Rooted in part upon the influence of computer science and cognitive psychology, in part upon structuralist world views, in part upon a commonsensical view of mathematics as something more than the learning of techniques to be reproduced on demand, there has emerged a constructivist stance towards the learning of mathematics that has placed problem solving in the forefront of the mathematics curriculum. In referring to the new emphasis however on knowledge as constructed rather than received, it is instructive to approach it not with a degree of amnesia, but an awareness of the influence of Piaget and his followers as well as of the progressive movement that we began to describe above. Noddings (1995) elaborates upon the relationship of the various forms of constructivism to the work of both Dewey and Piaget.

While it may be difficult to imagine a mathematics curriculum that is devoid of problem solving, the new perspective takes more seriously than was heretofore the case that what is at stake in problem solving is not primarily the application of already acquired techniques to arrive at an acceptable answer to a clearly formulated problem, but rather the effort to deal intelligently with what is not already known. Beginning in the early 1980's this theme so dominated the field that it was virtually impossible to read a journal or attend a conference in mathematics education anywhere in the world without having major focus explicitly devoted to problem solving and an analysis of associated heuristics (See Brown (1985) for an elaboration of this claim).

The theme of real world application became integrated with that of problem solving as there was an increased appreciation for a view of mathematics not only as a logically deductive axiomatic system, but as one that joined experience (rather than being conceived as a free floating entity with occasional serendipitous connections) through its inductive, pattern- seeking orientation as well.

These concerns are expressed in tone of almost nationalistic zeal in a document of the national organization of teachers of mathematics in North America (National Council of Teachers of Mathematics – NCTM) entitled, *An Agenda for Action: Recommendations for School Mathematics for the 1980's* (1980). We find the following:

> Problem solving must be the focus of school mathematics for the 1980's....Performance in problem solving will measure the effectiveness of our personal and national possession of mathematical competence.... Problem solving involves applying mathematics to the real world, serving theory and practice of current emerging sciences. (p.2).

The theme is elaborated in *The Curriculum Evaluation Standards For School Mathematics* (1989) and other related documents of the 1990's. We are told that:

> Problem solving should be the central focus of the mathematics curriculum. As such it is a primary goal of all mathematics instruction and an integral part of all mathematical activity.... Ideally, students should share their thinking and approaches with other students.... In addition, they should learn to value the process of solving problems as much as they value the solution. (p.23).

Problem solving thus begins to acquire a social context, – frequently referred to as 'communication' in addition to a continued focus upon 'real world' applications. Though the social context in the above document is more narrowly construed in the context of the classroom environment, there has been considerable interest in its broader implications in other documents that focus on the international scene. (See Keitel, Damerow, Bishop & Gerdes (1989)).

At the 7th International Congress of Mathematics Education (ICME) in Quebec in 1992, the theme of problem solving (and to a lesser extent applications of mathematics to the real world together with the social context of learning) had become so deeply entrenched among *au courant* educators that there were very few sessions that touted problem solving in their title. The focus however had become so well absorbed that it was implicit in a large number of the working and topic groups. (Compare Gaulin et. al. (1992) and Zweng et. al. (1983) for the explicit vs. implicit nature of the category at two ICME meetings that were about a decade apart).

From a pedagogical perspective, the centrality of problem solving translates in a variety of ways. Though not of one cloth, to the extent that a concern is with the heuristics of problem solving, there is an increased interest
1) in diagnosing how it is that students think,
2) in understanding what strategies they employ (both as a result of explicit teaching and as a consequence of their independent development) under what circumstances,
3) in acknowledging the power of error-making as an invitation for inquiry,
4) in encouraging them to operate in cooperative ways,
5) in seeking new ways of assessing the success of teaching that is commensurate with these emerging pedagogical strategies.

As part of the paradigm shift, there is a realization that if understanding is not a passive act, then one comes to understand ideas — mathematical and otherwise — in an effort to radically modifying them. That is, it is in the act of asking 'what if'? and 'what if not'? questions on emerging concepts that one gains power and understanding of these concepts.

This is a point of view expressed eloquently by Dewey (1957) not in focusing primarily upon matters of education, but in attempting to reconstruct the nature of philosophical inquiry in general. He comments,

Change in short is no longer looked upon as a fall from grace, as a lapse from reality or a sign of imperfection of Being. Modern science no longer tries to find some fixed form or essence behind each process of change. Rather, the experimental method tries to break down apparent fixities and to induce changes.... In short, the thing which is to be accepted and paid heed to is not what is originally given but that which emerges after the thing has been set under a variety of circumstances in order to see how it behaves (p. 113–114).

Consistent with this perspective, it has become popular recently for mathematics educators to advocate various forms of problem *posing* to be integrated with problem *solving*.[4]

It is a powerful insight that problem posing places both students and teachers in a position of genuine inquiry into problems that may not even be well formulated and whose form and substance may not signify difficulty of solution. Such engagement provides a climate in which one must attend to a host of emotional variables that transcend the notion of merely understanding what it is that is handed down in a more traditional classroom setting. From a conceptual point of view, we are presented with a view of mathematics that far outstrips the notion of mathematics as deductive logic.

4.3   Humanistic Mathematics Network

While it surely is not the case that there is a North American monopoly on the concept of *humanistic mathematics education*, there is an organization that was formed in the United States about a decade ago that defined itself exclusively by that theme. As such, an analysis of what has been produced by that group will not only be revealing, but it will provide a concrete backdrop for some of the criticism we will be offering in the next section. Though spawned as a US venture, the authors and readers of the resulting publication span the world. Now for the story of that organization.

In 1986, Alvin White convened about a dozen university mathematicians, mathematics educators and philosophers to discuss the relationship between mathematics and the humanities, and more generally to discover what was wrong with how the discipline of mathematics was being portrayed to its clients at elementary, secondary and university levels.

At that meeting, the group created a number of tenets that defined some of its subsequent exploration: Among them were:

a)   An appreciation of the role of intuition, not only in understanding, but in creating concepts that appear in their finished versions to be 'merely technical'.

b)   An appreciation for the human dimensions that motivate discovery – competition, cooperation, the urge for holistic pictures.

c)   An understanding of the value judgments implied in the growth of any discipline. Logic alone never completely accounts for *what* is investigated, *how* it is investigated and *why* it is investigated.

d)   A need for teaching. learning formats that will help wean our students from a view of knowledge as certain, to-be-received.

e)   The opportunity for students to think like a mathematician, including a chance to work on tasks of low definition, to generate new problems and to participate in controversy over mathematical issues.

f) Opportunity for faculty to do research on issues relating to teaching, and to be respected for that area of research.

Some of these are themes we already uncovered in our earlier discussions.

As a consequence of the enthusiasm of this small group, a publication entitled 'Humanistic Mathematics Newsletter' was begun in 1987. After seven editions, the Newsletter was transformed into a bona fide journal in April of 1992. (See White (1993) for a compilation of essays that apply and expand upon the themes in this journal).

In addition to the themes mentioned above (and sometimes cross-hatching them), the journal is devoted to an exploration of the relationship of mathematics to the humanities in a number of philosophically interesting ways. Among the questions explored are:

- Is mathematics a branch of the humanities?
- Can mathematics be reduced to one the humanities (e.g. poetry or literature or art)?
- What is the relationship mathematics and philosophy?
- How is mathematics expressed in the humanities (literature for example)?
- In what sense(s) is mathematics a language (and vice versa)?
- What does an awareness of the history of mathematics contribute to our understanding of the social and contextual nature of the discipline?

Consistent with the above tenets, pedagogical issues abound. Frequently these issues focus not upon a reconstruction for the student of the nature of mathematics as a humanistic enterprise but upon teaching in ways that honor the student's humanity. Lecturing is not necessarily relegated to Coventry, but thought is given to the purpose and manner of lecturing in relation to the students' minds (See for example Stein (1992)).

There are numerous descriptions of tutorial type programs at all educational levels. Articles by Stephens (1993) and Luttmann (1993) portray the astounding consequences of providing personal attention to undergraduates – challenging the assumption that mathematical talent is inborn and immune to an environment of cognitive and psychological support.

At the other extreme, there are several articles (reprinted) by Benezet (1991a; 1991b; 1991c) in which he describes a program that is radical by virtue of its omission rather than inclusion. He discusses the consequences of abandoning formal mathematics instruction all together below grade seven and focuses on language instruction instead. Subsequently, after one year of formal instruction, one could not tell the difference between those students who had been taught mathematics in earlier grades and those who had not.

What emerges in this journal is an intertwine of two themes that are sometimes treated separately and on some occasions integrated in the collection:

1) teaching mathematics humanistically (as in treating students with dignity and respect and concern for their awarenesses) and

2) teaching humanistic mathematics (as in teaching a view of mathematics as a meaningful human enterprise sharing many of the assumptions of other humanistic studies and experiences).

We turn now to a discussion of some unacknowledged legacies of traditional conceptions that reside in the humanistic mathematics education movement and some problematic issues generated by the multifaceted concept itself.

5. EXTENSIONS AND PROBLEMATICS OF HUMANISTIC MATHEMATICS EDUCATION

A problem solving/constructivist point of view would appear to inject a strong sense of personhood into the doing of mathematics. After all, there is a world of difference between thinking of mathematics as either following or offering a logically deductive pristine argument and creating or seeking heuristics that enable one to face what is unknown (maybe unknowable). Especially when we honor a form of pedagogy that encourages the posing of problems and that views errors not as experience to be avoided but as an invitation to create new knowledge, we would appear to have achieved the epitome of a humanistic orientation. What is there of personhood that has been left out? We shall explore the issue in the following two sections and will argue that the concept is in need of major surgery. We begin the next section with another anecdote.

5.1   Reason-Giving and Intentionality

Several years ago, I was tutoring a young man, Jordan, who wanted to know more about the famous 'ambiguous case' in trigonometry. That is, he wanted to know why such a fuss was being made about the problem of finding out information about the sides and angles of a triangle when one was given the measures of an angle, a side adjacent to the angle and a side opposite the angle. He had previously studied Euclidean geometry and in that context was able not only to solve problems but to talk about the strategies he used for their solution. I began the conversation by asking him to think once more about those circumstances under which a triangle was determined. Jordan, confused by the question, wanted to know why I was talking about triangles 'being determined'.

He reminded me that he had no difficulty with proving triangles congruent and that he had several strategies for doing so. He recalled that if three sides of one triangle are congruent to three sides of another triangle, then the triangles are congruent and the corresponding parts therefore also are in accord. He recalled how much he enjoyed figuring out which were the given corresponding sides when the information was not made explicit. In short, he enjoyed and was competent at problem solving with congruent triangles – defining problem solving in a variety of ways (adapted from Brown (1984)).

What has taken place here? Jordan was well accustomed to mathematics as *reason-giving*. What he had never been invited to see as problematic, however is the large scope within which domains of study fall. Doing many exercises of congruency for triangles may involve the student in clever problem solving activities. What it does not do, however is imbue those activities with a sense of *purpose*.

The issue is quite complicated, however. It is not possible for a number of good reasons to always involve students in *reason-giving* as seeking *purpose* and *intention*. First of all, the relationship between the big picture and the small exercise or activity is not always possible to explain at early stages of inquiry. That is, one frequently needs to acquire skills and accretions of information before being able to see the big picture.

Secondly, when too much of the story is told beforehand, much of the surprise is depleted from the account, and surprise is surely a valuable pedagogical tool. To be told when one is being introduced to the concept of irrational numbers, for example that not only are there an infinite number of such 'animals', but an uncountable number, removes the wonder and joy associated with the exploration to discover whether or not there is even *one* of them.

What is needed, however is enough sensitivity to the many different concepts of reason-giving so that teachers can entertain the possibility that seeking purpose is a larger category than reason-giving. It involves negotiation of goals to achieve as well as clever means to achieve them.

Another dimension of reason is not *reason-giving* but *reason-seeking* even after *reason-giving* has been established. That is, we have all had the experience of establishing relationships by careful reason-giving and yet remaining totally puzzled by the outcome. Why, for example, does it turn out that when we construct three equilateral triangles on the sides of a right triangle that the areas are additive as they are in the construction of three squares? It is possible to achieve that realization by calculation, but while such calculation allows us to be secure that the conclusion is correct, we are still left with the need to find out *why*. That is, the mystery frequently begins only after we have 'correctly' applied a chain of reasoning.

Frequently the first step in significant inquiry is not establishing an answer to a problem even with a justifiable litany of reason-giving. That is, to the extent that we are interested not only in establishing a proof or disproof of a conjectures and in solving problems, but in *understanding* something, we need to

1305

look at reason in a more multi-faceted way. It is possible as a consequence of producing proofs to achieve understanding that is as blind as when we operate only according to a set of rules.

There are many other interesting questions that arise in the context of reason-giving and reason-seeking. Though this issue is not frontally on the agenda of the humanistic mathematics education movement, it is worth pointing out that the focus on problem solving, student inquiry and student interest, subcutaneously generates issues of this sort in a way that more traditional approaches do not. We need a full fledged analysis of what it is we seek when we claim that we are interested in the relationship between mathematical thinking and reasoning.

What is needed for a further exploration is more full blown analysis of the concept of rationality rather than *reason-giving* alone in understanding how reasons function in a humanistic conception of mathematics education.

Having touted intentionality and purpose, it is important to realize that just as students construct mathematical knowledge and intentions for creating and exploring knowledge, so they have purposes and intentions with regard to their lives – mathematical and otherwise. Noddings (1993) reminds us of this truism in the following comment:

> Constructivists must attend to the fact that purposes are constructed as well as knowledge, and students have a wide variety of purposes. Just as we need to know how students think if we are to help them build powerful mathematical constructions, we need to know them as persons if we are to assist their construction of well chosen purposes. (p. 159).

How do we assist them in their construction of their own purposes? We address a part of the answer to that question in the next section.

5.2   History Revisited

Once more we begin with a brief anecdote. The purpose is to invite the reader to accompany the author along the pathway of a journey which led to a powerful insight.

> Several years ago I was telling my class of graduate students about Gauss' supposed encounter with the famous arithmetic series:
>
> $$1 + 2 + 3 + \ldots + 97 + 98 + 99 + 100$$
>
> The myth is passed down that he cleverly paired the two outside terms $(1 + 101)$, the two inner terms $(2 + 99)$, the two terms from each end $(3$

+ 98) and noticed that he had 50 pairs of 101, thus yielding 5050 as the sum. Algebraically, we can capture the strategy in general with the following (for n= 100):

$(n + 1) \times n/2$

I asked my students to spend a number of days investigating variations of this scheme (comparing for example what happens with an even and an odd last term). I also asked them to figure out as many different ways as possible to think about the problem — without using any specialized technical information. In addition to purely algebraic means, they worked on geometric schemes as well. Inspired by both geometric and algebraic, they came up with a number of different algebraic summations of the activity. In addition to the expected formulation, they came up with some rather messy ones such as:

$$\left[(n + 1) \times \frac{(n - 1)}{2}\right] + \left[\frac{(n + 1)}{2} \times \frac{1}{2}(n + 1)2\right] - \left[\frac{1}{2}(n + 1)\right]$$

When I asked them to discuss the many different formulations of the problem and to wonder about which approaches and which formulations they found most aesthetically appealing, I was surprised to find out that some of them preferred messy summaries (as above) which surely appeared to be more difficult to remember (revised from Brown (1973)).

Why would anyone have wanted to remember a messy formulation? It took a while for me to appreciate that messiness did a good job of encapsulating their personal history with the problem, and they wanted to remember the *struggle* more than the 'neat' *end-product*.

In this example, mathematical activity was viewed as an invitation to discuss issues of a far more general nature about self — issues having to do with one's view of how experience is best codified and remembered.

Thus the concept of history is one that may be expanded to include a student's (or a classes') reflection on quite idiosyncratic encounters with a problem over time. The historical sense of meaningfulness need not necessarily be relegated to a public history. In some ways it is possible for students to appreciate and create their own histories much as the women's movement is doing in an effort to compensate for the fact that their stories have been excluded from public accounts of history.

What the above anecdote illustrates is the value of personal awareness (how one wishes to honor the evolution of personal thought) as a goal that is accomplished by reflecting upon experiences in mathematics. Though the mathematical exploration was surely valuable in its own right, it is possible – from the perspective of an educator – to think of the mathematical experience as being instrumental in bringing that awareness about rather than as an end in its own right.

This insight not only enables us to speak of the potential of mathematics to address some of the issues of personhood suggested by Noddings, but it complicates the dichotomy we spoke about earlier in discussing The Humanistic Mathematics Network. We now turn to that issue.

5.3   Complicating a Dualistic View of Humanistic Mathematics

In the section on the Humanistic Mathematics Network, we discussed two different conceptions of humanistic mathematics:
1) teaching humanistic mathematics and
2) teaching mathematics humanistically.

The former involves a reconstructed vision of mathematics *per se*. That means that one would teach an alternative to a view of mathematics as absolute and certain. Students would be made familiar with the sense in which the discipline might be fallible. The history of ideas would reveal the sense in which both mathematical meaning and proof are socially constructed.

The latter has a different orientation. Here it is the student who is the focus rather than the discipline of mathematics per se. We pay particular attention to the interests of the students and to the way in which they acquire meaning.

There is something a bit artificial in establishing the dichotomy, since it is not hard to imagine a program which is aimed at accomplishing both (1) and (2). It is also possible of course to imagine a program that violates both (1) and (2). What may be particularly interesting to entertain, however are hybrid conceptions rather than pure programs of humanistic mathematics education. Such hybrids have the potential to sharpen what we might wish to accomplish in full fledged formulations. In order to do so, we consider a scheme depicted by the matrix below:

A full fledged humanistic program [incorporating both (1) and (2)] is depicted in box (D). A program that is lacking in both humanistic qualities is depicted box A. But what can we say about boxes (B) and (C)?

Looking at box (C), can we think of mathematics as absolute while learning as constructed? This is an enlightening category because it raises a number of fascinating issues that seem to be suppressed in the humanistic movement? Once explored, it opens up new options in the full fledged category of box (D) that we have barely begun to imagine.

	THE LEARNER	
	learning as received knowledge	learning as constructed knowledge
NATURE OF MATHEMATICS math as absolute	A	C
math as fallible	B	D

The question that impels me to explore this distinction is: What is the sort of learning that is allegedly being done in a constructive manner? The answer for the most part is that it is learning and doing of the discipline of mathematics. Most of the allusions to the interest of the student and to conceptions of understanding seem to make that assumption. The 'self' that is enhanced by engagement with mathematics is one that is seen in relation to the discipline.

Such a point of view neglects to take into consideration, however, that the concept of education is considerably broader than that of mathematics. It neglects to take into consideration that one can use mathematical experiences to view 'self' in a variety of ways that outstrip an interest in mathematics *per se*. In fact this is what we described in the Gauss example of the preceding subsection.

While it is true that the student described in that anecdote did in fact operate in a constructivist manner, the discussion was correctly silent with regard to the fallible vs. absolute nature of mathematics *per se*.

What is revealing about the self far outstrips an interest in and awareness of mathematics. One begins to face how it is that one wishes to keep track of the evolution of an idea and once the 'keeping track of' becomes part of the dialogue, it has the potential to take on a life of its own — independent of its source of inspiration.

But what sense can we make of box (B) in the above scheme? Does it make sense to focus upon the fallible nature of mathematical thought while viewing learning as knowledge to be received?

It was precisely this orientation that was one of the emblems of the progressive education movement of in the early 1930's. Most people associate progressive education exclusively with the child-centered approach to knowledge that we described earlier. They see the movement as concerned primarily with making the classroom a more interesting place to be.

In fact, Counts (1932), starting with the social context of education, took a totally different point of view – one that eventually created a schism in the movement. (See Cremin (1961) and Brown & Finn (1988) for an elaboration of this issue). His concern was not with the classroom as a social environment, but rather with society *writ large*. Seeing the amount of poverty and social injustice in the world, Counts' concern was not in using the classroom to titillate the interests of youngsters, but rather to do whatever was needed to use it for righting societal injustices.

Considerable debate ensued in the progressive education movement, much of it concerned with his total disregard not only for pedagogy but for the mind of his clients. Many people criticized him on the grounds that in using the classroom to work through his political agenda, he was indoctrinating rather than educating youngsters.

We need not go to the extremes suggested by Counts however, to seek an instructive analogy in mathematics education. It is possible to take the agenda of mathematics as lacking in certainty, having historical roots, filled with human dilemmas and possessing qualities of fallibilism as a central theme. What might we do with that observation other than use it for the purpose of exploring mathematics in a different way in the classroom? Could we be concerned with the urgency of that message in such a way that it acquires the force of a political movement as in the case of Counts?

There are many ways in which such an urgency might play itself out so that it becomes less of a pedagogical agenda and more one of commitment to revising the world order.

If we are concerned deeply with the way in which individuals, countries, societies think in dualistic terms – good and evil, right and wrong, family and other, we and they – in all of its different guises, then we might appropriately define the educational program as one of revamping the way in which students view knowledge and authority. Since one of the last bastions of a dualistic mind-set is the discipline of mathematics as it is conveyed in most educational settings, it might not be inappropriate to seek whatever means possible to use the classroom as a center for transforming that view of knowledge in society.

There may be certain ironies connected with offering such a viewpoint to students as a form of *received knowledge* itself, but we can imagine that what such a crusade would find appealing would be the reconstruction of society's view of knowledge and authority as opposed to using such a point of view for the purpose of making the classroom a more interesting place to be.[5] We can imagine establishing such an agenda without worrying about the here and now 'interests' of the students and without being concerned with justifying mathematical content in terms that are inherent in the discipline. Rather the goal would be messianic – passing along a transformed view of mathematics for the purpose of saving society.

Though the examples we used to illustrate the hybrid cases may appear a bit contrived – and even stretched conceptually – they have the advantage of calling our attention to the fact that in prioritizing humanistic curriculum concerns, we may need to distinguish among goals to be achieved. It is neither anti-intellectual nor anti-humanistic to appreciate that there are occasions upon which the mathematics agenda *per se* may serve educational and political purposes for which the discipline itself is viewed instrumentally.

We turn now to a final exploration of the two contrasting views of humanistic mathematics education discussed above – one which ultimately will offer a more sophisticated view of what might be involved in applying mathematics to the 'real world'.

5.4   Towards a More Robust View of History, Socialization and Application.

What are we doing when we pit view (1) against view (2) of humanistic mathematics education? Though the above examples were used to imagine that the two program could be driven by independent agendas, in what ways might we see them as relating? We could argue that though some programs might focus more upon the fallible nature of mathematics and the other upon the students as responsible for constructing their own meaning, most reasonable programs will seek some *rapprochement* via a compromise of sorts.

What such a compromise neglects to appreciate, however is that they are not so much different conceptions of the notion of humanistic mathematics education as they are glimpses of the same intellectual activity from different ends of the spectrum. The exploration of the novel use of history in seeking a candidate for box (C) is revealing. When we as teachers attend to the history of our students' own thinking as they encounter an idea that they explore over a protracted period of time, they themselves face dilemmas that are similar in some important ways to ones that 'the experts' faced when they originally encountered these concepts.[6]

Rather than impose standards for what constitutes a correct statement of a problem that is of interest to the students, and rather than pass judgment on the legitimacy of a proof, these matters can themselves become part of a continuous dialogue of the class. Just as Lakatos demonstrated that much of mathematics advances more by refutation of proofs of alleged theorems than by deductive proofs, so we as teachers can be patient for alleged truths and alleged proofs to be challenged and counterchallenged by our students. It is worth considering the possibility that this kind of activity might take place over a protracted period of time without feeling that one needs to set the record straight by imposing what are socially acceptable viewpoints about mathematical meaning on students.

As our students explore, we can direct them not only to cooperate but to think about how they have influenced each other, when they decided that an idea was worth honoring by some sort of naming activity, when they expressed the joy and frustration of discovery and of confusions as well, when they changed their minds about whose contributions were important and what questions were worthwhile. Attending to the emotional, intellectual and social climate of the classroom is not only a matter of observation by the teacher, but requires use of strategies that enable students themselves to become aware of when and how they operate. To the extent that they become part of the fabric of discourse, the students are experiencing and reflecting upon the qualities that are associated with the evolution of ideas.

Fawcett (1938) created and analyzed a fascinating teaching experiment in this spirit. He encouraged students of geometry to decide among themselves what they considered to be the most obvious, non-controversial statements about points, lines and figures in the plane. He then designed the course around their efforts to revise and expand upon these assumptions in their class effort to prove whatever they considered less obvious from these axioms of their own creation.

In addition to viewing activity in such a way that it heightens the students' awarenesses of their own thinking processes and potentially mirrors early stages of inquiry by mathematicians, there is another deep sense in which what we have called views (1) and (2) are connected. It is a view of mathematical thinking which connects the development of fundamental mathematical ideas with those that everyone experiences in the context of being human. It is not the pale coin of *applying mathematics to the real world*. That view assumes that the real world and mathematical thinking are in fact separate entities and that there is an occasional opportunity to seek their linkage. Mathematical language in fact has the potential to stand the 'application' issue on its head by offering metaphors for understanding the most fundamental qualities of human existence. Keyser (1916) depicts this connection. He says,

> Mathematics is precisely the ideal handling of the problems of life, and the central ideas of the science. The great concepts about which its stately doctrines have been built up, are precisely the chief ideas with which life must always deal, and which, as it tumbles and rolls about them through time and space, give it its interests and problems... (p. 77).

What does he identify in a specific way as the connecting links? Keyser comments,

> The mathematical concept of constant and variable are represented familiarly in life by the notions of fixedness and change. The concept of equation or that of an equational system, imposing restriction upon variability, is matched in life by the concept of natural and spiritual law, giving order to what were else chaotic change and providing partial freedom in lieu of none at all. What is known in mathematics under the

name of limit is everywhere present in life in the guise of some ideal, some excellence high-dwelling among the rocks, an 'ever flying perfect' as Emerson calls it.... The supreme concept of functionality finds its correlate in life in the all-pervasive sense of interdependence of mutual determination among the elements of the world. What is known in mathematics as transformation... is conceived in life as a process of transmutation by which, in the flux of the world, the content of the present has come out of the past and in its turn, in ceasing to be, gives birth to its successor. (p. 78).

Fischer (1993), an Austrian mathematician and educator, seeking the source of these metaphors, appreciates an underlying dualism that appears to account for mathematics as a *means* to explain complex situations and as a *system* of concepts that are inherent in us and that therefore affect how we see the world. He speaks of the inseparability of what he calls 'the aspect of means' and 'the aspect of system'. He comments,

[W]e have not yet learned to cope with the duality of means and systems in mathematics. We have especially not learned to recognize the reciprocal actions between these two aspects of mathematics.... I think we should study the duality of means and system with more effort and try to handle it – politics of science, education, and so forth – more constructively. (p. 114–5)

As in the case of the many dualities that Dewey exposed – the dualism of thought and action, the dualism of encouraging students to be interested vs. expecting them to exert effort, the dualism of mind and body – the most interesting resolution is not so much a practical compromise as it is a realization that the dualistic elements share hidden assumptions. By exposing these assumptions, the dualism does not dissolve; rather the competing forces are joined by a new conception that enables us to see each of the conflicting elements from a more robust point of view.[7]

5.5 The Location of the Concept of Problem in Humanistic Mathematics Education

We end this section with an analysis of a problem in relation to the concept of problem itself that has been implicit in much of our discussion in this section. Despite
1) its constructivist orientation,
2) its focus on interest of students,
3) its awareness of the various roles of the social context of education,
4) its challenge to the fallible nature of mathematics,

5) its awareness of the potential of history to illuminate the human agency in mathematics,

there has been a legacy from an earlier age that dominates much of curriculum. That is the field is still dominated by a rather narrow view of the purpose and uses of problem in mathematics.

A major fallacy that drives much of what we have criticized in earlier sections of this paper is based upon the definition of problem itself. That is, regardless of how we define a problem (and with the full realization that there are unsolved problems), it would be hard to imagine any definition of *problem* that would not invoke the concept of *solution* as part of the definition itself.

As a consequence, problems themselves are used for educational purposes in a way that exemplifies their definition. The desire for solution may be tempered or postponed or modified. This frequently is what happens in the case of problem generating or posing. By virtue of the definition of problem, however, we seem to have unwittingly imposed an educational agenda: an agenda that moves us in the direction of solving not only 'given' but self-selected problems.

Frequently problem posing disguises the fact that it is problem solving that is the ultimate goal. Thus, claims are made, for example, that if students select problems on their own, then they will be better motivated to try to solve them or that they will better understand the problem(s) they work on.

The fallacy resides in the fact that once we have a problem or a host of problems, there is much of educational value that can be set in motion other than the solution of those problems. One can invoke many alternatives to problem solving even when given a problem as a starting point. For example, one may:

1) Ask where the problem came from and wonder whether or not it is worth thinking more about.
2) Look at a collection of problems one has generated and become somewhat introspective. What are the kinds of problems one generates when one is given free reign? What does one find out about his or her view of the nature of mathematical thinking in thinking about these matters?
3) Reflect upon the extent to which one is inclined to create difficult problems? (notice how solving has snuck in again) and why. Also, one may ask to what extent s/he is inclined to create problems that have considerable clarity? Under what circumstances does one tend to create problems that appear to be vague and poorly defined.?
4) Inquire into the kinds of problems that generate fear, a feeling of helplessness, a feeling of largesse.
5) Investigate the kinds of problems one desires to share with others, to keep to oneself.

6) Inquire into how problems one has posed compare with those of others. To what does one attribute some of the differences?
7) Ask what are the many mathematical and extra-mathematical things that can be done when faced with a problem. [For example, one can 'de-problem' a problem or 'neutralize' it not by solving it, but by making it into a situation].
8) Ask how it is that substance and form of the solved and unsolved problems (associated with a unit of study) limit – sometimes unintentionally – the way we think of a field.

These may not all be magnificent directions to pursue of an educational nature, but they represent a beginning. They represent a different order of magnitude than those that we investigate when we accept implicitly that a problem points in an important way to a command to seek some potential solution. Some of the above questions do in fact suggest problems to solve. The point, however, is that the re-stated problems and their potential solutions are not necessarily derived from efforts to solve the mathematical problem that was given.

Which of these questions (and others of this kind) are in fact mathematical in nature and which ones are beside the point from a strictly mathematical point of view? I think it is necessary to be cautious in answering this question, lest we fall deeper into the isolationist trap that the humanistic mathematics education movement has come to challenge. We have suggested some pitfalls of an educational and mathematical nature that derive from an arrogant point of view that suggests that mathematics comes with an inherent definition and neither evolves nor is influenced by how it is that people experience the world and how they interact with each other. It is conceivable that inquiry of the sort described above will in fact not only enable more people to connect with the mathematical experience but may in fact generate some unexpected and interesting research mathematics along the way.

After all, it was only when people (in the spirit of question 8 above) began to wonder why researchers were posing and solving problems in a taken-for-granted way that entire fields of inquiry were born. The Erlanger Programme launched in 1872 by Felix Klein in geometry was born not out of problem solving alone, but out of wondering how the field was being defined by its existing assumptions and array of problems. Even when we focus on 'the field' and not the psyche of individuals, it is never problems and their solutions alone that enable us to classify the field of inquiry. Rather it is the human act of deciding what are pleasing, elegant, economical, challenging ways of viewing the field itself. We are never interested in solutions *per se*, but in solutions that are consistent with what one thinks the field is about, and as Toulmin (1977) has shown, 'aboutness' for fields has more to do with the questions asked of the field than with the objects themselves.

CONCLUSION

In seeking to elaborate upon the concept of humanistic mathematics education, we have used the helpful heuristic of seeking alternatives to the view of
mathematics as driven by logic alone. While it of course would be foolish to
disengage mathematics from logic, it is equally foolish not to inquire into
how that connection has distorted both pedagogical possibilities and a more
robust view of the nature of the discipline itself.

In closing, it is perhaps worth making explicit an important and mischie-
vous tenet of the view of liberal education that launched our exploration. The
problem is not only that deductive logic has been singled out as the defining
characteristic that distinguishes mathematics from other fields, but rather that
any *defining* characteristic has been sought. It is questionable on epistemological grounds alone that one can justify the separation of one discipline
from another as if they composed a mutually exclusive and exhaustive class.
To do so for the purpose of justifying its inclusion in an educational program
however, is to court an isolationist perspective that depletes that discipline of
some of its most human qualities. This essay has attempted to seek connections rather than divisions between mathematics and human experience.
What we have done has been illustrative and surely not exhaustive. A significant humanistic agenda might begin with an impulse to connect mathematics
curriculum with the deepest of human experiences and emotions. Such a program would not only seek to inculcate the view that mathematics influences
and is influenced by social and political factors, but would provide a vision
of mathematics filled with connectedness to other experiences. Categories
such as *problem solving, applications to the real world, social construction
of reality* and *historical perspective* may be a start, but there are others – both
supplementing and perhaps orthogonal to these – that imbue the field with
deep connections to personhood at all levels. Among such categories found
both in and about mathematics/education are the roles of narrative, joy, ap-
prehension, surprise, humor, poetry and even deception in teaching and learning as we all strive to create, justify and negotiate meaning.[8]

ENDNOTES

1. A modified form of this story appears in Brown (1981).
2. Ernest edits a British newsletter entitled POME (Philosophy of
    Mathematics Education) which explores many of the issues raised in a
    program which focuses upon challenges to the absolutist schools of
    mathematical philosophy. Many of the social issues generated by an
    awareness of the social construction of mathematical reality can be found
    in Nickson & Lehrman (1992).

3. For Dewey, an interest in the social context of learning was not so much a pedagogical ploy as it was a realization that all subject matter derives ultimately from a concern with social roots. Dewey (reprinted 1975) comments, 'The moment mathematical study is severed from the place which it occupies with reference to use in social life, it becomes unduly abstract.... It is presented as a matter of technical relations and formulae...'.(p. 41) Here he was not so much calling for 'practical applications' as we seem to be doing nowadays as he was inviting us to consider the ways in which people influence each other in the genesis of their thinking and in their motivation for defining areas of inquiry.

4. For a summary of issues raised in the categories of these last two paragraphs, see the following: Borasi (1987, 1994); Brown & Walter (1990); Confrey (1990); Fielker (1990); Silver (1994); Silver & Mamona (1989); von Glasersfeld (1994); Walter (1994).

5. There is the practical problem of imposing such a point of view on students who are not capable of hearing it precisely because they are at the very developmental level that one wishes to transform. See Perry (1970) for a discussion of such developmental problems. For an elaborated discussion of the social context of mathematics education that includes not only concern for the class room but the influence of mathematics broadly conceived on society, see Keitel (1989).

6. The word 'analogous' is important in this sentence. The argument here is not so much a genetic one (the child must reconstruct the development of the idea) as it is a search for what very well may be comparable intellectual hurdles by both groups.

7. See Dewey (1902) for a discussion of the relevant dualism of subject matter vs. interest of the child. It is elaborated upon in the Introduction of Brown & Finn (1988).

8. For a start in discussing some of these qualities, see Abbott (1963); Brown (1971); Brown, S. & Brown J. (1985); Brown (1996); Egan (1988); Egan & McEwan (1995); Hofstadter (1979); Johnson & Gazzard (1989); Knuth (1974); Lakatos (1976); Leacock (1956); Lipman (1977, 1988, 1991); Lipman, Sharp & Oscanyon (1977); Movshovitz-Hadar (1988); Nyberg (1993); Papy (1975); Paulos (1980); Pimm (1987); Plato (1976); Sfard (1994); Scheffler (1991).

REFERENCES

Abbott, E.A.: 1963, *Flatlands: A Romance of Many Dimensions,* Barnes and Noble, NY.
NCTM (eds.): 1980, *'An Agenda for Action'. Recommendations for School Mathematics of the 1980's.* National Council of Teachers of Mathematics, Reston, VA.
Benezet, L.P.: 1991a, 'The Teaching of Arithmetic I: The Story of an Experiment' *Humanistic Mathematics Network* 6, 2-6.

Benezet, L.P.: 1991b, 'The Teaching of Arithmetic II: The Story of an Experiment' *Humanistic Mathematics Network* 6, 7-10.

Benezet, L.P.: 1991c, 'The Teaching of Arithmetic II: The Story of an Experiment' *Humanistic Mathematics Network* 6, 11-14.

Bloor, D.: 1991, *Knowledge and Social Imagery,* University of Chicago Press, Chicago.

Borasi, R.,:1987, 'Exploring Mathematics Through the Analysis of Errors', *For the Learning of Mathematics* 7, 3, 2-8.

Borasi, R., 1994, 'Capitalizing on Errors as 'Springboards' for Inquiry: A Teaching Experiment', *Journal for Research in Mathematics Education,* 25, 3, 166--202.

Borasi, R.; Brown, S.I.: 1985, 'A Novel Approach to Texts', *For the Learning of Mathematics* 5, 1, 21-23.

Brown, S. I.: 1971. 'Rationality, Irrationality and Surprise', *Mathematics Teaching* 55, 13-19

Brown, S.I.: 1973, 'Mathematics and Humanistic Themes: *Sum* Considerations', *Educational Theory* 23, 3, 191-214.

Brown, S. I.: 1981, 'Ye Shall Be Known by Your Generations', *For The Learning of Mathematics* 3, 27-36.

Brown, S. I.: 1984, 'The Logic of Problem Generation: From Morality and Solving to Deposing and Rebellion', *For the Learning of Mathematics,* 4, 1, 9-20.

Brown, S. I.: 1985, 'Problem Solving and Teacher Education: The Humanism 'Twixt Models and *Muddles'*, in E. Jacobsen (ed.), *Studies in Mathematics Education,* Vol. 4, UNESCO Paris, 3-29.

Brown, S. I.: 1996, 'Posing Mathematically'. In T. Cooney, S. I. Brown, J. Dossey, G. Schrage, E. Wittmann (eds.), *Reconstituting the Frayed Braid: Teacher Education, Pedagogy and Mathematics,* Heinemann Publishing Co., Portsmouth, NH.

Brown, S. I., Brown, J.D.: 1985, review of 'Mathematics and Humor' by J. A. Paulos, 'Mathematics and Humor, Thinking' *The Journal of Philosophy for Children* 6, 1, 52-56.

Brown, S. I., Finn, M. (eds.): 1988, *Readings from Progressive Education: A Movement and its Professional Journal,* University Press of America, Lanham MD and London.

Brown, S. I., Walter, M.I.: 1990. *The Art of Problem Posing* (second edition), Lawrence Erlbaum, Hillsdale, NJ and London.

Buerk, D., 1982, 'An Experience With Some Able Women Who Avoid Mathematics', *For the Learning of Mathematics,* 3, 2, 19-24.

Confrey, J.: 1990, 'What Constructivism Implies for Teaching' In R. Davis, C. Maher, N. Noddings (eds.), *Constructivist Views on the Teaching and Learning of Mathematics,* National Council of the Teachers of Mathematics, Reston, VA.

Counts, G.: 1932, *Dare the School Build a New Social Order,* The John Day Co., New York.

Cremin, L.: 1961, *The Transformation of the School,* Alfred A. Knopf, New York.

Davis, P., Hersh, R.: 1986, *Descartes' Dream,* Houghton-Mifflin, Boston.

Dengler, P.: 1927, 'The New Education in Austria', *Progressive Education,* 4, 3, 237- 241.

Dewey, J.: 1957, *Reconstruction in Philosophy,* Beacon Press, Boston.

Dewey, J.: 1902, *The Child and the Curriculum,* University of Chicago Press, Chicago.

Dewey, J.: 1975, *Moral Principles in Education,* Southern Illinois University Press, Carbondale, Ill.

Dewey, J.: 1988, 'Progressive Education and the Science of Education'. In S. Brown and M. Finn (eds.) *Readings from Progressive Education: A Movement and its Professional Journal,* University Press of America, Lanham MD and London, 160-167.

Egan, K.: 1988, *Teaching as Story Telling,* Routledge, London.

Egan, K., McEwan, H. (eds.): 1995, *Narrative in Teaching, Learning and Research,* Teachers College Press, NY.

Ensor, B.: 1924, 'The New Education in Europe', *Progressive Education,* 1, 4, 222-229.

Ernest, P.: 1991, *The Philosophy of Mathematics Education,* Falmer, Washington DC

1318

Ernest, P., (ed.): 1994, *Mathematics Education and Philosophy: An International Perspective,* Falmer, Washington DC

Ernest, P., (ed.): 1994a, *Constructing Mathematical Knowledge: Epistemology and Mathematics Education,* Falmer, Washington DC

Fawcett, H.P.: 1938, *The Nature of Proof,* Teachers College, Columbia University, NY

Fielker, D.: 1990, 'Observation Lessons', *For the Learning of Mathematics* 10, 1, 16-22

Fischer, R.: 1993, 'Mathematics as a Means and as a System,' In P. Ernest (ed.), *Constructing Mathematical Knowledge,* Falmer, London, 113-133

Gaulin, C., Hodgson, B., Wheeler, D., Egsgard J. (eds.): 1994, *Proceedings of the 7th International Congress on Mathematical Education,* Les Presses de l'Université Laval, Quebec.

Gilbert, L.: 1933, 'A Visit to the Decroly School', *Progressive Education,* 10, 4, 199-203.

Hirst, P.H.: 1974, *Knowledge and the Curriculum: A Collection of Philosophical Papers.* Routledge and Keagan Paul, London.

Hofstadter, D.R.: 1979, *Gödel, Escher and Bach: An Eternal Golden Braid,* Vintage Books, New York

Hylla, E.: 1927, 'The New Education in Germany', *Progressive Education,* 4, 2, 164-168.

Keitel, C., Damerow, P., Bishop, A., Gerdes, P.(eds.) 1989, *Mathematics, Education and Society,:* Science and Technology Education Document Series No. 35, UNESCO, Paris.

Keyser, C.J.: 1916, 'Humanization of Teaching Mathematics', Chapter III in C.J. Keyser, *The Human Worth of Rigorous Thinking,* Columbia University Press, NY.

Kilpatrick, W.: 1928, 'Promising Educational Experiments in the Far East, *Progressive Education,* 3, 5, 246-250.

Kimball, B.: 1986, *Orators and Philosophers: A History of the Idea of a Liberal Education,* Teachers College Press, NY.

Kitcher, P.: 1988, *The Nature of Mathematical Knowledge,* Oxford University Press, Oxford.

Kolata, G.: 1989, 'A Program That Makes Conjectures', *New York Times Education Supplement,* June 18.

Knuth, D.E.: 1974, *The Rock: Surreal Numbers,* Addison Wesley, Reading, MA

Lakatos, I.: 1976, *Proofs and Refutations,* Cambridge University Press, Cambridge, England.

Leacock, S.: 1956, 'Mathematics for Golfers'. In J. R. Newman (Ed.) *The World of Mathematics,* Simon and Shuster, NY.

Lipman, M.: 1988, *Philosophy Goes to School,* Temple University Press, Philadelphia

Lipman, M.: 1991, *Thinking in Education,* Cambridge University Press, Cambridge.

Lipman, M., Sharp, A., Oscanyon, F.: 1977, *Philosophy in the Classroom,* Institute for the Advancement of Philosophy for Children, Upper Montclair, NJ.

Lipman, M., Johnson, T., Gazzard, A.: 1989. *Philosophy for Children: Where We Are Now,* Supplement No. 2. Institute for the Advancement of Philosophy for Children, Upper Montclair, NJ.

Luttmann, R.: 1993, 'The Basis for the Success of the Potsdam Program', *Humanistic Mathematics Network* 8, 44-45.

Movshovits-Hadar, N. 1988, 'School Mathematics Theorems: An Endless Source of Surprise.' *For the Learning of Mathematics* 8, 3, 34-39.

Nagel, J., Newman, J.: 1958, *Gödel's Proof,* New York University Press, NY.

NCTM (eds.): 1989, *Curriculum and Evaluation Standards for School Mathematics.,* National Council of Teachers of Mathematics, Reston, VA

Nickson, M., Lerman, S. (eds.): 1992, *The Social Context of Mathematics Education: Theory and Practice,* South Bank Press, London.

Noddings, N.: 1993, *Educating for Intelligent Belief or Unbelief,* Teachers College Press, NY.

Noddings, N.: 1993, 'Politicizing the Mathematics Classroom', In S. Restivo, J. Van Bendegem, R. Fischer (eds.): *Math Worlds: Philosophical and Social Studies of Mathematics and Mathematics Education,* SUNY Press, Albany, NY., 150-161.

Noddings, N.: 1995, *Philosophy of Education,* Westview Press, Boulder.

Nyberg, D.: 1993, *The Varnished Truth: Truth-telling and Deceiving in Ordinary Life,* Chicago University Press, Chicago.

Papy, F.: 1975, *The Little Dreamer,* Central Midwestern Regional Laboratory, St. Louis.

Paulos, J.A.: 1980, *Mathematics and Humor,* University of Chicago Press, Chicago.

Perry, W.G.: 1970, *Forms of Intellectual and Ethical Development in the College Years: A Scheme,* Holt, Rinehart and Winston, NY.

Phenix P.: 1964, *Realms of Meaning,* Mc-Graw Hill, NY.

Pimm, D.: 1987, *Speaking Mathematically: Communication in the Mathematics Classroom,* Routledge and Kegan, Paul, NY.

Plato: 1976, *Meno,* translated by G.M.A. Grube, Hackett Publishing Company, Indianapolis.

Roman, F.: 1924, 'The Hamburg System', *Progressive Education,* 1, 3, 148-150.

Scheffler, I. (ed.): 1958, *Philosophy and Education,* Allyn and Bacon, Inc. Boston.

Scheffler, I.: 1991, *In Praise of the Cognitive Emotions.* Routledge, Chapman and Hall, NY.

Seeger, F., Steinbring, H. (eds.): 1992, *The Dialogue Between Theory and Practice in Mathematics Education: Overcoming the Broadcast Metaphor,* Institut für Didaktik der Mathematik der Universität Bielefeld, Bielefeld.

Sfard, A.: 1994, 'Reification as the Birth of Metaphor,' *For the Learning of Mathematics* 14, 1, 44-55.

Silver, E.A.: 1994, 'On Mathematical Problem Posing', *For the Learning of Mathematics* 14, 1, 19-28.

Silver, E.A., Mamona, J.: 1989, 'Problem Posing by Middle School Teachers'. In C.A. Maher, G.A. Goldin, Davis, R.B. (eds.), *Proceedings of the Eleventh Annual Meeting of the North American Chapter of the International Group for the Psychology of Mathematics Education,* Rutgers-- The State University of New Jersey Press, New Brunswick, 263-269.

Stein, S.: 1992, 'Towards a Definition of Humanistic Mathematics', *Humanistic Mathematics Network* 7, 2-3.

Stephens, C.F.: 1993, 'A Humanistic Undergraduate Environment for Learning Undergraduate Mathematics, *Humanistic Mathematics Network* 8, 46-49.

Switzer, G.: 1928, 'The Red October School', *Progressive Education,* 5, 3, 246-250.

Toulmin, S.: 1977, *Human Understanding,* Princeton University Press, Princeton, NJ.

Tymoczko, T., 1985, *New Directions in the Philosophy of Mathematics,* Birkhäuser, Boston.

Tymoczko, T.: 1986, 'Making Room for Mathematicians in the Philosophy of Mathematics', *Mathematical Intelligencer* 8, 44-50.

Tymoczko, T.: 1994, 'Humanistic and Utilitarian Aspects of Mathematics', In C. Gaulin, B.R. Hodgson, D.H. Wheeler, J.C. Egsgard (eds.), *Proceedings of the 7th International Congress on Mathematical Education,* Les Presses de l'Université Laval, Quebec, 327-339.

Tymoczko, T.: 1993, 'Humanistic and Utilitarian Aspects of Mathematics', In A. White (ed.) *Essays in Humanistic Mathematics* Mathematical Association of America, Washington D.C.

Van Bendegem, J.P.: 1993, 'Foundations of Mathematics or Mathematical Practice: Is one Forced to Choose? In S. Restivo, J. Van Bendegem, R. Fischer (Eds.), *Math Worlds: Philosophical and Social Studies of Mathematics and Mathematics Education,* SUNY Press, Albany, NY. 21-38.

von Glasersfeld, E.: 1994, 'A Radical Constructivist View of Basic Mathematical Concepts', In P. Ernest (ed.), *Constructing Mathematical Knowledge,* Falmer London, 5-7.

Walter, M.: 1994, 'Developing Students' Problem-Posing Abilities by Deriving Questions from their Surroundings, Every day Materials and other Things' In C. Gaulin, B. Hodgson, D. Wheeler & J. Egsgard (eds.) *Proceedings of the 7th International Congress on Mathematical Education,* Les Presses de l'Université Laval, Quebec, 381- 382.

Wheeler, D.: 1982, 'Mathematization Matters', *For the Learning of Mathematics* 3, 1, 45-47.

White, A. (ed.): 1993, *Essays in Humanistic Mathematics,* The Mathematical Association of America, Washington, D.C.

Zweng, M., Green, T., Kilpatrick, J., Pollak, H., Suydam, M., (eds.): 1983, *Proceedings of the Fourth International Congress on Mathematical Education,* Birkhäuser, Berkeley.

NAME INDEX

A

Abbott, E.A. 1317
Abelson, H. 476
Aberg-Bengtsson, L. 223
Abraham, J. 1282
Abramovich, S. 316
Abrantes, P. 73, 89, 330
Abreu, G. 927
Acioly, N.M. 658, 659, 767
Adajian, L.B. 959, 963
Adams, V.M. 758
Adda, J. 964, 965
Adler, J. 402, 1094, 1187, 1195, 1196, 1197, 1199
Adorno, T.W. 1060, 1262, 1282
Agam, Y. 167, 169, 171, 175, 176, 201
Agassi, J. 839
Agnesi, M. 797
Ahlgren, A. 220, 222, 258
Ahmed, A. 525
Aichele, D.B. 1007
Aiken, L.R. 988
Ainley, J. 441, 464, 797
Albers, D.J. 51
Albis, V. 920
Albrecht, A. 965
Aldrich, M.L. 967
Ale, S. 925, 930
Alele-Williams, G. 1254
Alexanderson, G.L. 50
Ali, T. 704
Alibert, D. 885
Allaire, R. 961
Allen, R.A.B. 72, 73, 484
Allenby, R.B. 391
Alrø, H. 994, 995, 1277, 1278
Altet, M. 573
Altrichter, H. 1175, 1180
Anapolitanos, D.A. 888
Anderson 573
Anderson, B.T. 967, 968, 969, 970, 971, 973
Anderson, J.R. 478, 482, 483
Anderson, R.D. 289
Anderson, S. 931
Anegbi, C. 1022
Angelis, D. 1280
Anglin, W.S. 832
Anzinger, W. 1282
Appel, K. 881

Appelrath, K.H. 660
Apple, M.W. 1211, 1213, 1283
Arcavi, A. 1067
Archimedes 643
Arcidiacano, M.J. 213
Arfwedson, G. 1212
Aristotle 566, 889
Arnaud, R. 631
Arnold, G. 764
Arnold, S. 507
Arnold, S.M. 701, 731, 735
Arora, M.S. 587
Arrighi, G. 146
Arrigo 629
Arsac, G. 487, 526, 621, 856, 857, 858, 860
Arsac, J. 1107
Artigue, M. 296, 475, 488, 526, 551, 567, 630, 632, 677, 679, 682, 690, 691, 692, 694, 856, 863, 869, 1074, 1104, 1107
Arzarello, F. 1098, 1104, 1112
Ascham, R. 804
Ascher, M. 914, 915, 917, 919, 921, 922, 923, 925, 930, 932, 933, 1039, 1040, 1046
Ascher, R. 914, 915, 917, 919, 932, 1039
Atweh, B. 960, 994, 995
Augustine, St. 1074
Austin, J.L. 988
Ausubel, D.P. 885
Azcárate-Gimenez, C. 309

B

Babai, L. 882, 883
Bachelard, D. 1073
Bachelard, G. 197, 682, 684, 831, 843, 863
Bacon, F. 806, 1046
Bagnall, R. 772
Bailey, P. 924, 930, 1271, 1272
Bakar, M. 298, 299
Bakhtin, M. 1059, 1080, 1081
Balacheff, N. 9, 202, 469, 471, 480, 486, 488, 516, 526, 550, 684, 856, 858, 859, 885, 1104, 1107
Ball, D.L. 60, 526, 1094, 1123, 1151, 1192
Ball, G. 518, 525
Ball, J. 790, 791, 799

1333

Müller, G.N. 107, 897, 903
Mulligan, J. 1005, 1007
Münzinger, W. 1264, 1282
Mura, R. 962, 969, 975, 1161
Murray, F. 1151, 1152
Murray, H. 514, 515, 516
Murray, J.C. 403, 512, 526
Murtaugh, M. 657, 766
Mve Ondo, M. 925

N

Nadot, S. 1151
Nagarajan, V. 923
Nagasaki, E. 527, 528
Nagel, E. 1060
Nagel, J. 1295
Nahrgang, C. 989
Naidoo, A. 1283
Nathan, G. 1018
Nebres, B. 1158, 1166, 1255
Negt, O. 1263
Nelissen 107
Nello, M.S. 1005
Nelsen, R.B. 406
Nelson, D. 924, 930
Nelson, L.T. 213
Nemetz, T. 1221
Nemirovsky, R. 291, 475, 493
Nesher, P. 114, 127, 128, 129, 1005, 1043
Neubrand, M. 879
Neuman, D. 516
Neumann, J. von 51
Neuve 634
Nevile, L. 495
Newman, C.M. 211
Newman, D. 462
Newman, J. 1046, 1295
Newman, M.A. 1000, 1001, 1004
Newton, I. 806, 894, 895, 896
Newton-Raphson 316
Nicaud, J.F. 480
Nicholas, J. 767, 996, 1188, 1193
Nickson, M. 512, 838, 847, 890, 994, 1021,
    1150, 1277, 1282, 1316
Nicolas, P. 483
Niederdrenk-Felgner, C. 960, 962
Nielsen, L. 1095, 1257, 1284
Nightingale, F. 207, 215
Niss, M. 8, 11, 13, 21, 23, 27, 34, 55, 56, 61,
    66, 68, 86, 91, 336, 512, 545, 812,
    912, 1210, 1215, 1217, 1264, 1275,
    1282, 1283
Nissen, G. 1284
Nissen, P. 922
Njock, G. 913
Nobre, S. 920
Noddings, N. 954, 955, 1170, 1283, 1300,
    1306, 1308
Noether, E. 952
Noether, G.E. 260
Nogueira, A. 919
Nohda, N. 527, 528, 543, 997, 998
Noheda, N. 1195
Northam, J. 952
Noss, R. 487, 488, 524, 1280
Nunes, F. 448
Nunes, T. 60, 512, 515, 765, 920, 1044, 1071,
    1283
Nunokawa, K. 380
Nyagura, L. 1169
Nyberg, D. 1317
Nyhof-Young, J. 964

O

O'Barr, J.F. 954
O'Halloran, P. 1248
O'Shea, D. 691
Ockham, W. 1067
Odvárko, O. 965
Ogden, C.K. 841
Ohlsson, S. 473
Oldham, E. 703
Oldknow, A. 455
Olivier, A.I. 514, 515, 516, 526
Olmos, E.J. 800
Olssen, K. 1000
Omanson, S. 519
Orey, D. 921
Ormell, C. 55, 84
Orpen, B. 1197, 1198
Orr, E.W. 991
Orton, R. 1060, 1084
Osborne, A. 455
Oscanyon, F. 1317
Osta, I. 961
Oteiza, F. 1254
Otte, M. 372, 379, 381, 383, 384, 389, 390,
    392

Otten, W. 957
Ottosson, T. 223
Owen, E. 999
Owen, J. 1216
Owens, J. 1170

P

Pacioli, F.L. 413, 415
Paechter, C. 923, 930
Paffrath, F.H. 1282
Paine, L. 1133, 1152
Paivandi, S. 946
Pallascio, R. 961
Palmiter, J.R. 318, 319
Palumbo, D. 458
Panoff, M. 915
Papert, S. 406, 476, 482, 524
Papy, F. 1317
Paquin, L. 961
Parenti, L. 1093, 1097, 1107, 1117
Pargetter, R. 718
Parkin, B. 742, 743
Parzysz, B. 8, 161, 194, 196, 405, 476
Pascal 267
Pasquis, F. 956, 978
Passey, D. 330
Pateman, N. 550
Patronis, T. 1284
Paula, L. 920
Paulos, J.A. 226, 1317
Pavlou, M. 1003
Payan, C. 481
Payne, J.N. 106, 107, 108
Pea, R. 437
Peano 806, 889
Peard, R. 8, 239, 249, 922
Peck, F. 704, 705
Pedro, J.D. 956, 968, 970
Pehkonen, E. 997, 998
Peirce, C.S. 1060, 1065
Pepe, L. 634
Pereira-Mendoza, L. 223
Peretz, B 569
Pergola, M. 848
Perl, T. 968
Perlwitz, M. 850
Perraton, H. 722
Perrenoud, P. 573
Perrin, M. 915

Per.in-Glorian, M.J. 551, 860, 1074
Perry, M. 230
Perry, W.G. 703, 807, 808, 1083, 1084, 1317
Pestalozzi, J.H. 411, 415, 416, 417, 420, 518, 540
Peter, A. 552
Petersen, B. 989
Peterson, I. 289
Peterson, P.L. 114, 526, 1007, 1179, 1218
Petit, J.P. 788
Petitto, A. 920
Phenix, P. 1291
Phillips, B. 260, 261
Phillips, D.C. 89, 577
Piaget, J. 106, 224, 247, 293, 512, 514, 519, 677, 681, 684, 688, 695, 747, 748, 831, 834, 835, 842, 843, 844, 848, 852, 853, 860, 864, 865, 1060, 1068, 1070, 1073, 1074, 1077, 1080, 1082, 1299, 1300
Piatelli-Palmarini, M. 830
Pickert, G. 888
Pil, J. 925, 928
Pile, S. 805
Pimm, D. 8, 60, 371, 394, 991, 994, 997, 1317
Pine, J. 351
Pinxten, R. 919, 920, 932, 1036, 1039, 1040, 1042, 1044, 1049
Pirie, S. 886
Pisano, L. 635
Pitman, A.J. 1218
Plato 519, 716, 718, 831, 836, 893, 894, 897, 1046, 1071, 1079, 1081, 1317
Playfair, W. 215
Ploghaus, G. 665
Plunkett, St. 543
Poincaré, H. 51, 477, 831, 832
Poisson, S.D. 51, 207, 241, 242
Poitras, L. 968
Pollak, H.O. 53, 55, 56, 65, 66, 67, 799
Pollatsek, A. 223
Polya, G. 155, 618, 721, 839, 885
Ponte, de 1195
Ponte, J.P. 448, 617, 1099, 1174
Popova, A. 925
Popper, K.R. 89, 717, 830, 839
Porta, H. 318
Porter, N. 967
Posch, P. 1167, 1174, 1175, 1180
Posner, J. 914, 920

Wainer, H. 215
Waits, B. 302, 455, 459, 464
Walberg, H.J. 956
Walden, R. 953
Walker, D.F. 550
Walker, J.C. 718
Walker, M. 1195, 1197, 1198
Walkerdine, V. 805, 808, 850, 857, 953, 992
Wallbridge, M. 1003
Walle, J. van de 109, 110, 118
Walter, H. 1282
Walter, M.I. 418, 421, 1010, 1317
Walther, G. 542, 548
Wang, L.Q. 1219
Warry, M.C. 756
Waterhouse, P. 774
Watkins, A.E. 211, 212, 258
Watkins, K.B. 109, 110, 118
Watson, D.M. 524
Watson, H.R. 742, 922
Watson, I. 1001
Watson, J. 220, 228, 232, 272
Watson, K. 741
Watson, S. 793
Wattenberg, F. 693
Waxman, H. 522
Waywood, A. 824, 991, 1002, 1012, 1050, 1055, 1058
Weaver, J.F. 117
Webb, N.L. 545
Webber, V. 757
Weeler, E. 585
Weiser, W. 514, 519, 521, 1005
Weiss, I. 1162, 1166
Weissglass, J. 1213
Wells, G. 990
Wenger, E. 484, 658, 659, 765, 850, 1194
Werry, B. 1215, 1220
Wertsch, J. 144, 1073, 1194
West, B. 312
Westbury, I. 568, 571, 1255
Weyl, H. 716, 717
Whang, W.H. 1020
Wheatley, C. 456, 462
Wheeler, D. 45, 547, 989, 1290
Wheeler, M. 1162
White, A.M. 1046, 1048, 1302, 1303
White, B.Y. 472, 475
White, L.A. 909, 910, 911, 1036, 1046, 1047
Whitehead, A.N. 1069
Whitney, H. 516
Whorf 1078

Wiegel, H.G. 473, 845
Wilder, R.L. 909, 910, 911, 1038, 1039, 1047
Wildt, M. 763
Wiles, A. 786, 796
Williams, D. 1008
Williams, E. 901
Williams, J. 84, 924, 930
Williams, S.R. 306, 522
Williamson, P. 1011
Willis, G.B. 113, 131
Willis, S. 962, 1193
Wilson, B.J. 7, 722, 931, 1208, 1209, 1214, 1221
Wilson, P. 921
Wimbish, J. 692
Wing, T. 383
Winnicot, D. 1080
Winograd, K. 1011
Wise, L.L. 967
Withnall, A. 756, 757
Wittgenstein, L. 716, 717, 837, 838, 846, 847, 850, 852, 994, 1072, 1289
Wittmann, E.C. 107, 117, 126, 131, 521, 536, 537, 538, 540, 547, 548, 550, 551, 552, 897, 903, 1098, 1117, 1168, 1169, 1170
Wittrock, M. 1151
Wolf, C. 51
Wolfe, R. 1215
Wolfram, S. 474
Wolleat, P. 956, 968, 970
Womack, D. 811
Wong, N. 1211
Wood, D. 990
Wood, L.N. 767
Wood, N.G. 309
Wood, T. 131, 517, 525, 546, 850, 854, 1098
Woodrow, D. 1070
Woods, P. 866, 995
Wurm, S.A. 1222

Y

Yackel, E. 131, 525, 526, 850, 854, 887, 1098
Yanagimoto, A. 85
Yasukawa, K. 757
Yates, C. 713
Yates, W. 757
Yergeau, N. 968
Yerushalmy, M. 476, 477, 492

INDEX OF SUBJECTS